Advanced Financial Accounting

Sixth Edition

Thomas H. Beechy
Schulich School of Business, York University

V. Umashanker Trivedi
Schulich School of Business, York University

Kenneth E. MacAulay
Gerald Schwartz School of Business and Information Systems, St. Francis Xavier University

Pearson Canada
Toronto

Library and Archives Canada Cataloguing in Publication

Beechy, Thomas H., 1937–
Advanced financial accounting / Thomas H. Beechy, V. Umashanker Trivedi, Kenneth E. MacAulay.—6th ed.

Includes index.
First 3rd eds. published under title: Canadian advanced financial accounting.
ISBN 978-0-13-703038-5

1. Accounting—Textbooks. I. Trivedi, V. Umashanker (Viswanath Umashanker), 1965– II. MacAulay, Kenneth E. (Kenneth Eugene), 1962– III. Beechy, Thomas H., 1937– . Canadian advanced financial accounting. IV. °Title.

HF5636.B43 2010 657'.046 C2010-904549-1

ISBN 978-0-13-703038-5

Vice-President, Editorial Director: Gary Bennett
Editor-in-Chief: Nicole Lukach
Executive Marketing Manager: Cas Shields
Developmental Editor: John Lewis
Production Editor: Madhu Bhardwaj, Glyph International
Project Manager: Imee Salumbides
Copy Editor: Cat Haggert
Proofreader: Laurel Sparrow
Indexer: Belle Wong
Compositor: Glyph International
Permissions Researcher: Joanne Tang
Art Director: Miguel Acevedo
Cover and Interior Designer: Opus House/Sonya Thursby
Cover Image: Getty Images

1 2 3 4 5 14 13 12 11 10

Printed and bound in the United States of America.

PEARSON

Brief Contents

Contents

About the Authors

Thomas H. Beechy, DBA, CPA (Illinois)

Tom Beechy has been in the forefront of Canadian accounting publishing for many decades. This book represents the sixth edition of the first Canadian-authored advanced accounting university textbook, first published in 1984. Professor Beechy also is co-author of a major Canadian Intermediate Accounting text, now in its fifth edition. Tom migrated to Canada from the United States about forty years ago after acquiring degrees from George Washington University, Northwestern University, and Washington University (St. Louis) and teaching at Illinois Institute of Technology. Since his arrival in Canada, he has been at the Schulich School of Business where he is Professor Emeritus of Accounting as well as Director of International Academic Development. Tom loves to travel and can often be found in Europe or Asia (and especially in China). He is a classical music fanatic, and also enjoys dance, theatre, and movies.

V. Umashanker Trivedi, PhD

V. Umashanker Trivedi (Shanker) is an Associate Professor of Accounting at the Schulich School of Business, York University. He is a Chartered Accountant from India and obtained his Ph.D. from Arizona State University. Shanker's research interests are in financial accounting, the accounting profession, and tax. He has won research grants from the Canadian Institute of Chartered Accountants and the Canadian Academic Accounting Association. Shanker has published in journals such as *Experimental Economics*, *Behavioral Research in Accounting*, *Journal of Business Ethics*, and *Canadian Tax Journal*. Shanker has also published many cases in financial accounting. In the past 19 years Professor Trivedi has taught at York University, McMaster University, and Arizona State University and at all levels; bachelors, masters, and doctoral. His service at York University includes serving on the Senate and as the Chairman of the Senate Appeals Committee. Shanker enjoys smooth jazz, new age, and classical music.

Kenneth MacAulay, PhD, CA

Ken MacAulay is an associate professor of accounting in the Gerald Schwartz School of Business and Information Systems at St. Francis Xavier University. He is an active textbook author, co-authoring university-level introductory financial accounting and personal financial planning texts in addition to a high school financial planning text. He holds degrees from St. Francis Xavier University (BBA) and Queen's University (PhD). Before his academic career, Ken was a chartered accountant with Touche Ross (now Deloitte and Touche). He has continued to be active in the profession, having taught in the Atlantic School of Chartered Accountancy and having served as a member of the Nova Scotia Securities Commission from 2000 to 2009. He is a committed conservationist and can often be found flyfishing for trout and salmon in his spare time.

Preface

Welcome to the latest edition of *Advanced Financial Accounting!* Since 1984, this book has guided students through the complexities of business combinations, consolidations, and financial reporting for business enterprises, nonprofit organizations, and governments. This book is about more than just technical knowledge. Our goal is to help students develop a professional approach to accounting issues.

To help students demonstrate their professional competencies, we offer several realistic cases at the end of each chapter. Using these cases, students practise exercising professional judgment over a variety of issues in different contexts. As well, most chapters have at least one *multiple competency* case in which students are encouraged to apply their technical knowledge in a realistic setting and over a wide range of issues.

New Features

We have introduced many new features into this edition, including:

- **Learning objectives** to focus students' attention on the main issues of each chapter.
- **Reality check** boxes to highlight applications in practice as well as significant findings from empirical research.
- **Concept check** boxes to enable students to self-test their own understanding of important issues and concepts as they proceed through each chapter.
- **Proposed changes** boxes to highlight changes in current standards that are being proposed by the IASB.
- Compliance with **International Financial Reporting Standards** when relevant.
- **IFRS terminology** whenever applicable.
- **Accounting standards for private enterprises** in a separate section at the end of each chapter, where relevant.
- A renewed focus on the **direct method** of consolidation within each consolidation chapter.
- The **MEAR steps for consolidation,** a new method for remembering the steps in the consolidation process, are introduced in Chapter 3 and further developed in the succeeding consolidation chapters.
- New **graphic exhibits** in the consolidation chapters to complement and highlight the discussion in these chapters in a visually appealing manner.
- An increase in the number of **self-study problems.**
- Marginal icons directing students to a greatly enhanced **Companion Website (CW)**.
- A list of **relevant accounting standards** at the end of each chapter, for both IFRS and ASPE.
- **On-line appendices** covering fund accounting and specialized aspects of consolidation that are less essential for a thorough professional understanding of those topics.

Text Updating

Synopsis. The book begins with an overview of financial reporting objectives and the development of accounting standards. We fully explain the development of international accounting standards, but we also discuss standard-setting for Canadian private enterprises.

Chapters 2 through 9 are IFRS-compliant in all aspects relating to publicly accountable enterprises. Most of this material is common to both IFRS and the CICA's Accounting Standards for Private Enterprises (ASPE). In those few instances in which Canadian ASPE differs from IFRS, the differences are explained in a separate section at the end of the relevant chapter.

Chapter 10 explains accounting for nonprofit organizations, while Chapter 11 discusses governmental reporting. Vital organizational and accounting distinctions exist between nonprofit organizations and governments. Superficially, the accounting for these two groups may seem similar, however, not only are they are significantly different, but also their standards are set by two completely separate standard-setting organizations within the CICA.

Chapters 2 through 6 explain consolidations and business combinations. These chapters constitute the core of the book—for most people, this is what advanced accounting is all about. While we have thoroughly revised and updated these chapters, we have ensured that the text retains its highly readable quality. The main focus of these chapters is on the acquisition method required under IFRS and particularly on the entity method. This focus allows students first to obtain a clear and firm understanding of the consolidation process, and then to expand their understanding to the other complexities of consolidation. A supplementary discussion of the parent-company extension method (an available option within IFRS) is included later in each chapter. Throughout these chapters, the equity method is compared to the results of consolidation.

The direct method of consolidation is used throughout. A new and exciting feature of these chapters is our incorporation of a new step-by-step approach to the direct method of consolidation, the **MEAR steps to consolidation**. This approach takes the student through a logical progression of steps that will work in all consolidation situations. The MEAR steps divide the consolidation process into self-contained parts, allowing students to approach the process of consolidation in an organized and structured manner. Thus, these steps allow students to focus on a specific task, such as the calculation of the amortization of fair value increments in later years, retained earnings, net income of the subsidiary, or non-controlling interest etc. These self-contained sections replicate the types of problems that students will encounter on professional exams. We believe that students will find the *MEAR steps to consolidation* easy to follow and remember.

We believe that focusing on the direct method for illustrations within the text chapters is another feature that makes the difficult consolidation material manageable and easy to understand. However, the worksheet-method solutions for the chapter illustrations are now presented in the Companion Website for those students and instructors who prefer this method.

We have also incorporated many graphic exhibits in the consolidation chapters to complement and highlight the discussion in these chapters in a visually appealing manner. Further, the reality check boxes in each of the consolidation chapters have been carefully chosen to highlight the most recent examples from practice of how the material is implemented in real life and findings from current research on related topics.

Chapter 7 steps back from the consolidation process while we take a look at disaggregation—interim and segmented reporting. Segment reporting has been revised to be IFRS-compliant.

Chapters 8 and 9 deal with the second most important topic in the book—foreign currency. We have updated our discussions to include the most recent IFRS standards. The discussion in Chapter 8 on hedges has been substantially rewritten. The topic of hedge accounting focuses on anticipated transactions. Fair value and cash flow hedges are reviewed and examples provided. Two methods of recording hedges (the gross method and the net method) are illustrated for all examples involving hedges in the chapter.

In Chapter 9, the IFRS concept of functional currency replaces the concepts of integrated and self-sustaining subsidiaries. Both Chapters 8 and 9 conclude with a discussion of Canadian accounting standards for private enterprise. Finally, in both chapters almost all the problem material is either new or refreshed.

Chapter 10 presents the latest developments and financial accounting standards for not-for-profit organizations. This chapter has been revised extensively. The nature and characteristics of NFPs in Canada are introduced early in the chapter and used to provide additional insights in subsequent discussions of the accounting issues faced by NFPs. In addition, the on-line Appendix 10A, *Fund Accounting*, has been substantially lengthened to provide a fuller explanation of how fund accounting works. New material is introduced on recording encumbrances and budgetary accounts. The appendix now concludes with a comprehensive problem illustrating the use of the restricted fund method.

Chapter 11 discusses financial reporting for governments. It provides the only comprehensive introduction to public sector financial reporting among the major advanced accounting texts in Canada. Information on the nature and characteristics of governments is introduced early in the chapter and used to inform subsequent discussions. The types of government organizations and the major public sector accounting issues are discussed. The chapter concludes with a presentation and discussion of a comprehensive example of government financial statements.

Companion Website—www.pearsoned.ca/beechy

The book's Companion Website offers a considerable amount of additional assistance to students:

- **Excel® templates** for some problems.
- **Worksheet solutions** to supplement the direct method for all in-text consolidation examples.
- **Additional self-study problems,** with solutions.
- **Practice quizzes** for self-testing.
- **Appendices** of additional material on tangential issues that relate to some chapters.
- **IFRS Updates** as needed as the IASB reconsiders old standards and issues new ones.

Other Supplements

Instructor's Resource Manual with Solutions (ISBN: 978-0-13-248147-2). This supplement contains an overview of each chapter's main concepts and assignment material, as well as solutions for all review questions, cases (including detailed case notes), and problems. The Instructor's Resource Manual with Solutions is available to download from Pearson Education Canada's online catalogue at **http://vig.pearsoned.ca** and on the **Instructor's Resource CD-ROM (ISBN: 978-0-13-248145-8).**

Test Item File and TestGen Test Bank (TIF ISBN: 978-0-13-248143-4; TG ISBN: 978-0-13-249559-2). An expanded and improved set of multiple choice and short answer test questions is available to instructors as a Test Item File in Microsoft® Word and as a computerized test bank in Pearson Education Canada's TestGen software. TestGen allows instructors to custom design, generate, edit, and save classroom tests. It provides many options for organizing and displaying tests, along with search and sort features. The Test Item File and TestGen test bank are available to download from Pearson Education Canada's online catalogue at **http://vig.pearsoned.ca** and on the Instructor's Resource CD-ROM.

PowerPoint® Presentations (ISBN: 978-0-13-248148-9). New to the sixth edition, these slides highlight all of the important concepts in the text. The PowerPoint Presentations are available to download from Pearson Education Canada's online catalogue at **http://vig.pearsoned.ca** and on the Instructor's Resource CD-ROM.

CourseSmart (ISBN: 978-0-13-209192-3). CourseSmart goes beyond traditional expectations—providing instant, online access to the textbooks and course materials at a lower cost for students (average savings of 60%). With instant access from any computer and the ability to search the text, students will find the content they need quickly, no matter where they are. And with online tools like highlighting and note-taking, students can save time and study efficiently.

Instructors can save time and hassle with a digital eTextbook that allows them to search for the most relevant content at the very moment they need it. Whether it's about evaluating textbooks or creating lecture notes to help students with difficult concepts, CourseSmart can make life a little easier. See all the benefits at **www.coursesmart.com/instructors** or **www.coursesmart.com/students.**

Acknowledgments

As in the previous editions, much of the assignment material was drawn from the professional examination of Canada's three professional accounting bodies: CGA Canada, CICA, and SMA Canada. A few cases have also been included by the kind permission of the Institute of Chartered Accountants of Ontario. We are deeply indebted to all of these organizations for their cooperation and support in permitting us to use their copyrighted material. An acknowledgement appears at the end of each case or problem that was obtained from one of these four professional sources.

We are deeply indebted to the individuals who reviewed and provided valuable suggestions on the revision plan and the manuscript, including:

Talal Al-Hayale, University of Windsor

Walt Burton, Okanagan College

Han Donker, University of Northern British Columbia

Allan W. Foerster, Wilfrid Laurier University

Geoff Gatien, CA

Stuart H. Jones, University of Calgary

Julia Scott, McGill University

Catherine Seguin, University of Toronto

We are also grateful for the enthusiastic support and encouragement of the people at Pearson Canada. In particular, we would like to thank Nicole Lukach, Editor-in-Chief, Business and Economics, John Lewis, Developmental Editor, Imee Salumbides, Project Manager, Madhu Bhardwaj, Production Editor, Cat Haggert, Copy Editor, Laurel Sparrow, Proofreader, and Ross Meacher, Technical Checker.

On a personal note, we would like to thank our friends and families for their support and encouragement throughout the lengthy process of bringing this new edition to fruition.

Corrections

Despite the efforts of many people and reviews by many sets of eyes, errors have a nasty way of creeping into all books. Of course, we authors bear the responsibility for any errors that you may come across. We would greatly appreciate your bringing any and all errors to our attention, no matter how minor. We will place these corrections in the online *errata* section of the Companion Website as they come to our attention. Your corrections will also enable us to eliminate those errors prior to the next printing of the book, thereby making life a little easier for future students and instructors.

Please report errors by email to **tbeechy@schulich.yorku.ca.**

Thank you for using *Advanced Financial Accounting,* Sixth Edition. We hope you will find it an enjoyable book from which to learn these complex topics.

PEARSON The Pearson Canada **COMPANION WEBSITE**

A Great Way to Learn and Instruct Online

The Pearson Canada Companion Website is easy to navigate and is organized to correspond to the chapters in this textbook. Whether you are a student in the classroom or a distance learner you will discover helpful resources for in-depth study and research that empower you in your quest for greater knowledge and maximize your potential for success in the course.

Companion Website

www.pearsoned.ca/beechy

Enter

PEARSON

Jump to... http://www.pearsoned.ca/beechy | Home | Search | Help | Profile

Companion Website

Home >

Companion Website

Advanced Financial Accounting,
Sixth Edition, by Beechy, Trivedi, and MacAulay

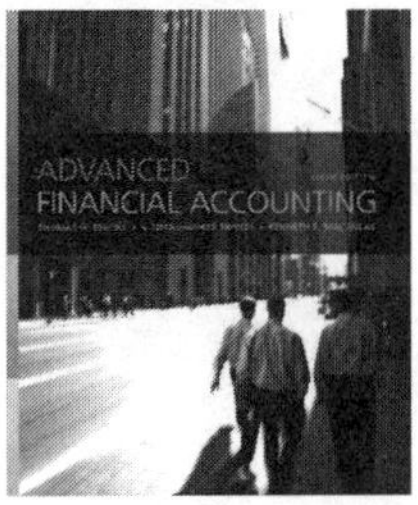

Student Resources

The modules in this section provide students with tools for learning course material. These modules include:

- Appendices 5A, 5B, 6A, 6B, and 10A
- Answers to the Concept Check Questions
- Worksheet solutions
- Excel templates
- Additional self-study problems
- Practice Quizzes

In the quiz modules students can send answers to the grader and receive instant feedback on their progress through the Results Reporter. Coaching comments and references to the textbook may be available to ensure that students take advantage of all available resources to enhance their learning experience.

Instructor Resources

Instructors can access additional teaching tools including PowerPoint slides, an Instructor's Resource Manual, and a testbank through Pearson Canada's online catalogue. To get a password, simply contact your Pearson Canada Representative or call Faculty Sales and Services at 1-800-850-5813.

1

Setting the Stage

LEARNING OBJECTIVES

After studying this chapter, students should be able to:

1. explain why companies have differing financial reporting objectives;
2. describe the process by which international financial accounting standards have been developed;
3. identify the obstacles to international comparability under IFRS; and
4. explain the Canadian approach for private enterprise reporting.

WHY STUDY ADVANCED ACCOUNTING?

Advanced Financial Accounting is the detailed study of three major topics:

- preparing consolidated financial statements;
- accounting for foreign currency transactions and foreign operations; and
- financial reporting by non-business organizations—not-for-profit organizations and governments.

The first topic is the main focus; it comprises five of the remaining ten chapters.

Consolidations

Almost certainly, every financial statement that you ever have seen is a *consolidated* statement. We're sure you've noticed the word "consolidated" in the statement title, such as *Consolidated Statement of Income*, and you undoubtedly have a general idea what it means: *consolidated statements include the assets, liabilities, revenues, expenses, and cash flows for the parent company plus all of its subsidiaries*. It may seem excessive to devote half (or more) of a course to this simple concept. However, that simple concept disguises the complexities that underlie consolidated statements.

Any professional accountant or qualified financial analyst should understand how consolidated statements are prepared. Many accounting estimates and assumptions are necessary to prepare financial statements for a "consolidated" entity that, legally, does not even exist! Consolidated statements are an accounting fiction, and every professional accountant must clearly understand why and how they are created. An accountant must also be able to explain the limitations of consolidated statements to potential users.

International Operations

We all are aware that the scope of business is increasingly international. Even relatively small companies are affected by international trade, even if it's only by purchasing inventory or raw materials from foreign suppliers in a foreign currency. Most large companies have substantial operations in one or more foreign countries. For example, Montreal-based Bombardier has annual revenues of about $20 billion, but only 4% of that revenue is from its Canadian operations. Bombardier does business around the world and operates factories in Germany, the United Kingdom, the United States, China, France, Spain, and many other countries.

How can Bombardier combine transactions and consolidate subsidiaries operating in US dollars, Canadian dollars, euros, British pounds sterling, and Chinese yuan? Not only are Bombardier's many "offshore" companies operating in host countries with different currencies, but each subsidiary also is operating internationally itself. The impacts of foreign operations show up in many ways in consolidated financial statements, some of which represent genuine risk exposure and some of which are just the mechanical results of the consolidation process. You need to know the difference.

Non-business Organizations

What happens when a corporation or organization is not driven by the profit motive? When profit ceases to be the motivation for an organization's existence, neither its operations nor its financial statements are driven by "bottom line" thinking.

This book's final two chapters are devoted to accounting in non-business organizations: (1) not-for-profit (or "nonprofit") organizations (NFPs) and (2) governments. It is likely that virtually all of your accounting education has focused on business enterprises. All business enterprises have similar accounting and reporting needs and can use a common private-enterprise accounting framework. Businesses comprise most of the world's economic activity. However, not-for-profit organizations and governments are substantial segments of economic activity, contributing 20–30% of employment in most countries.

An oft-heard comment is that "governments and NFPs should be run like a business." The difficulty with trying to run an NFP or government like a business is that they are *not* businesses. Business enterprises have identifiable products or services that are sold or delivered to specific identifiable customers or clients. There is nothing so specific about NFPs or governments. Certainly, there are "products" such as cancer research and road repair, but there is no identifiable "customer" to whom these products are sold. Nor do the "customers" normally pay for the product, at least not directly. Thus, the essential cost–revenue link that underlies all business activity does not exist in NFPs or governments.

While it is true that some segments of NFP and government activity *are* like businesses, such as a museum gift shop or a city electrical utility, these activities are a minor part of both

NFPs and governments. Those business-type enterprises can and should be accounted for as a business because they have the essential cost-revenue relationship.

Therefore the final two chapters discuss the nature of accounting for *non-business activities* of NFPs and governments. Many accounting graduates will find themselves involved in non-business organizations as professional accountants, as advisors, as board members, or simply as educated citizens who should be fully aware of NFP and government accounting issues.

A NEW WORLD ORDER IN ACCOUNTING

2011 is a pivotal year in accounting history. For the first time, most industrialized and developing countries will be using International Financial Reporting Standards (IFRS). Many nations (mostly in Europe) have been using IFRS for several years, but many more joined the user group in 2011, including Canada, China, India, and Japan. This commonality sounds wonderfully simple and consistent. As we will discuss a little later, however, international accounting standards do not necessarily provide the consistency and comparability that we might assume.

As well, despite the appearance of wide-spread commonality among nations, IFRS may have quite limited application in most countries:

- IFRS may be used only for preparing *consolidated* financial statements; *non*-consolidated statements may be required to comply with national laws governing corporate reporting.
- IFRS may apply only to *publicly accountable* companies—primarily companies with debt or equity securities traded on public markets; private companies may have a different reporting regime.
- IFRS does not apply to NFPs or governments.

In the next section, we will examine the standard-setting process in Canada and the post-2011 role of the Canadian Institute of Chartered Accountants' (CICA's) Accounting Standards Board (AcSB).

STANDARD-SETTING IN CANADA

Prior to adopting IFRS, the *CICA Handbook* contained the accounting standards for all Canadian companies, public and private, as well as for not-for-profit organizations. Those Canadian standards were generally applicable to all Canadian corporations because the national and provincial corporations acts require auditors to report in accordance with Generally Accepted Accounting Principles (GAAP), and GAAP was defined in the regulations as compliance with the *CICA Handbook*.

For a long time, the AcSB developed its own standards, although always with an eye on what other countries were doing, particularly the United States. For a while in the late twentieth century, the AcSB's official policy was to harmonize with the US standards. Keeping step with the US's Financial Accounting Standards Board (FASB) was intended to make life much easier for the very small proportion of Canadian companies that had to report to the US Securities and Exchange Commission (SEC) because their securities are traded in the USA. Those companies would then not have to reconcile their Canada-based statements with US standards.

At about the turn of the century, the AcSB realized that constantly adjusting Canadian standards to meet ever-changing US standards was a rather futile endeavour. Also, a series of huge US corporate accounting scandals (e.g., Enron; WorldCom) caused people around the world to realize that perhaps US standards weren't as "high quality" as had always been proclaimed. Simultaneously, the idea of worldwide acceptance of IFRS for multinational stock exchange listings began to take shape.

Consequently, the AcSB decided that Canada should also adopt IFRS. In a world increasingly characterized by international commerce, separate Canadian standards began to look like an anachronism. 2011 was chosen as the year of full conversion to IFRS for Canadian publicly accountable enterprises.

Does that mean Canada is out of the standard-setting business? No. It does mean that Canada has fully adopted IFRS for publicly accountable enterprises; but public companies and other publicly accountable enterprises constitute a very small proportion of Canadian corporations. Therefore, the CICA has a four-pronged approach to accounting standards:

1. Public and publicly accountable enterprises (e.g., fiduciary organizations like investment funds and private banks) will follow IFRS for their consolidated, general-purpose, publicly issued financial statements. The standards for publicly accountable enterprises are included in the *CICA Handbook, Part I.* The standards in Part I are exactly the same, word for word, as the IASB standards. They are included in the *CICA Handbook* only to satisfy certain legal reporting requirements that are contained in the various corporations acts and securities acts of the federal and provincial governments.
2. Canadian accounting standards for private enterprise are contained in the *CICA Handbook, Part II.*
3. NFP accounting standards are contained in the *CICA Handbook, Part III*, as previously was the case, with special sections devoted to the unique reporting requirements and issues of NFPs.
4. The Public Sector Accounting Board (PSAB) will continue to make recommendations for both senior (i.e., national, provincial, and territorial) and municipal governments, which are published by the CICA in the *Public Sector Accounting Handbook.*

Over the next ten chapters, this book will explain and illustrate the above four threads of Canadian financial reporting.

CONCEPT CHECK 1-1

Companion Website

1. Why might we refer to consolidated statements as *fictional* statements?
2. What standard-setting approaches are used in Canada? What are the four "threads" of Canadian financial reporting?

FINANCIAL REPORTING OBJECTIVES

Before we discuss IFRS, we need to review the role of financial reporting objectives. All accounting standards require *choices*—choices of accounting policies, accounting estimates, and disclosure. IFRS requires more estimates than previous Canadian standards, and estimates are particularly sensitive to implicit or explicit reporting objectives. Both the practice of accounting and the analysis of financial reports depend on being fully aware of the accounting implications of users' and preparers' objectives.

Financial reporting objectives are not vague and immeasurable, such as "to serve the general reader" or "to provide fair presentation"; general objectives like these are of no help at all. If several choices are available within IFRS (or private-company GAAP), how can an objective like "fair presentation" provide any guidance? Obviously, fair presentation is much better than unfair presentation, but unfair presentation basically is unethical and/or fraudulent reporting.

We will not discuss financial reporting objectives at length, you will be glad to know. But we will make a quick review. The importance of financial reporting objectives will become apparent in subsequent chapters when we discuss circumstances in which there is a choice of accounting policies or accounting estimates.

User Objectives

Financial statement readers use the statements as a basis for decisions. Users often want information that will help them to:

1. predict cash flows;
2. find out whether the company has complied with contractual requirements; and
3. evaluate management's performance.

Cash Flow Prediction Investors and creditors are often concerned about an organization's cash flow. Users are often keenly interested in the cash flow from operations, because the operating cash flow provides the cash for paying bills, paying dividends, and expansion. Users, therefore, often want accounting decisions made in a way that facilitates their *cash flow prediction*.

Under the **cash flow prediction objective**, financial statements should help users to predict future cash flows of the company based on past and current data. The statements should describe the current pattern of cash flows, and should indicate any expected alteration of those flows.

There are two principal accounting impacts when a cash flow prediction objective is adopted as the primary reporting objective:

1. net income will tend to be measured in a way that indicates long-run cash flow from operations; and
2. notes will be used to describe future cash flows not indicated in the body of the statements themselves, including expected changes in those flows that are reported.

The dominant impact of the cash flow prediction objective is that accounting choices will measure revenue and expenses in a way that most closely corresponds to accrual-basis cash flows. If a company uses many inter-period allocations of past costs and estimates of future costs in measuring earnings, the relationship between earnings and cash flow is unclear. When earnings relate closely to cash flows, prediction of future cash flows is easier than when earnings do not relate closely to cash flows.

Financial analysts refer to earnings that correspond closely to cash flows as **high-quality earnings**. *Low-quality* earnings, on the other hand, are those that are not reflected in cash flows from operations. Since investors tend to be interested in cash flows, *high-quality* earnings are preferred to low-quality earnings, and this preference often shows up in the market as higher share prices or a greater willingness of a bank to lend money.

Under the cash flow prediction objective, companies will opt for immediate recognition of costs rather than deferral and amortization (when they have that choice). An example is development costs that may be capitalized if they meet a set of criteria. Since the criteria all depend on management estimates, the defer-or-amortize decision basically rests with management.

A secondary impact of the cash flow prediction objective is that the notes to the financial statements may be used to disclose supplementary information about *future* cash flows. This is the reason that many accounting standards require disclosure of future cash flows relating to leases, debt repayments, etc. In addition, however, a company could also disclose information such as major expected changes in cost structure, the size of the order backlog, or the current value of inventories.

Contract Compliance Both *shareholders' agreements* and *loan agreements* (including bond indentures) usually contain specific requirements that involve accounting measurements. A **shareholders' agreement** is a contract among the shareholders. Shareholders' agreements are normal in a private company, but sometimes exist in a public company as well (e.g., to limit voting power).

Shareholders' agreements in private corporations often contain provisions about such matters as dividend entitlements, limitations on cash withdrawals, and valuation. Valuation is a particularly important issue in private companies because valuation provisions govern the way shares are valued if an investor wishes to buy additional shares or sell her or his shares. Valuation normally is determined on the basis of accounting measurements, usually book value per share, since there is no public market for the shares of private companies. Asset valuation and income measurement policies obviously have a significant impact on book values.

A **loan agreement** is the contract between a borrower and a lender. Lenders usually include *covenants* or *maintenance tests* in loan agreements, which are requirements that the borrower must meet to keep the loan in good standing. Examples include limits on additional debt, a minimum times-interest-earned ratio, and limitations on dividend payout.

The level of the maintenance tests is (or should be) determined by the lender after taking into consideration the accounting policies used by the borrower. Therefore, the lender is concerned not only with the level of the ratios but also whether consistent accounting policies have been used as the basis for their calculation.

Performance Evaluation Frequently, financial statement readers want to know how well management is running the business. Indeed, managers themselves usually need a report card to see how they are doing. In a small business, the managers may have a good idea of the success of their management, but may need the financial statements to show creditors or silent partners how the business is going. On the other hand, managers may think they are doing all right, but need the statements to verify their perceptions.

When performance evaluation is the primary objective of the financial statements, the accounting policies should, as much as possible, reflect the way in which decisions are made.

For example, suppose that a private company manages a chain of hotels. Management wants to issue financial statements that show investors how well management is doing its job. The chain opens new hotels fairly regularly, and it has a policy of renovating older hotels. Suppose that management decides to build a new hotel based on an analysis of the future market in the area, and on the potential net cash flow and present value of the project. Start-up costs will be substantial, but management believes that future revenues will recover these costs. Since the decision was made by offsetting the start-up costs against revenues in future periods, the performance evaluation objective would call for capitalizing the costs and amortizing them against the future revenues.

The treatment of hotel start-up costs would be quite different under the cash flow prediction alternative. For cash flow prediction, it would be better to expense the costs immediately because the cash outflow occurred immediately and because start-up costs are a routine part of doing business and opening new hotels.

One problem with the performance evaluation objective is that it is sometimes indistinguishable from an approach that seeks simply to maximize reported earnings. Statement users who are close to the company (such as managers, directors, owners of private corporations, or controlling shareholders of public companies) are frequently in a position to know which objective is being followed. But for an external user, it is sometimes hard to tell the two apart. Clues may be gained by closely scrutinizing the accounting policies relating to revenue and expense recognition in the notes to the financial statements.

Preparer Objectives

The preceding objectives relate to users' decision needs. The preparers of the statements are likely to have their own set of priorities when they select accounting policies. "Preparers" refers to the *managers*, not to their accounting staff. Remember that the financial statements are the responsibility of management. The accountant provides the expertise to assist the managers in meeting their reporting objectives, but the statements are management's.

The policies that management chooses will have an impact on the reported results and therefore can affect users' perceptions. The policies may also have a more direct impact on the managers themselves—compensation levels often are tied to accounting measurements, and the managers' future job prospects may be enhanced by reporting the "right" results.

In the following sections, we will discuss five major reporting objectives of the preparers. These are:

1. income tax deferral;
2. net income maximization or minimization;
3. earnings management–the big bath
4. income smoothing; and
5. contract compliance.

Some accountants would prefer to refer to these preparer reporting objectives as preparer *motivations* rather than as objectives, reserving the term "objectives" to relate to the legitimate decision needs of the users.

Income Tax Deferral One of the responsibilities of management is to maximize the discounted net present value of the enterprise's future cash flow. One way of doing this is to delay the liability for income taxes. Money has a time value—a dollar of taxes paid in the future has a smaller present value than a dollar of taxes paid currently. Thus deferral of tax payments increases the present value of the company.

In general, the objective of tax deferral (sometimes known as tax *minimization*) leads to accounting policies that delay revenue recognition and/or speed up expense recognition. The result is net income that is lower than would be reported under alternative acceptable accounting policies. The policies must be long-term in scope; the accounting treatment cannot be changed from year to year. Bear in mind that shifting relatively small amounts of revenue or expense from one period to another can have a substantial impact on *net* income. If net income is 10% of revenue, shifting just 2% of revenue or expense will have an impact of up to 20% on net income.

For some companies, particularly small private corporations, tax deferral may be the only objective of financial reporting. The managers know that net income is on the low side of the permissible range of accounting net income figures, and they can explain the situation to bankers or other major creditors who might be using the statements. Since tax deferral reduces the current cash flow drain on the company, bankers may welcome the astute tax management and may evaluate the company's reported performance more favourably.

Tax deferral might seem to be a desirable objective for all companies. But, for many enterprises, minimizing net income is incompatible with other reporting objectives. If the company is trying to attract investors, for example, a low reported net income will not help. Bear in mind that the company cannot say in its annual report that the accounting figures should be taken with a grain of salt because they are tax-influenced amounts. Therefore, many companies choose not to emphasize tax deferral as an objective of financial reporting, but rather adopt other objectives that are more important to the overall corporate goals.

Maximization or Minimization of Earnings Sometimes management's financial reporting objective is to *maximize* or *minimize* the enterprise's reported net income. Management may wish to maximize earnings to attract new investors or to allay the fears of present investors. If bond indentures or loan agreements contain covenants concerning dividend payout ratios, times-interest-earned ratios, etc., a high level of earnings will make it easier to comply with the restrictions. Other companies may be in satisfactory financial health, but wish to look even better to be well perceived in a competitive financial and business market.

On the other hand, management may wish to minimize reported earnings (for reasons other than tax deferral). Management may feel that the company's earnings are embarrassingly high and may wish to discourage the entry of new competitors or to avoid attracting public or political attention, or higher wage demands by employees. Management may hope to discourage takeover bids if control is not firmly held by friendly shareholders.

Earnings can be minimized by delaying revenue recognition as long as possible and by expensing (rather than deferring) as many costs as possible, a practice often defended as being "conservative."

Earnings Management—The "Big Bath" One aspect of earnings management that merits special mention is the practice of taking a **big bath** in a loss year. This is an observed tendency of companies to load all possible losses and write-downs into a year that is going to be a low-earnings or loss year anyway, especially if new management is taking over and wishes to make themselves look good in future years. Management's view is that if they're going to report a loss, they might as well report a large one and "clean up the balance sheet."

Companies often take the opportunity offered by a loss year to write down assets of doubtful future benefit, especially intangible assets. Sometimes, the write-down is very substantial, and there have been cases in which the auditors have objected that the company is writing its assets down to an amount that is well below recoverable cost. Another strategy is to make substantial provisions for future costs related to current decisions and actions, such as restructuring costs or reclamation costs.

The earnings management objective of the big bath is that, by writing down assets, the company has less amortization in future years. Hence, future earnings are enhanced. This is why the big bath strategy can be part of an earnings maximization objective. New management finds this especially attractive since they can blame the poor performance on prior management while setting the stage for higher profits in the future. Similarly, when a company makes provisions for future costs that are at the high end of the feasible range of estimates, the current provision reduces the amount of expense that is charged in future years. Indeed, if the current charge turns out to be excessive, the company can recognize a gain in future years when it reduces the recorded liability.

The big bath motivation treads very close to the line of ethical reporting. The intent, either conscious or unconscious, is to increase future earnings by stretching the limits of accounting estimates. Taken far enough, a big bath can result in deliberate misstatement of accounting results, in both the current and future periods. If all of the charges in a big bath are legitimate, then one wonders whether the prior years' financial statements were misstated because they included assets that had no future benefit.

Income Smoothing Investors and creditors are concerned not only with the level of earnings, but also with the business risk of a company. The level of risk is equated with the volatility of earnings and cash flows. In attempting to influence users' perceptions about the company, managers may wish to select accounting policies that not only increase the apparent *level* of earnings but also decrease the apparent *volatility* of earnings. Accounting policies can have the effect of smoothing earnings, even though the IFRS attempts to limit income smoothing by stressing current recognition of current economic events, such as changes in the pension liability and changes in the fair value of certain assets. IFRS also discourages the matching concept, which often has been used as the rationale for smoothing.

Smoothing may be accomplished through either revenue or expense recognition policies, or both. Revenue can be smoothed by spreading its recognition over an earnings cycle, such as by allocating part of revenue in a multiple-service contract to future services rather than immediate recognition. Also, management may time the recognition of irregular lumps of revenue to fall into periods of low economic activity. In some situations, expenses can be smoothed by amortizing costs over a period of years rather than by recognizing them at inception; a prime example is development costs.

The smoothing of expenses is most effective if the expenses can be related to levels of revenue, since smoothing of expenses will not in itself necessarily lead to the smoothing of net income. For example, if net revenue fluctuates substantially, the smoothing of an expense will tend to lower the entire level of earnings over a period of years but will not decrease the fluctuation. Indeed, if the same volatility exists but at a lower overall level of earnings, the relative risk will appear to increase rather than to decrease.

Contract Compliance Financial reporting often is influenced by a goal of optimizing compliance with the terms of contracts. This objective of contract compliance may be observed when managers choose accounting policies that will most readily enable the company to meet covenants imposed by major lenders in loan agreements. Often, the desire to meet contract provisions leads to other reporting objectives such as income maximization or smoothing. The real motivation may be the contract provisions, however.

Other Objectives

The user and preparer objectives discussed above are only some of the most common objectives. There can be a wide array of other objectives, depending on the nature of the enterprise and its reporting environment.

Regulated companies, for example, normally are permitted to earn a maximum percentage return on their invested capital. As a result, a regulated company will tend to use accounting policies that maximize the book value of the asset base to maximize the permitted dollar return on investment (and, after financial leverage, on the shareholders' equity).

Similarly, a company that is subsidized by some level of government is apt to use accounting policies that maximize the amount of subsidy to which the company is legally and ethically entitled.

Parent Company GAAP Canadian companies that are wholly owned subsidiaries of foreign parents usually must comply with the accounting mandates of their parents. Often, that means complying with US GAAP. About 65% of the wholly owned foreign subsidiaries in the *Financial Post 500* have US parents, and US GAAP will prevail in those subsidiaries. For subsidiaries of non-US parent companies, IFRS usually is used.

In addition, a wholly owned subsidiary of a foreign parent derives its reporting objectives from its parent, and the parent's reporting objectives may be driven by factors that are quite different from anything encountered in Canada. Therefore, an accountant who is working for such a subsidiary must be sensitive to and familiar with its specific reporting context.

Prioritizing Objectives

In any financial reporting situation, there is a potential conflict between user objectives and preparer motivations. Since the managers are preparing the statements, it would appear that preparer motivations would dominate the selection of objectives.

However, users are not without power:

- Canada Revenue Agency (CRA) has the power to assess taxes on taxable income determined independently of reported accounting income.
- Major shareholders can, through the board of directors and its audit committee, have an influence on reporting objectives.
- Public shareholders have little direct influence, but security analysts and the financial press can put pressure on corporations to provide financial information that is most useful to outsiders rather than self-serving to managers.
- Major lenders have direct power to demand attention to their reporting needs, although competitive forces temper this power—bankers sometimes worry that if they are too insistent, the customer will go to another bank.

All financial reporting situations therefore involve a trade-off between users and preparers in determining the reporting objectives. The relative strength of the two groups will influence the selection of accounting policies.

When choosing from alternative accounting policies and feasible estimates, management will not be able to make choices that satisfy all of these objectives simultaneously. Therefore it is necessary to prioritize the objectives by deciding which is the most important, which is the next most important, and so forth.

The prioritizing of reporting objectives involves ranking the objectives in order of importance. A ranking of objectives must be tailored to each reporting enterprise; there is no generalized ranking. When there is a conflict in the accounting policies indicated by the various objectives, the objective(s) at the top of the ranking will win out over those farther down.

CONCEPT CHECK 1-2

Companion Website

1. Explain how someone can be both a *user* and a *preparer* of financial statements.
2. Why wouldn't all taxable enterprises choose to follow income tax minimization as their primary reporting goal?
3. How might management's "big bath" objective lead to an ethical quandary for an accountant?
4. An enterprise may have several reporting objectives. Explain what difficulty arises in this situation and how it is resolved.

INTERNATIONAL ACCOUNTING STANDARDS

The Beginning

The creation of international accounting standards began in 1973 with the founding of the International Accounting Standards Committee (IASC). The IASC was a volunteer organization; the members were representatives of national professional accounting bodies (e.g., the

American Institute of Certified Public Accountants, AICPA, and the CICA). The intent of the IASC was to establish an international forum for discussing financial accounting issues and standard-setting. The objective was to reduce the range of accounting options so as to achieve some degree of similarity or *harmonization* among different nations' accounting standards. The ultimate goal was comparability between financial statements issued in different jurisdictions.

Over a period of almost 30 years, the IASC membership grew from nine professional associations to more than 200. The standard-setting body within the IASC was the IASC Board, which continued to operate with a somewhat rotating membership of nine members. By 2001, the IASC Board had issued 41 International Accounting Standards (IAS). These IASs had no direct authority, however; essentially, they were suggestions for other national standard-setters. However, some nations that emerged from central control (particularly countries of the former Soviet bloc) adopted IASs as their accounting standards because there was no established standard-setting body in those countries.

The Emergence of International Financial Markets

In the 1990s, international financial markets were becoming far more focussed on a few cities such as New York, London, Frankfurt, Hong Kong, and Tokyo. Competitive pressures on regional stock exchanges such as the Toronto Stock Exchange (TSX) increased. All exchanges were eager to attract more foreign companies as listed companies to gain a greater market share. A barrier to foreign listings was the widespread requirement to use local accounting standards for reporting to local investors. For example, if a German company listed on the TSX, the company would need to prepare financial statements using Canadian GAAP, or at least to prepare a reconciliation. That is an onerous task, one that is hardly worth the effort just to gain access to the small Canadian securities market.

Given the general drive for foreign listings, the work of the IASC attracted the attention of an important industry group, the International Organization of Securities Commissions (IOSCO). IOSCO told the IASC that if the IASC was able to develop a solid set of "quality" accounting standards, IOSCO would recommend to all national security commissions that each nation's stock exchanges accept foreign registrants' statements using international standards instead of local national standards. A major step in this direction occurred in the mid-1990s when Germany's Minister of Finance ruled that all public German corporations should prepare their *consolidated* statements in accordance with international GAAP.

The IASC worked hard to develop an improved set of standards, which IOSCO ultimately accepted. In 2002, the European Parliament mandated that all EU consolidated financial statements must be prepared in accordance with international GAAP, starting in 2005. At that point, international standards were well on their way toward universal application for consolidated statements.

Restructuring the IASC

As the IASC worked on improving standards, it became obvious that it needed to become an independent professional group. It was no longer feasible to operate effectively as a volunteer organization. Therefore, a new structure came into effect in 2002 (revised in 2009), shown in Exhibit 1-1.

EXHIBIT 1-1

IASC Organization Chart

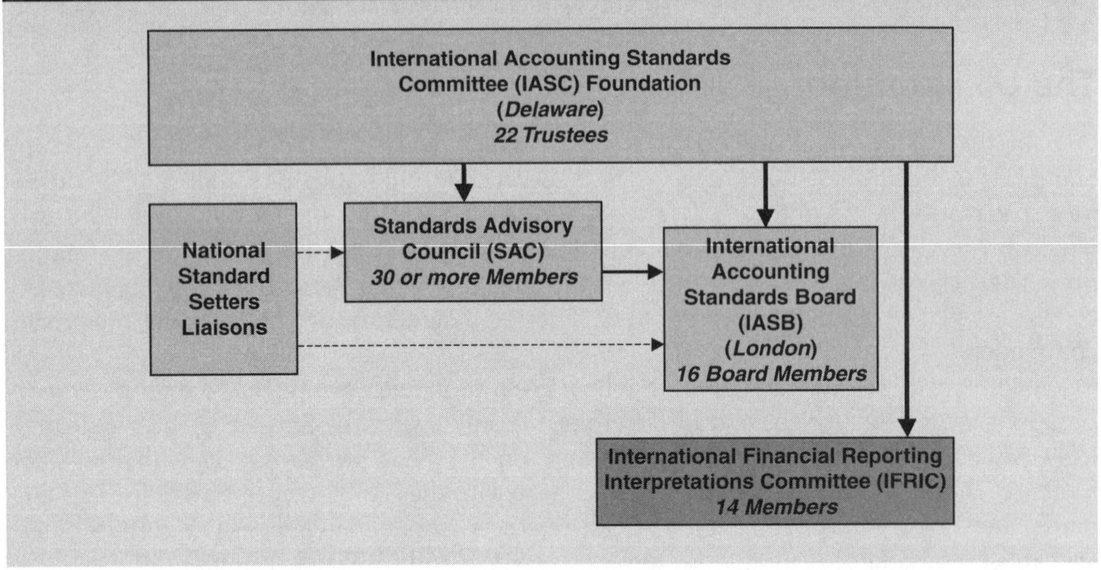

The structure has the following components:

- The umbrella organization is a not-for-profit foundation incorporated in the US state of Delaware that consists of 22 trustees; a primary responsibility of the trustees is to appoint the IASB board members.
- The International Accounting Standards Board (IASB), based in London, is the standard-setting body. The Board has been expanded from nine to 16 members, and may be expanded again in the future as more countries convert to international standards.
- A Standards Advisory Council (SAC) offers advice to the Board concerning agenda issues; the SAC must have a minimum of 30 members, chosen mainly to represent different types of organizations and in different countries around the world. At the time of writing this text, the SAC had 45 members.
- A 14-member International Financial Reporting Interpretations Committee (IFRIC) issues interpretations of existing standards.

International standards follow the general approach of issuing new standards on topics not previously addressed by existing IASs, and also revising existing standards when necessary. Thus, international public-company GAAP consists of two series of standards:

- Forty-one International Accounting Standards issued by the old IASC, revised as necessary by the current IASB; and
- International Financial Reporting Standards (IFRS), which are new standards on topics not previously covered by IASs.

Both sets together comprise international GAAP and are collectively referred to as **International Financial Reporting Standards** or **IFRS**.

A very important aspect of the new structure is that Board members often are direct liaisons with the standard-setters in their countries. This arrangement enables a much closer level of cooperation between the IASB and some of the crucial national standard-setters.

The US Situation

One of the world's most important standard-setting bodies is the Financial Accounting Standards Board in the United States, which sets accounting standards for all public companies. The real authority of the FASB is derived from the Securities and Exchange Commission, which regulates the US securities markets. Public companies must report in the US market on whatever basis is specified by the SEC, and thus the FASB's standards are given authority by virtue of their acceptance by the SEC. The FASB standards are not binding on private companies.

The SEC requires US companies to follow FASB pronouncements, but foreign-based corporations (whose securities are traded in the US) can file with the SEC using IFRS instead of US GAAP. This fact has placed great pressure on the FASB to harmonize with the IASB. Similarly, the IASB is under pressure to harmonize with the FASB because "international standards" aren't truly international if the world's largest securities market doesn't use IFRS. There also are several other forces at work to push the FASB and IASB to harmonize.

As a result, the FASB and IASB have been working diligently to reach agreement on many issues, including a new conceptual framework. IFRS has adopted many aspects of US standards, such as "comprehensive income," while the FASB has modified many of its standards to agree with IFRS. The two Boards meet regularly to find common ground among many contentious issues. At present, there are still many differences between the two sets of standards. However, the goal is to complete harmonization by 2015, although some delay can be expected. Quite possibly, US and international GAAPs could be completely harmonized and in effect by 2017—then we would truly have a single set of accounting standards around the world.

Be careful, though. Even though the *standards* may be the same, national differences still will affect *reported results*. We'll discuss this important issue below.

Increased Judgment

Applying accounting standards has always required a high level of professional judgment. This is especially true of principle-based standards such as the pre-2011 Canadian standards. Now that we've switched to the even more principle-based IFRS, judgment plays an even greater role. International standards expand the need for judgment in three ways:

- IFRS requires many judgmental decisions for selecting the appropriate accounting *policies*.
- IFRS expands the number of management estimates, such as estimates of fair value, in a wider variety of circumstances.
- IFRS reduces the limitations on management's estimates, relying more on principle-based standards and generally eliminating numerical "bright lines" that limit management's flexibility somewhat, such as the numerical guidelines for treating a lease as a capital lease.

The cases in this book are intended to help you develop your professional judgment.

Professional judgment must be based on generally-accepted criteria, such as the qualitative characteristics of accounting that you already have learned in prior courses—qualities such as timeliness, relevance, and verifiability. Most importantly, professional judgment rests on the foundation of reporting objectives.

CONCEPT CHECK 1-3

1. What was the major force that accelerated development of international standards in the 1990s?
2. Explain the relationship between the IASB and individual national standard-setting bodies such as the CICA and the FASB.

INTERNATIONAL STANDARDS—AN ILLUSION OF COMPARABILITY

The driving force behind adopting international standards has been the *international financial markets*—to enable companies to list their securities on multiple exchanges around the world. The underlying logic is that if every country adopts international accounting standards it will be easy to compare the financial results of companies based in different countries.

The logic is attractive. If we all use the same reporting standards, the barriers of diverse national standards will fall. That logic is correct to a certain extent. However, interpretation of financial statements under international standards will still be difficult. To some extent, comparability is an illusion. There are three factors that limit comparability:

1. While IFRS may be accepted in hundreds of countries around the world, they are not accepted to the same extent in every country.
2. The quality of reporting under IFRS depends on the quality of the accounting and auditing profession in that country, as well as on the effectiveness of the country's financial reporting enforcement mechanism.
3. Even when the full IFRS are formally adopted by a nation, some standards will inevitably be applied differently in different nations due to local circumstances.

When each nation used home-grown financial standards, users were automatically forewarned that the statements were not directly comparable. Statements from other countries looked different, used different terminology, were arranged differently, and some statements were "missing"—for example, a cash flow statement was not generally required outside of Anglo-Saxon countries such as the United States, United Kingdom, Canada, and Australia. The new hazard is that, with international standards, users will be misled into thinking that internation comparison is simple. Comparability is certainly much better with IFRS, but a financial statement user must be aware of many factors in a corporation's host country that will affect the company's financial reporting.

In the following sections, we will briefly discuss these four limiting factors:

1. some jurisdictions may accept IFRS, but not *all* of IFRS;
2. the quality of the accounting infrastructure varies among nations;
3. national factors can have a significant effect on proper interpretation of financial statements; and
4. IFRS may apply only to public corporations—those that come under the jurisdiction of national securities regulators.

We will place primary emphasis on the fourth factor because the vast majority of corporations in Canada are private, not public.

Uneven Adoption of IFRS

There are two basic ways in which national accounting standards are established:

1. By law or by government regulation. Examples include most European countries, the EU, and China. These are known as *code-law* countries.
2. By the country's accounting profession or by an independent non-government authority established within that country. Examples include the USA, UK, Canada, and Japan. These are known as *common-law* countries.

Under either approach, a nation may not adopt IFRS completely:

- In code-law countries, a change to international standards requires legislation. When the IASB changes or amends international standards, a code-law country must pass new legislation before the change can become effective. New legislation may be slow in coming or may not be proposed at all for some IFRS revisions.
- In common-law countries, legislation is not required, but the local standard-setter may balk at one or more aspects of an international standard and refuse to put that standard into effect.

When acceptance of IFRS is incomplete, we really don't have truly international standards. Instead we have something a little different, as indicated by this statement in the 2009 annual report of the large Australian mining group, Rio Tinto:

> The Group's financial statements have been prepared in accordance with IFRS as adopted by the European Union ('EU IFRS'), which differs in certain respects from the version of IFRS that is applicable in Australia ('Australian IFRS').[1]

Rio Tinto then explains what the difference is, as required by IFRS.

---

1. Rio Tinto, *Annual Report 2009,* (March 2010), http://www.riotinto.com/annualreport2009/financial_statements/reconciliation_with_australian_ifrs.html. The accounting difference relates to the treatment of *goodwill*, a topic that you will see a lot over the next six chapters.

Institutional Quality

To apply international standards effectively, a nation must have:

- professional and experienced preparers;
- quality auditing; and
- an effective enforcement mechanism.

As well, corporate senior managers must be honest and ethical, and not attempt to hide things from the auditors (or internal auditors). If any one of these factors is missing, the financial statements may not be a fair and true indicator of the financial health of the company.

Preparer Professionalism To apply complex international standards, preparers (i.e., internal accounting staff) must possess a high level of professional judgment. Preparers need to make many judgments concerning issues such as asset lives, residual values, fair values, impairments, account collectability, inventory obsolescence, and so forth. Professional judgment requires training and the internalization of judgmental criteria (e.g., reliability, verifiability, relevance); otherwise, there is no difference between *professional* judgment and *amateur* judgment.

In developing countries, professionally trained accountants are often in short supply. As a result, accounting estimates become inconsistent and/or arbitrary; international comparisons are not valid.

Audit Quality Audits are not of consistently high quality around the world. It is easy to think of the "Big Four" auditing firms extending their knowledgeable and ethical arms around the world, but a majority of audits are not carried out by the Big Four. In any case, those large firms are not international partnerships; each one is an association of affiliated national partnerships, and not all of the national offices are equally strong. For example, one of the Big Four firms was very embarrassed when its Italian affiliate failed to detect a massive fraud taking place in an Italy-based international dairy company, Parmalat—the auditor didn't even discover the simple fact that a supposed $4 billion dollar bank account did not exist! Not surprisingly, the Big Four firm quickly disassociated itself from that Italian auditing affiliate.

In some countries, there has historically been a close association between a company and its auditors. For example, in China prior to 1992, the auditors of state-owned enterprises (SOEs) were directly affiliated with the corporation. When China introduced capitalism, the government began requiring *independent* auditing, but no tradition of independent auditing existed. Consequently, the government made strenuous efforts to strengthen the professionalism of the auditing profession. One step was to require the public financial statements of companies with non-Chinese investors to be audited by an international auditing firm, even if the statements submitted to the government were audited by a Chinese auditing firm. Another was to establish three very large National Institutes of Accounting (in Beijing, Shanghai, and Xiamen) to provide mandatory professional development not only for auditors, but also for senior managers of large state-owned enterprises.

A sophisticated auditing profession does not exist in many small countries. Even if well-trained auditors are imported from other countries to add expertise, those imported auditors may not understand the local environment and ways of doing business, which is fundamental to performing a good audit.

REALITY CHECK 1-1

Importance of the Accounting Infrastructure

Some Chinese public companies prepare two sets of financial statements, for reporting to two different shareholder groups. An empirical study into financial reporting in China during the 1990s found large differences in reported net income *for the same company in the same year* depending on whether the audit was by (1) a local audit firm reporting to government and local investors, or (2) an international audit firm reporting to foreign investors. The researchers concluded that the disparity was due to the lack of "an effective financial-reporting infrastructure, including preparer professionalism, quality auditing, and effective enforcement. Developing countries often lack such infrastructure to make accounting standards work as originally intended."

Source: S. Chen, Z. Sun, and Y. Wang, "Evidence from China on Whether Harmonized Accounting Standards Harmonize Accounting Practices." *Accounting Horizons* 16:3 (September 2002) p. 193.

Enforcement What good are accounting standards if there is no one to enforce them? Laws can demand that companies use international accounting standards, but there must also be a body that is responsible for challenging a company's questionable application of accounting standards.

Enforcement can be the responsibility of (1) an independent or semi-independent agency, usually in the form of a securities commission that supervises the securities exchanges in that country, or (2) a government department, such as a Ministry of Finance. In either case, the enforcement body must have sufficient staff and budget to carry out its responsibility.

For example, the Securities and Exchange Commission carries that "big stick" in the United States and has not been afraid to challenge companies. In Canada, enforcement has largely been carried out by the Ontario Securities Commission (OSC). The authority of these two enforcement agencies comes from their legal responsibility to supervise stock exchanges that are under their jurisdiction:

- for the SEC, all stock exchanges in the United States, and
- for the OSC, the Toronto Stock Exchange (TSX).

The SEC can be a vigilant and sometimes aggressive enforcer of quality accounting. However, its strength is only as good as the budget that the US Congress gives it. The SEC can be weakened by inadequate financing, as happened in much of the latter part of the twentieth century prior to the accounting scandals of Enron and WorldCom, among others. Inadequate financing is also alleged to have been the reason that a decade of SEC investigations of Bernard Madoff failed to reveal that he was running a giant pyramid (known as a "Ponzi scheme") that bilked investors of an estimated US$48 *billion*.

In many other countries, the enforcement body is seriously underfunded and understaffed. An inadequately staffed body will not be able to enforce accounting standards for companies based in that country, companies that may well be listed on multiple exchanges around the world. Regulators of other exchanges don't have the legal authority to investigate a company that is based in another jurisdiction. For example, the OSC does not have the right to investigate a company based in Russia, even if it is listed on the TSX; the OSC cannot subpoena documents and statements from outside Canada. Thus, reliable international accounting requires effective enforcement in all nations that have public companies. We will talk about private companies toward the end of this chapter.

Comparisons Made Simple—Or Are They?

As we mentioned earlier, the primary driving force for adopting international standards was internationalization of the securities markets. If companies use a common set of accounting standards, securities exchanges can solicit listings from companies anywhere in the world and not be restricted to listings only from domestic companies using local GAAP. International companies such as German auto giant Daimler could (and did) list its shares on dozens of exchanges around the world without using different accounting standards in each country. If German, American, Japanese, and Korean auto companies all use international standards, it should be possible to compare the financial statements of those companies without learning the accounting peculiarities of each nation.

However, it is not quite so simple. A common international set of accounting standards does achieve a much greater surface similarity. Companies from all nations will have similar financial statements, statement components, disclosures, and measurement methods. The invisible differences lie in the underlying economic, political, legal, and environmental differences between countries, as well as simply the ways of doing business.

Legal Factors In many countries such as Italy or France, taxable income must be the same as accounting net income. In other countries (e.g., Canada and the United States), taxable income can be different (in limited ways) from accounting income. When tax–book conformity is required, managers have strong motivation to use accounting options that reduce earnings.

Another entirely different type of legal factor may arise from religious considerations. Some countries require application of Islamic principles in business. Islamic principles forbid interest. Banks that follow Islamic principles earn their return by taking an equity stake instead of charging interest. The equity stake is designed to achieve essentially the same return as would interest, but without violating Islamic principles. The bank receives payment in the form of dividends or profit-sharing; no interest expense will appear on the books of the "borrower." Under such a system a calculation of "times interest earned" or similar ratios will be meaningless.

Ways of Doing Business In Germany, employees and bankers play a major role in corporate management. Both have representatives on the board of supervisors (that is, directors). There are significant financial reporting implications. One major difference is the way of viewing high debt. In North America, a high debt load is normally viewed as a bad indicator while a conservative no-debt structure indicates a safer company. In Germany, however, the presence of high debt and bank representation on the board indicates that the banks are supporting the company. In contrast, the absence of debt in a company's capital structure often indicates that the banks have no faith in that company—a very bad indicator.

Japan offers another example. In North America, publicly issued financial statements must be consolidated statements. Until recently, Japan did not issue consolidated statements. Now that Japan does require consolidated statements, it should be possible to see the resources under control of those huge corporate groups (such as Mitsubishi). Good step forward for comparability, right? Wrong!

Japanese corporate structure is very different from that in Western countries. Conglomerates in the United States, Canada, and Europe operate through a parent company and a multitude of controlled subsidiaries. In contrast, a Japanese conglomerate of hundreds of companies has no parent company. Instead, each company in the group owns a tiny percentage of the other companies in the group, no more than 2% or 3%. A majority of the shares of any one company is owned within the group through these multiple inter-company holdings, thereby rendering hostile takeovers impossible. But since there is no pyramid of companies with a parent company at the top, Japanese consolidated statements don't include the assets and liabilities of other companies in the group—they include only a miscellany of controlled subsidiaries, usually those in foreign countries.

Economic and Political Factors When we compare the financial statements of Canadian companies we can be assured that the economic and political environment affects all companies more or less equally. When we compare across borders, that consistency may disappear. Inflation and exchange rate fluctuations vary by country. Even a relatively small difference in inflation rates can have a long-term impact on prospective earnings of companies in different countries. The higher the inflation rate, the more likely that assets will be revalued. Also, high inflation leads companies away from holding monetary investments, but may increase reliance on monetary liabilities, especially if financed from a low-inflation country.

Another important economic/political factor is the extent of state control or regulation in a company's home country. State control and/or regulation always entails prescriptive accounting, either directly or indirectly. An example of indirect accounting influence is regulatory rate-of-return guidelines. Rate-of-return regulations always base the permitted level of operating earnings as a percentage of the asset base. A company that is subject to rate-of-return limitations will (1) capitalize as many costs as possible, thereby increasing the asset base, and (2) use high levels of debt financing to increase the residual rate of return to shareholders.

Japan provides another example. Large companies are subject to regulatory oversight for violations of the anti-monopoly law. Therefore, companies may try to "lie low" by adopting accounting policies and estimates that make them seem less dominant and profitable. A comparative study of major construction companies in Japan and the United States discovered that while US companies almost always used percentage-of-completion accounting, Japanese companies used the completed-contract method to delay revenue recognition unless they were weak companies and were trying to reassure investors and banks with higher assets and earnings.[2]

---

2. Kazuyuki Suda, "International Accounting Standards and Japanese Corporate Accounting: An Empirical Research of Accounting for Construction Contracts." *Kansai University Review of Economics and Business* 23:1–2 (March 1995), pp. 95–123. Completed-contract accounting is not permitted under IFRS; Japan committed to IFRS compliance by 2011.

REALITY CHECK 1-2

Evidence on the Limits of International Comparability

Empirical studies of cross-country accounting comparisons have always found that using a common set of standards does not completely solve the comparability problem. For example:

- An extensive international interview study of international investors concluded that:

  Based on our survey, investors who make the effort to understand the firms in a foreign country on their own terms, that is, familiarize themselves with local environmental norms and develop skills in interpreting foreign accounts in their original form, are least likely to encounter problems caused by accounting differences.[a]

- Another comparison of "matched" Japanese and American companies discovered that a common GAAP (US, in this study) didn't solve the problem of comparison between countries:

  Analysts are likely to perceive inaccurately that the financial statements of Japanese companies listing in the United States are directly comparable to those of US companies because they are both based on US GAAP. . . . [R]estated Japanese numbers are easily misinterpreted, as US investors may not fully understand the difference in environmental factors and business practices between the two countries.[b]

  Japanese financial statements, restated according to US GAAP, are more comparable to the financial statements of Japanese companies, using Japanese GAAP, than to the financial statements of US companies.[c]

In other words, it is possible to create uniform accounting standards, but not uniform economic, political, legal, or business environments. Financial reporting is a function of its environment, not just of accounting standards.

a. Frederick D. S. Choi and Richard M. Levich, *The Capital Market Effects of International Accounting Diversity* (1990: Dow Jones-Irwin), p. 82.

b. Don Herrmann, Tatsuo Inuoe, and Wayne B. Bertrand, "Are There Benefits to Restating Japanese Financial Statements According to US GAAP?", *The Journal of Financial Statement Analysis* (Fall 1996), p. 7.

c. *Ibid.*

Private Companies

Private companies have a much smaller and more easily identifiable user group than do public companies. Public companies are reporting to the worldwide community of investors, investors who have no other direct access to information about the company. In contrast, a private company is reporting to a small user group, often only to its bankers. Both banks and private equity investors (if any) have the ability to demand additional information directly from a company if they are not satisfied with the annual financial statements. Since the user group is easily identified and has more specific information needs, there is no need for a private corporation to issue "general purpose" financial statements.

Therefore, nations generally exempt private companies from applying IFRS, or at least from applying the full set of IFRS. In practice, there are five different possible sets of GAAP that a private company might use, depending on its home country:

1. IFRS for small and medium enterprises (SMEs);
2. full IFRS, the same as for public companies;

3. a national GAAP for SMEs or private companies;
4. a code-law requirement to satisfy legal reporting requirements; or
5. a disclosed basis of accounting.

The first category is used by countries that have no well-established standard-setting mechanism, which includes most of the world's smaller nations. The IASB has developed a somewhat simplified version of "IFRS for SMEs" (sometimes nicknamed "IFRS-lite"). IFRS-SME is based on full IFRS, but has less complex reporting requirements.

The second approach, to use full IFRS, is never a *requirement* but may be an appropriate *choice* by large private companies that are competing with public companies for debt or equity financing in the private financial markets. A large private company may fear that its cost of capital will be higher if it reports on a basis different from competing public companies.

Canada falls into the third category—countries that develop their own standards for private enterprises. While these national reporting standards have many similarities to IFRS, they usually are simpler and may provide additional guidance to special industries (e.g., mining) that the IFRS doesn't cover well.[3] We will discuss the Canadian approach to accounting standards for private enterprises (ASPE) more fully in the next section.

The fourth approach, following a country's legally required accounting requirements, may apply to smaller companies that do not need external capital. This choice may also be used for individual companies within a consolidated group to meet local reporting requirements.

The fifth approach applies in countries (such as the United States) that have no mandated reporting requirements for private companies. In these countries many companies may choose not to use IFRS or IFRS-lite, but instead use the fifth option—a **disclosed basis of accounting** (DBA). If there is no imposed set of GAAP for private companies, they can use accounting policies that are "tailored" to their needs, also known as **tailored accounting policies**.

DBA doesn't imply that a company can throw out all of inherited GAAP, but only that it may choose to modify or ignore some parts of GAAP, such as accounting for deferred income taxes or employee retirement benefits. Large private companies need to keep their bankers and private investors happy, so they tend to use accounting that serves the users' needs, perhaps by stressing the transparency of cash flows rather than complex allocations. They may also choose to maintain all accounts on a historical cost basis and ignore fair values.

The point is that when we compare a public company with a private company, the two companies may be using different accounting principles, thereby partially defeating the broader purpose of international standards.

---

3. For example, IFRS deals with agriculture quite extensively, since agriculture looms large in the European consciousness. However, IFRS doesn't deal with gold or diamond mining or oil sands development at all because there aren't a lot of those things going on in Europe.

CONCEPT CHECK 1-4

1. Explain briefly why the effective application of IFRS depends on the quality of professional accountants worldwide.
2. Why is *enforcement* a major factor affecting the credibility of financial statements prepared in different countries, even when all are prepared on the basis of IFRS?
3. The wide acceptance of IFRS around the world is intended to improve comparability between companies based in different countries. Explain briefly which national and institutional factors may affect the *real* comparability as opposed to *apparent* comparability.
4. If a private company is not required to use IFRS by law or by the national standard-setter in its home country, why would that company voluntarily adopt IFRS as its reporting basis?

CANADIAN ACCOUNTING STANDARDS FOR PRIVATE ENTERPRISES

Public companies comprise a very small proportion of business enterprises in Canada. The CICA has estimated that less than 1% of all Canadian corporations are public; the remaining 99% are private. Private companies have a small user group, usually only the owners and managers and sometimes a bank or two. Therefore, Canadian standard-setters decided to permit Canadian private companies to choose either one of two GAAPs:

- full IFRS, just like a public company; or
- Canadian GAAP for non-publicly accountable enterprises, known as Accounting Standards for Private Enterprises (ASPE).

A private company may choose to use full IFRS if it is competing in the non-public capital markets for funds. For example, a large private company will often negotiate with bankers, investment funds, pension funds, and other suppliers of debt and private-equity financing. If a company uses a simplified private-company GAAP, it runs a risk that potential capital providers will assess the risk as higher because it is not using IFRS. Therefore, despite the additional cost of using full IFRS, a private company may elect to do so in hopes of achieving a lower cost of capital.

Accounting Standards for Private Enterprises

In developing accounting standards for private enterprises, the Accounting Standards Board had three choices:

- adopt IFRS-SME, perhaps modified for the Canadian environment;
- modify or simplify the full IFRS; or

- use the pre-2011 Canadian accounting standards and modify those standards to suit private companies.

The AcSB chose the third option. ASPE is largely a continuation of Canadian GAAP prior to 2011, although it has been modified for greater consistency with IFRS.

Why did the AcSB choose that option? There were several reasons:

- Most private companies were already using Canadian accounting standards, with or without the then-existing differential reporting options, and therefore were familiar with their content and application.
- Using a homemade set of standards based on previously existing Canadian standards maintains a consistency of reporting; companies will not have the heavy burden of re-educating their financial statement users (or themselves) about the financial reporting impact of a new set of accounting standards.
- The AcSB can adapt Canadian private enterprise standards to the Canadian economic and business environment much more readily than would be possible with an IFRS-derived set of standards.

It may seem strange to have two different sets of accounting standards. However, this situation already existed to some extent prior to 2011. Canadian standards had, for many years, included *differential reporting standards* that exempted private (i.e., non-publicly-accountable) enterprises from a few standards and from selected requirements of others.

Thus, having a somewhat different set of standards for private companies has been a fact of life for many years. Simultaneously adopting IFRS for publicly accountable enterprises and similar-but-different accounting standards for non-PAE private companies is nothing extraordinary.

How Will I Learn *Two* Sets of Standards?

Throughout this textbook, each chapter will be based on IFRS accounting. At the end of each chapter, when relevant, there will be a section describing how Canadian ASPE differs from IFRS. The differences are always to make the accounting simpler, never more complex. Once you've learned IFRS, you only have to remember those few aspects that don't apply to private companies in Canada. We believe that you will not be confused by the differences.

A SPECIAL NOTE ON FINANCIAL STATEMENT PRESENTATION

In 2008, the IASB issued a discussion paper on financial statement presentation. This paper proposed a new format for financial statements under IFRS. The implementation date is uncertain, but probably won't happen before 2013.

In this book, we continue to use the traditional North American financial statement formats. Learning about consolidations can be difficult enough without also having to cope with a new reporting format. If and when they are adopted, the new formats will change presentation, but they will not affect the process and procedures of consolidation.

You will notice that we use "statement of financial position" (SFP) throughout the text, in conformity with IFRS terminology. This is not compulsory. "Balance sheet" will continue to be a completely acceptable statement title, and probably the most commonly used title in Canada. Indeed, ASPE uses "balance sheet" as its dominant terminology.

Summary of Key Points

1. There are four types of accounting standards in Canada: those for (1) publicly accountable enterprises, (2) private companies, (3) not-for-profit organizations, and (4) governments. The first three are included in different parts of the *CICA Handbook* while governmental reporting standards are issued by the Public Sector Accounting Board.
2. International Financial Reporting Standards (IFRS) are developed by the International Accounting Standards Board (IASB). IFRS is the required basis of accounting for Canada-based companies that have publicly traded securities, and also for private companies that have a fiduciary responsibility, such as investment companies.
3. The application of accounting standards in any reporting enterprise depends on the company's financial reporting objectives; the reporting objectives influence management's selection of accounting policies and affect the many accounting estimates that underlie the amounts reported on the financial statements. IFRS requires a very large number of management estimates.
4. There are two general types of financial reporting objectives: (1) those that are relevant for users such as shareholders, bankers, and employees, and (2) those that reflect motivations of managers.
5. The primary impetus for the development and acceptance of international standards was the emergence of international financial markets, and especially of stock exchanges competing for company listings.
6. IFRS is designed for publicly accountable companies—those that have publicly issued equity and/or debt securities, plus other companies that have a fiduciary responsibility by holding resources belonging to others, such as banks, trust companies, and mutual funds. However, private companies may also use IFRS if they choose, or if their home country requires them to use IFRS or the version of IFRS that is designed specifically for private enterprises.
7. Financial statement quality depends on the quality of the accounting infrastructure in the home country of the reporting company—an adequate supply of trained accountants, quality auditing, and effective enforcement. IFRS increases the importance of a strong accounting infrastructure.
8. Despite the general worldwide acceptance of IFRS, it is very difficult to compare companies across national borders. Nations have significantly differing legal, economic, and political environments, and different ways of doing business. Common standards do not adjust for different reporting environments.

9. Standards for private companies are established by their home country. Some nations may use the SME standards being developed by the IASB, while others may use full IFRS. Some other nations may use their own national standards. The CICA's Accounting Standards Board has developed Canadian accounting standards for private enterprise (ASPE) on the basis of the pre-2011 *CICA Handbook*, modified somewhat to be consistent with IFRS. ASPE is a somewhat simplified version of pre-existing standards, based largely on historical cost, and contains fewer required disclosures than IFRS.

Companion Website

Visit the text's website at www.pearsoned.ca/beechy for practice quizzes, additional problems, Excel® templates, answers to Concept Check questions, and important IFRS updates.

Review Questions

1-1 What distinguishes professional judgment from non-professional judgment?

1-2 Why is it necessary for the accountant to define the objectives of financial reporting for the enterprise for which he or she is preparing financial statements?

1-3 Since most externally reported financial statements are required to be in accordance with IFRS, how can the existence of specific objectives of financial reporting affect the preparation of the statements?

1-4 Explain what is meant by high-quality earnings.

1-5 Explain the difference between user objectives and preparer objectives. Give three examples of each.

1-6 What is a shareholders' agreement?

1-7 What is a covenant? Give four examples.

1-8 How can a manager be both a preparer and a user of financial statements?

1-9 International standards are intended to provide uniformity, and yet some countries may not adopt IFRS in their entirety. Explain why this may happen.

1-10 What are the three components of a nation's accounting infrastructure? How can these components affect the quality of financial reporting in that country?

1-11 You wish to compare the financial statements of three automobile manufacturers, one each in the United States, Germany, and Japan. All use IFRS. What national business environment factors may make comparison difficult? Give at least two examples.

1-12 In Canada, what reporting options are available to non-publicly accountable enterprises? When would each be used?

CASES

CASE 1-1 EASTERN BAY CORP.; HARBINGER LTD.

Helen Hook is president and chief executive officer of Eastern Bay Corp., a large, diversified corporation with its head office in Halifax and its executive offices in Toronto. The corporation controls 27 other corporations in Canada, USA, and Europe. Eastern Bay's common shares are traded on both the Toronto Stock Exchange and the London Stock Exchange. Its preferred shares are held by a group of US life insurance companies that purchased the shares in a private offering several years ago. The same insurance companies hold about half of Eastern Bay's bonds, while the rest are held by pension plans.

Helen's brother, Harvey, is president of Harbinger Ltd., a chain of employment offices operating in western Canada. The company was founded by Harvey Hook in 1981 after he left the personnel services division of a national consulting firm. Harvey owns 67% of the shares of Harbinger. His father, Henry, owns the other 33%. Henry has been an important source of capital for Harvey, lending Harbinger $175,000 at its inception and, in 1986, accepting a 33% ownership interest in lieu of repayment of the debt. Harbinger has no other major creditors, although a line of credit has recently been negotiated with the Royal Bank of Canada.

Required

Explain how the objectives of financial reporting would differ between Eastern Bay Corp. and Harbinger Ltd. Be as specific as possible.

CASE 1-2 CARLISLE CARPET CORPORATION

Carlisle Carpet Corporation (CCC) is a manufacturer of broadloom carpeting, located in Winnipeg, Manitoba. The company enjoys a good reputation for its product, but unfortunately has not been very profitable in recent years owing to increasing imports of cheaper carpeting. To combat this threat, CCC has invested substantial sums of money in new equipment to improve efficiency. Although efficiency picked up as a result, the improvement seemed only to keep the profit picture from getting any worse, rather than to actually increase net income. It is unclear whether CCC will recover its investment in the new equipment and therefore it recorded an impairment of value at the end of the prior fiscal year.

CCC is a private Canadian corporation, with 60% of the shares held by Professors Pension Plan (PPP). The other 40% is held by the original founders of CCC, now retired. Three months ago, PPP sold its 60% interest in CCC to Upper Lip Enterprises Ltd., a publicly owned British carpet manufacturer. Upper Lip planned to integrate CCC into its own operations, so that CCC would both (1) manufacture certain types of carpet sold through Upper Lip's distributors and (2) be the North American distributor of Upper Lip's British-made carpets.

Last week, the financial vice-president of Upper Lip sent a letter to David Blase, the controller of CCC, in which he detailed certain changes in accounting policy that CCC should institute to make its reporting practices consistent with those of Upper Lip, for purposes of consolidation and divisional performance appraisal. Included in the letter were the following:

1. Inventories, both raw materials and finished goods, should be valued on the average-cost basis rather than on the FIFO basis previously used by CCC.
2. Carpeting sold to Upper Lip and its other subsidiaries should be billed at standard cost plus 10%, rather than at full list price less 15%, as is now the case. In effect, the gross margin on the intercompany transfers would be reduced from 35% of cost to 10% of cost. Carpet purchased by CCC from the Upper Lip group of companies would also be invoiced to CCC at cost plus 10%.
3. CCC should restore the equipment write-down before the end of the current fiscal year, since the takeover of CCC by Upper Lip will enhance the value of the equipment.
4. Depreciation on the new equipment should be increased from 8% per year (straight-line) to 12.5% per year. Standard costs would be adjusted to reflect the higher rate.

The financial vice-president, in his letter to David, has asked for a report to specifically identify and describe any problems in implementing the suggested changes in accounting, and provide solutions to any problems that exist.

Required

Assume that you are David Blase. Draft the report for the vice-president on the suggested changes to the accounting policies.

CASE 1-3 RENAUD DEVELOPMENT CORPORATION

Renaud Development Corporation (RDC) is a real estate development company that is 60% owned by Bertrand Renaud. RDC has three shareholders: (1) Bertrand Renaud, a major figure in real property development, owns 60%; (2) Ascher's Inc., a privately owned Canadian department store chain, owns 30%; and (3) the TransCanada Bank owns 10%. RDC engages in two types of development—residential land sites and commercial retail space.

Mr. Renaud has been considering issuing a new class of RDC non-voting common shares to a small group of private investors. The purpose would be to provide a larger equity base so that RDC could be more aggressive in its commercial division. Like all real estate development companies, RDC is very highly leveraged; about 80% of the assets are financed by debt, most of which is provided by or through TransCanada Bank. The issue price of the new shares would be determined on the basis of the net market value equity of the company's properties (that is, the total appraised values minus the company's outstanding debt). Since the company will continue to be private, a shareholders' agreement will govern the company's buyback of the new shares if any investor decides in the future to sell his or her shares. The buyback price of the non-voting shares is to be determined as the original issue price of the shares plus a proportionate share in the increase in the net book value of the common share equity from the date of issue to the date of repurchase, based on the most recent audited financial statements.

The shareholders' agreement places no restrictions on the potential resale price of the voting shares held by Mr. Renaud, Ascher's Inc., and the bank; should any of these shares be sold, they would be sold at their fair market value (which, for real estate developments, is normally based on the present value of future cash flows).

Mr. Renaud is interested in the implications of the proposed non-voting share issue for financial reporting. He is aware that Canada has recently moved to international accounting standards but is uncertain how or if the change will affect RDC. Therefore he has engaged an accounting advisor to offer advice on the most desirable general accounting approach as well as on the most suitable specific accounting policies. A description of the business of the company follows.

RESIDENTIAL DEVELOPMENT

In the residential division, RDC buys large tracts of land near major Canadian cities and holds the land for a few years until the growth of the city makes the land attractive for residential development. The purchase of the land is financed at least 90% by bank loans, and the loans provide for a line of credit to enable the company to borrow from the bank to pay the interest on the loans for up to five years after the land purchase; this holding period is considered by the bank to be the development period. When the time seems right (but usually within five years), RDC develops the land by providing services (e.g., sewer, water, electrical, and telephone mains and connections), laying out roads, and subdividing the land into home sites. The development process takes less than a year.

The sites are then advertised and sold to customers; about 25% of the sales are for cash, but more often they are for a 10–20% down payment with RDC accepting a mortgage for the remainder. The mortgages are usually for a five-year term and a 20-year amortization, bearing interest at a fixed rate that is one or two percentage points below the market rate of mortgage interest (but above the cost of RDC's borrowing). The prices charged to customers for the land vary within an individual tract. Some locations are considered more desirable than others and may therefore carry a price that is as much as double that of the less desirable locations within the same development.

RDC does no residential building; the company only sells the sites. Purchasers must arrange for construction of the houses themselves. Usually, however, RDC enters into an exclusive contract with one (or sometimes two) house builder(s) to construct houses on the sites. The builders erect model homes on the front sites (i.e., on the major access road), and then negotiate individually with the customers for construction of their homes. RDC charges the builders rent for the properties occupied by the model homes. When sales of the sites are complete, RDC sells the property under the model homes to the purchasers of the model homes or to the builder.

RDC has been quite successful in its residential land development business. However, there is one land tract outside of Calgary that it has been unable to sell as quickly as desired. Purchased eight years ago and developed two years ago, only about 30% of the tract has been sold. Defaults by purchasers have been high, and the proceeds from the land sales have not been sufficient to pay the interest on the bank loan; the company has had to use cash from other developments to service the loan.

COMMERCIAL DEVELOPMENT

The commercial division builds and leases retail developments in urban and suburban locations. Sometimes the shopping centres are built on a part of the residential development areas described above, but usually the sites are completely independent of the residential division.

There is little lag between acquisition and development of a retail site, although the project can take up to six years from land assembly to final grand opening. The acquisition and development costs are financed by the bank, although in very large developments the bank will syndicate its participation (that is, bring in other banks to share the cost and the risk). Syndicate members demand audited financial statements from RDC.

RDC's general policy is to hold and operate the properties, although the company will sell if the price is right. Each property usually has an Ascher's store as an "anchor" store (a major retailer that occupies a large space and provides much of the attractiveness of the development to shoppers and thereby to smaller retail lessees). There is a long-term lease agreement between the Ascher's store and RDC that locks the store into the development for at least 30 years. Similar leases bind other major anchor stores, but smaller retailers usually sign five-year leases that are cancellable by either party at the end of the lease term.

The long-term leases are for fixed lease payments, with provision for increases due to inflation and due to increases in operating costs. Shorter-term (e.g., five-year) leases are for a minimum monthly amount plus a percentage of the gross sales of the store. Smaller lessees also pay a large amount, equivalent to 50% of one year's minimum lease payments, at the inception of the lease; this payment is not repeated for lease renewals. RDC's cash flow from the lease payments is used to operate the developments and to service the bank debt that financed them. RDC has not had to pay any income taxes in the commercial division because capital cost allowance on the properties is more than enough to offset lease income. Excess CCA from the commercial division cannot be used to offset profits in the residential division for income tax purposes, however.

Most of the retail developments have been very successful; the insurable value of the properties is, in aggregate, four times the depreciated historical cost of the properties. There are three recently built shopping centres that have not yet reached their full potential but are expected to do so within the next two years. Four other developments were built in recent years in parts of the country that were hit hard by the economic recession in those years and they have never fully recovered; these properties are unable to recover their full operating and carrying costs.

Required

Outline the accounting policies that would seem to best serve the reporting objectives of RDC, assuming that the new share issue is to occur. Your recommendations should include (but not be limited to) recognition of the revenues for each division, treatment of costs (including development costs and interest), and valuation of properties under development and after development. You also should advise Mr. Renaud as to whether RDC should follow international accounting standards from now on.

[ICAO, adapted]

CASE 1-4 SMITH AND STEWART

Smith and Stewart (Stewart) is a partnership of lawyers. It was recently formed from a merger of Becker and Brackman (Becker) and Copp and Copp (Copp). Stewart has 38 partners—including 6 from Becker and 32 from Copp—and 75 employees. At the date of the merger, Stewart purchased land and an office building for $2 million, and fully computerized its offices. The partners have agreed to have the annual financial statements audited even though this was not done in the past.

The partnership agreement requires an annual valuation of the assets and liabilities of the firm. This valuation will be used to determine the amount an existing partner will receive from the partnership when exiting the partnership, and the amount a new partner will pay to enter the partnership.

The partners have been busy getting the new partnership up and running and have paid little attention to accounting policies.

Prior to the merger, Becker recorded revenue when it invoiced the client. Daily time reports were used to keep track of the number of hours worked for each client. This information was not recorded in the accounting system and in general the accounting records were not kept up-to-date.

Copp also recorded revenue at the time the client was invoiced. This was based on partner hours, which were determined based on work in progress and recorded for employees at their regular billing rate, based on the hours worked. At year-end, an adjustment was made to reduce work in progress to reflect the actual costs incurred by Copp.

The new partnership agreement requires a valuation of work in progress at the merger date. This amount, which has yet to be determined, will be recorded as goodwill.

Stewart has arranged a line of credit with a bank that allows the partnership to borrow up to 75% of the carrying value of accounts receivable and 40% of the carrying value of work in progress based on the partnership's monthly financial statements. The bank has also provided mortgage financing of $950,000 for Stewart's land and building. The bank requires unaudited monthly financial statements as well as the annual audited financial statements.

As at the date of the merger, capital assets owned by the predecessor firms were transferred to the new partnership.

Each partner receives a monthly "draw" payment, which is an advance on his or her share of annual profit.

Your auditing firm has been hired by Stewart to prepare a report advising the partnership on accounting policies—identifying alternatives and making specific supported recommendations. A partner in your auditing firm has asked you to prepare the report. In addition, the partner has asked you to prepare a memo detailing the important auditing issues that are likely to arise and how they could be resolved.

Required

Prepare the requested report and the memo.

[CICA, adapted]

CASE 1-5 W&K GARDENS

Lindsay Kay approached her friend Michael Wait about going into business together as co-owners of a gardening centre. Lindsay loved gardening and had some skills as an accountant. Michael was a landscape architect. Lindsay and Michael agreed to become business partners and open a new garden centre to be called W&K Gardens (W&K). There were only two existing nurseries in the local area, and Lindsay and Michael felt that there would be sufficient customer demand from continued residential expansion to support another gardening centre.

The pair decided that Lindsay would assume responsibility for the accounting and Michael would complete gardening layouts for customers. In addition, Michael would design a website where customers could order plants for pickup or delivery, and on which Lindsay could eventually provide online gardening tips and advice. Michael suggested that they initially pay a flat fee to an Internet service provider for hosting their website. Michael would register their Internet domain name, develop the webpage, and create the initial graphics.

They developed a business plan for the gardening centre and Lindsay applied for a loan from the provincial Ministry of Agriculture and Education, which was offering forgivable loans for up to $500,000 to promote small businesses in the province. Lindsay and Michael soon received a letter from the provincial government that started with the words, "Congratulations—you have met all the criteria to receive a forgivable loan of $500,000." (Further details on the loan are provided in Exhibit A.)

Although there were many details to work out, they felt that they could be open for business by the first week of June. They already had start-up funds from the forgivable loan, and a business plan. Michael knew of a large plot of land (20 hectares) with a small but suitable building in a nearby location that was available for lease. Lindsay and Michael reviewed the terms of the lease (Exhibit B) received from a real estate agent and agreed that although the payments were considerable, the location would be well worth it and they would have plenty of space to carry a full assortment of annuals, perennials, shrubs, trees, and garden accessories. They were willing to pay a higher fee for the ability to expand in the future. Lindsay's notes concerning the inventory of plants and care that would be needed are included in Exhibit C.

The old building would have to be renovated before it could be used as a storefront and they agreed to hire someone to complete the necessary work on time. They estimated the cost of the renovation to be about $125,000 but realized that they would have to meet with a contractor to get a formal estimate for the work to be done.

Lindsay also noted that they would need an operating loan for approximately $100,000 in addition to the government loan. Lindsay arranged to meet with her bank manager as soon as possible. With her business plan in hand, she was going to approach the bank for additional financing for the initial costs and purchase of inventory. Lindsay's personal borrowing rate was currently 11%. However, she had been advised that the new business would be able to borrow at 2% below this rate, assuming that W&K would be able to maintain an adequate amount of assets to cover liabilities by the second year of operation. Lindsay now began to gather the details needed to finalize the business plan for the bank.

Michael determined that they would have to purchase a small truck and some equipment to carry out the landscape design service. Since he had been in charge of purchasing at Green Thumb Landscapers, he had a good idea of the type and cost of this equipment (Exhibit D).

To provide income during the off-season, Michael suggested they submit a bid for a tender that he had seen advertised in the paper. The town was accepting bids for snow removal from municipal parking lots and storage of snow from street removal. Last year, the town had had difficulty finding contractors for the snow removal since it was a small job. The town also needed space to "store" the removed snow and, with this new location, Michael and Lindsay would certainly have the capability to store snow. Michael was concerned, though, that the snow would contain chemical contaminants acquired from the town's roads. Michael believed that they could win the snow removal contract for a flat fee of $30,000 and an additional flat fee of $50,000 for storage of snow for one "snow season."

Michael suggested that they should discuss the details of the business partnership at a meeting the following morning to avoid future disputes. They had already agreed that Michael would contribute his personally owned landscaping equipment (fair value $18,000), a small used truck (fair value $12,000) and cash of $5,000. Lindsay would contribute computer equipment (fair value $8,500), office furniture (fair value $6,500) and cash of $20,000. Each partner would receive an equal interest in both capital and income. Michael also stated that he wanted Lindsay's opinion on the appropriate accounting policies that should be selected so he could anticipate earnings. He also wanted an outline of any matters related to the set-up of the business and Lindsay's opinion about whether a partnership would be the best structure for their business.

Required

Assume the role of Lindsay Kay. Prepare notes to summarize your analysis in preparation for a meeting between Lindsay and Michael.

Exhibit A Forgivable Loan from Ministry of Agriculture and Education

Clause 1: Lindsay Kay will receive a forgivable loan of $500,000 for the development and operation of W&K Gardens as described in the attached business plan.

Clause 2: The government will provide $500,000 on May 20, 20X6, which is forgivable on May 20, 20X11, if the following conditions are met:

- three university students are hired for the period June 1 to August 31 each year;
- all produce is grown on-site or purchased from local growers; and
- audited financial statements are provided to the government three months after year-end.

Clause 3: If any of the above terms is not met, the loan is repayable with interest of 10% by the end of the fiscal year in which the term is broken.

Clause 4: The government has the right to inspect the premises and financial records to ensure that all conditions of the loan have been met at any time.

Exhibit B Terms of the Lease

Addison Ltd. agrees to rent to W&K the land site and building that it requires in starting up its new business. The lease agreement calls for five annual lease payments of $300,000 (including executory costs of $19,506) at the beginning of each year; the details surrounding the agreement are as follows:

Commissions and legal fees (incurred by Addison)	$60,000
Building:	
Addison's carrying value of building	$340,000
Fair value of the building	$400,000
Economic life of building	6 years
Guaranteed residual value at end of lease term	$75,000
Land:	
Addison's carrying value of land	$375,000
Fair value of the land	$1,000,000
Residual value at end of lease term	$1,000,000
Rate implicit in the lease (known by W&K)	10%

Addison contacted its building contractor, who promised to have the renovations completed on time at a price very close to the estimated amount of $125,000. The renovation work would have a useful life of approximately eight years.

Addison stated that the lease will be non-cancellable but is willing to provide an option to renew the lease at the end of the five-year term.

Exhibit C **Inventory Requirements**

W&K would be open for business all year but the amount and type of inventory would fluctuate depending on the time of the year. The garden centre would consist of a greenhouse, outdoor tents, a store, and a small outdoor nursery. The storefront would be open year-round and would sell fertilizers, planters, garden tools, and accessories. Gift baskets would be brought in for special occasions such as Mother's Day, Halloween, Thanksgiving, and Christmas.

To attract customers to the store, Michael would provide customized landscape designs for a flat fee of $500. The customer would then receive a credit for the same amount at the store. The credit would have no cash value, but could be used for the purchase of shrubs, flowers, etc., at the store over the next two years.

Annual plants (such as geraniums, petunias, and many more varieties) would be purchased from local growing farms each spring. These plants would all have to be sold before the end of summer. Perennial plants (including bellflowers, day lilies, and hostas) would be grown in W&K's greenhouse and transferred to the outdoor store protected by large tents. Those plants not sold by September 30 would be returned to the greenhouse for winter storage and care. It was expected that most perennial plants would be sold, especially if Lindsay discounted the price to encourage customers to buy and plant in the fall instead of waiting for the following spring.

Shrubs and trees would be purchased from local nurseries early in the spring. It was expected that about 80% of these purchases would be sold during the growing season. The remaining 20% would be transferred to the outdoor nursery to be replanted and would remain there until the next season. To be competitive with the other two garden centres, Lindsay thought that they should offer a one-year warranty on all shrubs and trees returned by customers with a valid sales receipt.

The outdoor nursery would be used primarily for Christmas trees, which would be grown from seedling stock and could remain in the ground for a number of years. In the initial years, mature trees would be bought from a local supplier.

Exhibit D **Capital Asset Requirements**

Michael estimated that the following capital assets would be required for the first year of operations. Part of the government loan would be used to purchase these items.

Three small used trucks (in addition to the one contributed by Michael)	$40,000
Landscaping equipment (backhoe, rototiller, etc.)	$60,000
Small power tools	$15,000
Display shelves for the store	$12,000

[ICAO, adapted]

CASE 1-6 **MILTONICS POTIONS LTD.**

Miltonics Potions Ltd. (MPL) is a privately held Ontario corporation engaged in the development and marketing of patent medicines. In early 20X1 the company's research chemists began working on a project to develop a patent remedy for colitis (a disease that causes inflammation of the bowel). During the year, $200,000 was spent in research on this project without developing a useful product.

Work continued in 20X2, with an additional $100,000 being spent. By the end of 20X2, an apparently feasible product had been developed and was being considered by MPL's top management for further development and exploitation. On February 14, 20X3 (prior to completion and issuance of the 20X2 financial statements), the managers reached the decision to proceed with further development, production, and marketing of the product, barring adverse medical results (i.e., unacceptable side effects) from tests then underway. Such adverse results were possible, but were considered unlikely since nothing untoward had occurred to date in the testing program.

During 20X3, the product was refined and the mass production formulation was developed (at a cost of $150,000). Production facilities were prepared (at a cost of $300,000), and patent number 381–1003-86 was obtained on the product. Legal expenses totalled $32,000.

In early 20X4, production and distribution began. Sales in the first year were modest, totalling only $450,000. However, $500,000 was spent on promotion, mainly in print media advertising and in sending free samples to doctors and clinics. Only in 20X5 did the sales reach forecast levels, thereby indicating that MPL had a successful product.

However, the success of the product spawned an imitator and, in 20X5, MPL sued a competitor for patent infringement. MPL demanded that the competitor cease production and marketing of the competing product and requested $2,000,000 in damages. Legal costs of $50,000 were incurred in this action in 20X5; the case was still pending at the end of the year.

In July 20X6, after MPL had spent an additional $20,000 in legal fees, the case was dismissed in court, thereby rendering MPL's patent indefensible. Since the competitor was a well-known pharmaceutical firm, MPL's sales suffered considerably from the competition.

Required

a) On a year-by-year basis, describe the alternative accounting methods that MPL could use for the costs incurred in developing, patenting, and defending the new product. Do not use hindsight in arriving at your alternatives.

b) Explain what additional information you would need and what criteria you would use to make a decision on the alternative to adopt for each year.

2

Intercorporate Equity Investments: An Introduction

LEARNING OBJECTIVES

After studying this chapter, students should be able to:

1. explain the difference between passive equity investments and strategic investments;
2. identify the proper accounting treatment for investments in controlled entities, associates, and joint ventures;
3. understand the relationship between consolidation and equity reporting;
4. describe the basic principles of consolidation; and
5. apply both the direct and worksheet methods of consolidation in simple situations.

INTRODUCTION

Onex Corporation is a diversified Canadian company that operates through a wide variety of operating companies that Onex controls or can significantly influence. Onex has significant investments in 18 different companies, including Celestica (an Ontario-based global electronic systems company) and Cineplex Entertainment (Canada's dominant movie exhibitor).

The objective of financial reporting is to show the assets and liabilities that are under the control of the shareholders of a corporation. When a reporting entity such as Onex owns shares in other companies, the reporting entity may control not only the assets it legally owns, but also the assets that are owned by other companies in the group. How can financial statements reflect this economic reality underlying intercorporate share ownership? That is the main focus of this text.

CLASSIFICATION OF INTERCORPORATE INVESTMENTS

An **intercorporate investment** is any purchase by one corporation of the securities of another corporation. Broadly speaking, the investment may be either in debt securities or in equity securities—preferred or common shares. You have already studied investments in debt securities in your intermediate accounting courses. Therefore, our focus in this text is on equity investments.

A corporation may invest in the equity of other corporations for two reasons—passive and strategic:

1. A **passive investment** is an investment in another company's shares to earn dividends or to earn profits by actively trading the shares for short-term profit.
2. A **strategic investment** is one that the investor makes to be able to *control* or *significantly influence* the operations of the investee corporation.

Passive Investments

Accounting for passive investments poses no particular problems. They are initially recorded at cost and are reported at fair market value on each period's statement of financial position (SFP).

The treatment of gains and losses depends on how the company has elected to classify the investment—a choice that the reporting entity makes for each separate passive equity investment when the investment is first made. The choices available under IFRS 9, *Financial Instruments*, are to report the investment at either:

1. fair value through profit or loss (FVTPL),[1] or
2. fair value through other comprehensive income (FVTOCI).

If an equity investment is classified as "fair value through profit and loss" (FVTPL), both (1) dividends and (2) the change in fair value from one period to another are reported in the net income section of the statement of comprehensive income (SCI).

If, on the other hand, an equity investment is classified as "fair value through other comprehensive income" (FVTOCI), (1) dividends from that investment are recognized in net income but (2) changes in the fair value of the investment are reported as *other comprehensive income* (OCI); the accumulated gains and losses are reported as a separate component of shareholders' equity. The choice to classify an equity investment as "fair value through other comprehensive income" is irrevocable—the classification cannot be changed subsequently.

The fair value gains and losses of FVTOCI investments can never be transferred from their separate component of equity to net income. However, the company can move the accumulated gains and losses *within* shareholders' equity. That means that the company can transfer the gains and losses directly to retained earnings at any time, *but not via the profit and loss section of the statement of comprehensive income*.

Strategic Investments

Strategic investments provide strategic or a long-term advantage by giving the investor the ability to either significantly influence or control the operating or financing decisions of the

1. The term "held for trading" was used previously under IFRS to refer to fair value through profit or loss (FVTPL) investments. IFRS 9 becomes mandatory in 2013 but permits early adoption. Many Canadian public companies early-adopted IFRS 9, thereby avoiding the necessity of restating prior years' financial statements. Also, we don't describe the pre-2013 approach because our focus here is on strategic investments.

investee. Strategic equity investments can take several different forms depending on the investor's strategic objectives:

- Controlled entities:
  - Subsidiaries
  - Special purpose entities
- Associated companies
- Joint ventures

Generally, investments are considered strategic if a company owns either directly or indirectly 20% or more of the voting shares of the investee, unless it can clearly be demonstrated that the investments are passive.

Debt instruments can also be used strategically by giving the investor leverage over the investee corporation, especially in start-up or developing investee corporations. In those cases, the investor can provide capital to the investee while still gaining the greater security that comes with being a creditor rather than a shareholder. Although the investor may use debt instruments as an effective strategic tool, the investment in debt itself is not accounted for as a strategic investment, but instead is accounted for at amortized cost as an investment in debt securities being held to maturity.

In the following sections, we will explain these various types of strategic equity investments and the appropriate method of accounting for each. Along the way, we also will discuss the two basic concepts that underlie accounting for strategic investments—(1) control and (2) significant influence.

CONCEPT CHECK 2-1

Companion Website

1. Why are the two categories of *passive* and *strategic* used to classify equity investments?
2. What are the major types of strategic investments?

CONTROLLED ENTITIES

According to IAS 27, *Consolidated and Separate Financial Statements*, **control** exists when one entity has *the power to direct the financing and operating activities of another entity to derive benefits from that entity*. Both the power to direct the activities of the other entity and the benefits derived from that entity must be considered when determining whether or not control exists. Further, notice that the definition cites the *power* to control and does not require that the controlling entity actively use that power. Often, the controlling entity is quite happy to let the controlled entity continue to manage its own affairs without direct interference by the parent.

There are many aspects of control that accountants must be aware of. We'll give a broad view first, and then return later to examine some of the nuances of the concept of *control*.

REALITY CHECK 2-1

Porsche SE Group

Porsche SE obtained control of Volkswagen AG on January 5, 2009, by securing 50.76% of Volkswagen's ordinary shares. The 2008–2009 annual report of Porsche SE shows the consolidated financial results under IFRS of the Porsche SE group, which comprises 84 companies in Germany and 353 companies internationally. Many of the companies are marketing subsidiaries in the countries in which the group sells its products. Others are engineering and R&D, financial services, or manufacturing companies. The manufacturing subsidiaries include those devoted to individual products or product lines, such as Porsche, Volkswagen, Audi, Bentley, Bugatti, Lamborghini, and Skoda cars.

Source: Porsche SE, *Annual Report 2008/09*, http://www.porsche-se.com/filestore.aspx/default.pdf?pool=pho&type=download&id=anualreport0809-complete&lang=en&filetype=default&version=2.

Subsidiaries

By far, the most common type of controlled entity is a *subsidiary*. A **subsidiary** is a corporation (or a partnership) that is controlled by a **parent** company that owns, usually, a majority of the voting shares/rights of the subsidiary. Since shareholders elect a corporation's board of directors, holding most of the shares enables the parent company to control the composition of the subsidiary's board. Since the board determines a corporation's strategic, operating, and financing policies, the parent corporation can control those policies through its power to elect the subsidiary's board.

Virtually all business corporations operate through a structure that consists of a parent company and many subsidiary corporations, the vast majority of which were formed by the parent company to carry out part of its business operations. A parent corporation will establish subsidiaries for three principal reasons:

1. To isolate risk; if one subsidiary fails, it does not jeopardize the overall corporate structure and functioning.
2. To develop different management teams for essentially different functions or types of business, such as manufacturing vs. sales.
3. To comply with local legal requirements, including tax compliance.

To the public the most "famous" subsidiaries are those that are the result of one corporation buying another, known as a *business combination*. Business combinations often get lots of public attention, and yet their number is really quite small when compared with the vast numbers of parent-founded subsidiaries. Onex Corporation, mentioned in the first paragraph of this chapter, is an example of a company specializing in buying other companies; Onex is known as a *turn-around company*, whose specialty is buying faltering companies and restoring them to health.

Although business combinations are a relatively minor source of subsidiaries, they bring with them many accounting issues that will be explained in the following chapters.

Special Purpose Entities

A second type of controlled enterprise is a *special purpose entity*, also known as a *variable interest entity* or a *structured entity*.[2] In an interpretation, SIC 12 *Consolidation—Special Purpose Entities*, the IASB provides guidance on when a **special purpose entity (SPE)** should be consolidated. An SPE is set up by the reporting enterprise (or "sponsor") to perform a very specific and narrow function. The difference between a subsidiary and an SPE is that an SPE is not controlled through voting power. Indeed, an SPE may not even be a corporation but could instead be a partnership or simply a delegation of powers to certain individuals to act on behalf of the "sponsoring" corporation.

Three examples of SPEs are:

- A corporation (the "sponsor") may set up an SPE to buy assets (e.g., buildings, equipment) on behalf of the sponsor. The SPE will arrange the purchase financing and then collect rent from the sponsor for use of the assets (and thereby pay down the debt). This arrangement often is intended to keep both the assets and the related debt financing off the books of the sponsor, thereby achieving off-balance-sheet financing.
- The controlling shareholders of a corporation may form a separate "lending agency" to provide secured loans to the corporation. The shareholders give their own money to the SPE, which in turn lends it to the corporation. Effectively, the shareholders are contributing additional capital to the corporation, but instead of bearing risk, they are entitled to receive interest and loan repayments. If the corporation goes bankrupt, the shareholders get first claim on the assets (over other creditors) because they are secured.
- A not-for-profit organization that is engaged in active public fund-raising efforts may set up a separate not-for-profit SPE, usually called a "foundation." Major donations may be channelled into the foundation instead of into the main organization so that the main organization can claim to be under-funded.

All of these three examples have been used extensively by organizations that aren't very attentive to ethical financial reporting standards.

On the other hand, there are uses for SPEs that don't attempt to mislead anyone. For example, a separate corporation (i.e., an SPE) may be established to *securitize* a company's receivables. **Securitization** is the process of transferring receivables into an SPE and then issuing securities to private or public investors as a means of financing those receivables. That is, the company sells the receivables to an SPE, and the SPE gets the money (or the vast majority of the money) to pay for the receivables by selling bonds or similar financial instruments to other investors.

SPEs are not usually controlled through shareholdings. Instead, control is exercised by other means, such as through interlocking management. The crucial question in deciding on *control* is "who benefits most"? If the activities of an SPE are for the primary benefit of the sponsoring corporation, whether financial, operational, or for financial reporting chicanery,

2. Terminology is inconsistent. SPE is the commonly used term and is used in SIC 12. *Variable interest entity* is the phrase used by the FASB and in pre-2011 Canadian standards. *Structured entity* is the term favoured by the IASB in Exposure Draft 10, *Consolidated Financial Statements*.

REALITY CHECK 2-2

Use of SPEs by Porsche SE

Porsche SE makes use of SPEs for refinancing its financial services business. The company consolidates such SPEs in its consolidated financial statements. The company's 2008–2009 annual report states:

> Asset backed securities transactions accomplished via special purpose entities to refinance the financial services business are included in the bonds, commercial paper and notes, loan liabilities and other financial obligation with an amount of €13,561 million.

Source: Porsche SE, Note 29, Non-current and current financial liabilities to the consolidated balance sheet, *Annual Report 2008/09*, p. 208, http://www.porsche-se.com/filestore.aspx/default.pdf?pool= pho&type=download&id=anualreport0809-complete&lang=en&filetype=default&version=2.

then the SPE must be *consolidated* in the same manner as a subsidiary. This relatively recent requirement in accounting standards clearly tends to undercut the unethical use of SPEs to manipulate a company's financial statements.

Accounting for Controlled Entities

IAS 27 requires a parent to present consolidated financial statements in which it consolidates all its subsidiaries. SIC 12 requires an SPE to be consolidated when an entity "in substance" controls that SPE. SIC 12 provides guidance on deciding when such "in substance" control exists.

Under both IFRS and US standards, a corporation's publicly issued financial statements *must* be **consolidated**—all entities controlled by the reporting entity, including subsidiaries and controlled SPEs, must be included in the consolidated statements. With consolidated statements, all of the assets and all of the liabilities are reported as a single *economic* entity, as though the combined companies were a single legal entity.

PROPOSED CHANGE

The IASB has circulated an exposure draft, ED 10, Consolidated Financial Statements, in which it has proposed the following common definition of control applicable to both subsidiaries and SPEs:

> A reporting entity controls another entity when the reporting entity has the power to direct the activities of that other entity to generate returns for the reporting entity.

The IASB is planning to issue the final standard by 2011.

Source: ED 10, Consolidated Financial Statements, http://www.iasb.org/NR/rdonlyres/DAEA5425-4ABE-4217-8429-DB395333E8CC/0/ED10_STANDARD_1208.pdf.

In many other countries, the parent company is permitted (or required) to issue its own separate-entity, unconsolidated statements. If you look at the financial statements of a European company, be sure to find out whether you're looking at the consolidated statements or just at the parent company's separate-entity statements.

Consolidated financial statements are designed to report on the **economic entity** formed by the parent and all of its subsidiaries (and controlled SPEs). There is no legal entity that corresponds with a consolidated economic entity, and therefore consolidated statements are sometimes referred to as an *accounting fiction*. "Fiction" is not derogatory—it merely is intended to convey the fact that the statements do not portray a "real" company but instead comprise many separate legal entities. Financial statement readers should be aware of this fact.

Understanding this accounting fiction is important for anyone who is lending money to (or doing business with) a parent company based on its consolidated statements. Lending agreements are with individual legal entities; the parent corporation may control its subsidiaries, but most of the assets on the consolidated statements are out of reach of the parent company's creditors because they don't legally belong to the parent company.

CONCEPT CHECK 2-2

Companion Website

1. What two factors determine the existence of control of subsidiaries?
2. What are the two major types of controlled entities?
3. How do publicly accountable entities commonly report entities controlled by them?
4. Why are SPEs required to be consolidated?

ASSOCIATES

IAS 28, *Investments in Associates*, defines **associates** as companies (investees) over whom the investor has the ability to exert *significant influence* but not the ability to exert control either solely or jointly with other entities. **Significant influence** is the ability to *participate* in the operating and financial policy decisions of the investee without being able to control them.

Significant Influence

A holding, either directly or indirectly through subsidiaries, of 20% or more of the voting shares of another entity is taken as evidence that significant influence exists, unless evidence exists to prove otherwise. Likewise, a holding of less than 20% of the voting shares is indicative of lack of significant influence unless evidence exists to prove otherwise. However, the 20% threshold should not be given undue weight. A shareholding of 35% may not provide significant influence to an investor if it is prevented from exercising influence by another shareholder holding the remaining 65%. Conversely, the existence of another shareholder holding the majority of the shares of the investee may not preclude significant influence from

REALITY CHECK 2-3

Onex Corporation

Onex Corporation has substantial investments in 18 operating companies. Of the 18, 13 are controlled through voting share ownership and are consolidated. The other five are as follows:

Investee corporation	Onex ownership share
Cineplex Entertainment	23%
Res-Care, Inc.	6%
Allison Transmission, Inc.	15%
Hawker Beechcraft Corporation	20%
RSI Home Products, Inc.	20%

Two of the five investments are below the normal 20% threshold, but the company states that "Onex exerts significant influence over these . . . investments through its right to appoint members to the Board of Directors (or Board of Trustees)."

Source: Onex Corporation annual financial statements, posted on SEDAR, February 26, 2009.

existing. The following additional evidence should be considered for deciding whether or not significant evidence exists:

- representation on the board of directors or other equivalent governing body of the investee;
- participation in the policy-making process of the investee;
- material transactions between the investor and the investee;
- interchange of managerial personnel between the investor and investee; or
- provision of essential technical information by the investor to the investee.

Additionally, potential voting rights are a factor to be considered in deciding whether significant influence exists.

Reporting Method

Significant influence gives the investor the power to play a major role in the investee's earnings process. Since the investor is a participant in the investee's earnings process, under IAS 28, the investor's proportionate share of the investee's earnings should be reported in the investor's SCI. This is known as the **equity method of reporting**. Under the equity method, the investor doesn't report dividends as income. Instead, the investor calculates its share of the associate's net income (or loss), and then adds that amount to the investment account and includes it in determining the investor's net income.

For example, assume that Helmut Corporation owns 25% of Aaron Ltd. Helmut's 25% share of Aaron's $400,000 in earnings is $100,000. At the end of the reporting period, Helmut will record the earnings as follows:

Investment in Aaron (SFP)	100,000	
Helmut share of earnings of Aaron (SCI, net income section)		100,000

If Aaron declares dividends of $60,000, Helmut will record its 25% share as a reduction in the investment account:

Dividends receivable (SFP)	15,000	
Investment in Aaron (SFP)		15,000

The receipt of dividends has no effect on Helmut's net income because Aaron's earnings have already been recognized in Helmut's accounts.

As you will see later, Helmut's share is not necessarily the same as Aaron's net income × 25%; there are usually some adjustments that must be made first. The equity method is illustrated further below.

CONCEPT CHECK 2-3

Companion Website

1. Why is a 20% or more shareholding in an entity insufficient by itself to determine whether or not significant influence exists?
2. Why are investments in associates reported under the equity method?

JOINT VENTURES

A **joint venture** is defined in IAS 31, *Interests in Joint Ventures*, as an agreement between two or more entities to enter into business together by, usually, creating a new venture (corporation or partnership) under *joint control*. Joint ventures are common in certain industries (such as resource exploration); they are common in global competition when two otherwise competing companies join forces to establish operations in another country or when one company joins with the host country's government in establishing a new venture.

The **joint venture agreement** specifies each co-venturer's capital contribution, representation on the board of directors, and involvement in management, plus other relevant matters. An essential and distinguishing characteristic of a joint venture is that no one investor can make major strategic decisions unilaterally; major decisions require the consent of all of the co-venturers. This is known as **joint control**.

Usually joint ventures are carried on as separate private corporations. The joint venture agreement is similar to the shareholders' agreement in private corporations that clarifies the rights and responsibilities of the various shareholders. The difference is that, in private corporations, a single shareholder or a small group may exercise control. In a joint venture no one investor (or subgroup of investors) can control the joint venture even though that investor may contribute a majority of the capital or hold the majority of shares. Joint ventures require agreement among the co-venturers, not voting power.

Joint control should not be confused with profit sharing. Control is joint, but profit sharing is not necessarily equal. The joint venture agreement stipulates how the risks and benefits of the venture will be shared, including the distribution of profits and dividends.

Reporting Methods

Joint ventures can be reporting using either of two methods:

- equity method;
- proportionate consolidation.

The equity method has been discussed above, for associates. For joint ventures, it is applied in essentially the same manner.

In **proportionate consolidation**, only the investor's proportionate share of the joint venture assets, liabilities, revenues, and expenses is added to the investee's consolidated financial statements. If the investor has a 30% share in a joint venture, then only 30% of the joint venture's financial statement amounts are consolidated in the parent's statements. The investment in joint venture account on the SFP is eliminated. The adjustments required to the earnings of the joint venture under the proportionate consolidation method are identical to the consolidation adjustments required under consolidation.

PROPOSED CHANGE

Since the joint venturer is entitled only to the outcome from the joint venture and not to the assets and liabilities of the joint venture, the IASB has proposed that joint ventures should be reported only under the equity method. However, the Board is experiencing some opposition to the elimination of proportionate consolidation. The latest news on the IASB website indicates that the board is planning to issue the final standard sometime in the third quarter of 2010. The effective date of the proposed standard has not yet been decided. Until explicitly prohibited, proportionate consolidation remains an acceptable alternative.

CONCEPT CHECK 2-4

Companion Website

1. What differentiates an investment in a *joint venture* from investments in (1) an *associate* and (2) a *subsidiary*, respectively?
2. Why does the IASB feel that the equity method, compared to the proportionate consolidation method, is a better method for reporting an investment in a joint venture?

SUMMARY OF REPORTING METHODS

Exhibit 2-1 summarizes the reporting methods for intercorporate strategic investments for publicly issued statements. In the following sections, we will illustrate both consolidation and equity reporting.

EXHIBIT 2-1

Accounting for Strategic Intercorporate Investments

Investment Type	Publicly Accountable Enterprises				Private Enterprises
	Method of Accounting	SFP	Impact on Net Income	OCI	
Subsidiaries & controlled SPEs	Consolidation	Investment account replaced by assets & liabilities of investee	Revenue and expense items of investee added to investor's revenue and expense items on SCI adjusted for amortizations and intercompany unrealized profits	OCI items of investee added to OCI of investor	In addition to consolidation can use either the cost or equity method; same method should be used for all subsidiaries
Significantly influenced associate companies	Equity method	Initial cost plus adjusted cumulative unremitted earnings	Share of investee's earnings adjusted for amortizations and intercompany unrealized profits Realized gains/ losses on sale (fair value – carrying value)	NA	Equity method not required; can use the cost method; same method should be used for all investments
Joint ventures	Equity method or proportionate consolidation	Same as above for each method	Same as above for each method	Same as above for each method	Proportionate consolidation, cost, or equity method; same method should be used for all joint ventures

As we review consolidation, it is crucial to understand that *reporting* is not the same as *recording*. Consolidated amounts *never appear on the parent company's books*—reported numbers are the result of spreadsheet analysis, either computer-based or manual.

Similarly, investments *reported* on the equity basis are usually *recorded* on the cost basis on the investor's books. The adjustments to determine the equity-basis investment amount for the SFP are normally made on the accountant's working papers but are not necessarily recorded on the parent's books. To convert the cost-basis investment account to the equity basis requires a simple adjusting entry at the end of each year (or quarter).

ILLUSTRATION OF CONSOLIDATION

Consolidated statements are prepared from the point of view of the shareholders of the parent company. Consolidation adds the elements in the financial statements of subsidiaries to those of the parent. On the SFP there will be no investment account for the consolidated subsidiaries. Instead, the assets and liabilities of the subsidiaries will be added to those of the parent to show the economic resources of the entire economic entity. On the SCI, the revenues and expenses will be the totals for each item for the parent plus the subsidiaries. The effects of any intercompany transactions will be eliminated to avoid double-counting.

Eliminations and Adjustments

To prepare its consolidated financial statements, a parent will add together the financial statement amounts for itself and its subsidiaries. In the process, however, some changes to the pre-consolidation reported balances must be made. There are two types of changes that are made when statements are consolidated: (1) *eliminations* and (2) *adjustments*:

- **Eliminations** are changes that prevent certain amounts on the separate-entity statements from appearing on the consolidated statements. Eliminations are necessary to avoid double-counting (such as intercompany sales) and to cancel out offsetting balances (such as intercompany receivables and payables).
- **Adjustments**, on the other hand, are made to alter reported amounts to reflect the economic substance of transactions rather than their nominal amount.

Direct Versus Worksheet Approach to Consolidation

Direct Approach There are two general approaches to preparing consolidated financial statements, the *direct approach* and the *worksheet approach*. The **direct approach** prepares the consolidated statements by setting up the SCI and SFP formats and computing each consolidated balance directly. Each asset, liability, revenue, and expense is separately calculated and entered into the consolidated statement. The direct approach works from the separate-entity financial statements of the parent and the subsidiary.

Worksheet Approach The alternative method is the **worksheet approach**. The worksheet (or spreadsheet) approach uses a multi-columnar worksheet to enter the trial balances of the parent and each subsidiary. Then eliminations and adjustments are entered onto the worksheet, and the accounts are cross-added to determine the consolidated balances. The finished consolidated statements are then prepared from the consolidated trial balance.

Which Approach to Use? The direct approach is intuitively appealing because we are working directly with the statements and can see clearly what is happening to the consolidated statements as we make eliminations and adjustments. When the statements to be consolidated are fairly simple, it is quite feasible to compile the consolidated statements by the direct method.

In more complex situations, it becomes difficult to keep track of the many adjustments, with the frustrating result that the financial statements won't balance!

The worksheet approach is less intuitive, but is more methodical and keeps better track of the eliminations and adjustments, some of which get very complicated. In complex situations, therefore, accountants in practice find it easier to use a worksheet (usually computerized) to summarize the necessary eliminations and adjustments. The worksheet also provides the management trail (or audit trail) that explains how the consolidated statements were derived.

In this chapter we will illustrate both approaches. The direct approach will be presented first and the worksheet approach second. Both approaches yield the same result. It doesn't matter which approach is used—what is important is the result, not the method used to derive the result. In later chapters of the text, however, we will only use the direct approach. The worksheet approach becomes unwieldy to illustrate in the text when more complicated problems are involved (even though it helps keep better track of the various adjustments and eliminations). Therefore, illustrations for later chapters using the worksheet approach will be available only online on the Companion Website for this text at www.pearsoned.ca/beechy.

Companion Website

CONSOLIDATION: COST METHOD RECORDING

Consolidating a Parent-Founded Subsidiary—Simple Example

The condensed SFP of a parent before setting up its subsidiary is shown below:

Parent Statement of Financial Position
December 31, 20X9

Assets	
Cash	$10,000
TOTAL ASSETS	$10,000
Liabilities and shareholders' equity	
Share capital	$ 5,000
Retained earnings	5,000
TOTAL LIABILITIES AND SHAREHOLDERS' EQUITY	$10,000

New Subsidiary Founded Assume that the parent founded a subsidiary by investing $1,000. The separate statements of financial position for each company are provided below. Notice that we introduced an "investment in subsidiary" account for $1,000 in the parent's SFP and a counterbalancing share capital account for $1,000 in the subsidiary's SFP. From the parent's point of view, no new owner's equity was created by the formation of the subsidiary. All that happened is that one asset (cash) decreased by $1,000 while another account, investment in subsidiary, increased by the same amount of $1,000. Its total equity continued to be $10,000.

Separate Statements of Financial Position
December 31, 20X9

	Parent	Subsidiary
Assets		
Cash	$ 9,000	$1,000
Investment in subsidiary	**1,000**	—
TOTAL ASSETS	$10,000	$1,000
Liabilities and shareholders' equity		
Share capital	$ 5,000	**$1,000**
Retained earnings	5,000	—
TOTAL LIABILITIES AND SHAREHOLDERS' EQUITY	$10,000	$1,000

Direct Approach—Consolidation Immediately After Founding the Subsidiary

Both the investment in subsidiary account of $1,000 in the parent's SFP and the share capital account of $1,000 in the subsidiary's SFP are eliminated. From the consolidated perspective one asset, cash, went up $1,000 while another asset, investment in subsidiary, went down by $1,000. *The subsidiary's share capital is not added to the parent's share capital since it is already reflected in the parent's total equity of $10,000.* If we consolidate the subsidiary immediately after its creation, with the parent, we should get back the original SFP of the parent.

Parent Consolidated Statement of Financial Position
December 31, 20X9

Assets	
Cash ($9,000 + **$1,000**)	$10,000
Investment in subsidiary ($1,000 − **$1,000**)	0
TOTAL ASSETS	$10,000
Liabilities and shareholders' equity	
Share capital	$ 5,000
Retained earnings	5,000
TOTAL LIABILITIES AND SHAREHOLDERS' EQUITY	$10,000

Worksheet Approach—Consolidation upon Founding the Subsidiary

The entries to eliminate the investment in subsidiary account in the parent's books and the share capital in the subsidiary's books and the parent's consolidation worksheet are provided below. The consolidated SFP under the worksheet approach will be identical to the SFP derived under the direct approach above:

Share capital (of subsidiary)	1,000	
Investment in subsidiary (of parent)		1,000

	December 31, 20X9			
	Trial Balances		Adjustments	
	Parent	Subsidiary	Dr/(Cr)	Consolidated
Cash	$ 9,000	$ 1,000	—	$10,000
Investment in subsidiary	1,000	—	$ (1,000)	0
Share capital	(5,000)	(1,000)	1,000	(5,000)
Retained earnings	(5,000)	—	—	(5,000)
	$ —	$ —	$ —	$ —

Example with Intercompany Transactions and Balances

Assume that Parco established a subsidiary in 20X0 by creating a new corporation named Subco. Subco issued 100 common shares to Parco in return for $80,000 cash paid by Parco for the shares. Parco has remained the sole shareholder of Subco in succeeding years.

On December 31, 20X8, several years after the incorporation of Subco, the trial balances for the two companies are as shown in Exhibit 2-2. The 20X8 separate-entity

EXHIBIT 2-2

Separate-Entity Trial Balances

	December 31, 20X8			
	Parco		Subco	
	Dr	Cr	Dr	Cr
Cash	$ 70,000		$ 40,000	
Accounts receivable	200,000		110,000	
Receivable from Subco	60,000		—	
Inventories	150,000		120,000	
Land	100,000		—	
Buildings and equipment	1,000,000		450,000	
Accumulated depreciation		$ 300,000		$ 100,000
Investment in Subco (at cost)	80,000			
Accounts payable		120,000		80,000
Due to Parco		—		60,000
Long-term notes payable		—		300,000
Deferred income taxes		140,000		30,000
Common shares		300,000		80,000
Dividends declared	30,000		20,000	
Retained earnings, December 31, 20X7		762,000		60,000
Sales revenue		800,000		400,000
Dividend income		20,000		—
Cost of sales	480,000		280,000	
Depreciation expense	130,000		30,000	
Income tax expense	32,000		20,000	
Other expenses	110,000		40,000	
	$ 2,442,000	$ 2,442,000	$ 1,110,000	$ 1,110,000

financial statements of the two companies (derived from the trial balances) are presented in Exhibit 2-3, prior to any adjustments related to Parco's investment in Subco. In Exhibit 2-3, we have boldfaced and highlighted those elements that are of particular interest for consolidation purposes.

To prepare the consolidated statements we first need to know the nature and extent of financial interactions between the two. Important facts relating to the 20X8 statements are as follows:

1. Parco uses the *cost method* to account for its investment in Subco ($80,000). Under the **cost method**, the value of the investment is retained at the original cost paid for the investment, without adjusting it for the investor's share of the investee's earnings. Dividends received by the parent from the subsidiary are reported as income in the separate-entity SCI of the parent.
2. The two statements of financial position include $60,000 that is owed by Subco to Parco. The amount is a current asset for Parco and a current liability for Subco.
3. Dividends received from Subco during the year are shown as dividend income on Parco's SCI.
4. The sales of Parco include $100,000 of merchandise sold to Subco, all of which was sold by Subco to outside customers during the year.

Overall Analysis of the Example We can arrive at the following conclusions based on the facts provided in the example:

- In this example, consolidation requires only eliminations; adjustments are not required.
- We need to make eliminations to remove double-counting for the following two issues:
  - the sale of $100,000 by Parco to Subco; and
  - the dividend income of $20,000 of Parco received from Subco.
- We need to make eliminations to remove offsetting balances for the following two issues:
  - the investment in Subco of $80,000; and
  - $60,000 owed by Subco to Parco.
- *Finally, but very importantly, the retained earnings of Subco are not eliminated during the consolidation process.*

In-Depth Analysis of the Example We will elaborate on each of the above issues in further detail below:

- The sale of $100,000 by Parco to Subco. When Parco sold these goods to Subco it would have recognized a sale of $100,000 and the cost of purchasing those goods (amount not provided in the problem) as cost of goods sold in its SCI. Subco in turn sold the same goods to outsiders. Therefore, it would recognize the amount at which it sold the goods to outsiders (amount not provided in the problem) as a sale, while recognizing the cost of purchasing these goods from Parco at $100,000 as cost of goods sold in its SCI.

EXHIBIT 2-3

Separate-Entity Financial Statements

Statements of Financial Position
December 31, 20X8

	Parco	Subco
Assets		
Current assets:		
Cash	$ 70,000	$ 40,000
Accounts receivable	200,000	110,000
Receivable from Subco	**60,000**	—
Inventories	150,000	120,000
	480,000	270,000
Property, plant, and equipment:		
Land	100,000	—
Buildings and equipment	1,000,000	450,000
Accumulated depreciation	(300,000)	(100,000)
	800,000	350,000
Other assets:		
Investment in Subco (at cost)	**80,000**	—
TOTAL ASSETS	$1,360,000	$ 620,000
Liabilities and shareholders' equity		
Current liabilities:		
Accounts payable	$ 120,000	$ 80,000
Due to Parco	—	**60,000**
	120,000	140,000
Long-term notes payable	—	300,000
Deferred income taxes	140,000	30,000
Total liabilities	260,000	470,000
Shareholders' equity:		
Common shares	300,000	**80,000**
Retained earnings	800,000	70,000
Total shareholders' equity	1,100,000	150,000
TOTAL LIABILITIES AND SHAREHOLDERS' EQUITY	$1,360,000	$ 620,000

Statements of Comprehensive Income
Year Ended December 31, 20X8

	Parco	Subco
Sales revenue	$ 800,000	$ 400,000
Dividend income	**20,000**	—
	820,000	400,000
Operating expenses:		
Cost of sales	480,000	280,000
Depreciation expense	130,000	30,000
Income tax expense	32,000	20,000
Other expenses	110,000	40,000
	752,000	370,000
NET INCOME	68,000	30,000

Statements of Changes in Equity-Retained Earnings Section
Year Ended December 31, 20X8

	Parco	Subco
Retained earnings, December 31, 20X7	762,000	60,000
Net income	68,000	30,000
Dividends declared	(30,000)	**(20,000)**
Retained earnings, December 31, 20X8	$ 800,000	$ 70,000

Therefore, from a consolidated perspective both the sales figure and the cost of goods sold figure are overstated by $100,000. Only the results of transactions with outsiders should be included in the consolidated financial statements. As a result, we need to subtract $100,000 from both sales and cost of goods sold when preparing the consolidated statements.

- The dividend income of $20,000 of Parco received from Subco. This $20,000 is already included in Subco's income. Therefore, from a consolidated perspective, including the same $20,000 as both Parco's dividend income and Subco's net income would be double-counting. Only the results of transactions with outsiders should be included in the consolidated financial statements.

  Therefore, we need to subtract $20,000 from both dividend income and dividends declared. Doing so will decrease Parco's income by $20,000 but increase Subco's retained earnings by that amount. Since we are going to add Subco's retained earnings to Parco's retained earnings (as discussed in detail further below), the overall impact of this elimination on the consolidated retained earnings is nil.
- The investment in Subco of $80,000. The investment account is really just an aggregate that represents the net assets of the subsidiary; instead of showing the net investment in the subsidiary as an asset, the consolidated statements show all of the assets and liabilities of the subsidiary that underlie the investment. Parco accounts for its investment in Subco at cost. Therefore, the balance in the investment account will match the share capital of Subco. We need to eliminate both amounts.

  As we pointed out in our first consolidation example, *the subsidiary's share capital is not added to the parent's share capital since Subco's net assets are already included in the parent's total net assets (and shareholders' equity) of $1,100,000*. The net assets and shareholders' equity that will be shown in Parco's consolidated SFP will be the net assets (and shareholders' equity) *from the point of view of the Parco shareholders*. The common share equity that is outstanding for Parco is the $300,000 shown in Parco's SFP.
- $60,000 owed by Subco to Parco. From a consolidated point of view you cannot lend and owe money to yourself. Therefore, "Receivable from Subco" and "Due to Parco" are both reduced by $60,000 respectively.
- Retained earnings of Subco. Because Parco accounts for its investment in Subco at cost, Parco recorded only the dividend income received from Subco; Parco did not record the rest of Subco's earnings from the time of its establishment. Therefore, Parco's retained earnings do not reflect the retained earnings of Subco. Hence, during consolidation, Subco's retained earnings should be added to Parco's retained earnings.

  We will modify this conclusion later (1) in the presence of non-controlling interest, (2) when the subsidiary is not established by the parent but is purchased, and (3) when the parent uses the equity method to record its subsidiary in its separate-entity financial statements. Stay tuned!

Direct Approach—Consolidation Involving Intercompany Transactions and Balances The Parco consolidated financial statements for 20X8 are shown in Exhibit 2-4. In this exhibit, the statements have been prepared by the direct method. The consolidated financial statements are obtained by (1) adding together the individual amounts on the parent and subsidiaries' financial statements;

EXHIBIT 2-4

Parco Consolidated Financial Statements

Consolidated Statement of Financial Position
December 31, 20X8

Assets	
Current assets:	
Cash [70,000 + 40,000]	$ 110,000
Accounts receivable [200,000 + 110,000]	310,000
Receivable from Subco [60,000 + 0 – **60,000**]	—
Inventories [150,000 + 120,000]	270,000
	690,000
Property, plant, and equipment:	
Land [100,000 + 0]	100,000
Buildings and equipment [1,000,000 + 450,000]	1,450,000
Accumulated depreciation [300,000 + 100,000]	(400,000)
	1,150,000
Other assets:	
Investment in Subco (at cost) [80,000 + 0 – **80,000**]	—
TOTAL ASSETS	$1,840,000
Liabilities and shareholders' equity	
Current liabilities:	
Accounts payable [120,000 + 80,000]	$ 200,000
Due to Parco [0 + 60,000 – **60,000**]	—
	200,000
Long-term notes payable [0 + 300,000]	300,000
Deferred income taxes [140,000 + 30,000]	170,000
Total liabilities	670,000
Shareholders' equity:	
Common shares [300,000 + 80,000 – **80,000**]	300,000
Retained earnings [800,000 + 70,000]	870,000
Total shareholders' equity	1,170,000
TOTAL LIABILITIES AND SHAREHOLDERS' EQUITY	$1,840,000

Consolidated Statement of Comprehensive Income
Year Ended December 31, 20X8

Revenue:	
Sales revenue [800,000 + 400,000 – **100,000**]	$1,100,000
Dividend income [20,000 + 0 – **20,000**]	—
	1,100,000
Operating expenses:	
Cost of sales [480,000 + 280,000 – **100,000**]	660,000
Depreciation expense [130,000 + 30,000]	160,000
Income tax expense [32,000 + 20,000]	52,000
Other expenses [110,000 + 40,000]	150,000
	1,022,000
NET INCOME	$ 78,000

Statements of Changes in Equity-Retained Earnings Section
Year Ended December 31, 20X8

Retained earnings, December 31, 20X7 [762,000 + 60,000]	822,000
Net income	$ 78,000
Dividends declared [30,000 + 20,000 – **20,000**]	(30,000)
Retained earnings, December 31, 20X8	$ 870,000

EXHIBIT 2-5

Parco Consolidated Worksheet—Cost Basis of Recording

December 31, 20X8

	Trial balances			
	Parco Dr/(Cr)	**Subco Dr/(Cr)**	**Adjustments Dr/(Cr)**	**Parco consolidated trial balance**
Cash	$ 70,000	$ 40,000		$ 110,000
Accounts receivable	200,000	110,000		310,000
Receivable from Subco	60,000	—	$ (60,000) **b**	—
Inventories	150,000	120,000		270,000
Land	100,000	—		100,000
Buildings and equipment	1,000,000	450,000		1,450,000
Accumulated depreciation	(300,000)	(100,000)		(400,000)
Investment in Subco (at cost)	80,000	—	(80,000) **a**	—
Accounts payable	(120,000)	(80,000)		(200,000)
Due to Parco	—	(60,000)	60,000 **b**	—
Long-term notes payable	—	(300,000)		(300,000)
Deferred income taxes	(140,000)	(30,000)		(170,000)
Common shares	(300,000)	(80,000)	80,000 **a**	(300,000)
Dividends declared	30,000	20,000	(20,000) **d**	30,000
Retained earnings, December 31, 20X7	(762,000)	(60,000)		(822,000)
Sales revenue	(800,000)	(400,000)	100,000 **c**	(1,100,000)
Dividend income	(20,000)	—	20,000 **d**	—
Cost of sales	480,000	280,000	(100,000) **c**	660,000
Depreciation expense	130,000	30,000		160,000
Income tax expense	32,000	20,000		52,000
Other expenses	110,000	40,000		150,000
	$ —	$ —	$ —	$ —

(2) subtracting amounts as necessary for eliminations; and then (3) entering the resulting amounts directly into consolidated financial statements.

Worksheet Approach—Consolidation Involving Intercompany Transactions and Balances Exhibit 2-5 illustrates a worksheet based on the separate-entity trial balances for each company. The trial balances of the parent and the subsidiary (or subsidiaries) are listed in the first columns of the worksheet, and the eliminations and adjustments are inserted in the next column. Cross-adding the rows yields the amounts that will be used to prepare the consolidated statements.

The eliminations that were made in preparing Parco's consolidated statements can be summarized as follows, in general journal format. The parentheses indicate the company on whose statements the accounts being adjusted appear:

(a) Common shares (of Subco)	80,000	
Investment in Subco (by Parco)		80,000
(b) Due to Parco (Subco)	60,000	
Receivable from Subco (Parco)		60,000

(c) Sales (Parco)	100,000	
Cost of sales (Subco)		100,000
(d) Dividend income (Parco)	20,000	
Dividends declared (Subco)		20,000

In each of the eliminations, one side eliminates an amount on Subco's financial statements, while the other side of the entry eliminates an amount on Parco's statements. There is no way that these entries can or should be recorded on either company's books. Consolidation elimination "entries" are entered only on working papers to prepare the consolidated statements, and they are never entered on the formal books of account of either the parent or the subsidiary.

REPORTING SUBSIDIARIES USING THE EQUITY METHOD

Separate-Entity Financial Statements

The preparation of consolidated financial statements does not eliminate the need for each separate legal entity to prepare its own financial statements. Each corporation is taxed individually, and unconsolidated statements are necessary for income tax reporting if for no other purpose.

Consolidated statements may not be adequate for the needs of creditors or other users of financial statements. Creditors have claims on the resources of specific corporations, not on the resources of other corporations within a consolidated group of companies. Therefore it may be of little benefit to a creditor to see the consolidated assets and liabilities when the credit risk is associated with the financial position of a single company.

Under IFRS, when a parent prepares its separate-entity statements for public use, investments in unconsolidated subsidiaries are required to be reported at cost or as financial instruments. However, often such investments may be reported on the equity basis when the separate-entity financial statements are prepared for the use of a specific user, such as a bank or other major lender, who is interested in the net assets, earnings, and cash flow of the individual corporation. The equity basis permits the financial statement user to discern the full economic impact of the operations of the overall economic entity (i.e., the parent corporation and its subsidiaries) and yet still see the assets, liabilities, results of operations, and cash flows for the parent company alone.

Subsidiaries Recorded on the Cost Method but Reported by the Equity Method

A parent company almost invariably carries its subsidiaries' investment accounts on the cost basis, even if the investments will be reported on the equity method for unconsolidated reporting. The reason is that the process of consolidation is much simpler if the investments are carried at cost instead of equity. We shall illustrate this fact in a following section. Thus, normally, a parent company will choose to *record* its investment in a subsidiary using the cost method even if it *reports* unconsolidated subsidiaries on the equity method.

It is vital to remember that, with strategic investments, an investor's *recording* usually does not coincide with its *reporting*. Adjustments and eliminations appear only on working papers for preparing financial statements and are not recorded in the investor corporation's accounts.

In our present example, the following adjustments can be made *on Parco's working papers* to convert the investment in Subco from the cost to the equity method for *reporting* purposes:

Dividend income	20,000	
Investment in Subco		20,000
(to eliminate the dividends recognized as income under the cost method)		
Investment in Subco	30,000	
Equity in earnings of Subco		30,000
(to recognize Parco's share of the subsidiary's current year's earnings as income)		
Investment in Subco	60,000	
Retained earnings		60,000
(to recognize Parco's share of the unremitted earnings of Subco from prior years)		

It is important to remember that these entries are worksheet entries only—they will not be recorded on Parco's books because the account is maintained on the cost basis.

Recording a Subsidiary by the Equity Method

It is possible, but rare, for a parent company to carry a subsidiary's investment account on its books by using the equity basis. Therefore, for completeness, we will now assume that Parco does record its investment in Subco using the equity method.

Exhibit 2-6 shows the various components of the carrying value of Subco under the equity method of accounting. In the current year, the entries required in Parco's books relating to its share of Subco's earnings in the current year are as follows.

Investment in Subco	30,000	
Equity in earnings of Subco		30,000
Cash (or Dividends Receivable)	20,000	
Investment in Subco		20,000

The first entry above recognizes Parco's 100% share of Subco's current year earnings of $30,000 and increases the investment in Subco account by that amount. The equity in earnings of Subco will be included as an income item in Parco's current year SCI. The dividend of $20,000 is deducted from the investment in Subco account, offset by an increase in the cash (or dividends receivable) account.

Under the equity method, Parco would have made similar entries in earlier years to recognize its share of Subco's prior years' earnings. Thus, Parco's books will already reflect its share of Subco's unremitted earnings. Therefore, no further entries are required in the current year in relation to Subco's prior years' earnings.

EXHIBIT 2-6

Investment in Subco in Separate-Entity Financial Statements of Parco Using Equity Basis of Recording

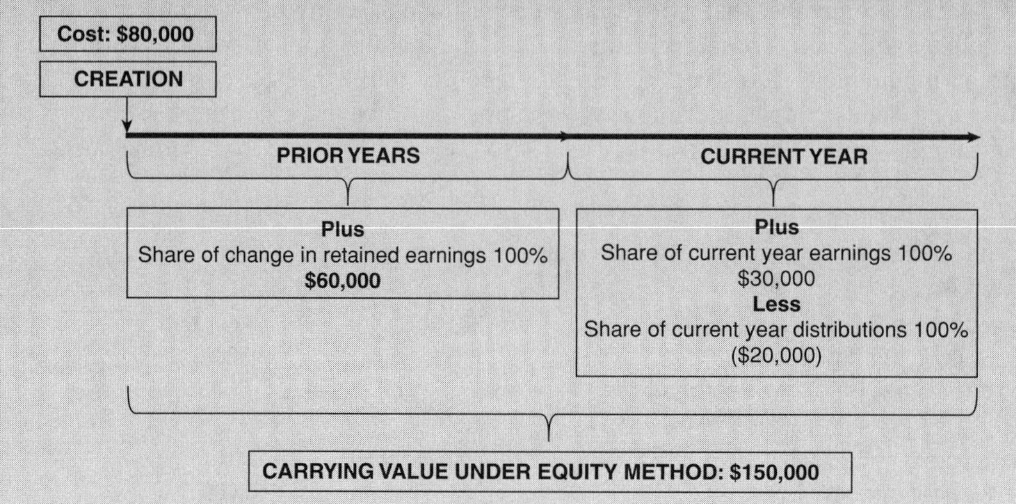

Note that under the equity method it is *not* necessary to eliminate intercompany transactions such as the $100,000 sales by Parco to Subco. The necessary adjustments are only for items that affect net income—the intercompany transaction washes out in its effect on net income.

COMPARISON OF COST, EQUITY, AND CONSOLIDATION METHODS

Exhibit 2-7 provides a comparison of the financial statements of Parco under the three different policies for reporting the investment in Subco. The first column shows Parco's separate-entity financial statements with the investment in Subco reported on the cost basis. These financial statements are derived from the first column of Exhibit 2-3.

The second column shows Parco's separate-entity financial statements prepared on the equity basis. Note that the first two columns are identical except for the investment in Subco and reported earnings from Subco. As a result, the reported net income and retained earnings of Parco differ significantly between the first and second columns.

The third column of Exhibit 2-7 shows Parco's consolidated financial statements. Almost all of the amounts in the third column are different from those in the first two columns. The assets, liabilities, revenues, and expenses include those of both Parco and Subco, while the investment account in Subco and the receivable from Subco accounts have disappeared and the long-term notes payable account has been added.

EXHIBIT 2-7

Parco Financial Statements using Different Reporting Practices

Statement of Financial Position, December 31, 20X8

	Cost basis	Equity basis	Consolidated
Assets			
Current assets:			
Cash	$ 70,000	$ 70,000	$ 110,000
Accounts receivable	200,000	200,000	310,000
Receivable from Subco	60,000	60,000	—
Inventories	150,000	150,000	270,000
	480,000	480,000	690,000
Property, plant, and equipment:			
Land	100,000	100,000	100,000
Buildings and equipment	1,000,000	1,000,000	1,450,000
Accumulated depreciation	(300,000)	(300,000)	(400,000)
	800,000	800,000	1,150,000
Other assets:			
Investment in Subco	80,000	150,000	—
TOTAL ASSETS	$1,360,000	$1,430,000	$1,840,000
Liabilities and shareholders' equity			
Liabilities:			
Current accounts payable	$ 120,000	$ 120,000	$ 200,000
Long-term notes payable	—	—	300,000
Deferred income taxes	140,000	140,000	170,000
Total liabilities	260,000	260,000	670,000
Shareholders' equity:			
Common shares	300,000	300,000	300,000
Retained earnings	800,000	870,000	870,000
Total shareholders' equity	1,100,000	1,170,000	1,170,000
TOTAL LIABILITIES AND SHAREHOLDERS' EQUITY	$1,360,000	$1,430,000	$1,840,000

Statement of Comprehensive Income
Year Ended December 31, 20X8

	Cost basis	Equity basis	Consolidated
Sales revenue	$ 800,000	$ 800,000	$1,100,000
Operating expenses:			
Cost of sales	480,000	480,000	660,000
Depreciation expense	130,000	130,000	160,000
Income tax expense	32,000	32,000	52,000
Other expenses	110,000	110,000	150,000
	752,000	752,000	1,022,000
Net income from operations	48,000	48,000	78,000
Dividend income	20,000		
Equity in earnings of Subco		30,000	
NET INCOME	$ 68,000	$ 78,000	$ 78,000

Statement of Changes in Equity-Retained Earnings Section
Year Ended December 31, 20X8

	Cost basis	Equity basis	Consolidated
Retained earnings, December 31, 20X7	762,000	822,000	822,000
Net income	$ 68,000	$ 78,000	$ 78,000
Dividends declared	(30,000)	(30,000)	(30,000)
Retained earnings, December 31, 20X8	$ 800,000	$ 870,000	$ 870,000

It is impossible to tell from the third column which of the assets and liabilities are those of Parco, since the two corporations are reported as a single economic entity. If a lender were to extend a line of credit to Parco based on (for example) 75% of Parco's accounts receivable, the lender would not be able to tell from the consolidated statements just how much of the $310,000 reported accounts receivable is an asset of Parco.

While most of the consolidated amounts differ from those in the first two columns of Exhibit 2-7, two items are the same in the second and third columns but different from the first column: *Retained earnings* and *Net income*. A basic and important attribute of the equity method is that the parent's reported net income and net assets (shareholders' equity) will be the same as when the subsidiaries are consolidated. The effect of consolidation is to disaggregate the net investment in the subsidiary into the component assets and liabilities, and to disaggregate the parent's equity in the earnings of the subsidiary into its components of revenue and expense.

The equity method is frequently referred to as **single-line consolidation** because the equity method and consolidation both result in the same net income and shareholders' equity for the parent. There is one line on the SFP that shows the net asset value of the subsidiary, and one line on the SCI that shows the net earnings derived from the subsidiary.[3]

The one-line adjustment to the parent's earnings is commonly known as the **equity pick-up** of the subsidiary's earnings.

CONCEPT CHECK 2-5

Companion Website

1. Why is the retained earnings balance of the subsidiary not eliminated during consolidation when a parent-founded subsidiary is recorded under the cost method?
2. Why are inter-company transactions and balances not eliminated under the equity method of reporting?

CONSOLIDATION: EQUITY METHOD RECORDING

In our earlier illustration of direct consolidation and of the consolidation worksheet we assumed that the parent company carried the investment in Subco at cost. While the cost method is most commonly used for internal recordkeeping, the equity method may also be

3. An exception arises for the investor's share of any discontinued operations of the investee. The investor's proportionate share of discontinued operations will be reported net of related taxes on the investor's SCI after net income from continuing operations.

EXHIBIT 2-8

Parco Consolidation Worksheet—Equity Basis of Recording

December 31, 20X8

	Trial balances		Elimination and	Parco
	Parco Dr/(Cr)	Subco Dr/(Cr)	adjustments Dr/(Cr)	consolidated trial balance
Cash	$ 70,000	$ 40,000		$ 110,000
Accounts receivable	200,000	110,000		310,000
Receivable from Subco	60,000	—	$ (60,000) **c**	—
Inventories	150,000	120,000		270,000
Land	100,000	—		100,000
Buildings and equipment	1,000,000	450,000		1,450,000
Accumulated depreciation	(300,000)	(100,000)		(400,000)
Investment in Subco (at equity)	**150,000**	—	**(140,000) a** **(10,000) b**	
Accounts payable	(120,000)	(80,000)		(200,000)
Due to Parco	—	(60,000)	60,000 **c**	—
Long-term notes payable	—	(300,000)		(300,000)
Deferred income taxes	(140,000)	(30,000)		(170,000)
Common shares	(300,000)	(80,000)	80,000 **a**	(300,000)
Dividends declared	30,000	20,000	(20,000) **b**	30,000
Retained earnings, December 31, 20X7	**(822,000)**	(60,000)	**60,000 a**	(822,000)
Sales revenue	(800,000)	(400,000)	100,000 **d**	(1,100,000)
Equity in earnings of Subco	**(30,000)**	—	**30,000 b**	—
Cost of sales	480,000	280,000	(100,000) **d**	660,000
Depreciation expense	130,000	30,000		160,000
Income tax expense	32,000	20,000		52,000
Other expenses	110,000	40,000		150,000
	$ —	$ —	$ —	$ —

used. Therefore, we will now illustrate how consolidation works when Parco uses the equity method in its separate-entity financial statements to record its investment in Subco. However, given that such a practice is rare in real life, later chapters will not illustrate consolidation under equity recording.

If Parco had been using the equity method, (1) the investment account would be $150,000 at the end of 20X8; (2) Parco's opening retained earnings would be $822,000 instead of $762,000; and (3) the SCI accounts would include the $30,000 equity in the earnings of Subco rather than dividend income of $20,000.

The first column of Exhibit 2-8 shows the condensed financial statements for Parco, assuming that the investment has been recorded by use of the equity method. The accounts and amounts that are affected by using the equity method rather than the cost method are highlighted in bold. When the eliminating entries are prepared, the two entries to eliminate the balance of the investment account differ from those shown in Exhibit 2-5 because the composition of the balance in the investment account is different.

Under the cost method, only the original cost of the investment is included in the investment account, and the only elimination necessary is to offset the cost of the investment against the common share account of the subsidiary.

Under the equity method, however, the investment account includes both the original cost of the investment and the unremitted earnings of the subsidiary. Both of these amounts must be eliminated. The parent's retained earnings also include the earnings of the subsidiary, since the subsidiary's earnings are taken into the parent's income each year. If we added the retained earnings of Subco to the retained earnings of Parco, as we did under the cost method, we would be double-counting Subco's retained earnings. Therefore, the worksheet entries to eliminate the investment account are shown as follows when the equity method of recording the investment has been used:

(a)	Common shares (of Subco)	80,000	
	Retained earnings (of Subco)	60,000	
	Investment in Subco (by Parco)		140,000
(b)	Equity in earnings of subsidiary (of Parco)	30,000	
	Dividends declared (by Subco)		20,000
	Investment in Subco (of Parco)		10,000

Worksheet entry (a) eliminates the original investment and the accumulated retained (and unremitted) earnings of Subco of prior years. Entry (b) eliminates the dividends and the double-counting of Subco's earnings for the current year. In effect, the two adjustments reverse the entries that were originally made by Parco to record its interest in the earnings of Subco and to record the original investment.

The process of consolidation cancels out entries made for the equity pick-up of the subsidiaries' earnings. This is why companies virtually always use the cost basis of recording their strategic investments—the process of consolidation requires that the equity-basis adjustments be eliminated, and thus most companies simply record the investment on the cost basis. It is simpler *not* to use the equity method for *recording* the investment. The remaining two eliminations, for the intercompany debt and the intercompany sales, are unaffected by the method of recording the investment.

The net effect of the eliminations to the SCI and retained earnings section of the statement of changes in equity (SCE/RE) is to reduce the combined ending retained earnings by $70,000, thereby preventing the double-counting of Subco's ending retained earnings. This net change of $70,000 is transferred to the SFP to complete the worksheet.

Exhibit 2-9 below graphically depicts the impact on the separate-entity SCI and SFP of the parent of using the cost and equity method respectively to record its investment in its 100% owned subsidiary. Exhibit 2-9 also shows the impact of consolidation on the consolidated SCI and SFP. Further, Exhibit 2-9 briefly summarizes the changes needed to convert from the cost method of reporting the investment in the subsidiary to the equity method and consolidation respectively; and likewise from the equity method to consolidation.

EXHIBIT 2-9

Cost, Equity, and Consolidation Methods to Report 100% Owned Subsidiary

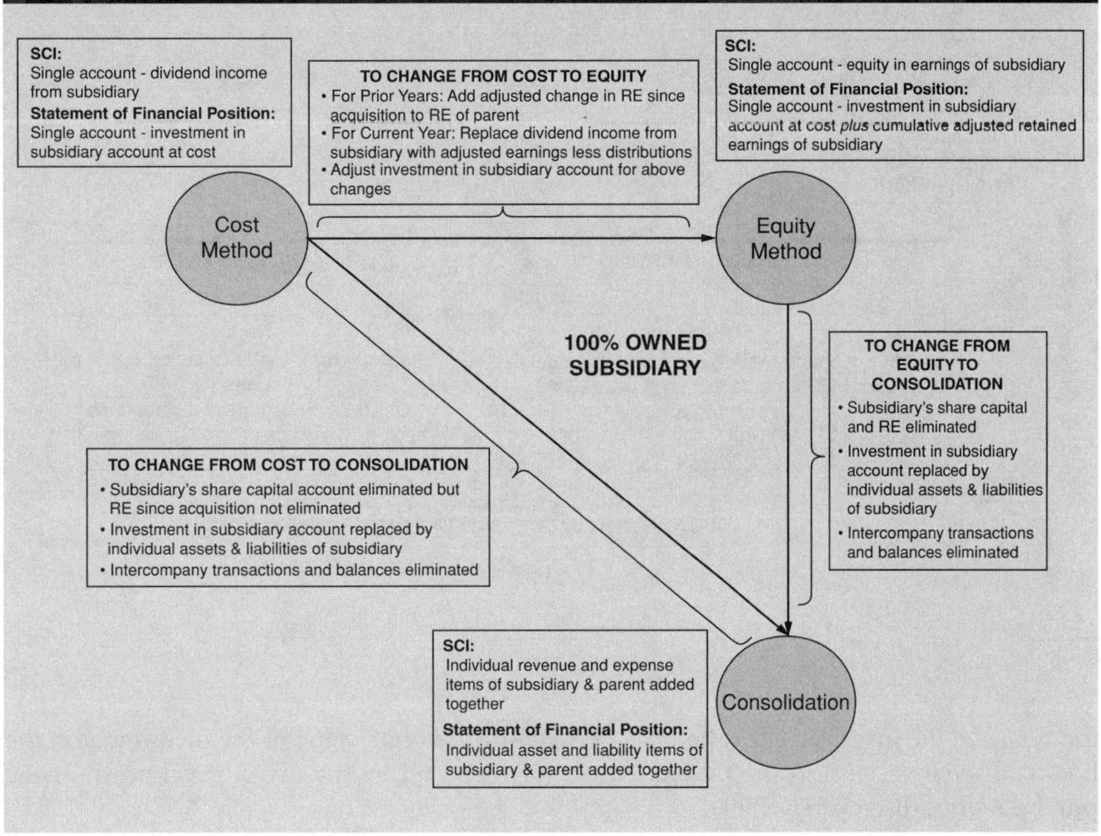

CONCEPT CHECK 2-6

1. When might a parent, which otherwise must consolidate its subsidiaries, report them under the equity method?
2. Why is the consolidated retained earnings balance of the parent equal to its retained earnings balance under the equity method of reporting investments in subsidiaries?

EQUITY METHOD: A CONCEPTUAL ELABORATION

Under the **equity method** the investor records the investment initially at its cost or purchase price. Usually, the purchase price equals the fair or market value of the investment at the time of the purchase. The purchase price rarely is equal to the carrying value of the investment in

EXHIBIT 2-10

Common Adjustments under the Equity Method

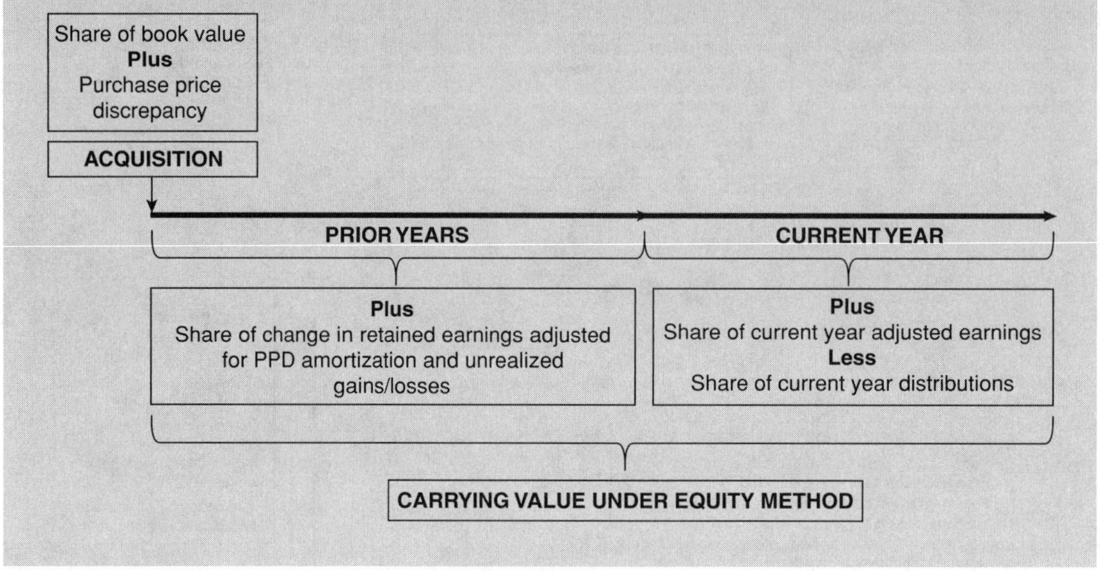

the books of the investee. The difference between the carrying value of the investment in the books of the investee and the purchase price or cost paid by the investor is known as the purchase price discrepancy (PPD).

In subsequent years the carrying value of the investment is adjusted to recognize the investor's share of the investee's adjusted earnings after the date of acquisition. The investor makes two major types of adjustments to the investee's earnings before calculating its share of such earnings: (1) amortization of the PPD; and (2) elimination by reducing unrealized gains/losses on intercompany transactions.

The adjustments to the investee's earnings are similar to the adjustments required when consolidating the financial statements of subsidiaries with the financial statement of the parent; therefore, these adjustments are called **consolidating adjustments**. The carrying value of the investment is also reduced by any distributions such as dividends made by the investee.

Exhibit 2-10 provides an overview of how the carrying value is calculated under the equity method, focusing on the most common adjustments (1) at time of acquisition, (2) in prior years, and (3) in the current year. These adjustments will be the subject of our discussion in the next few chapters.

The investor's share of the investee's adjusted net income or loss is included as a single line item of profit or loss in the investor's SCI. The investment is included at its carrying value as a single line item on the investor's SFP. Therefore, the equity method is also known as *single-line consolidation*. Additional adjustments to the carrying value of the investment are also necessary for the investor's proportionate share of the investee's OCI.

Share of Losses Exceeds Investor's Interest in Associate or Joint Venture

Sometimes the investor's share of the adjusted losses of the investee (i.e., associate or joint venture) exceeds its interest in the investee. In such circumstances, the investor stops recognizing further losses in its net income. Here "investor's interest in the investee" refers to the carrying value of the investment in the investee calculated using the equity method and including long-term interests in the investee that are deemed to constitute additional investments. Examples of such long-term interests include preferred shares and long-term receivables. There should be no plans for settlement of such additional investments in the near future. If the investor provides further commitments or guarantees on behalf of the investee, losses are recognized only as provision (liability) to the extent of those commitments or guarantees. When the investee resumes making profits, the investor starts recognizing its portion of such profits only when they exceed the losses not recognized previously.

A CLOSER LOOK AT CONTROL

A corporation's strategic operating and financing policies are normally determined by its board of directors. The members of the board of directors are elected by the shareholders. Therefore, if an investor owns a majority of the voting shares, the investor normally will possess the power to elect a majority of the board of directors and thus will have the power of control.

Note that we said a majority of the *voting shares*. Many corporations, especially in Canada, have dual-share structures wherein one class of common shares has more votes than another. For example, Onex Corporation owns only 13% of the total outstanding shares of Celestica Inc. but has 79% of the votes. Celestica has (at the end of 2008) about 200 million shares that get one vote each and about 30 million shares that have 25 votes each. Thus, the multiple-voting shares get a total of 750 million votes as compared to 200 million for the single-voting shares. Guess which class of shares Onex owns!

On the other hand, having a majority of the votes does not always ensure control. An investor's ability to elect a majority of an investee's board of directors may be restricted by contractual agreements, regulatory requirements, or legal restrictions.

Determining whether control exists is not a formulaic process. Instead, the accountant must determine whether or not control exists by looking at many factors. Control may be direct or indirect, and may be exercised through factors other than just share ownership. For example:

- Does the investor have an agreement with other investors that guarantees control?
- Does the investor have the ability to appoint, hire, transfer, or fire key members of the investee's management?

- Do the investor and investee corporation have **interlocking boards**, wherein a majority of the board members are on both companies' boards?
- Does the investor provide retractable debt financing to the investee that is crucial to the investee's financial health?

Indirect Control

Control need not be direct. **Indirect control** exists when a subsidiary is controlled by one or more other subsidiaries rather than by the parent company. Exhibit 2-11 shows three examples of indirect control.

In Case 1, the parent (**P**) controls subsidiary **A** by owning 70% of **A**'s voting shares, and **A** controls **C** by owning 60% of **C**'s voting shares. Since **P** controls **A**, **P** can control **A**'s votes for **C**'s board of directors. Therefore, **P** has indirect control of **C**. **C** is a subsidiary of **A**, and both **C** and **A** are subsidiaries of **P**.

Voting control is a yes–no matter, not multiplicative. **P** controls 60% of the votes for **C**'s board of directors, not just 42% (i.e., 70% × 60%). **P** controls **A**, and **A** controls **C**; therefore **P** controls **C**. Ownership of 60%, whether direct or indirect, gives **P** virtually complete control over the strategic policies of **C**.

In Case 2, control of **P** over **C** is achieved indirectly through two direct subsidiaries of **P**: **A** and **B**. Neither **A** nor **B** has control of **C** because each has less than a majority of **C**'s voting shares. However, **P** can control **C** because **P** controls 70% of the votes in **C** through its control of **A** and **B** (40% + 30%). In this example, **A**, **B**, and **C** are all subsidiaries of **P**, but **C** is *not* a subsidiary of either **A** or **B**.

In Case 3, **P** has both direct and indirect ownership interests in **C**. Control is achieved only by virtue of the shares of **C** that are owned by both **P** and **A**, and thus **P**'s control of **C** is still indirect, despite **P**'s direct ownership of 15% of **C**'s voting shares. The sum of one corporation's direct and indirect interest in another corporation is known as the **beneficial interest**. **P** has a 55% beneficial interest in **C**. **A** and **C** are subsidiaries of **P**; **C** is *not* a subsidiary of **A**.

EXHIBIT 2-11

Examples of Indirect Control

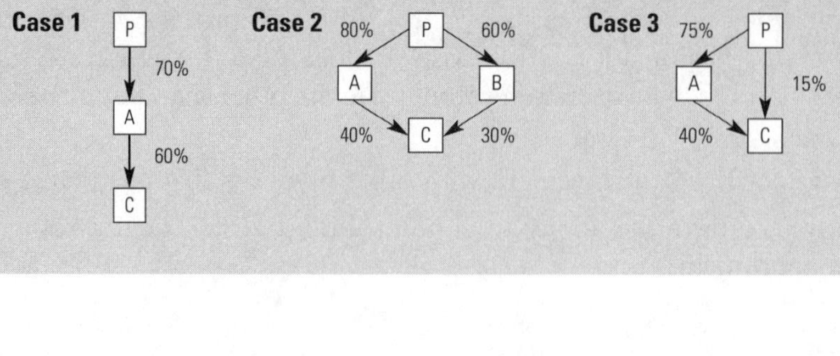

Other types of ownership arrangements can exist; these three examples are merely illustrative. Some intercorporate ownerships are very complex, and require careful analysis to determine who controls whom.

Consolidation of Indirect Holdings

When there are several layers of subsidiaries, consolidated statements will normally be prepared at each level, particularly when there are non-controlling shareholders in the intermediate layers. For example, assume that Corporation A owns 70% of Corporation B, and Corporation B owns 60% of C. The following financial statements will be prepared.

- C will prepare its own separate-entity financial statements, which will be used by C's minority shareholders and for income tax purposes.
- B will prepare separate-entity (i.e., non-consolidated) statements for tax purposes, internal purposes, and perhaps for specific users, such as the bank. In the non-consolidated statements, the investment in C will be shown as an asset.
- For issuance to the general public, B will also prepare consolidated statements that include the assets, liabilities, revenue, expenses, and cash flows of C. These statements are relevant for B's non-controlling shareholders.
- A will prepare consolidated statements that include all of the assets, liabilities, revenues, expenses, and cash flows of the consolidated statements of B, which includes C. A's consolidated statements are relevant to the shareholders of A, and of A only. A will also prepare non-consolidated statements for tax purposes and perhaps as special-purpose statements for bankers and creditors.

Non-controlling shareholders are interested only in the statements of the company in which they own shares. B's non-controlling shareholders are not entitled to the statements of A, even though B is controlled by A, because they are not shareholders of A.

PRIVATE ENTERPRISE REPORTING AND UNCONSOLIDATED STATEMENTS

In addition to presenting accounting methods for publicly accountable enterprises, Exhibit 2-1 provided the private-enterprise reporting alternatives for various types of strategic investments available under Canadian Accounting Standards for Private Enterprises (ASPE). An investor corporation must use the chosen method of accounting uniformly for all investments within each category of investment (i.e., subsidiaries, controlled SPEs, significantly influenced associate companies, and joint ventures).

Private enterprises are not required to prepare consolidated statements. The users of private–enterprise financial statements often prefer to see non-consolidated statements to evaluate the creditworthiness, management performance, or dividend-paying ability of the separate entity. If consolidated statements are forced upon these users, the additional costs

REALITY CHECK 2-4

Proportionate Consolidation Versus Equity Method of Reporting

Even though IASB is proposing to eliminate proportional consolidation, there is some empirical evidence suggesting that it provides useful information to investors that is lost with equity reporting. Under proportional consolidation, the investor's proportionate shares of the investee's assets and liabilities are brought onto the investor's statement of financial position. This is not required under the equity method of reporting. Therefore, the equity method of accounting can be used as an off-balance-sheet financing technique to reduce the debt-to-equity ratio of the investor. One study found that financial statements prepared using proportionate consolidation provide better predictions of future profitability than statements prepared using the equity method.[a] Another study, using US data, found that proportionately consolidated financial statements have greater relevance than statements using the equity method for explaining bond ratings.[b] Surprisingly, a third study, using Canadian data, found that financial statement measures based on the equity method are more relevant for bond ratings than are similar measures based on proportionate consolidation.[c]

The lack of information provided by the equity method of reporting can be alleviated by requiring the investor to provide adequate disclosure regarding its share of the investee's assets and liabilities. A UK study of mandated disclosures by UK firms of their share of the liabilities of their equity-accounted associates and joint ventures finds that such disclosures are useful to the market when valuing the shares of the investing firms.[d] International accounting standards also require similar disclosures relating to the assets and liabilities of associates and joint ventures.

a. R. C. Graham, R. D. King, and C. K. J. Morrill, "Decision usefulness of alternative joint venture reporting methods." *Accounting Horizons* 17:2 (June 2003), p. 123.
b. M. P. Bauman, "Proportionate consolidation versus the equity method: Additional evidence on the association with bond ratings." *International Review of Financial Analysis* 16 (2007), p. 496.
c. K. Kothavala, "Proportionate consolidation versus the equity method: A risk measurement perspective on reporting interests in joint ventures." *Journal of Accounting and Public Policy* 22 (2003), p. 517.
d. J. O'Hanlon and P. Taylor, "The value relevance of disclosures of liabilities of equity-accounted investees: UK evidence." *Accounting and Business Research* 37:4 (2007), p. 267.

of consolidation will be pointless and will violate the basic concept that user benefits should exceed the preparation cost.

Either the cost or equity method may be used to report non consolidated subsidiaries and SPEs of private enterprises. A company cannot choose to consolidate some subsidiaries and not others. The investor corporation should use the same method to report all of its subsidiaries.

For significant-influence investments, it is not necessary to use the equity method. The cost method may be used instead. All investments in significantly influenced companies must be reported on the same basis, either all by the cost method or all by the equity method.

For joint ventures the investor can use the proportionate consolidation, cost method, or the equity method. All joint ventures must be reported on the same basis.

Finally, Reality Check 2-4 provides findings from empirical research on the issue of proportionate consolidation versus the equity method.

Relevant Standards

IASB

Standards

IAS 1 Presentation of Financial Statements
IAS 27 Consolidated and Separate Financial Statements
IAS 28 Investments in Associates
IAS 31 Interests in Joint Ventures
IFRS 3 Business Combinations

Standing Interpretations Committee Interpretations

SIC 12 Consolidations—Special Purpose Entities

Exposure Drafts by IASB

ED 9 Joint Arrangements
ED 10 Consolidated Financial Statements

Accounting Standards for Private Enterprises

1582 Business Combinations
1601 Consolidated Financial Statements
1602 Non-controlling Interests
1590 Subsidiaries
3051 Investments
3055 Joint Ventures
3856 Financial Instruments

Summary of Key Points

1. An intercorporate investment is any investment by one corporation in the debt or equity securities of another.
2. A passive investment is an intercorporate investment in debt, non-voting shares, or a relatively small number of voting shares in another corporation. Passive investments do not have the ability to influence the strategies of the investee corporation. All passive equity investments are reported at fair values. While all gains (realized as well as unrealized) relating to passive investments classified as "fair value through profit and loss" are taken to net income, all gains relating to passive investments irrevocably classified as "fair value through other comprehensive income" are taken directly to equity through OCI. Such gains can never be reclassified into net income.
3. A strategic intercorporate investment is intended to enable the investor to control or significantly influence the strategic operating and financing policies of the investee. If the

investor has the ability to determine the strategic operating and financing policies of the investee, then the investor controls the investee. The controlled company is deemed to be a subsidiary of the investor, or parent, corporation.

4. Most subsidiaries are created by the parent company to carry on some aspect of the company's business. These are known as parent-founded subsidiaries. Other subsidiaries are acquired by buying voting control from the subsidiary's former shareholders. When a parent controls a subsidiary by owning less than 100% of the shares, a non-controlling interest exists.
5. A special purpose entity (SPE) is a business venture that is established by a corporation but that is not controlled by the corporation through share ownership. The following factors should be considered to decide whether or not an SPE should or should not be consolidated: (1) the purpose and design of the SPE, (2) the reporting entity's returns from its involvement with the SPE, (3) the activities of the SPE and the extent to which its policies have been predetermined, and (4) the reporting entity's ability to change any restrictions or predetermined strategic operating and financing policies.
6. Significant influence may exist if the investor holds less than voting control, but more than a nominal amount. The general guideline is that ownership of between 20% and 50% of the voting shares gives the investor significant influence. Equity-basis reporting is normally used to report investments in significantly influenced companies.
7. A joint venture is a co-operative venture undertaken together with one or more other investors. No one investor controls a joint venture. All of the co-venturers must agree on strategic policies. Joint ventures are reported using either the equity method or proportionate consolidation. Equity-basis reporting is sometimes called one-line consolidation.
8. Parent companies should prepare consolidated statements that report on the total economic entity that is controlled by the parent. All subsidiaries should be consolidated.
9. The *recording* and *reporting* of strategic intercorporate investments are two different things. Intercorporate investments are usually recorded on the books of the investor on the cost basis. If the equity basis is used for reporting, the adjustments from cost to equity are entered on working papers and are not recorded in the investor's books. Consolidated financial statements are always prepared on working papers. The working papers may use either a direct approach or a worksheet approach. It is not possible to record the adjustments needed for consolidation, because there is no set of books that corresponds to the consolidated economic entity.
10. Canadian businesses commonly operate through a multi-corporate structure, with a parent company controlling several subsidiaries. Each legal corporate entity must prepare its own separate-entity financial statements for tax and other special purposes. Corporations that issue general purpose financial statements must issue only consolidated financial statements to the general public.
11. Control can be either direct or indirect. Indirect control exists when the parent company controls an intermediate company that controls another company. *Control* does not imply *absolute* control. The parent company can have complete control over the subsidiary only by owning 100% of the subsidiary's shares.
12. Exceptions to the consolidation policy can occur when the reporting enterprise is a private corporation (and not otherwise accountable to the public).

Companion Website

Visit the text's website at www.pearsoned.ca/beechy for practice quizzes, additional problems, Excel® templates, answers to Concept Check questions, and important IFRS updates.

Self-Study Problem[4] 2-1

Bunker Ltd. is a wholly owned subsidiary of Archie Corp. Bunker was formed by Archie with an initial investment of $1,000,000. Bunker produces some of the merchandise sold by Archie in its retail stores. Bunker also sells some of its output to other unrelated companies. The December 31, 20X6, trial balances for Archie and Bunker are shown in Exhibit 2-12. The condensed SFP, SCI, and the SCE/RE for both companies are shown in Exhibit 2-13. Additional information is as follows:

1. During 20X6, Bunker sold goods with a production cost of $2,600,000 to Archie for $4,000,000. Archie subsequently sold the goods to its customers for $7,000,000.
2. Included in Archie's current receivables is $80,000 in dividends receivable from Bunker.

EXHIBIT 2-12

Separate-Entity Trial Balances

December 31, 20X6

	Archie Corp.		Bunker Ltd.	
	Dr	**Cr**	**Dr**	**Cr**
Cash and current receivables	$ 200,000		$ 400,000	
Inventories	900,000		500,000	
Furniture, fixtures, and equipment (net)	2,000,000		1,700,000	
Buildings under capital leases (net)	6,000,000		3,000,000	
Investment in Bunker Ltd. (at cost)	1,000,000			
Current liabilities		1,500,000		400,000
Long-term liabilities		4,000,000		2,000,000
Common shares		1,500,000		1,000,000
Retained earnings, December 31, 20X5		2,100,000		1,600,000
Dividends declared	2,000,000		500,000	
Sales revenue		13,000,000		5,000,000
Dividend income		500,000		—
Cost of sales	7,000,000		3,200,000	
Other expenses	3,500,000		700,000	
	$22,600,000	$22,600,000	$10,000,000	$10,000,000

4. The solutions to all of the Self-Study Problems are at the end of the text, following Chapter 11.

3. Included in Bunker's current receivables is $200,000 due from Archie for merchandise purchases.
4. During 20X6, Archie declared dividends of $2,000,000 and Bunker declared dividends of $500,000.

Required

Prepare a consolidated SFP and a consolidated SCI and SCE/RE for Archie Corp. for the year ended December 31, 20X6. Use either the direct method or the worksheet method (or both!).

EXHIBIT 2-13

Separate-Entity Financial Statements

Statements of Financial Position
December 31, 20X6

	Archie Corp.	Bunker Ltd.
Assets		
Cash and current receivables	$ 200,000	$ 400,000
Inventories	900,000	500,000
Furniture, fixtures, and equipment (net of accumulated depreciation)	2,000,000	1,700,000
Buildings under capital lease (net of related amortization)	6,000,000	3,000,000
Investment in Bunker Ltd. (at cost)	1,000,000	—
	$10,100,000	$5,600,000
Liabilities and shareholders' equity		
Current liabilities	$ 1,500,000	$ 400,000
Long-term liabilities	4,000,000	2,000,000
Common shares	1,500,000	1,000,000
Retained earnings	3,100,000	2,200,000
	$10,100,000	$5,600,000

Statements of Comprehensive Income
Year Ended December 31, 20X6

	Archie Corp.	Bunker Ltd.
Revenue		
Sales	$13,000,000	$5,000,000
Dividend income	500,000	—
	13,500,000	5,000,000
Expenses		
Cost of sales	7,000,000	3,200,000
Other expenses	3,500,000	700,000
	10,500,000	3,900,000
Net income	$ 3,000,000	$1,100,000

Statements of Changes in Equity-Retained Earnings Section
Year Ended December 31, 20X6

Retained earnings, December 31, 20X5	2,100,000	1,600,000
Net income	$ 3,000,000	$1,100,000
Dividends declared	(2,000,000)	(500,000)
Retained earnings, December 31, 20X6	$ 3,100,000	$2,200,000

EXHIBIT 2-14

Statements of Comprehensive Income
Year Ended December 31, 20X7
(000 omitted)

	Brad Corp.	Pitt Ltd.
Revenue		
Sales revenue	$ 7,100	$3,400
Other income	235	840
Total revenue	7,335	4,240
Operating expenses		
Cost of goods sold	4,175	1,900
Selling expenses	435	560
General and administrative expenses	995	770
Interest and other expenses	1,015	30
Total operating expenses	6,620	3,260
Earnings before income taxes	715	980
Income tax expense	215	290
Net earnings	$ 500	$ 690

Statements of Changes in Equity—Retained Earnings Section
Year Ended December 31, 20X7
(000 omitted)

	Brad Corp.	Pitt Ltd.
Retained earnings, December 31, 20X6	$39,500	$6,410
Net earnings	500	690
Dividends declared	(160)	(100)
Retained earnings, December 31, 20X7	$39,840	$7,000

Self-Study Problem 2-2

In 20X1, Brad Corporation established a wholly owned subsidiary, Pitt Limited, with an initial investment of $20,000,000. Brad is a Winnipeg-based appliance manufacturer. Brad established Pitt as a retail chain to sell Brad's appliances under several different brand names, as well as some lines of kitchen appliances imported from Europe. Both Brad and Pitt are Canadian corporations.

The separate-entity statements of comprehensive income and the retained earnings section of the statements of changes in equity for the year ended December 31, 20X7, are shown in Exhibit 2-14. The statements of financial position for December 31, 20X7, are shown in Exhibit 2-15. Additional information is as follows:

1. During 20X7, Pitt purchased merchandise from Brad for a total price of $1,400,000. Brad's cost of goods sold for this merchandise was $1,100,000. Pitt sold all of the merchandise to unrelated customers for $2,100,000.

EXHIBIT 2-15

Statements of Financial Position
December 31, 20X7
(000 omitted)

	Brad Corp.	Pitt Ltd.
Assets		
Cash and temporary investments	$ 1,500	$ 450
Current receivables and accrued expenses	3,400	1,890
Inventories	10,640	5,210
Current assets	15,540	7,550
Loan receivable	1,000	
Land	18,000	
Buildings and equipment (net)	37,700	22,450
Investment in Pitt Limited	20,000	
TOTAL ASSETS	$92,240	$30,000
Liabilities and shareholders' equity		
Current payables and accrued liabilities	$ 2,820	$ 1,540
Income tax payable	180	85
Current liabilities	3,000	1,625
Long-term debt payable	33,750	1,000
Deferred tax liability	2,650	375
Total liabilities	39,400	3,000
Common shares	13,000	20,000
Retained earnings	39,840	7,000
Total shareholders' equity	52,840	27,000
TOTAL LIABILITIES AND SHAREHOLDERS' EQUITY	$92,240	$30,000

2. At year-end 20X7, Pitt owed $200,000 to Brad for merchandise purchases.
3. On December 17, 20X7, Pitt's board of directors declared dividends of $100,000, payable on January 10, 20X8.
4. On July 1, 20X7, Pitt borrowed $1,000,000 from Brad, interest to be paid annually at a rate of 6% per annum.
5. Brad Corporation uses the cost method for recording the investment in Pitt Limited.

Required

Prepare a consolidated SFP at December 31, 20X7, and a consolidated SCI and SCE/RE for the year then ended.

Review Questions

2-1 What are the two types of passive equity investments? What is the appropriate method of accounting for these investments?

2-2 What is the difference between *fair value through profit and loss* (FVTPL) investments and *fair value through other comprehensive income* (FVTOCI) investments?

2-3 ABC Corporation owns 12% of XYZ's common shares. Is the cost method of reporting the investment necessarily appropriate? Explain.

2-4 What factors should be examined to determine whether significant influence exists?

2-5 What is a *joint venture*?

2-6 Is profit sharing equal in a joint venture? Explain.

2-7 How are dividends received from an investee corporation reported by an investor corporation if the investor is using the equity method?

2-8 "The extent of share ownership does not necessarily coincide with the extent of control exercised." Explain.

2-9 Under what circumstance can one corporation control another without owning a majority of the controlled corporation's voting shares?

2-10 P Corporation owns 75% of S Corporation, and S Corporation owns 55% of T Corporation. Is T a subsidiary of P?

2-11 P Corporation owns 55% of Q Corp. and 58% of R Corp. Q and R each own 30% of W Ltd. Is W a subsidiary of one or more of the other three companies? If so, which one(s)?

2-12 Why do many parent corporations prefer to own 100% of the shares of their subsidiaries, rather than smaller proportions? What advantages are there to a parent in owning *less* than 100% of its subsidiaries?

2-13 Why do many corporations carry out their operations through multiple subsidiaries?

2-14 Why would a company purchase a subsidiary rather than simply establishing a new subsidiary of its own? Why would a corporation want to keep a purchased subsidiary as a separate legal entity?

2-15 Explain one legitimate use for a *special purpose entity* (SPE).

2-16 When should an investor corporation report its investment in the shares of another corporation on the equity basis?

2-17 What is the objective of preparing consolidated financial statements?

2-18 Why might a corporation use the cost method of *recording* an intercorporate investment while using the equity method or consolidation for *reporting*?

2-19 What are the two general approaches to preparing consolidated financial statements? Do the different approaches provide different results?

2-20 When intercompany sales are eliminated during consolidation, why is cost of sales reduced by the amount of intercompany sales?

2-21 Are consolidation eliminating and adjusting entries entered on the books of the parent or of the subsidiary? Explain.

2-22 Why is the equity method often referred to as *one-line consolidation*?

2-23 Why might it be necessary for a parent company to prepare *unconsolidated* financial statements as well as consolidated statements?

2-24 How does the process of consolidation differ when the parent company has used the equity method of recording its investment in a subsidiary, as compared to consolidation when the cost method of recording has been used?

2-25 When might consolidated statements be misleading?

2-26 Is it possible for a parent company to go bankrupt while its operating subsidiaries stay healthy?

2-27 To what extent do the creditors of a subsidiary have a claim on the assets of the parent company?

2-28 Why do users of private-company financial statements often prefer non-consolidated financial statements?

2-29 How are strategic investments reported under accounting standards for private enterprises?

2-30 Under what circumstances is the cost method used to account for strategic investments?

CASES

CASE 2-1 MULTI-CORPORATION

Multi-Corporation has been following a growth and diversification strategy for the past two years. To accomplish this goal, it has been making a series of strategic investments. This growth has been financed through the bank and private investors. Next year, the company is going to issue shares to the public.

You have just finished a meeting with Catherine, the controller of Multi-Corporation. She has asked you to provide recommendations on how to report the following investments that were made in 20X6.

1. Multi-Corporation purchased all of the 100,000 outstanding B shares of Suds Limited. Each share has one vote. The previous owner of the B shares, Megan, retained all of the 80,000 outstanding A shares of Suds Limited. Each share also has one vote. To avoid sudden changes to the business, Megan stipulated in the sales agreement that she was to retain the right to refuse the appointment of management for Suds Limited and to approve any significant transactions of Suds Limited.
2. Multi-Corporation owns 37% of the voting common shares of Berry Corporation. The remaining 63% of the shares are held by members of the family of the company founder.

To date, the family has elected all members of the board of directors, and Multi-Corporation has not been able to obtain a seat on the board. Multi-Corporation is hoping eventually to buy a block of shares from an elderly family member and eventually own 60% of the shares.

Required

Provide a report to Catherine outlining the appropriate method of accounting for these investments.

[CICA, adapted]

CASE 2-2 SALIERI LTD.

Salieri Ltd. is a manufacturer of musical instruments that is controlled by Tony Antonio. Salieri Ltd. was originally a private company, but it became public in 20X0 when a substantial public share issue occurred. The Antonio family now holds 68% of the shares of Salieri; the remaining 32% are widely distributed throughout Canada.

Although Salieri is an operating company, it also has substantial investments in a number of other Canadian corporations. One such investment is its ownership of 80% of the shares of Bach Burgers, Inc., a chain of fast-food outlets. Salieri acquired its shares in Bach from the original founder of the company, John Sebastian, in 20X9. Bach Burgers is run completely independently; Teresa Antonio (Tony's wife) is one of the members of Bach Burgers' 12-person board of directors, but otherwise Salieri exercises no direction over the operations of Bach Burgers.

Another investment of Salieri Ltd. is its 45% interest in Pits Mining Corporation. This investment was the outcome of a takeover attempt by Salieri two years ago. Salieri was frustrated in its attempt by a coalition of other companies in the extraction industry, which effectively blocked Salieri's bid for control. Salieri was left with the 45% interest that it had managed to acquire. Although Salieri's block of Pits shares is by far the largest single block, Salieri has not been able to gain representation on the Pits board of directors. Salieri Ltd. has instituted court action against Pits Mining to force the other shareholders to admit Salieri nominees to the board.

Mozart Piano Corporation is a piano manufacturer that is 20% owned by Salieri Ltd. Although Salieri does manufacture musical instruments, it does not produce pianos, and Salieri and Mozart frequently conduct joint marketing efforts since their products are complementary and not competitive. Mozart is a private company; all of the other shares are held by the Amadeus family. Mozart has an 80%-owned subsidiary, Leopold Klaviers, Inc., which manufactures harpsichords and clavichords to be sold domestically through Mozart and internationally through other agents.

Salieri Ltd. also owns 15% of Frix Flutes, Ltd. The 15% share was acquired several years ago to provide Frix with some new financing at a time when the company was experiencing financial difficulties. Salieri also assisted Frix by licensing to Frix the rights to use patents owned by Salieri. The licensing agreement can be cancelled by Salieri upon six months' written notice.

The only other corporate share investment held by Salieri is its 100% ownership of Salieri Acceptance Corporation (SAC). SAC was formed by Salieri to aid its customers in purchasing

Salieri instruments on an installment basis. Six of the nine SAC directors are also directors of Salieri Ltd. The other three are representatives of the financial institutions that finance SAC's operations.

Required

Discuss the manner in which Salieri should account for its various investments when issuing its annual financial statements. Specify what additional information you would like to have, if any. Recommend an accounting approach for each investment, stating any assumptions that you make in arriving at your recommendations.

CASE 2-3 HEAVENLY HAKKA, NATURE'S HARVEST, AND CRYSTAL

1. Vincent Hzu is the sole owner of a successful chain of Hakka Indian–Chinese restaurants, Heavenly Hakka Inc., in Canada. Vincent (through Heavenly Hakka) and his two friends, Ibrahim Khan and Venkat Gupta, started a company, Szechwan Samosas Inc. (SS), 15 years ago to manufacture and sell Hakka-style samosas. Heavenly Hakka, Ibrahim, and Venkat each own one-third of the shares of SS. However, given Vincent's experience running restaurants, it was agreed that the profits would be shared as follows—Heavenly Hakka, 40%, and the other two friends, 30% each. Further, Heavenly Hakka is the sole supplier of all the Hakka-style filling that goes into the samosas of SS. SS has become a great success in Ontario, in no small part due to the invaluable contribution of Vincent and Heavenly Hakka. The relationship between the friends had, by and large, been friendly in the past. However, during the past year differences have cropped up among the three on the future direction of SS. Vincent feels that the successful concept of SS should be expanded to other provinces in Canada. In contrast, both Ibrahim and Venkat feel that doing so might divert their attention from the Ontario operation, thereby potentially jeopardizing it. In the interest of maintaining amity among friends, Vincent has not pressed on the issue of expansion. However, clearly, Vincent has been unhappy these past few months, so much so that he has stopped visiting the SS restaurants completely.
2. Nature's Harvest (NH) is a petroleum exploration company incorporated in Benezuela; 60% of its voting shares are owned by Mid-West Petroleum, a publicly listed, Alberta-based company. The new nationalistic government of Benezuela recently decided that Benezuelan companies should be managed by Benezuelans and that their profits should be reinvested within Benezuela. Consequently, the Benezuelan government nominated the majority of the board of directors of NH with its own appointees. However, two of Mid-West's nominees still continue on the board of directors of NH. Further, the government of Benezuela legislated a ban on the repatriation of profits by Benezuelan companies to their foreign shareholders. All technical expertise to NH is, however, still being provided by Mid-West.
3. Premier Inc., a Canada-based public limited company and one of the world's top manufacturers of manual scooters, holds a 19% equity interest in Crystal Inc., a manufacturer of automatic motor scooters. Premier is represented on Crystal's board of directors. Further, Premier also has veto and blocking rights in Crystal as set forth in the partnership agreement between them. Premier is planning to divest its shares in Crystal by the end of next year.

Required

Discuss the accounting alternatives available to report the investment in each of the three independent situations above. Specify what additional information you would like to have, if any. Recommend an accounting approach and disclosures required for each investment, stating any assumptions that you make in arriving at your recommendations. Refer to appropriate standards for appropriate disclosures relating to each situation above.

CASE 2-4 XYZ LTD.

During 20X5, XYZ Ltd. purchased for cash all of the 100,000 Class B shares of Sub Limited. Each share carries one vote. The previous owner, Mr. Bill, retained all 20,000 outstanding Class A shares of Sub Limited, each carrying four votes. To avoid sudden changes, Mr. Bill stipulated in the sale agreement that he was to retain the right to refuse the appointment of management for Sub Limited and to approve any significant transactions of Sub Limited.

Required

Should XYZ Ltd. consolidate the operations of Sub Limited in its 20X5 financial statements, which are to be issued in accordance with IFRS? Provide support for your recommendation.

[CICA]

CASE 2-5 JACKSON CAPITAL INC.

Jackson Capital Inc. (JCI) is a new private investment company that provides capital to business ventures. JCI's business mission is to support companies to allow them to compete successfully in domestic and international markets. JCI aims to increase the value of its investments, thereby creating wealth for its shareholders.

Funds to finance the investments were obtained through a private offering of share capital, conventional long-term loans payable, and a bond issue that is indexed to the TSX Composite. Annual operating expenses are expected to be $1 million before bonuses, interest, and taxes.

Over the past year, JCI has accumulated a diversified investment portfolio. Depending on the needs of the borrower, JCI provides capital in many different forms, including demand loans, short-term equity investments, fixed-term loans, and loans convertible into share capital. JCI also purchases preferred and common shares in new business ventures where JCI management anticipates a significant return. Any excess funds not committed to a particular investment are held temporarily in money market funds.

JCI has hired three investment managers to review financing applications. These managers visit the applicant's premises to meet with management and review the operations and business plans. They then prepare a report stating their reasons for supporting or rejecting the application. JCI's senior executives review these reports at their monthly meetings and decide whether to invest and what types of investments to make.

Once the investments are made, the investment managers are expected to monitor the investments and review detailed monthly financial reports submitted by the investees. The investment managers' performance bonuses are based on the returns generated by the investments they have recommended.

It is now August 20X6. JCI's first fiscal year ended on June 30, 20X6. JCI's draft statement of financial position and other financial information is included in Exhibits A, B, and C. An annual audit is required under the terms of the bond issue. Potter and Cook, Chartered

Accountants, has been appointed auditor of JCI. You are employed by Potter and Cook and are the in-charge accountant on this engagement. Mr. Potter has asked you to prepare a memo discussing the significant accounting issues, audit risks, and related audit procedures for this engagement.

Required

Prepare the memo requested by Mr. Potter.

Exhibit A

DRAFT SFP (JUNE 30, 20X6) (THOUSANDS)

Assets	
Cash and marketable securities	$ 1,670
Investments (at cost)	21,300
Interest receivable	60
Furniture and fixtures (net of amortization)	50
	$23,080
Liabilities	
Accounts payable and accrued liabilities	$ 20
Accrued interest payable	180
Loans payable	12,000
	$12,200
Equity	
Share capital	$12,000
Deficit	(1,120)
	$23,080

Exhibit B

SUMMARY OF INVESTMENT PORTFOLIO (JUNE 30, 20X6)

The SFP for June 30, 20X6, shows a total of $21.3 million in long-term investments. The breakdown of these investments is as follows:

Investments	**Cost**
15% common share investment in Fairex Resource Inc., a company listed on the TSX Venture Exchange. Management intends to monitor the performance of this mining company over the next six months and to make a hold/sell decision based on reported reserves and production costs.	$3.8 million
25% interest in common shares of Hellon Ltd., a private Canadian real estate company, plus 7.5% convertible debentures with a face value of $2 million acquired at 98% of maturity value. The debentures are convertible into common shares at the option of the holder.	$6.2 million
Five-year loan denominated in Brazilian currency (reals) to Ipanema Ltd., a Brazilian company formed to build a power generating station. Interest at 7% per annum is due semiannually. 75% of the loan balance is secured by the power generating station under construction. The balance is unsecured.	$8 million
50% interest in Western Gas, a jointly owned gas exploration project operating in Western Canada. One of JCI's investment managers sits on the three-member board of directors.	$2 million
50,000 stock warrants in Toronto Hydrocarbons Ltd., expiring March 22, 20X8. The underlying common shares trade publicly.	$1.3 million

Exhibit C

CAPITAL STRUCTURE (JUNE 30, 20X6)

The SFP for June 30, 20X6, shows a total of $12 million in share capital and $12 million in loans payable.

Loans Payable

The Company has $2 million in demand loans payable with floating interest rates, and $4 million in loans due September 1, 20X8, with fixed interest rates.

In addition, the Company has long-term 5% stock-indexed bonds payable. Interest at the stated rate is to be paid semiannually, commencing September 1, 20X6. The principal repayment on March 1, 20X9, is indexed to changes in the TSX Composite as follows: the $6 million original balance of the bonds at the issue date of March 1, 20X6, is to be multiplied by the stock index at March 1, 20X9, and then divided by the stock index as at March 1, 20X6. The stock-indexed bonds are secured by the Company's investments.

Share Capital

Issued share capital consists of:

– 1 million 8% Class A (non-voting) shares redeemable at the holders' option on or after August 10, 20X8	$7 million
– 10,000 common shares	$5 million

[CICA]

Problems

P2-1

Alex Corporation acquired a 40% interest in Calvin Company on June 1, 20X8, for $425,000. The management of Alex Corporation is now preparing the first set of financial statements since the acquisition and is unsure about the method of accounting most appropriate for the investment. You are asked for advice.

Required

a) Can Alex report the investment in Calvin using the equity method or the proportionate consolidation method? Under what circumstances would each be appropriate? Are there circumstances under which Alex can use the cost method to report its investment in Calvin? Finally, under which circumstances can Alex use the fair value method to report its investment in Calvin? In each case, fully support your answer by providing all supporting factors.

b) What are the circumstances under which it would be appropriate for Alex to prepare consolidated financial statements? Identify the extent of control that would be implied by the use of consolidation and give examples of factors that would make consolidation appropriate.

P2-2

On January 1, 20X6, LJ Corporation purchased 20% of the outstanding shares of XYZ Corporation at a cost of $150,000. During the next two fiscal years, XYZ reported net income and dividends as follows:

Year	Net Income	Dividends
20X6	$45,000	$30,000
20X7	20,000	50,000

Required

a) If LJ uses the cost method to account for its investments in XYZ, what would be the balance in the investment account at the end of fiscal year 20X7?

b) If LJ uses the equity method to account for its investment in XYZ, what would be the balance in LJ's account called "Investment in XYZ" at December 31, 20X7?
[CGA–Canada adapted]

P2-3

On April 30, 20X4, Large Inc. established a subsidiary known as Small Inc. Large invested $500,000 in the shares of Small. Small has no other shares outstanding. Since its establishment, Small has had the following earnings and paid the following dividends:

Year	Net Income (Loss)	Dividends
20X4	$(50,000)	—
20X5	60,000	$16,000
20X6	56,000	38,000
20X7	104,000	44,000

Required

a) Determine the amount of Small Inc.'s earnings that will be reported as investment income by Large Inc. in 20X7, under the equity method.

b) Calculate the balance of the investment in Small Inc. account on Large Inc.'s books at December 31, 20X7, assuming that Large Inc. maintains the investment account on the equity basis.

P2-4

Harry Inc., a publicly traded company, purchased 1,000 shares, constituting a 40% ownership interest, in Sally Inc. on January 1, 20X1 for $150,000. Harry Inc.'s income under the cost basis for 20X1 is $80,000. Sally's income per its separate-entity financial statements is $15,000 and it paid a total dividend of $20,000 in 20X1. Both companies have the same year-end. At year-end, each share of Sally was trading at $100 in the market.

Required

a) Based on the above information, calculate/show (i) journal entries made by Harry in its books relating to its investment in Sally, and (ii) the balance in its investment in Sally account at year-end, assuming that Harry treats its investment in Sally as a FVTOCI investment.

b) Based on the above information, calculate/show the (i) journal entries made by Harry in its books relating to its investment in Sally (ii) total income of Harry for the year, and (iii) balance in its investment in Sally account at year-end, assuming that Harry treats its investment in Sally as a significantly influenced investment.

P2-5

Take Inc. invested $50,000 for its 15% share in Give Inc. on January 1, 20X1, by purchasing 10,000 shares of Give Inc. The following table provides pertinent details relating to Give Inc for the next four years. Take Inc. has a December 31 year-end.

Year	Income	Dividends Declared	Share Price on December 31
20X1	$150,000	$120,000	$4.70
20X2	60,000	110,000	4.60
20X3	100,000	80,000	5.00
20X4	80,000	120,000	5.50

Required

Calculate the dividend income and unrealized gains/losses recognized by Take Inc. in each of the four years, and the carrying value of its investment in Give Inc. Assume that Take Inc. accounts for its investment in Give Inc. as a FVTOCI investment.

P2-6

Max Corporation has a wholly owned subsidiary, Min Ltd., which was formed several years ago. Both Max and Min are in the same business, but in different geographic areas. Min's initial capital was provided by Max, which purchased all of Min's shares for $500,000. At December 31, 20X6, the SFP accounts of Max and Min appeared as follows:

Statements of Financial Position of Max and Min as at December 31, 20X6

	Max	Min
Cash	$ 90,000	$ 30,000
Accounts receivable	200,000	130,000
Receivable from Min	80,000	—
Property, plant, and equipment	2,500,000	1,400,000
Accumulated depreciation	(670,000)	(360,000)
Investment in Min	500,000	—
TOTAL ASSETS	$2,700,000	$1,200,000
Accounts payable	$ 300,000	$ 200,000
Payable to Max	—	80,000
Bonds payable	1,000,000	—
Deferred tax liability	100,000	50,000
Common shares	400,000	500,000
Retained earnings	900,000	370,000
TOTAL LIABILITIES AND EQUITY	$2,700,000	$1,200,000

During 20X6, Min paid dividends of $80,000 to Max, and purchased goods from Max at a total price of $1,200,000. All of the purchases from Max were subsequently sold to third parties during the year.

Required

Prepare a consolidated SFP for Max Corporation at December 31, 20X6.

P2-7

Hook Corp. is a wholly owned, parent-founded subsidiary of Chappell Inc. The unconsolidated statement of comprehensive income and the retained earnings section of the statement of changes in equity for the two companies for the year ended December 31, 20X6, are as follows:

Separate-Entity Financial Statements
Statements of Comprehensive Income
Year Ended December 31, 20X6

	Chappell Inc.	Hook Corp.
REVENUES:		
Sales	$6,500,000	$2,100,000
Interest	200,000	60,000
Dividends	100,000	—
Total revenue	6,800,000	2,160,000
EXPENSES:		
Cost of goods sold	3,300,000	1,300,000
Depreciation expense	600,000	160,000
Administrative expense	900,000	300,000
Income tax expense	780,000	170,000
Other operating expenses	290,000	40,000
Total expense	5,870,000	1,970,000
Net earnings	$ 930,000	$ 190,000

Statements of Changes in Equity—Retained Earnings Section
Year Ended December 31, 20X6

	Chappell Inc.	Hook Corp.
Retained earnings, January 1, 20X6	$1,920,000	$ 520,000
Net earnings	930,000	190,000
Dividends declared	(330,000)	(100,000)
Retained earnings, December 1, 20X6	$2,520,000	$ 610,000

Additional Information

1. During the year, Hook acquired merchandise from Chappell at a total sale price of $900,000. None of the merchandise was in Hook's inventory at year-end.
2. At the beginning of the year, Hook borrowed $800,000 from Chappell at 10% interest per annum. The loan (and accrued interest) was still outstanding at the end of the year.
3. Chappell carries its investment in Hook at the cost basis in its accounts.

Required

Prepare a consolidated statement of comprehensive income and the retained earnings section of the statement of changes in equity for Chappell Inc., for the year ended December 31, 20X6.

P2-8

Thorne Ltd. is a wholly owned subsidiary of Fellows Corporation. The SFP, statement of comprehensive income, and the retained earnings section of the statement of changes in equity for each company are shown below. Additional information is as follows:

1. Thorne sells most of its output to Fellows. During 20X6, intercompany sales amounted to $3,500,000. Fellows has accounts payable to Thorne for $20,000.
2. Fellows owns the land on which Thorne's building is situated. Fellows leases the land to Thorne for $30,000 per month.
3. The long-term note payable on Thorne's books represents a loan from Fellows. The note bears interest at 10% per annum.
4. Both companies declare dividends quarterly. The last quarter's dividends were declared on December 31, 20X6, payable on January 10, 20X7.
5. Fellows uses the cost method to account for its investment in Thorne.

Required

1. Prepare a consolidated SFP, SCI, and the SCE/RE for Fellows Corporation.
2. What are the adjusting entries required if Fellows wishes to convert from the cost to the equity method to account for its investment in Thorne? How would Fellows' separate-entity financial statements appear if it accounts for its investment in Thorne under the equity method?
3. Using Fellows' separate-entity financial statements under the equity method, prepare a consolidated SFP, a consolidated SCI, and consolidated SCE/RE for Fellows Corporation.

Separate-Entity Financial Statements
Statements of Comprehensive Income
Year Ended December 31, 20X6

	Fellows	Thorne
REVENUES:		
Sales	$5,600,000	$4,700,000
Interest, dividend and lease	850,000	15,000
	6,450,000	4,715,000
EXPENSES:		
Cost of goods sold	4,400,000	2,500,000
Interest expense	—	70,000
Other expenses	1,300,000	1,795,000
	5,700,000	4,365,000
Net income	$ 750,000	$ 350,000

Statements of Changes in Equity—Retained Earnings Section
Year Ended December 31, 20X6

	Fellows	Thorne
Retained earnings, January 1, 20X6	$1,330,000	$ 100,000
Net income	750,000	350,000
Dividends declared	(700,000)	(200,000)
Retained earnings, December 31, 20X6	$1,380,000	$ 250,000

Statements of Financial Position
December 31, 20X6

	Fellows	Thorne
ASSETS		
Current assets:		
Cash	$ 180,000	$ 25,000
Accounts receivable	700,000	135,000
Temporary investments and accrued investment income	360,000	90,000
Inventories	—	330,000
	1,240,000	580,000
PROPERTY, PLANT, AND EQUIPMENT:		
Land	900,000	—
Buildings and equipment	—	1,500,000
Accumulated depreciation	—	(500,000)
	900,000	1,000,000
Long-term note receivable	700,000	—
Investment in Thorne	500,000	—
TOTAL ASSETS	$3,340,000	$1,580,000
EQUITIES		
Current liabilities:		
Accounts payable and accrued liabilities	$ 240,000	$ 80,000
Dividends payable	120,000	50,000
	360,000	130,000
Long-term note payable	—	700,000
Total liabilities	360,000	830,000
Shareholders' equity		
Common shares	1,600,000	500,000
Retained earnings	1,380,000	250,000
TOTAL LIABILITIES AND SHAREHOLDERS' EQUITY	$3,340,000	$1,580,000

P2-9

Empire Optical Co., Ltd. is a chain of eyeglass outlets. Empire owns 100% of Class Glass Ltd., a competing chain that Empire established to serve a different market segment. To obtain the best deal from suppliers, Empire buys most of the materials and frames for both chains, and resells to Class whatever that chain needs.

During 20X6, Empire sold materials costing $2,000,000 to Class at cost. At the end of the year, Class still owed Empire $250,000 for purchases of the materials.

Empire records its investment in Class on the equity basis. During 20X6, Class declared and paid dividends totalling $200,000. Empire has not yet recorded its equity in the earnings of Class for 20X6. The pre-consolidation trial balances for the two companies are shown below. An Excel spreadsheet relating to this problem appears on the Companion Website.

Required

Prepare a consolidated SFP and SCI for Empire Optical Co., Ltd. for 20X6.

Trial Balances
Dr (Cr)

	Empire	Class
Cash	$ 400,000	$ 50,000
Accounts receivable	300,000	150,000
Inventory	1,200,000	600,000
Fixtures and equipment (net)	5,000,000	1,400,000
Investment in Class Glass Ltd.	2,100,000	—
Other investments	500,000	—
Accounts payable	(700,000)	(500,000)
Common shares	(1,600,000)	(1,000,000)
Retained earnings	(5,700,000)	(1,300,000)
Dividends paid	600,000	200,000
Sales	(16,000,000)	(7,100,000)
Cost of goods sold	11,000,000	5,000,000
Other operating expenses	3,000,000	2,500,000
Dividend and interest income	(100,000)	—
	$ 0	$ 0

3

Business Combinations

LEARNING OBJECTIVES

After studying this chapter, students should be able to:

1. define a business combination;
2. identify the different types of business combinations;
3. explain the general accounting approach to business combinations;
4. measure the fair values of the consideration transferred and the assets and liabilities acquired; and
5. demonstrate the mechanics of consolidating a purchased subsidiary at the time of acquisition.

INTRODUCTION

Live Nation Inc. and Ticketmaster Entertainment announced the completion of their merger on January 25, 2010. Live Nation is the largest producer of live concerts in the world, and Ticketmaster is a leading live entertainment ticketing and marketing company. The merged entity will operate under the Live Nation Entertainment name. The merger was effected by an exchange of shares—Ticketmaster shareholders received approximately 1.474 shares of Live Nation common stock for each share of Ticketmaster common stock. After the merger, Ticketmaster's previous shareholders own approximately 50.1% and Live Nation's shareholders own the remaining 49.9% of the merged company.

In the previous chapter we pointed out that most subsidiaries are established by the parent corporation to carry out some part of the parent's operations. The merger of Live Nation and Ticketmaster illustrates a different way of obtaining a subsidiary—by a *business combination*, in which one corporation acquires another functioning business as a going concern.

A second example of a business combination is the January 2010 reverse merger of Artek Exploration Ltd. (a junior oil and gas exploration company based in Calgary) with COSTA Energy Inc. COSTA has a stock listing and so Artek was able to become a public company by merging with COSTA and then changing the name of the merged company to Artek Exploration. That's a quick way to become a public company.

In Chapter 2, we discussed the various reasons that a parent may want to purchase a subsidiary. In this chapter, we will examine the accounting issues that arise when one corporation acquires another company as a going concern rather than by establishing a new subsidiary.

The consolidation procedures that we illustrate in this chapter are at the simplest level—a consolidated statement of financial position (SFP) at the date of acquisition. However, consolidations after the acquisition date are much more complicated. Chapters 4, 5, and 6 will deal with these post-acquisition complexities.

DEFINITION OF A BUSINESS COMBINATION

A **business combination** is a transaction or other event in which one corporate entity obtains control of one or more operating businesses. The first key aspect of the definition is that the buyer obtains **control**. Control can usually be obtained either by:

1. buying the assets themselves (which automatically gives control to the buyer), or
2. buying enough shares in the corporation that owns the assets to enable the investor to control the investee corporation (which makes the purchased corporation a subsidiary).

Thus, (1) forming a *joint venture* or (2) combining two entities that already are under *common control* (discussed later in the chapter) do not fit the definition of a business combination.

A second key aspect of the definition is that the acquirer obtains control of a *business*. The term **business** means an organized group of activities and assets that can be carried on or managed for the purpose of providing returns. Returns can be in terms of dividends, lowering of costs, or other economic benefits to investors. Thus, a business consists of inputs (i.e., assets) and processes (i.e., organized group of activities) applied to those inputs that have the ability to create outputs either currently or reasonably expected in the future.[1]

When the purchase is accomplished by buying control over another corporation, liabilities are automatically part of the package. But when the purchaser buys a group of assets that constitutes a business, there may or may not be liabilities attached, such as when one corporation sells an operating division to another company. The acquired business does not need to be a separate corporate entity. An acquirer can buy a portion of a corporation, such as an operating division or a sales group that can function as a stand-alone business. However, in any discussion of business combinations, remember that **net assets**, i.e., assets less liabilities, includes any related liabilities.

Not all business combinations result in a parent–subsidiary relationship. When a business combination is a direct purchase of net assets, the acquired assets and liabilities are recorded directly on the books of the acquirer, as we shall discuss shortly. Exhibit 3-1 below graphically depicts some common types of business combinations that do and do not lead to consolidation. We will discuss some of these business combinations further later in the chapter.

It also is possible for an acquirer to purchase a group of assets that does not meet the definition of a business combination. This kind of purchase is called an "asset group acquisition." When an asset group is acquired, the cost of purchasing the asset group is apportioned to the individual identifiable assets and liabilities on the basis of their individual fair values. An asset group can have no goodwill because it is not a functioning business and cannot have goodwill

1. The presence of outputs is not essential for a business to exist; for example, a business in a developmental stage will not have outputs.

EXHIBIT 3-1

Common Types of Business Combinations

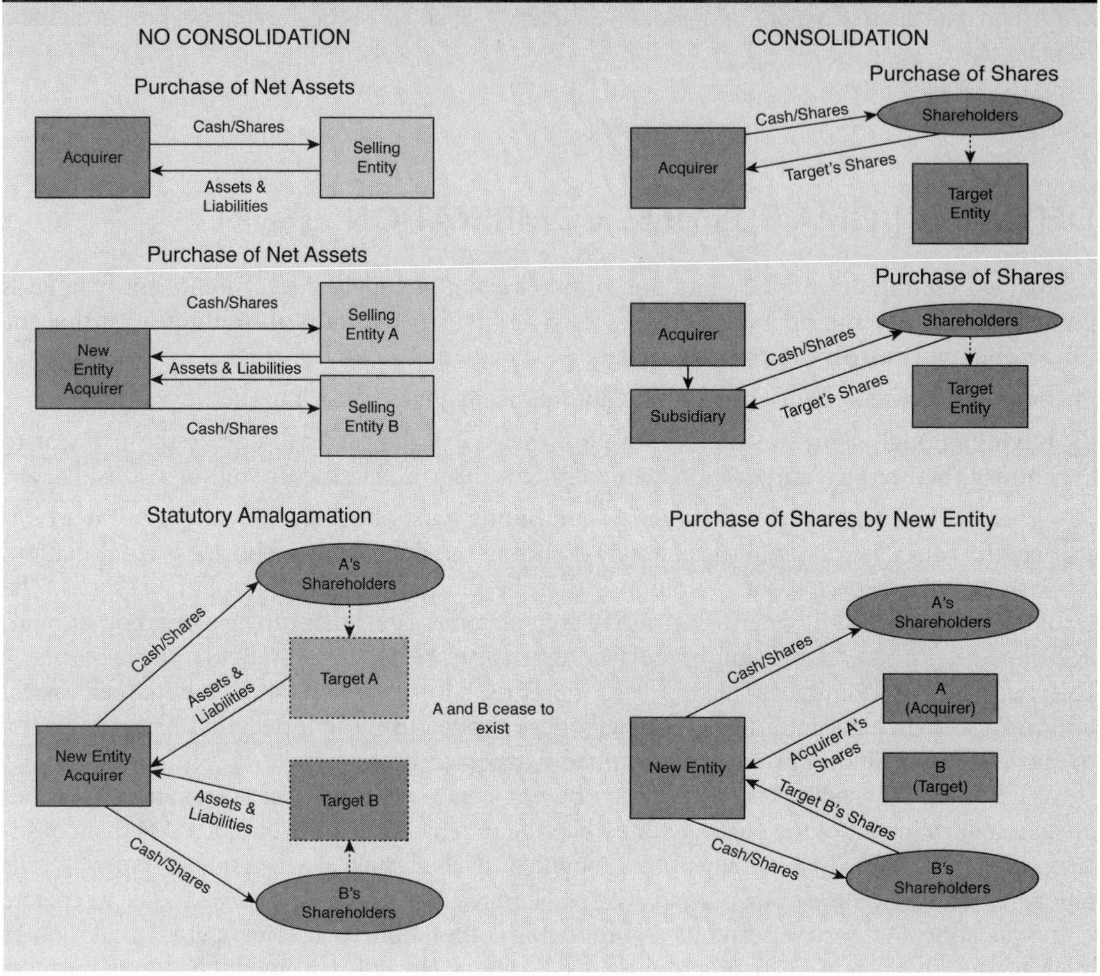

that generates higher returns. This type of transaction is often called a "basket purchase" of assets. Accounting for an acquisition of an asset group is covered in intermediate accounting textbooks.

ACCOUNTING FOR BUSINESS COMBINATIONS—GENERAL APPROACH

Several theoretically different methods for reporting business combinations are possible. Various countries' national accounting standards have used some of these methods in the fairly recent past. Currently, however, IFRS 3, *Business Combinations*, requires the *acquisition method* to report all business combinations.

REALITY CHECK 3-1

Benefits of Mergers and Reasons for Mergers

Empirical research on mergers and acquisitions indicates that while mergers do appear to create value, most of the associated gains appear to go to the shareholders of the target company or acquiree.[a] Mergers appear to occur in waves and to cluster by industry. This evidence suggests that mergers occur in reaction to sudden and unexpected shocks within a particular industry. Empirical research also supports other theoretical reasons about why mergers occur: (1) efficiency-related reasons such as economies of scale or some other synergy, (2) creation of market power by forming monopolies or oligopolies, (3) market discipline in the form of the removal of incompetent target management, (4) self-serving reasons on the part of management such as "empire building," and (5) diversification to reduce risk.

In contrast, a survey of chief financial officers (CFOs) of US firms that had acquired other firms during the 1990–2001 period, the largest merger wave in history,[b] found that the top-ranked reason given for mergers was operating synergies. They also found that CFOs viewed achieving diversification, especially as a means of reducing losses during economic downturns, as being a legitimate reason for mergers.

a. A. Gregor, M. Mitchell, and E. Stafford, "New evidence and perspectives on mergers." *The Journal of Economic Perspectives* 15:2 (Spring 2001), p. 103.

b. T. K. Mukherjee, H. Kiymaz, and H. K. Baker, "Merger motives and target valuation: A survey of evidence from CFOs." *Journal of Applied Finance* 14:2 (Fall 2004), p. 7.

The acquisition method approaches a business combination from the perspective of the acquirer, the entity that obtains control of the other entity(ies) in the business combination. Under the **acquisition method**, all assets and liabilities are identified and reported at their fair values. The buyer may have acquired more than just the assets reported on the acquired company's books—for example the buyer may have acquired other valuable *identifiable* assets (such as license rights or customer lists) that clearly have a fair value but are not reported on the acquired company's books. A major advantage of recognizing these previously unidentified assets is that it will allow users to more accurately assess the value of the investment and its subsequent performance and compare it against other alternative investments or entities and their performance.

Recall that a business combination may occur through (1) the direct purchase of net assets, or (2) by obtaining control over the net assets of a corporation, usually through the purchase of shares. Under the acquisition method, the general approach to accounting for both types of business combinations is a five-step process:

1. identify the *acquirer*;
2. determine the *acquisition date*;
3. calculate the *fair value of the purchase consideration* transferred (i.e., the *cost* of the purchase);
4. recognize and measure the identifiable assets and liabilities of the acquired business; and
5. recognize and measure either *goodwill* or a *gain from a bargain purchase*, if either exists in the transaction.

If an acquirer gains control by purchasing less than 100% of the acquired entity, then the fourth step includes measuring and recognizing the *non-controlling interest*. We will delay our discussion of non-controlling interests until Chapter 5.

The *mechanics* of accounting for the acquisition will depend on the nature of the purchase, particularly on whether the purchase was of the net assets directly or of *control* over the net assets through acquisition of shares of the company that owns the assets. Let's look at the general features that apply to all business combinations before we worry about the acquisition method used.

Identifying the Acquirer

The **acquirer** in a business combination is the corporation whose shareholders control the combined economic entity. When the purchase is for cash (or other assets or by incurring liabilities), it is obvious that the acquirer is the company that pays to acquire the other (or the assets of the other). When the combination is effected by an exchange of shares, the acquirer may not be so obvious.

The corporation that issues the shares is usually, but not always, the acquirer. Therefore, it is necessary to examine which shareholder group gets control of the combined economic entity to determine who the acquirer is.

Voting control may appear to be evenly split between the shareholders of the two combining companies. If that is the case, other factors must be examined to determine who the acquirer is. Examples of other factors include:

- the relative voting rights in the combined entity of the owners of the combining entities;
- in the absence of any group with significant voting interest, the presence of a group with a large minority voting interest;
- the composition of the board of directors;
- the composition of the senior management team; and
- the terms relating to the exchange of the equity shares, with the group paying a premium being the acquirer.

Determining the Acquisition Date

The acquisition date is the date on which the acquirer obtains control over the acquired company. Usually, the closing date, the date on which the purchase consideration is transferred and the assets and liabilities of the acquiree are acquired, constitutes the acquisition date. However, the acquirer and the acquiree can, through a written agreement, arrange for control to be transferred on a date other than the closing date. In such a case, the date on which the control is transferred, and not the closing date, will constitute the date of acquisition.

Calculating the Fair Value of the Consideration

Usually the purchase consideration for the assets acquired is in the form of (1) cash or other assets, (2) shares issued by the acquirer as consideration for the net assets acquired, or (3) a combination of cash and shares. Specifically, the purchase consideration transferred can include cash, other assets, a business or a subsidiary, ordinary and preferred shares, options, warrants, liabilities incurred to former owners, or contingent consideration. On occasion, it is possible to acquire control without actually transferring any consideration, such as by contract alone.

The general principle is that the consideration transferred should be measured at its fair value on the *date of the acquisition*. When the purchase is by cash, it is not difficult to determine the fair value of the consideration transferred. When the purchase is paid for with other assets or liabilities of the acquirer, the purchase consideration is measured by the fair value of those assets and liabilities on the date of the acquisition.

In many cases the acquirer issues its own shares in full or partial payment to acquire the net assets of another company. Theoretically, the value of the consideration is the market value of the shares issued by the acquirer. In practice, it may be a little more complicated. For example, the fair value of the *acquiree's* shares may be more reliably measurable than the fair value of the acquirer's shares. A prime example occurs when the acquiree is a public company but the acquirer is a private company. In such cases, fair value should be measured using the acquisition date fair value of the transferred equity interest of the acquiree.

Acquisition-Related Costs **Acquisition-related costs** are costs incurred to achieve the business combination and are not considered part of the purchase consideration. These costs are treated as expenses of the period in which they are incurred and services are received. Examples of such costs are finder's fees; professional or consulting fees (e.g., advisory, legal, accounting, and valuation fees); and general administrative costs, including costs incurred for maintaining an acquisitions department. The exceptions are costs of issuing debt or shares. Costs of issuing debt are deducted from the value of the debt originally recognized. Transaction costs relating to the issue of shares are deducted from shareholders' equity, net of any related income tax benefit.

Measurement Period The **measurement period** is a period after the acquisition date during which certain adjustments are permitted. The measurement period cannot be more than one year. Sometimes, it takes a while to determine the fair value of the acquiree's assets and liabilities. Indeed, it sometimes takes a while just to determine what all of the identifiable assets are, especially for intangible assets such as intellectual property and license rights. The amount of purchase consideration may also be uncertain at the date of acquisition.

When it is not feasible to fully determine either the purchase price and/or the fair values at the date of acquisition, the acquiring company uses estimated values or *provisional amounts*. Once the acquirer does determine the consideration and/or fair values, these "final" amounts are used as though they had been known at the date of acquisition.

There always is some lag between the date of acquisition and final measurement because the acquirer has other things to worry about during the acquisition phase—fair values are assigned later. In most cases, the final measurements are determined by the time that the financial statements are prepared, two or three months after the end of the fiscal year. If final determination happens after financial statements for the acquisition date have been issued, some restatement of the acquisition year's statements may be necessary when the next period's statements are issued.

Reality Check 3-2 below provides an example of how the measurement period was used by Spyker Cars, a Netherlands-based manufacturer of exclusive premium sports cars, to finalize the purchase price allocation (PPA) relating to its purchase of a Formula One racing team.

REALITY CHECK 3-2

Spyker F1 Team Ltd.: Finalization of Purchase Price Allocation During Measurement Period

In a press release on October 10, 2007, Dutch automaker Spyker Cars N.V. announced that, following IFRS, it had that day finalized the PPA relating to its acquisition of Midland F1 Team Ltd., (changed to Spyker F1 Team Ltd. after the acquisition), a Formula One racing team. The final PPA differed from the provisional PPA included in the annual accounts for 2006. The comparative 2006 financial statements in the 2007 annual report were restated to reflect the final PPA.

The difference between the provisional and final PPA had a negative impact of €3.099 million on the operating results of 2006. As a consequence, the comparative 2006 operating result incorporated in the 2007 annual report was for €0.831 million as opposed to the operating result of €3.930 million in the original 2006 annual report.

In its annual accounts for 2006, Spyker Cars N.V. stated (page 87 of the 2006 Annual Report):

> Due to amongst other things the specific nature of F1 Racing the purchase price allocation ("PPA") has proven to be complex. The management has used several fair value methods to calculate to the best of their knowledge the right PPA values. This is the first PPA of a Formula One team under IFRS regulations and therefore no comparable information was found for some fair value calculations and management had to estimate the value to their best knowledge using common business sense.

The press release also indicates that the management arrived at the provisional and final PPA based on the advice of an internationally renowned independent valuator.

The Spyker F1 Team, however, had a short life. At the end of the 2007 racing season it was sold and was renamed as Force India Formula One.

Source: Spyker Cars N.V., "Spyker cars N.V. determines final purchase price allocation ("PPA") in connection with the 2006 acquisition of Midland F1 team," press release, October 10, 2007.

Contingent Consideration A business combination may include a provision for contingent consideration. **Contingent consideration** is an add-on to the base acquisition price that is based on events occurring or conditions being met some time after the purchase takes place. The amount of contingent consideration can be based on a number of factors, such as:

- a fuller assessment of the finances and operations of the acquired company;
- the outcome of renegotiating agreements with debt holders;
- achievement of stated earnings objectives in accounting periods *following* the change of control; or
- achievement of a target market price for the acquirer's shares by a specified future date.

Contingent consideration is paid in future periods but is considered as being part of the consideration transferred for the acquisition. The fair value of contingent consideration is estimated on the acquisition date and is included as part of the total consideration. The value of contingent consideration normally will change as the future unfolds.

Recognition of these changes depends on whether those changes relate to (1) additional information obtained *during* the measurement period, or (2) events occurring *after* the acquisition date. In the first instance, the changes are considered part of the original purchase consideration transferred and the original accounting of the acquisition is adjusted accordingly. In the latter case, the changes are recognized separately from the business combination and usually are adjusted as gains or losses in the acquirer's SCI (net income section).

Business Combinations with no Transfer of Consideration A business combination can occur without the transfer of any consideration by the acquirer. Examples include circumstances such as:

- when the acquiree repurchases a sufficient quantity of its shares from other shareholders such that the acquirer, who previously was a minority owner of the acquiree, now is the majority shareholder of the acquiree and controls it;
- when the acquirer owns the majority of the acquiree's voting shares but had previously been prevented from exercising control by regulation or by contract—if that restriction lapses or is removed, the acquirer now gains control over the acquiree; and
- by contract alone.

A business combination by contract alone, as the name denotes, occurs when the acquirer and acquiree agree to a business combination solely via contract. No consideration is exchanged for obtaining control, and the acquirer does not own any equity interest in the acquiree both previous to the acquisition and on the date of acquisition. For example, often companies that manage the medical practice of physicians enter into formal management agreements with physicians or with physician practice companies to manage the latter's medical practices. Such agreements give control of the medical practice to the management companies, despite the absence of any consideration being exchanged and the absence of share ownership. In such cases a business combination is deemed to have occurred solely via contract. Ownership of the medical practice stays with the original shareholders/physicians.

Recognizing and Measuring Identifiable Assets and Liabilities

Under the acquisition method, the acquirer is required to:

1. *recognize* identifiable assets and liabilities separately from goodwill; and
2. *measure* such assets and liabilities at their fair values on the *date of the acquisition*.

A key word is **identifiable**. The acquirer may be able to identify many more assets and liabilities than those shown on the acquiree's SFP. This is particularly true for intangible assets. An identifiable intangible asset is one that either is *separable* or *arises from contractual rights*. In addition, the fair value of any identifiable intangible asset must be measurable. The acquirer cannot ignore these assets and just assume they are part of the acquiree's goodwill.

Similarly, contingent liabilities should be separately identified if (1) they are a present obligation that arises from past events, and (2) their fair values can be reliably measured.

Categorization and Measurement of Identifiable Intangibles

Identification As pointed out earlier, an acquired company often has intangible assets that are not reported on its SFP because the acquired company did not originally incur a cost to buy those assets. For example, suppose that Snowball Corporation has developed a valuable trademark over the course of its business. That trademark has not been reported as an asset on Snowball's SFP because the company did not incur any direct cost to acquire it. Subsequently, Icicle Limited buys Snowball. The trademark "Snowball" has been purchased by Icicle as part of the basket of Snowball's net assets. Icicle must recognize the trademark even though it does not appear on Snowball's books or SFP.

In addition to the trademarks, other identifiable intangible assets such as patents and copyrights are often not shown on the acquired company's SFP. Easily overlooked assets also include customer lists, employment contracts, favourable lease agreements, secret formulas (e.g., Coca-Cola, KFC), Internet domain names, and order backlogs. Goodwill should not be used as a catch-all to include identifiable intangible assets.

IFRS 3 classifies intangibles assets into five types: artistic-related, contract-based, customer-related, market-related, and technology-based. IFRS 3 provides illustrative examples for each type. While these examples are not exhaustive, they do provide a useful structure for identifying intangible assets.

Measurement The measurement principle requires that all identifiable assets and liabilities be measured at their fair values on the date of acquisition. Therefore, the carrying values of the acquired assets and liabilities are completely irrelevant to the acquiring corporation's consolidated financial statements. Fair value measurements clearly are judgmental, often being a combination of different methods of valuation—a bit of a hodgepodge, really. This problem is especially severe in the case of intangible assets. There are three general types of valuation methods or models used for valuing intangible assets:

1. *Market-based*—based on prices in an active market, or prices of similar assets (analogy or benchmark approach);
2. *Income-based*—based on future economic benefit derived from owning the asset; and
3. *Cost-based*, although the result may not reflect fair value.

The market-based approach is the best approach; however, such data frequently are not available. Therefore, the most often-used methods are income-based. All of these methods provide a great deal of latitude for management judgment in determining such fair values, especially in the case of intangible assets. As we shall see in the next chapter, measurement judgments can have significant consequences for reporting in future periods.

Exceptions to the Fair-Value Measurement Principle There are some exceptions to the fair-valuation rule: (1) deferred income taxes, (2) employee benefits, (3) indemnification assets, (4) reacquired assets, (5) share-based payment awards, and (6) assets held for sale. Most of these items are measured in accordance with the usual requirements under other applicable IFRS standards. Therefore, except for deferred income taxes, we will not discuss them in further detail in the text.

The deferred tax amounts that appear on the acquiree's SFP are not assets and liabilities from the standpoint of the buyer, since they relate solely to the differences between tax bases and accounting carrying values on the books of the acquiree.[2] We don't escape the complications of income tax allocation, however. Deferred tax accounting is a factor in the purchaser's financial reporting for purchased subsidiaries. Acquiring companies must determine their own deferred tax balances based on the difference between the asset and liability values they show on their consolidated financial statements and the tax bases. Deferred tax considerations tend to confuse students who are trying to understand the complex issues in business combinations and consolidations. Therefore, we treat deferred tax implications separately in Appendix 3A.

Measuring and Recognizing Goodwill or a Gain from a Bargain Purchase

The price paid for the operating unit will be determined in part by its earnings ability. The acquirer may or may not choose to continue to operate the unit in the same manner; but regardless of the acquirer's plans, the price to be paid will take into account the acquiree's estimated future net earnings stream.

If the unit has been successful and has demonstrated an ability to generate above-average earnings, then the acquirer may have to pay a price that is higher than the aggregate fair value of the identifiable net assets. On the other hand, if the unit has not been successful, the price may be less than the fair value of the net identifiable assets (but not normally less than the liquidating value of the net assets including tax effects).

The difference between the fair value of the net identifiable assets (identifiable assets acquired less liabilities assumed) and the purchase consideration transferred is known as **goodwill** when the purchase consideration is higher than the fair value of the net identifiable assets, and as a **gain from a bargain purchase** (also known as **negative goodwill**) when the purchase consideration is less.

Goodwill acquired in a purchase of net assets is recorded on the acquirer's books, along with the fair values of the other assets and liabilities acquired. It is important to understand that goodwill *is* a purchased asset. The purchaser paid good money (or shares) for the goodwill just as surely as for buildings and inventory. In some circles, goodwill is called a "nothing," which derives from the fact that it does not represent any specific asset, either tangible or intangible. But the fact that we can't point at an object (as for a tangible asset) or a specific right (as for an intangible or financial asset) does not make its cost any less real.

The gain from a bargain purchase or negative goodwill is recognized by the acquirer as a gain in its consolidated SCI. A bargain purchase typically happens when there is a forced sale on the part of the seller who is acting under compulsion from creditors or courts. To ensure that a gain on a bargain purchase is genuine, the acquirer must review all the assets and liabilities acquired and identify and recognize any unrecognized assets and liabilities noted during the review.[3]

---

2. This refers to the results of the inter-period income tax allocation process—deferred tax accounting. Any current taxes receivable or payable are assigned their fair value.
3. Negative goodwill is discussed more fully at the end of this chapter.

Now that we have a good overview of the acquisition method we can next focus on the actual mechanics of accounting for business combinations. In the following two sections we will (1) illustrate the accounting of a direct purchase of net assets, and then (2) discuss and illustrate the accounting for purchase of shares.

CONCEPT CHECK 3-1

Companion Website

1. Under the acquisition method, what are the five steps required to be followed to account for business combinations?
2. Why is determining the acquisition date important under the acquisition method of accounting for business combinations?

ILLUSTRATION OF DIRECT PURCHASE OF NET ASSETS

To illustrate the accounting for a direct purchase of net assets, assume that on December 31, 20X5, Purchase Ltd. acquires all of the assets and liabilities of Target Ltd. by issuing 40,000 Purchase Ltd. common shares to Target Ltd. Before the transaction, Purchase Ltd. had 160,000 common shares outstanding. After the transaction, 200,000 Purchase Ltd. shares are outstanding, of which Target Ltd. owns 20%. The pre-transaction statements of financial position of both companies are shown in Exhibit 3-2.

The estimated fair values of Target Ltd.'s assets and liabilities are shown at the bottom of Exhibit 3-2. Their aggregate fair value is $1,100,000. If we assume that the market value of Purchase Ltd.'s shares is $30 each, then the total purchase consideration transferred for the acquisition is $1,200,000. Therefore, the goodwill relating to the acquisition is $100,000. The transaction will be recorded *on the books of Purchase Ltd.* as follows:

Cash and receivables	200,000	
Inventory	50,000	
Land	400,000	
Buildings and equipment	550,000	
Goodwill	100,000	
Accounts payable		100,000
Common shares		1,200,000

The selling company, Target Ltd., will record the transaction by writing off all of its assets and liabilities and entering the new asset of Purchase Ltd.'s shares, recognizing a gain of $400,000 on the transaction. Note that from the perspective of the parent, this same $400,000 represents the **purchase price discrepancy** (PPD), i.e., the difference between the purchase consideration of $1,200,000 and the carrying value of the net identifiable assets acquired of $800,000. The difference of $400,000 also represents the **fair value increment** (FVI), the difference between the fair value of all of the assets of Target Ltd. including goodwill

EXHIBIT 3-2

Pre-Transaction Statements of Financial Position

December 31, 20X5

	Purchase Ltd.	Target Ltd.
Cash	$1,000,000	$ 50,000
Accounts receivable	2,000,000	150,000
Inventory	200,000	50,000
Land	1,000,000	300,000
Buildings and equipment	3,000,000	500,000
Accumulated depreciation	(1,200,000)	(150,000)
TOTAL ASSETS	$6,000,000	$ 900,000
Accounts payable	$1,000,000	$ 100,000
Long-term notes payable	400,000	—
Common shares*	2,600,000	200,000
Retained earnings	2,000,000	600,000
TOTAL LIABILITIES AND SHAREHOLDERS' EQUITY	$6,000,000	$ 900,000

*for Purchase Ltd.—160,000 shares outstanding

Fair values of Target Ltd.'s net assets:	
Cash	$ 50,000
Accounts receivable	150,000
Inventory	50,000
Land	400,000
Buildings and equipment	550,000
Accounts payable	(100,000)
TOTAL	$1,100,000

purchased by Parent Ltd. of $1,200,000, and the carrying value of those assets in the books of Target Ltd. of $800,000.

The post-transaction statements of financial position for the two companies will appear as shown in Exhibit 3-3. Purchase Ltd.'s assets and liabilities increase by the amount of the fair values of the acquired assets and the goodwill arising from the purchase, while Target Ltd.'s previous net assets have been replaced by its sole remaining asset, the shares in Purchase Ltd. If the transaction had been for cash instead of Purchase Ltd. shares, Target Ltd.'s sole remaining asset would have been the cash received.

The purchase of Target Ltd.'s net assets by Purchase Ltd. is a business combination, but it is not an intercorporate investment by Purchase Ltd. because Purchase Ltd. is not investing in the *shares* of Target Ltd. Since Purchase Ltd. is acquiring the assets and liabilities directly instead of indirectly through the purchase of Target Ltd. shares, Purchase Ltd. records the assets and liabilities directly on its books and there is no need for consolidated statements; Target Ltd. is *not* a subsidiary of Purchase Ltd.

After the net asset purchase has been recorded, Purchase Ltd. will account for the assets as it would any new asset group. There is no special treatment required.

EXHIBIT 3-3

Post-Transaction Statements of Financial Position

December 31, 20X5

	Purchase Ltd.	Target Ltd.
Cash	$1,050,000	$ —
Accounts receivable	2,150,000	—
Inventory	250,000	—
Land	1,400,000	—
Buildings and equipment	3,550,000	—
Accumulated depreciation	(1,200,000)	—
Goodwill	100,000	—
Investment in Purchase Ltd. shares	—	1,200,000
TOTAL ASSETS	$7,300,000	$1,200,000
Accounts payable	$1,100,000	$ —
Long-term notes payable	400,000	—
Common shares*	3,800,000	200,000
Retained earnings	2,000,000	1,000,000
TOTAL LIABILITIES AND SHAREHOLDERS' EQUITY	$7,300,000	$1,200,000

* for Purchase Ltd.—200,000 shares outstanding

PURCHASE OF SHARES

Buying the *assets* (or *net assets*) of another company is one way to accomplish a business combination. However, a much more common method of acquiring control over the assets of another company is to buy the *voting shares* of the other business. If one company buys a controlling block of the shares of another company, then control over the assets has been achieved, and the acquirer has a new subsidiary.

An acquirer can obtain a controlling share interest by any one or a combination of three methods:

- buying sufficient shares on the open market;
- entering into private sale agreements with major shareholders; or
- issuing a public tender offer to buy the shares.

Regardless of the purchase method used, the acquirer buys shares already outstanding. *The transaction is with the existing shareholders, not with the target company.* The buyer does not need the co-operation of the acquired company itself. Sometimes the target company's board of directors opposes a takeover attempt and tries to persuade the shareholders not to sell their shares to the acquirer—the takeover attempt in this instance is known as a **hostile takeover**. Nevertheless, if the purchaser can convince enough of the target company's shareholders to sell their shares, a business combination will occur.

Unlike a direct purchase of assets, a business combination that is achieved by an acquisition of shares has no impact on the asset and equity structure of the acquired company.[4] The acquired company continues to carry its assets and liabilities on its own books. The purchaser has acquired *control* over the assets, but has not acquired the assets themselves.

Advantages of Share Purchase

The purchase of shares rather than assets has the obvious advantage that control can be obtained by buying considerably less than 100% of the shares. Thus control can be obtained at substantially less cost than if the acquirer purchased the assets directly.

There are several other advantages to buying shares rather than the net assets themselves:

- The shares may be selling at a price on the market that is less than the fair value per share (or even carrying value per share) of the net assets. The acquirer can therefore obtain control over the assets at a lower price than could be negotiated for the assets themselves.
- By buying shares rather than assets, the acquirer ends up with an asset that is more easily saleable than the assets themselves, in case the acquirer later decides to divest itself of the acquired business, or a portion thereof.
- The acquirer may prefer to retain the newly acquired business as a separate entity for legal, tax, and business reasons. The acquired business's liabilities need not be assumed directly, and there is no interruption of the business relationships built up by the acquired corporation.
- Income tax impacts can be a major factor in the choice between purchasing assets and purchasing shares. A purchase of shares may benefit the seller because any gain to the seller on a sale of shares will be taxed as a capital gain. However, if the assets are sold, gains may be subject to tax at full rates, such as (1) CCA (capital cost allowance) recapture, (2) a sale of inventory, or (3) a sale of intangibles that were fully deducted for tax purposes when paid for initially. Also, the acquiree may have substantial tax loss carryforwards that the company is unlikely to utilize. The purchaser may be able to take advantage of these carryforwards, say by transferring income-bearing assets to the acquired subsidiary.

For the buyer, however, a purchase of assets may be more desirable than a purchase of shares from a tax viewpoint. When the assets are purchased directly, their cost to the acquiring company becomes the basis for their tax treatment. For example, depreciable assets are recorded on the acquiring company's books at fair values, and CCA will be based on those fair values. Similarly, goodwill purchased is treated as *eligible capital property* for tax purposes and 75% of the goodwill is subject to CCA (the other 25% is not deductible).

If control over the assets is obtained via a share purchase, on the other hand, there is no change in the tax basis for the assets because there is no change in the assets' ownership. Thus the buyer cannot take advantage of any increased tax shields if net assets are purchased at fair values that are greater than carrying values.

Another advantage of buying control over another company is that the acquirer does not automatically assume the contingent liabilities of the target company, such as lawsuits or

4. An exception occurs when "push-down" accounting is used. We will discuss this concept towards the end of the chapter.

environmental liabilities. If large unexpected liabilities arise, the controlling company can let the subsidiary go bankrupt—the parent loses its investment, but that's better than being pulled down by overwhelming and unexpected liabilities associated with assets purchased directly.

Obviously, the decision on acquisition method is subject to many variables. In a friendly takeover, the method of purchase and the purchase price are subject to negotiation, taking into account the various factors affecting both parties, including income tax. If the takeover is hostile, then a purchase of shares is the only alternative.

Share Exchanges

There are many different ways in which shares can be exchanged to accomplish a business combination.[5] Some of the more common and straightforward methods include the following.

- **Direct exchange.** The acquirer issues new shares to the shareholders of the acquired company in exchange for the shares of the target company (the acquiree).
- **Indirect exchange.** *Subsidiaries* of the acquirer issue shares in exchange for the acquiree's shares.
- **Holding company.** A new corporation is formed; the new corporation issues shares to the shareholders of both the acquirer and the acquiree in exchange for the outstanding shares of both companies.
- **Statutory amalgamation.** The shareholders of the two corporations agree to a *statutory amalgamation*.
- **Reverse takeover.** The acquiree issues new shares to the shareholders of the acquirer in exchange for the acquirer's outstanding shares.

Direct Exchange The first method listed above is the most common approach. What happens is:

- the acquirer issues new shares to the shareholders of the acquiree, and therefore has more shares outstanding after the acquisition than before the acquisition;
- the pre-acquisition shareholders of the acquiree become shareholders in the acquirer, so that the acquirer's post-acquisition shareholders consist of both its original shareholders *and* the former shareholders of the acquiree; and
- the acquiree's shares are now held by the acquiring *corporation* instead of external shareholders.

Indirect Exchange The second approach is similar to the first, except that the acquirer does not issue its own shares to acquire the company directly. Instead, the acquirer obtains indirect control by having its subsidiaries issue new shares to acquire the company. This approach is useful when the acquirer does not want to alter the ownership percentages of the existing shareholders by issuance of additional shares. For example, if the controlling shareholder of the acquirer owns 51% of the acquirer's shares, the issuance of additional shares would

5. Some share exchanges may also include cash as part of the purchase consideration.

decrease the controlling shareholder's interest to below 50%, and control could be lost. But if the acquirer has a subsidiary that is, say, 70% owned, quite a number of additional shares could be issued by the subsidiary without jeopardizing the parent's control.

Holding Company Under the third method, a new company is created that will hold the shares of both of the combining companies. The holding company issues its new shares in exchange for the shares of both the acquiree and the acquirer. After the exchange, the shares of both operating companies are held by the holding company, while the shares of the holding company are held by the former shareholders of both the acquiree and the acquirer.

The third method is not likely to be used by public companies. If the acquirer has a stock exchange listing, that listing would not automatically transfer to the newly formed company. The new company would have to apply for a new listing, which would disrupt trading in the acquirer's shares. The interruption in trading would likely have an adverse effect on the acquirer's share price.

Statutory Amalgamation In a statutory amalgamation, the shareholders of two or more corporations approve the combination or amalgamation of their companies into a single surviving corporation. Statutory amalgamations are governed by the provincial or federal corporations acts under which the companies are incorporated. For two or more corporations to amalgamate, they must be incorporated under the same act. The shareholders of the combined company are the former shareholders of the combining companies.

Statutory amalgamation is the only method of combination in which the combining companies cease to exist as separate legal entities. It is also the only method of share exchange in which the assets of both companies end up being recorded on the books of one company, similar to the recording of assets in a direct purchase of net assets.

In all other forms of share exchange, there is no transfer of assets and thus no recording of the acquiree's assets on the acquirer's books—the results of the combination are reported by means of consolidated financial statements, as we discussed in the previous chapter. In contrast, consolidated statements are not needed for the combined companies after a statutory amalgamation because only one company survives. Of course, if either amalgamating company has subsidiaries, it would still be necessary to prepare consolidated statements that includes those subsidiaries.

Reverse Takeover It is obvious in the previous four methods of exchanging shares which corporation is the acquirer in the business combination. Simply, the acquirer is the corporation that obtains control over the other entity. However, it is possible to arrange the combination in such a way that the company that legally appears to be the acquirer is, in substance, the acquiree (the fifth method).

For example, suppose that LesserLimited has 100,000 shares outstanding before the combination, and issues 200,000 new shares to acquire all of GreaterCorp's shares. LesserLimited will own all of the shares of GreaterCorp and thus will legally control GreaterCorp. However, two-thirds of the shares of LesserLimited will be owned by the former shareholders of GreaterCorp, and the former shareholders of GreaterCorp will have voting control of LesserLimited after the combination. The substance of the combination is that control resides with GreaterCorp's shareholders even though the legal form of the combination is that

LesserLimited acquired GreaterCorp. This form of business combination is called a **reverse takeover**.

After a reverse takeover, the consolidated financial statements will be issued under the name of the legal parent (in this example, LesserLimited) but should reflect the substance of the combination as a continuation of the financial statements of the legal subsidiary (i.e., GreaterCorp). Pre-combination comparative statements and historical data should be those of the legal subsidiary (and in-substance acquirer) rather than of the legal parent (and in-substance acquiree).[6]

Because of the potential confusion from reporting the substance of the activities of the legal subsidiary under the name of the legal parent, it is common for reverse takeovers to be accompanied by a company name change so that the name of the legal parent becomes almost indistinguishable from that of the legal subsidiary. This is what happened in the COSTA Energy Inc. example that we cited in the chapter introduction.

One of the main reasons for a reverse takeover is to acquire a stock exchange listing. If LesserLimited had a Toronto Stock Exchange (TSX) listing and GreaterCorp wanted one, a reverse takeover could be arranged instead of going to the trouble and expense of applying to the Ontario Securities Commission (OSC) and the TSX for a new listing. After a reverse takeover, LesserLimited would legally own GreaterCorp and could continue to use the TSX listing. However, to preserve the substance of the transaction as a continuance of GreaterCorp, LesserLimited would legally change its name to GreaterCorp and continue trading with the same TSX listing but under the name of the in-substance acquirer.

In some instances, the legal acquirer (and in-substance acquiree) is just a **shell company** that has an exchange listing but no assets. In that case, no business combination has really occurred because the shell company is not a "business" within the definitions used for business combinations.

The accounting problem in any business combination is to report in accordance with the *substance* of the combination, and not to be misled by its legal form. Accountants must be sensitive to the objectives of managers and owners in arranging business combinations, and must examine the end result to determine who purchased what and for how much.

Illustration of a Share Exchange

To illustrate the acquirer's accounting for a purchase of shares, assume that on December 31, 20X5, Purchase Ltd. acquires all of the outstanding shares of Target Ltd. by issuing 40,000 Purchase Ltd. shares with a market value of $30, or $1,200,000 total, in exchange.[7] After the exchange of shares, all of the Target Ltd. shares will be held by the corporate entity of Purchase Ltd., while the newly issued shares of Purchase Ltd. will be held by the former shareholders of Target Ltd. and *not* by Target Ltd. as a corporate entity. Target Ltd. will have no shareholders external to the combined entity, while the shareholder base and the number of shares outstanding for Purchase Ltd. have increased.

6. A detailed description of reverse takeover accounting is beyond the scope of this book. IFRS 3 provides guidance on reverse takeovers.
7. This transaction has the same value as the illustration used earlier in the chapter for a direct purchase of net assets.

EXHIBIT 3-4

Statements of Financial Position, December 31, 20X5

	Before the exchange of shares		After the exchange of shares	
	Purchase Ltd.	Target Ltd.	Purchase Ltd.	Target Ltd.
Cash	$1,000,000	$ 50,000	$1,000,000	$ 50,000
Accounts receivable	2,000,000	150,000	2,000,000	150,000
Inventory	200,000	50,000	200,000	50,000
Land	1,000,000	300,000	1,000,000	300,000
Buildings and equipment	3,000,000	500,000	3,000,000	500,000
Accumulated depreciation	(1,200,000)	(150,000)	(1,200,000)	(150,000)
Investment in Target Ltd.	—	—	1,200,000	—
TOTAL ASSETS	$6,000,000	$900,000	$7,200,000	$900,000
Accounts payable	$1,000,000	$100,000	$1,000,000	$100,000
Long-term notes payable	400,000	—	400,000	—
Common shares*	2,600,000	200,000	3,800,000	200,000
Retained earnings	2,000,000	600,000	2,000,000	600,000
TOTAL LIABILITIES AND SHARE EQUITY	$6,000,000	$900,000	$7,200,000	$900,000

*For Purchase Ltd., 160,000 shares before the exchange; 200,000 shares after the exchange.

When Purchase Ltd. acquires the shares, the entry to record the purchase on the books of Purchase Ltd. will be as follows:

Investment in Target Ltd.	1,200,000	
Common shares		1,200,000

There will be no entry on Target Ltd.'s books, because Target Ltd. is not a party to the transaction; the transaction is with the shareholders of Target Ltd. and not with the company itself. After the original purchase is recorded, the investment is accounted for on Purchase Ltd.'s books by either the cost or equity method, as discussed in Chapter 2.

Exhibit 3-4 shows the statements of financial position of Purchase Ltd. and Target Ltd. on December 31, 20X5, both before and after the purchase of Target Ltd.'s shares by Purchase Ltd. The pre-transaction amounts are the same as were shown in Exhibit 3-2, when Purchase Ltd. purchased the net assets of Target Ltd.

The post-transaction amounts on Purchase Ltd.'s separate-entity SFP differ from the pre-transaction amounts only in one respect—Purchase Ltd. now has an account, "Investment in Target Ltd.," that reflects the cost of buying Target Ltd.'s shares, offset by an equal increase in Purchase Ltd.'s common share account. The purchase price was $1,200,000, determined by the value of the 40,000 Purchase Ltd. common shares given to Target Ltd.'s shareholders in exchange for their shares in Target Ltd.

Target Ltd.'s SFP is completely unaffected by the exchange of shares. Target Ltd.'s *owner* has changed, but nothing has changed in the company's accounts. Target Ltd.'s net asset carrying value was $800,000 prior to the change of ownership, and remains $800,000 after the change of ownership.

However, Target Ltd. is now a subsidiary of Purchase Ltd., and therefore Purchase Ltd. will prepare consolidated financial statements for public reporting purposes. The preparation of consolidated statements for a purchased subsidiary is somewhat more complex than for parent-founded subsidiaries, and involves choices from among several optional approaches. Consolidation of a purchased subsidiary at the date of acquisition will be illustrated shortly.

CONCEPT CHECK 3-2

Companion Website

1. Why would a company buy the shares of another company to obtain control of the net assets of that company rather than directly buying the net assets of that company?
2. What are the common methods of share exchange used in business combinations?

ALTERNATIVE APPROACHES TO REPORTING MERGERS

Alternative Approaches to Reporting Business Combinations

In Chapter 2 we demonstrated the preparation of consolidated statements for Parco. To obtain the Parco consolidated SFP, we simply added the balances of Subco's assets and liabilities to those of Parco, after eliminating the intercompany balances. It might seem logical to use the same procedure to prepare Purchase Ltd.'s consolidated SFP, adding the carrying values of the two companies' assets and liabilities together to get the consolidated amounts.

However, in Chapter 2 we were demonstrating consolidation of a *parent-founded* subsidiary. In wholly owned parent-founded subsidiaries, the carrying values of the subsidiary's net assets represent the costs of the assets to the consolidated economic entity, because it was the parent's investment that provided the funds to purchase the assets. When a subsidiary is purchased, however, the purchase price of the net assets acquired will almost certainly be different from the carrying value of those assets on the subsidiary's books.

There are four general alternative approaches to consolidation after one company acquires control over another.

Pooling-of-Interests Method The **pooling-of-interests method** involves adding together the *carrying values* of the assets and liabilities of the two companies. The assumption underlying the pooling method is that the combined economic entity is a continuation under common ownership of two previously separate going concerns, and that the operations of both companies will continue without substantial change. If the companies continue to function as separate entities—although now under common ownership—then it is presumed that there should be no change in the basis of accounting for the assets and liabilities as a result of the combination. The pooling method completely ignores the fair value of both companies' assets and liabilities. As a result, its use can have a significant impact on the results reported in the company's financial statements.

Acquisition Method The **acquisition method** adds the *fair values* of Target Ltd.'s assets and liabilities at the date of acquisition to the *carrying values* of Purchase Ltd.'s assets and liabilities. This method is now used in Canada and will be fully demonstrated later in this chapter.

Purchase Method The **purchase method** adds the *purchase cost allocated* to Target Ltd.'s assets and liabilities at the date of acquisition to the *carrying values* of Purchase Ltd.'s assets and liabilities. Notice the subtle distinction between this method and the acquisition method just above. The acquisition method uses fair values, while the purchase method uses the purchase cost allocation to the acquiree's assets and liabilities. In the case of a *wholly owned subsidiary*, the purchase method will be identical to the acquisition method when the purchase price is equal to or greater than the fair values of the net identifiable assets of Target Ltd.

For non-wholly owned subsidiaries, however, the purchase method can yield results quite different from the acquisition method because of the difference between the two methods in how the non-controlling interest is valued. We will illustrate the application of the acquisition method to the acquisition of non-wholly owned subsidiaries in Chapter 5.

New-Entity Method The acquisition and purchase methods can be criticized because the consolidated SFP contains a mixture of old carrying values (for Purchase Ltd.'s assets) and date-of-acquisition fair values (for Target Ltd.'s assets). One can argue that when a business combination occurs, a new economic entity is formed, and that a new basis of accountability should be established for *all* of the assets.

Under the **new-entity method**, in contrast, all of the assets and liabilities of *both* Target Ltd. and Purchase Ltd. are revalued to fair value, so that the consolidated SFP will disclose the current fair values (on the date of the combination) of all of the assets for the combined entity.

Under certain circumstances, there is merit in the arguments for the new-entity method. If the combining enterprises are of roughly comparable size, and if the operations of the newly combined enterprises are going to be substantially different from the predecessor operations, then a case can be made for establishing a new basis of accountability. However, there are significant practical problems in implementing the method. Obtaining fair values for all of the assets is likely to be an expensive and time-consuming project, unless the acquiring company already uses current values for internal reporting purposes. In addition, a substantial degree of subjectivity would inevitably exist in the fair-value determination.

Summary of Methods

The two variables that vary among the four methods outlined above are (1) the valuation of the parent's net assets; and (2) the valuation of the subsidiary's net assets. The alternatives can be summarized as follows:

Method	Net Assets of Parent Company	Net Assets of Subsidiary	Applicability of Method in Canada
Pooling of interests	Carrying value	Carrying value	Prior to 2001 in limited cases
Acquisition	Carrying value	Fair value	Mandatory after January 1, 2011
Purchase	Carrying value	Purchase price paid*	Widely used prior to January 1, 2011
New entity	Fair value	Fair value	Discussed, but never used in practice

* In the case of a 100% owned subsidiary if purchase price paid is equal to or greater than the fair value of the net identifiable assets of the subsidiary, the purchase and acquisition methods are identical.

Although the acquisition method is now the "approved" method of accounting for business combinations, it is useful to have at least "name recognition" of the alternative approaches. Accounting for business combinations has been contentious for a long time—it's never really been a settled issue. Indeed, standard-setters had quite recently given serious consideration to the new entity method, but eventually settled on the acquisition method. Who knows what may lie ahead?

With one exception, we will not discuss or illustrate the application of the alternative approaches because they are not currently used for business combinations. However, the pooling-of-interests approach is used in corporate restructurings. We will discuss pooling briefly in the next section, and then move on to applying the acquisition method for business combinations.

Corporate Restructurings

The acquisition-method requirement of IFRS 3 does not apply to combinations of companies under **common control**, wherein two or more subsidiaries are controlled by the same owners both before and after the combination. The owners can be either the same parent company or the same controlling shareholders. The primary type of control is a parent company that combines two or more of its controlled subsidiaries. Common control can also be exerted through contractual arrangements.[8] *Common control transactions* are also commonly known as **corporate restructurings**.

A parent company (or its owners) may decide to rearrange the intercorporate ownerships of the economic entity comprising the parent and its several subsidiaries. New subsidiaries may be formed, or parts of the economic entity may be combined or otherwise regrouped or redefined. When a corporate restructuring takes place, it is not an arm's-length transaction because all of the individual corporations are ultimately controlled by the same shareholders. Since there is no arm's-length transaction, the assets cannot be revalued for reporting on either the separate-entity or the consolidated financial statements.

Common control transactions are quite common in both public and private companies in Canada. There is no guidance in IFRS for how such transactions should be reported because these corporate reshufflings have no impact on *consolidated* statements. Corporate restructurings are accounted for in the same manner as pooling of interests; since there is no substantive change to control or ownership interests, a corporate restructuring is accounted for strictly on the basis of carrying values—fair values are never used because they are not arm's length transactions. Therefore, it is necessary to understand the pooling method even though it is not used for business combinations under IFRS.

8. Sometimes, pursuant to contractual agreements, a group of individuals may collectively control two companies by having the power over their financial and operating policies and thereby obtaining benefits from the activities of those companies. A combination of these two companies will not therefore lead to a change in the ultimate collective control over the combined entity. Therefore, such a combination will be deemed to be a common control transaction and not a business combination.

CONCEPT CHECK 3-3

1. What general alternative approaches to reporting business combinations are available, and how do they differ from each other?
2. How do corporate restructurings differ from business combinations?

CONSOLIDATION PROCEDURES USING THE ACQUISITION METHOD

General Approach

Before plunging into the greater complexities of consolidation in the following chapters, we will more carefully illustrate the general procedure for consolidating subsidiaries that were acquired through a business combination. The key factor that differentiates the procedure is that, for business combinations, consolidation mechanics must adjust for fair values, whereas fair values are not an issue for parent-founded subsidiaries.

The reporting objective is *substance over form*. Although the parent and its subsidiaries are separate *legal* entities and prepare separate, individual financial statements, the overall *economic* entity is the group of companies. Indeed, consolidated statements are called **group accounts** in most parts of the world, even though there are no formal "accounts" for the group—just consolidation working papers and financial statements.

In theory, acquisition-method accounting combines the carrying values of the parent with the fair values (*at date of acquisition*) of the purchased subsidiaries. In practice, consolidation actually begins with *carrying values* of both companies. At the date of acquisition, it is clear that the carrying values and the fair values relate to the same assets and liabilities. As time moves on, however, assets will enter and leave the SFP of the purchased subsidiary, and the asset base will change.

Therefore, broadly speaking, consolidation takes the carrying values of both companies and adds the fair-value increment (FVI) relating to each asset. A **fair-value increment** (or decrement) is the difference between the carrying values and fair values of the acquiree's identifiable assets and liabilities at the date of acquisition, plus any goodwill. Specifically, the FVI is first allocated to the various identifiable assets and liabilities of the acquiree to the *full extent* of their *fair-value increments (or decrements)*. Any excess of the FVI after the allocation process is allocated to goodwill.

In this and the later chapters, we follow a sequence of steps that we call the **MEAR steps to consolidation**. MEAR is a mnenomic (a memory aid) that stands for the four steps required in a typical consolidation: **M**easure, **E**liminate, **A**mortize FVIs, and **R**ecognize non-controlling interest's share of earnings. We hope that this simple memory device will help you to remember the sequence in the consolidation process, which can become rather complex at times.

EXHIBIT 3-5

MEAR Steps to Consolidation—Phase 1

Consolidation Steps	At Acquisition
1. Measure	• Calculate cost and fair-value increments (FVI) • Allocate FVI
2. Eliminate	• Eliminate parent's investment account and sub's share equity accounts

The MEAR steps to consolidation help us approach the consolidation process in a systematic and organized fashion, qualities indispensable for solving the more complicated consolidation problems that will come later in the text. Hopefully, they will save countless hours of frustration. In our experience, students who approach consolidations systematically will obtain a better understanding of the topic and consequently also perform better on exams. At the same time these steps are like the training wheels on a bicycle. They are needed at the beginning when you are becoming comfortable with the consolidation process. However, you may feel comfortable enough to dispense with them in the course of time.

We will develop the full sequence of steps (and sub-steps) in subsequent chapters. However, since this chapter focuses only on consolidation at the date of acquisition, we need be concerned here with only the first two steps, **M**easure and **E**liminate, These steps are always required at the date of acquisition as well as for all subsequent reporting dates. Exhibit 3-5 elaborates on the steps required under **M**easure and **E**liminate.

Illustration

An analysis of the purchase price for Target Ltd. is illustrated in Exhibit 3-6. Of the $1,200,000 purchase price, $800,000 is attributed to the carrying value of the net assets acquired, and the difference of $400,000 represents the FVI. The FVI of $400,000 is allocated to the various identifiable assets of Target Ltd to the extent of the total of their fair-value increment of $300,000, the residual of $100,000 being allocated to goodwill.

Sometimes the PPD is less than the total of the fair value increments relating to the net identifiable assets. In such a case we have a negative goodwill or a bargain purchase. In such a situation, the difference is recognized as a gain from a bargain purchase in the consolidated financial statements by the acquirer as discussed in further detail below. Irrespective of the presence or absence of a bargain purchase, the allocation of the FVI to the various assets and liabilities acquired is carried out as usual following the **M**easure step of the MEAR steps to consolidation.

Exhibit 3-7 shows the derivation of Purchase Ltd.'s consolidated SFP at December 31, 20X5, using the direct method. For each item on the SFP, we take the carrying value for Purchase Ltd., add the carrying value of Target Ltd., and add the fair-value increment. The fair-value increment (and goodwill) adjustments are indicated with an "**a**." Also, we must eliminate Purchase Ltd.'s investment account and Target's shareholders' equity accounts (indicated with a "**b**").

EXHIBIT 3-6

Allocation of Fair Value Increment

100% Purchase of Target Ltd., December 31, 20X5

	Carrying value (a)	Fair value (b)	Fair value Increment (c) = (b) – (a)	FVI Allocated	
Purchase price					$1,200,000
Less carrying value of Target's net identifiable assets (100%)					(800,000)
= Fair Value Increment, allocated below					400,000
Cash	$ 50,000	$ 50,000	—		
Accounts receivable	150,000	150,000	—		
Inventory	50,000	50,000	—		
Land	300,000	400,000	$100,000	$100,000	
Buildings and equipment	500,000	550,000	50,000	50,000	
Accumulated depreciation	(150,000)	—	150,000	150,000	
Accounts payable	(100,000)	(100,000)	—		
Total fair-value increment					(300,000)
Net asset carrying value	$800,000				
Fair value of assets acquired		$1,100,000			
Balance of FVI allocated to goodwill					$ 100,000

There is one aspect of Exhibit 3-7 that merits explanation. You'll notice that *accumulated depreciation* is calculated by adding the two companies' amounts together, and then *subtracting Target Ltd.'s accumulated depreciation at the date of acquisition*. We subtract Target Ltd.'s accumulated depreciation because we want to show the fair value of Target Ltd.'s depreciable assets at the date of acquisition. This amount is included in the capital asset account itself. If we carried Target's accumulated depreciation forward, we would be reducing the fair value. In effect, we would be combining fair value in the asset account with written-off cost in the accumulated depreciation.

Although we have indicated which adjustments on Exhibit 3-7 are for fair-value increments and which are eliminations, bear in mind that these purchase adjustments and eliminations are not independent. Essentially, all of the adjustments shown in Exhibit 3-7 are allocations of the $1,200,000 fair value. In future years, all of the components of this fair value adjustment must be made simultaneously, as we will illustrate in the following chapters.

The consolidation procedures under the worksheet method are provided on this textbook's Companion Website.

Companion Website

CONCEPT CHECK 3-4

1. What consolidation procedures are required at the time of acquisition under the acquisition method?
2. Under the acquisition method, why must fair-value increments be allocated to various assets and liabilities?

EXHIBIT 3-7

Purchase Ltd. Consolidated SFP

Consolidated Statement of Financial Position
December 31, 20X5

ASSETS	
Current assets:	
Cash [1,000,000 + 50,000]	$1,050,000
Accounts receivable [2,000,000 + 150,000]	2,150,000
Inventory [200,000 + 50,000]	250,000
	3,450,000
Property, Plant, and Equipment:	
Land [1,000,000 + 300,000 + **100,000a**]	1,400,000
Buildings and equipment [3,000,000 + 500,000 + **50,000a**]	3,550,000
Accumulated depreciation [1,200,000 + 150,000 – **150,000a**]	(1,200,000)
	3,750,000
Other Assets:	
Investment in Target Ltd. [1,200,000 – **400,000a** – **800,000b**]	—
Goodwill [+ **100,000a**]	100,000
TOTAL ASSETS	$7,300,000
LIABILITIES AND SHAREHOLDERS' EQUITY	
Liabilities:	
Current: accounts payable [1,000,000 + 100,000]	$1,100,000
Long-term: notes payable [400,000 + 0]	400,000
	1,500,000
Shareholders' Equity:	
Common shares [3,800,000 + 200,000 – **200,000b**]	3,800,000
Retained earnings [2,000,000 + 600,000 – **600,000b**]	2,000,000
	5,800,000
TOTAL LIABILITIES AND SHAREHOLDERS' EQUITY	$7,300,000

NEGATIVE GOODWILL

In the business combination used in the previous example, control over net assets with a fair value of $1,100,000 was acquired for $1,200,000. The difference between the purchase price and the fair value of the acquired net assets is treated as goodwill.

It is not unusual, however, for the total fair value of the assets and liabilities to be *greater* than the purchase price. This excess of fair values over the purchase price is commonly known as negative goodwill, although the term is not particularly indicative of the accounting treatment of the amount. The total of the net debits (to record the fair values) is greater than the credits (to record the consideration paid), and therefore there are more debits than credits in the consolidated statements—not a tolerable situation in a double-entry system. The task is to correct the balance by either increasing the credits or decreasing the debits.

In previous years, it was common practice to increase the credits by establishing an account to credit for the amount of negative goodwill. It was not normally called "negative goodwill," of course. Usually a more opaque title was chosen, such as "excess of fair value over cost of assets acquired." This was prohibited by prior Canadian standards and is also prohibited under IFRS. Instead of creating a credit for negative goodwill, debits and credits must be balanced by recognizing a *gain on bargain purchase* in the consolidated SCI issued by the acquirer.

A bargain purchase is possible for a variety of reasons. If the acquisition is by a purchase of shares, then the market price of the acquiree's shares may be well below the net asset value per share. Or if the acquiree is a private company, an acquirer may make a bargain purchase if the present owners are anxious to sell, perhaps due to the death of the founder-manager, a divorce, changed family financial position, or simply an inability to manage effectively—family-owned businesses are infamous for failing after the third generation takes over.

Continuing our example, suppose that Purchase Ltd. acquired all of the shares of Target Ltd., as above, but at a cost of only $1,050,000. Since the fair value of Target's net assets is $1,100,000, negative goodwill of $50,000 exists. Under the acquisition method the identifiable assets and liabilities of the acquiree are *always* reported at their fair values regardless of the purchase consideration transferred. Therefore, in our example Target Ltd.'s assets and liabilities will be reported on Purchase Ltd.'s consolidated SFP at a total amount of $1,100,000, their fair value. The PPD in this case will be $250,000 ($1,050,000 purchase consideration less $800,000 carrying value of the net identifiable assets). However, the fair value increment continues to be $300,000. The difference of $50,000 ($300,000 fair value increment less $250,000 PPD) represents a negative goodwill and will be recognized as a gain on bargain purchase in the consolidated SCI issued by Purchase Ltd.

DISCLOSURE

Business combinations are significant events. They often change the nature of operations of a company and thus change the components of the earnings stream. All users' financial reporting objectives are affected by substantial business combinations. At a minimum, the asset and liability structure of the reporting enterprise is changed. Disclosure of business combinations therefore is quite important.

IFRS 3 recommends a long list of disclosures for business combinations completed during a reporting period. The acquirer is required to disclose information that enables users to evaluate the:

- nature and financial effect of business combinations that occurred either during the reporting period or after the end of the reporting period but before the date on which the financial statements for that period are authorized for issue; and
- financial effects of the adjustments made in the current reporting period relating to a business combination that occurred either in that reporting period or in previous reporting periods.

We will not reproduce the complete list of disclosures here, but the disclosures should cover essential aspects such as:

- a description, including the name of the acquired subsidiary, the date of acquisition, percentage of the voting shares acquired, primary reason for the business combination, and how control was obtained;
- a qualitative description of the factors giving rise to the goodwill and intangible assets not separately identifiable from goodwill;
- the amount of any contingent consideration recognized, and the arrangement and basis for arriving at such amount;
- amounts of the major classes of assets and liabilities acquired;
- fair value on the acquisition date of the purchase consideration transferred and of each major class of consideration;
- the amount and reason for a gain from bargain purchase if present; and
- the amount and measurement basis of the non-controlling interest if less than 100% of the acquiree is acquired.

For acquisitions that are individually immaterial, similar information should be disclosed in the aggregate.

Exhibit 3-8 shows the 2008 disclosure note relating to business combinations made by Tesco PLC, a UK-based grocery chain. Exhibit 3-8 focuses mainly on Tesco's acquisition of Dobbies Garden Centres PLC, a UK retailer. You can see several pieces of information in this note:

- Tesco made several acquisitions during the year; the most significant acquisition (Dobbies) has been disclosed separately, while the rest are shown in aggregate.
- Acquisition accounting has been applied for all acquisitions.
- Goodwill relates mainly to location, assembled workforce, and synergies expected to be achieved from the business combinations.
- The fair values relating to the acquisitions are provisional and will be reviewed based on additional information up to one year from the date of the acquisition.
- Dobbies is a publicly listed garden centre retailer in the United Kingdom. Tesco did not buy the assets and liabilities of Dobbies directly. Instead, it bought 65.5% of the share capital of Dobbies in 2007.
- The purchase was for cash, and the total purchase consideration paid is cash of £103 million. Note that the costs associated with the acquisition of £3 million have been added to the total consideration. This practice was allowed by earlier IFRS standards. IFRS 3 no longer allows these costs to be added to the cost of the acquisition but rather requires them to be expensed by the acquirer in the year they are incurred and services received.
- Of the total cost, £61 million was allocated to goodwill, which is 57.5% of the total purchase price.
- In the subsequent year, specifically July 31, 2008, Tesco completed the acquisition of the remaining 34.5% of the share capital of Dobbies for total consideration of £43million. This resulted in additional goodwill of £18million.

EXHIBIT 3-8

Disclosure of Acquisitions

TESCO PLC

Note 27 Business combinations

The Group has made a number of acquisitions in the year, of which the most significant acquisition has been disclosed separately and the remainder shown in aggregate.

The net assets and results of the acquired businesses are included in the consolidated accounts of the Group from the date of acquisition. Acquisition accounting has been applied and the goodwill arising has been capitalised and is subject to annual impairment testing.

The goodwill acquired in the business combinations listed below has been allocated to the single group of cash-generating units represented by the acquired businesses, as this is the lowest level within the Group at which the goodwill is monitored internally. Goodwill arising on acquisitions in the year is attributable mainly to location, the assembled workforce and the synergies expected to be achieved.

The fair values currently established for acquisitions made in the year to 23 February 2008 are provisional. Fair values will be reviewed based on additional information up to one year from the date of acquisition. The Directors do not believe that any net adjustments resulting from such a review would have a material effect on the Group.

DOBBIES GARDEN CENTRES PLC

In 2007, the Group acquired 65.5% of the share capital of Dobbies Garden Centres PLC, a retailer in the United Kingdom.

The fair value of the identifiable assets and liabilities of Dobbies Garden Centres PLC as at the date of acquisition were:

	Pre-acquisition carrying amounts £m	Fair value adjustments £m	Recognised values on acquisition £m
Property, plant and equipment	132	31	163
Brand	—	8	8
Goodwill	2	(2)	—
Inventories	11	—	11
Trade and other receivables	(12)	(3)	(15)
Cash and cash equivalents	1	—	1
Trade and other payables	3	3	6
Bank loans and overdraft	(87)	1	(86)
Deferred tax liability	(3)	(15)	(18)
Post-employment benefit obligation	(1)	—	(1)
Net assets	46	23	69
Minority interest			(24)
Net assets acquired			45
Goodwill arising on acquisition			61
Consideration:			106
Cash consideration			103
Costs associated with the acquisition			3
Total consideration			106

EXHIBIT 3-8 *(Continued)*

Disclosure of Acquisitions

The trading results of Dobbies Garden Centres PLC during the period since acquisition of the majority share and details of the results had the acquisition taken place at the beginning of the financial year have not been disclosed as it is impracticable to do so. Dobbies Garden Centres PLC remains listed on the Alternative Investment Market, and therefore we are unable to disclose information until it has been released to the market. The results of Dobbies Garden Centres PLC are not material in the context of the Group.

Source: Tesco PLC, Note 27, Business Combinations, to the group financial statements of Tesco PLC for the period ended February 23, 2008. *Annual Report and Financial Statements*, p. 90. **http://www.tescoplc.com/plc/ir/ar/archive/ar2008/arfs_08/2008_TESCO_REPORT_COMPLETE.pdf**

FAIR VALUES, REVALUATIONS, AND PUSH-DOWN ACCOUNTING

We have emphasized that the fair values of the net assets of the acquiree are never recorded in the books of the acquirer; the full purchase price is simply recorded in an investment account on the acquirer's books. We have also stated that when a business combination is accomplished by a purchase of shares (rather than by a direct purchase of assets), the acquiree continues to exist as a separate legal and reporting entity. The carrying values of the acquiree's net assets are not affected by the acquisition or by the fair values attributed to the assets by the acquirer.

However, IAS 16 allows entities to choose between the cost model and the revaluation model to measure property, plant, and equipment (PPE) after initial recognition. The choice between the two models must be made for an entire class of PPE. The revaluation model can be used for PPE whose fair value can be measured reliably. Under the revaluation model the assets have to be carried at their revaluated amount, which is, their fair values at the date of the revaluation less any subsequent accumulated depreciation and impairment losses. Importantly, under the revaluation model, the assets have to be revaluated at sufficient regularity to ensure that their carrying values are not materially different from their values if fair values were used at the end of the reporting period.

Similarly, IAS 38 also allows the use of the revaluation model to measure intangible assets that have an active market. Therefore, when a subsidiary chooses the revaluation model to measure its assets, the difference between the carrying values of its assets on its books and their corresponding acquisition date fair values may be minor or immaterial. If the parent and the subsidiary adopt the revaluation model for the latter's assets, the carrying values of those assets in the subsidiary's books will remain identical to their values on the consolidated financial statements. This practice will achieve results similar to the results obtained under push-down accounting, described below.

An exception to the general rule that the acquiree's carrying values are unaffected by the purchase may arise when the acquirer directs the acquiree to restate its assets to fair value. This practice is known as **push-down accounting** because the fair values are "pushed down" to the acquiree's books. The net effect is the same as though the acquirer had formed a new subsidiary, which then purchased all of the assets and liabilities of the acquiree.

While IFRS does not address the issue of push-down accounting, in the United States the SEC *requires* its registrants to use the practice when an acquired subsidiary is "substantially" wholly owned (roughly 90%) and there is no publicly held debt or senior shares. Push-down accounting was allowed but not required in Canada before the adoption of international standards. In any event, if push-down accounting was used by a Canadian company previously, such push-down accounting values can be used as **deemed cost** while adopting IFRS for the first time.

Advantages of Push-Down Accounting

There are two advantages to push-down accounting. The first is that the financial position and results of operations of the acquiree will be reported on the same economic basis in both the consolidated statements and its own separate-entity statements. Without push-down accounting, for example, it would be possible for the subsidiary to report a profit on its own and yet contribute an operating loss to the parent's consolidated results if the consolidation adjustments were sufficient to tip the balance between profit and loss.

The second advantage is that the process of consolidation will be greatly simplified for the parent. Since the carrying values will be the same as the acquisition fair values, there will be no need for many of the consolidation adjustments that otherwise will be required every time consolidated statements are prepared.

A special case of push-down accounting arises in a reverse takeover. In a reverse takeover, it is the legal acquirer that is really the in-substance acquiree—the fair values reported on the consolidated statements will be those of the company issuing the statements (the legal parent but in-substance subsidiary). In that case, it makes little sense for the in-substance acquiree to be carrying its assets and liabilities at carrying values that will never be reported in its own financial statements. It is more logical simply to put the fair values on the books of the in-substance acquiree.

Canadian Accounting Standards for Private Enterprises Prior to 2011, the *CICA Handbook* had already been harmonized with IFRS 3. Therefore, the basic definitions and reporting approaches described above apply to private enterprises as well. However, there still are some significant differences that reflect the fact that, by definition, a private enterprise is not issuing general-purpose financial statements. The significant differences are as follows:

- Private enterprises are not required to issue consolidated statements. Consolidated reporting is a *choice*, not a requirement. When subsidiaries are not consolidated, they can be reported on either the cost or equity basis. However, all subsidiaries should be reported on the same basis. A company cannot choose to consolidate some subsidiaries but not others.
- Sometimes, a private enterprise will have a subsidiary that is a public company. For example, a private company may own a majority of the public company's shares. In that case, the subsidiary's shares may be reported either (1) by the equity method or (2) at fair value

with gains and losses from changes in fair value taken directly into earnings. If the equity method is chosen, the parent must disclose the fair value of the investment in the notes.

If the class of shares owned by the parent (e.g., a special class of multiple-voting shares) are not traded publicly, then the equity method of reporting should be used.

- Both investments in and earnings from non-consolidated subsidiaries should be separately disclosed in the parent's financial statements.

CONCEPT CHECK 3-5

Companion Website

1. How does negative goodwill arise? How does negative goodwill affect the allocation of the PPD?
2. Explain what is meant by "push-down accounting." What are two possible benefits that arise from using this method?
3. Suppose that a private company holds a controlling interest in a public company. How, if at all, should the fair value of those shares be reported in the private company's financial statements?

Relevant Standards

IASB

Standards

IFRS 3	Business Combinations
IAS 16	Property, Plant and Equipment
IAS 27	Consolidated and Separate Financial Statements
IAS 38	Intangible Assets

Summary of Key Points

1. A business combination is the acquisition of net assets or *control* over net assets that constitute a functioning business. Control over net assets is usually obtained by buying a majority of the shares in the company that owns the assets. When control is acquired, the acquired net assets remain the property of the controlled subsidiary. Therefore, consolidated financial statements are necessary.

2. Business combinations have to be accounted using the acquisition method, which requires five steps: (1) identify the acquirer, (2) determine the acquisition date, (3) calculate the fair value of the purchase consideration transferred, (4) recognize and measure net identifiable assets acquired and liabilities assumed, and (5) measure and recognize goodwill or a gain from a bargain purchase.

   The acquired identifiable assets and liabilities are recognized at their fair values. If the purchase price is less than the aggregate fair value of the net assets, negative goodwill or gain from bargain purchase arises. A gain from a bargain purchase is recognized in the consolidated SCI issued by the acquirer in the period of the acquisition.

3. A purchase of net assets may be accomplished (1) by paying cash or other assets or (2) by issuing shares. A combination of cash and shares may be used. When shares are issued, the purchase price is based on the market value of the shares on the acquisition date.

4. If the net assets are purchased directly, the fair values of the acquired assets and liabilities are recorded on the books of the acquirer. There is no parent–subsidiary relationship because the acquirer did not buy another corporation; it bought the net assets instead.

5. Acquisition of majority control over another company enables the investor to obtain control over the assets without having to pay the full fair value of the assets. Shares can be purchased for cash or other assets. Alternatively, the purchaser can issue its own shares in exchange for the shares of the acquiree. If there is an exchange of shares, the acquirer does not have to give up any cash. The previous holders of the acquiree's shares now hold shares in the acquirer instead.

6. Theoretically, there are four approaches to reporting consolidated financial statements following purchase of control over another corporation: pooling of interests, acquisition, purchase, and new entity.

   Under the pooling method, the carrying values of the parent and the subsidiary are simply added together and reported as the consolidated amounts.

   Under acquisition accounting, the subsidiary's assets and liabilities are added to the parent's carrying values at their fair values on the date of acquisition.

   Under purchase accounting, the subsidiary's assets and liabilities are added to the parent's carrying values at the purchase price paid for them. If the purchase price is equal to or greater than the date-of-acquisition fair values of the subsidiary's identifiable assets and liabilities, then such assets and liabilities are added at their fair values to the parent's carrying values. In this latter situation, the purchase method of consolidation gives the same results as if the net assets had been purchased directly. When the purchase price paid is greater than the fair value of the identifiable assets and liabilities, the difference constitutes goodwill.

   With the new-entity method, the fair values of the parent and the subsidiary are added together to form a new basis of accountability for the ongoing economic entity.

7. The pooling method is not permitted for arm's-length business combinations by International Financial Reporting Standards or by FASB standards in the United States. However, the pooling method must be applied to non-arm's-length corporate restructurings, including the combining of companies under common control.

8. Normally, fair values are not recorded on the books of the acquiree; adjustments are made solely on working papers to prepare consolidated financial statements. However, fair values

may be recorded on the books of the acquired company if the investor corporation has acquired substantially all of the shares of the subsidiary. This practice is known as *push-down accounting*. Push-down accounting was allowed in the past in Canada, and continues to be allowed in the United States. IFRS is silent on push-down accounting. Nevertheless, if push-down accounting was used previously by a Canadian entity, the push-down accounting values can be used as deemed cost while adopting IFRS for the first time.

Companion Website

Visit the text's website at www.pearsoned.ca/beechy for practice quizzes, additional problems, Excel® templates, answers to Concept Check questions, and important IFRS updates.

Self-Study Problem 3-1

Ace Corporation acquired Blue Corporation on August 31, 20X6. Both corporations have fiscal years ending on August 31. Exhibit 3-9 shows the SFP for each corporation as of August 31, 20X6, immediately *prior* to the combination, and net income amounts for each corporation for the fiscal year ended August 31, 20X6.

The fair values of the assets and liabilities of the two companies at the date of acquisition are shown in Exhibit 3-10. The deferred development costs represent the unamortized balance of the development costs of the companies' leading-edge products. There is no observable market value for this identifiable intangible asset, but Ace expects to fully recover the costs in future years.

Before the combination, Ace had 1,200,000 common shares issued and outstanding. Blue had 750,000 common shares issued and outstanding.

EXHIBIT 3-9

Pre-Combination Statements of Financial Position, August 31, 20X6

	Ace	Blue
Cash and cash equivalents	$ 2,350,000	$ 1,200,000
Accounts receivable	2,000,000	1,800,000
Land	5,000,000	—
Machinery and equipment, net	13,500,000	8,400,000
Deferred development costs	600,000	3,100,000
	$23,450,000	$14,500,000
Accounts payable	$ 650,000	$ 1,100,000
Notes payable, long-term	2,000,000	1,000,000
Common shares	15,000,000	6,950,000
Retained earnings	5,800,000	5,450,000
	$23,450,000	$14,500,000
Net income, year ended August 31, 20X6	$ 2,450,000	$ 1,300,000

EXHIBIT 3-10

Fair Values, August 31, 20X6

	Ace	Blue
Cash and cash equivalents	$ 2,350,000	$ 1,200,000
Accounts receivable	2,000,000	1,800,000
Land	8,500,000	—
Machinery and equipment, net	11,000,000	11,000,000
Deferred development costs	750,000	4,000,000
Accounts payable	(650,000)	(1,100,000)
Notes payable, long-term	(2,000,000)	(900,000)
Net asset fair value	$21,950,000	$16,000,000

Required

Prepare the Ace Corporation post-combination SFP under each of the following *independent* situations:

1. Ace Corporation purchased the assets and assumed the liabilities of Blue Corporation by paying $2,000,000 cash and issuing long-term instalment notes payable of $18,000,000.
2. Ace issued 400,000 common shares for all of the outstanding common shares of Blue. The market value of Ace's shares was $50 per share.
3. Ace purchased 100% of Blue's outstanding common shares from Blue's previous shareholders. As consideration, Ace issued 270,000 common shares and paid $1,000,000 in cash. The market value of Ace's shares was $50 per share.

Self-Study Problem 3-2

On January 1, 20X6, Patricia Ltd. acquired 100% of the shares of Shelley Inc. The acquisition took place by issuing new Patricia Ltd. shares to the Shelley Inc. shareholders in a one-to-one exchange for their shares of Shelley Inc. The value of the newly issued Patricia Ltd. shares was estimated at $850,000. At the date of acquisition, the statements of financial position for the companies were as shown in Exhibit 3-11.

At the date of acquisition, the fair values of Shelley's assets and liabilities differed from carrying values as follows:

	Carrying value	Fair value
Land	$180,000	$300,000
Buildings	430,000	450,000
Equipment	120,000	180,000

Required

Prepare the post-acquisition consolidated SFP for Patricia Ltd. at January 1, 20X6, using the acquisition method.

EXHIBIT 3-11

Pre-Combination Statements of Financial Position, January 1, 20X6

	Patricia Ltd.	Shelley Inc.
Assets		
Cash	$ 80,000	$ 55,000
Accounts receivable	220,000	135,000
Inventories	100,000	90,000
Total current assets	400,000	280,000
Land	800,000	180,000
Buildings (net)	1,100,000	430,000
Equipment (net)	720,000	120,000
TOTAL ASSETS	$3,020,000	$1,010,000
Liabilities and shareholders' equity		
Accounts payable	$ 120,000	$ 140,000
Long-term debt payable	400,000	420,000
Total liabilities	520,000	560,000
Common shares	1,000,000	200,000
Retained earnings	1,500,000	250,000
Total shareholders' equity	2,500,000	450,000
TOTAL LIABILITIES AND SHAREHOLDERS' EQUITY	$3,020,000	$1,010,000

Review Questions

3-1 Describe the two basic types of acquisitions that can result in a business combination.

3-2 What consideration can be used in a business combination?

3-3 When one corporation buys the assets or assets and liabilities of another company, at what values are the acquired items recorded on the buyer's books?

3-4 In general, how would fair values be determined for productive assets?

3-5 In general, how would fair values be determined for liabilities?

3-6 What is *negative goodwill*? How should it be reported in the consolidated statements?

3-7 When an acquirer buys the net assets of another company by issuing shares, what is the relationship between the two companies after the transaction has taken place?

3-8 What are the advantages for the acquirer of obtaining control over assets by a purchase of shares rather than by a direct purchase of assets?

3-9 What are the disadvantages for the acquirer of obtaining control by a purchase of shares?

3-10 How can an acquirer obtain control if the management of the acquiree is hostile to the business combination?

3-11 From an income tax standpoint, what may be the disadvantages for an acquirer in obtaining control through a purchase of shares rather than by a direct purchase of net assets?

3-12 If an acquirer issues a tender offer, is it necessary for the offering company to buy all of the shares tendered?

3-13 Company P issues its shares in exchange for the shares of Company S. After the exchange, who owns the newly issued shares of P?

3-14 In an exchange of shares, how can the acquirer be identified?

3-15 What is the most common reason for a combination of a public company and a private company accomplished by means of a reverse takeover?

3-16 In consolidated statements following a reverse takeover, which company's net assets are reported at fair values: the legal acquirer or the legal subsidiary?

3-17 Why is a reverse takeover often immediately followed by a name change of the legal parent corporation?

3-18 In what form(s) of business combination do the combining companies cease to exist as separate legal entities?

3-19 What is a corporate restructuring? How are restructurings accounted for?

3-20 Under what circumstances is push-down accounting most likely to be used?

CASES

CASE 3-1 AMES BROTHERS LTD.

Ames Brothers Ltd. (ABL) is a relatively small producer of petrochemicals located in Sarnia. The common shares of the firm are publicly traded on the Toronto Stock Exchange, while the non-voting preferred shares are traded on the over-the-counter market. Because of the strategic competitive position of the firm, there was considerable recent interest in the shares of the company. During 20X6, much active trading occurred, pushing the price of the common shares from less than $8 to more than $20 by the end of the year. Similarly, the trading interest in the preferred shares pushed the dividend yield from 12% to only 9%.

Shortly after the end of 20X6, three other firms made public announcements about the extent of their holdings in ABL shares. Silverman Mines announced that it had acquired, on the open market, 32% of the common shares of ABL; Hislop Industries announced that it had acquired 24% of ABL's common shares in a private transaction with an individual who had previously been ABL's major shareholder; and Render Resources announced that it had accumulated a total of 58% of ABL's preferred shares.

However, Silverman Mines and Hislop Industries are related. The Patterson Power Corporation owns 72% of the voting shares of Silverman Mines and 38% of the voting shares of Hislop Mines. There are no other large holdings of stock of either Silverman or Hislop. Render Resources is not related to Silverman, Hislop, or Patterson.

Required

a) Has a business combination occurred in 20X6, with respect to ABL, as the term "business combination" is used in IFRS? Explain fully.

b) What implications do the various accumulations of ABL shares have for the financial reporting (for 20X6 and following years) for:

1. Silverman Mines
2. Hislop Industries
3. Render Resources
4. Patterson Power Corporation

CASE 3-2 SUDAIR LTD. AND ALBERTAIR LTD.

On February 7, 20X6, Sudair Ltd. and Albertair Ltd. jointly announced a merger of the two regional airlines. Sudair had assets totalling $500 million and had 1,000,000 common shares outstanding. Albertair had assets amounting to $400 million and 600,000 shares outstanding. Under the terms of the merger, Sudair will issue two new Sudair shares for each share of Albertair outstanding. The two companies will then merge their administrative and operating structures and will coordinate their routes and schedules to improve interchange between the two lines and to enable the combined fleet of nine jet aircraft to be more efficiently used. Both companies are publicly owned.

Required

How should the merger of Sudair and Albertair be reported?

CASE 3-3 POOL INC. AND SPARTIN LTD.

Pool Inc. and Spartin Ltd. are both public companies. The common shares of Pool have been selling in a range of $30 to $43 per share over the past year. Spartin's common shares have been selling at between $18 and $23.

The two companies are in related lines of business. In view of the increasing exposure of the companies to world competition arising from the reduction in tariff barriers, the boards of directors have approved an agreement in principle to combine the two businesses. The boards have also agreed that the combination should take the form of a share exchange, with one share of Pool equivalent to two shares of Spartin in the exchange. On the date of acquisition each share of Pool was worth $33 while each share of Spartin was worth $20.

The manner of executing the combination has not yet been decided. Three possibilities are under consideration:

1. Pool could issue one new share in exchange for two of Spartin's shares.
2. Spartin could issue two new shares in exchange for each of Pool's shares.
3. A new corporation could be formed, PS Enterprises Inc., which would issue one share in exchange for each share of Spartin and two shares in exchange for each share of Pool.

The directors are uncertain as to the accounting implications of the three alternatives. They believe that the fair values of the assets and liabilities of both companies are approximately equal to their carrying values. They have asked you to prepare a report in which you explain how the accounting results would differ under the three share exchange alternatives. They have provided you with the condensed statements of financial position of both companies as shown in Exhibit A. Pool Inc. currently has 1,600,000 common shares outstanding, and Spartin Ltd. has 1,200,000 shares outstanding.

Required

Prepare the report requested by the boards of directors.

Exhibit A Condensed Statements of Financial Position

	Pool Inc.	Spartin Ltd.
Current assets	$ 7,000,000	$ 4,500,000
Capital assets	63,000,000	22,500,000
	$70,000,000	$27,000,000
Current liabilities	$ 6,000,000	$ 1,500,000
Long-term debt	14,000,000	5,500,000
Common shares	17,000,000	16,000,000
Retained earnings	33,000,000	4,000,000
	$70,000,000	$27,000,000

CASE 3-4 BOATSMAN BOATS LIMITED AND STICKNEY SKATE CORPORATION

Boatsman Boats Limited (BBL) is a dealer in pleasure boats located in Kingston, Ontario. The company is incorporated under the *Ontario Business Corporations Act* and is wholly owned by its founder and president, Jim Boatsman. In 20X5, BBL had revenues of $2,500,000 with total assets of about $1,000,000 at year-end.

Late in 20X6, Jim Boatsman reached an agreement with Clyde Stickney for the combination of BBL and Stickney Skate Corporation (SSC). SSC is a manufacturer of ice skates and is located in Ottawa, Ontario. SSC's 20X5 revenue totalled $2,000,000 and year-end assets totalled $1,500,000. Clyde Stickney is president and general manager of SSC, and he owns 65% of the SSC shares. The other 35% is owned by Clyde's former partner, who left the business several years previously because of a policy disagreement with Clyde.

Clyde and Jim decided to combine the two businesses because their seasonal business cycles were complementary. Common ownership would permit working capital to be shifted from one company to the other, and the larger asset base and more stable financial performance of the combined company would probably increase the total debt capacity.

Under the terms of the agreement, BBL would issue common shares to Clyde Stickney in exchange for Clyde's shares in SSC. As a result of the exchange, Jim's share of BBL would drop to 60% of the outstanding BBL shares, and Clyde would hold the remaining 40%. Clyde and Jim signed a shareholders' agreement that gave each of them equal representation on the BBL board of directors.

As the end of 20X6 approached, Jim, Clyde, and CA (the BBL auditor) were discussing the appropriate treatment of the business combination on BBL's 20X6 financial statements. Clyde was of the opinion that CA should simply add together the assets and liabilities of the two companies at their carrying values (after eliminating intercompany balances and transactions, of course). Jim, on the other hand, thought that the combination had resulted in a new, stronger entity, and that the financial statements should reflect that fact by revaluing the net assets of both BBL and SSC to reflect fair values at the date of the combination. CA, however, insisted that only SSC's net assets should be revalued, and then only to the extent of the 65% of the assets that were represented by BBL's shareholdings in SSC.

While Jim and Clyde disagreed with each other on the appropriate valuation of the assets, both disagreed with CA's proposal. Jim and Clyde clearly controlled SSC through BBL, they argued; that was the whole point of the combination. In their opinion it would be inappropriate to value the same assets on two different bases, 65% current value and 35% carrying value. If only SSC's assets were to be revalued, then they reasoned that the assets at least should be valued consistently, at 100% of fair value.

In an effort to resolve the impasse that was developing, Jim and Clyde hired an independent consultant to advise them. The consultant was asked (1) to advise the shareholders on the pros and cons of each alternative in BBL's specific case, and (2) to make a recommendation on a preferred approach. The consultant was supplied with the condensed statements of financial position of BBL and SSC as shown in Exhibit B, and with CA's estimate of fair values (Exhibit C).

Required

Prepare the consultant's report. Assume that the business combination took place on December 31, 20X6.

Exhibit B Condensed Statements of Financial Position of BBL and SSC

Condensed Statements of Financial Position
December 31, 20X6

	Boatsman Boats Ltd.	Stickney Skate Corp.
Current assets	$ 600,000	$ 350,000
Land	—	250,000
Buildings and equipment	—	2,500,000
Accumulated depreciation	—	(1,500,000)
Furniture and fixtures	800,000	300,000
Accumulated depreciation	(330,000)	(100,000)
Investment in Stickney Skate Corp.	1,300,000	—
TOTAL ASSETS	$2,370,000	$1,800,000
Current liabilities	$ 370,000	$ 400,000
Long-term liabilities	300,000	900,000
Common shares	1,500,000	200,000
Retained earnings	200,000	300,000
TOTAL LIABILITIES AND EQUITIES	$2,370,000	$1,800,000

Exhibit C Estimated Fair Values of BBL and SSC

Net Asset Fair Values
December 31, 20X6

	Boatsman Boats Ltd.	Stickney Skate Corp.
Current assets	$ 600,000	$ 350,000
Land	—	700,000
Buildings and equipment:		
estimated replacement cost new	—	5,000,000
less depreciation	—	(3,000,000)
Furniture and fixtures:		
estimated replacement cost new	1,300,000	500,000
less depreciation	(520,000)	(240,000)
Current liabilities	(370,000)	(400,000)
Long-term liabilities*	(270,000)	(930,000)
Net asset fair value	$ 740,000	$1,980,000

* Discounted at current long-term interest rates.

[ICAO]

CASE 3-5 GROWTH INC. AND MINOR LTD.

Growth Inc. has just acquired control of Minor Ltd. by buying 100% of Minor's outstanding shares for $6,500,000 cash. The condensed SFP for Minor on the date of acquisition is shown below.

Growth is a public company. Currently, it has two bank covenants. The first requires Growth to maintain a specific debt-to-equity ratio and the second requires a specific current ratio. If these covenants are violated, the bank loan will be payable on demand. Growth is in a very competitive business. To encourage its employees to stay, it has adopted a new business plan that provides managers a bonus based on a percentage of net income.

The president of Growth Inc., Teresa, has hired you, CA, to assist her with the accounting for Minor.

To account for the acquisition, Growth's management has had all of Minor's capital assets appraised by two separate, independent, engineering consultants. One consultant appraised the capital assets at $7,800,000 in their present state. The other consultant arrived at a lower figure of $7,100,000, based on the assumption that imminent technological changes would soon decrease the value-in-use of Minor's capital assets by about 10%.

The asset amount for the leased building is the discounted present value of the remaining lease payments on a warehouse that Minor leased to Growth Inc. five years ago. The lease is non-cancellable and title to the building will transfer to Growth at the end of the lease term. The lease has 15 years yet to run, and the annual lease payments are $500,000 per year. The interest rate implicit in the lease was 9%.

Minor's debentures are thinly traded on the open market. Recent sales have indicated that these bonds are currently yielding about 14%. The bonds mature in 10 years.

The deferred income tax balance is the accumulated balance of CCA/depreciation temporary differences. The management of Minor sees no likelihood of the balance being reduced in the foreseeable future, because projected capital expenditures will enter the CCA classes in amounts that will more than offset the amount of depreciation for the older assets.

The carrying value of Minor's inventory appears to approximate replacement cost. However, an overstock of some items of finished goods may require temporary price reductions of about 10% to reduce inventory to more manageable levels.

Required

Provide a report for Teresa outlining how the assets of Minor Ltd. should be valued for purposes of preparing consolidated financial statements. She wants you to identify alternatives and support your decision.

Minor Ltd.
Condensed Statement of Financial Position

Cash	$ 200,000
Accounts receivable	770,000
Inventories	1,000,000
Capital assets (net)	5,000,000
Leased building	4,030,000
	$11,000,000
Accounts payable	$ 300,000
8% debentures payable	7,000,000
Deferred income taxes	700,000
Common shares	1,000,000
Retained earnings	2,000,000
	$11,000,000

CASE 3-6 WONDER AMUSEMENTS

Wonder Amusements Limited (WAL) was incorporated over 40 years ago as an amusement park and golf course. Over time, a nearby city has grown to the point where it borders on WAL's properties. In recent years WAL's owners, who are all members of one family, have seen WAL's land values increase significantly. WAL's majority shareholder, Howard Smith, owns 55% of the outstanding shares and is not active in WAL's day-to-day activities.

Last year, Howard hired a new chief executive officer, Leo Titan, who has a reputation for being an aggressive risk taker. Howard is committed, and has the personal financial resources required, to support Leo's plans.

Eight months ago, WAL became the successful bidder for a new sports franchise, in conjunction with a minority partner. Under the terms of the franchise agreement, WAL is required to build a sports arena, which is currently being constructed on a section of the amusement park. Another section of the amusement park is being relocated to ensure that the entrances to the arena are close to public transportation and parking. Consequently, some of the rides will be relocated. WAL is the sole owner of the arena at present.

The sports franchise is separately incorporated as Northern Sports Limited (NSL); WAL holds 75% of the shares in the company. Another bid is being prepared by NSL to obtain a second sports franchise so that the arena can be used more often. NSL will be required to lease space from WAL when the arena is completed in about 22 months.

For the first two sports seasons, NSL will have to lease arena space from Aggressive Limited (AL). During this time, NSL does not expect to be profitable because:

- it may take time to build a competitive team;
- AL is charging a high rent, and is not giving NSL a share of concession revenue;

- AL cannot make the better dates (e.g., Saturday nights) available to NSL to attract sports fans; and
- as a newcomer to the league, NSL is restricted with regard to the players who are available to it and the days of the week it can play in its home city.

Consequently, NSL has arranged to borrow funds from WAL and from others to finance costs and losses.

Your employer, Fabio & Fox, Chartered Accountants, has conducted the audit of WAL for several years. WAL has tended to be marginally profitable one year and then have losses the next year. The company has continued to operate because the directors knew the real estate holdings were becoming increasingly valuable.

Leo is expected to oversee the expanded accounting and finance functions in the company. Leo has met with you and the partner in charge of the WAL audit and has discussed various issues related to the year ending September 30, 20X6. His comments are provided in Exhibit D.

You have been asked by the partner to prepare for him a report, which will be used for the next meeting with Leo. He would like you to discuss the accounting and audit implications related to your discussion with Leo. The partner wants a thorough analysis of all important issues as well as support for your position.

In your review of documents, and as a result of various conversations, you have learned the following:

1. The arena will be mortgaged, but only for about 50% of its expected cost. Lenders are concerned about the special-use nature of the arena and whether it will be successfully rented for other events, such as concerts.
2. The mortgage lenders to WAL and the minority shareholders in NSL are both expected to want to see appraisals and financial statements before deciding to invest. Covenants will be required by the lenders to ensure that excessive expenditures are not undertaken and that cash is preserved.
3. Leo does not intend to consolidate NSL until it is profitable. The investment in NSL will be reported on WAL's financial statements at cost. Thus, the WAL financial statements will also be used for income tax purposes.
4. WAL's minority shareholders are not active in the business and want quarterly financial statements to monitor progress and assess Leo's performance. The minority shareholders have all expressed concern over Leo's growth strategy over the past year. Many are approaching their retirement years and are relying on WAL to supplement their retirement income.

Required

Prepare the report.

Exhibit D Notes From Discussions With Leo Titan

1. To build a road to the arena's parking lot, two holes of the 18-hole golf course will be relocated next spring. Costs of $140,000 are expected to be incurred this year in design, tree planting, ground preparation, and grass seeding to have the arena ready for next spring. These costs are to be capitalized as part of the golf course lands, along with the related property taxes of $13,000 and interest of $15,000.

2. In May 20X6, WAL acquired for $4.25 million all of the shares of an amusement park in a different city, when its land lease expired. The amusement park company was wound up and the equipment, rides, concessions, and other assets are being transported to WAL at a cost of $350,000. The estimated fair value of the assets and liabilities (according to Leo) is as follows:

Concession prizes (e.g., stuffed animals)	$ 22,500
Rides and games	4,200,000
Equipment and parts	1,650,000
Electrical supplies	75,000
Lighting and signs	100,000
Estimated present value of tax loss carryforward	700,000
	6,747,500
Liabilities	1,200,000
Net Assets	$5,547,500

   WAL expects to spend approximately $400,000 in getting the assets in operating order and $500,000 on foundations and site preparations for the rides. Leo wants to "capitalize as much as possible."
3. Approximately $600,000 will be used to relocate rides that are currently on land that is needed for the arena. This amount is to be capitalized, net of scrap recovery on dismantled and redundant equipment of $60,000. Virtually all of the rides were fully depreciated years ago.
4. To assist in financing the new ventures, WAL sold excess land to developers who intend to construct a shopping centre, office buildings, and expensive homes that will be adjunct to the golf course and away from the amusement park. The developers and WAL agreed to these terms:

Paid to WAL on May 1, 20X6	$ 6,000,000
To be paid to WAL on March 1, 20X7	10,000,000
To be paid to WAL on March 1, 20X8	8,000,000
	$24,000,000

   The land is to be turned over to the developers on or about February 1, 20X7, but the sale is to be reported in 20X6.
5. An additional "contingent profit" will accrue to WAL if the developers earn a return on investment of more than 25% when they resell the newly constructed buildings. Leo wants a note to the 20X6 financial statements that describes the potential of a contingent gain.
6. The excess land that was sold to the developers was carried on WAL's books at $1.35 million, on a pro rata cost basis. Leo would like to revalue the remaining land from $5.4 million to about $100 million in the 20X6 financial statements.
7. The golf course has been unprofitable in recent years. However, green fees are to be raised and specific tee-off times will be allotted to a private club, which is currently being organized. Members of the private club will pay a non-refundable entrance fee of $2,000 per member plus $100 per month for five years. The $2,000 is to be recorded as revenue on receipt. Approximately $350,000 is to be spent to upgrade club facilities.
8. Leo wants to capitalize all costs of NSL on NSL's books until it has completed its first year of operations. In addition to the franchise fee, $20 million will have to be spent on the following:

Acquisition of player contracts	$12,000,000
Advertising and promotion	1,500,000
Equipment	3,200,000
Wages, benefits, and bonuses	6,800,000
Other operating costs	3,300,000
	26,800,000
Less:	
Revenue—ticket sales	(6,000,000)
Revenue—other	(800,000)
	$20,000,000

   The value of players can change quickly, depending on their performance, injuries, and other factors.

9. The new sports arena will have private boxes in which a company can entertain groups of clients. The boxes are leased on a five-year contract basis, and they must be occupied for a minimum price per night. To date, 12 boxes have been leased for $15,000 per box for a five-year period, exclusive of nightly charges. A down payment of $3,000 was required; the payments have been recorded as revenue.
10. Three senior officers of WAL, including Leo, receive bonuses based on income before income taxes. The three have agreed to have their fiscal 20X6 bonus accrued in 20X7 along with their 20X7 bonuses. Actual payments to them are scheduled for January 20X8.
11. Insurance premiums on the construction activity that is taking place total $1.4 million in fiscal 20X6, and to date they have been capitalized.
12. A $500,000 fee was paid to a mortgage broker to arrange financing for WAL. This amount has been recorded as "other assets." No financing has been arranged to date.

[CICA]

CASE 3-7 MAJOR DEVELOPMENTS CORPORATION

John "Calc" Gossling is one of Canada's foremost real estate investment analysts. He works for the firm of Bouchard Wiener Securities Inc. (BWS). His job is to do research and make recommendations on the stock of publicly traded companies, independent of any interest his employer may have in the companies. The research gets published and is used by investors in making their investment decisions. He is noted for his superb number-crunching ability, scathing comments, and accurate analysis. In late 19X4, he correctly predicted the end of the real estate bubble, which occurred about two years later. His writing style is in marked contrast to the traditional dry prose of most investment analysts.

Major Developments Corporation (Major) is a publicly traded company operating primarily in the real estate sector. Major has a March 31 year-end and in 20X5 reported revenues of $704 million and after-tax income of $118 million. The company buys and sells commercial real estate properties and manufactures commercial elevator components (its original business before it got into real estate). Major survived the recession of the 19X0s, and during that time purchased a number of commercial "jewels" at bargain prices. In 20X4, Major ventured overseas, acquiring properties in three Asian countries.

Major's share price climbed steadily from 19X9 until July 11, 20X5. On that date BWS released a stunning research report by Gossling on Major (see extracts in Exhibit E). The report caused an uproar, as it claimed that many of Major's accounting policies in 20X5 were misleading and therefore not in accordance with IFRS principles. It further claimed that the company was overvalued and had poor prospects because of its real estate portfolio mix.

The stock had been trading in the $15–16 range but immediately dropped to around $9. BWS profited from the decline in the stock price because it held a significant short position in Major's stock. Within four days, lawyers working for Major launched a legal suit against BWS, claiming damages plus a full retraction of all statements made to be published in a national newspaper.

BWS's legal counsel is now examining various courses of action. To help prepare for the case, counsel has hired Brick & Mortar, Chartered Accountants, to provide a report on the validity of the positions of each of the parties on the disagreements over accounting policies as well as any other relevant advice. You, CA, work for Brick & Mortar. You have obtained a copy of Major's 20X5 annual report (see extracts in Exhibit F). Major's lawyers have provided the information in Exhibit G.

Required

Prepare a draft report to legal counsel for the partner to review.

Exhibit E Extracts from John Gossling's Research Report

—I have done a detailed review of Major's 20X5 annual report. I approached management of the company with a detailed list of further questions, but management did not respond in the four days that I gave them.
—It is my contention that in 20X5, Major clearly violated IFRS principles on a number of issues. I am saying that the accounting is wrong, not just aggressive.
—Major's accounting for its real estate loans really takes the cake for non-compliance. The company consolidates the assets and results of two corporations to whom it has granted loans when it does not own any shares in either of the two companies.
—I don't like the accounting in Major's non-real-estate business. There is no question it is misleading. Starting in 20X5, the company specifically states in the financial statement notes that revenue (and profit, I might add) is recognized on product that is still sitting in the company's warehouse.
—How can Rely Holdings—a company that lost $750,000, in which Major had acquired an additional 25% interest for $5 million—be valued at over $29 million? The valuation of Rely Holdings makes no sense.
—How can a company capitalize costs incurred for properties that were never acquired? Clearly these costs cannot be considered assets, and it is misleading to do so.
—It is absurd that Major continues to recognize the revenue from properties in certain economically unstable Asian countries. It is unlikely that the money will be collected. Major should write off these buildings immediately instead of recognizing revenue from them.

Recommendation on Major Developments Corp.

Price earnings multiplier based on last fiscal year	12.7
Overall rating on their stock	underperform
Recommendation	sell

Exhibit F Extracts from Major Developments Corporation's 20X5 Annual Report

NOTE 1: ACCOUNTING POLICIES

The company incurs significant costs in investigating new properties for purchase. Costs incurred in investigating any and all properties, whether or not these properties are ultimately purchased by the company, are capitalized as part of the cost of properties actually acquired. These costs are amortized over the useful lives of the properties acquired.

Economic problems in certain Asian countries where the company owns properties have made collection of rental revenues from these properties difficult at this time. The company expects that, once the difficulties in these countries have been resolved, amounts owed will be collected in full. It is the company's policy to accrue the revenue from these properties.

Revenue on product sales is recognized when the goods are shipped to the customer. In the case of "bill and hold" sales, revenue is recognized when the goods are placed in the company's designated storage area.

The consolidated financial statements include the accounts of Major and its majority-owned subsidiaries and, commencing prospectively in fiscal 20X5, the accounts of companies in which Major has no common share ownership but to which it has advanced loans that are currently in default. The equity method is used for investments in which there is significant influence, considered to be voting ownership of 20% to 50%.

NOTE 14: INVESTMENTS

	20X5	20X4
Rely Holdings Inc.	$29,640,000	$25,000,000

In 20X0, Major purchased an additional 25% interest in Rely Holdings Inc. for $5 million. Major now owns 48% of Rely Holdings Inc. Major accounts for its investment on an equity basis. In 20X5, Major recorded a loss of $750,000 from Rely Holdings Inc.

Exhibit G **Extracts from Information Provided by Major's Lawyers**

1. Major's auditor has always provided an unqualified report on the audited financial statements of Major, including the 20X5 financial statements.
2. Major has a legal opinion that the two loans are in default (Item A), and a third-party opinion (Item B) that the default permits consolidation of these companies.
   Item A ". . . In my opinion, loan 323 to Skyscraper Inc. and loan 324 to Wenon Corporation are in default as of February 1, 20X4, under the aforesaid terms of default of the respective loan agreements, dated the 12th day of August, 20X1. The lender has the right under law and contract to repossess said aforementioned properties, for the purposes of realization on the loans, subject to restrictions of right under clause 43.(b) . . . " [Matthew Krebs, Q.C.]
   Item B "Based on facts set out in the attached document, we concur that it is acceptable, under international standards, for Major to consolidate Skyscraper Inc. and Wenon Corporation." [Jesse & Mitchell, Chartered Accountants]
3. "Bill and hold" refers to a practice whereby a customer purchases goods but the seller retains physical possession until the customer requests shipment. Delivery is delayed at the purchaser's request, but the purchaser accepts both the title to the goods and the related billing.

[CICA]

Problems

P3-1

Pond Ltd. and Stream Inc. have reached agreement in principle to combine their operations. However, the boards of directors are undecided as to the best way to accomplish the combination. Several alternatives are under consideration:

1. Pond acquires the net assets of Stream (including the liabilities) for $2,000,000 cash.
2. Pond acquires all of the assets of Stream (but not the liabilities) for $2,800,000 cash.
3. Pond acquires the net assets of Stream by issuing 120,000 shares in Pond, valued at $2,000,000.
4. Pond acquires all of the shares of Stream by exchanging them for 120,000 newly issued shares in Pond.

The reported carrying values of Pond and Stream are shown below, together with the fair values at the date of combination. Prior to the combination, Pond has 480,000 shares outstanding and Stream has 60,000 shares outstanding.

Required

a) In a comparative, columnar format, show how the consolidated SFP of Pond Ltd. would appear immediately after the combination under each of the four alternatives using the acquisition method.
b) For each of the four alternatives, briefly state who owns the shares of each corporation and whether Pond Ltd. and Stream Inc. are related companies.

Condensed Statements of Financial Position
(thousands of dollars)

	Pond Ltd.		Stream Inc.	
	Carrying values	Fair values	Carrying values	Fair values
Current assets	$ 8,000	$ 8,000	$ 600	$ 600
Capital assets	12,000	16,000	800	1,400
Investments	—	—	600	400
	$20,000		$2,000	
Current liabilities	$ 4,000	6,000	$ 200	200
Long-term liabilities	6,000	6,000	800	600
Deferred income taxes	2,000	2,000	200	—
Common shares	2,000		400	
Retained earnings	6,000		400	
	$20,000		$2,000	

P3-2

South Ltd. acquired 100% of the voting shares of North Ltd. In exchange, South Ltd. issued 50,000 common shares, with a market value of $10 per share, to the common shareholders of North Ltd. Both companies have a December 31 year-end, and this transaction occurred on December 31, 20X6. The outstanding preferred shares of North Ltd. did not change hands. The call price of the North Ltd. preferred shares is equal to their carrying value.

Following are the statements of financial position of the two companies at December 31, 20X6, before the transactions took place:

Statements of Financial Position
As at December 31, 20X6

	South Ltd.		North Ltd.	
	Carrying values	Fair values	Carrying values	Fair values
Current assets	$ 150,000	$200,000	$210,000	$260,000
Capital assets, net	950,000	820,000	780,000	860,000
Goodwill	110,000		—	
TOTAL	$1,210,000		$990,000	
Current liabilities	$ 100,000	$ 90,000	$165,000	185,000
Long-term liabilities	500,000	520,000	200,000	230,000
Preferred shares	—		270,000	270,000
Common shares	300,000		100,000	
Retained earnings	310,000		255,000	
TOTAL	$1,210,000		$990,000	

Required

Prepare the consolidated SFP for the date of acquisition, December 31, 20X6, under the acquisition method.

[CGA–Canada, adapted]

P3-3

On December 31, 20X6, the statements of financial position of Bee Ltd. and See Corp. are as follows:

	Bee Ltd.	See Corp.
Cash	$ 400,000	$ 700,000
Accounts receivable	1,600,000	1,800,000
Inventories	1,000,000	500,000
Plant and equipment(net)	3,500,000	5,000,000
TOTAL ASSETS	$6,500,000	$8,000,000
Current liabilities	$ 600,000	$ 300,000
Long-term liabilities	900,000	600,000
Common shares	2,500,000	1,000,000
Retained earnings	2,500,000	6,100,000
TOTAL LIABILITIES AND EQUITIES	$6,500,000	$8,000,000

Bee Ltd. has 100,000 common shares outstanding, and See Corp. has 45,000 shares outstanding. On January 1, 20X7, Bee Ltd. issues an additional 90,000 common shares to See Corp. at $90 per share in return for all of the assets and liabilities of that company. See Corp. distributes Bee Ltd.'s common shares to its shareholders in return for their outstanding common shares, and ceases to exist as a separate legal entity. At the time of this transaction, the cash, accounts receivable, inventories, and current liabilities of both companies have fair values equal to their carrying values. The plant and equipment and long-term liabilities have fair values as follows:

	Bee Ltd.	See Corp.
Plant and equipment (net)	$3,900,000	$5,300,000
Long-term liabilities	600,000	500,000

In addition, See Corp. has a patent worth $100,000.

Required

1. What is the amount of goodwill that would be recorded for this business combination?
2. In completing the fair value increment allocation, what other intangible assets could potentially exist that a value could be allocated to instead of (or in addition to) goodwill?
3. Prepare an SFP at January 1, 20X7, for Bee Ltd. after the purchase.
   [SMA, adapted]

P3-4

On December 31, 20X6, Retail Ltd. purchased 100% of the outstanding shares of Supply Corporation by issuing Retail Ltd. shares worth $960,000 at current market prices. Supply Corporation was a supplier of merchandise to Retail Ltd.; Retail had purchased over 80% of Supply's total output in 20X6. Supply had experienced declining profitability for many years, and in 20X4 began experiencing losses. By December 31, 20X6, Supply had accumulated tax-loss carryforwards amounting to $140,000. In contrast, Retail Ltd. was quite profitable, and analysts predicted that Retail's positioning in the retail market was well suited to weather economic downturns without undue deterioration in profit levels.

The SFP for Supply Corporation at the date of acquisition is shown below, together with estimates of the fair values of Supply's recorded assets and liabilities. In addition, Supply held exclusive Canadian rights to certain production processes; the fair value of these rights was estimated to be $200,000.

Required

Explain what values should be assigned to Supply Corporation's assets and liabilities when Retail Ltd. prepares its consolidated financial statements (including goodwill, if any).

Supply Corporation

	Statement of Financial Position December 31, 20X6		Fair values
Assets			
CURRENT ASSETS:			
Cash	$ 20,000		$ 20,000
Accounts receivable (net)	40,000		40,000
Inventories	210,000		200,000
		270,000	
PLANT, PROPERTY, AND EQUIPMENT:			
Buildings	600,000		500,000
Machinery and equipment	500,000		370,000
Accumulated depreciation	(450,000)		
	650,000		
Land	200,000		360,000
		850,000	
Investments in shares		100,000	110,000
TOTAL ASSETS		$1,220,000	
Liabilities and shareholders' equity			
CURRENT LIABILITIES:			
Accounts payable	$ 60,000		60,000
Unearned revenue	170,000		150,000
Current portion of long-term debt	100,000		100,000
		330,000	
Bonds payable		400,000	380,000
SHAREHOLDERS' EQUITY:			
Common shares	150,000		
Retained earnings	340,000		
		490,000	
TOTAL LIABILITIES AND SHAREHOLDERS' EQUITY		$1,220,000	

P3-5

Askill Corporation (Askill), a public corporation, has concluded negotiations with Basket Corporation (Basket) for the purchase of all of Basket's net assets at fair value, effective January 1, 20X7. An examination at that date by independent experts disclosed that the fair value of Basket's inventories was $300,000; the fair value of its machinery and equipment was $320,000.

Additional Information:

- The fair value of the patent was $62,000. The values of the accounts receivable and of the current and long-term liabilities were equal to their carrying value.
- The purchase agreement stated that the purchase price of all the net assets will be $540,000 payable in cash.
- Both corporations have December 31 year-ends. The statements of financial position of both corporations, as at the date of the implementation of the purchase agreement (January 1, 20X7), are as follows:

	Askill Corp.	Basket Corp.
Cash	$ 700,000	$ —
Accounts receivable	288,000	224,000
Inventories at cost	270,000	248,000
Machinery and equipment—net	412,000	200,000
Patent	—	40,000
TOTAL ASSETS	$1,670,000	$712,000
Current liabilities	$ 60,000	$ 70,000
Long-term liabilities	520,000	300,000
Capital–common shares	200,000	100,000
Retained earnings	890,000	242,000
TOTAL LIABILITIES AND SHAREHOLDERS' EQUITY	$1,670,000	$712,000

Required

1. What is the amount of goodwill that would be recorded for the business combination?
2. Prepare Askill's SFP at January 1, 20X7.
   [CICA]

P3-6

Parch Ltd. purchased 100% of the voting shares of Subbet Ltd. for $1,400,000 on October 1, 20X6. The SFP of Subbet Ltd. at that date was:

Subbet Ltd.
Statement of Financial Position
October 1, 20X6

	Net Carrying value	Fair value
Cash	$ 300,000	$300,000
Receivables	410,000	370,000
Inventory	560,000	750,000
Capital assets, net	1,220,000	920,000
	$2,490,000	
Current liabilities	$ 340,000	370,000
Long-term liability	700,000	700,000
Common shares	400,000	
Retained earnings	1,050,000	
	$2,490,000	

Required

What are the eliminations and adjustments required *at the date of acquisition* that would be necessary to consolidate the financial statements of Subbet Ltd. with those of Parch Ltd.?

[CGA–Canada, adapted]

P3-7

On December 31, 20X6, Prager Limited acquired 100% of the outstanding voting shares of Sabre Limited for $2 million in cash; 75% of the cash was obtained by issuing a five-year note payable. The statements of financial position of Prager and Sabre and the fair values of Sabre's identifiable assets and liabilities immediately before the acquisition transaction were as follows:

		Sabre Limited	
	Prager Limited	Carrying value	Fair value
ASSETS:			
Cash	$ 800,000	$ 100,000	$ 100,000
Accounts receivable	500,000	300,000	300,000
Inventory	600,000	600,000	662,500
Land	900,000	800,000	900,000
Buildings and equipment	6,000,000	1,400,000	1,200,000
Accumulated depreciation	(2,950,000)	(400,000)	
Patents	—	200,000	150,000
	$5,850,000	$3,000,000	
LIABILITIES AND SHAREHOLDERS' EQUITY:			
Accounts payable	$1,000,000	$ 500,000	500,000
Long-term debt	2,000,000	1,000,000	900,000
Common shares	1,500,000	950,000	
Retained earnings	1,350,000	550,000	
	$5,850,000	$3,000,000	

Required

Prepare the consolidated SFP for Prager Limited immediately following the acquisition of Sabre Limited.

[SMA, adapted]

P3-8

Companion Website

On January 4, 20X7, Pradeesh Corp. acquired 100% of the outstanding common shares of Serena Inc. by a share-for-share exchange of its own shares valued at $1,000,000. The statements of financial position of both companies just prior to the share exchange are shown below. Serena has patents that are not shown on the SFP, but that have an estimated fair value of $200,000 and an estimated remaining productive life of four years. Serena's buildings and equipment have an estimated fair value that is $300,000 in excess of carrying value, and the deferred charges are assumed to have a fair value of zero. Serena's buildings and equipment are being depreciated on the straight-line basis and have a remaining useful life of 10 years. The deferred charges are being amortized over the following three years. Please note that the spreadsheet relating to the problem is available on the companion website for this text.

Statements of Financial Position
December 31, 20X6

	Pradeesh	Serena
Cash	$ 110,000	$ 85,000
Accounts and other receivables	140,000	80,000
Inventories	110,000	55,000
Buildings and equipment	1,500,000	800,000
Accumulated depreciation	(700,000)	(400,000)
Deferred charges	—	120,000
	$1,160,000	$740,000
Accounts and other payables	$ 200,000	$100,000
Bonds payable	—	200,000
Deferred income taxes	60,000	40,000
Common shares*	600,000	150,000
Retained earnings	300,000	250,000
	$1,160,000	$740,000

*Pradeesh = 300,000 shares; Serena = 150,000 shares.

Required

Prepare a consolidated SFP for Pradeesh Corp., immediately following the share exchange.

APPENDIX 3A

Income Tax Allocation

INTRODUCTION

In your intermediate accounting course you undoubtedly studied the topic of income tax allocation. The effects of income tax allocation show up as "deferred tax" on almost all statements of financial position. Deferred tax also is a component of income tax expense. Deferred income tax arises from two causes:

1. temporary differences between accounting income and taxable income; and
2. carrying forward of available but unused tax losses and tax credits.

In the main body of Chapter 3, we avoided any discussion of deferred tax as it relates to business combinations. However, it does play a part in the allocation of the fair value increment and the calculation of goodwill. We have left this topic to an appendix because we do not want to obscure the principal issues of accounting for business combinations. Income taxes are not irrelevant, but they are not central to an understanding of business combinations and the reporting of strategic equity investments.

Temporary Differences in Business Combinations

In general, temporary differences arise because the carrying values of assets (and liabilities) differ from their tax bases. The most common type of temporary difference relates to depreciable tangible capital assets—book depreciation methods *(accounting method)* are usually different from CCA *(tax method)*, and therefore an asset's carrying value is different from its tax basis.

A similar situation arises in business combinations. The cost allocated to an asset in a business combination is based on the asset's fair value. The fair value then becomes its carrying value on the *consolidated* SFP. However, the Canada Revenue Agency doesn't care about an asset's fair value—only its tax basis matters. The tax basis hasn't changed as the result of the business combination; the acquired company still exists as a separate corporate entity unless there has been a statutory amalgamation. Therefore, a temporary difference exists between the asset's carrying value (at fair value) *on the post-acquisition consolidated statements* and its pre-existing tax basis for the acquired company as a separate taxable entity. This difference must be dealt with.

Exhibit 3A-1 attempts to clarify the situation. Suppose that a newly acquired subsidiary, S, has an asset with a tax basis of $70 and a carrying value *on S's books* of $100. The temporary difference is $30. If S's tax rate is 40%, the deferred tax liability pertaining to that asset is $30 × 40% = $12 on *S's separate-entity SFP*.

However, suppose the fair value of that asset is $150. P, the parent company, will show the asset on P's *consolidated* SFP at $150. For P's consolidated statements, the temporary difference is $150 − $70 = $80. At a 40% tax rate, the deferred tax liability pertaining to that asset is $80 × 40% = $32 *on P's consolidated SFP*.

EXHIBIT 3A-1

Temporary Differences in Business Combinations

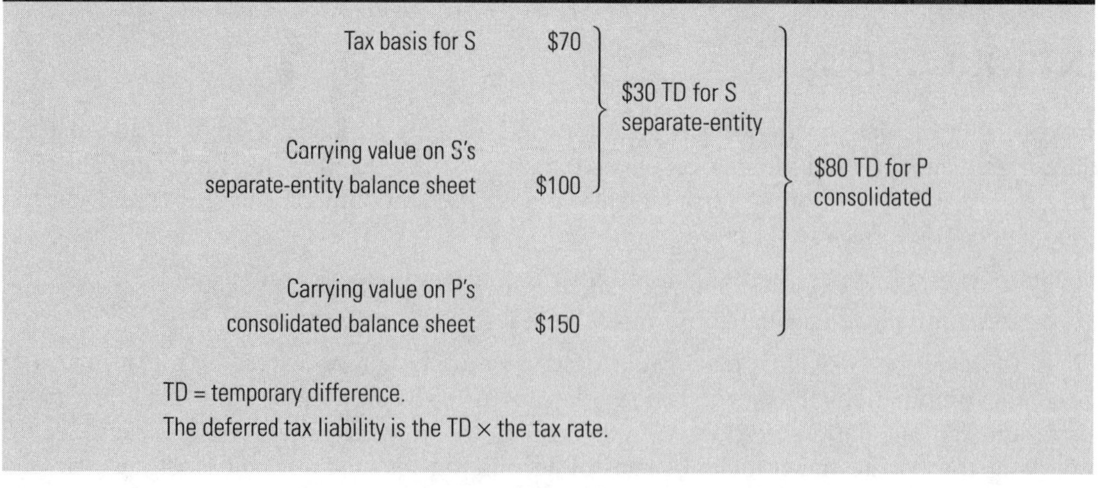

The amount shown as the deferred tax liability on P's consolidated SFP does not affect the tax status of S. Each of S and P is taxed as a separate corporate entity.

Now, let's apply income tax allocation to the example in the main body of this chapter.

- Purchase Ltd. acquired 100% of the shares of Target Ltd. for $1,200,000.
- The carrying value of Target Ltd.'s net assets *on Target Ltd.'s books* was $800,000.
- Fair-value increments totalled $300,000: $100,000 for land plus $200,000 for buildings and equipment.
- Goodwill was $100,000.

Let's make some additional assumptions:

- The tax basis for the land is equal to its carrying value on Target Ltd.'s books of $300,000.
- The tax basis of Target Ltd.'s buildings and equipment is $250,000.
- The tax basis for all other Target Ltd. assets and liabilities is equal to their carrying values.
- The tax rate for both Target Ltd. and Purchase Ltd. is 40%.

The relevant amounts can be summarized as follows.

	Land	Buildings & Equipment	Total
Tax basis	$300,000	$250,000	$550,000
Target Ltd.'s carrying value	300,000	350,000	650,000
Fair value to Purchase Ltd.	400,000	550,000	950,000

For Target Ltd., the total temporary difference is $650,000 – $550,000 = $100,000. The deferred tax liability is $100,000 × 40% = $40,000. For simplicity's sake, we did not include this amount among the net assets shown in the main body of the chapter.

For Purchase Ltd.'s consolidated statements, the temporary difference is $400,000, and the deferred tax liability (at 40%) is $160,000. Exhibit 3A-2 shows the allocation of the fair value increment with the deferred tax liability included. We have fudged the original amounts a bit by subdividing accounts payable and shifting $40,000 to a deferred tax liability account, to be consistent with our calculation of Target Ltd.'s temporary differences. This slight adjustment to the original numbers maintains the total amount of Target Ltd.'s net assets at $800,000. Thus we can clearly see what impact deferred tax has on the allocation of the fair value increment.

Notice what happens to goodwill. Because we now are recognizing a liability that we did not recognize in Exhibit 3-6, the amount of the purchase price that is allocated to the net assets goes down. This forces the difference between the purchase price and the net carrying value to go up, thereby increasing the residual. The residual is goodwill. Therefore, the net result of recognizing the deferred tax is to increase liabilities with an offsetting increase in goodwill.

The recognition of deferred tax based on consolidation fair values has been subject to some criticism. In earlier years, fair-value increments were viewed as permanent differences because the fair-value increments never flow through to the income tax return. Fair-value increments are purely an accounting construct and are irrelevant for tax purposes.

Under IFRS, however, temporary differences are recognized in this situation because the current approach to income tax accounting requires a deferred tax liability to be recognized on the assumption that assets are sold *at their carrying values*, thereby attracting taxation.

EXHIBIT 3A-2

Allocation of Fair Value Increment, Including Deferred Taxes

100% Purchase of Target Ltd., December 31, 20X5

Purchase price					$1,200,000
Less carrying value of Target's net identifiable assets (100%)					(800,000)
= Fair Value Increment, allocated below					400,000
	Carrying value (a)	Fair value (b)	Fair value Increment (c) = (b) − (a)	FVI Allocated	
Cash	$ 50,000	$ 50,000	—		
Accounts receivable	150,000	`150,000	—		
Inventory	50,000	50,000	—		
Land	300,000	400,000	$100,000	$ 100,000	
Buildings and equipment	500,000	550,000	50,000	50,000	
Accumulated depreciation	(150,000)	—	150,000	150,000	
Accounts payable	(60,000)	(60,000)	—		
Deferred tax liability	**(40,000)**	**(160,000)**	**(120,000)**	**(120,000)**	
Total fair value increment					(180,000)
Net asset carrying value	$800,000				
Fair value of assets acquired		$980,000			
Balance of FVI allocated to goodwill					$ 220,000

Since the carrying values for a purchased subsidiary are the fair values at date of acquisition, strict application of the concept results in the recognition of deferred tax liabilities for what are sometimes called "phantom" values.

What happens to these amounts? We shall see in the following chapters that the fair-value increments must be amortized (except for land and goodwill). As the fair values are amortized, the temporary difference goes down and the deferred tax liability is comparably reduced. As well, goodwill (at its heightened amount) is subjected to an impairment test. Therefore, the recognition of deferred tax liabilities based on fair values triggers three types of inter-period allocation in following years. Such complexity is the reason that we have chosen to put income tax allocation factors in appendices rather than in the main body of each chapter.

Unrecognized Tax Loss and Credit Carryforwards

Some companies have tax loss and credit carryforwards. Sometimes this is a target company's most attractive asset. When substantial amounts of unused tax loss and credit carryforwards exist, a purchaser may be willing to pay quite a lot for those benefits even if the target company appears to be a real loser. To obtain the benefit of tax loss and credit carryforwards, the business combination must be accomplished through an exchange of shares, not by paying cash (or other assets).

The target company may or may not have already recognized the full amounts of those benefits on its SFP. The amount recognized depends on a two-step procedure under which deferred tax assets are recognized in full, less a valuation allowance, if applicable, to reduce the net carrying amount to the highest amount which is more likely than not to be realizable. If the target company had serious financial difficulties, the "more likely than not" criterion would not have been met and therefore the tax losses and credits that were recorded as a deferred tax asset would have been completely reduced by the valuation allowance. However, the acquisition may make the realizability of the tax losses and credits more likely than not. Therefore, these tax losses and credits now have value to the parent company. The losses and credits will be recognized at their full fair value in the fair value increment allocation (i.e., without the valuation allowance) and be identified as a deferred tax asset in the purchaser's consolidated SFP.

Using the following data we will consider what will happen in a business combination under two scenarios. Suppose that XYZ Corporation purchased 100% of the shares of ABC Corporation for $2,000,000 and that the fair value of the net assets (excluding tax losses) totalled $1,400,000. In addition, unused tax loss carryforwards that the target company had assigned zero value in its books have a fair value of $200,000.

If it is more than 50% likely that the benefit will occur, then the purchase price/fair value increment will be allocated as follows:

Purchase price		$2,000,000
Fair value of net assets acquired (excluding tax loss benefits)	$1,400,000	
Deferred tax asset	200,000	1,600,000
Goodwill		$ 400,000

If the "more likely than not" criterion has *not* been met, the purchase price will be recorded as:

Purchase price	$2,000,000	
Fair value of net assets acquired (excluding tax loss benefits)	$1,400,000	
Deferred tax asset	0	1,400,000
Goodwill		$ 600,000

Note the difference in the goodwill amount depending on whether the probability criterion has been met. If the deferred tax asset is recognized, it is considered a temporary difference.

Equity-Basis Reporting

The preceding brief discussion focussed on business combinations. However, exactly the same process is followed for investments that are reported on the equity basis, whether they are unconsolidated subsidiaries or significantly influenced affiliates. Temporary differences and future tax loss and credit carryforward benefits must enter the allocation of the purchase price exactly as illustrated above. The next chapter explains the adjustments that are necessary under the equity method.

4

Wholly Owned Subsidiaries: Reporting Subsequent to Acquisition

LEARNING OBJECTIVES

After studying this chapter students should be able to:

1. consolidate wholly owned subsidiaries;
2. eliminate transactions that occur between a parent and its subsidiaries;
3. eliminate unrealized profit on upstream and downstream sales of inventory between a subsidiary and parent;
4. recognize profits realized in current year on upstream sale of inventory in the previous year;
5. amortize fair-value increments; and
6. report non-consolidated subsidiaries under the equity basis.

INTRODUCTION

The technology industry is particularly prone to mergers and acquisitions. Larger companies acquire smaller specialized firms as a way of entering a sector. KLA-Tencor, one of the largest semiconductor equipment companies in the world, is no exception. During 2009, the company finalized its acquisition of ICOS Vision Systems Corporation N.V. for a total cash consideration of US$489 million (net of US$130 million in cash held by ICOS). Of that purchase price, US$474 million was allocated to identifiable intangible assets and goodwill—97% of the total fair values was assigned to non-tangible assets (i.e., net of cash acquired).

All those acquired intangible assets are amortizable or must be tested for impairment, or both. The amortization and/or impairment losses won't occur on the subsidiary's books because the fair value appears only on KLA-Tencor's *consolidated* statements. Therefore, KLA-Tencor must make consolidation-related amortization and impairment adjustments, which can significantly impact the consolidated operating results subsequent to an acquisition. Indeed, in 2009, KLA-Tencor reported "goodwill and purchased intangible asset impairment" of US$447 million, which is 74% of the company's pre-tax earnings! Fair-value amortization and impairment can have a substantial impact on earnings per share.

OVERVIEW

After a business combination has occurred, the acquirer must prepare its subsequent-years' consolidated statements on the basis of the fair values allocated to the acquiree's assets and liabilities. Those fair values are not static; short-term items flow through the statements, and most long-term assets must be depreciated or amortized. As well, the acquired assets must be subjected to regular impairment tests and written down if impaired.

Date-of-acquisition consolidation happens only once, and then only for internal reporting. The real issues arise in post-acquisition consolidation. In this chapter, things get more realistic—and more complex! This chapter explains the basics of consolidation for the statement of comprehensive income (SCI) and statement of financial position (SFP) after acquisition. We will do so in the context of wholly owned subsidiaries. We illustrate the following aspects of consolidation for the first and second years after acquisition:

- eliminating transactions that occur between a parent and its subsidiaries;
- eliminating unrealized profit on intercompany sales of inventory;
- recognizing profit realized in the current year on upstream sales of inventory in the previous year;
- amortizing fair-value increments; and
- reporting non-consolidated subsidiaries on the equity basis.

We will, as usual, illustrate only the direct method in the text. For the worksheet method, refer to this textbook's Companion Website.

In the main body of the chapter, we focus on the core issues of post-acquisition consolidation of a wholly owned subsidiary, illustrated for the first and second reporting periods following its creation or acquisition. This chapter also has two appendices. The appendices cover issues that are relevant only for subsidiaries acquired in a business combination:

- deferred tax calculations (Appendix 4A);
- goodwill impairment testing (Appendix 4B).

Bear in mind that the vast majority of subsidiaries are parent-founded. These two issues do not arise when consolidating parent-founded subsidiaries because any deferred taxes and/or impairment losses will already have been recorded directly on the subsidiaries' books. The process of consolidation makes no changes in the values of a wholly owned subsidiary's assets or liabilities.

In this chapter, we deal only with wholly owned subsidiaries. Subsequent chapters will relax that simplifying assumption, thereby introducing further complexities.

Now, sit back, pay attention, and enjoy the ride!

CONSOLIDATION ONE YEAR AFTER ACQUISITION

Before we begin, we must point out that each corporation—the parent and each of its subsidiaries—will continue to prepare its own financial statements. These separate-entity financial statements will have no fair values (except when required under specific national GAAP), and will include all intercompany transactions that occur between the related companies; e.g., sales of inventory by one company to the other will be reported as revenue by the selling company and inventory purchases by the other.

When we talk about *consolidated* statements, we are referring to the set of statements that a publicly held parent company prepares for distribution to its shareholders in accordance with GAAP. For a public company in Canada, the relevant GAAP is IFRS. These statements are based on the concept of the *economic entity*—there is no corresponding legal entity. Remember that consolidated statements comprise only one set of financial statements, intended for a specific purpose—every corporation still prepares its own individual statements for the tax authorities, for its bankers, for its own performance evaluation, and so forth.

Chapter 3 used an example of Purchase Ltd.'s acquisition of 100% of the shares of Target Ltd. To prepare Purchase Ltd.'s consolidated financial statements *after* the date of acquisition, we will need four types of information:

1. the details of the purchase transaction;
2. the amortization or depreciation policy for capital assets;
3. the nature and extent of intercompany transactions between the two companies, including intercompany receivables and payables; and
4. the disposition of assets that have been sold intercompany (including the assets in the original acquisition).

Over this and the following two chapters we will add various types of transactions to our basic example of Purchase Ltd. and Target Ltd. We will not attempt to be exhaustive—though this is an advanced accounting textbook, it is not an all-inclusive consolidation handbook. By the time you finish with Chapter 6, however, you should have a thorough understanding of the consolidation process and of the types of interactions that must be accounted for.

Basic Information

Assume that on December 31, 20X5, Purchase Ltd. purchased all of the outstanding shares of Target Ltd. by issuing 40,000 new shares of Purchase Ltd. in exchange for the shares of Target Ltd. The newly issued Purchase Ltd. shares had a market value of $30 per share—a total purchase cost of $1,200,000. The total cost was allocated to the fair values of Target Ltd.'s assets and liabilities and to goodwill *at the date of acquisition* as shown in Exhibit 4-1.[1] These fair values and goodwill are the same amounts used in the illustration in the previous chapter.

At every reporting date after December 31, 20X5, Purchase Ltd. will have to include the fair-value increments (and/or decrements) and goodwill in its *consolidated* net assets. However:

- The carrying values of most fair-valued assets flow to income, either directly through cost of sales (for current assets such as inventories) or indirectly, through amortization or depreciation for tangible and intangible capital assets (except goodwill and other intangible assets with indefinite lives).

1. Exhibit 4-1 is identical to Exhibit 3–6. The same example is used throughout Chapters 3 to 6 to help readers with comparisons and to make it easier to see the impact of additional complexities.

EXHIBIT 4-1

Allocation of Purchase Price

100% Purchase of Target Ltd., December 31, 20X5

Purchase price					$1,200,000
Less carrying value of Target's net identifiable assets (100%)					(800,000)
= Fair-Value Increment, allocated below					400,000
	Carrying value (a)	Fair value (b)	Fair-Value increment (c) = (b) − (a)	FVI allocated	
Cash	$ 50,000	$ 50,000	—		
Accounts receivable	150,000	150,000	—		
Inventory	50,000	50,000	—		
Land	300,000	400,000	$100,000	$100,000	
Buildings and equipment	500,000	550,000	50,000	50,000	
Accumulated depreciation	(150,000)	—	150,000	150,000	
Accounts payable	(100,000)	(100,000)	—		
Total fair-value increment					(300,000)
Net asset carrying value	$800,000				
Fair value of assets acquired		$1,100,000			
Balance of FVI allocated to goodwill					$ 100,000

- Assets included in the purchase transaction may have been sold or retired at some time following Purchase's acquisition of Target.

When either of these events happens, we must make adjustments to the initial fair-value increments at every reporting date.

Other adjustments are needed to eliminate or "back out" intercompany transactions. For the year ended December 31, 20X6, we will assume the following:

1. Target Ltd.'s buildings and equipment will be depreciated over 10 years after the date of acquisition, using straight-line depreciation.
2. During 20X6, Target Ltd. sold goods of $55,000 to Purchase Ltd. Target Ltd.'s gross margin is 40% of sales.
3. On December 31, 20X6, $20,000 of the goods acquired by Purchase Ltd. from Target Ltd. are still in Purchase Ltd.'s inventory.
4. During 20X6, Target Ltd. paid dividends totalling $30,000 to Purchase Ltd., Target Ltd.'s sole shareholder. Purchase Ltd. maintains its investment in Target Ltd. account on the cost basis, and therefore the dividends received were recorded as dividend income.

Chapter 2 illustrated the basic approach to eliminating intercompany transactions and balances. Chapter 3 explained the eliminations that are required when a subsidiary is purchased. The example in this chapter will combine these two types of adjustments, and will add four more issues that are essential to understanding consolidations:

1. amortization of fair-value increments;
2. impairment testing for goodwill;

3. elimination of unrealized profit on intercompany sales; and
4. recognition of the profit realized in the current year on intercompany sales made in the previous year.

The next three sections will discuss the first three issues, while the fourth issue will be discussed later on in the chapter.

Amortization/Impairment of Fair-Value Increments

A large part of the purchase price in a business combination may be allocated to fair-value increments. A study of 756 US business combinations revealed that the purchase price discrepancy—fair-value increments and goodwill—equalled, on average, almost 200% of carrying value. The aggregate purchase price was $404 billion, comprising $137 billion in carrying value and $267 billion in purchase price discrepancy.[2]

Therefore, fair-value increments (or decrements) most likely will significantly impact consolidated earnings subsequent to the purchase. Each of the major categories of assets is discussed below.

Inventory Fair-value increments for inventory will flow through cost of sales to decrease net income when the inventory is sold to third parties. In the period in which the inventory is sold, which typically is assumed to be the period after acquisition, the fair-value increment is added to cost of sales instead of to inventory on the consolidation working papers.

Tangible Capital Assets A purchased subsidiary will continue to amortize the depreciable capital assets that are recorded on its books. However, the subsidiary's depreciation will be based on the *carrying value* of the assets on its books. The depreciation on the *subsidiary's separate-entity* financial statements will not reflect the higher prices paid by the parent in the business combination.

When the *parent's consolidated statements* are prepared, the fair-value increments/decrements on depreciable assets must be amortized in accordance with the depreciation policy being used by the subsidiary. If, for example, a building has a 20-year estimated remaining useful life from the date of the business combination, the fair-value increment must be amortized over the 20-year remaining period.

For example, suppose a subsidiary has a four-year-old asset with an original cost of $100,000. This asset is being amortized on the subsidiary's books by the straight-line method over 20 years. At the date that the parent bought the subsidiary, the carrying value of the asset was:

Cost	$100,000
Accumulated amortization [($100,000 ÷ 20) × 4]	20,000
	$ 80,000

Fair value at the date of acquisition was $120,000. Therefore, the fair-value increment is $40,000. Following acquisition, the subsidiary will continue to amortize the asset at $5,000 per year: $100,000 ÷ 20 = $5,000. The fair-value increment will be amortized over the remaining expected useful life of the asset, which is 16 years after acquisition: ($120,000 − $80,000) ÷ 16 = $2,500 per year. Amortization of this asset on the *consolidated* SCI will be $7,500:

2. Benjamin C. Ayers, Craig E. Lefanowicz, and John R. Robinson, "The Financial Statement Effects of Eliminating the Pooling-of-Interest Method of Acquisition Accounting," *Accounting Horizons*, 14:1 (March 2000), pp. 1–19.

Subsidiary's amortization	$100,000 ÷ 20 =	$5,000
Fair-value increment	$ 40,000 ÷ 16 =	2,500
Consolidated amortization		$7,500

Intangible Capital Assets A company recognizes an intangible asset on its books only when the asset has been purchased or when capitalizable costs were incurred to develop the asset. As a result, a company often has intangible assets that are not reported on its books. Examples include trademarks, customer lists, franchises, and so forth. When one company is acquired by another in a business combination, the acquirer should identify any specific intangible assets that have not been reported on the acquiree's SFP. When intangible assets can be identified, *whether or not they appear on the acquired company's SFP*, they must be assigned a fair value.

After initial recognition, an intangible asset is carried at cost less any accumulated amortization and impairment losses. If the intangible asset's life is indefinite, it is not amortized but tested for impairment.

If the identifiable intangible asset is already reported on the subsidiary's SFP, the fair-value increment is accounted for in the same way. If the intangible asset is not already reported on the subsidiary's SFP, the asset's useful life must be determined. If the asset's life is not indefinite, the fair-value increment is amortized over its useful life.

If it becomes apparent that an intangible asset's value has become impaired (i.e., declined to below its consolidated carrying value), fair value must be written down to the impaired value.

GOODWILL

Goodwill is not amortized. Since goodwill is not amortized, it must be subjected to an annual impairment test. To apply the impairment test, goodwill must be attributed to each **cash-generating unit** or group of cash generating units, provided that each unit (or group of units) (1) constitutes the lowest level within the entity at which goodwill is monitored for internal management purposes, and (2) is not larger than the related operating segment as reported in the annual disclosure of operating segments.[3] A cash-generating unit is not necessarily the same as a corporate entity. Therefore, when goodwill arises in a business combination, that goodwill must be allocated to individual cash-generating units if there is more than one within the acquired corporation.

Once goodwill has been attributed to cash-generating units, an impairment test for each unit is applied by comparing the recoverable amount of the unit with its carrying value, including goodwill. Any excess of carrying value over the recoverable amount is treated as an *impairment loss* in the SCI.

It is obvious that the impairment test involves a lot of management estimation and judgment. Recoverable value of a cash-generating unit is a function of its future earnings, and there is a lot of subjectivity involved in estimating future earnings. The application of impairment tests for goodwill seems to give management a lot of opportunity for write-downs to contribute to a "big bath."

Appendix 4B explains the IFRS impairment test more extensively.

3. Segments and segment reporting are discussed in Chapter 7.

Unrealized Profits

One of the more challenging aspects of consolidated statements is that we must keep track of assets that were sold by one company in the group to another. Sales from a parent to a subsidiary are **downstream sales**, while sales from a subsidiary to a parent are called **upstream sales**. Sales between subsidiaries are treated as upstream sales.

In the facts for Purchase Ltd. and Target Ltd. listed above, there are three points relating to the intercompany sales:

- Target Ltd. had sales to Purchase Ltd. (i.e., *upstream* sales) of $55,000;
- $20,000 of those goods are still in Purchase Ltd.'s inventory at year-end; and
- Target Ltd.'s gross margin on sales is 40%.

The $20,000 of goods in Purchase Ltd.'s inventory are stated at their acquisition price to Purchase Ltd. However, they cost Target Ltd. less than that to produce. Target Ltd.'s gross margin is 40%, which means that the $20,000 inventory contains a gross profit margin of $20,000 × 40% = $8,000; the goods cost $12,000 to produce.

Consolidated statements must show only the results of transactions between the consolidated entity and those companies and individuals outside the combined economic entity. In substance, the $8,000 gross profit is only an internal transaction, not external. Therefore, consolidated inventory must be reduced by eliminating the $8,000 *unrealized profit* on the upstream sales of inventory. This treatment remains the same regardless of whether the sale is made by a 100% (wholly) owned subsidiary or a *non*-wholly owned subsidiary to its parent [IAS 27, ¶21]. We always eliminate the entire unrealized profit relating to any intercompany sale during consolidation.

Obviously, the consolidated inventory must be reduced by $8,000, but what happens to the offset? When we compute cost of sales, beginning inventory and purchases are added together, and ending inventory is subtracted. The SCI effect of an *overstated ending inventory* is to *understate cost of sales*. Therefore, we must not only reduce consolidated inventory by $8,000, but also we must increase cost of sales by $8,000. If this seems confusing, just remember that *increasing* a cost will *reduce* net income, thereby eliminating the unrealized profit.

In summary, two adjustments are necessary:

1. eliminate the intercompany sale transaction; and
2. eliminate the unrealized profit.

We will illustrate these adjustments shortly.

Unrealized profit arises any time one corporation sells assets to another and those assets stay within the consolidated economic entity instead of being sold externally. Inventory is the most common type of intercompany sale, but capital assets or investments may also be sold. The same principles apply, regardless of the nature of the asset(s) involved.

Direct Method

The unconsolidated financial statements for Purchase Ltd. and Target Ltd. are shown in Exhibit 4-2. We have assumed that Purchase Ltd. *records* its investment in Target Ltd. on the cost basis in its accounts, as is almost always the case. Therefore, the separate-entity financial

EXHIBIT 4-2

Separate-Entity Financial Statements for 20X6

Statements of Comprehensive Income
Year Ended December 31, 20X6

	Purchase Ltd.	Target Ltd.
Revenue:		
Sales	$2,400,000	$ 300,000
Dividend income	30,000	—
	2,430,000	300,000
Expenses:		
Cost of sales	1,750,000	180,000
Depreciation expense	100,000	35,000
Other expenses	250,000	20,000
	2,100,000	235,000
NET INCOME	$ 330,000	$ 65,000

Statements of Changes in Equity—Retained Earnings Section
Year Ended December 31, 20X6

	Purchase Ltd.	Target Ltd.
Retained earnings, December 31, 20X5	$2,000,000	$ 600,000
Net income	330,000	65,000
Dividends declared	—	(30,000)
Retained earnings, December 31, 20X6	$2,330,000	$ 635,000

Statements of Financial Position
December 31, 20X6

	Purchase Ltd.	Target Ltd.
ASSETS		
Current Assets:		
Cash	$ 980,000	$ 100,000
Accounts receivable	2,200,000	250,000
Inventory	250,000	70,000
	3,430,000	420,000
Property, Plant, and Equipment:		
Land	1,000,000	300,000
Buildings and equipment	3,000,000	500,000
Accumulated depreciation	(1,300,000)	(185,000)
	2,700,000	615,000
Other Assets:		
Investments (at cost)	1,200,000	—
TOTAL ASSETS	$7,330,000	$1,035,000
LIABILITIES AND SHAREHOLDERS' EQUITY		
Liabilities:		
Current: accounts payable	$ 800,000	$ 200,000
Long-term: notes payable	400,000	—
	1,200,000	200,000
Shareholders' Equity:		
Common shares	3,800,000	200,000
Retained earnings	2,330,000	635,000
	6,130,000	835,000
TOTAL LIABILITIES AND SHAREHOLDERS' EQUITY	$7,330,000	$1,035,000

EXHIBIT 4-3

MEAR Steps to Consolidation at the End of the First Year Following Acquisition

Consolidation Steps	Acquisition Related	Relating to First Year Following Acquisition
1. Measure	• Calculate cost and fair-value increments (FVI) • Allocate FVI	
2. Eliminate	• Eliminate parent's investment account and sub's share equity accounts	
		• Eliminate intercompany transactions and balances • Eliminate unrealized profits
3. Amortize		• Amortize FVIs • Recognize impairments

statements show (1) the investment at the purchase price of $1,200,000, and (2) the dividends of $30,000 received by Purchase Ltd. from Target Ltd. as dividend income.

MEAR Steps to Consolidation—Phase 2 In Chapter 3, we introduced the MEAR approach to consolidating subsidiaries that were acquired via a business combination. In that chapter, we introduced the *Measure* step and, to a limited extent, the *Eliminate* step. In this chapter, we extend the MEAR concept further. We will enlarge upon the Eliminate step and introduce the *Amortize* step. Indeed, you may already have noticed that we expanded the Eliminate step when we discussed intercompany transactions in the preceding section—intercompany transactions and unrealized profits must be eliminated.

Exhibit 4-3 provides the MEAR steps to consolidation required at the end of the first year following acquisition.

The **Measure** step and part of the **Eliminate** step are sufficient when consolidation is occurring on the date of acquisition, since both relate to acquisition-related adjustments and eliminations. However, when consolidation is occurring in the first year subsequent to the date of acquisition, we need to add additional steps to the Eliminate step and add the **Amortize** step. Note that throughout the chapters on consolidation we will present the consolidation process in terms of the MEAR steps. As we cover new issues, existing MEAR steps will be amplified and new steps added. In addition, the last step of every iteration will always be to consolidate the statements.

In our current example, the Eliminate and Amortize steps relate to current year adjustments and eliminations. Specifically:

1. The **Eliminate** step requires us to:
   a) identify and eliminate all inter-company transactions and balances;
   b) calculate and eliminate any *unrealized* profit (or loss) relating to the intercompany sale of inventory and other assets in the current period.
2. The **Amortize** step requires us to:
   a) amortize the FVI allocated to the various identifiable assets and liabilities, as appropriate;

b) write off any impairment of goodwill and other intangible assets with indeterminate useful lives;

c) determine the balance of the FVI allocated that remains unamortized or unimpaired at the end of the period.

Exhibit 4-1 already illustrates the Measure step for our example as well as the first aspect of Eliminate. We will now illustrate the additional steps of Eliminate and Amortize.

Eliminate

Intercompany Transactions and Balances There were two intercompany transactions in 20X6 requiring eliminations:[4]

Upstream sale by Target Ltd.	(55,000)
Dividend income of Purchase Ltd. and dividends declared by Target Ltd.	(30,000)

These both must be eliminated. The first item relates to the sale by Target Ltd. of $55,000 worth of goods to Purchase Ltd. We need to eliminate $55,000 from both sales (of Target) and cost of goods sold (of Purchase). The second item relates to Purchase Ltd.'s *share* of $30,000 of the dividends declared by Target Ltd. that have been recognized by Purchase Ltd. as dividend income. Since Purchase owns 100% of Target, we must eliminate $30,000 from both dividend income (of Purchase) and dividends declared (by Target).

Notice that each of these eliminations involves an elimination of something recorded on Target's books, offset by elimination of something on Purchase's books. This should reinforce the fact that consolidation adjustments cannot be recorded on any company's books—these are purely worksheet adjustments for consolidated financial reporting. You also should always keep in mind that nothing that we do during consolidation affects anything on the books of either company. Their individual separate-entity statements are not affected at all.

Unrealized Profits In our example there is only one source of unrealized profits, unrealized profit on the upstream sale of inventory. As explained earlier, we need to increase cost of goods sold and decrease ending inventory by that amount.

Unrealized profit on upstream sale of inventory	(8,000)

Amortize Before we start adjusting for amortization and depreciation, it is helpful to prepare a schedule of what needs to be done. A schedule for Purchase Ltd.'s acquisition of Target Ltd. would be as follows:

	FVI allocated	Amortization period	Amortization per year	Amortization/ impairment loss during 20X6	Balance of FVI remaining at the end of 20X6
Land	$100,000	—		—	$100,000
Building & Equipment	200,000	10	$20,000	$20,000	180,000
Goodwill	100,000	—		—	100,000
Total	$400,000			$20,000	$380,000

4. In this and remaining consolidation-related chapters in the text, eliminations and negative adjustments are in parentheses.

From the schedule above we know that the total amortization/impairment loss adjustment that needs to be recognized in the consolidated financial statements in the current period is $20,000. Specifically, this adjustment pertains to the depreciation expense relating to the fair-value increment allocated to property, plant, and equipment.

We also know from the schedule above that the balance of the FVI adjustment that needs to be added to the carrying values of the parent and subsidiary is $380,000, made up of an increase to land for $100,000, building and equipment for $180,000, and goodwill for $100,000. Note that the adjustment for building and equipment of $180,000 is the result of the initial FVI allocated to buildings and equipment of $200,000 less the $20,000 depreciation adjustment required in the current year.

Prepare the Consolidated Statements We can start the consolidation process by adding the carrying values of both companies and making the various adjustments and eliminations identified in the previous steps. If necessary we need to make appropriate adjustments to eliminate the accumulated depreciation of the subsidiary at the time of acquisition. We also need to remember to eliminate the common shares of $200,000 and retained earnings at the time of acquisition of $600,000 of Target Ltd., and the investment at cost of $1,200,000.

To do the above, we can go down the SCI and SFP and insert the correct amounts on a line-by-line basis. In Exhibit 4-4, we have added together the separate-entity amounts, and made the required additional adjustments and eliminations. The necessary adjustments and eliminations are listed below once again, now by each financial statement, starting with the SCI.

The starting point, as always, is to enter the carrying values of both companies' assets, liabilities, and shareholders' equity. Then we can add the FVIs, eliminate the investment (and Target's share equity accounts), and proceed with our other eliminations and adjustments. You will notice that we placed a superscript "U" for "upstream" next to both (1) the eliminated $55,000 upstream inventory sale and cost of goods, and (2) the $8,000 unrealized gain relating to the sale, both on the SFP and the SCI. This is to help us keep track of what we're doing. As we build additional complexities into our example, anything we can do to remind ourselves of what the adjustments are for will help us be clear about what we're doing (for example, placing a subscript "D" for "downstream").

Statement of Comprehensive Income and SCE/RE

- *Sales revenue*. The combined sales total is $2,700,000. We must eliminate the intercompany sales of $\$55{,}000^{U}$. The result is consolidated sales of $2,645,000.
- *Dividend income*. We need to eliminate the entire $30,000 dividend income both from the dividend income line item on the SCI and the dividend declared line item in the retained earnings section of the statement of changes in equity (SCE/RE).
- *Cost of sales*. The combined unadjusted cost of sales is $1,750,000 + $180,000 = $1,930,000. This amount must be decreased by the full amount of the intercompany sales of $\$55{,}000^{U}$ and increased by the unrealized profit of $\$8{,}000^{U}$ that is in Purchase Ltd.'s ending inventory.
- *Depreciation expense*. The depreciation expense amount should be increased by the $20,000 depreciation of the fair-value increment allocated to Target Ltd.'s buildings and equipment.

EXHIBIT 4-4

Purchase Ltd. Consolidated Financial Statements (Direct Method)

Consolidated Statement of Comprehensive Income
Year Ended December 31, 20X6

Sales revenue [2,400,000 + 300,000 − **55,000^U**]	$2,645,000
Dividend income [30,000 + 0 − **30,000**]	—
Operating Expenses:	
Cost of sales [1,750,000 + 180,000 − **55,000^U** + **8,000^U**]	1,883,000
Depreciation expense [100,000 + 35,000 + **20,000**]	155,000
Other expenses [250,000 + 20,000]	270,000
	2,308,000
NET INCOME	$ 337,000

Consolidated Statement of Changes in Equity—Retained Earnings Section
Year Ended December 31, 20X6

Retained earnings, December 31, 20X5 [2,000,000 + 600,000 − **600,000**]	$2,000,000
Net income	337,000
Dividends declared [0 + 30,000 − **30,000**]	—
Retained earnings, December 31, 20X6	$2,337,000

Consolidated Statement of Financial Position
December 31, 20X6

ASSETS	
Current assets:	
Cash [980,000 + 100,000]	$1,080,000
Accounts receivable [2,200,000 + 250,000]	2,450,000
Inventory [250,000 + 70,000 − **8,000^U**]	312,000
	3,842,000
Property, Plant, and Equipment:	
Land [1,000,000 + 300,000 + **100,000**]	1,400,000
Buildings and equipment [3,000,000 + 500,000 + **50,000**]	3,550,000
Accumulated depreciation [1,300,000 + 185,000 − **150,000** + **20,000**]	(1,355,000)
	3,595,000
Other Assets:	
Investments [1,200,000 + 0 − **1,200,000**]	—
Goodwill [100,000]	100,000
TOTAL ASSETS	$7,537,000
LIABILITIES AND SHAREHOLDERS' EQUITY	
Liabilities:	
Current: accounts payable [800,000 + 200,000]	$1,000,000
Long-term: notes payable [400,000 + 0]	400,000
	1,400,000
Shareholders' Equity:	
Common shares **[Purchase Ltd. shares only]**	3,800,000
Retained earnings	
[2,330,000 + 635,000 − **600,000** − **8,000^U** − **20,000**]	2,337,000
	6,137,000
TOTAL LIABILITIES AND SHAREHOLDERS' EQUITY	$7,537,000

- The combined, unadjusted, net income of the two companies is \$330,000 + \$65,000 = \$395,000. After adjustment for amortization of fair-value increments, and after eliminating unrealized profit, consolidated net income drops to \$337,000. The total reduction is \$58,000. Remember this number—you will see it again shortly!

Statement of Financial Position

- *Inventory*. Combined inventories must be reduced by the unrealized profit of \$8,000^U from intercompany sales.
- *Land*. The fair-value increment of \$100,000 must be added.
- *Buildings and equipment*. The total fair-value increment for Target Ltd.'s buildings and equipment is \$200,000. The increase is recognized in the consolidated statements by (1) eliminating Target Ltd.'s date-of-acquisition accumulated depreciation of \$150,000, and (2) increasing the buildings and equipment asset account by \$50,000. Therefore, only \$50,000 is added to the asset account.
- *Accumulated depreciation*. Target Ltd.'s accumulated depreciation at December 31, 20X6, is \$185,000. This amount includes the \$150,000 accumulated at the date of acquisition plus \$35,000 additional depreciation expense for 20X6. The \$150,000 must be eliminated—the acquired company's accumulated depreciation at the date of acquisition should not be carried forward. The \$35,000 remains, because it represents depreciation *after* the date of acquisition. But the \$35,000 represents depreciation on Target Ltd.'s *carrying value*. To reflect depreciation on the *fair* value, the \$20,000 amortization of the fair-value increment must be added.
- *Investments*. The investment account must be reduced by the cost of Purchase Ltd.'s investment in Target Ltd. In this example, there are no other investments. In many situations, however, there will be other investments that will *not* be eliminated.
- *Common shares*. Only Purchase Ltd.'s common shares are included.
- *Retained earnings* (at year-end). This is the challenging one! We start by adding the two companies' retained earnings together. Next, we must eliminate Target Ltd.'s date-of-acquisition retained earnings (\$600,000). Then we make the adjustments that were necessary for the consolidated SCI:
  - eliminate the unrealized profit of \$8,000^U, and
  - reduce retained earnings by the amount of additional fair-value amortization—\$20,000.

There is one SCI adjustment that is missing from the list above relating to the ending retained earnings-—dividend income. The reason that it doesn't show up among our adjustments on the retained earnings line of the SFP is that the amount has already washed out. Our adjustment relating to dividend income decreased both the dividend income amount on the SCI by \$30,000 and the dividend declared amount in the SCE/RE by \$30,000. The net impact on the consolidated ending retained earnings is zero, and thus there is no need for an adjustment to the ending retained earnings balance on the SFP.

Remember the \$58,000 decrease in net income from separate-entity to consolidated net income? That consists of two amounts: \$30,000 dividend income shown as revenue to Purchase Ltd. but *not as an expense to Target Ltd.*, plus the \$28,000 (i.e., \$8,000^U + \$20,000) in other adjustments to consolidated net income. *When deriving consolidated retained earnings on the SFP, all adjustments on the consolidated SCI and consolidated SCE/RE are made* except *for intercompany dividends.*

You might wonder why we don't simply take the ending consolidated retained earnings amount from the statement of changes in retained earnings and put that amount in the SFP. The answer is that we must be able to derive the retained earnings independently, to make sure that the statements balance and that we haven't overlooked anything.[5]

Worksheet Approach

For the illustration of how the worksheet approach applies to our example, please refer to the Companion Website.

Equity-Basis Reporting of Non-Consolidated Subsidiaries

A Canadian publicly accountable parent company will issue *only* consolidated statements as its general purpose financial statements. A private company may or may not choose to issue consolidated statements to its limited group of statement users.

In addition to the consolidated statements, every parent company will also prepare non-consolidated statements. Non-consolidated statements are used for income tax reporting, for a bank's credit analysis, and for the shareholders of a private company.

In non-consolidated statements, the subsidiaries can be reported on either the cost or the equity basis. When the equity method of reporting is used, the parent corporation includes in its net income the parent's share of the subsidiary's earnings. Target Ltd.'s 20X6 separate-entity net income is $65,000, as shown in Exhibit 4-2. Using the equity method, Target Ltd.'s net income (after adjustment) will be reported in Purchase Ltd.'s SCI as a single amount.

The Target Ltd. net income cannot be reported by Purchase Ltd. simply as $65,000, because to do so would ignore the substance of the purchase transaction. Since Purchase Ltd. has acquired control over the assets and liabilities of Target Ltd., the earnings of Target Ltd. must be reported in Purchase Ltd.'s statements *as though the net assets of Target Ltd. had been purchased directly by Purchase Ltd.*

If the assets and liabilities had been purchased directly, then they would have been recorded at their fair values, and goodwill of $100,000 would have been recorded. The fair values are amortized and any transactions between the Target Ltd. division and the rest of the company will not appear on the financial statements of Purchase Ltd. In other words, it is necessary to adjust the earnings of Target Ltd. to reflect *all of the same adjustments that would be made if Target Ltd. were consolidated.*

Part A of Exhibit 4-5 shows the computation of Target Ltd.'s adjusted earnings. Starting with the Target Ltd. reported net income of $65,000, deductions are made for (1) depreciation of the fair-value increment on buildings and equipment, and (2) elimination of the unrealized profit on intercompany sales.

The adjusted Target Ltd. earnings amount to $37,000. Purchase Ltd. owns 100% of the shares of Target Ltd., so Purchase Ltd. will report this entire amount on Purchase Ltd.'s SCI as equity in the earnings of Target Ltd. (the *equity pick-up*).

5. From a very practical student standpoint, it is also useful to be able to derive consolidated retained earnings without having to work through a consolidated statement of comprehensive income. That is a favourite examination question, both in coursework and in professional examinations!

EXHIBIT 4-5

Equity Basis of Reporting Purchase Ltd.'s Investment in Target Ltd.

Year Ended December 31, 20X6	
A. Equity in earnings of Target Ltd.:	
Earnings as reported by Target	$ 65,000
Adjustments:	
1. Amortization of fair-value increment on buildings and equipment: $200,000/10 years	(20,000)
2. Elimination of unrealized profit on upstream sales: $20,000 × 40% gross margin	(8,000)
Adjusted Target Ltd. earnings, equity basis	$ 37,000
B. Investment in Target Ltd.:	
Balance, December 31, 20X5	$1,200,000
Plus Purchase's share of Target's equity basis earnings: $37,000 × 100%	37,000
Less dividends received from Target	(30,000)
Balance, December 31, 20X6	$1,207,000

Part B of Exhibit 4-5 summarizes the impact of the equity method on the investment account. The year-end balance of $1,207,000 will be reported on Purchase Ltd.'s unconsolidated SFP. The investment account reflects (1) the cost of the investment plus (2) the cumulative amount of unremitted adjusted earnings since the date of acquisition.

The adjustments made to Target Ltd.'s net income are made only for *reporting* on Purchase Ltd.'s statements. Target Ltd. will report net income of $65,000 on its own separate-entity financial statements, even though Purchase Ltd.'s equity-basis SCI will report the lesser amount of $37,000 in earnings from Target Ltd.

Purchase Ltd. may choose to *record* the equity-basis earnings of Target in its accounts, in which case the adjustment will appear as follows:

Investment in Target Ltd.	37,000	
Equity in earnings of Target Ltd.		37,000

The credit to the SCI account is offset by a debit to increase the investment account. When Target Ltd. declares dividends, the declaration will be recorded as follows:

Dividends receivable	30,000	
Investment in Target Ltd.		30,000

When the dividends are paid, Purchase Ltd. will debit cash and credit the dividends receivable account.

It is not necessary for Purchase Ltd. to *record* its investment in Target Ltd. on the equity basis, even though it may *report* the investment on the equity basis. As a bookkeeping convenience, it is most common for the investor to maintain the investment account on the cost basis.

Comparison of Consolidation Versus Equity Reporting Exhibit 4-6 shows the SFP and SCI for Purchase Ltd. for the year ended December 31, 20X6. The first column shows the results of reporting Target on the equity basis, while the second column shows consolidated statements.

EXHIBIT 4-6

Comparing Equity-Basis Reporting and Consolidation

Purchase Ltd.
Statement of Consolidated Income
Year Ended December 31, 20X6

	Equity Basis	Consolidated
Sales revenue	$2,400,000	$2,645,000
Equity in earnings of Target Ltd.	37,000	—
	2,437,000	2,645,000
Operating Expenses:		
Cost of sales	1,750,000	1,883,000
Depreciation expense	100,000	155,000
Other expenses	250,000	270,000
	2,100,000	2,308,000
NET INCOME	$ 337,000	$ 337,000

Statement of Changes in Equity—Retained Earnings Section
Year Ended December 31, 20X6

	Equity Basis	Consolidated
Retained earnings, December 31, 20X5	$2,000,000	$2,000,000
Net income	337,000	337,000
Dividends declared	—	—
Retained earnings, December 31, 20X6	$2,337,000	$2,337,000

Purchase Ltd.
Statement of Financial Position, December 31, 20X6

	Equity Basis	Consolidated
ASSETS		
Current Assets:		
Cash	$ 980,000	$1,080,000
Accounts receivable	2,200,000	2,450,000
Inventory	250,000	312,000
	3,430,000	3,842,000
Property, Plant, and Equipment:		
Land	1,000,000	1,400,000
Buildings and equipment	3,000,000	3,550,000
Accumulated depreciation	(1,300,000)	(1,355,000)
	2,700,000	3,595,000
Other Assets:		
Investments	1,207,000	—
Goodwill	—	100,000
TOTAL ASSETS	$7,337,000	$7,537,000
LIABILITIES AND SHAREHOLDERS' EQUITY		
Liabilities:		
Current: accounts payable	$ 800,000	$1,000,000
Long-term: notes payable	400,000	400,000
	1,200,000	1,400,000
Shareholders' Equity:		
Common shares	3,800,000	3,800,000
Retained earnings	2,337,000	2,337,000
	6,137,000	6,137,000
TOTAL LIABILITIES AND SHAREHOLDERS' EQUITY	$7,337,000	$7,537,000

In the unconsolidated statements, the assets and liabilities are only those of Purchase Ltd., and the revenues and expenses are also only those generated or incurred by Purchase Ltd. One of the assets of Purchase Ltd. is the investment in Target Ltd., which appears as a non-current asset on the SFP. Similarly, the SCI shows Purchase Ltd.'s equity in the earnings of Target Ltd. as a separate item.

When we consolidate Purchase Ltd. and Target Ltd., however, we eliminate the investment in the Target Ltd. account on the SFP and instead show all of the individual assets and liabilities of Target Ltd. that the investment represents. The shareholders' equity accounts are exactly the same in both columns. The total net asset value of Purchase Ltd. is not altered by the process of consolidation; all that happens is that the investment account is disaggregated so that the readers of Purchase Ltd.'s financial statements can see the total resources (of both Purchase Ltd. and Target Ltd.) that are under the control of the management of Purchase Ltd.

The unconsolidated SCI includes the net equity-basis earnings of Target Ltd. on a single line. Upon consolidation, that line disappears and the net amount thereof ($37,000) is disaggregated by including the revenues and expenses of Target Ltd. in the main body of the statement, along with those of Purchase Ltd. The consolidated net income is exactly the same as the unconsolidated net income of Purchase Ltd., since the investment in Target Ltd. has been reported on the equity basis.

The equity-basis investment account is increased by the $37,000 equity pick-up of Target Ltd.'s earnings, minus the $30,000 dividends received from Target Ltd. As a result, the investment account is shown at $1,207,000 in the equity basis column.

The equity-basis investment account and equity-in-earnings account summarize the investor's interest in the net assets and earnings from operations of the investee corporation in a single line on the financial statements of the investor. Therefore the equity method is often referred to as **one-line consolidation** and also as the *consolidation method of equity reporting*. The net income and the shareholders' equity on the equity-basis unconsolidated statements are the same as they are on the consolidated statements.

CONCEPT CHECK 4-1

Companion Website

1. Why should acquisition-related fair-value increments and decrements be amortized in subsequent consolidated financial statements?
2. Why does the unrealized profit on the intercompany sale of assets have to be eliminated when preparing consolidated financial statements?

DISCONTINUED OPERATIONS

Under the equity method of accounting, an investor is required to include its share of the profit or loss of its associates as a separate line item in its SCI. Similarly, the investor's share of its associates' other comprehensive income must also be shown separately in the investor's statement of other comprehensive income.

However, it would be rare for an associate company's discontinued operation to qualify as a discontinued operation of the investor. Under IFRS 5, a discontinued operation is defined as a component of an entity that either (1) has been disposed of, or (2) is classified as held for sale, *and*

a) represents a separate major line of business or geographical area of operations;
b) is part of a single coordinated plan to dispose of a separate major line of business or geographical area of operations; or
c) is a subsidiary acquired exclusively with a view to resale.

Therefore, the discontinued operations of an associate will not normally constitute a discontinued operation of the investor. Nevertheless, to provide users of financial statements with adequate information, IAS 28 requires an investor to separately disclose its share of any discontinued operations of its associates.

Similarly, the discontinued operations of a subsidiary should be reported separately, *only if the items represent discontinued operations to the parent* by satisfying the requirements at the level of the parent.

Suppose that a subsidiary discontinues its major line of business. The subsidiary will report the gain or loss as a discontinued operation in its own separate-entity SCI. However, suppose also that the parent company has similar operations of its own or in other subsidiaries. From the point of view of the parent corporation, the subsidiary's discontinuance is just one of many similar lines of business. In that case, the parent would report the gain or loss as a normal operating activity.

For example, think about a parent company that has several retail clothing subsidiaries. If one subsidiary ceases operations, that is big news for the subsidiary but not for the parent. The parent will still be in the retail clothing business, even though one subsidiary has left the business. The retail clothing business line continues for the parent and therefore is not a discontinued operation for consolidated financial reporting.

In contrast to the discontinued operations of a subsidiary above, the complete discontinuance of business by an associate or subsidiary may very well satisfy the requirements for treatment as a discontinued operation of the investor. In such cases, the discontinued operation of the associate or subsidiary is presented separately as a discontinued operation in the investor's financial statements.

CONSOLIDATION IN SECOND SUBSEQUENT YEAR

Basic Information

Before we generalize the approach to preparing consolidated financial statements (in Chapter 6), we will extend this example for one more year. The two companies' financial statements for the year ended December 31, 20X7, are shown in Exhibit 4-7. Additional information is as follows:

1. Target Ltd. had sales of $60,000 to Purchase Ltd. (i.e., upstream); Target Ltd.'s 20X7 gross margin was 45%; $10,000 (sales price) of the goods are in Purchase Ltd.'s

EXHIBIT 4-7

Separate-Entity Financial Statements for 20X7

Statements of Comprehensive Income
Year Ended December 31, 20X7

	Purchase Ltd.	Target Ltd.
Revenue:		
Sales	$3,000,000	$ 400,000
Dividend income	20,000	—
Gain on sale of land	—	150,000
	3,020,000	550,000
Expenses:		
Cost of sales	2,100,000	220,000
Depreciation expense	100,000	35,000
Other expenses	440,000	75,000
	2,640,000	330,000
NET INCOME	$ 380,000	$ 220,000

Statements of Changes in Equity—Retained Earnings Section
Year Ended December 31, 20X7

	Purchase Ltd.	Target Ltd.
Retained earnings, December 31, 20X6	$2,330,000	$ 635,000
Net income	380,000	220,000
Dividends declared	(135,000)	(20,000)
Retained earnings, December 31, 20X7	$2,575,000	$ 835,000

Statements of Financial Position—December 31, 20X7

	Purchase Ltd.	Target Ltd.
ASSETS		
Current Assets:		
Cash	$ 490,000	$ 70,000
Accounts receivable	1,900,000	275,000
Note receivable	—	500,000
Inventory	300,000	60,000
	2,690,000	905,000
Property, Plant, and Equipment:		
Land	1,450,000	—
Buildings and equipment	3,800,000	500,000
Accumulated depreciation	(1,400,000)	(220,000)
	3,850,000	280,000
Other assets:		
Investments (at cost)	1,200,000	—
TOTAL ASSETS	$7,740,000	$1,185,000
LIABILITIES AND SHAREHOLDERS' EQUITY		
Current Liabilities:		
Accounts payable	$ 515,000	$ 150,000
Note payable	500,000	—
Long-term: notes payable	350,000	—
	1,365,000	150,000
Shareholders' Equity:		
Common shares	3,800,000	200,000
Retained earnings	2,575,000	835,000
	6,375,000	1,035,000
TOTAL LIABILITIES AND SHAREHOLDERS' EQUITY	$7,740,000	$1,185,000

inventory on December 31, 20X7. Unrealized upstream profit therefore is $10,000 × 45% = $4,500^U$.

2. Purchase had sales of $20,000 to Target Ltd. (i.e., downstream); Purchase Ltd.'s 20X7 gross margin was 30%; $6,000 (sales price) of the goods sold to Target Ltd. are in Target Ltd.'s 20X7 ending inventory. Unrealized downstream profit is $6,000 × 30% = $1,800$_D$.
3. Purchase Ltd. borrowed $500,000 from Target Ltd. on December 29, 20X7. Both companies have reported this as a current amount on their individual separate-entity SFPs.
4. Target Ltd. sold its land to Purchase Ltd. for $450,000. The land originally cost Target Ltd. $300,000, and its fair value at the date of Purchase Ltd.'s acquisition of Target Ltd. was $400,000. The gain on the sale ($150,000^U) is separately disclosed as an item of revenue on Target Ltd.'s SCI.

Our current example on consolidation at the end of the second year following acquisition, in addition to illustrating all the eliminations and adjustments discussed previously, will also illustrate the following two consolidation related issues:

- elimination of unrealized profit on downstream sales;
- recognition of the profit realized in the current year on upstream sales made in the previous year.

These issues will expand our MEAR analysis by another step. The next two sections will discuss these two issues.

Eliminating Unrealized Profit on Downstream Sales

No special complication arises when a downstream sale is made by a parent to its 100% owned subsidiary. In such a case, the treatment accorded to the unrealized profit is identical to the treatment, as discussed previously, accorded to unrealized profits relating to upstream sales of assets. Things get a bit more complicated when there is a downstream sale by a parent to a *non*-wholly owned subsidiary. We will discuss this issue in greater depth in Chapter 5, when we discuss the topic of consolidating non-wholly owned subsidiaries.

Recognition of Profit Realized in Current Year on Intercompany Sales Made in Previous Year

In our example on consolidation at the end of 20X6, we had an $8,000 unrealized gain on the upstream sale of inventory. The continuation of our example in 20X7 is silent on what happened to the unsold portion of the inventory and the related $8,000 unrealized gain in 20X7. That does not pose a problem. As a computational convenience, unrealized intercompany profits at the end of one year are automatically assumed to have been fully realized during the next year.

Therefore, a suitable adjustment to recognize such realization has to be made at the *beginning* of the second year. To the extent there remain unrealized profits in the ending inventory of the second year, whether emanating from the intercompany sales of that year or years prior, an independent adjustment at the *end* of the second year will take care of such unrealized profits.

Consequently, the related profit, which was treated as *unrealized* during consolidation in the previous year, should now be treated as having been *realized* in the current year. Recall that we increased the cost of goods sold account by $8,000 in 20X6 to reflect the fact that the $8,000 was unrealized at the end of the year. Now that the $8,000 is assumed to be realized, we should reflect that fact by decreasing the cost of goods sold by $8,000. What about the offset? To find the answer to this question, remember that consolidation-related eliminations and adjustments are made only in working papers and are not recorded anywhere. Hence, they do not carry over to later years. Consequently, in these later years, we have to capture the cumulative impact of consolidation-related adjustments and eliminations made in earlier years.

In our example, we increased the cost of goods sold of 20X6 by $8,000, which had the effect of decreasing net income by $8,000 and, consequently, the ending SCE/RE of 20X6 by $8,000. The adjustment necessary now in 20X7, to capture the cumulative impact of the above adjustment made in 20X6, requires us to decrease SCE/RE by $8,000. Therefore, the offset for decreasing the cost of goods sold of 20X7 by $8,000 will be to decrease beginning SCE/RE of 20X7 by $8,000.

Unrealized gains can also arise from intercompany sales of assets other than inventory. The treatment of such other unrealized gains is similar to the treatment of unrealized inventory gains. We will discuss this issue later in the chapter as we further develop our continuing example. However, the main discussion of unrealized gains on assets other than inventory is deferred to Chapter 6.

Direct Method

The MEAR steps listed previously in Exhibit 4-3 relate to acquisition and current period adjustments and eliminations. These steps are no longer sufficient when consolidation is occurring in the second or later years after acquisition. Now we have to make adjustments and eliminations relating to three time periods: (1) the period of acquisition, (2) period(s) following acquisition but prior to the current period, and (3) the current period. To achieve the above objective we need a modified set of MEAR steps for phase 3. Exhibit 4-8 provides the MEAR steps modified for consolidating a wholly owned subsidiary in the second or later year following acquisition.

The Measure step remains unchanged and we will not repeat it here. However, the Eliminate and Amortize steps will produce different results since we are now consolidating at the end of the second year after acquisition. The current year now is 20X7, while 20X6 is the previous year. In contrast, in our previous example, 20X6 was the current year. Therefore, in our current example, the Eliminate and Amortize steps relate to current year *as well as prior year(s)* adjustments and eliminations. Specifically:

1. the Eliminate step adds a third step to the two from before:
   a) Identify and eliminate all inter-company transactions and balances.
   b) Calculate and eliminate the *unrealized* profit (or loss) relating to the sale of inventory and other assets in the current period.
   c) Calculate and recognize the profit (or loss) realized in the current year on the sale of inventory and other assets in previous periods.

EXHIBIT 4-8

MEAR Steps to Consolidation at the End of the Second or Later Year Following Acquisition

Consolidation Steps	Acquisition Related	Relating to First Year Following Acquisition	Relating to Following Years
1. Measure	• Calculate cost and fair-value increments (FVI) • Allocate FVI		
2. Eliminate and recognize	• Eliminate parent's investment account and sub's share equity accounts		
		• Eliminate intercompany transactions and balances • Eliminate unrealized profits	
			• Recognize realized profits
3. Amortize		• Amortize FVIs • Recognize impairments	
			• Recognize cumulative amortization of FVIs • Recognize cumulative impairments

2. the Amortize steps now require that we:
   a) Amortize the FVI allocated to the various identifiable assets and liabilities (i.e., the fair-value increments and decrements relating to those assets and liabilities) *in the current and previous periods*.
   b) Write off any impairment of goodwill and other intangible assets with indeterminate useful lives *in the current and previous periods*.
   c) Find the balance of the allocated FVI remaining unamortized or unimpaired at the end of the *current* period.

We will now perform these two steps for consolidation at the end of the second year after acquisition.

Eliminate

Intercompany Transactions and Balances

The schedule of adjustments for 20X7 is as follows:

Upstream sale by Target Ltd.	(60,000)
Downstream sale by Purchase Ltd.	(20,000)
Dividend income of Purchase Ltd. and dividends declared by Target Ltd.	(20,000)
Note receivable of Target Ltd., and note payable of Purchase Ltd.	(500,000)

In our illustration, in 20X7, there are four intercompany items that need to be eliminated.

1. Target Ltd. sold $60,000 worth of goods to Purchase Ltd. We need to eliminate $60,000 from both sales and cost of goods sold.
2. Purchase Ltd. sold $20,000 worth of goods to Target Ltd. We need to eliminate this $20,000 from both sales and cost of goods sold.

3. Purchase Ltd. recognized its share of $20,000 of the dividends declared by Target Ltd., as dividend income. In this example, Target is a 100% owned subsidiary, and thus the entire $20,000 dividend is Target Ltd.'s "share." We must eliminate this $20,000 from both dividend income and dividends declared.
4. Purchase Ltd. borrowed $500,000 from Target Ltd. on December 29, 20X7. We need to eliminate the associated note receivable and note payable at the time of consolidation. The example does not mention any interest rate attached to the loan. Furthermore, the loan occurred only on December 29. Therefore, we can disregard any associated interest as immaterial. Otherwise, we would have had to eliminate the associated interest income and interest expense that may have been recognized by Target Ltd. and Purchase Ltd., respectively.

Unrealized and Realized Profits

Realized profit on upstream sale of inventory in previous year	8,000
Unrealized profit on upstream sale of inventory in the current year	(4,500)
Unrealized profit on downstream sale of inventory in the current year	(1,800)
Unrealized gain on sale of land by Target Ltd. to Purchase Ltd.	(150,000)

In our illustration we have one source of realized profit, two sources of unrealized profit, and one source of unrealized gain. Remember that in 20X6 we had $8,000 of unrealized profit on the upstream sale of inventory, which we eliminated by increasing the cost of goods sold of 20X6 and decreasing the ending inventory of 20X6 respectively by that amount. The profit was unrealized since the corresponding goods were still with Purchase Ltd. at the end of the year. Now, in 20X7, these goods are assumed to have been sold to an outside party and therefore the associated profits are now realized.

The ending 20X6 inventory is also the beginning 20X7 inventory. Purchase Ltd. would have included the unadjusted beginning inventory in its cost of sales calculation in the current year; from the consolidation point of view, that results in *overstating* opening inventory by $8,000, and consequently *overstating* cost of sales by the same amount. Therefore, we must *reduce* consolidated cost of sales by $8,000 to account for the realization of the profits in 20X7.

We should increase the cost of goods sold of 20X7 and decrease the ending inventory of 20X7 by $4,500 and $1,800 to eliminate the unrealized profits on the upstream and downstream sale of inventory respectively this year. The underlying logic is identical to the logic underlying the elimination of the unrealized profit on the upstream sale of inventory in 20X6.

Finally, Target Ltd. sold its land to Purchase Ltd. during the year for a gain of $150,000. However, the land is still owned within the consolidated entity, therefore, the associated gain is unrealized, and therefore has to be eliminated.

Amortize

	FVI allocated	Amortization period	Amortization per year	Amortization/ impairment loss during previous periods	Amortization/ impairment loss during 20X7	Balance of FVI remaining at the end of 20X7
Land	$100,000	—			—	$100,000
Building and Equipment	200,000	10	$20,000	$20,000	$20,000	160,000
Goodwill	100,000	—			—	100,000
Total	$400,000			$20,000	$20,000	$360,000

From the schedule above we can see that we need to recognize a total amortization/impairment loss adjustment of $20,000 in the previous year (as explained in greater detail further below) and a similar adjustment in the current year.

We can also see from the schedule above that the balance of the FVI adjustment to be added to the carrying values of the parent and subsidiary is $360,000, consisting of increases to land of $100,000, building and equipment of $160,000, and goodwill of $100,000. Note that the adjustment for building and equipment of $160,000 is the result of the initial FVI allocated to building and equipment of $200,000 minus the $40,000 depreciation adjustment required in total over the previous and current year.

Recall that in our earlier discussion we said that all consolidation-related adjustments or eliminations are made only in the consolidation-related working papers and not recorded on either company's books. Therefore, these adjustments do not carry over to later years. Consequently, every time we consolidate subsequent to the date of acquisition, we need to either (1) replicate those adjustments and eliminations made in previous years, or (2) capture their cumulative impact with suitable but different cumulative adjustments.

Now, we will illustrate the second type of adjustments—adjustments required to capture the cumulative impact of adjustments and eliminations made in prior years. Such adjustments are naturally made to the opening retained earnings of the year, since retained earnings represent the cumulative impact of prior years' operations.

In our current example, we have to adjust the opening retained earnings for the impact of two prior years' adjustments:

Amortization/impairment loss adjustment of $20,000 pertaining to 20X6	(20,000)
Unrealized profit on upstream sale of inventory in 20X6	(8,000)

The first item is the $20,000 amortization or depreciation expense adjustment made in 20X6 relating to the fair-value increment allocated to buildings and equipment. This amortization expense adjustment would have decreased the consolidated income of 20X6 and, consequently, the ending consolidated retained earnings of 20X6 by $20,000. However, this decrease will not be reflected in the opening book retained earnings in 20X7 of either Target Ltd. or Purchase Ltd.

Therefore, at the time of consolidation in 20X7, to capture the impact of this prior-year amortization adjustment, we now have to adjust the beginning consolidated retained earnings of 20X7 by $20,000. If we were to extend our example to 20X8, and the facts remained the same, we would need to adjust the consolidated opening retained earnings balance of 20X8 by $40,000: $20,000 for the amortization expense adjustment relating to 20X6 and another $20,000 for the amortization expense adjustment relating to 20X7.

The second item above relates to the elimination of the unrealized profit of $8,000 on the upstream sale of inventory in 20X6. This elimination would have reduced the consolidated income of 20X6 and the ending retained earnings of 20X6 by $8,000. Again, to capture the impact of this prior-year elimination, we have to adjust the opening retained earnings of 20X7 by $8,000.

Recall that we adjusted the 20X7 cost of goods sold by reducing it by the same $8,000. We did this because the inventory in question was sold in 20X7 and thus the $8,000 became realized in 20X7. The impact will be to increase both (1) 20X7 consolidated income and (2) 20X7 ending retained earnings by $8,000. The net effect of the combination of the $8,000

EXHIBIT 4-9

Purchase Ltd. Statement of Comprehensive Income (Direct Method)

Consolidated Statement of Comprehensive Income
Year Ended December 31, 20X7

Revenue:	
Sales revenue [3,000,000 + 400,000 − 60,000^U − 20,000$_D$]	$3,320,000
Dividend income [20,000 + 0 − 20,000]	—
Gain on sale of land [0 + 150,000 − 150,000^U]	—
	3,320,000
Operating expenses:	
Cost of sales [2,100,000 + 220,000 − 60,000^U − 20,000$_D$ + 4,500^U + 1,800$_D$ − 8,000^U]	2,238,300
Depreciation expense [100,000 + 35,000 + 20,000]	155,000
Other expenses [440,000 + 75,000]	515,000
	2,908,300
NET INCOME	$ 411,700

Consolidated Statement of Changes in Equity—Retained Earnings Section
Year Ended December 31, 20X7

Retained earnings, December 31, 20X6 [2,330,000 + 635,000 − 600,000 − 20,000 − 8,000^U]	$2,337,000
Net income	411,700
Dividends declared [135,000 + 20,000 − 20,000]	(135,000)
Retained earnings, December 31, 20X7	$2,613,700

reduction of the opening retained earnings balance and the increase by $8,000 of the ending retained earnings balance on the final ending retained earnings balance on the SFP is zero. The impact of the series of adjustments relating to the upstream sale of inventory in 20X6 was to defer recognizing the profits relating to such inventory from 20X6 to 20X7, the period in which the profit was actually realized by the consolidated entity. This is an example of the inter-period allocation of profits.

Now we have all the ingredients required to carry out the actual consolidation. Again, we will go down the SCI and SFP and insert the correct amounts on a line-by-line basis.

Statement of Comprehensive Income and SCE/RE The consolidated statement of income and retained earnings is shown in Exhibit 4-9. The amounts that require adjustment are as follows:

- *Sales*. The two companies' combined sales of $3,400,000 must be adjusted for the intercompany sales. In 20X7, there were upstream sales (Target Ltd. to Purchase Ltd.) of $60,000 and downstream sales (Purchase Ltd. to Target Ltd.) of $20,000. The sum of these amounts must be removed from sales revenue: $60,000^U + $20,000$_D$ = $80,000.
- *Dividend income*. We need to eliminate the entire $20,000 dividend income both from the dividend income line item on the SCI and the dividend declared line item on the SCE/RE.
- *Gain on sale of land*. The $150,000^U unrealized gain on the sale of land by Target Ltd. to Purchase Ltd. in 20X7 must be eliminated.

- *Cost of sales*. Cost of sales must also be reduced by the \$80,000 (\$60,000^{U} + \$20,000$_{D}$) of inter-company sales. Some of the goods sold from one company to the other are still in inventory. Therefore, we must also adjust cost of sales by increasing it for the unrealized profit of \$4,500^{U} in Purchase Ltd.'s year-end inventory and of \$1,800$_{D}$ in Target Ltd.'s year-end inventory. Finally, we must adjust cost of sales by decreasing it for the realized profit of \$8,000^{U} from the previous year's upstream sale of inventory.
- *Depreciation expense*. We must continue to amortize the fair-value increment on Target Ltd.'s buildings and equipment. As in 20X6, the amortization is \$200,000 ÷ 10 years, or \$20,000. This amount is added to the depreciation expense.
- *Dividends declared*. Target Ltd.'s \$20,000 in dividends paid to Purchase Ltd. must be eliminated.
- *Opening retained earnings*. The opening balances (i.e., the December 31, 20X6, balances) must be adjusted for two things: (1) Target Ltd.'s retained earnings balance at the date of acquisition and (2) adjustments to earnings since the date of acquisition. The 20X6 earnings adjustments were for \$20,000 amortization of the fair-value increment and for \$8,000^{U} unrealized profit on intercompany inventory sales in that year. Both of these amounts are subtracted from the opening retained earnings to get the correct, adjusted, beginning balance.

Statement of Financial Position The consolidated SFP is shown in Exhibit 4-10. Adjustments are as follows:

- *Note receivable*. The intercompany receivable of \$500,000 that is included on Target Ltd.'s books must be eliminated.
- *Inventory*. The unrealized profits from both the upstream and downstream sales of \$4,500^{U} and \$1,800$_{D}$ embedded in the closing inventory of Purchase Ltd. and Target Ltd., respectively, must be eliminated.
- *Land*. Target Ltd.'s land has been sold to Purchase Ltd. Target Ltd. recorded a gain of \$150,000^{U} on the sale. This is an intercompany unrealized profit that must be eliminated. However, there was a fair-value increment of \$100,000 on the land at the date of purchase. This FVI still must be added, even though legal title to the land has now been transferred from Target Ltd. to Purchase Ltd. In a consolidated statement, it doesn't matter which company actually owns it.
- *Buildings and equipment*. The date-of-acquisition FVI of \$50,000 must be added, just as in 20X6.
- *Accumulated depreciation*. Target Ltd.'s date-of-acquisition accumulated depreciation of \$150,000 is eliminated; two years' worth of FVI amortization of \$20,000 per year is added.
- *Current note payable*. Purchase Ltd.'s payables include the \$500,000 owed to Target Ltd. This intercompany balance must be eliminated.
- *Common shares*. As usual, only the parent's shares are reported on the consolidated statement of financial position.

EXHIBIT 4-10

Purchase Ltd. Consolidated Statement of Financial Position (Direct Method)

Consolidated Statement of Financial Position
December 31, 20X7

ASSETS	
Current assets:	
Cash [490,000 + 70,000]	$ 560,000
Accounts receivable [1,900,000 + 275,000]	2,175,000
Note receivable [0 + 500,000 − **500,000**]	—
Inventory [300,000 + 60,000 − **$4,500^U$** − **$1,800_D$**]	353,700
	3,088,700
Property, Plant, and Equipment:	
Land [1,450,000 + 0 **+ 100,000** − **$150,000^U$**]	1,400,000
Buildings and equipment [3,800,000 + 500,000 **+ 50,000**]	4,350,000
Accumulated depreciation [1,400,000 + 220,000 − **150,000** **+ 40,000**]	(1,510,000)
	4,240,000
Other Assets:	
Investments [1,200,000 + 0 − **1,200,000**]	—
Goodwill	100,000
TOTAL ASSETS	$7,428,700
LIABILITIES AND SHAREHOLDERS' EQUITY	
Current liabilities:	
Accounts payable [515,000 + 150,000]	$ 665,000
Note payable [500,000 + 0 − **500,000**]	—
Long-term liability: notes payable [350,000 + 0]	350,000
	1,015,000
Shareholders' Equity:	
Common shares **[Purchase Ltd. shares only]**	3,800,000
Retained earnings [2,575,000 + 835,000 − **600,000** − **$150,000^U$** − **$4,500^U$** − **$1,800_D$** − **(20,000 × 2)**]	2,613,700
	6,413,700
TOTAL LIABILITIES AND SHAREHOLDERS' EQUITY	$7,428,700

- *Retained earnings*. Consolidated retained earnings is calculated by starting with the book balances of the two companies, and then:
  (1) subtracting Target Ltd.'s date-of-acquisition retained earnings,
  (2) subtracting year-end unrealized profits, and
  (3) subtracting the cumulative amount of FVI amortization since the date of acquisition (i.e., $20,000 × 2 years).

Notice, as discussed earlier, that it is not necessary to adjust for the unrealized profit in the beginning inventory when we compute the ending consolidated retained earnings. Target Ltd.'s separate-entity retained earnings already includes the $8,000 previously unrealized profit from 20X6, and by *not* making any adjustment, we permit it to flow through to consolidated retained earnings as a now-realized amount. Of course, we are assuming that the beginning inventory has been sold during the period. This is the normal assumption; we only need to be told how much of the intercompany sales is still in ending inventory each year (and the relevant gross margin percentage) to make the adjustments for unrealized year-end profit, regardless of which year the intercompany sales occurred.

"Proving" Retained Earnings It is wise to calculate the closing balance of the consolidated retained earnings on the SFP at the time of every consolidation. As we observed earlier in the chapter, we could have obtained the year-end consolidated retained earnings from the bottom of the statement of changes in retained earnings, or simply by treating retained earnings as a "plug" once we had calculated all of the other balances. However, it is useful to be able to derive closing retained earnings directly from information given, rather than going through the whole process of constructing a consolidated SCI. And "plugs" are always dangerous—there is no way to tell if the SFP really is in balance. Purchase Ltd.'s consolidated retained earnings figure for December 31, 20X7, is as follows:

Purchase Ltd.'s separate-entity retained earnings	$2,575,000
Target Ltd.'s separate-entity retained earnings	835,000
Target Ltd.'s date-of-acquisition retained earnings	(600,000)
Unrealized profit on sale of land	(150,000)
Unrealized upstream profit in ending inventory	(4,500)
Unrealized downstream profit in ending inventory	(1,800)
Two years' amortization of FVI in buildings and equipment	(40,000)
Purchase Ltd.'s consolidated retained earnings	**$2,613,700**

Worksheet Approach

Companion Website

As usual, the worksheet approach of consolidation two years after acquisition is available on the Companion Website.

Completed Consolidated Financial Statements

Exhibits 4-11 through 4-13 present the complete consolidated financial statements for Purchase Ltd. as of December 31, 20X7. Since financial statements should be comparative statements, the 20X7 statements also include the amounts for 20X6. A complete set of financial statements must include a cash flow statement. Exhibit 4-13 illustrates a cash flow statement.

The preparation of a consolidated cash flow statement involves no particular challenges. The statement can be prepared by combining the cash flow statements of the separate entities and eliminating intercompany transactions. Alternatively, the statement can be prepared directly from the consolidated SCI, SFP, and SCE/RE in exactly the same manner as from any other set of financial statements.

EXHIBIT 4-11

Purchase Ltd. Consolidated Statement of Comprehensive Income and SCE/RE

Consolidated Statement of Comprehensive Income
Years Ended December 31

	20X7	20X6
SALES REVENUE	$3,320,000	$2,645,000
Operating Expenses:		
Cost of sales	2,238,300	1,883,000
Depreciation expense	155,000	155,000
Other expenses	515,000	270,000
	2,908,300	2,308,000
NET INCOME	$ 411,700	$ 337,000

Consolidated Statement of Changes in Equity—Retained Earnings Section
Years Ended December 31

	20X7	20X6
Retained earnings, January 1	$2,337,000	$2,000,000
Net income	411,700	337,000
Dividends declared	(135,000)	—
Retained earnings, December 31	$2,613,700	$2,337,000

EXHIBIT 4-12

Purchase Ltd. Consolidated Statement of Financial Position

Consolidated Statement of Financial Position
December 31

	20X7	20X6
ASSETS		
Current Assets:		
Cash	$ 560,000	$1,080,000
Accounts receivable	2,175,000	2,450,000
Inventory	353,700	312,000
	3,088,700	3,842,000
Property, Plant, and Equipment:		
Land	1,400,000	1,400,000
Buildings and equipment	4,350,000	3,550,000
Accumulated depreciation	(1,510,000)	(1,355,000)
	4,240,000	3,595,000
Other Assets:		
Goodwill	100,000	100,000
TOTAL ASSETS	$7,428,700	$7,537,000

EXHIBIT 4-12 (*Continued*)

Purchase Ltd. Consolidated Statement of Financial Position

LIABILITIES AND SHAREHOLDERS' EQUITY		
Liabilities:		
Current: accounts payable	$ 665,000	$1,000,000
Long-term: notes payable	350,000	400,000
	1,015,000	1,400,000
Shareholders' Equity:		
Common shares	3,800,000	3,800,000
Retained earnings	2,613,700	2,337,000
	6,413,700	6,137,000
TOTAL LIABILITIES AND SHAREHOLDERS' EQUITY	$7,428,700	$7,537,000

Note Disclosure

While Exhibits 4-11 through 4-13 do present the complete set of statements, they do not present the notes thereto. The notes should contain detailed disclosure of Purchase Ltd.'s acquisition of Target Ltd., as we discussed at the end of Chapter 3.

In practice, there exists considerable variation in the extent of disclosure made by Canadian companies about business combinations. One possible reason for the relative lack of disclosure could be the absence of materiality. Reality Check 4-1 summarizes results from a research study on the various reasons and causes of management's disclosures relating to business combinations.

EXHIBIT 4-13

Consolidated Cash Flow Statement

Years Ended December 31	20X7	20X6
OPERATING ACTIVITIES		
Consolidated net income, as reported	$ 411,700	$337,000
Add Expenses Not Requiring Cash:		
Depreciation on capital assets	155,000	155,000
Changes in Working Capital Items:		
Current accounts receivable	275,000	(300,000)
Inventory	(41,700)	(62,000)
Accounts payable	(335,000)	(100,000)
Net cash from operating activities	465,000	30,000
FINANCING ACTIVITIES		
Decrease in long-term notes payable	(50,000)	—
Dividends declared and paid	(135,000)	—
	(185,000)	—
INVESTING ACTIVITIES		
Purchase of buildings and equipment	(800,000)	—
INCREASE (DECREASE) IN CASH	$(520,000)	$ 30,000
Cash at the beginning of the year	1,080,000	1,050,000
Cash at the end of the year	560,000	1,080,000

REALITY CHECK 4-1

Management's Disclosures about Business Combinations

The 2007 edition of *Financial Reporting in Canada* reported that about 45% of the companies (of the 200 surveyed companies) disclosed business combinations in each of the five years, 2002–2006, ranging from 42.5% in 2005 and 2006 to 47.5% in 2003. Most disclosures were made about the cost of the purchase, followed by disclosures of the name of the acquiree and of the fair value of the major class of assets and liabilities acquired respectively.[a]

A more recent empirical analysis of business combination disclosure found that management's level of disclosure decreases when an abnormally high level of the purchase price is allocated to goodwill. Goodwill is the residual remaining after allocating the purchase price to net identifiable assets. Therefore, if an acquirer overpays for an acquisition, the excess is absorbed by goodwill. Furthermore, since goodwill is not subject to amortization, increasing the portion of the purchase price allocated to goodwill reduces the amount allocated to assets that are subject to amortization and thereby increases future earnings.

The research also found that the level of disclosure appears to be related to two measures of earnings management—(1) frequency of unexpected accruals, and (2) the frequency of exactly meeting quarterly analysts' forecasts in the five years leading to the business combination. Better disclosure of business combinations was also found to be related to a more positive change in return on assets in the two years following the business combination as well as to increased stock returns.

The author's analysis also indicates that investors do not fully adjust for the difference in disclosure levels; that is, they seem to be fooled by the level of accounting disclosures provided on business combinations by the managers.

a *Financial Reporting in Canada 2007*, Thirty-second Edition (Toronto: CICA, 2007).

Source: R. Shalev, "The information content of business combination disclosure level," *The Accounting Review* 84:1 (2009), p. 239.

Consolidating Parent-Founded Subsidiaries

The example used throughout this chapter is that of a business combination. Purchase Ltd. acquired control over the net assets of Target Ltd. at a price that included both fair-value increments and goodwill. By using a business combination as the basis for the example, we can fairly comprehensively illustrate the major types of adjustments that may be required when consolidated statements are prepared.

However, we pointed out in Chapter 2 that most subsidiaries are not the result of one corporation's acquiring another in a business combination. Instead, most subsidiaries are formed by their parent to conduct or facilitate some component of the parent's business. The process of consolidation for a subsidiary that was founded and wholly owned by its parent is much easier than for a subsidiary that was acquired as a going concern.

Since the investment by the parent was directly in the subsidiary (rather than by buying the subsidiary's shares from another shareholder), the paid-in capital accounts of the subsidiary directly offset the original investment in the investment account of the parent. There are no fair-value increments or goodwill to worry about. The lack of fair-value increments means that there is no periodic amortization of those amounts to adjust for. Consolidating a wholly owned, parent-founded subsidiary simply requires:

1. adjusting for intercompany transactions;
2. eliminating any unrealized profits or losses; and
3. eliminating intercompany receivable and payable balances.

Indirect Holdings

In Chapter 2 we pointed out that a parent company might control a subsidiary indirectly through other subsidiaries, rather than by direct ownership. When the parent prepares its consolidated financial statements, both the direct and the indirect subsidiaries are consolidated.

Procedurally, indirect subsidiaries can be consolidated in either of two ways. The first is to consolidate by steps, from the bottom up. If P controls A, and A controls B and C, then consolidated statements for A can be prepared that include its direct subsidiaries, B and C. A's *consolidated* statements will then include all of the assets and liabilities of B and C just as if A owned them directly, and the investment accounts will have been eliminated. The next step is then to consolidate A's *consolidated* statements with P's statements. If the consolidation is being performed by the direct approach without a worksheet, then the step method is almost certainly the best one to use.

The second approach is to perform the consolidation of all subsidiaries, direct and indirect, on a single worksheet. A single-step worksheet approach may be easiest for those who are performing the consolidation on a computer spreadsheet, since it is relatively easy to include all of the subsidiaries on the worksheet with adequate space for explanatory notes.

Whichever procedural approach is used, the elimination and adjustment process is no different from that illustrated in this chapter for directly owned subsidiaries.

IAS 27 requires that consolidated financial statements be prepared using uniform accounting policies for like transactions and events of similar nature. It simplifies the process of consolidation when all subsidiaries use the same accounting policies as the parent. When the same accounting policies are used, there will be no need for the parent to adjust the accounts of the subsidiaries for accounting policy differences. This is fairly easily accomplished with wholly owned subsidiaries—the parent company's management can specify the subsidiaries' accounting policies. Otherwise, appropriate adjustments must be made in the financial statements while preparing consolidated financial statements.

CONCEPT CHECK 4-2

Companion Website

1. What is the current year adjustment for the unrealized profit on the intercompany sale of inventory in the previous year? What is the underlying rationale for such a treatment?
2. What, in general, is the current year adjustment for consolidation-related adjustments and eliminations made in previous year(s)?

IMPAIRMENT TESTING OF GOODWILL BY PRIVATE ENTERPRISES

Private enterprises (i.e., companies without public accountability) are not required to apply an annual impairment test. Private companies should apply an impairment test only when a specific event or circumstance indicates that impairment might have happened. Further, the impairment test need be performed only at the *reporting unit* level rather than at the level of the cash-generating unit.

Basically, a *reporting unit* is defined by the internal reporting system of the corporation. A **reporting unit** is any part of the corporation that is evaluated regularly by the corporation's principal decision maker (normally the chief operating officer) for resource allocation decisions. Appendix 4B provides further details on the requirements for impairment testing of goodwill under ASPE.

Relevant Standards

IASB

IFRS 5 Non-current Assets Held for Sale and Discontinued Operations
IFRS 8 Operating Segments
IAS 1 Presentation of Financial Statements
IAS 27 Consolidated and Separate Financial Statements
IAS 28 Investments in Associates
IAS 36 Impairment of Assets

Summary of Key Points

1. The parent company and each of its subsidiaries will prepare individual, separate-entity, financial statements. These statements are independent of the consolidated statements. Consolidated statements are prepared only for the shareholders of the parent company. The existence of consolidated statements does not eliminate the need for separate-entity statements.

2. Only a statement of financial position is necessary when a parent and its purchased subsidiary are consolidated at the date of acquisition. At all subsequent reporting dates, consolidation involves a full set of financial statements.

3. At reporting dates following acquisition, consolidated net income must be adjusted for amortization of fair-value increments, adjustments to goodwill, and elimination of unrealized profits on intercompany sales. Amortization of fair-value increments on tangible and intangible assets should be based on the estimated remaining useful life of the asset. Goodwill must be written down if its value for generating future earnings is impaired.
4. Sales of current and non-current assets between a parent and its subsidiaries, or between subsidiaries, should be eliminated. Profits on intercompany sales of assets should be eliminated, unless the assets have been sold to outside third parties.
5. If consolidated statements are not prepared, the parent can report its investment in the subsidiary on either the cost or the equity basis. If the equity basis is used for reporting non-consolidated subsidiaries, the parent company's reported net income and retained earnings will be exactly the same as though the statements had been consolidated.
6. A subsidiary's discontinued operation will not normally constitute a discontinued operation for the parent in a consolidated SCI. Discontinued operations arising in consolidated subsidiaries are reported as such in the parent's SCI only *if the items qualify as discontinued operations to the parent.*
7. A complete set of consolidated financial statements should include a cash flow statement. The cash flow statement can be prepared for consolidated statements in exactly the same manner as for separate-entity statements.

Companion Website

Visit the text's website at www.pearsoned.ca/beechy for practice quizzes, additional problems, Excel® templates, answers to Concept Check questions, and important IFRS updates.

Self-Study Problem 4-1

Early in 20X5, Parco acquired 100% of the shares of Subco by issuing Parco shares worth $10 million. The carrying value of Subco's net assets at the date of acquisition was $7,000,000. The fair values of Subco's assets were deemed to be equal to their carrying values on Subco's books with one exception: the aggregate fair value of Subco's buildings was $1,400,000 higher than their carrying value.

Parco and Subco enjoyed a trading relationship for many years prior to the combination. In 20X4, for example, Subco had sold $1 million of goods to Parco (at a gross margin of 20% on sales), and Parco had billed Subco $300,000 for management services. However, the two companies had no common ownership interest and were not related companies prior to the 20X5 business combination.

In 20X5, following the business combination, Subco had sales of $1.2 million to Parco. Subco's gross margin remained at 20%. Of the amount sold, $200,000 remained in Parco's inventory at the end of 20X5. Parco billed Subco $400,000 for management fees, of which $100,000 remained unpaid at the end of the year. Other information is as follows:

- Subco reported separate-entity net income of $350,000 for 20X5. Subco declared and paid dividends of $150,000 during the year.
- Parco reported separate-entity net income of $680,000 for 20X5, including the dividend income from Subco. Parco declared dividends of $200,000, of which one-quarter were unpaid at year-end.
- Retained earnings at the date of acquisition were $3,450,000 for Parco and $1,250,000 for Subco.
- Subco's buildings have an estimated remaining useful life of 14 years. Subco uses straight-line depreciation.
- There has been no impairment of goodwill.

Required

Determine the following amounts:

1. Parco's consolidated net income for the year ended December 31, 20X5.
2. Parco's consolidated retained earnings at December 31, 20X5.
3. Parco's equity-basis earnings from Subco for 20X5.

Self-Study Problem 4-2

On January 1, 20X8, Parent Ltd. (Par) bought 100% of the shares of Subsidiary Inc. (Sub) for $1,084,000 cash. Sub's statement of financial position at the date of acquisition is shown in Exhibit 4-14, together with the estimated fair values of Sub's assets and liabilities.

EXHIBIT 4-14

Subsidiary Inc. Statement of Financial Position

January 1, 20X8	Carrying values	Fair values
Cash	$ 80,000	$ 80,000
Accounts receivable	99,000	99,000
Inventory	178,000	195,000
Property, plant, and equipment	800,000	740,000
Accumulated depreciation	(200,000)	
Total assets	$957,000	
Accounts payable	$ 70,000	70,000
Long-term notes payable	200,000	200,000
Common shares	250,000	
Retained earnings	437,000	
Total liabilities and shareholders' equity	$957,000	

EXHIBIT 4-15

Separate-Entity Financial Statements for 20X9

Statements of Comprehensive Income
Year Ended December 31, 20X9

	Parent Ltd.	Subsidiary Inc.
Sales revenue	$1,200,000	$ 987,000
Cost of goods sold	(800,000)	(650,000)
	400,000	337,000
Other operating expenses	(235,000)	(147,000)
NET INCOME	$ 165,000	$ 190,000

Statements of Changes in Equity—Retained Earnings Section
Year Ended December 31, 20X9

Retained earnings, December 31, 20X8	$1,153,000	$ 330,000
Net income	165,000	190,000
Retained earnings, December 31, 20X9	$1,318,000	$ 520,000

Statements of Financial Position
December 31, 20X9

	Parent Ltd.	Subsidiary Inc.
ASSETS		
Current Assets:		
Cash	$ 120,000	$ 110,000
Accounts receivable	150,000	135,000
Inventory	240,000	195,000
	510,000	440,000
Property, plant, and equipment	1,400,000	910,000
Accumulated depreciation	(510,000)	(320,000)
	890,000	590,000
Other Assets:		
Investments (at cost)	1,084,000	—
Goodwill	76,000	—
	1,160,000	—
TOTAL ASSETS	$2,560,000	$1,030,000
LIABILITIES AND SHAREHOLDERS' EQUITY		
Liabilities:		
Accounts payable	$ 142,000	$ 60,000
Long-term notes payable	600,000	200,000
	742,000	260,000
Shareholders' Equity:		
Common shares	500,000	250,000
Retained earnings	1,318,000	520,000
	1,818,000	770,000
TOTAL LIABILITIES AND SHAREHOLDERS' EQUITY	$2,560,000	$1,030,000

Additional information is as follows:

- Sub depreciates its tangible capital assets over 10 years on a straight-line basis, assuming zero residual value.
- During 20X9, Par sold goods with a cost of $300,000 to Sub for $390,000. At the end of 20X9, 20% of those goods remain in Sub's inventory.
- Sub sold goods costing $100,000 to Par for $150,000 in 20X9. At the end of the year, 40% of these goods remain in Par's inventory.
- Par sold land to Sub on January 1, 20X9, for $710,000. The original cost of the land was $500,000 to Par. The gain was netted to "other expenses."
- On January 1, 20X9, Par had inventory on hand that it had bought from Sub for $45,000. Intercompany profit of $12,000 was included in that price.

The separate-entity financial statements for Par and Sub for the year ended December 31, 20X9, are shown in Exhibit 4-15.

Required

Prepare the consolidated financial statements for 20X9.

Review Questions

4-1 What is accomplished by the acquisition adjustment when consolidated statements are prepared?

4-2 How would the acquisition adjustment for an acquired subsidiary differ from that for a parent-founded subsidiary?

4-3 How is goodwill arising from a business combination accounted for in years following the combination?

4-4 Why are the fair-value increments and decrements on depreciable capital assets amortized? What is the basis for determining the amount of amortization?

4-5 When is it necessary to eliminate the profit on intercompany transactions?

4-6 How does management judgment impact on the impairment test for goodwill?

4-7 What is the reporting option available to private enterprises for the goodwill impairment test?

4-8 Explain why the adjustment for unrealized profit in ending inventories appears to *increase* cost of goods sold.

4-9 Explain the difference between the acquisition adjustment and the operations adjustments.

4-10 Why is the equity method of reporting sometimes called the consolidation method of equity reporting?

4-11 How does a parent company's total net assets amount differ under consolidated reporting as compared to equity reporting for a subsidiary?

4-12 Under equity reporting, how do discontinued operations of an investee corporation affect the SCI of the investor corporation?

4-13 How does unrealized profit in the beginning inventories affect the consolidated net income, if the inventories have been sold during the year?

4-14 What disclosure should be made in the financial statements of an acquirer as to the details of a business combination?

4-15 In what general ways will consolidation of a parent-founded subsidiary differ from consolidation of a purchased subsidiary?

4-16 Are consolidated statements required after one corporation directly acquires the net assets of another corporation?

CASES

CASE 4-1 GROWTH LIMITED

You are the CA appointed as the new auditor of Growth Limited (GL), a private company, for the next three years. The requirement for an audit is specified in GL's debt covenant with the bank. This is the first year that an audit will be completed.

As part of an ongoing expansion program, GL added two new sizes to its line of fish-crate products. The president of GL is pleased with the continuing expansion program. Annual sales are $1,800,000, the highest level in GL's history and a real achievement for a firm of its size. The president attributes the increase in sales to the exacting standards of quality incorporated in its new products and made the following comments.

"We have never amortized or tested goodwill for impairment since goodwill is being built up in our business, not used. In fact, I can never see it going down in value since our business is continuing to grow. This year for the first time we acquired another company that provides additional products to add to our line. That increased our goodwill even more than we have now."

"We also wrote off the deferred tax balance this year because it doesn't mean anything. In fact, our banker adds the accumulated deferred tax balance to retained earnings when he reviews our annual financing proposals. I just couldn't think of any reason why we should pay you to calculate deferred taxes when no one uses them."

Required

Discuss the president's comments.

[CICA]

CASE 4-2 PELICAN SYSTEMS INC.

Pelican Systems Inc. (PSI), a public company, develops and manufactures equipment that is sold to technology, communications, and airline enterprises, and designs and installs customized information networks for customers. The chief executive officer (CEO) of PSI retired on December 31, 20X4, and Gerald Cinco was hired as his replacement. An executive search firm recommended Cinco and he signed a three-year employment contract with PSI that includes performance bonuses. At the annual shareholders' meeting held on March 6, 20X5, Cinco predicted strong growth in revenue and in earnings per share, which would result in a healthy increase in the value of PSI's shares.

Cinco's predictions were validated by PSI's results as reflected in its audited financial statements for the fiscal year ended December 31, 20X5, and a substantial increase in the share value from the preceding year-end share value.

Following its policy of appointing new auditors every five years, at the annual shareholders' meeting held on March 5, 20X6, Sharp & Ipson, Chartered Accountants LLP (S&I), was appointed as auditor for the year ending December 31, 20X6.

It is now March 17, 20X6. You are a CA with S&I and have been assigned the responsibility for the PSI audit engagement. You have obtained the extracts from the consolidated financial statements for the year ended December 31, 20X5 (Exhibit A), information pertaining to the operations and accounting policies of PSI gathered through interviews with company employees (Exhibit B), and extracts from the audit working papers prepared by the predecessor auditor (Exhibit C).

The partner responsible for the PSI audit will be attending a meeting of the board of directors on March 26, 20X6. The partner has asked you to prepare a memo to help her understand the impact of the accounting policies followed in the prior year.

Required

Prepare the memo requested by the partner.

Exhibit A Extracts from Consolidated Financial Statements

Pelican Systems Inc.
Consolidated Statement of Financial Position as at December 31
(in thousands of dollars)

	20X5	20X4
ASSETS		
Current Assets		
Cash	$ 2,080	$ 1,090
Accounts receivable	11,300	10,200
Inventory	8,400	7,350
Prepaids	720	690
	22,500	19,330
Property, plant, and equipment (net)	40,400	44,800
Long-term investments	2,500	—
Deferred charges	2,604	870
Goodwill and other intangible assets	3,956	—
	$71,960	$65,000

LIABILITIES AND SHAREHOLDERS' EQUITY		
Current Liabilities		
Bank indebtedness	$ 8,850	$12,000
Accounts payable and accruals	3,110	3,160
Current portion of long-term debt	4,750	4,000
	16,710	19,160
Long-term debt	33,250	28,000
Deferred income taxes	1,090	980
	51,050	48,140
Common shares	12,000	12,000
Retained earnings	8,910	4,860
	20,910	16,860
	$71,960	$65,000

Pelican Systems Inc.
Consolidated Statement of Comprehensive Income
Years ended December 31
(in thousands of dollars)

	20X5	20X4
Revenues	$80,000	$73,000
Cost of generating revenues	49,600	44,100
Gross margin	30,400	28,900
Selling, general and administrative expenses	14,400	14,600
Interest and financing charges	2,650	2,380
Amortization expense	5,850	6,420
	22,900	23,400
Income before taxes	7,500	5,500
Income taxes	2,850	2,090
Net income	$ 4,650	$ 3,410

Exhibit B Information Pertaining to the Operations and Accounting Policies of PSI

SALES LEASING PROGRAM

To stimulate sales, PSI sells customized equipment on a leasing basis, whereby an unrelated financial institution purchases the equipment from PSI and leases this equipment to PSI's customers. PSI arranges sales on this basis for higher credit-risk customers. This sales practice was adopted effective April 1, 20X5, as directed by the CEO "to expand our customer base to meet our objective of sales and earnings growth."

PSI pays a financing arrangement fee of 10% of the selling price of the equipment to the financial institution as compensation for extending a lower interest rate to the customer than would be typical for the credit risk related to the customer. PSI guarantees the payments of the customers. The financial institution holds title to the equipment until the final lease payment is made, at which time title is transferred to the lessee. PSI has the right to purchase each of the lease receivables from the financial institution at any time for the amount of the outstanding balance. The financing arrangement fee is not refundable.

During the fiscal year ended December 31, 20X5, sales totalling $12,000,000 were made under the terms of this leasing program, which provided PSI with a cash flow of $10,800,000 net of the financing arrangement fee paid to the financial institution. PSI's gross margin on these sales, before the financing arrangement fee, was $5,400,000.

PSI's director of marketing stated that, in January 20X6, the financial institution advised PSI that $1,600,000 of the $2,000,000 principal portion of the payments due by December 31, 20X5, had been made by the lessees and requested compensation of $400,000 plus interest of $24,000 for payments in arrears.

ACQUISITION OF EQUIPMENT

On July 1, 20X5, PSI acquired state-of-the-art technology equipment that is being used to manufacture a new product line under a special financing arrangement. PSI is required to pay to the seller 15% of the profit, defined as gross margin, realized from sales of this product line during the three years ending August 31, 20X8. PSI is required to remit the amount due annually no later than November 30 of each year, with the amount supported by "a certification by PSI's auditor that PSI has remitted in full the amount due under the terms of the financing arrangement."

According to PSI's director of procurements, the cost to PSI to purchase the equipment for cash would have been $3,000,000. Revenue from sales of the new product line is projected to total $65,000,000 for the three years ending August 31, 20X8, as follows: first year, $19,500,000; second year, $27,300,000; third year, $18,200,000; and for the fourth and fifth years combined, $25,000,000. The life of the product line is estimated to be five years. The projected gross margin is 40%. Sales of the new product line commenced on September 1, 20X5, and totalled $6,500,000 for the four months ended December 31, 20X5, and generated a gross margin of $2,600,000. This product line is often included in a "bundle of equipment" sold to customers and a portion of the selling price of the "bundle" is allocated internally to this product line.

PSI's accounting policy is to recognize the amount payable to the seller annually on August 31 as a charge to the cost of generating revenues. No amount was accrued at December 31, 20X5.

SALE OF SUBSIDIARY

On November 1, 20X5, PSI sold a wholly owned subsidiary, Ersatz Technologies Inc. (ETI), and realized a gain of $1,600,000 on the sale. The gain was included in selling, general, and administrative expense (SG&A) in PSI's SCI and was not separately disclosed. PSI's annual report for fiscal 20X5 included a statement that the corporation had "achieved its goal of improvements in efficiency and cost control by reducing SG&A to 18% of sales revenue from its previous level of 20%."

INVESTMENT IN H&P

In February 20X5, PSI invested $2,500,000 in Hope & Pratt Ltd. (H&P), a publicly traded dot-com enterprise. This represented a 10% stake in the 25,000,000 shares issued. By May 20X5, H&P's shares were trading at a market price of $60 per share. On December 31, 20X5, H&P's shares were trading at $20 per share and had dropped to $5 per share by February 1, 20X6, as a result of financial warnings issued by H&P. H&P's shares are currently trading at $4 per share. H&P reported a loss of $9,800,000 for the year ended December 31, 20X5.

ACQUISITION OF ATI

Effective September 1, 20X5, PSI acquired 100% ownership of AvanTemps Inc. (ATI) at a cost of $6,000,000. PSI determined its offering price as follows:

- fair value of ATI's net tangible assets, $2,044,000;
- $1,500,000 payment to Ethan Brodsky (who owned 51% of the shares of ATI, is the founder of ATI, and is responsible for the development of ATI's advanced technologies) for entering into a three-year employment contract with PSI;
- $456,000 for unused non-capital losses totalling $1,200,000 at a tax rate of 38%; and
- $2,000,000 to reflect the value of ATI's business.

Brodsky was also granted stock options for shares of PSI.
Based on ATI's profitability in the first quarter of fiscal 20X6 and on projected profitability in the future, the treasurer advised you that the benefit of the unused tax losses will be recognized as a reduction in income tax expense in fiscal 20X6.

Exhibit C **Extracts from Working Papers Prepared by Predecessor Auditor**

1. Materiality was set at $1,000,000 based on projected revenue for fiscal 20X5.
2. Inherent risk was noted as "greater than in previous years for fiscal 20X5 because of the new CEO's objective of reporting earnings growth and because of the risk of manipulation of earnings to maximize his bonus."

3. The working papers pertaining to the new sales leasing program include the following information:
   - PSI's accounting policy is to recognize the profit on these sales at the date of sale to the financial institution that acts as a lessor to PSI's customers and to recognize the cost of the payment guarantees as paid to the financial institution. PSI accrued a $424,000 liability on December 31, 20X5, and included this amount in accounts payable based on notification by the financial institution of customer payments in arrears. PSI remitted this amount, which includes interest of $24,000, to the financial institution on January 31, 20X6. The CA concluded that PSI's accounting policy is acceptable because title to the equipment is transferred to the financial institution and the cost of the payment guarantee is reflected in PSI's financial statements.
   - PSI's accounting policy is to defer and amortize the financing arrangement fee over the three-year term of the leases. Amortization of $200,000 of the $1,200,000 in fees incurred in fiscal 20X5 is included in the "interest and financing charges" SCI account and the unamortized balance of $1,000,000 is included in the "deferred charges" SFP account.
4. A working paper noted that the determination of the gain on the sale of ETI had been verified and that PSI had received the full amount of the proceeds from the sale.
5. A working paper noted that the treasurer had informed the auditor that "it is too early to determine whether or not the loss in value of the H&P investment is other than a temporary decline." He is hopeful for a turnaround by H&P.
6. A working paper pertaining to the acquisition of ATI includes the following information:

   An intangible asset in the amount of $1,500,000 has been recognized for the employment contract and is considered to have an indefinite life until such time as Brodsky announces his intention to leave PSI.

[ICAO]

CASE 4-3 BRAND DRUG LIMITED

In the course of the audit of Brand Drug Limited (BDL), the CA, while reviewing the draft financial statements for the year ended August 31, 20X6, noticed that BDL's investment in National Pharmaceuticals Limited (NPL) was valued on the cost basis. In 20X5, it had been valued on the equity basis. Representing a 22% interest in NPL, this investment had been made 10 years ago to infuse fresh equity into NPL, with a view to protecting BDL's source of supply for drugs.

BDL's controller informed CA that NPL had suffered a large loss in 20X6, as shown by the May interim financial statements. BDL's representative on NPL's board of directors had resigned because BDL's purchases from NPL now constituted less than 5% of its total purchases. In addition, NPL had been uncooperative in providing profit data in time to make the year-end equity adjustment. Consequently, BDL's controller had revised the method of accounting for the investment in NPL.

CA then found out that BDL's managers are planning a share issue in 20X7 and do not want their earnings impaired by NPL's poor performance. However, they are reluctant to divest themselves of NPL in case the rumoured development by NPL of a new drug to reduce the impact of colitis materializes.

When CA approached NPL's managers, they refused to disclose any information on NPL's operations. CA then learned from a stockbroker friend that NPL's poor results were due to its market being undercut by generic drug manufacturers. The loss had been increased when NPL's management wrote off most of NPL's intangible assets. CA summarized the relevant information on the treatment of the investment for his audit file (Exhibit D).

Exhibit D CA's Notes on Investment in NPL's Shares

Extracts from BDL's draft financial statements for the year ended August 31, 20X6, in thousands of dollars:

	20X6 (Draft)		20X5 (Actual)	
INVESTMENT IN NPL (NOTE 3)	$25,000	(1)	$27,400	(2)
Retained Earnings:				
Opening balance	$ 6,500		$ 2,350	
plus: net earnings	4,500		7,300	
	11,000		9,650	
less: prior period adjustment (Note 1)	(2,400)		—	
Dividends	(2,250)		(3,150)	
Closing balance	$ 6,350		$ 6,500	

Note 1: Represents original cost. The 20X5 balance has been reduced by the amount of previously recorded equity interest of $2.4 million. In the nine months ended May 31, 20X6, NPL reported a net loss of $140 million after writing off development and patent costs as extraordinary items.

Note 2: Valued on equity basis. Equity adjustment for 20X5 involved the elimination of $5.5 million unrealized profit included in ending inventory, on sales from NPL to BDL. The unrealized profit in BDL's ending inventory for 20X6 amounts to $1.5 million.

Note 3: Stock market trading in NPL's common shares has been heavy in 20X6. Prices for the year are as follows:

August 31, 20X5:	$22.00
February 28, 20X6:	$ 4.00
August 31, 20X6:	$12.00

BDL owns 2,000,000 common shares of NPL; in neither 20X5 nor 20X6 did NPL declare or pay any dividends.

Required

Discuss the matters raised above.

[CICA]

Problems

P4-1

Companion Website

OfficePlus Corporation is a retailer of office supplies and equipment in Vancouver. On March 5, 20X6, OfficePlus formed a new corporation in Calgary to operate the same type of business. OfficePlus invested $200,000 cash in exchange for 10,000 common shares in the new subsidiary, to be known as Plus Limited.

During 20X6, Plus Limited commenced operations. Most of Plus's initial inventory came from OfficePlus. In total, goods that had cost OfficePlus $200,000 were sold to Plus at an assigned value of $250,000. These goods were re-priced by Plus to sell for $500,000 at retail. At year-end, 30% of the merchandise acquired from OfficePlus was still in Plus's inventory.

OfficePlus also extended a loan to Plus to finance the start-up costs. A total of $150,000 was lent during the year, of which $80,000 was still owing at year-end. Interest of $10,000 on the loan had been accrued by both companies, of which only $8,000 had actually been paid during 20X6.

Condensed statements of financial position and statements of comprehensive income of the two companies are presented below, as of December 31, 20X6.

Required

Prepare a consolidated SFP and SCI for OfficePlus Corporation at December 31, 20X6.

Statements of Financial Position
December 31, 20X6

	OfficePlus	Plus
Cash	$ 85,000	$ 10,000
Accounts and other receivables	275,000	130,000
Inventories	440,000	60,000
Capital assets	500,000	400,000
Accumulated amortization	(200,000)	(30,000)
Investment in Plus (at cost)	200,000	—
	$1,300,000	$570,000
Accounts and other payables	$ 300,000	$150,000
Long-term liabilities	270,000	200,000
Common shares	50,000	200,000
Retained earnings	680,000	20,000
	$1,300,000	$570,000

Statements of Comprehensive Income
Year Ended December 31, 20X6

	OfficePlus	Plus
Sales	$2,000,000	$600,000
Other income	70,000	—
	2,070,000	600,000
Expenses	1,700,000	540,000
Net income	$ 370,000	$ 60,000

Statements of Changes in Equity—Retained Earnings Section
Year Ended December 31, 20X6

	OfficePlus	Plus
Retained earnings, December 31, 20X5	$ 510,000	—
Net income	370,000	$ 60,000
Dividends	(200,000)	(40,000)
Retained earnings, December 31, 20X6	$ 680,000	$ 20,000

P4-2

At the end of 20X7, the condensed statements of financial position and statements of comprehensive income of OfficePlus Corporation and Plus Limited were as they appear below. Intercompany activities were as follows:

1. Plus sold all of its opening (i.e., December 31, 20X6) inventory including that acquired from OfficePlus (see P4-1).
2. Plus purchased merchandise from OfficePlus for $400,000. This price included a 25% markup over the cost to OfficePlus. At year-end, 40% of these goods were still in Plus's inventory.
3. Plus sold to OfficePlus some merchandise for $120,000. Plus had acquired the merchandise for $100,000. The merchandise was all in OfficePlus's inventory at year-end, but is expected to sell for $150,000 in 20X8.

4. Plus fully repaid OfficePlus the $80,000 loan that had been outstanding at the beginning of the year, plus $7,000 in interest ($2,000 of the interest pertained to 20X6).
5. OfficePlus purchased a plot of land in Calgary for $100,000 and resold it to Plus for $140,000.

Required

Prepare a consolidated statement of income and retained earnings and a consolidated SFP for OfficePlus Corporation for 20X7.

Statements of Financial Position
December 31, 20X7

	OfficePlus	Plus
Cash	$ 50,000	$ 10,000
Accounts and other receivables	230,000	60,000
Inventories	470,000	195,000
Capital assets	560,000	520,000
Accumulated depreciation	(230,000)	(60,000)
Investment in Plus	200,000	—
Other investments	140,000	—
	$1,420,000	$725,000
Accounts and other payables	$ 360,000	$250,000
Long-term liabilities	250,000	230,000
Common shares	50,000	200,000
Retained earnings	760,000	45,000
	$1,420,000	$725,000

Statements of Comprehensive Income
Year Ended December 31, 20X7

	OfficePlus	Plus
Sales	$2,300,000	$720,000
Other income	100,000	—
	2,400,000	720,000
Expenses	2,100,000	650,000
Net income	$ 300,000	$ 70,000

Statements of Changes in Equity—Retained Earnings Section
Year Ended December 31, 20X7

	OfficePlus	Plus
Retained earnings, December 31, 20X6	$ 680,000	$ 20,000
Net income	300,000	70,000
Dividends	(220,000)	(45,000)
Retained earnings, December 31, 20X7	$ 760,000	$ 45,000

P4-3

On January 1, 20X6, Big Inc. acquired 100% of the outstanding shares of Small Corp. for $10,000,000 cash. On this date, Small had shareholders' equity of $8,000,000, including $4,000,000 in retained earnings. Small had buildings and equipment that had a fair value of $1,200,000 less than carrying value, inventory that had a fair value of $300,000 greater than carrying value, and investments that had a fair value of $1,300,000 greater than carrying value.

The statements of financial position of the two companies on December 31, 20X6, are shown below.

Additional Information

1. The goodwill on Small's books arose from the purchase of another company several years ago, a company that has since been amalgamated into Small. The goodwill was assumed to have a fair value of zero on January 1, 20X6.
2. Small's plant and equipment has an estimated average remaining life of 10 years from January 1, 20X6. The net carrying value of the plant and equipment was $10,000,000 on that date, after deducting $4,000,000 of accumulated depreciation.
3. On January 1, 20X6, Big held inventory of $800,000 that had been purchased from Small. Small had sold the merchandise to Big at a 100% markup over cost.
4. On December 31, 20X6, Big held inventory of $1,000,000 that had been purchased from Small during 20X6 at 100% above Small's cost.
5. At the end of 20X6, Big owed Small $400,000 for merchandise purchased on account.
6. During 20X6, Small sold an investment for $800,000. The investment had cost Small $360,000, and had a fair value of $600,000 on January 1, 20X6.
7. Big's retained earnings on December 31, 20X6, include dividend income received from Small. Small declared dividends of $400,000 in 20X6.

Required

Prepare a consolidated statement of financial position for Big Inc. at December 31, 20X6.

Statements of Financial Position
December 31, 20X6

	Big	Small
Cash	$ 2,000,000	$ 600,000
Accounts receivable	3,200,000	800,000
Inventories	4,800,000	1,400,000
Plant and equipment	42,000,000	14,000,000
Accumulated depreciation	(12,000,000)	(5,000,000)
Goodwill	—	800,000
Long-term investments (cost)	10,000,000	3,200,000
Total assets	$50,000,000	$15,800,000
Accounts payable	$ 6,000,000	$ 1,000,000
Bonds payable	10,000,000	6,000,000
Common shares	14,000,000	4,000,000
Retained earnings	20,000,000	4,800,000
	$50,000,000	$15,800,000

P4-4

Companion Website

On January 1, 20X6, Parent Ltd. purchased 100% of the outstanding voting common shares of Sub Ltd. for $2,800,000. Any revaluation arising from the purchase of depreciable assets is to be amortized over 10 years.

During 20X6, the following events occurred:

1. No dividends were paid on the shares by either company.
2. Sub Ltd. sold inventory costing $494,000 to Parent Ltd. for $682,000, 30% of which was not sold at year-end.

3. During 20X6, all of the current assets that had a fair market value greater than carrying value were sold to outside parties or were collected.
4. Parent Ltd. has made no entries in the investment in Sub Ltd. account following the acquisition.
   Condensed trial balance information for Sub Ltd. and Parent Ltd. is shown below.

Required

Prepare a consolidated statement of comprehensive income and retained earnings and a consolidated statement of financial position for Parent Ltd. for the year ended December 31, 20X6.

[CGA–Canada, adapted]

		Sub Limited	
	Post-closing trial balance January 1, 20X6	Fair market value January 1, 20X6	Pre-closing trial balance December 31, 20X6
Cash	$ 185,000	$ 185,000	$ 135,000
Accounts receivable, net	432,000	450,000	385,000
Inventory	690,000	730,000	730,000
Land	510,000	570,000	510,000
Buildings and equipment, net	974,000	850,000	963,000
Goodwill	110,000	—	110,000
	$2,901,000		$2,833,000
Current liabilities	$ 320,000	$ 320,000	$ 310,000
Bonds payable, 10%	215,000	215,000	215,000
Common shares	400,000	—	400,000
Retained earnings	1,966,000	—	1,966,000
Sales	—	—	1,430,000
Cost of goods sold	—	—	(867,000)
Depreciation	—	—	(11,000)
Other expenses	—	—	(588,500)
Bond interest expense	—	—	(21,500)
	$2,901,000		$2,833,000

Parent Ltd.
Pre-closing trial balance
December 31, 20X6

Cash	$ 275,000
Accounts receivable, net	384,000
Marketable securities	129,000
Inventory	860,000
Land	730,000
Buildings and equipment, net	862,000
Goodwill*	140,000
Investment in Sub Ltd.	2,800,000
	$6,180,000

*Not related to Sub Ltd.

Current liabilities	$ 395,000
Bonds payable	685,000
Common shares	1,100,000
Retained earnings	3,757,000
Sales	1,930,000
Cost of goods sold	(1,463,000)
Depreciation	(27,000)
Other expenses	(203,450)
Bond interest income	6,450
	$6,180,000

P4-5

Persaud Ltd. acquired 100% of the voting shares of Singh Ltd. on January 1, 20X6, for $1,255,000. The financial statement of Singh Ltd. on the date of acquisition was as follows:

Singh Ltd.
Statement of Financial Position
January 1, 20X6

	Carrying value	Fair market value
Cash	$ 40,000	$ 40,000
Accounts receivable	110,000	130,000
Inventory	280,000	320,000
Land	310,000	400,000
Depreciable capital assets, net	460,000	495,000
Total	$1,200,000	
Current liabilities	$ 250,000	250,000
Common shares	400,000	—
Retained earnings	550,000	—
Total	$1,200,000	

The inventory will be sold and the accounts receivable collected within seven months, and the depreciable capital assets will be depreciated over 10 years, straight-line, with no salvage value.

During 20X6, Singh Ltd. sold inventory to Persaud Ltd. for $150,000 with a 20% markup on retail. At the end of 20X6, $30,000 (at retail) of these goods were still in the inventory. Persaud Ltd. sold $200,000 of goods to Singh Ltd. during 20X6, with a 25% markup on retail, and $40,000 (at retail) of these were still in inventory at the end of 20X6. All of these goods remaining in inventory were sold during 20X7.

During 20X7, Persaud Ltd. sold $180,000 of goods to Singh Ltd. with a 25% markup on retail, and $50,000 (at retail) of these goods were in inventory at the end of 20X7. In addition, Singh Ltd. sold goods to Persaud Ltd. for $220,000 with a 20% markup on retail, and $60,000 (at retail) of these were still in inventory at the end of 20X7. All of these remaining goods were sold during 20X8.

The following are the financial statements of the two companies at December 31, 20X7:

Statements of Financial Position
December 31, 20X7

	Persaud Ltd.	Singh Ltd.
Cash	$ 55,000	$ 40,000
Accounts receivable	140,000	110,000
Inventory	400,000	320,000
Land	670,000	385,000
Depreciable capital assets, net	864,000	520,000
Investment in Singh Ltd.	1,255,000	—
Total	$3,384,000	$1,375,000
Current liabilities	$ 248,000	$ 180,000
Common shares	1,136,000	400,000
Retained earnings	2,000,000	795,000
Total	$3,384,000	$1,375,000

Statements of Comprehensive Income
Year Ended December 31, 20X7

	Persaud Ltd.	Singh Ltd.
Sales	$ 900,000	$ 845,000
Cost of goods sold	542,000	479,000
Depreciation	120,000	110,000
Other expenses	128,000	126,000
	790,000	715,000
Net income	$ 110,000	$ 130,000

Neither company paid dividends during 20X6 or 20X7.

Required

Calculate the following, considering all dates carefully:

1. Investment income, under the equity method, for 20X6.
2. Consolidated net income for 20X7.
3. Consolidated balance of accounts receivable at December 31, 20X7.
4. Consolidated balance of depreciable capital assets at December 31, 20X7.
5. Consolidated balance of inventory at December 31, 20X7.

[CGA–Canada, adapted]

P4-6 PRADEESH AND SERENA 20X7

Companion Website

On January 4, 20X7, Pradeesh Corp. acquired 100% of the outstanding common shares of Serena Inc. by a share-for-share exchange of its own shares valued at $1,000,000 (**P3–8**). The statements of financial position of both companies just prior to the share exchange are shown below. Serena had patents, not shown on the SFP, that had an estimated fair value of $200,000 and an estimated remaining productive life of four years. Serena's buildings and equipment had an estimated fair value $300,000 in excess of carrying value, and the deferred charges were assumed to have a fair value of zero. Serena's buildings and equipment are being depreciated on the straight-line basis and have a remaining useful life of 10 years. The deferred charges are being amortized over three years.

Statements of Financial Position
December 31, 20X6

	Pradeesh	Serena
Cash	$ 110,000	$ 85,000
Accounts and other receivables	140,000	80,000
Inventories	110,000	55,000
Buildings and equipment	1,500,000	800,000
Accumulated depreciation	(700,000)	(400,000)
Deferred charges	—	120,000
	$1,160,000	$740,000
Accounts and other payables	$ 200,000	$100,000
Bonds payable	—	200,000
Deferred income taxes	60,000	40,000
Common shares*	600,000	150,000
Retained earnings	300,000	250,000
	$1,160,000	$740,000

*Pradeesh = 300,000 shares; Serena = 150,000 shares.

During 20X7, the year following the acquisition, Serena borrowed $100,000 from Pradeesh; $40,000 was repaid and $60,000 is still outstanding at year-end. No interest is being charged on the loan. Through the year, Serena sold goods to Pradeesh totalling $400,000. Serena's gross margin is 40% of selling price, and its tax rate is 25%. Three-quarters of these goods were resold by Pradeesh to its customers for $450,000. Dividend declarations amounted to $80,000 by Pradeesh and $50,000 by Serena. There were no other intercompany transactions. The year-end 20X7 SFPs and SCIs for Pradeesh and Serena are shown below.

Required

1. How would the SCI and SFP for Pradeesh Corp. differ from those shown below if Pradeesh reported its investment in Serena on the equity basis? Show all calculations.
2. Prepare a complete set of consolidated financial statements for Pradeesh Corp. for 20X7.

Statements of Financial Position
December 31, 20X7

	Pradeesh	Serena
Cash	$ 50,000	$ 25,000
Accounts and other receivables	240,000	90,000
Inventories	150,000	80,000
Buildings and equipment	1,300,000	900,000
Accumulated depreciation	(570,000)	(445,000)
Land	—	60,000
Investment in Serena (at cost)	1,000,000	—
Other investments	70,000	30,000
Deferred charges	—	80,000
	$2,240,000	$820,000

Accounts and other payables	$ 150,000	$180,000
Bonds payable	—	170,000
Deferred income taxes	70,000	45,000
Common shares	1,600,000	150,000
Retained earnings	420,000	275,000
	$2,240,000	$820,000

Statements of Comprehensive Income
Year Ended December 31, 20X7

	Pradeesh	Serena
Sales	$1,500,000	$900,000
Dividend income	50,000	—
	1,550,000	900,000
Cost of sales	1,000,000	540,000
Depreciation expense	70,000	45,000
Amortization expense	—	40,000
Income tax expense	50,000	25,000
Other expenses	230,000	175,000
	1,350,000	825,000
Net income	$ 200,000	$ 75,000

Statements of Changes in Equity—Retained Earnings Section
Year Ended December 31, 20X7

	Pradeesh	Serena
Retained earnings, December 31, 20X6	$ 300,000	$250,000
Net income	200,000	75,000
Dividends declared	(80,000)	(50,000)
Retained earnings, December 31, 20X7	$ 420,000	$275,000

P4-7

Refer to **P4-6**. During 20X8, the following events occurred:

1. Serena Inc. had sales of $800,000 to Pradeesh Corp. Serena's gross margin was still 40% of selling price, and its income tax rate continued to be 25%. At year-end, $120,000 of these goods were still in Pradeesh's inventory.
2. On October 1, 20X8, Serena sold its land to Pradeesh for $185,000 (on which income taxes were due for $20,000). Pradeesh paid Serena $85,000 and gave a promissory note for $100,000 that was due in three years at 10% interest per year, simple interest to be paid at maturity.
3. $60,000 that Serena owed to Pradeesh at the beginning of the year was repaid during 20X8.
4. Pradeesh paid dividends of $100,000 during the year; Serena paid dividends of $70,000.

The pre-closing trial balances of Pradeesh and Serena at December 31, 20X8, are shown below.

Required

1. Determine Pradeesh Corp.'s equity in the earnings of Serena Inc. for 20X8. Determine the balance of the Investment in Serena account on Pradeesh's books at December 31, 20X8, assuming that Pradeesh recorded its investment on the equity basis.

2. Prepare a comparative consolidated SFP and SCI for Pradeesh Corp. for 20X8.

Trial Balances
December 31, 20X8

	Pradeesh	Serena
Cash	$ 55,500	$ 45,000
Accounts and other receivables	160,000	116,000
Inventories	140,000	75,000
Buildings and equipment	1,700,000	900,000
Accumulated depreciation	(655,000)	(495,000)
Land	185,000	—
Investment in Serena	1,000,000	—
Due from Pradeesh	—	102,500
Other investments	100,000	50,000
Deferred charges	—	40,000
Accounts and other payables	(225,000)	(215,000)
Payable to Serena	(102,500)	—
Deferred income taxes	(75,000)	(47,500)
Common shares	(1,800,000)	(150,000)
Retained earnings	(420,000)	(275,000)
Dividends paid	100,000	70,000
Sales	(1,680,000)	(1,200,000)
Cost of sales	1,120,000	720,000
Depreciation expense	85,000	50,000
Amortization expense	—	40,000
Income tax expense	31,000	57,000
Other expenses	351,000	244,500
Gain on sale of land	—	(125,000)
Other income	(70,000)	(2,500)
	$ 0	$ 0

P4-8

On January 1, 20X5, Piper Ltd. purchased 100% of the shares of Sutton Ltd. for $1,085,000. At that time Sutton Ltd. had the following SFP:

Sutton Ltd.
Statement of Financial Position
January 1, 20X5

	Net carrying value	Fair value
Cash	$ 60,000	$ 60,000
Accounts receivable	120,000	150,000
Inventory—FIFO	180,000	230,000
Capital assets, net	1,500,000	1,350,000
Goodwill	100,000	—
	$1,960,000	
Current liabilities	$ 140,000	140,000
Bonds payable	800,000	850,000
Common shares	400,000	—
Retained earnings	620,000	—
	$1,960,000	

The bonds were issued at par and will mature in 10 years. Sutton Ltd. has a receivables and inventory turnover of greater than six times per year. The capital assets have an average of 10 years of remaining life and are being amortized straight-line.

In 20X5, Sutton Ltd. sold inventory to Piper Ltd. for $260,000; the inventory had cost $320,000. At the end of 20X5, 25% was still in Piper's inventory but was all sold in 20X6.

In 20X6, Piper Ltd. sold inventory to Sutton Ltd. for $275,000; the inventory had cost $200,000. At the end of 20X6, 35% was left in Sutton's inventory.

During 20X5, the subsidiary earned $875,000 and paid dividends of $50,000. During 20X6, the subsidiary incurred a loss of $180,000 and paid dividends of $60,000.

Piper uses the cost method for the investment in subsidiary and nets almost everything to "Other expenses."

At December 31, 20X6, the following financial statements were available:

Statement of Financial Position
December 31, 20X6

	Piper Ltd.	Sutton Ltd.
Cash	$ 290,000	$ 75,000
Accounts receivable	850,000	179,000
Inventory	970,000	245,000
Capital assets, net	2,631,000	1,863,000
Goodwill	—	100,000
Investment in Sutton Ltd.	1,085,000	—
	$5,826,000	$2,462,000
Current liabilities	$ 450,000	$ 49,000
Bonds payable	—	800,000
Common shares	1,000,000	400,000
Retained earnings	3,026,000	1,385,000
Net income (loss)	1,350,000	(172,000)
	$5,826,000	$2,462,000

Statement of Comprehensive Income
Year Ended December 31, 20X6

	Piper Ltd.	Sutton Ltd.
Sales	$9,865,000	$1,650,000
Cost of sales	8,040,000	1,140,000
Gross profit	1,825,000	510,000
Depreciation	(106,000)	(96,000)
Other expenses	(369,000)	(816,000)
Gain on sale of building	—	230,000
Net income	$1,350,000	$ (172,000)

Required

1. Prepare a consolidated statement of comprehensive income for 20X6.
2. Calculate the amounts that would appear on the consolidated SFP at December 31, 20X6, for:
   a) Capital assets, net
   b) Bonds payable

[CGA–Canada, adapted]

APPENDIX 4A

Income Tax Allocation Subsequent to Acquisition

INTRODUCTION AND REVIEW

Appendix 3A discussed the issue of income tax allocation in a business combination and illustrated the calculation of deferred tax (DT) at acquisition. The essence of tax allocation for business combinations is that the buyer, *on its consolidated SFP*, must calculate DT as part of the purchase equation. The DT for each asset and liability is based on its temporary difference. The temporary difference is the difference between (1) the tax basis of the asset to the *subsidiary*; and (2) the fair value of the asset as it is included on the *parent's* consolidated statement.

For the purchase transaction in Chapter 3, which also pertains to this chapter, the amounts are as follows:

	Target Ltd.'s carrying value (1)	Tax basis for Target (2)	Fair value to Purchase (3)	Temporary difference (3) – (2)
Land	$300,000	$300,000	$400,000	$100,000
Buildings and equipment	350,000	250,000	550,000	300,000
Total	$650,000	$550,000	$950,000	$400,000

Target Ltd.'s carrying values are included as column (1), but they really are irrelevant for determining the amount of DT. They are irrelevant because we need to compare the fair values with the assets' *tax bases*, not with their carrying values on the subsidiary's books. We have put them in the table to emphasize that the tax bases of Target Ltd.'s assets may be different from their carrying values. For tax allocation, the relevant figures are those in columns (2) and (3).

The temporary differences are shown in the last column. The tax basis for each asset is subtracted from its fair value. If we assume that Purchase Ltd.'s income tax rate is 40%, we must include $400,000 × 40% = $160,000 as a DT liability when we allocate the purchase price. As we explained in Appendix 3A, the effect of including the DT liability is to increase the amount of the purchase price that is allocated to goodwill.

POST-ACQUISITION TAX ACCOUNTING FOR FAIR-VALUE INCREMENTS

The balance in the DT account is a function of the temporary differences at each SFP date. In a business combination, the temporary difference is the difference between the tax basis of an asset to the tax-paying entity (that is, to the *subsidiary* that legally owns the asset and that deducts the CCA) and its value as reported *on the parent company's consolidated SFP*.

In a business combination, we must focus on the fair-value increments relating to amortizable capital assets, both tangible and intangible. Residual goodwill in a purchase of shares is not a capital asset, and it is not deductible for tax purposes.

For amortizable capital assets, in years subsequent to the acquisition, (1) the fair-value increments are amortized and flow into expense, thereby reducing their carrying value, and (2) the assets' tax bases change as the assets are recognized in taxable income (e.g., through CCA). Therefore, the temporary differences change. The change in temporary differences arising from fair-value increment (FVI) amortization must be recognized on the consolidated SFP.

In this chapter, we amortized the fair-value increment relating to buildings and equipment. The amortization for each of 20X6 and 20X7 was $20,000. Therefore, the fair-value increment declined from $200,000 at the date of acquisition to $180,000 at the end of 20X6 and $160,000 at the end of 20X7.

The change in the FVI is only half of the situation. The other half is the tax basis. The tax basis changes because Target Ltd. continues taking CCA on its buildings and equipment. The overall temporary difference depends on both the FVI amortization and the change in the tax basis. Fortunately, however, we really don't need to know the tax basis of all of the subsidiary's assets to adjust for the change in temporary differences during each year.

Remember that the starting point for consolidation is the companies' separate-entity financial statements (or trial balances). The subsidiary will be using tax allocation procedures on its own books. Therefore, the subsidiary will already have recorded the DT that relates to temporary differences between its assets' tax bases and their carrying values. All we have to do for consolidation is to supplement that already-reported DT amount by recognizing the additional change to the temporary difference that relates to the FVI:

Tax basis of Target assets	} *Recorded* on Target's books
Carrying value on Target's books	} Added as a consolidation *adjustment*
Consolidation value = carrying value + FVI	

In essence, therefore, we only have to make a DT adjustment for the change in the temporary difference that is caused by the FVI amortization. In each of 20X6 and 20X7, the amortization is $20,000. At an assumed income tax rate of 40%, each year's worksheet adjustment for the additional change in consolidated DT will be:

Deferred tax liability—long-term	8,000	
Income tax expense ($20,000 × 40%)		8,000

The adjustment always will be to *reduce* the DT liability because FVIs will never increase—they will only decrease. This does not mean that the *overall* temporary difference may not increase. Instead, it means that an increase that might have been recorded on Target Ltd.'s books will be reduced by the additional adjustment in consolidation.

For example, suppose that in 20X6, Target Ltd. recorded depreciation of $35,000 on its buildings and equipment and took CCA of $65,000. The carrying value of buildings and equipment *on Target Ltd.'s books* will be $350,000 − $35,000 = $315,000. The tax basis will be $250,000 − $65,000 = $185,000. The changes can be summarized as follows:

	20X5	20X6
Tax basis	$250,000	$185,000
Target's carrying value	350,000	315,000
Temporary difference	$100,000	$130,000

From 20X5 to 20X6, Target Ltd.'s temporary difference for the buildings and equipment increased by $30,000. Target Ltd. will have *recorded* the appropriate increase in the DT liability of $12,000 (that is, $30,000 × 40% = $12,000) resulting from the increase in the temporary difference.

Looking now at Purchase Ltd.'s consolidated amounts (i.e., including FVI), the consolidated temporary difference is as follows:

	20X5	20X6
Tax basis	$250,000	$185,000
Purchase's consolidated value	550,000	495,000
Temporary difference	$300,000	$310,000

The consolidated value of the buildings and equipment acquired in the business combination was initially a Target Ltd. carrying value of $350,000 plus FVI of $200,000, for a total fair value of $550,000. One year later, the Target Ltd. carrying value has been depreciated to $315,000 and the FVI has been amortized to $180,000—the sum of these two amounts equals the $495,000 shown above.

Overall, the temporary difference relating to the fair values shown on Purchase Ltd.'s consolidated SFP is increased by $10,000. The related increase in the consolidated DT liability is $10,000 × 40% = $4,000. The change in consolidated DT liability relating to Target Ltd.'s buildings and equipment can be summarized as follows:

	Temporary Difference	Deferred Tax Liability
Increase recorded on Target Ltd.'s books	$30,000	$12,000 Cr
Decrease from FVI amortization upon consolidation	20,000	8,000 Dr
Net change in consolidated amounts	$10,000	$ 4,000 Cr

Therefore, when we make the consolidation adjustments relating to DT, we need concern ourselves only with the changes in the fair-value increments. We can safely assume that the subsidiary has already recorded the DT arising from the timing differences between the tax basis and the carrying value of its assets and liabilities.

UNREALIZED PROFIT

The only other income tax aspect that we need to worry about is that relating to unrealized profit. At the end of 20X6, there is unrealized upstream profit of $8,000 in inventory. This profit is unrealized only from the viewpoint of the consolidated entity. So far as the Canada Revenue Agency is concerned, Target Ltd. has earned this profit and will be taxed on it in 20X6. The tax, at 40%, will amount to $3,200.

On consolidation, the unrealized profit is eliminated. Since the profit is removed from net income, tax allocation requires that the related taxes also be removed from net income. The adjustment to achieve this is quite straightforward:

Deferred tax	3,200	
Income tax expense ($8,000 × 40%)		3,200

All unrealized profit eliminations must be accompanied by an adjustment for income tax, deferring recognition of the income taxes paid by the selling company to the period in which the profit is realized.

In 20X7, the beginning-of-year unrealized profit is recognized in consolidated net income, and therefore the income tax expense also is recognized:

Income tax expense ($8,000 × 40%)	3,200	
Deferred tax		3,200

Of course, the year-end 20X7 unrealized profit must be eliminated, and those eliminations must be accompanied by adjustments to defer recognition of the related income tax expense.

SUMMARY

Income tax allocation affects consolidation in two ways:

1. Amortization of the fair-value increments changes the consolidated reporting values of tangible and intangible capital assets (except land), and therefore the temporary differences are affected.
2. The tax relating to unrealized profits must be removed from consolidated net income and deferred as part of the DT balance(s) on the SFP.

Fortunately, we need not worry about making the full adjustment for the changes in consolidated temporary differences for capital assets. The subsidiary company will have recorded the effects of changes in temporary differences between their carrying values and the tax bases. On consolidation, we need only to adjust for the income tax effect of the FVI amortization.

APPENDIX 4B

Goodwill Impairment Test

ALLOCATION OF GOODWILL TO CASH-GENERATING UNITS

Goodwill does not generate cash flows on its own, but contributes to the cash-generation potential of other assets or groups of assets. Therefore, the *recoverable value* of goodwill cannot be calculated independently of the *recoverable value* of other assets or groups of assets. To facilitate subsequent impairment testing of goodwill, acquisition-related goodwill must be allocated to each of the corporation's *cash-generating units*, or *groups* of cash-generating units, that are expected to profit from the synergies of the business combination. This requirement must be followed even if none of the acquiree's other assets or liabilities are allocated to such unit(s).

The unit or groups of units to which goodwill is allocated should (1) be the lowest level within the corporation at which goodwill is monitored internally, and (2) not be larger than an operating segment as reported in the annual financial statements.[6] The allocation process ensures that testing for impairment of goodwill occurs at a level at which the corporation manages its operations and to which goodwill can naturally be associated.

For impairment testing, goodwill should be allocated to each of a company's cash-generating units from the date of acquisition. However, if the initial allocation of goodwill cannot be completed by the end of the year in which the business combination occurs, the allocation of goodwill to cash-generating units should be completed before the first annual period beginning after the acquisition date (that is, by the end of the subsequent annual period).

APPLYING THE IMPAIRMENT TEST

The impairment test for goodwill is conducted by comparing the carrying value of the related *cash-generating unit(s)*, including the goodwill allocated, with their *recoverable values*. If the *recoverable value* is greater than the carrying value, including goodwill, there is no impairment. Conversely, if the *recoverable value* is less than the carrying value there is an impairment loss. Such an impairment loss is used to reduce the carrying values of the goodwill and the other assets in the *cash-generating unit(s)* in the following order:

- first to reduce the carrying value of the goodwill allocated to the cash-generating unit or group of units; and
- next to reduce the other assets of the unit or group of units on a prorated basis, based on the carrying value of each such asset.

Impairment losses should be recognized immediately in profit or loss unless such losses relate to revalued assets. In the latter case, the impairment losses are treated as a revaluation decrease and are recognized in other comprehensive income to the extent the losses do not exceed the revaluation surplus relating to the same asset. Impairment losses reduce the value of the revaluation surplus for that asset.

A **cash-generating unit** is the corporation's smallest identifiable group of assets that generates cash inflows that are largely independent of the cash inflows of other assets or groups

6. The classification and reporting of segments is discussed in Chapter 7.

of assets. Goodwill often contributes to the cash-generation potential of multiple units as opposed to a single unit. Therefore, in such circumstances it may not be possible to allocate goodwill in a non-arbitrary manner to a single cash-generating unit to which it relates but only to a group of such cash-generating units.

Impairment testing of goodwill is carried out at the level of the group of cash-generating units to which the goodwill has been allocated. However, before doing so, the individual cash-generating unit to which the goodwill relates (but to which goodwill could not be allocated) should first be tested for impairment. The impairment test should be conducted by comparing the carrying value of the unit, disregarding any related goodwill, to its recoverable value. Impairment testing of the goodwill allocated is carried out next in the usual fashion as described in the previous paragraph.

Here, **recoverable value** of a cash-generating unit represents the higher of its (1) fair value less costs to sell, and (2) *value in use*. **Value in use** of the cash-generating unit represents the present value of the estimated future cash flows expected to be generated from the continuing use of the unit, and from its disposal at the end of its useful life. It is not necessary for a corporation to determine both the fair value less costs to sell and the value in use of a cash-generating unit. As long as one of these values exceeds the carrying value of the unit, including the allocated goodwill, there is no impairment.

The most recent detailed calculation from the preceding period of the recoverable value of the cash-generating unit(s) to which goodwill has been allocated can be used in the current period (instead of making a fresh calculation) if *all* of the following three criteria are satisfied:

1. the cash-generating unit's assets and liabilities have not changed significantly since the most recent calculation of the recoverable value; *and*
2. the most recent recoverable value estimate exceeds the carrying amount of the unit by a substantial amount; *and*
3. events and circumstances since the most recent recoverable value estimation indicate that the probability of impairment is remote.

An impairment loss recognized in relation to goodwill cannot be reversed in later periods.

TIMING OF IMPAIRMENT TESTS

Goodwill acquired in relation to a business combination should be tested for impairment annually regardless of whether or not there is any indication of impairment. While the annual impairment test can be conducted at any time in the year, it should be performed at the same time every year.

To test for impairment in goodwill, the cash-generating units(s) to which goodwill has been allocated must be tested for impairment. The impairment testing of the cash-generating unit(s), in addition to being carried out annually, should be done whenever there is an indication that the unit(s) may be impaired.

PRIVATE ENTERPRISES

Accounting standards for private enterprises require a private corporation that is not otherwise publicly accountable to test goodwill for impairment only when events or changes in circumstances indicate that the carrying value of a *reporting unit* to which the goodwill has been assigned exceeds its fair value. Thus, private enterprises are exempt from the burden of conducting an annual test of impairment of goodwill. Further, the testing of impairment at the reporting unit level obviates the need to allocate fair values to individual assets. Examples of events and circumstances indicating that the carrying value exceeds the fair value include:

- a significant change in the legal or business environment of the enterprise;
- an unfavourable assessment or action by a regulator;
- unexpected competition;
- loss of key personnel;
- a more likely than not probability that a significant portion or all of a *reporting unit* will be sold or otherwise disposed of;
- testing for impairment or write-down of a significant asset group within a *reporting unit*; or
- recognition of a goodwill impairment loss by a subsidiary that is a component of the *reporting unit* in its separate-entity financial statements.

The above list is not exhaustive; there may be other factors that indicate impairment in goodwill.

Notice that the requirements for impairment testing of goodwill under accounting standards for private enterprises differ from their counterparts under international standards in:

1. the use of the term *reporting unit* instead of *cash-generating unit*; and
2. the use of *fair value* instead of *recoverable value*.

The reason for these differences can be attributed to the fact that accounting standards for private enterprises are based on Canadian GAAP in existence before the adoption of international standards.

When the carrying value of a reporting unit, including the allocated goodwill, exceeds its fair value, such excess should be recognized as an impairment loss in the period in which such impairment occurs. Impairment losses, once recognized, cannot be reversed when the fair value of the related reporting unit increases in value subsequently.

Relevant Standards

Accounting Standards for Private Enterprises

Section 3064 Goodwill and Intangible Assets

5

Consolidation of Non-Wholly Owned Subsidiaries

LEARNING OBJECTIVES

After studying this chapter, students should be able to:

1. explain why some subsidiaries are not wholly owned;
2. identify the conceptual alternatives for consolidating non-wholly owned subsidiaries;
3. describe the different principles of accounting provided by IFRS for reporting non-wholly owned subsidiaries; and
4. consolidate a non-wholly owned subsidiary:
   a) at the date of acquisition;
   b) one year after acquisition; and
   c) two years after acquisition.

INTRODUCTION

Platmin Limited is a mineral exploration company incorporated in Canada; its shares trade on the TSX. Platmin focuses on the exploration and development of platinum deposits in South Africa. The company states its consolidation policy as follows:

> These consolidated financial statements include the accounts of the Company and its subsidiaries over which control is exercised. Where shareholding is below 50%, but control is exercised, the entity is consolidated.

Platmin consolidates more than 30 controlled subsidiaries in its consolidated financial statements for 2009. Not all of the subsidiaries are 100% owned. Indeed, Platmin controls several companies in which its ownership share is less than a majority:

Name of Consolidated Entity	% Ownership as of February 28, 2009
Born Free Investments 330 Ltd.	35.5
Dream World Investments 226 Ltd.	35.5
Sengani Family Mining and Exploration Ltd. ("Sengani")	35.5
Setseka Mining Ltd. ("Setseka")	37.9
Taung Platinum Exploration Ltd. ("Taung Platinum")	29.0

Clearly, some subsidiaries have other shareholders in addition to the parent. Such subsidiaries are known simply as **non-wholly owned subsidiaries**. As we will see in this chapter, there are often good reasons for owning less than 100%.

The previous two chapters dealt with the preparation of consolidated statements when the parent company owns 100% of the shares of the subsidiary. This chapter focuses on the consolidated statements of a parent that owns less than 100% of its subsidiary.

The numerical example in this chapter exactly parallels the example we used in Chapters 3 and 4, except that now we assume the parent buys *less* than 100% of the subsidiary's shares.

WHY OWN LESS THAN 100%?

A parent's ownership interest may be less than 100% for either of two reasons:

- in a business combination, the acquiring company (the parent) may buy a majority of the shares, but less than 100%; or
- a parent may form a new subsidiary with the involvement of a non-controlling partner who is providing specialized expertise, management ability, market access, governmental support, etc.

Some parent corporations prefer to purchase significantly less than 100% of the shares in a business combination. The parent then need not invest the full value of the subsidiary's net assets. A less-than-100% investment conserves the parent's liquid resources (if the purchase was for cash) or reduces its share dilution (if the purchase was an exchange of shares). In addition, the maintenance of a significant **non-controlling interest** (NCI) in the subsidiary can spread the ownership risk, can provide valuable links with other corporate shareholders, and can maintain a market for the subsidiary's shares.

Non-controlling interests may also exist if the parent initially establishes the subsidiary, but subsequently sells shares in the subsidiary to others. The sale may be of shares originally owned by the parent (i.e., a secondary offering by the parent) or may be of new shares (i.e., a direct or primary offering by the subsidiary). In either case, the parent ends up holding less than 100% of the subsidiary. Subsequent changes in ownership interest are discussed in Appendices 5A and 5B on the Companion Website.

Companion Website

CONCEPTUAL ALTERNATIVES

As is the case with most aspects of accounting, there is no single theoretical approach to accounting for subsidiaries when an NCI exists. Three consecutive questions arise.

1. Should the NCI's share of net assets be included in the consolidated statement of financial position (SFP)?
2. If included, should the net assets be shown at their carrying value on the subsidiary's books (i.e., carrying value) or at their fair value as of the date of acquisition?
3. If the NCI's share of net assets is included at fair value, should such net assets also include the NCI's share of goodwill?

The answers to these three questions flow from two major competing theories of consolidation applicable to non-wholly owned subsidiaries—the *proprietary theory* and the *entity theory*.

The **proprietary theory** views the consolidated group from the viewpoint of the owners of the parent. Therefore, the goal of consolidation is to report only the total interest owned by the shareholders of the parent. The **proportionate consolidation method** is an application of proprietary theory.

In contrast, the **entity theory** views the consolidated group as a single economic entity, and the goal of consolidation is to report all of the interests *controlled* by that entity, regardless of the interest owned by the shareholders of the parent. The **entity method** (also known as *full goodwill method*) of consolidation is an application of entity theory.

Two other methods of consolidation lie between the proprietary and entity methods—the *parent-company method* and the *parent-company extension method*. The **parent-company method** consolidates (1) the parent's share of the *fair values* of the subsidiary's assets and liabilities plus (2) the NCI's share of the *carrying values* of the subsidiary's assets and liabilities. The **parent-company extension method** (also known as the *purchased goodwill method*) includes 100% of the *fair value* of the subsidiary's net identifiable assets and liabilities, but only the parent's share of goodwill. The four alternatives are summarized below—Exhibit 5-1 summarizes them pictorially:

1. **Proportionate consolidation method**: Include only the parent's share of the fair value of the subsidiary's assets and liabilities, and revenues and expenses (i.e., exclude the NCI entirely). The consolidated SCI would include only the parent's share of the subsidiary's revenues and expenses.
2. **Parent-company method**: Include the parent's share of the fair values of the subsidiary's assets and liabilities, plus the carrying value (i.e. book value) of the NCI's share. The consolidated SCI would include 100% of the subsidiary's revenues and expenses.
3. **Parent-company extension** or **purchased goodwill method**: Include 100% of the *fair value* of the subsidiary's net identifiable assets and liabilities, but only the parent's share of goodwill, and 100% of all revenues and expenses. Thus, under this method only the goodwill on the portion paid by the parent in excess of the proportionate net fair value acquired is included. On the SFP, the non-controlling interest is valued at its proportionate share of the fair value of the net identifiable assets of the subsidiary.
4. **Entity** or **full goodwill method**: Include 100% of the *fair value* of the subsidiary's assets and liabilities *and goodwill*, and 100% of all revenues and expenses. This method includes the entire implicit goodwill for the enterprise as a whole, including the NCI's share. On the SFP, the NCI is valued at its proportionate share of the full fair value of the subsidiary.

Required Methods for Reporting Business Combinations

In principle, the IASB believes that the only correct method of measuring NCI is the fourth method above, i.e., the entity or full goodwill method. The board also believes that allowing alternative methods of measurement reduces comparability. Nevertheless, because not

EXHIBIT 5-1

Consolidation Approaches to Reporting NCI

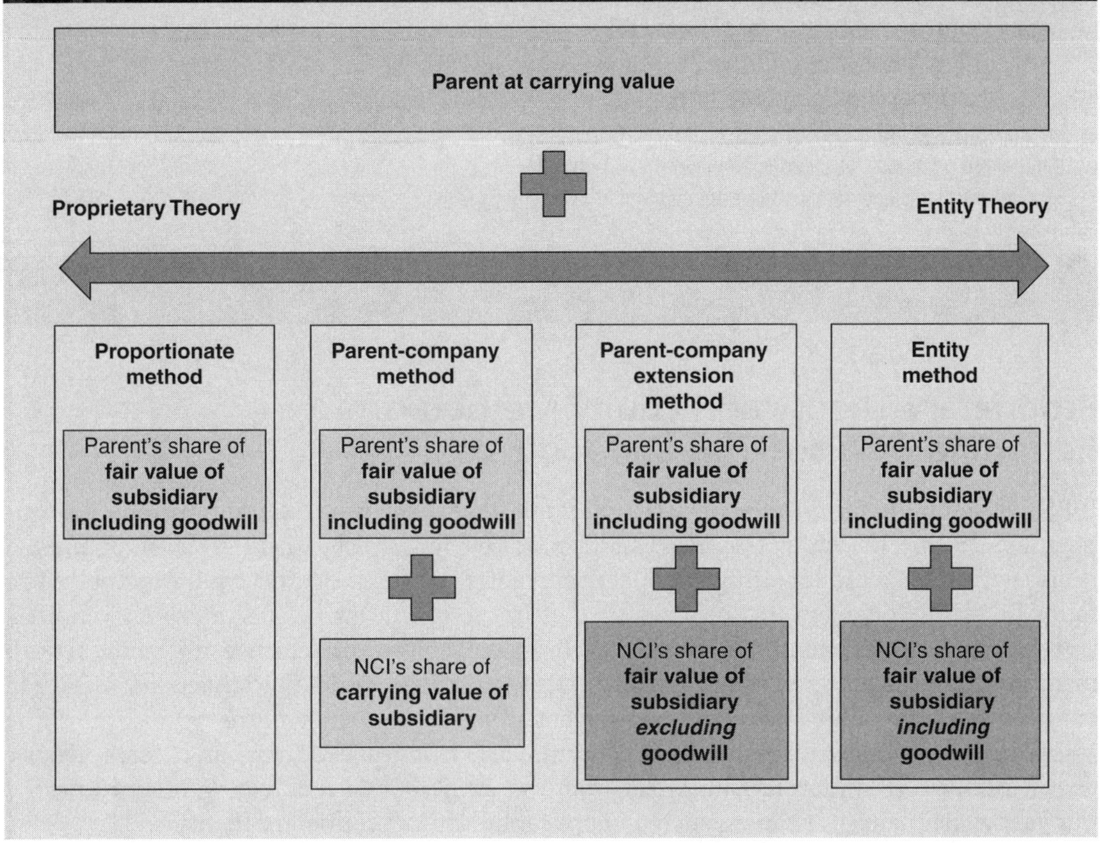

enough members of the IASB supported method 4 above, IFRS 3 *Business Combinations* allows the use of either method 3 or method 4 above on a transaction-by-transaction basis. That is, each business combination can be viewed as a separate transaction that can be accounted for by either method. Consistency is not required.

Until recently a variant of the parent-company method, the **purchase method**, was required in Canada to report business combinations. The purchase method limits the assigned total fair values of the acquired assets and liabilities to the purchase price paid. Pre-2011 business combinations that were initially reported using the purchase method can continue to be reported using that method.

The proportionate consolidation method was required in the past in Canada to report investments in joint ventures. Under IAS 31 *Interests in Joint Ventures,* joint ventures can be reported using either the equity method or the proportionate consolidation method.

We will focus solely on the entity method in our illustrations in the main body of Chapters 5 and 6. We will point out the difference between the entity and the parent-company extension method in a separate section toward the end of each chapter.

REALITY CHECK 5-1

Application of the Proprietary Theory While Reporting Associates and Joint Ventures Under the Equity Method

Transactions eliminated on consolidation

Unrealized gains on transactions between the Group and its associates and joint ventures are eliminated to the extent of the Group's interest in the associates and joint ventures.

Source: Walters Kluwer, *Annual Report* (2009) p. 77.

Proprietary Theory and Equity Method of Reporting of Associates and Joint Ventures

IFRS 3 favours the use of the entity theory while reporting business combinations. In contrast, IAS 28 (*Investments in Associates*) and IAS 31 (*Interests in Joint Ventures*) both require the proprietary theory for reporting associates and joint ventures on the equity method. The rationale for the divergence appears to be that in the case of associates and joint ventures, since control or sole control is lacking, there is less chance of the investor being able to manipulate profits reported by it by suitably arranging intercompany transactions with such entities. Therefore, under IFRS the investing entity includes its share of the net income of the associate adjusted *only* for its share of any unrealized or realized gains and losses. Reality Check 5-1 provides the relevant extract from the 2009 annual report of Walters Kluwer, a publishing company, illustrating such an application of the proprietary theory.

As the extract in Reality Check 5-1 makes clear, when unrealized gains (and losses) exist on transactions between an entity and its associates and joint ventures, such gains and losses are eliminated *only* to the extent of the entity's ownership interest. It does not matter whether the transaction is downstream from the entity to its associates/joint ventures or upstream from the associates/joint ventures to the entity. This is a clear example of the application of the proprietary theory.

However, as you will discover later in the chapter, unrealized gains/losses on downstream sales are not treated the same as unrealized gain/losses on upstream sales when such sales occur between an entity and its non-wholly owned subsidiaries. The entity theory applies in the latter case. We will elaborate on these differences in greater detail further into the chapter.

CONCEPT CHECK 5-1

Companion Website

1. How do the four methods of consolidation (proportionate, parent-company, parent-company extension and entity) apply the two theories of consolidation (proprietary and entity)?
2. Why does IFRS require the use of the entity theory while consolidating *subsidiaries* but require the use of the proprietary theory while reporting an *associate* or *joint venture* under the equity method?

EXHIBIT 5-2

Business Combination—Purchase of 70% of Target

Post-acquisition asset positions, December 31, 20X5
Statements of Financial Position

	Purchase Ltd.	Target Ltd.	Target fair values
Cash	$ 1,000,000	$ 50,000	$ 50,000
Accounts receivable	2,000,000	150,000	150,000
Inventory	200,000	50,000	50,000
Land	1,000,000	300,000	400,000
Buildings and equipment	3,000,000	500,000	550,000
Accumulated depreciation	(1,200,000)	(150,000)	
Investment in Target Ltd.	840,000		
Total assets	$ 6,840,000	$ 900,000	
Current: accounts payable	$ 1,000,000	$ 100,000	(100,000)
Long-term: notes payable	400,000	—	
Common shares	3,440,000	200,000	
Retained earnings	2,000,000	600,000	
Total liabilities and shareholders' equity	$ 6,840,000	$ 900,000	
Net fair value of Target assets and liabilities			$ 1,100,000

CONSOLIDATION AT DATE OF ACQUISITION

To illustrate consolidation of a non-wholly owned subsidiary at the date of acquisition, we will use the same basic facts as we used in the Chapter 3 example.

Assume that Purchase Ltd. buys only 70% of the outstanding shares of Target Ltd. on December 31, 20X5, giving 28,000 Purchase Ltd. shares in exchange. If we assume that the market value of Purchase Ltd.'s shares is $30 per share, then the total cost of the acquisition is $840,000. The post-acquisition SFP of Purchase Ltd. and Target Ltd., and the fair values of Target Ltd.'s assets and liabilities, are shown in Exhibit 5-2.

We will use our MEAR steps for consolidation under the direct method from Chapter 4, now modified for consolidating a non-wholly owned subsidiary. The updated phase 4 steps are presented in Exhibit 5-3.

Since we are now consolidating at the time of acquisition, we need to carry out only those adjustments and eliminations listed under the column titled "Acquisition Related," in Exhibit 5-3. Exhibit 5-4 applies the first step of Measure, which requires us to calculate the purchase price, the 100% fair value, and FVI; first allocating the FVI to the various identifiable assets and liabilities, while allocating the balance to goodwill. To reiterate, under the entity method, the goodwill of $100,000 represents the sum of Purchase Ltd.'s share of $70,000 and NCI's share of $30,000.

EXHIBIT 5-3

MEAR Steps for Consolidating a Non-Wholly Owned Subsidiary

Consolidation Steps	Acquisition Related	Relating to First Year Following Acquisition	Relating to Following Years
1. Measure	• Calculate cost and fair-value increments (FVI) • Allocate FVI • Determine NCI balance		
2. Eliminate and recognize	• Eliminate parent's investment account and sub's share equity accounts		
		• Eliminate intercompany transactions and balances • Eliminate unrealized profits	
			• Recognize realized profits
3. Amortize		• Amortize FVIs • Recognize impairments	
			• Recognize cumulative amortization of FVIs • Recognize cumulative impairments
4. Recognize NCI share of earnings		• Recognize NCI share of earnings • Calculate NCI SFP balance • Calculate RE balance	
5. Check • Independent calculation of RE balances • Independent calculation of NCI balances			

You will notice that in Exhibit 5-4 we calculate 100% of the fair value of Target Ltd. based on the purchase price of $840,000 paid by Purchase Ltd. for its 70% share. This is a very quick and uncomplicated method of calculating the full fair value of the acquisition. However, this calculation won't yield the correct result if the buyer pays less than its proportionate fair value of the target company's net assets, which is known as a *bargain purchase*. We will illustrate the correct method for a bargain purchase in a separate section toward the end of this chapter.

Under the entity method, the NCI is measured at its share of 100% of the fair value of Target Ltd. including the full value of goodwill, i.e., 30% of $1,200,000, or $360,000. Included in the $360,000 is the NCI's share of goodwill, which is 30% of $100,000 or $30,000.

We are now ready to prepare the consolidated SFP at the date of acquisition for our illustration. Exhibit 5-5 shows the Purchase Ltd. consolidated SFP immediately after the business combination, prepared (by the direct approach) under the entity method.

EXHIBIT 5-4

Allocation of Fair-Value Increment

70% Purchase of Target Ltd., December 31, 20X5

Purchase price				$840,000	
100% fair value based on purchase price [$840,000 × (100% / 70%)]					$1,200,000
Less carrying value of Target's net identifiable assets					(800,000)
= Fair-value increment, allocated below					400,000
	Carrying value (a)	Fair value (b)	Fair-value increment (c) = (b) − (a)	FVI allocated	
Cash	$ 50,000	$ 50,000	—		
Accounts receivable	150,000	150,000	—		
Inventory	50,000	50,000	—		
Land	300,000	400,000	$100,000	$100,000	
Buildings and equipment	500,000	550,000	50,000	50,000	
Accumulated depreciation	(150,000)	—	150,000	150,000	
Accounts payable	(100,000)	(100,000)	—		
Total fair-value increment					(300,000)
Net asset carrying value	$800,000				
Fair value of assets acquired		$1,100,000			
Balance of FVI allocated to goodwill @ 100%					$ 100,000

The derivation of Purchase Ltd.'s consolidated SFP at December 31, 20X5, in Exhibit 5-5 is very similar to the derivation in Exhibit 3-10 of Chapter 3. For each item on the SFP, we take the carrying value for Purchase Ltd., add the carrying value of Target Ltd., and add the fair-value increment. The fair-value increment (and goodwill) is indicated with an "**a**." Also, as required under the Eliminate step applicable to consolidation at the time of acquisition, we must also eliminate Purchase Ltd.'s investment account and Target's shareholders' equity accounts (indicated with a "**b**").

In Chapter 3, Target Ltd. was a wholly owned subsidiary of Purchase Ltd. In the present illustration, Purchase Ltd. owns only 70% of Target Ltd. Nevertheless, the consolidated total assets and total liabilities and shareholders' equity are the same in both cases, $7,300,000. Under the entity method we need to include the full fair value of Target Ltd.'s assets and liabilities in the Purchase Ltd. consolidated SFP, rather than just the fair-value increments that relate to Purchase Ltd.'s 70% share. Therefore, to balance the SFP, we need to allocate to NCI its 30% share of the carrying value (i.e., $800,000 × 30% = $240,000) and fair-value increment ($400,000 × 30% = $120,000, including goodwill) of Target Ltd.'s net assets.

The total fair value of Target Ltd.'s identifiable net assets is $1,100,000, as shown in Exhibit 5-2. The total amount of Purchase Ltd.'s identifiable net assets is increased by that amount upon consolidation. The total goodwill of $100,000 relating to the acquisition of Target Ltd. is made up of the $70,000 paid by Purchase Ltd. for its 70% share and $30,000,

EXHIBIT 5-5

Consolidation at Date of Acquisition, Non-Wholly Owned Subsidiary

Purchase Ltd.
Consolidated Statement of Financial Position
December 31, 20X5

ASSETS	
Current Assets:	
Cash [1,000,000 + 50,000]	$1,050,000
Accounts receivable [2,000,000 + 150,000]	2,150,000
Inventory [200,000 + 50,000]	250,000
	3,450,000
Property, Plant, and Equipment:	
Land [1,000,000 + 300,000 + **100,000a**]	1,400,000
Buildings and equipment [3,000,000 + 500,000 + **50,000a**]	3,550,000
Accumulated depreciation [1,200,000 + 150,000 − **150,000a**]	(1,200,000)
	3,750,000
Other Assets:	
Investment in Target Ltd. [840,000 − **560,000b** − **280,000b**]	—
Goodwill [+ **100,000a**]	100,000
TOTAL ASSETS	$7,300,000
LIABILITIES AND SHAREHOLDERS' EQUITY	
Liabilities:	
Current: accounts payable [1,000,000 + 100,000]	$1,100,000
Long-term: notes payable [400,000 + 0]	400,000
	1,500,000
Shareholders' Equity:	
Common shares [3,440,000 + 200,000 − **200,000b**]	3,440,000
Retained earnings [2,000,000 + 600,000 − **600,000b**]	2,000,000
NCI [+ **240,000a** + **120,000a**]	360,000
	5,800,000
TOTAL LIABILITIES AND SHAREHOLDERS' EQUITY	$7,300,000

the NCI's share allocated to it. Therefore, the non-controlling interest is $360,000, which is: (30% × $1,100,000) + (30% × $100,000).

Assigning goodwill to the non-controlling shareholders' interest can be defended because if 70% of Target Ltd. is worth $840,000, then 30% must be worth three-sevenths of that amount, or $360,000. Canadian securities laws give some support to this approach. When there has been a block purchase of shares in certain publicly traded companies,[1] an offer to buy non-controlling shareholders' shares must be at least as attractive as the price paid for the majority shares.

1. For example, those covered by the *Ontario Securities Act* (Section 91).

Amortization in Subsequent Years

In Chapter 4, the parent owned 100% of the subsidiary. Therefore, we amortized 100% of the fair-value increments over the expected useful lives of the assets. We also would have recognized losses resulting from the impairment of the full value of the goodwill. Under the entity method, even when the parent does not own 100% of the subsidiary, the consolidated assets and liabilities (and consequently the NCI) continue to include the NCI's share of the subsidiary's fair-value increments, including goodwill. Therefore, we should continue to amortize 100% of the fair-value increments and recognize a loss on the impairment of 100% of the goodwill. However, to the extent these expenses and losses relate to the NCI's share in the subsidiary, we need to charge such expenses and losses against the NCI's interest on the consolidated SFP.

We will now illustrate consolidation of a non-wholly owned subsidiary (1) one year after acquisition, and (2) two years after acquisition.

CONCEPT CHECK 5-2

Companion Website

1. For the same subsidiary, how would the consolidated SFP at the date of acquisition differ if the subsidiary were non-wholly owned rather than wholly owned?
2. Under the entity method, what does the value of the NCI on the consolidated SFP represent?

CONSOLIDATION ONE YEAR AFTER ACQUISITION

Basic Information

For the year ended December 31, 20X6 (i.e., one year following the business combination), the following occurred:

- Target Ltd.'s buildings and equipment will be depreciated over 10 years after the date of acquisition, using straight-line depreciation.
- During 20X6, Target sold goods of $55,000^U to Purchase Ltd. Target Ltd.'s gross margin is 40% of sales.
- On December 31, 20X6, $20,000 of the goods acquired by Purchase Ltd. from Target Ltd. are still in Purchase Ltd.'s inventory. Unrealized profit is $20,000 × 40% = $8,000^U.
- During 20X6, Target Ltd. paid dividends totalling $30,000. Of this amount, 70% (i.e., $21,000) were received by Purchase Ltd. Purchase Ltd. maintains its investment in Target Ltd. on the cost basis; therefore, the dividends were recorded as dividend income.

EXHIBIT 5-6

Separate-Entity Financial Statements for 20X6

Statements of Comprehensive Income
Year Ended December 31, 20X6

	Purchase Ltd.	Target Ltd.
Revenue:		
Sales	$2,400,000	$ 300,000
Dividend income	21,000	—
	2,421,000	300,000
Expenses:		
Cost of sales	1,750,000	180,000
Depreciation expense	100,000	35,000
Other expenses	250,000	20,000
	2,100,000	235,000
NET INCOME AND COMPREHENSIVE INCOME	$ 321,000	$ 65,000

Statement of Changes in Equity—Retained Earnings Section
Year Ended December 31, 20X6

	Purchase Ltd.	Target Ltd.
Retained earnings, December 31, 20X5	$2,000,000	$ 600,000
Net income	321,000	65,000
Dividends declared	—	(30,000)
Retained earnings, December 31, 20X6	$2,321,000	$ 635,000

Statements of Financial Position
December 31, 20X6

	Purchase Ltd.	Target Ltd.
ASSETS		
Current Assets:		
Cash	$ 971,000	$ 100,000
Accounts receivable	2,200,000	250,000
Inventory	250,000	70,000
	3,421,000	420,000
Property, Plant, and Equipment:		
Land	1,000,000	300,000
Buildings and equipment	3,000,000	500,000
Accumulated depreciation	(1,300,000)	(185,000)
	2,700,000	615,000
Other Assets:		
Investments (at cost)	840,000	—
TOTAL ASSETS	$6,961,000	$1,035,000
LIABILITIES		
Liabilities and Shareholders' Equity		
Current liability: accounts payable	$ 800,000	$ 200,000
Long-term liability: note payable	400,000	—
	1,200,000	200,000
Shareholders' Equity:		
Common shares	3,440,000	200,000
Retained earnings	2,321,000	635,000
	5,761,000	835,000
TOTAL LIABILITIES AND SHAREHOLDERS' EQUITY	$6,961,000	$1,035,000

Direct Method

Exhibit 5-6 shows the separate-entity financial statements for 20X6. We assume that Purchase Ltd. is using the cost basis of *recording* its investment in Target Ltd. These statements are very similar to those shown in Exhibit 4-2. The differences are due to two factors:

1. Purchase Ltd. acquired 70% instead of 100%, and therefore:
   - investment in Target Ltd. is smaller by $360,000 (i.e., $1,200,000 − $840,000); and
   - Purchase Ltd.'s common share account is less by $360,000 due to the lower value of the shares issued in the acquisition.
2. Although Target declared and paid $30,000 in dividends (just as in 20X6 in Chapter 4), Purchase Ltd. received only 70% of Target Ltd.'s dividends. Therefore, Purchase Ltd.'s dividend income, closing retained earnings, and cash balance are all less by 30% × $30,000 = $9,000.

Since consolidation is now occurring in the first year after acquisition, we must carry out all the adjustments and eliminations required under the column titled "Relating to First Year Following Acquisition," in Exhibit 5-3. Exhibit 5-4 has already illustrated the first step of Measure. Therefore, we will not repeat that step here. Now, we will go ahead and illustrate the remaining steps.

Eliminate

Intercompany Transactions and Balances

Upstream sale by Target Ltd.	(55,000)
Dividends declared by Target Ltd.	(30,000)

In our illustration there are two intercompany items that need to be eliminated. The first item relates to the sale by Target Ltd. of $55,000^U$ worth of goods to Purchase Ltd. Our analysis relating to the sale of $55,000^U$ remains unchanged from our analysis in Chapter 4. We need to eliminate $55,000^U$ from both sales and cost of goods sold.

The second item relates to the $30,000 worth of dividends declared by Target Ltd. Our analysis and conclusion relating to this item will now differ slightly compared to our analysis in Chapter 4. Remember that of the $30,000 dividends declared by Target Ltd., Purchase Ltd.'s share is only $21,000; the remaining $9,000 belongs to the NCI. Therefore, while we eliminate the dividends declared amount of $30,000, we need to eliminate only $21,000 from dividend income. The NCI's share of $9,000 will be subtracted from the NCI balance on the SFP.

Unrealized and Realized Profits

Unrealized profit on upstream sale of inventory	(8,000)

There is only one adjustment required to eliminate unrealized earnings—the same adjustment as the one in Chapter 4 required for eliminating the unrealized profit on upstream sale of inventory. As explained earlier, we need to increase cost of goods sold and decrease ending inventory by that amount. Since this is the first year after acquisition, there are no profits on intercompany sale of inventory or other assets in prior period(s) that have been realized in the current period.

Amortize

	FVI allocated	Amortization period	Amortization per year	Amortization/ impairment loss during 20X6	Balance of FVI remaining at the end of 20X6
Land	$100,000	—		—	$100,000
Building and Equipment	200,000	10	$20,000	$20,000	180,000
Goodwill	100,000	—		—	100,000
Total	$400,000			$20,000	$380,000

The schedule above is identical to the schedule in Chapter 4. Therefore, the inferences we can draw from it are identical to the ones in Chapter 4. Specifically, from the schedule above we know that there is a $20,000 amortization/impairment loss; this loss must be recognized in the consolidated financial statements in the current period. This adjustment pertains to the depreciation expense relating to the fair-value increment allocated to property, plant, and equipment.

We also know from the schedule above that the balance of the FVI adjustment that needs to be added to the carrying values of the parent and subsidiary is $380,000, made up of an increase to land for $100,000, buildings and equipment for $180,000, and goodwill for $100,000. Note that the adjustment for buildings and equipment of $180,000 is the result of the initial FVI allocated to buildings and equipment of $200,000 less the $20,000 depreciation adjustment required in the current year.

Recognize NCI Share of Earnings In every consolidation of a controlled subsidiary, 100% of the subsidiary's revenues and expenses are added to those of the parent. The consolidated SCI shows the total combined revenues and expenses and by extension the total net income for the entire economic entity.

However, if all of the subsidiary's earnings were distributed to the shareholders as dividends, the parent would receive only the proportion relating to its ownership interest in the subsidiary—the remainder would go to the people or institutions that hold the remaining (or non-controlling) shares. Therefore, we need to show the parent's shareholders the portion of consolidated net income that belongs to them and the portion that "belongs" to the NCI. This is done by allocating the net income between the parent's shareholders and the NCI. Such an apportionment of the net income of the consolidated entity will appear immediately below the net income line item on the consolidated SCI whenever the parent owns less than 100% of the shares. The net income allocated to the NCI represents the net income accruing to the minority or NCI.

Be careful here—*accrue* and *belong* in this sense do not mean that the earnings are recorded on anyone's books the way we usually use the word. Each term is used simply to indicate that the parent corporation does not have the right to receive the benefits of shares it does not own.

Note that the amount apportioned as the non-controlling share is based on the subsidiary's separate-entity net income, *adjusted for unrealized profits and other expenses*. However, the consolidated SCI of Purchase Ltd. will provide only a final net income number for the consolidated entity as a whole. It will not provide us with a breakdown of that amount, such that we can identify the amount of the adjusted income of Target Ltd. Without this detail we cannot apportion the consolidated net income amount between the shareholders of Purchase Ltd. and the NCI.

From the previous steps we already know the various adjustments required to be made to Target Ltd.'s income. Further, Target Ltd.'s income on its separate-entity financial statements is $65,000. Therefore, we have all the information necessary to calculate the amount of income to be apportioned to the NCI on the SCI as shown in the schedule below:

Details	Amount
Net income of Target Ltd. for 20X6 (from separate-entity financial statement)	$65,000
Less:	
Unrealized gains on upstream sale of inventory	(8,000)
Amortization of fair-value increment during the year	(20,000)
Adjusted net income of Target Ltd. for 20X6	**37,000**
NCI's share @ 30%	**11,100**
Purchase Ltd.'s share @ 70%	**$25,900**

In the schedule above we first start with the unadjusted net income of Target Ltd. for the year 20X6, taken from its separate-entity financial statements. Target Ltd. reported separate-entity earnings of $65,000. Before calculating the NCI's share of Target Ltd.'s earnings, we need to adjust the $65,000 amount for the unrealized profits and amortization expenses identified in the previous steps.

Specifically, there are two adjustments to the net income of Target Ltd.—(1) elimination of the unrealized gain of $8,000^U on the upstream sale of inventory, and (2) recognition of a $20,000 expense relating to the amortization of the fair-value increment during the year. Both of these adjustments reduce the net income of Target Ltd., which results in an adjusted net income of $37,000. On Purchase Ltd.'s consolidated SCI, 30% of this amount (i.e., $11,100) should be allocated to the NCI as its share of income for the year. Naturally, the remaining 70% of the adjusted net income of Target Ltd for 20X6, that is, $25,900 ($37,000 – $11,100), flows to the benefit of Purchase Ltd. shareholders.

Why Reduce NCI's Earnings? Why do the earnings of the NCI get reduced just because Purchase Ltd. failed to sell its entire inventory and for the excess amortization charged relating to the fair-value increment? They don't! These deductions for NCI have nothing to do with the NCI's real entitlement to the subsidiary's earnings and dividends. The non-controlling shareholders look at the *subsidiary's* financial statements and receive the *subsidiary's* dividends.

In preparing Purchase Ltd.'s *consolidated* statements, we adjusted the consolidated cost of sales and depreciation expense for 100% of the unrealized profit and amortization of fair-value increment. Now we need to reduce the NCI by the NCI's 30% share of the unrealized upstream profit and the amortization expense so that only 70% of that effect shows up in Purchase Ltd.'s consolidated earnings. Bear in mind that the calculation of NCI is only an adjustment to the *parent's* consolidated statements, not to the subsidiary's separate-entity statements.

Prepare the Consolidated Statements We now have all the information necessary for preparing the consolidated financial statements of Purchase Ltd. at the end of 20X6. Therefore, we will now prepare the consolidated statement of income and the retained earnings section of the consolidated statement of changes in equity and the consolidated SFP for Purchase Ltd. for the year 20X6. We start the consolidation process by adding the carrying values of both companies and making the various adjustments identified in the previous steps. We also need to remember to eliminate the common shares of $200,000 and retained earnings at the time of acquisition of $600,000 of Target Ltd., and the investment at cost of $840,000.

To do the above, following our practice in earlier chapters, we can go down the SCI and SFP and insert the correct amounts on a line-by-line basis. In Exhibit 5-7, we have added together the separate-entity amounts, and made the required additional adjustments and eliminations. The necessary adjustments and eliminations are listed below once again, now by each financial statement starting with the SCI. Exhibit 5-7 illustrates consolidation under the entity method.

Statement of Comprehensive Income and SCE/RE

- *Sales*. The upstream intercompany sales of $\$55{,}000^{U}$ are eliminated.
- *Dividend income*. The dividends paid by Target Ltd. to Purchase Ltd. are eliminated: $30,000 × 70% = $21,000.
- *Cost of sales*. Cost of sales is reduced by $\$55{,}000^{U}$ to avoid counting the intercompany sales in cost of goods sold twice. However, this elimination is partially offset by the unrealized profit in Purchase Ltd.'s ending inventory: $20,000 × 40% = $\$8{,}000^{U}$.
- *Depreciation expense*. As usual, the FVI for buildings and equipment must be amortized. The amortization is of the full FVI of $200,000. The FVI amortization therefore is $200,000 ÷ 10 = $20,000.
- *Allocation of net income*. The net income of $337,000 has to be allocated between the owners of the parent and the NCI. Note however that only the NCI's share of the adjusted income of Target Ltd. is allocated to it. The NCI does not share in the profits from the operations of Purchase Ltd. Further, as pointed out earlier, this allocation process is done solely for the purpose of reporting the financial affairs of Purchase Ltd. to its shareholders. The NCI shareholders of Target Ltd. will not be using the financial statements of Purchase Ltd. Instead, they will use the separate-entity financial statements issued by Target Ltd. to its shareholders. The NCI's share of the adjusted income of Target Ltd. of $11,100 is allocated to it, while Purchase Ltd.'s income from its operations and its share of the adjusted income of Target Ltd. totalling $325,900 is allocated to its owners.
- *Beginning consolidated retained earnings*. The beginning consolidated retained earnings balance includes the retained earnings of only Purchase Ltd., since the beginning retained earnings balance of Target Ltd. represents its retained earnings on the date of its acquisition by Purchase Ltd.

Statement of Financial Position

- *Inventory*. Inventory is reduced by the $\$8{,}000^{U}$ unrealized profit on upstream sales. This adjustment is the counterpart of the $\$8{,}000^{U}$ increase to cost of goods sold on the SCI. Therefore, in essence what we have done is that we first reduced the ending inventory value by $\$8{,}000^{U}$ and, next, treated such a reduction as an expense on the SCI by appropriately

EXHIBIT 5-7

Purchase Ltd. Consolidated Financial Statements

[Purchase owns 70% of Target Ltd.—Direct Method]
Consolidated Statement of Comprehensive Income
Year Ended December 31, 20X6

Sales revenue [2,400,000 + 300,000 − **55,000**[U]]	$2,645,000
Dividend income [21,000 + 0 − **21,000**]	
Operating Expenses:	
Cost of sales [1,750,000 + 180,000 − **55,000**[U] **+ 8,000**[U]]	1,883,000
Depreciation expense [100,000 + 35,000 + **20,000**]	155,000
Other expenses [250,000 + 20,000]	270,000
	2,308,000
NET INCOME AND COMPREHENSIVE INCOME	$ 337,000
Net Income Attributable to:	
Owners of the parent	$ 325,900
Non-controlling interests	11,100

Consolidated Statement of Changes in Equity—Retained Earnings Section
Year Ended December 31, 20X6

Retained earnings, December 31, 20X5 [2,000,000 + 600,000 − **600,000**]	2,000,000
Net income	325,900
Dividends declared [0 + 30,000 − **30,000**]	—
Retained earnings, December 31, 20X6	$2,325,900

Consolidated Statement of Financial Position
December 31, 20X6

ASSETS	
Current Assets:	
Cash [971,000 + 100,000]	$1,071,000
Accounts receivable [2,200,000 + 250,000]	2,450,000
Inventory [250,000 + 70,000 − **8,000**[U]]	312,000
	3,833,000
Property, Plant, and Equipment:	
Land [1,000,000 + 300,000 **+ 100,000**]	1,400,000
Buildings and equipment [3,000,000 + 500,000 **+ 50,000**]	3,550,000
Accumulated depreciation [1,300,000 + 185,000 − **150,000 + 20,000**]	(1,355,000)
	3,595,000
Other Assets:	
Investments [840,000 + 0 − **840,000**]	—
Goodwill [0 + **100,000**]	100,000
TOTAL ASSETS	$7,528,000
LIABILITIES AND SHAREHOLDERS' EQUITY	
Liabilities:	
Current: accounts payable [800,000 + 200,000]	$1,000,000
Long-term: notes payable [400,000 + 0]	400,000
	1,400,000

EXHIBIT 5-7 (*Continued*)

Purchase Ltd. Consolidated Financial Statements

Shareholders' Equity:	
Common shares [**Purchase Ltd. shares only**]	3,440,000
Retained earnings [2,321,000 + 635,000 − **600,000** − **10,500** − (**8,000^U × 70%**) − (**20,000 × 70%**)]*	2,325,900
	5,765,900
NCI in net assets of Target Ltd. [**360,000** + **11,100** − **9,000**]	362,100
Total equity	6,128,000
TOTAL LIABILITIES AND SHAREHOLDERS' EQUITY	$7,528,000

*The $10,500 is the portion of the increase in retained earnings that is allocable to the NCI. Retained earnings increased by $35,000 ($635,000 − $600,000) and 30% of this increase is $10,500 ($35,000 × 30%). The adjustments to retained earnings are explained in more detail later.

increasing the cost of goods sold. Alternatively, we can arrive at the same conclusion by using the following equation:

Beginning Inventory + Purchases = Cost of Goods Sold + Ending Inventory

If we hold constant the beginning inventory and purchases, to maintain equality, any decrease in the ending inventory must be matched by an equal increase in the cost of goods sold account.

- *Land*. The FVI of $100,000 is added.
- *Buildings and equipment*. Buildings and equipment is *increased* by $50,000 to reflect the fair value at the date of acquisition, as was the case for consolidation at the date of acquisition.
- *Accumulated depreciation*. Target Ltd.'s date-of-acquisition accumulated depreciation is not carried forward on the consolidated SFP. The elimination is for the full amount of the date-of-acquisition accumulated depreciation of $150,000. There are two effects to this adjustment:
  - The net date-of-acquisition value assigned to Target Ltd.'s buildings and equipment is increased by $200,000 (that is, $150,000 + $50,000): (1) the elimination of accumulated depreciation, plus (2) the increase in value assigned to the asset account.
  - The amount remaining in Target Ltd.'s accumulated depreciation is only the depreciation taken *since the date of acquisition*, which is one year's amortization of the FVI: $200,000 ÷ 10 = $20,000.
- *Investment in Target Ltd*. This account is eliminated completely, of course.
- *Common shares*. Only Purchase Ltd.'s shares are included.
- *Retained earnings*. Refer to the double-check step below for a detailed discussion of the calculation of the ending consolidated retained earnings balance.
- *Non-controlling interest*. Again, refer to the double-check step below for a detailed discussion of the calculation of the ending balance of the NCI.

Classification of NCI on the SFP Throughout this text, following IAS 27, the NCI will be shown on the SFP within equity, but separately from the parent shareholders' equity.

In the past, North American practice was to present the NCI on the SFP as a separate item between the liabilities and shareholders' equity. However, in the accounting profession worldwide, there was always some unease about this method of presenting the NCI. Theoretically, items on the equities side of the SFP should be a part of either creditors' equity (i.e., liabilities) or shareholders' equity. Having an unidentified floating object between liabilities and shareholders' equity seems contrary to the basic concept of the SFP. Therefore, the present practice of presenting the NCI within equity removes this source of unease. It also is the method previously used in Japan, as well as in some other countries.

Check We automatically arrived at the NCI and retained earnings balances at the end of 20X6 during the consolidation process. However, it is prudent to independently calculate the NCI and retained earnings balances at the end of the year as a double-check. We will first start with the NCI balance.

To do so, we update the beginning NCI balance with all items affecting NCI that occurred during the year. The NCI balance at the beginning of 20X6 is $360,000. In our example there are two items pertaining to 20X6 which affect the NCI balance—(1) the net income allocated to the NCI as calculated previously, and (2) the NCI's share of the dividends declared by Target Ltd. As the schedule below demonstrates, it is relatively straightforward to calculate the ending NCI balance using the above information:

NCI Balance at the End of 20X6

Balance of NCI at the time of acquisition	$360,000
Add: NCI's share of Target Ltd.'s adjusted net income in 20X6	11,100
Less: NCI's share of dividends declared by Target Ltd. in 20X6	(9,000)
Ending balance of NCI in 20X6	$362,100

Similarly, it is relatively straightforward to calculate the retained earnings balance of Parent Ltd. on the date of consolidation as demonstrated below:

Ending retained earnings balance of Purchase Ltd. from its separate-entity SFP	$2,321,000
Less dividend income from Target Ltd.	(21,000)
= Adjusted separate-entity ending retained earnings balance of Purchase Ltd.	2,300,000
Add Purchase Ltd.'s share of Target Ltd.'s adjusted income	25,900
Ending consolidated retained earnings of Purchase Ltd.	$2,325,900

We will demonstrate an alternative calculation of ending consolidated retained earnings a little later in the chapter, one that begins with *consolidated* retained earnings rather than *separate-entity* retained earnings. For examination purposes, it is useful to understand both approaches, depending on the format of the information presented in an examination question.

Notice that the first thing we did in the schedule above while calculating the ending retained earnings was to subtract the $21,000 dividend income recognized in the separate-entity financial statements of Purchase Ltd., under the cost method. In contrast, the consolidated retained earnings balance of Purchase Ltd. will include the full portion of Purchase Ltd.'s share of the adjusted income of Target Ltd. of $25,900, not just the portion distributed as dividends. Therefore, to avoid double-counting we need to first subtract the dividend income recognized, before adding $25,900 to get the ending consolidated retained earnings of Purchase Ltd. of $2,325,900.

An alternative method of calculating the ending consolidated retained earnings balance is provided below. During consolidations there are conceptually different methods of calculating a particular answer. The suitability of a particular method will depend on the information available. You should try to understand the various alternative methods available to arrive at an answer. Such an exercise will go a long way in furthering your understanding of the consolidation process.

Purchase's separate-entity retained earnings		$2,321,000
Purchase's share of increase in Target's retained earnings		
Target's separate-entity retained earnings	635,000	
Less Target's date-of-acquisition retained earnings	(600,000)	
Less NCI's portion of Target's increased retained earnings [(635,000 − 600,000) × 30%]	(10,500)	
Net increase to Purchase		24,500
Purchase's share of unrealized upstream profit (8,000 × 70%)		(5,600)
Purchase's share of 20X6 amortization of FVI on buildings and equipment ($20,000 × 70%)		(14,000)
Consolidated retained earnings, December 31, 20X6		$2,325,900

In the alternative method, we first start with Purchase Ltd.'s separate-entity retained earnings of $2,321,000. To this amount we need to add Purchase Ltd.'s share of the change in the separate-entity retained earnings of Target Ltd. from the time of acquisition to the date of consolidation, i.e., during 20X6, which is $635,000 − $600,000 − $10,500. $10,500 represents the NCI's 30% share of the change in the separate-entity retained earnings of Target Ltd. of $35,000 ($635,000 − $600,000).

Additionally, we need to adjust Purchase Ltd.'s share of the change in the separate-entity retained earnings of Target Ltd. with Purchase Ltd.'s share of the unrealized profit on upstream sale of $5,600[U] and of the 20X6 amortization of FVI on buildings and equipment of $14,000. The result represents the consolidated retained earnings balance on December 31, 20X6, of $2,325,900. We have used this alternative method while preparing the consolidated financial statements below.

Worksheet Approach

For the illustration of how the worksheet approach applies to our example, please refer to the Companion Website.

CONCEPT CHECK 5-3

1. In the case of non-wholly owned subsidiaries, why are the eliminations relating to unrealized gains/losses on downstream transactions different from the eliminations relating to unrealized gains/losses on upstream transactions?
2. During the consolidation process, why does the NCI get allocated its share of the net income of the subsidiary and its share of the adjustments to the net income of the subsidiary?

CONSOLIDATION IN SECOND SUBSEQUENT YEAR

The separate-entity financial statements for the two companies are shown in Exhibit 5-8. Assume that during 20X7, the following occurred.

1. Target Ltd. had sales of $60,000^U$ to Purchase Ltd.; Target Ltd.'s 20X7 gross margin was 45%; $10,000 (sales price) of the goods is in Purchase Ltd.'s inventory on December 31, 20X7. Unrealized upstream profit therefore is $10,000 × 45% = $4,500^U$.
2. Purchase Ltd. had sales of $20,000_D$ to Target Ltd.; Purchase Ltd.'s 20X7 gross margin was 30%; $6,000 (sales price) of the goods sold to Target Ltd. is in Target Ltd.'s 20X7 ending inventory. Unrealized downstream profit is $6,000 × 30% = $1,800_D$.
3. Purchase Ltd. borrowed $500,000 from Target Ltd. on December 29, 20X7. Both companies have reported this as a current item on their separate-entity statements of financial position.
4. Target Ltd. sold its land to Purchase Ltd. for $450,000. The land originally cost Target Ltd. $300,000, and its fair value at the date of Purchase Ltd.'s acquisition of Target Ltd. was $400,000. The gain on the sale ($150,000^U$) is separately disclosed on Target Ltd.'s SCI as an unusual item.

EXHIBIT 5-8

Separate-Entity Financial Statements for 20X7

Statements of Comprehensive Income
Year Ended December 31, 20X7

	Purchase Ltd.	Target Ltd.
Revenue:		
Sales	$3,000,000	$400,000
Dividend income	14,000	—
Gain on sale of land	—	150,000
	3,014,000	550,000
Expenses:		
Cost of sales	2,100,000	220,000
Depreciation expense	100,000	35,000
Other expenses	440,000	75,000
	2,640,000	330,000
NET INCOME AND COMPREHENSIVE INCOME	$ 374,000	$220,000

Statements of Changes in Equity—Retained Earnings Section
Year Ended December 31, 20X7

	Purchase Ltd.	Target Ltd.
Retained earnings, December 31, 20X6	$2,321,000	$635,000
Net income	374,000	220,000
Dividends declared	(135,000)	(20,000)
Retained earnings, December 31, 20X7	$2,560,000	$835,000

EXHIBIT 5-8 (*Continued*)

Separate-Entity Financial Statements for 20X7

Statements of Financial Position
December 31, 20X7

	Purchase Ltd.	Target Ltd.
ASSETS		
Current Assets:		
Cash	$ 475,000	$ 70,000
Accounts receivable	1,900,000	275,000
Note receivable	—	500,000
Inventory	300,000	60,000
	2,675,000	905,000
Property, Plant, and Equipment:		
Land	1,450,000	—
Buildings and equipment	3,800,000	500,000
Accumulated depreciation	(1,400,000)	(220,000)
	3,850,000	280,000
Other Assets:		
Investments (at cost)	840,000	—
TOTAL ASSETS	$7,365,000	$1,185,000
LIABILITIES AND SHAREHOLDERS' EQUITY		
LIABILITIES:		
Current Liabilities:		
Accounts payable	$ 515,000	$ 150,000
Note payable	500,000	—
Long-term: note payable	350,000	—
	1,365,000	150,000
Shareholders' Equity:		
Common shares	3,440,000	200,000
Retained earnings	2,560,000	835,000
	6,000,000	1,035,000
TOTAL LIABILITIES AND SHAREHOLDERS' EQUITY	$7,365,000	$1,185,000

These facts are exactly the same as those used in Chapter 4; they are repeated here for convenience.

Direct Method

In our illustration we are now at the end of the second year after acquisition. Therefore, we must now carry out all the adjustments and eliminations listed under the last column titled "Relating to Following Years" in Exhibit 5-3.

The first step of Measure remains unchanged from what it was earlier in the chapter when we illustrated consolidation at the time of acquisition; therefore, we will not repeat it here. Instead, we will now move to the next step of Eliminate.

Eliminate Intercompany Transactions and Balances

Upstream sale by Target Ltd.	(60,000)
Downstream sale by Purchase Ltd.	(20,000)
Dividends declared by Target Ltd.	(20,000)
Note receivable of Target Ltd., and note payable of Purchase Ltd.	(500,000)

In 20X7 there are four intercompany items. Our analysis of these steps remains unchanged from our analysis in Chapter 4 in relation to consolidation in the second subsequent year, except for the dividends declared by Target Ltd.

1. Target Ltd. sold $\$60,000^U$ worth of goods to Purchase Ltd. We need to eliminate $\$60,000^U$ from both sales and cost of goods sold.
2. Purchase Ltd. sold $\$20,000_D$ worth of goods to Target Ltd. We must eliminate $\$20,000_D$ from both sales and cost of goods sold as well.
3. Dividends of $20,000 were declared by Target Ltd. Our analysis of the dividends of $20,000 declared by Target Ltd in 20X7 is the same as our analysis of the dividends declared in 20X6. Of the $20,000 dividends declared by Target Ltd. in 20X7, Purchase Ltd.'s share is only $14,000; the remaining $6,000 belongs to the NCI. Therefore, while we eliminate the dividends declared amount of $20,000, we need to eliminate only $14,000 from dividend income. The NCI's share of $6,000 will be subtracted from the NCI balance on the SFP.
4. Purchase Ltd. borrowed $500,000 from Target Ltd. on December 29, 20X7. We need to eliminate Target Ltd.'s note receivable and Purchase Ltd.'s note payable at the time of consolidation. The loan occurred at the end of the year, and thus we can disregard any associated interest as immaterial. Otherwise, we would have had to eliminate the associated interest income and interest expense which may have been recognized by Target Ltd. and Purchase Ltd., respectively.

Unrealized and Realized Profits

Realized profit on upstream sale of inventory in previous year	8,000
Unrealized profit on upstream sale of inventory in the current year	(4,500)
Unrealized profit on downstream sale of inventory in the current year	(1,800)
Unrealized gain on sale of land by Target Ltd. to Purchase Ltd.	(150,000)

Again, the unrealized and realized profits are the same as in Chapter 4 in the year 20X7. We have one source of realized profit, two sources of unrealized profit, and one source of unrealized gain. Remember that in 20X6 we had $\$8,000^U$ of unrealized profit on the upstream sale of inventory, which we eliminated by increasing the cost of goods sold of 20X6 and decreasing the ending inventory of 20X6 respectively by that amount. The profit was unrealized since the corresponding goods were still with Purchase Ltd. at the end of the year. These adjustments would have decreased ending retained earnings and NCI by $\$5,600^U$ and $\$2,400^U$ respectively. Now, in 20X7, these goods have been sold to an outside party and therefore the associated profits are now realized.

The ending 20X6 inventory is also the beginning 20X7 inventory. Purchase Ltd. would have included the unadjusted beginning inventory in its cost of sales calculation in the current year; from the consolidation point of view that results in *overstating* opening inventory by

$\$8{,}000^{U}$, and *overstating* cost of sales by the same amount. Therefore, we must *reduce* consolidated cost of sales by $\$8{,}000^{U}$ to account for the realization of the profits in 20X7. In summary, therefore, we should decrease the opening retained earnings and NCI balance of 20X7 by $\$5{,}600^{U}$ and $\$2{,}400^{U}$ respectively, while decreasing cost of goods sold of 20X7 by $\$8{,}000^{U}$.

We should increase the cost of goods sold of 20X7 and decrease the ending inventory of 20X7 by $\$4{,}500^{U}$ and $\$1{,}800_{D}$ to eliminate the unrealized profits on the upstream and downstream sales of inventory, respectively, this year. The underlying logic is identical to the logic underlying the elimination of the unrealized profit on the upstream sale of inventory in 20X6.

Finally, Target Ltd. sold its land to Purchase Ltd. during the year for a gain of $\$150{,}000^{U}$. However, the land is still owned within the consolidated entity; therefore, the associated gain is unrealized, and must be eliminated.

Amortize The step of "Amortize" will produce different results in 20X7 as compared to the results in 20X6 in the chapter; however, the results will be the same as those obtained in 20X7 in Chapter 4.

	FVI allocated	Amortization period	Amortization per year	Amortization/ impairment loss during previous periods	Amortization/ impairment loss during 20X7	Balance of FVI remaining at the end of 20X7
Land	$100,000	—			—	$100,000
Building and Equipment	200,000	10	$20,000	$20,000	$20,000	160,000
Goodwill	100,000	—			—	100,000
Total	$400,000			$20,000	$20,000	$360,000

The inferences from the schedule above remain identical to those obtained in Chapter 4 for the second subsequent year. From the schedule above we can see that we need to recognize a total amortization/impairment loss adjustment of $20,000 in the previous year (as explained in greater detail in the following section) and a similar adjustment in the current year.

We can also see from the schedule above that the balance of the FVI adjustment that needs to be added to the carrying values of the parent and subsidiary is $360,000, made up of an increase to land for $100,000, buildings and equipment for $160,000, and goodwill for $100,000. Note that the adjustment for buildings and equipment of $160,000 is the result of the initial FVI allocated to buildings and equipment of $200,000 minus the $40,000 depreciation adjustment required in total over the previous and current year.

Recognize NCI Share of Earnings Before we can determine our year-end balance in retained earnings and NCI, we must first determine how much of the subsidiary's net income is to be allocated to the NCI. The process is relatively simple. We start by calculating the adjusted income of the subsidiary. The income is adjusted to remove profits that are unrealized in the current year and include profits unrealized in previous years that have been realized in the current year. In addition, any amortization or impairment of FVI has to be subtracted from the subsidiary's income. This will provide a measure of the subsidiary's adjusted income. After determining the adjusted income, we calculate the NCI's share of the adjusted income.

With the NCI's share of the adjusted income known, it is again a relatively simple process to determine the ending balance in NCI. We simply start with the balance in the NCI at the beginning of the year and add to it its share of the adjusted income and subtract its share of the dividends declared by the subsidiary. These steps are illustrated in detail below for our example.

We will first focus on the NCI's share of Target's adjusted income in 20X7. We already know the various adjustments that need to be made to the earnings of Target Ltd. in 20X7. We also know that Target Ltd.'s income in 20X7 is $220,000. Therefore, we can easily calculate the share of income that should be apportioned to the NCI. The calculation of the adjusted net income of Target Ltd. in 20X7, and the NCI's share of adjusted income, is presented in the schedule below:

Details	Amount
Net income of Target Ltd. for 20X7 (from separate-entity financial statement)	$220,000
Add:	
Realized profit on upstream sale of inventory in previous year	8,000
Less:	
Unrealized profit on upstream sale of inventory in the current year	(4,500)
Unrealized gain on sale of land by Target Ltd. to Purchase Ltd.	(150,000)
Amortization of FVI during the year	(20,000)
Adjusted net income of Target Ltd. for 20X7	**$ 53,500**
NCI's share @ 30%	**$ 16,050**

In the schedule above we first start with the unadjusted net income of Target Ltd. for the year 20X7 of $220,000, taken from its separate-entity financial statements. Before calculating the NCI in Target Ltd.'s earnings, we need to adjust the $220,000 amount for realized and unrealized profits and other expenses.

Specifically, there are four adjustments required to be made to the net income of Target Ltd.—one relating to a realized profit, two related to unrealized profit amounts, and one related to the amortization of the fair-value increment. All four of these adjustments were already identified in the previous Eliminate and Amortize steps. Note that we did not include the unrealized profit on the downstream sale of inventory of $\$1,800_D$, identified in the Eliminate step. This profit exists in the hands of Purchase Ltd., and not in the hands of Target Ltd. Therefore, following entity theory, the NCI balance should not be adjusted for this amount. Instead of adjusting the net income of Target Ltd., we should adjust the separate-entity income of Purchase Ltd. by the $\$1,800_D$ unrealized gain relating to the downstream sale of inventory.

The adjusted net income of Target Ltd. for 20X7, after making all the above adjustments, is $53,500. Therefore, the NCI's share is $16,050. Naturally, Purchase Ltd.'s share of Target Ltd.'s adjusted income is $37,450. We also need to adjust Purchase Ltd.'s separate-entity net income by the $\$1,800_D$ unrealized gain relating to the downstream sale of inventory.

It is now easy to calculate the ending balance in the NCI as demonstrated below. Note that our beginning balance of NCI is obtained from last year's consolidated financial statements, which we completed earlier in the chapter.

NCI Balance at the End of 20X7

Balance of NCI at the beginning of 20X7	$362,100
Add: NCI's share of Target Ltd.'s adjusted net income in 20X7	16,050
Less: NCI's share of dividends declared by Target Ltd. in 20X7	(6,000)
Ending balance of NCI in 20X7	$372,150

It is also relatively easy to calculate the ending balance in retained earnings. Again we start with the beginning balance in retained earnings, obtained from last year's consolidated financial statements. To it we add the parent's net income and the parent's share of its subsidiary's net income. Note that both the income of the parent and the income of the subsidiary have been adjusted for the various items we discussed above. You should also note that because we recorded our investment in Target using the cost method, we will have to reduce Purchase's net income by the amount of dividends that were received from Target and included in net income.

Consolidated Retained Earnings Balance at the End of 20X7

Beginning balance of consolidated retained earnings		$2,325,900
Add: Purchase Ltd.'s adjusted income		
Purchase Ltd.'s net income		374,000
Less unrealized profit on downstream sale of inventory		(1,800)
Less dividend income from Target Ltd.		(14,000)
Purchase Ltd.'s adjusted income		358,200
Add: Purchase Ltd.'s share of Target Ltd.'s adjusted income:		
Adjusted net income of Target Ltd. for 20X7	53,500	
Purchase Ltd.'s share @ 70%		37,450
Less: Dividends declared by Purchase Ltd.		135,000
Ending balance of consolidated retained earnings		$2,586,550

The opening NCI and consolidated retained earnings balances for 20X7 were obtained from the ending NCI and consolidated retained earnings balances for 20X6, calculated previously. If all that we wanted was these balances and if we would always have problems that provided us with these balances, then, when using the direct method, we could stop here. However, we will rarely encounter a problem that requires consolidation for two successive years, much less for the first two years after consolidation.

Instead, most problems will require consolidation a few years after acquisition and these problems will usually not provide the ending consolidated balances of NCI and retained earnings from the previous year. In such a case, we will need the information necessary to calculate the opening NCI and retained earnings balances for that year without being able to refer to the ending balances of the previous year. The calculations that follow illustrate that process. In this case, given that we already know these balances, we can view these calculations as a double-check on the beginning balances. Furthermore, the same process can be used in any year to check that the ending balances calculated for NCI and retained earnings are correct. However, it is important to remember that if the beginning balances are not provided, then these calculations become a necessary step in the consolidation process using the direct method.

Information Necessary for Calculating NCI and Retained Earnings at the Beginning of the Year There is no NCI balance on the separate-entity financial statements of the parent. Therefore, we will have to re-calculate the beginning NCI balance every year when we prepare consolidated financial statements of the parent. It is important for students to understand the adjustments involved in this calculation because they reflect the adjustments that are made in practice by firms when they roll forward their consolidation worksheet for the current year's consolidation. As we will see, we need to allocate to the NCI its share of the adjusted earnings of the subsidiary for previous years to be able to calculate the beginning NCI and retained earnings balances.

Recognize NCI Share of Prior-Year Earnings To calculate the NCI balance at the beginning of 20X7, we need to allocate to it its share of the adjusted change in the retained earnings of the subsidiary in the prior year of 20X6.

The opening retained earnings balance of Target Ltd. on its separate-entity SFP for 20X7 is $635,000. The retained earnings balance of Target Ltd. at the time of its acquisition is $600,000. Therefore, the change in the retained earnings of Target Ltd. from the time of acquisition until the beginning of 20X7 is $35,000. The NCI's share is $10,500. Therefore, the NCI balance at the beginning of 20X7 will be $370,500 before allocating to it its share of the consolidation-related adjustments and eliminations pertaining to prior years.

Recall our earlier statement that every time we consolidate subsequent to the date of acquisition, we need to either (1) repeat the individual adjustments and eliminations made in each previous year, or (2) capture their cumulative impact with cumulative adjustments. We will focus on the second type of adjustments—cumulative adjustments.

We are consolidating a non-wholly owned subsidiary. Therefore, the cumulative adjustments in 20X7 required to capture the cumulative impact of adjustments and eliminations made in prior years will have an impact not only on the opening retained earnings of the year, but also on the opening balance of NCI since we are now consolidating a non-wholly owned subsidiary.

In our current example, we must adjust the opening retained earnings and the opening NCI for the impact of two prior years' adjustments:

Amortization/impairment loss adjustment of $20,000 pertaining to 20X6	(20,000)
Unrealized profit on upstream sale of inventory in 20X6	(8,000)

The first item is the $20,000 amortization or depreciation expense adjustment made in 20X6 relating to the fair-value increment allocated to buildings and equipment. This amortization expense adjustment would have decreased the consolidated income of 20X6 and consequently decreased the 20X6 ending consolidated retained earnings by $14,000 and the ending NCI by $6,000. However, this decrease will not be reflected in the opening retained earnings in 20X7 of the separate-entity statements of either Target Ltd., or Purchase Ltd. As well, there is no NCI account in either of the separate-entity statements of financial position of Purchase Ltd. or Target Ltd.

Therefore, we now have to adjust the 20X7 beginning consolidated retained earnings by $14,000 and the beginning NCI by $6,000. If we were to extend our example to 20X8 and the facts remained the same, we would need to adjust the 20X8 opening consolidated retained earnings balance by $28,000: $14,000 for the amortization expense adjustment relating to 20X6 and another $14,000 for the amortization expense adjustment relating to 20X7. Similarly, the 20X8 opening NCI would need to be adjusted by $12,000: $6,000 for the amortization expense adjustment relating to 20X6 and another $6,000 for the amortization expense adjustment relating to 20X7.

NCI Balance at the Beginning of 20X7		
Balance of NCI at the time of acquisition		$ 360,000
Add: NCI's share of the adjusted change in retained earnings in prior years		
Retained earnings balance of Target Ltd. at the end of 20X6	$635,000	
Retained earnings balance of Target Ltd. at the time of acquisition	600,000	
Change in carrying value of Target Ltd. in previous years	35,000	
Less:		
Amortization of fair-value increment in previous years	(20,000)	
Unrealized profit on upstream sale of inventory in 20X6	(8,000)	
Adjusted change in retained earnings of Target Ltd. in prior years	7,000	
NCI's share @ 30%		2,100
Opening balance of NCI on January 1, 20X7		$ 362,100

Opening Consolidated Retained Earnings Balance at the Beginning of 20X7		
Opening retained earnings balance from separate-entity financial statements of Purchase Ltd. on January 1, 20X7		$2,321,000
Add: Purchase Ltd.'s share of the adjusted change in retained earnings in prior years:		
Cumulative adjusted change in retained earnings of Target Ltd. in prior years (as calculated in the first section above)	$ 7,000	
Purchase Ltd.'s share @ 70%		4,900
Opening consolidated retained earnings balance on January 1, 20X7		$2,325,900

In addition, we will use the same process to calculate the beginning balances of retained earnings and NCI for the consolidated financial statements of Purchase Ltd. for 20X7. Furthermore, we already know the share of the adjusted income attributable to Purchase Ltd. and the NCI for 20X7. Therefore, now, we have all the ingredients required to carry out the actual consolidation. Again, we will go down the SCI and SFP and insert the correct amounts on a line-by-line basis.

Consolidated Statement of Comprehensive Income and SCE/RE The consolidated statement of comprehensive income and SCE/RE are as shown in Exhibit 5-9. The amounts that require adjustment are as follows:

- *Sales*. The two companies' combined sales of $3,400,000 are adjusted for the $80,000 ($60,000^U and $20,000$_D$) in intercompany sales.
- *Dividend income*. The intercompany dividends are eliminated.
- *Gain on sale of land*. The $150,000^U unrealized gain is eliminated.
- *Cost of sales*. The unrealized profit adjustments to cost of sales are identical to those shown in Chapter 4 for 20X7. The entire unrealized profit in opening inventory ($8,000^U) must be subtracted from cost of sales (thereby increasing net income), and the unrealized profits in the ending inventory ($4,500^U and $1,800$_D$) must be added.
- *Depreciation expense*. Amortization of the FVI on Target Ltd.'s buildings and equipment is added to the carrying amount of depreciation. As in 20X6, the amortization is $200,000 ÷ 10 years, or $20,000.
- *Allocation of net income*. The net income of $411,700 has to be allocated between the owners of the parent and the NCI. Remember that only the NCI's share of the adjusted income of Target Ltd. is allocated to it. Therefore, we allocate $16,050 to NCI as its share of Target

EXHIBIT 5-9

Purchase Ltd. Consolidated Statement of Comprehensive Income (Direct Method)

Purchase Ltd.
Consolidated Statement of Comprehensive Income
Year Ended December 31, 20X7

Revenue:	
Sales revenue [3,000,000 + 400,000 − 60,000^{U} − 20,000$_{D}$]	$3,320,000
Dividend income [14,000 + 0 − 14,000]	—
Gain on sale of land [0 + 150,000 − 150,000^{U}]	—
	3,320,000
Operating Expenses:	
Cost of sales [2,100,000 + 220,000 − 60,000^{U} − 20,000 − 8,000^{U} + 4,500^{U} + 1,800$_{D}$]	2,238,300
Depreciation expense [100,000 + 35,000 + 20,000]	155,000
Other expenses [440,000 + 75,000]	515,000
	2,908,300
NET INCOME AND COMPREHENSIVE INCOME	$ 411,700
Net income attributable to:	
Owners of the parent	$ 395,650
Non-controlling interest	16,050

Purchase Ltd.
Consolidated Statement of Changes in Equity—Retained Earnings Section
Year Ended December 31, 20X7

Retained earnings, December 31, 20X6 [2,321,000 + 635,000 − 600,000 − (35,000 × 0.30) − (8,000^{U} × 0.70) − (20,000 × 0.70)]	$2,325,900
Net income	395,650
Dividends declared [135,000 + 20,000 − 20,000]	(135,000)
Retained earnings, December 31, 20X7	$2,586,550

Ltd's. adjusted income, while $395,650 is allocated to Purchase Ltd.'s owners, which includes its share of the adjusted income of Target Ltd.

- *Opening retained earnings.* The 20X7 opening retained earnings is, obviously, the same as the year-end 20X6 retained earnings. The sum of the carrying balances is reduced by (1) Target Ltd.'s date-of-acquisition retained earnings; (2) NCI's share of Target Ltd.'s unadjusted earnings since acquisition; (3) Purchase Ltd.'s share of unrealized upstream profits; and (4) pre-20X7 amortization of FVI. Note that we have used the same information here as we will in the double-check step later to calculate the retained earnings balances; it's just arranged differently here.
- *Dividends declared.* Target Ltd.'s declared dividends of $20,000 are eliminated. This reduction is matched by the elimination of the $14,000 dividend income of Purchase Ltd. and the $6,000 reduction that we will make to the NCI balance on the SFP.

Statement of Financial Position The consolidated SFP is shown in Exhibit 5-10. Adjustments are as follows:

- *Note receivable.* The intercompany note receivable of $500,000 is eliminated.

- *Inventory*. The unrealized profits from both the upstream and downstream sales are eliminated: $4,500^{U} and $1,800$_{D}$.
- *Land*. We add the FVI for land, and then subtract the $150,000^{U} unrealized gain on the intercompany sale.
- *Buildings and equipment*. The balance is increased by $50,000, to reflect fair value.
- *Accumulated depreciation*. Target Ltd.'s date-of-acquisition accumulated depreciation of $150,000 is eliminated; two years' worth of FVI amortization of $20,000 per year is added.
- *Investments*. Purchase Ltd.'s $840,000 investment in Target Ltd. is eliminated.
- *Note payable*. The intercompany balance of $500,000 is eliminated.
- *Common shares*. Only Purchase Ltd.'s shares are included.
- *Retained earnings*. We start with the carrying balances of the two companies, and then:
  1. subtract Target Ltd.'s date-of-acquisition retained earnings;
  2. subtract the NCI's share of the change in retained earnings since the date of acquisition: ($835,000 − $600,000) × 30% = $70,500;
  3. subtract Purchase Ltd.'s 70% share of upstream unrealized profits in land and in ending inventory;
  4. subtract 100% of unrealized downstream profits;
  5. subtract Purchase Ltd.'s cumulative amount of FVI amortization since the date of acquisition (i.e., $20,000 × 70% × 2 years).
     Again, we used the same information as we will use in the double-check step later, but arranged differently, to arrive at the closing consolidated retained earnings balance.
- *Non-controlling interest*. We start with the carrying balance of NCI, and then:
  1. add the NCI's share of the adjusted change in the retained earnings of Target Ltd. in the prior year of 20X6 of $2,100;
  2. add the NCI's share of the adjusted income of Target Ltd. in the current year of $16,050;
  3. subtract the NCI's share of the dividends declared by Target Ltd. of $6,000.

Check The NCI and retained earnings balances calculated below provide independent checks of the ending NCI and ending consolidated retained earnings. These will be useful checks of the accuracy of our work.

NCI Balance at the End of 20X7

Balance of NCI at the time of acquisition		$360,000
Add: NCI's share of the adjusted change in retained earnings in prior years		
Retained earnings balance of Target Ltd. at the end of 20X7	$835,000	
Retained earnings balance of Target Ltd. at the time of acquisition	600,000	
Change in carrying value of Target Ltd. since acquisition	235,000	
Less:		
Amortization of fair-value increment	(40,000)	
Unrealized profit on upstream sale of inventory in 20X7	(4,500)	
Unrealized gain on sale of land in 20X7	(150,000)	
Adjusted change in retained earnings of Target Ltd. since acquisition	40,500	
NCI's share @ 30%		12,150
Ending balance of NCI on December 31, 20X7		$372,150

Consolidated Retained Earnings Balance at the End of 20X7

20X7 separate-entity ending retained earnings balance of Purchase Ltd.		$2,560,000
Less unrealized profit on downstream sale of inventory		(1,800)
Adjusted separate-entity retained earnings balance of Purchase		2,558,200
Add: Purchase Ltd.'s share of the adjusted change in retained earnings since acquisition		
Adjusted change in retained earnings of Target Ltd. since acquisition (as calculated in the section just above)	$40,500	
Purchase Ltd.'s share @ 70%		28,350
20X7 ending consolidated retained earnings balance of Purchase Ltd.		$2,586,550

EXHIBIT 5-10

Purchase Ltd. Consolidated Statement of Financial Position (Direct Method)

Statement of Financial Position
December 31, 20X7

ASSETS	
Current Assets:	
Cash [475,000 + 70,000]	$ 545,000
Accounts receivable [1,900,000 + 275,000]	2,175,000
Note receivable [0 + 500,000 − **500,000**]	—
Inventory [300,000 + 60,000 − **4,500^U** − **1,800$_D$**]	353,700
	3,073,700
Property, Plant, and Equipment:	
Land [1,450,000 + 0 + **100,000** − **150,000^U**]	1,400,000
Buildings and equipment [3,800,000 + 500,000 + **50,000**]	4,350,000
Accumulated depreciation [1,400,000 + 220,000 − **150,000** + **20,000** + **20,000**]	(1,510,000)
	4,240,000
Other Assets:	
Investments [840,000 + 0 − **840,000**]	—
Goodwill	100,000
TOTAL ASSETS	$7,413,700
LIABILITIES AND SHAREHOLDERS' EQUITY	
Current Liabilities:	
Accounts payable [515,000 + 150,000]	$ 665,000
Note payable [500,000 + 0 − **500,000**]	—
Long-term liability: notes payable [350,000 + 0]	350,000
	1,015,000
Shareholders' Equity:	
Common shares **[Purchase Ltd. shares only]**	3,440,000
Retained earnings [2,560,000 + 835,000 − **600,000** − **(235,000 × 0.30)** − **(150,000^U × 0.70)** − **(4,500^U × 0.70)** − **1,800$_D$** − **(20,000 × 0.70 × 2)**]	2,586,550
	6,026,550
NCI **[360,000 + 2,100 + 16,050 − 6,000]**	372,150
TOTAL SHAREHOLDERS' EQUITY	6,398,700
Total liabilities and shareholders' equity	$7,413,700

Notice that there is one new adjustment required for calculating the adjusted separate-entity retained earnings of Purchase Ltd—the adjustment relating to the unrealized profit on the downstream sale of inventory. As we pointed out earlier, this profit is unrealized in the hands of Purchase Ltd., and therefore should be fully attributed to Purchase Ltd.'s shareholders.

The remaining adjustment of $28,350 required to obtain the ending consolidated retained earnings has a relatively simple explanation. We already know that the adjusted change in the retained earnings of Target Ltd. to December 31, 20X7, is $40,500. Therefore, Purchase Ltd.'s share of that amount is 70% or $28,350. Consequently, we also do not need to make an eliminating adjustment for the $14,000 dividend income already recognized by Purchase Ltd. in 20X7. The consolidated retained earnings balance of Purchase Ltd. at the end of 20X7 is therefore $2,586,550.

CONCEPT CHECK 5-4

Companion Website

1. How do the adjustments relating to prior periods differ when a subsidiary is non-wholly owned compared to similar adjustments when a subsidiary is wholly owned?
2. What is the rationale for reporting the NCI as part of equity on the SFP?

OTHER ISSUES

Consolidated Statements under the Parent-Company Extension Method

In our illustration, under the entity method the NCI was allocated its share of $30,000 of the goodwill of $100,000 based on the $70,000 paid by Purchase Ltd. for its share of the goodwill. However, an acquiring company may be willing to pay a bonus to gain control, and it may be *control* of the assets that gives rise to goodwill. That control gives rise to goodwill is shown by the fact that many takeover bids propose a high price, but offer to buy only enough of the outstanding shares (e.g., 51%) to gain control.

Therefore, when control of assets is what gives rise to goodwill, it may not be appropriate to attribute goodwill to the NCI. Even otherwise, the full value of the goodwill of Target Ltd. and the NCI's share of goodwill may not bear a linear relationship to the price paid by the parent for its share of goodwill. Therefore, in such a circumstance, given the uncertainty surrounding the value of the NCI's share of the goodwill, it may be prudent to include only the parent's portion of the goodwill in the consolidated SFP and not the entire 100% value of the goodwill. The parent-company extension method below follows this approach.

Parent-Company Extension Method The parent-company extension method is identical to the entity method except that only the goodwill actually purchased by the parent is shown on the consolidated SFP—no goodwill is assigned to the NCI. Therefore, in our illustration, under the parent-company extension method, at the time of acquisition (1) the amount shown for goodwill will be $70,000; and (2) the NCI will be valued at its share of the fair value of the net identifiable assets, i.e., at $330,000 (30% of $1,100,000).

Since under the parent-company extension method the goodwill on the consolidated SFP represents only the parent's share of goodwill, it naturally follows that any loss related to the impairment of such goodwill should be attributed solely to the parent. The NCI should not share in such impairment losses. Of course, the amortization expenses relating to the NCI's share of fair-value increments should continue to be charged against the NCI on the consolidated SFP. In our illustration, there was no impairment in the value of the goodwill in either 20X6 or 20X7. Therefore, for our illustration, the only difference to the consolidated financial statements under the parent-company extension method at all three points in time—at the time of acquisition, one year, and two years after acquisition—will be: (1) goodwill at $70,000 instead of at $100,000, and (2) an NCI balance lower by $30,000.

Bargain Purchase

The acquisition method requires the acquiree to be valued at its full fair value on the date of its acquisition. When there is a bargain purchase, the purchase consideration paid by the parent for its share of the acquiree will be less than the fair value of its share. Therefore, in such a case, the full fair value of the acquiree cannot be determined by simply grossing up the purchase price paid by the parent. Consequently, the Measure step in our MEAR steps to consolidation is inappropriate when there is a bargain purchase. We will now provide an alternative calculation for the Measure step where there is a bargain purchase.

Let us alter our illustration by assuming that Purchase Ltd. paid only $759,500 for its 70% share of Target Ltd. in a bargain purchase. However, Purchase Ltd.'s share of the fair value of the net identifiable assets of Target Ltd. is $1,100,000 × 70% = $770,000. Therefore, the gain on the bargain purchase is $10,500 as calculated below:

Parent Ltd.'s share of fair value of net identifiable assets [$1,100,000 × 70%]	$770,000
Purchase price	759,500
Gain on bargain purchase allocated fully to Parent Ltd.	$ 10,500

This gain on the bargain purchase belongs fully to Parent Ltd. and is recognized as a gain in the consolidated SCI issued by Parent Ltd. in the year of acquisition. Since we cannot assume that the NCI has or will also be capable of buying its share at a bargain, we cannot attribute a similar gain to the NCI. The correct value of NCI is calculated by ignoring the bargain purchase and is therefore 30% of $1,100,000, i.e., $330,000.[2]

2. You will notice that the calculated value of $330,000 of NCI is identical to its value under the parent-company extension method. This is no coincidence but due to the fact that in both cases NCI's value depends only on the fair value of the net identifiable assets of Target Ltd. Specifically, in the case of a bargain purchase the NCI is calculated ignoring any gain on such bargain purchase, while in the case of the parent-company extension method it is calculated ignoring the value of goodwill.

EXHIBIT 5-11

Allocation of Fair-Value Increment

70% Bargain Purchase of Target Ltd., December 31, 20X5

100% fair value of Target Ltd.					$1,100,000
Less carrying value of Target's net identifiable assets					(800,000)
= Fair-Value Increment, allocated below					300,000
	Carrying value (a)	Fair value (b)	Fair-value increment (c) = (b) − (a)	FVI allocated	
Cash	$ 50,000	$ 50,000	—		
Accounts receivable	150,000	150,000	—		
Inventory	50,000	50,000	—		
Land	300,000	400,000	$100,000	$100,000	
Buildings and equipment	500,000	550,000	50,000	50,000	
Accumulated depreciation	(150,000)	—	150,000	150,000	
Accounts payable	(100,000)	(100,000)	—		
Total fair-value increment					(300,000)
Net asset carrying value	$800,000				
Fair value of assets acquired		$1,100,000			
Balance of FVI					$ —

Since goodwill is absent, the fair value of 100% of Target Ltd. is equal to the full value of its net identifiable assets of $1,100,000. Therefore, the fair-value increment is $300,000, which is fully allocated to the various identifiable assets and liabilities in the usual manner as demonstrated in Exhibit 5-11.

The remaining MEAR steps to consolidation remain unchanged, and thus can be followed while consolidating a subsidiary purchased in a bargain purchase.

Application of Proprietary Theory When Using Equity Method to Report Associates and Joint Ventures

If Target Ltd. were an associate or joint venture instead of being a subsidiary of Purchase Ltd., IFRS would require us to use the proprietary theory while reporting Purchase Ltd.'s share of Target Ltd.'s adjusted net income under the equity method. The altered calculation required under the proprietary theory is provided below:

Details	Amount
Net income of Target Ltd. for 20X7 (from separate-entity financial statement)	$220,000
Add:	
Realized profit on upstream sale of inventory in previous year	8,000
Less:	
Unrealized profit on upstream sale of inventory in the current year	(4,500)
Unrealized profit on downstream sale of inventory in the current year	**(1,800)**
Unrealized gain on sale of land by Target Ltd. to Purchase Ltd.	(150,000)
Amortization of FVI during the year	(20,000)
Adjusted net income of Target Ltd. for 20X7	$ 51,700
Purchase's share @ 70%	$ 36,190

The only difference now, highlighted in bold above, is that while calculating Purchase Ltd.'s 70% share of Target Ltd.'s adjusted income, we also include the $\$1,800_D$ unrealized gain on the downstream sale. Therefore, Purchase Ltd.'s share is reduced by only its 70% share and not the full amount of the unrealized gain of $\$1,800_D$ as done previously in our main example, when Target was assumed to be a subsidiary. Thus, in our example, for the same set of facts, Purchase Ltd. will recognize an extra $540 income if Target is its associate or joint venture instead of being its subsidiary.

CONCEPT CHECK 5-5

Companion Website

1. How is the value of the NCI on the SFP different under the parent-company extension method as compared to its value under the entity method?
2. Why is the calculation of the gain on a bargain purchase different from the calculation of goodwill in the absence of a bargain purchase?
3. How is the treatment of unrealized gains and losses different under the proprietary theory compared to under the entity theory?

Reality Check 5-2 provides findings from academic studies on the prevalence and implications of the existence of differences between ownership and control.

THE NEXT STEPS

Chapters 4 and 5 have worked methodically through the consolidation process at three points in time: the date of acquisition, one year after acquisition, and two years after acquisition. Chapter 4 assumed that the parent owned 100% of the subsidiary shares. Chapter 5 relaxed that assumption and illustrated consolidation when the subsidiary is *not* wholly owned. Through the course of these two chapters, most of the major aspects of consolidation have been illustrated.

The next chapter covers the one remaining major aspect of consolidations—intercompany sale of depreciable or amortizable assets. In fact, it is quite possible that an item that is an inventory item to the seller is a depreciable asset to the buyer. Don't worry, however; we will not be discussing this issue in the text! Chapter 6 also presents a general set of steps to approach the consolidation process that can be used at any point in time, freeing us from the methodical process of year-by-year consolidations. We also will take a third and final look at the equity basis of reporting. We'll bet you can hardly wait!

REALITY CHECK 5-2

Ownership Versus Control

The common perception about corporations is that their ownership is widely held. However, research has found that this holds true only for large firms in the richest common-law countries.[a] In their analysis of the shareholding pattern of the largest corporations in 23 wealthy countries, the authors find that outside of the United States, especially in countries with poor shareholder protection, even the largest firms have controlling shareholders; sometimes it is the state but often it is the family of the founder. The authors find that the controlling shareholders typically have power over the firm significantly in excess of their ownership rights (excess control), typically through the use of pyramids (a chain of companies) and participation in management.

Another study found that even in developed countries there is diversion of corporate resources from the corporation and non-controlling shareholders to the controlling shareholders (known as tunnelling).[b] They also find that most of the tunnelling is legal, using mechanisms such as expropriation of corporate opportunities, favourable transfer pricing, transferring assets at non-market prices, and loans at non-market rates. They also find in their analysis of law cases that civil-law countries, compared to common-law countries, are less protective of non-controlling shareholders.

Finally, a third study analysed the ultimate shareholding pattern of a large sample of publicly traded firms in Canada and found that small investors in publicly traded firms are vulnerable to the expropriation of the resources of those firms because of excess control.[c] This problem is especially severe in Quebec, which follows civil law, as compared to the rest of Canada, which follows common law.

a. R. La Porta, F. Lopez-de-Silanes, and A. Shleifer. "Corporate ownership around the world." *The Journal of Finance* 54: 2 (April 1999), p. 471.
b. S. Johnson, R. La Porta, F. Lopez-de-Silanes, and A. Shleifer. "Tunneling." *The American Economic Review* 90:2 (May 2000), p. 22.
c. N. Attig, "Excess control and the risk of corporate expropriation: Canadian evidence." *Canadian Journal of Administrative Sciences* 24: 2 (June 2007), p. 94.

Relevant Standards

IASB

Standards

IAS 27 Consolidated and Separate Financial Statements
IAS 28 Investments in Associates
IAS 31 Interests in Joint Ventures
IFRS 3 Business Combinations

IASB Exposure Draft

ED 10 Consolidated Financial Statements

Summary of Key Points

1. When a parent company purchases control of a subsidiary but acquires less than 100% of the subsidiary's shares, the portion not owned by the parent is called the "non-controlling interest."
2. Different conceptual alternatives exist for accounting for the NCI in the consolidated financial statements of the parent. These alternatives flow from two major competing theories of consolidation, which are at either end of a continuum— the proprietary theory and the entity theory.
3. Based on the degree to which each of these two theories of consolidation—the proprietary theory and the entity theory—are applied, we have four methods of consolidating a non-wholly owned subsidiary—proportionate method, parent-company method, parent-company extension method, and entity method.
4. IFRS require either the *entity* or the *parent-company extension* method to be used on a transaction-by-transaction basis for consolidating non-wholly owned subsidiaries. Under the entity method the subsidiary's assets and liabilities are consolidated with those of the parent at 100% of their fair values. In contrast, under the parent-company extension method the subsidiary's assets and liabilities, *excluding the NCI's share of goodwill*, are consolidated with those of the parent at 100% of their fair values. Under both methods, the parent's assets and liabilities are consolidated at their carrying value on the parent's separate-entity SFP.
5. IFRS require the application of the proprietary theory when reporting investments in an associate or joint venture under the equity method. Consequently, unrealized gains or losses on inter-company transactions between an entity and its associates or joint ventures are eliminated *only* to the extent of the entity's ownership share in those associates/joint ventures.
6. All of the subsidiary's assets and liabilities are consolidated on the parent's SFP, but part of those net assets represents the equity of the non-controlling interest. On the parent's SFP, there must be an amount shown for the NCI's share of the subsidiary's net assets. IFRS require this amount to be shown under the equity section, separately from the parent's shareholders' equity.
7. All of the subsidiary's revenues and expenses are included in the parent's SCI, but part of the subsidiary's earnings accrues to the NCI. Therefore, the parent must allocate such share to the NCI on the consolidated SCI.
8. All unrealized gains relating to transactions between the parent and the subsidiary have to be eliminated and the NCI's share of such gains should be allocated to it.

Companion Website

Visit the text's website at www.pearsoned.ca/beechy for practice quizzes, additional problems, Excel® templates, answers to Concept Check questions, and important IFRS updates.

EXHIBIT 5-12

Regina Ltd.

Statement of Financial Position
December 31, 20X4

Current Assets:	
Cash	$ 50,000
Accounts and other receivables	70,000
Inventory	80,000
	200,000
Capital Assets:	
Building	260,000
Accumulated depreciation	(40,000)
Equipment	175,000
Accumulated depreciation	(70,000)
	325,000
TOTAL ASSETS	$525,000
Liabilities:	
Current accounts payable and accrued liabilities	$ 80,000
Shareholders' Equity:	
Common shares	220,000
Retained earnings	225,000
	445,000
TOTAL LIABILITIES AND SHAREHOLDERS' EQUITY	$525,000

Self-Study Problem 5-1

On January 10, 20X5, Regina Ltd. acquired 60% of the shares of Dakota Ltd. by issuing common shares valued at $150,000. Prior to the acquisition of Dakota, Regina's SFP appeared as shown in Exhibit 5-12. The SFP of Dakota Ltd. at the date of acquisition is shown in Exhibit 5-13.

Required

Prepare a consolidated SFP for Regina Ltd., as it would appear immediately following the acquisition of Dakota.

Self-Study Problem 5-2

During 20X5, the following transactions occurred between Regina Ltd. and Dakota Ltd. (see SSP 5-1):

a) Regina lent $50,000 at 10% interest to Dakota Ltd. on July 1, 20X5, for one year. The interest was unpaid at December 31, 20X5.

EXHIBIT 5-13

Dakota Ltd.

Statement of Financial Position
January 10, 20X5

	Carrying value	Fair value
Current Assets:		
Cash	$ 10,000	$10,000
Accounts and other receivables	20,000	20,000
Inventory	30,000	30,000
	60,000	
Capital Assets:		
Land	45,000	80,000
Building	150,000	130,000
Accumulated depreciation	(50,000)	
Equipment	130,000	10,000
Accumulated depreciation	(80,000)	
	195,000	
TOTAL ASSETS	$255,000	
Liabilities:		
Current accounts payable	$ 40,000	40,000
Long-term debenture payable	50,000	50,000
	90,000	
Shareholders' Equity:		
Common shares	100,000	
Retained earnings	65,000	
	165,000	
TOTAL LIABILITIES AND SHAREHOLDERS' EQUITY	$255,000	

b) During 20X5, Regina purchased inventory from Dakota at a cost of $400,000; $100,000 of that amount was still in Regina's inventory at the end of 20X5. [Hint: look at Dakota's SCI to compute Dakota's gross profit percentage.]
c) During 20X5, Dakota purchased inventory of $200,000 from Regina; $40,000 of that amount was still in Dakota's inventory at the end of 20X5.

Other Information

d) Dakota's building and equipment were estimated to have remaining useful lives from January 10, 20X5, of 10 and 5 years, respectively. Straight-line depreciation is being used.
e) There has been no impairment of goodwill.
f) No fixed assets were sold or written off during 20X5.

The December 31, 20X5, separate-entity financial statements for both companies are shown in Exhibit 5-14.

EXHIBIT 5-14

Regina Ltd. and Dakota Ltd.

Statements of Financial Position
December 31, 20X5

	Regina Ltd.	Dakota Ltd.
Current Assets:		
Cash	$ 28,000	$ 10,000
Accounts and other receivables	110,000	30,000
Inventories	160,000	60,000
	298,000	100,000
Capital Assets:		
Land	—	135,000
Buildings	300,000	150,000
Accumulated depreciation	(45,000)	(60,000)
Equipment	200,000	130,000
Accumulated depreciation	(80,000)	(90,000)
	375,000	265,000
Other Assets:		
Investment in Dakota Ltd. (at cost)	150,000	—
TOTAL ASSETS	$823,000	$365,000
Liabilities:		
Current accounts payable and accrued liabilities	$ 40,000	$ 80,000
Long-term liabilities	65,000	50,000
	105,000	130,000
Shareholders' Equity:		
Common shares	370,000	100,000
Retained earnings	348,000	135,000
	718,000	235,000
TOTAL LIABILITIES AND SHAREHOLDERS' EQUITY	$823,000	$365,000

Statements of Comprehensive Income
Year Ended December 31, 20X5

	Regina Ltd.	Dakota Ltd.
Sales	$2,000,000	$1,000,000
Dividend income	24,000	—
Other income	7,000	—
	2,031,000	1,000,000
Cost of sales	1,000,000	600,000
Other operating expenses	886,000	280,000
Interest expense	2,000	10,000
	1,888,000	890,000
NET INCOME AND COMPREHENSIVE INCOME	$ 143,000	$ 110,000

Statements of Changes in Equity—Retained Earnings Section
Year Ended December 31, 20X5

	Regina Ltd.	Dakota Ltd.
Retained earnings, December 31, 20X4	$225,000	$ 65,000
Net income	143,000	110,000
Dividends declared	(20,000)	(40,000)
Retained earnings, December 31, 20X5	$348,000	$135,000

Required

Prepare the consolidated statement of income and retained earnings and the consolidated SFP for Regina Ltd. for the year ended December 31, 20X5.

Self-Study Problem 5-3

Regina Ltd. owns 60% of the common shares of Dakota Ltd., acquired on January 10, 20X5. The details of the purchase are given in SSP 5-1, and the trial balances for December 31, 20X5, and selected transactions for 20X5 are shown in SSP 5-2. The financial statements of both companies (unconsolidated) at December 31, 20X6, are shown in Exhibit 5-15.

Additional Information

1. At the beginning of 20X6, unrealized upstream profits in inventory amounted to $40,000 held in Regina's inventory (i.e., from upstream sales) and $20,000 in Dakota's inventory (i.e., downstream).
2. During 20X6, Dakota sold inventory to Regina for $160,000 at the normal gross margin. One-half of that amount is still in Regina's inventory at year-end.
3. Late in 20X6, Regina sold inventory to Dakota at a special price of $40,000. All of these goods are still in Dakota's inventory on December 31, 20X6. The cost to Regina of the goods sold to Dakota was $20,000, a 50% gross margin on the selling price.
4. The one-year, $50,000 loan that Regina extended to Dakota on July 1, 20X5, was extended for two more years (to July 1, 20X8). Simple interest (at 10%) has been accrued by both companies, but no interest will be paid until the principal is repaid.

Required

Calculate the following amounts for the year ended December 31, 20X6:

1. NCI in earnings (i.e., on Regina's consolidated SCI).
2. NCI (on Regina's consolidated SFP), December 31, 20X6.
3. Regina's year-end consolidated retained earnings.

Review Questions

5-1 Define the following terms:

a) NCI

b) Minority interest

EXHIBIT 5-15

Regina Ltd. and Dakota Ltd.

Statements of Financial Position
December 31, 20X6

	Regina Ltd.	Dakota Ltd.
Current Assets:		
Cash	$ 63,800	$ 52,500
Accounts and other receivables	120,000	77,000
Inventories	130,000	55,000
	313,800	184,500
Capital Assets:		
Land	—	135,000
Buildings	380,000	150,000
Accumulated depreciation	(56,200)	(70,000)
Equipment	230,000	170,000
Accumulated depreciation	(68,000)	(47,000)
	485,800	338,000
Other Assets:		
Investment in Dakota Ltd. (at cost)	150,000	—
TOTAL ASSETS	$949,600	$522,500
Liabilities:		
Current accounts payable and accrued liabilities	$ 51,600	$ 97,500
Long-term liabilities	180,000	120,000
	231,600	217,500
Shareholders' Equity:		
Common shares	370,000	100,000
Retained earnings	348,000	205,000
	718,000	305,000
TOTAL LIABILITIES AND SHAREHOLDERS' EQUITY	$949,600	$522,500

Statements of Comprehensive Income
Year Ended December 31, 20X6

	Regina Ltd.	Dakota Ltd.
Sales	$2,200,000	$1,100,000
Dividend income	36,000	—
Gain on sale of equipment	10,000	—
Other income	12,000	—
	2,258,000	1,100,000
Cost of sales	1,300,000	660,000
Other operating expenses	864,000	292,000
Interest expense	20,000	18,000
	2,184,000	970,000
NET INCOME AND COMPREHENSIVE INCOME	$ 74,000	$ 130,000

Statements of Changes in Equity—Retained Earnings Section
Year Ended December 31, 20X6

	Regina Ltd.	Dakota Ltd.
Retained earnings, December 31, 20X5	$ 348,000	$ 135,000
Net income	74,000	130,000
Dividends declared	(74,000)	(60,000)
Retained earnings, December 31, 20X6	$ 348,000	$ 205,000

c) Proportionate consolidation

d) Parent-company method

e) Parent-company extension method

f) Entity method

5-2 Why do some corporations prefer to control their subsidiaries with less than full ownership?

5-3 How can the inclusion of 100% of a subsidiary's assets on the consolidated SFP be justified when the parent owns less than 100% of the subsidiary's shares?

5-4 When all of a non-wholly owned subsidiary's revenues and expenses are consolidated, what recognition is given to the fact that the parent's share of the subsidiary's earnings is less than 100%?

5-5 Under the entity approach of reporting non-controlling interest, what value is assigned to goodwill?

5-6 How does the parent-company extension method modify the entity approach? What is the rationale for this modification?

5-7 Explain why a subsidiary's assets and liabilities are consolidated using two different valuations (fair value and carrying value) under the parent-company method.

5-8 At the date of acquisition, how is the amount of non-controlling interest measured under the entity method and the parent-company extension method, respectively?

5-9 One year after the date of acquisition, how is the amount of non-controlling interest on the SFP measured under the entity method and the parent-company extension method, respectively?

5-10 How do unrealized profits on upstream sales affect the non-controlling interest's share of a subsidiary's earnings?

5-11 How do unrealized profits on downstream sales affect the non-controlling interest's share of a subsidiary's earnings?

5-12 How are non-controlling shareholders likely to react to the reduction of their share of the subsidiary's earnings as a result of unrealized profits?

5-13 What is the impact on the non-controlling interest of unrealized profits in *beginning* inventories?

5-14 Why are a non-wholly owned subsidiary's dividend payments completely eliminated even though the parent does not receive all of the dividends?

5-15 Under the parent-company and parent-company extension methods, all of a subsidiary's assets and liabilities are consolidated regardless of the ownership percentage of the parent. Nevertheless, the ownership percentage may affect the amount of the reported (consolidated) assets. Explain.

CASES

CASE 5-1 MCINTOSH INVESTMENTS LTD.

McIntosh Investments Ltd. (MIL) is a diversified public company. Loraine McIntosh, the president, owns 40% of the common shares of MIL. Another 30% are owned jointly by Loraine's brothers, Blair and Bill. The 70% ownership by Loraine and her brothers gives her control of the company. The remaining 30% of the shares are widely distributed.

On April 1, 20X6, the first day of MIL's fiscal year, Loraine succeeded in negotiating the acquisition by MIL of 30% of the outstanding common shares of Efrim Auto Parts, Inc. (EAPI). EAPI was an important supplier of parts to Candide Cars Corporation (CCC), a maker of specialty automobiles ("the best of all possible cars"), which was 40% owned by MIL. Loraine was particularly pleased at being able to arrange the purchase of the shares of EAPI because she was certain that great efficiency could be obtained by having the operations of EAPI and CCC more closely coordinated.

The EAPI shares were purchased from a descendant of the founder of EAPI, Jeffrey Efrim. The shares were purchased for a consideration of $600,000 cash and the issuance of 10,000 shares of MIL common stock. MIL shares were currently being traded on the TSX at $40 per share. Exhibit A presents the SFP of EAPI as of March 31, 20X6, the end of EAPI's fiscal year.

During the following year, Loraine and her fellow managers took an active interest in the affairs of both CCC and EAPI. CCC became EAPI's major customer, and purchased $2,000,000 of parts from EAPI during fiscal 20X7. At the end of fiscal 20X7, CCC had

EXHIBIT A

EAPI Statement of Financial Position

Statement of Financial Position
March 31, 20X6

	Carrying value	Fair value
Cash	$ 200,000	$ 200,000
Accounts receivable	300,000	300,000
Inventories	400,000	440,000
Equipment (net)	2,100,000	2,400,000
Long-term investment (cost)	300,000	360,000
	$3,300,000	
Accounts payable and accrued liabilities	600,000	500,000
Debentures outstanding	700,000	600,000
Common shares (60,000 shares)	500,000	—
Retained earnings	1,500,000	—
	$3,300,000	

parts in inventory that were purchased from EAPI at a cost (to CCC) of $300,000, as compared to only $100,000 of such parts in inventory a year earlier. The attention of MIL management had increased EAPI's efficiency so that average gross profit on sales rose to 35% in fiscal 20X7. EAPI's net income after tax in fiscal 20X7 reached a record high of $300,000 after tax, enabling EAPI to declare a dividend of $1.50 per common share on March 31, 20X7.

Required

Determine what impact MIL's investment in EAPI shares and EAPI's fiscal 20X7 activities will have on the financial statements of MIL. Where alternatives are possible, state them and briefly explain the alternatives you chose. State any assumptions that you find it necessary to make.

CASE 5-2 SIMPSON LTD.

Simpson Ltd. is a private Ontario corporation controlled by Ted Simpson. The company owns a series of chocolate chip cookie stores throughout Ontario, and also has a wholly owned Quebec subsidiary that operates stores in Montreal and Quebec City. Because of its lack of stores in Western Canada and its managers' lack of knowledge about that part of the country, Simpson Ltd. has just acquired 70% of the outstanding class A voting shares of Ong Inc. for $6,000,000 cash. Ong Inc. is another cookie store chain that is headquartered in Vancouver and has stores throughout Vancouver and Victoria, as well as in Edmonton, Saskatoon, and Winnipeg.

Ted expects that the acquisition will greatly help the Simpson Ltd. "bottom line," which in turn will help Simpson Ltd. to obtain expanded debt financing because of the greater net income and cash flow. The management of Ong Inc. will not change as a result of the purchase; the former sole owner, John Ong, retains the remaining 30% of the Ong Inc. shares and has agreed to continue as CEO of Ong Inc. for at least five years after the change in control. The president and chief operating officer, Travis Hubner, will also stay on, so there is no reason that the acquired company should not continue to be highly profitable. The condensed SFP of Ong Inc. at the date of acquisition is shown in Exhibit B.

The acquisition was financed mainly by debt; $4,500,000 was borrowed by Simpson Ltd. from the Western Bank of British Columbia, secured by the assets of both Simpson Ltd. and Ong Inc. The bank has requested audited financial statements of both companies on an annual basis, supplemented by unaudited quarterly statements.

Ong Inc. owns the buildings in which some of its stores are located, but most are leased. None of the land is owned. The buildings are being depreciated over 30 years. John has obtained two separate appraisals of the owned buildings; one appraisal firm has placed the aggregate current value at $9,500,000, while the second firm arrived at a value of $8,400,000. Ong Inc. owns all of the equipment in its stores; the equipment is being depreciated over 10 years, and is, on average, 40% depreciated. It would cost $3,300,000 to replace the existing equipment with new equipment of similar capacity. Inventories are generally worth their carrying values, except that the replacement cost of the stock of

EXHIBIT B

Ong Inc. Condensed Statement of Financial Position

Condensed Statement of Financial Position
May 8, 20X5

Assets		
Cash		$ 200,000
Accounts receivable		100,000
Inventories—raw materials and supplies		1,200,000
Buildings	$7,000,000	
Accumulated depreciation	(1,400,000)	5,600,000
Equipment	3,000,000	
Accumulated depreciation	(1,200,000)	1,800,000
TOTAL ASSETS		$8,900,000
LIABILITIES AND SHAREHOLDERS' EQUITY		
Liabilities:		
Accounts payable	$ 350,000	
Accrued expenses	50,000	
Total current liabilities		$ 400,000
Bank loan payable, due May 3, 20X7		2,700,000
Deferred income taxes		1,100,000
Total liabilities		4,200,000
Shareholders' Equity:		
Common shares—Class A voting	1,000,000	
Retained earnings	3,700,000	4,700,000
TOTAL LIABILITIES AND SHARE EQUITY		$8,900,000

imported Belgian chocolate in the Vancouver warehouse is $20,000 less than carrying value because of the strengthening Canadian dollar. On the other hand, the accounts payable shown in Exhibit B include an unrealized gain of $10,000 because much of the liability is denominated in Belgian francs.

Required

Determine, on a line-by-line basis, the impact on Simpson Ltd.'s consolidated assets and liabilities as a result of the acquisition, in accordance with Ted Simpson's objectives in acquiring Ong. Where alternative values could be used, explain the reasons for your selection.

[ICAO]

CASE 5-3 PROCTOR INDUSTRIES

You, CA, are the senior in charge of an audit of Proctor Industries (PI), a public company in the business of selling plumbing parts wholesale. It is now November 3, 20X5—five weeks after PI's year-end of September 30, 20X5, and one week before your firm has been asked to discuss the financial statements for PI, including any significant accounting issues, with PI's audit committee.

PI's unconsolidated annual sales approximate $36 million. It operates through six regional branches with approximately equal sales volumes at each branch.

PI has a 60% interest in Minor Inc., a company located in the United Kingdom. Minor Inc. also has a September 30 year-end and is audited by a firm of chartered accountants in the United Kingdom.

You are at the client's premises reviewing the year-end working papers for Proctor Industries, and you note the following items:

1. PI's unconsolidated net income before income taxes is normally about $2 million.
2. The allowance for doubtful accounts in PI is $200,000. Based on the work performed in this section of the audit, the audit assistant concluded that the allowance should be at least $250,000, and could be as high as $350,000.
3. You have contacted the auditors for Minor Inc. (MI) to obtain its financial statements. However, they are unable to provide you with the audited financial statements since the president of MI refused to sign the management representation letter. He disagrees with the revenue recognition policy insisted on by the auditors of MI and intends to obtain opinions from other audit firms on this issue. The financial statements, under the policy supported by the auditors, show a net loss of $320,000 for the year. MI's current policy for revenue recognition is when items are produced, based on the support that there is a ready market for MI's supplies, which are currently in short supply. PI's revenue recognition policy is when goods are shipped to the customer.
4. There is a new item on PI's SFP called "Investments." The working papers indicate that this represents a cash payment in June 20X5 of $100,000 for all the common shares of Chemicals Inc. (CI). This company has an August 31 year-end. Although CI has previously never been audited, PI requested, and you have completed, an audit of CI for its August 31, 20X5 year-end. The audited financial statements for CI appear in Exhibit C. CI manufactures household cleaning products. The equipment used in the manufacturing process is not complex and is inexpensive to replace. CI has earned large profits in the past, mainly from government contracts. This year, the financial statements show an after-tax profit of $100,000.
5. An extract of the agreement to purchase CI states that if the company earns more than $1 million per year in any of the next five years, the vendor may buy back the common shares for a price to be determined.
6. One of the legal letters for PI was returned with the following comment:

   Chemicals Inc. may be liable for damages arising from the alleged dumping of hazardous chemicals from its Bedford plant into the nearby Black River. As of the current date, a statement of claim has been filed. CI denies these allegations.

The partner has asked you to prepare a memo on the above items for his use in discussions with the audit committee.

Required

Prepare the memo requested by the partner.

EXHIBIT C

Chemicals Inc. Extracts from Audited Statement of Financial Position

Extracts from Audited Statement of Financial Position
As at August 31, 20X5

Assets	
Accounts receivable	$ 900,000
Prepaid expenses	100,000
Inventory	400,000
Capital assets, net	400,000
	$1,800,000
Liabilities and Shareholders' Equity	
Accounts payable	$ 500,000
Common shares (100 issued)	50,000
Retained earnings	1,250,000
	$1,800,000

[CICA]

CASE 5-4 FLORAL IMPRESSIONS LTD.

You, CA, are employed at Beaulieu & Beauregard, Chartered Accountants. On November 20, 20X5, Domenic Jones, a partner in your firm, sent you the following email:

> Our firm has been reappointed auditors of Floral Impressions Ltd. (FIL) for the year ending December 31, 20X5. I met with the president and major shareholder of FIL, Liz Holtby, last week. I have prepared some background information on FIL for you to review, including the company's October 31, 20X5, internal non-consolidated financial statements (Exhibit D). FIL is increasing the amount of business it does on the internet, and Liz would like us to provide comments on the direction in which FIL is moving. I made notes on her plans for FIL's increasing use of the internet (Exhibit E). I also met with Craig Albertson, the controller, and I made notes from that meeting (Exhibit F).
>
> Once you have reviewed the material, I would like you to draft an audit planning memo identifying the new accounting and audit issues for the 20X5 audit. I would also like the memo to address Liz's specific requests.
>
> I'd like to receive something by next week. Let me know if you have any questions.

Required

Prepare the memo requested by the partner.

Exhibit D Background Information

Floral Impressions Ltd. (FIL), a small public company listed on a Canadian stock exchange, is a wholesaler of silk plants with three warehouses located in Ontario, Alberta, and British Columbia. It imports its inventory of silk flowers and accessories from Indonesia. FIL employees arrange bouquets, trees, wreaths, and decorative floral products for sale in Canada to flower shops, grocery stores, and other retailers.

The silk plant concept was novel when FIL was incorporated in 19X4. For the first three fiscal years, sales grew at approximately 40% per year, and FIL expanded to meet the demand. However, increased competition resulted in declining sales and operating losses over the next six years. Liz inherited the shares of the company in 20X3. She had just completed a marketing course and was very excited about becoming involved in the business and applying her new skills. The fiscal year ended December 31, 20X4, brought a return to higher sales levels and a modest net income. Liz's management contract, which was negotiated in 20X4, provides for stock options to be granted to her each year based on the percentage increase of FIL's revenue from one year to the next. On October 31, 20X5, Liz was granted stock options for the first time. She received 4,500 stock options at $2.50 each, the market price at that date.

On January 15, 20X5, when shares were trading at $4 each, FIL announced an agreement with the shareholders of Rest-EZE Wreath Corporation (RWC) whereby FIL would acquire 100% of the voting shares of RWC by issuing 200,000 FIL common shares. The acquisition of RWC was completed on October 31, 20X5. The market value of FIL's shares has declined significantly since the announcement. RWC, a small private Canadian corporation, sells funeral wreaths, made with fresh flowers, on the internet. The suppliers, florists throughout Canada, advertise their wreath models on RWC's website, which is targeted at funeral homes and their customers. These clients order their flowers through RWC's website. RWC records 100% of the sales, invoices the client for the same amount, and remits 85% of the proceeds to the supplier. RWC absorbs any bad debts. RWC is in the process of installing a billing system on its website that would allow customers to pay by credit card, but is still working out some bugs. RWC's assets (mainly accounts receivable and office equipment) less the liabilities have a fair market value of $150,000, as established by an independent evaluator. RWC has never been audited and its year-end is November 30.

Floral Impressions Ltd.
Non-Consolidated Statement of Financial Position
(in thousands of dollars)

	October 31, 20X5 (unaudited)	December 31, 20X4 (audited)
Assets		
Current assets		
Accounts receivable	$2,003	$1,610
Inventory	610	420
	2,613	2,030
Property, plant, and equipment	216	239
Computer development costs	32	22
Intangibles—customer list	20	0
	$2,881	$2,291
Liabilities		
Current liabilities		
Bank indebtedness	$1,850	$1,520
Accounts payable	1,253	1,199
	3,103	2,719
Shareholders' deficiency		
Common shares (20X5: 600,000; 20X4: 400,000)	400	400
Deficit	(622)	(828)
	(222)	(428)
	$2,881	$2,291

Floral Impressions Ltd.
Non-Consolidated Statement of Consolidated Income
(in thousands of dollars)

	Ten months Ended October 31, 20X5 (unaudited)	Year Ended December 31, 20X4 (audited)
Sales	$24,950	$22,119
Cost of goods sold	20,630	18,801
Gross margin	4,320	3,318
General and administrative expenses	4,114	3,229
Income before income taxes	206	89
Income taxes	—	—
Net income	$ 206	$ 89

Exhibit E Notes from Domenic Jones' Conversation with Liz Holtby

Liz believes the acquisition of RWC provides an opportunity to expand into a less cyclical market and to sell on the internet. RWC has well established relationships with two major funeral home chains. Liz is excited about benefiting from RWC's website because the site fits perfectly with FIL's new direction and allows FIL to gain access to the internet immediately. So far, the site has not generated significant new business for FIL, but Liz is confident that, with time, sales will increase. As soon as RWC's billing system allows payments by credit card, FIL also intends to link directly into RWC's accounting system to invoice its own clients. Liz anticipates that RWC will account for about 40% of FIL's consolidated revenue this year. Liz plans to exercise her stock options and sell the shares acquired as soon as the share price reaches $9 or more.

To gain greater exposure on the internet, FIL is also developing its own website. FIL will pay for the costs of running the site by selling advertising spots on the site to home decorating companies. Liz believes she can generate $80,000 in advertising revenue over a 12-month period once the site is up and running. So far, FIL has pre-sold 10 spots for $200 each. The advertisements are to run for one month. Unfortunately, the site delays have caused some advertisers to cancel their contracts. Others are threatening to cancel their contracts unless FIL gets the site up and running within the next month. The controller has recorded the advertising revenue as sales.

FIL has two technicians working in its computer department. Most of their time is spent keeping the network up and running. Since an intranet was developed two months ago to give all employees access to the internet, the network has been bombarded with junk mail and has slowed down or crashed regularly. As a result, the two technicians have not had time to develop the website or to upgrade the firewall as planned. Liz wants the website up and running right away and has threatened to hire RWC's programmers to develop the website if FIL's technicians don't do it quickly enough.

Very recently, Liz spoke to a representative from a company offering to perform all of FIL's accounting over the internet. Now Liz's vision for FIL is to do everything on the internet. The representative says that a company will maintain, on its own website, the latest version of whatever standard accounting package FIL uses. FIl would access the site and post the transactions (accounts receivable, accounts payable, and payroll). His company would generate the accounting books and records and would generate FIL's monthly financial statements. Liz likes the plan because she could reduce both administrative staffing costs and the amount of time she spends managing the administration group. It would allow Liz to better focus her efforts on developing FIL's internet site and related sales.

Exhibit F Notes from Domenic Jones' Conversation with Craig Albertson

Craig Albertson was hired by FIL in September 20X5 as the controller. FIL's previous controller resigned in June 20X5 due to illness and the position was temporarily filled by the accounts payable clerk. Craig anticipates that he will have all year-end information ready for our audit team by March 15, 20X6.

In February 20X5, Liz outsourced FIL's payroll function to a service bureau that offered an exceptional price if FIL signed a five-year contract. The payroll consists of 50 employees. Craig has heard rumours that the service bureau is experiencing financial difficulties.

Historically, FIL's sales are highest during February and March, and August to October. Accounts receivable consist of a large number of small dollar value accounts, with the exception of five large chain store customers that account for approximately 40% of the total accounts receivable. The allowance returns typically have been 1% of fourth-quarter sales.

Management counts inventory at the end of each quarter and cost of goods sold is adjusted accordingly. At September 30, 20X5, the inventories held at each location were as follows: 55% of the total dollar value in British Columbia, 35% in Alberta, and 10% in Ontario. By year-end Craig expects inventory at all sites to be at much lower levels. While visiting the warehouse, I observed that the physical security over inventory was tight. Craig commented that FIL has never written down inventory in the past and that he estimates about 2% of the current inventory is obsolete because it is out of style.

During the year, management negotiated an operating line of credit with a new financial institution. The amount authorized is limited to 75% of accounts receivable under 90 days old and 50% of inventory, to a maximum of $2 million. The loans bear interest at prime plus 3%. Under this agreement, FIL is required to provide audited financial statements within 90 days of the fiscal year-end.

Craig did not record the investment in RWC, since the only change was in the number of common shares issued.

On October 1, 20X5, FIL purchased a customer list for $20,000 from a former competitor that was going out of business. FIL has not yet determined an amortization policy for this purchase.

Some employees and board members have questioned FIL's sudden focus on the internet when other companies seem to be moving away from it and back to traditional sales methods. Craig raised the same concern. He doesn't understand why FIL is changing direction when the new management's marketing changes produced such good results in 20X4.

[CICA, adapted]

Problems

P5-1

On December 30, 20X5, the statements of financial position of the Perk Company and the Scent Company are as follows:

	Perk Company	Scent Company
Cash	$ 7,000,000	$ 200,000
Accounts receivable	1,000,000	600,000
Inventory	1,300,000	800,000
Capital assets, net	6,700,000	3,400,000
	$16,000,000	$5,000,000
Current liabilities	$ 3,000,000	$ 200,000
Long-term liabilities	4,000,000	800,000
Common shares	5,000,000	1,000,000
Contributed surplus	—	1,000,000
Retained earnings	4,000,000	2,000,000
	$16,000,000	$5,000,000

For both companies, the fair values of their identifiable assets and liabilities are equal to their carrying values except for the following fair values:

	Perk	Scent
Inventories	$1,000,000	$ 600,000
Capital assets (net)	7,000,000	5,000,000
Long-term liabilities	3,800,000	1,100,000

The following cases are *independent*:

1. On December 31, 20X5, Perk Company purchases the net assets of Scent Company for $5.5 million in cash. Scent Company distributes the proceeds to its shareholders in return for their shares, cancels the shares, and ceases to exist as a separate legal entity.
2. On December 31, 20X5, Perk Company purchases 75% of the outstanding voting shares of Scent Company for $4.5 million in cash. Scent Company continues to operate as a separate legal entity.

Required

For each of the two independent cases, prepare a consolidated SFP for Perk Company at December 31, 20X5, subsequent to the business combination. For the second case, prepare a consolidated SFP using *each* of the following four methods.

1. Proportionate consolidation
2. Parent-company
3. Parent-company extension
4. Entity
   [SMA, adapted]

P5-2

Zoe Ltd. has the following SFP at December 31, 20X5:

Zoe Ltd.
Statement of Financial Position
December 31, 20X5

Current assets		$ 80,000
Capital assets:		
Land	$ 30,000	
Building, net	100,000	
Equipment, net	50,000	180,000
Goodwill		20,000
		$280,000
Current liabilities		$ 55,000
Bonds payable		80,000
Common shares		100,000
Retained earnings, January 1, 20X5		60,000
Net loss for 20X5		(15,000)
		$280,000

On December 31, 20X5, Halifax Ltd. bought 70% of the outstanding shares of Zoe Ltd. and paid $190,000. The current fair values of the net assets of Zoe Ltd. on December 31, 20X5, are:

Current assets	$ 80,000	Current liabilities	$55,000
Land	180,000	Bonds payable	70,000
Building	160,000		
Equipment	20,000		

Halifax Ltd. is an investment company that has assets composed only of cash and short-term marketable investments.

Required

Calculate the following items, as they would appear on the Halifax Ltd. consolidated SFP at December 31, 20X5, under the entity method and the parent-company extension method respectively:

a) Land
b) Goodwill
c) NCI

[CGA—Canada, adapted]

P5-3

Calgary Ltd. acquired a subsidiary, Ottawa Ltd., on July 1, 20X5, by paying $200,000 for 70% of the outstanding shares. The fiscal year-end for both companies is December 31. The statements of financial position of Ottawa Ltd. and Calgary Ltd. are shown below.

Required

Prepare the consolidated SFP as at July 1, 20X5, for Calgary Ltd., under the entity method and the parent-company extension method respectively.

[CGA—Canada, adapted]

Ottawa Ltd.
Statement of Financial Position
July 1, 20X5

	Carrying value	Fair market value
Current assets	$140,000	$140,000
Capital assets:		
Land	90,000	150,000
Building, net	215,000	200,000
Equipment, net	60,000	90,000
	$505,000	
Current liabilities	$ 70,000	70,000
Bonds payable	210,000	225,000
Common shares	100,000	
Retained earnings, January 1, 20X5	70,000	
Net income (January 1—July 1)	55,000	
	$505,000	

Calgary Ltd.
Statement of Financial Position
July 1, 20X5

	Carrying value	Fair market value
Current assets	$ 150,000	$100,000
Capital assets:		
Land	400,000	700,000
Building, net	550,000	400,000
Equipment, net	360,000	200,000
Investment in Ottawa Ltd.	200,000	
Goodwill	400,000	
	$2,060,000	
Current liabilities	$ 60,000	60,000
Bonds payable	200,000	170,000
Common shares	1,000,000	
Retained earnings, July 1, 20X5	800,000	
	$2,060,000	

P5-4

Qorp Ltd. has the following SFP at December 31, 20X5.

Qorp Ltd.
Statement of Financial Position
December 31, 20X5

Current assets		$ 85,000
Capital assets:		
Land	$ 30,000	
Building, net	120,000	
Equipment, net	50,000	200,000
Goodwill		50,000
		$335,000
Current liabilities		$ 65,000
Bonds payable, 18-year duration, due 20X23		70,000
Common shares		120,000
Retained earnings, January 1, 20X5		140,000
Net loss for 20X5		(60,000)
		$335,000

On January 1, 20X6, Zip Ltd., whose assets are composed entirely of share investments and cash, paid $185,000 for 70% of the outstanding shares of Qorp Ltd. The current fair values of the net assets of Qorp Ltd. on January 1, 20X6, were:

Current assets	$85,000	Current liabilities	$65,000
Land	75,000	Bonds payable	70,000
Building (net)	180,000		
Equipment (net)	30,000		

Zip Ltd. had the following shareholders' equity on January 1, 20X6:

Common shares	$ 480,000
Retained earnings	710,000
	$1,190,000

Required

1. Assume a consolidated SFP is prepared on January 1, 20X6. Calculate the dollar amounts for the following items as they would appear on that consolidated SFP under the entity method:

   a) Goodwill
   b) Land
   c) Equipment
   d) Common shares
   e) Retained earnings
   f) NCI

2. What does NCI represent on the consolidated SFP?
   [CGA—Canada, adapted]

P5-5

On January 1, 20X5, Big Ltd. purchased 80% of the shares of Small Ltd. for $1,400,000 and, on the same day, Small Ltd. purchased 60% of the shares of Smaller Ltd. for $930,000. Any excess of the purchase price was allocated to goodwill.

	Big Ltd.	Small Ltd.	Smaller Ltd.
	At January 1, 20X5		
Shares	$1,950,000	$1,600,000	$ 500,000
Retained earnings	2,300,000	1,910,000	730,000
	$4,250,000	$3,510,000	$1,230,000
	During 20X5		
Net income (cost basis)	$800,000	$600,000	$300,000
Dividends paid	120,000	100,000	40,000

There were no intercompany transactions.

Required

Calculate the balance of non-controlling interest as it would be shown on the consolidated SFP of Big Ltd., at December 31, 20X5, under the entity method.
[CGA—Canada, adapted]

P5-6

Parent Ltd. pays $550,000 cash for 70% of the outstanding voting shares of Sub Ltd. on January 1, 20X5. The following information was available:

Sub Ltd.
Statement of Financial Position
January 1, 20X5

	Carrying value	Fair value
Cash	$ 40,000	$40,000
Inventory	40,000	30,000
Equipment, net	120,000	100,000
Building, net	300,000	360,000
Land	50,000	160,000
	$550,000	
Liabilities	$ 10,000	14,000
Common shares	250,000	—
Retained earnings	290,000	—
	$550,000	

During 20X5, Sub Ltd. earned $180,000 and paid no dividends. The inventory on hand at January 1, 20X5, was sold during 20X5. The equipment will be depreciated over 10 years straight-line; the building will be depreciated over 20 years straight-line. The liabilities were paid during 20X5. Parent Ltd. uses the cost method of accounting for its investment.

Required

Prepare the consolidation-related eliminations required at December 31, 20X5, based on the above information under the entity method.

[CGA—Canada, adapted]

P5-7

On January 1, 20X5, Par Ltd. purchased 80% of the voting shares of Sub Ltd. for $906,400. The SFP of Sub Ltd. on that date was as follows:

Sub Ltd.
Statement of Financial Position
January 1, 20X5

	Net carrying value	Fair value
Cash	$ 160,000	$160,000
Accounts receivable	200,000	240,000
Inventory	300,000	380,000
Capital assets, net	900,000	750,000
	$1,560,000	
Current liabilities	$ 150,000	130,000
Bonds payable	362,000	362,000
Common shares	200,000	—
Retained earnings	848,000	—
	$1,560,000	

The accounts receivable, inventory, and current liabilities have "turned over" by December 31, 20X5, and the net capital assets will be amortized over 10 years, on a straight-line basis.

Additional Information

1. During 20X5, Par Ltd. sold goods costing $100,000 to Sub Ltd. for $140,000. At December 31, 20X5, 20% of these goods were still in the inventory of Sub Ltd.
2. In 20X5, Sub Ltd. sold goods costing $200,000 to Par Ltd. for $250,000. At December 31, 20X5, 30% of these goods were still in the inventory of Par Ltd.
3. In 20X5, Sub Ltd. sold land to Par Ltd. for $300,000. The land had cost Sub $240,000.
4. Both companies pay income taxes at the rate of 40%.

The statements of financial position and statements of comprehensive income for Par Ltd. and Sub Ltd. at December 31, 20X5, are presented below.

Statements of Financial Position
December 31, 20X5

	Par Ltd.	Sub Ltd.
Cash	$ 200,000	$ 140,000
Accounts receivable	300,000	190,000
Inventory	500,000	460,000
Buildings and equipment (net)	1,200,000	900,000
Investment in Sub Ltd.	906,400	—
Other investments	417,600	—
TOTAL ASSETS	$3,524,000	$1,690,000
Current liabilities	$ 300,000	$ 206,000
Bonds payable	513,000	362,000
Common shares	500,000	200,000
Retained earnings	2,211,000	922,000
TOTAL LIABILITIES AND SHARE EQUITY	$3,524,000	$1,690,000

Statements of Comprehensive Income
Year Ended December 31, 20X5

	Par Ltd.	Sub Ltd.
Sales	$2,000,000	$2,000,000
Cost of sales	1,400,000	1,700,000
Gross margin	600,000	300,000
Depreciation expense	100,000	90,000
Interest expense	63,000	44,000
Income tax expense	140,000	74,000
Other expenses	124,000	78,000
Investment income	(37,000)	(60,000)
NET INCOME AND COMPREHENSIVE INCOME	$ 210,000	$ 74,000

Required under the entity method

1. Prepare the consolidated statement of comprehensive income for the year ended December 31, 20X5.
2. Present the following as they would appear on the consolidated SFP at December 31, 20X5:
   a) Net capital assets
   b) Goodwill
   c) Retained earnings

[CGA—Canada, adapted]

P5-8

On January 1, 20X4, Parent Ltd. purchased 90% of the shares of Sub Ltd. for $975,000. At that time Sub Ltd. had the following SFP:

Sub Ltd.
Statement of Financial Position
January 1, 20X4

	Carrying value	Fair value
Cash	$ 60,000	$ 60,000
Accounts receivable	120,000	150,000
Inventory—FIFO	180,000	230,000
Capital assets, net	1,500,000	1,350,000
Goodwill	100,000	—
	$1,960,000	
Current liabilities	$ 140,000	140,000
Bonds payable	800,000	850,000
Common shares	400,000	—
Retained earnings	620,000	—
	$1,960,000	

The bonds were issued at par and will mature in 10 years. Sub Ltd. has a receivables and inventory turnover of greater than six times per year. The capital assets have an average of 10 years of remaining life and are being amortized straight-line. The annual tests for goodwill impairment have indicated no impairment of goodwill since the date of acquisition.

In 20X4, Sub Ltd. sold inventory to Parent Ltd. for $320,000; the inventory had cost $260,000. At the end of 20X4, 25% was still in Parent's inventory but it was all sold in 20X5.

In 20X5, Parent Ltd. sold inventory to Sub Ltd. for $275,000; the inventory had cost $200,000. At the end of 20X5, 35% was left in Sub's inventory.

During 20X4, the subsidiary earned $875,000 and paid dividends of $60,000. During 20X5, the subsidiary incurred a loss of $172,000 and paid dividends of $60,000.

The parent company used the cost method for the investment in subsidiary and netted almost everything to "Other expenses."

At December 31, 20X5, the following financial statements were available:

Statements of Financial Position
December 31, 20X5

	Parent Ltd.	Sub Ltd.
Cash	$ 400,000	$ 75,000
Accounts receivable	850,000	179,000
Inventory	970,000	245,000
Capital assets, net	2,631,000	1,863,000
Goodwill	—	100,000
Investment in Sub Ltd.	975,000	—
	$5,826,000	$2,462,000
Current liabilities	$ 450,000	$ 49,000
Bonds payable	—	800,000
Common shares	1,000,000	400,000
Retained earnings, January 1, 20X5	3,026,000	1,385,000
Net income (loss)	1,350,000	(172,000)
	$5,826,000	$2,462,000

Statements of Comprehensive Income
Year Ended December 31, 20X5

	Parent Ltd.	Sub Ltd.
Sales	$9,865,000	$1,650,000
Cost of sales	8,040,000	1,140,000
Gross profit	1,825,000	510,000
Depreciation	(106,000)	(104,000)
Other expenses	(369,000)	(808,000)
Gain on sale of building	—	230,000
Net income and comprehensive income	$1,350,000	$ (172,000)

Required under the entity method

1. Prepare a consolidated statement of comprehensive income for 20X5.
2. Calculate the amounts that would appear on the consolidated SFP at December 31, 20X5, for:
   a) Goodwill
   b) Capital assets, net
   c) Bonds payable
   d) NCI

[CGA—Canada, adapted]

P5-9

The consolidated statement of comprehensive income of Top Corporation (TOP) and its subsidiary Bottom Company (BTM) was prepared incorrectly by an inexperienced accounting clerk. You have now been hired by TOP and you are asked to prepare a corrected consolidated SCI for an upcoming meeting. TOP owns 80% of the outstanding shares of BTM, and BTM declared and paid a dividend of $25,000 on December 15, 20X6. The following is the preliminary consolidated SCI of TOP, as prepared by the accounting clerk, for the year ended December 31, 20X6.

Statements of Comprehensive Income
Year Ended December 31, 20X6

	Top Corporation	Bottom Company	Consolidated
Sales	$900,000	$400,000	$1,300,000
Gain on sale of capital assets	—	50,000	50,000
Investment income	20,000	—	20,000
	920,000	450,000	1,370,000
Cost of goods sold	600,000	200,000	800,000
Gross profit	320,000	250,000	570,000
Expenses			
Selling and administrative	120,000	90,000	210,000
Amortization	50,000	40,000	90,000
Income taxes	60,000	48,000	108,000
Net income and comprehensive income	$ 90,000	$ 72,000	$ 162,000

Additional Information

Your discussions with other management personnel provided you with the following additional information:

1. The gain on sale of capital assets resulted from BTM selling equipment to TOP on January 1, 20X6. At the time of the sale, the equipment was recorded on BTM's books with a cost of $120,000 and net carrying value of $60,000. The equipment was purchased on January 1, 20X0, and has been amortized on a straight-line basis over its estimated useful life of 12 years. There was no change in the estimated useful life of the equipment upon acquisition by TOP. Amortization in the year of acquisition/sale is based on the number of months owned, for both companies.
2. TOP and BTM had never had any intercompany sales prior to January 1, 20X6. However, on October 31, 20X6, TOP sold BTM inventory for $60,000, which originally cost TOP $40,000. By December 31, 20X6, 50% of this inventory was resold by BTM to its retail customers.
3. TOP and BTM both pay income taxes at a rate of 40%, including taxes for gains on sales of capital assets.
4. TOP uses the cost method of accounting to record its investment in BTM.
5. At the date of acquisition of the common shares of BTM there was no fair-value increment.

Required

Prepare a corrected consolidated SCI for the year ended December 31, 20X5, under the entity method.

[CGA–Canada, adapted]

P5-10

Mallik Ltd. purchased 30,000 shares or 25% of Lee Chan Inc.'s shares on January 1, 20X8, for $300,000 and classified the investment as a fair value through OCI investment. Lee Chan Inc. reported a loss of $(100,000) in 20X8, and a profit of $200,000 in 20X9, and paid dividends of $50,000 in 20X8 and $25,000 in 20X9. On December 31, 20X8, 50% of the $100,000 worth of goods sold by Lee Chan to Mallik in 20X8 still remained in Mallik's ending inventory. Lee Chan's gross margin is 50%. Lee Chan's shares traded at $15 per share on December 31, 20X8, and January 1, 20X9.

On January 1, 20X9, Mallik obtained significant influence over the operating and investing decisions of Lee Chan when the controlling shareholder sold some shares in Lee Chan in the open market. Accordingly, the investment in Lee Chan was reclassified by Mallik to a significant-influence investment. On January 1, 20X9, Lee Chan's shareholders' equity was $1,500,000, Lee Chan had inventory that was overvalued by $100,000, and the balance of the FVI was allocated to a building that had a remaining useful life of 10 years.

Mallik sold the inventory purchased from Lee Chan in 20X8 by the end of 20X9. However, $50,000 worth of inventory purchased by Mallik from Lee Chan during 20X9 remained in its ending inventory at the end of 20X9. Lee Chan's gross profit ratio continued to be 50% in 20X9 as well.

On December 31, 20X9, Mallik sold its investment in Lee Chan for $12 per share.

Required

Prepare all journal entries relating to Mallik's investment in Lee Chan chronologically by date for 20X8 and 20X9. Show all supporting calculations.

P5-11 PENNY LTD. AND SZABO INC.

Penny Ltd. acquired a 75% interest in Szabo Inc., on December 31, 20X0, for $637,500. On that date Szabo had common stock of $550,000 and retained earnings of $125,000. Szabo's inventory was overvalued by $85,000 on that date, and the balance of the FVI was allocated to buildings. The carrying value of Szabo's buildings (net) on that date was $75,000. Penny's buildings had a carrying value of $150,000 on that date. While Szabo's buildings had a future life of 10 years, Penny's buildings had a future life of 15 years on December 31, 20X0.

Szabo reported net income of $50,000 in 20X1 and $65,000 in 20X2. While Szabo declared $30,000 dividends in 20X1, it declared $20,000 dividends in 20X2.

Penny, which uses the equity method, reported net income of $60,000 in 20X1 and $70,000 in 20X2. Penny declared $40,000 dividends in 20X1, and $60,000 dividends in 20X2. Penny's retained earnings under the equity method on December 31, 20X2, were $250,000.

Required

Compute the following, showing all supporting calculations:

1. Non-controlling interest in net income for years 20X1 and 20X2, respectively.
2. Separate-entity net income of Penny under the cost method for 20X1 and 20X2.
3. Separate-entity retained earnings of Penny under the cost method on December 31, 20X1.
4. Non-controlling interest at December 31, 20X2.
5. Investment in Szabo at December 31, 20X2, under the equity method
6. Using the investment in Szabo balance calculated in part 5 above, calculate the consolidated buildings (net) at December 31, 20X2.

6

Subsequent-Year Consolidations: General Approach

LEARNING OBJECTIVES

After studying this chapter, students should be able to:

1. adjust for intercompany sale of long-term assets;
2. use the general approach to consolidation in the years after founding or buying a subsidiary;
3. report non-consolidated subsidiaries and investment in associates and jointly controlled entities under the equity basis in the years after the initial investment; and
4. report discontinued operations in consolidated financial statements.

INTRODUCTION

The notes to the consolidated financial statements for 2008–2009 of Porsche SE, the holding company of the Porsche group, prepared under IFRS, includes the following disclosure relating to the principles followed during consolidation:

> Expenses and income as well as receivables, liabilities and provisions between the consolidated entities are offset. Intercompany profits from the disposal of assets within the group which have not yet been resold to third parties are eliminated.

The disclosure by Porsche SE above is typical of disclosures relating to consolidation by companies following IFRS. Inventec, a Taiwanese company that manufactures notebook computers, servers, and mobile devices, provides the following additional information relating to unrealized gains on the intercompany sale of depreciable assets:

> Gains and losses resulting from transactions involving depreciable assets are recognized rateably over their economic lives.

We discussed and illustrated the elimination of intercompany balances and unrealized gains in the previous chapters. The Inventec quote indicates the additional complication created by intercompany sales of long-term amortizable assets—amortization of long-term assets sold intercompany. In this chapter, among other issues, we will discuss the adjustments required to report intercompany sales of long-term depreciable assets in the consolidated financial statements.

It has been a long journey since we first started our discussion of consolidations in Chapter 2. At last, in this chapter, we reach the end of our exploration of the major facets of consolidated financial statements. We do not intend to be exhaustive (even though you may feel exhausted!). There are many additional complications to preparing consolidated statements. It is easy to imagine "what if . . . ?" scenarios. But additional complications are rare and should not be your focus. Once you understand Chapters 3 through 6, you will understand all of the significant issues in consolidation.

In Chapter 6, as well as illustrating intercompany sale of long-term amortizable assets, we will also discuss:

- the MEAR steps under the general approach to consolidation in the years after founding or buying a subsidiary;
- equity-basis reporting;
- briefly, consolidation when the parent uses the equity method to record its investment in its subsidiary; and
- consolidated reporting of discontinued operations.

In addition, we provide two appendices on the textbook's Companion Website:

- Parent corporations may invest in non-voting or preferred shares in addition to voting shares. Appendix 6A will briefly discuss the impact that such investments have on control and on consolidation.
- Intercompany bond holdings also are possible. In the vast majority of cases, intercompany debt can be eliminated by a simple adjustment, as shown in earlier chapters. In rare instances (*extremely* rare in Canada, where there is no organized exchange for bonds), there may be intercompany bond holdings involving premiums and discounts. Appendix 6B illustrates the adjustments for a bond premium or discount.

Readers who are not interested in some of the more obscure aspects of consolidation are encouraged to skip online Appendices 6A and 6B and proceed directly to Chapter 7.

INTERCOMPANY SALE OF LONG-TERM ASSETS

General Concept

We have repeatedly illustrated that unrealized profits on intercompany sales must be removed from consolidated net income. The concept of eliminating unrealized intercorporate profits or gains is applicable to *any* sale between members of a group of controlled, jointly controlled, or significantly influenced companies. The sale need not involve the parent or investor corporation; sales from one subsidiary to another or from one significantly influenced investee corporation to another require elimination of unrealized profit.

However, as pointed out earlier in Chapter 5, the extent to which unrealized gains and losses relating to downstream transactions are eliminated depends on whether such transactions are with a subsidiary or with an associate/joint venture. We will illustrate this difference later in the chapter. First, however, we will focus on unrealized gains relating to transactions with subsidiaries.

Downstream Sales of Amortizable Assets

Suppose that at the end of 20X6, Company P, (PC), buys a piece of equipment for $200,000 and sells it to its wholly owned subsidiary, Company S, (SC), for $250,000$_D$. SC will depreciate the asset's cost of $250,000 (assuming zero residual value) over the remaining useful life of the asset of 10 years on a straight-line basis, beginning in 20X7.

The cost of the asset to the consolidated entity is the original cost of the equipment to PC of $200,000. Therefore, when consolidating the financial statements for 20X6, we must reduce the reported value of the equipment from its carrying value on SC's books of $250,000 to the actual cost to the consolidated entity (that is, to PC) of $200,000. To prepare the consolidated statements, we must:

- eliminate the $50,000$_D$ gain on the intercompany sale from PC's revenue; and
- reduce the equipment account by the $50,000$_D$ unrealized gain.

These adjustments will reduce the consolidated retained earnings balance at the end of 20X6 by $50,000. Remember that these adjustments are not actually recorded on any company's books—those of PC or those of SC. Hence, PC's opening retained earnings balance in 20X7 will be overstated by $50,000$_D$. Therefore, the cumulative consolidation adjustment required while calculating the opening consolidated retained earnings balance in 20X7 in relation to the unrealized gain in the prior year of 20X6 is a negative adjustment of $50,000.

In 20X7, SC will begin to depreciate the equipment at the rate of $25,000 per year. From the viewpoint of the consolidated entity, depreciation expense is overstated because SC's carrying value of the equipment includes the unrealized profit of $50,000$_D$. Based on the actual cost of the equipment of $200,000, depreciation expense should only be $20,000 per year. Therefore, the excess depreciation of $5,000 in the books of SC must be reversed via a depreciation adjustment in PC's consolidated statements.

This reversal of $5,000 also represents the realization of 1/10th of the unrealized gain of $50,000$_D$ in 20X7. Thus, the unrealized gains will be realized on a straight-line basis over the 10-year useful life of the equipment. The following schedule summarizes the effect of the difference in depreciation on the unrealized gain relating to the equipment at the end of 20X7:

	Cost	Useful life	Depreciation/ realized gain per year	Carrying value/ unrealized gain at the end of 20X7
In SC's books	$250,000	10	$ 25,000	$225,000
In consolidated statements	200,000	10	20,000	180,000
Unrealized/realized gain	$ 50,000	10	$ 5,000	$ 45,000

By the end of 20X7, the consolidation adjustments will:

- reduce the cost of the equipment on the statement of financial position from $250,000 to $200,000 (to eliminate the $50,000 overstatement of equipment in SC's books);

- eliminate the unrealized gain of $\$50{,}000_D$ in the opening retained earnings of PC, with a negative adjustment of $50,000;
- decrease depreciation expense by $5,000 (to eliminate the excess depreciation charged by SC); and
- reduce accumulated depreciation by $5,000.

The reduction of the *opening* retained earnings by $50,000 and the partially offsetting decrease in depreciation expense of the *current year* by $5,000 will have a net reducing effect on the *ending* retained earnings of $45,000.

On intercompany *inventory* sales, the profit is realized when the inventory is eventually *sold* to an outside party. On *depreciable assets*, the profit is realized not by direct sale to outsiders, but rather by *using* the asset to produce goods or services to be sold to outsiders.

In 20X8, the *unrealized gain in prior years* must be eliminated from the opening consolidated retained earnings. So far, the unrealized gain at the end of 20X6 (and therefore at the beginning of 20X7) was $\$50{,}000_D$. However, $5,000, one-tenth of the unrealized profit of $\$50{,}000_D$, was realized by the end of 20X7 when we decreased the consolidated depreciation expense of that year by that amount. Therefore, the unrealized gain at the *beginning* of 20X8 of $\$50{,}000 \times 9/10 = \$45{,}000_D$, is adjusted via a negative cumulative adjustment to the opening consolidated retained earnings of 20X8 for that amount. To summarize, the following adjustments should be made in the consolidated financial statements of PC at the beginning of 20X8:

- reduce retained earnings by $45,000, which is $\$50{,}000 \times 9/10$;
- reduce accumulated depreciation by the $5,000 depreciation in previous years (one year, 20X7, so far); and
- reduce the equipment account by the full intercompany profit of $\$50{,}000_D$.

In 20X8, SC will again recognize an excess amortization of $5,000, while another $5,000 of the unrealized gains in prior years becomes realized. Therefore, when we prepare the year-end 20X8 consolidated statements, we will make exactly the same additional adjustment for 20X8 as we made for 20X7's depreciation:

- decrease depreciation expense by $5,000; and
- reduce accumulated depreciation by $5,000.

In subsequent years, the adjustment for the remaining unrealized gain will reflect the depreciation taken to date. For example, in 20X13 we will recognize the fact that the equipment has already been depreciated for six years (20X7 through 20X12, inclusive). The situation by the end of 20X13 is summarized below:

	Cost	Depreciation/ realized gains in prior years (20X7–20X12)	Depreciation/ realized gain in 20X13	Carrying value/ unrealized gain at the end of 20X13
In SC's books	$250,000	$150,000	$25,000	$75,000
In consolidated statements	200,000	120,000	20,000	60,000
Unrealized/realized gain	$ 50,000	$ 30,000	$ 5,000	$15,000

Therefore, using the direct approach to consolidation, the line-by-line adjustments during 20X13 will be as follows:

- equipment—reduce by the full unrealized profit of $\$50{,}000_D$;
- *opening* consolidated retained earnings (on the retained earnings section of the statement of changes in equity)—reduce by the four years' unrealized gain on the transaction that remains at the start of the year: $\$50{,}000 \times 4/10 = \$20{,}000_D$;
- depreciation expense—reduce by the current year's depreciation of the unrealized profit ($\$50{,}000 \times 1/10$) = \$5,000;
- accumulated depreciation—multiply the unrealized gain by the fraction of years elapsed since the intercompany sale (i.e., $\$50{,}000 \times 7/10 = \$35{,}000_D$), and subtract that amount from the accumulated depreciation balance;
- *closing* consolidated retained earnings—reduce by the remaining three years' unrealized gain on the transaction: $\$50{,}000 \times 3/10 = \$15{,}000_D$—which will happen automatically when the adjustments to the opening consolidated retained earnings and current year consolidated earnings flow through to the closing retained earnings.

By the end of 20X16, the asset is fully depreciated and there will be no depreciation expense in subsequent years. The only consolidation adjustment that will be made in 20X17 and thereafter (until the asset is retired and written off) will be a cumulative adjustment that has no impact on either consolidated net income or consolidated retained earnings:

- equipment—reduce by the full unrealized gain of $\$50{,}000_D$
- accumulated depreciation—reduce by the full realized gain of $\$50{,}000_D$

Upstream Sales of Amortizable Assets

When the intercompany sale of an amortizable asset is upstream or is horizontal (i.e., between two subsidiaries), the consolidation eliminations are exactly the same as those shown above *if* the selling subsidiary is 100% owned by the parent.

If the selling subsidiary is not wholly owned, the adjustments are complicated somewhat by the presence of the non-controlling interest (NCI). The adjustments will now affect both consolidated retained earnings and NCI to the extent of their respective ownership share in SC.

For example, assume the same situation as above except that SC sells the equipment to PC, and PC owns 75% of the shares of SC. The non-controlling interest will have a 25% interest in the $\$50{,}000^U$ gain.

The full $\$50{,}000^U$ will be eliminated from consolidated net income in 20X6, and the annual amortization of \$5,000 will also be eliminated in each of the following 10 years. However, the non-controlling interest will also have to be adjusted for elimination of the unrealized profit.

When non-controlling interest is computed for the consolidated statement of financial position, the unrealized profit *at the end of the year* must be deducted from the subsidiary's net carrying value before we calculate the non-controlling interest's share. The impact on the year-end 20X6 statement of financial position can be shown as follows:

- equipment—reduce by the full unrealized gain of $\$50{,}000^U$;

- ending non-controlling interest—reduce by its share of the unrealized gain ($50,000 × 25%) = $12,500[U]; and
- ending consolidated retained earnings—reduce by its share of the unrealized gain ($50,000 × 75%) = $37,500[U].

Notice that both the retained earnings and the non-controlling interest are reduced by negative adjustments. That will always be the case, because they are simply the allocated proportions of the unrealized gain.

In 20X7, we make the same unrealized gain adjustment again to the opening balances, since none of the unrealized gain had been recognized by the beginning of the year. In addition, we also must make the statement of comprehensive income adjustment, including the portion allocated to the non-controlling interest. The adjustments for 20X7 are as follows:

- equipment—reduce by the full unrealized gain of $50,000[U];
- *opening* non-controlling interest—reduce by its share of the unrealized gain ($50,000 × 25%) = $12,500[U];
- *opening* retained earnings—reduce by its share of the unrealized gain ($50,000 × 75%) = $37,500[U];
- depreciation expense—reduce by $5,000; and
- accumulated depreciation—reduce by $5,000.

The adjustments to the opening NCI and retained earnings respectively, coupled with the reduction in the depreciation expense by $5,000 during the year, will have the net effect of reducing the *ending* NCI by $11,250 [$12,500 − (25% of $5,000)] and *ending* retained earnings by $33,750 [$37,500 − (75% of $5,000)].

Because of the above adjustments, by the end of 20X7, one-tenth of the unrealized gain (i.e., $5,000) will have been recognized. Therefore, given that consolidation-related adjustments do not carry over to the next year, the following adjustments should be made as cumulative adjustments to opening balances in 20X8:

- equipment—reduce by the full unrealized gain of $50,000[U];
- *opening* non-controlling interest—reduce by its share of the unrealized gain ($45,000 × 25%) = $11,250[U];
- *opening* consolidated retained earnings—reduce by its share of the unrealized gain ($45,000 × 75%) = $33,750[U]; and
- accumulated depreciation—reduce by $5,000.

During 20X8 we should make the following additional current-year adjustments:

- decrease depreciation expense by $5,000; and
- reduce accumulated depreciation by $5,000.

The decrease in depreciation expense will flow through to *ending* retained earnings and *ending* NCI in the ratio of 75:25. In summary, by the end of 20X8, the net impact on the *ending* retained earnings and *ending* NCI will be a negative adjustment of $30,000 and $10,000 respectively.

Jumping ahead to 20X13, the adjustments will be:

1. Cumulative adjustments
   - equipment—reduce by the full unrealized gain of $50,000^U;
   - *opening* non-controlling interest—reduce by its share of the unrealized gain ($50,000 × 25% × 4/10) = $5,000^U;
   - *opening* consolidated retained earnings—reduce by its share of the unrealized gain ($50,000 × 75% × 4/10) = $15,000^U; and
   - accumulated depreciation—reduce by $30,000.
2. Current-year adjustments
   - decrease depreciation expense by $5,000; and
   - reduce accumulated depreciation by $5,000.

By year-end the cumulative impact of the above adjustments will be to reduce *ending* consolidated retained earnings by $11,250 and *ending* NCI by $3,750.

Each year, the current operations adjustment is the same as long as depreciation is being charged. The cumulative adjustment, however, gradually shifts the total net gain from unrealized (as deductions from consolidated retained earnings and non-controlling interest) to realized (as a reduction in accumulated depreciation).

We have been explaining intercompany sales of depreciable assets outside of the broader context of the consolidation process. To isolate and highlight the effects of the unrealized profit elimination, we have shown the direct impact on the *consolidated retained earnings* and *non-controlling interest*. In practice, this adjustment is included in the overall adjustment for consolidated retained earnings and non-controlling interest, just as we did in earlier chapters for unrealized profits in intercompany inventory transactions. The next major section of this chapter will illustrate the broader approach to calculating the non-controlling interest in earnings.

Losses on Intercompany Sales

Losses on intercompany sales may or may not be eliminated. The key question is whether or not the loss reflects impairment in that asset. If there is no evidence of impairment of the value of the asset sold, then the intercompany loss on the sale should be eliminated. But if the sale price reflects impairment in the asset, then the asset should have been written down even without the sale; the loss on the sale simply reflects an impairment that should be reflected by a reduction in the carrying value of the asset anyway. Thus, the crucial question in deciding whether or not to eliminate a loss is whether the asset should have been written down even if it had *not* been sold.

Under IAS 36 *Impairment of Assets,* an impairment loss exists when the carrying value of the asset exceeds its recoverable value. The recoverable value of an asset represents the higher of its (1) fair value less costs to sell; and (2) value in use. **Value in use** of an asset represents the present value of the estimated future cash flows expected to be generated from the continuing use of the unit and from its disposal at the end of its useful life. However, it is not necessary to determine *both* the fair value less costs to sell and the value in use of an asset. As long as one of these values exceeds the carrying value of the asset, there is no impairment.

Subsequent Sale of Intercompany Acquired Capital Assets

One company may buy a depreciable asset from another in the consolidated group, and then later sell that asset to a third party in an arm's-length transaction.

For example, suppose PC sells the equipment, previously acquired from SC, for $220,000 at the beginning of 20X10. PC will recognize a gain of $45,000, the $220,000 proceeds from sale minus the remaining net carrying value to PC of $175,000 (i.e., $250,000 cost to PC × 70% remaining useful life). The current example is a continuation of our original example wherein PC owns 100% of SC; therefore, there is no NCI.

At the beginning of 20X10, there will be 70% of the original gain from the intercompany sale still unrealized. Therefore, the cumulative adjustment required to opening retained earnings to recognize this unrealized gain is:

- *opening* consolidated retained earnings—reduce by $35,000[U].

Once the asset has been sold to a third party, the entire remaining unrealized gain must be recognized and added to the gain (or deducted from the loss) on the third-party sale:

- gain on sale of equipment—increase by $35,000.

Therefore, in essence we simultaneously decreased opening retained earnings by $35,000 and increased gain on sale of equipment by $35,000. This should seem familiar, since we encountered a similar pair of adjustments in earlier chapters when the unrealized gain on intercompany sale of inventory was realized in the subsequent year on the sale of such inventory to a third party. In earlier chapters, instead of increasing gain on sale of equipment, we decreased cost of goods sold to recognize the realization of the gain on the sale of the inventory.

Thus, the gain on PC's sale will be increased by the remaining unrealized profit on SC's sale, reflecting the fact that for the consolidated entity as a whole, a profit of $80,000 was realized on the sale of the equipment to an unrelated party:

Sale price		$220,000
Consolidated carrying value:		
Cost to SC	$200,000	
Depreciation (3 years @ $20,000)	60,000	140,000
Gain to consolidated entity		$ 80,000

CONCEPT CHECK 6-1

1. What are the different types of consolidation-related adjustments required relating to the intercompany sale of a depreciable asset in a previous period?
2. What consolidation-related adjustments are required when a depreciable asset sold intercompany in a previous year is sold to a third party in a subsequent year?

SUBSEQUENT-YEAR CONSOLIDATIONS—GENERAL APPROACH

So far we have discussed the process of preparing consolidated financial statements (1) at the date of acquisition, (2) one year subsequent to acquisition, and (3) two years subsequent to acquisition. We have explored the basic concepts underlying consolidation and the treatment of non-controlling interest. The major procedural aspects of consolidation have also been presented. In this section, we discuss the general approach to preparing consolidated financial statements at any reporting date subsequent to acquisition, regardless of how long ago the business combination occurred.

Basic Conceptual Approach and Consolidation Steps under Direct Method

Previous chapters have emphasized that consolidated financial statements must reflect adjustments for three types of events: (1) the acquisition transaction, (2) the cumulative effects of amortization and transactions to the beginning of the current reporting period, and (3) the effects of amortization and transactions in the current period. It doesn't matter whether the three types of adjustments are kept separate or combined.

The general nature of these adjustments is portrayed in Exhibit 6-1 with a timeline. The first point of interest on the timeline is point A, the date of acquisition of the parent's controlling interest in the subsidiary. The consolidation adjustments for this event are a constant, and have been thoroughly discussed.

Point C on the timeline is the most recent point, which is the current SFP date. The adjustments for point C and for the year then ended (the time between point B and point C) have been reviewed several times in the previous chapters and should be reasonably clear by now.

The more problematic adjustment is apt to be that for the time between acquisition (point A) and the beginning of the current year (point B). We have pointed out that the consolidation adjustments for the intervening period (points A to B) are *cumulative* adjustments. We can simply accumulate the effects of each year's current operations adjustments, bearing in mind that the net effect of all adjustments to statement of comprehensive income accounts and to previous years' current nonmonetary accounts (e.g., inventories) will usually be reflected in retained earnings. The result will then be the point A-to-B adjustment when we prepare the consolidated statements for the next accounting period (point B to C).

If we have the task of preparing only a year-end consolidated SFP, then we don't have to worry about point B but can adjust the SFP amounts directly to year-end balances. For example, there would be no reason to distinguish between fair-value amortizations in the current year and those relating to prior years. Although SFP-only consolidations may be encountered in student examination situations, actual accounting practice calls for preparing a full set of financial statements and not just a non-comparative year-end SFP. In preparing a full set of financial statements, we need to isolate the adjustments relating to the current period so that we can prepare the SCI as well as the comparative SFP.

EXHIBIT 6-1

Overview of Consolidation Adjustments

(1) Acquisition adjustments

a) Eliminate subsidiary's share equity accounts; establish non-controlling interest.

b) Add fair value increments and goodwill.

c) Offset subsidiary's accumulated depreciation against the asset account(s).

(2) Cumulative operations adjustments to start of the current year (i.e., affecting current year's *beginning*-of-year SFP amounts).

a) Recognize the non-controlling interest's share of subsidiary retained earnings from date of acquisition to *start* of the current year.

b) Recognize the cumulative amortization of fair-value increments (or decrements) and goodwill.

c) Eliminate the impact of intercompany transactions that affect carrying values:

i) Gains and losses from intercompany transactions that are still unrealized at the start of the year.

ii) Flow-through to retained earnings of fair-valued assets and liabilities that have since been sold to third parties.

(3) Current year operations adjustments.

a) Amortize fair-value increments (decrements) and goodwill.

b) Eliminate the current year's intercompany transactions.

c) Realize previously unrealized profits (losses), if they are realized or partially realized in the current year.

d) Eliminate unrealized profits (losses) arising from intercompany transactions in the current year.

e) Recognize the non-controlling interest in earnings.

f) Eliminate year-end intercompany balances.

The general MEAR steps to consolidation, which accomplish the consolidation adjustments in Exhibit 6-1, and thus can be used in any year subsequent to acquisition, are provided in Exhibit 6-2.

To illustrate the preparation of consolidated financial statements in *any* year, we will use a different example than the one used in previous chapters. This example will include an intercompany sale of capital assets to illustrate the adjustments described in the first part of this chapter.

EXHIBIT 6-2

MEAR Steps Under the General Approach to Consolidation

<table>
<tr><th>Consolidation Steps</th><th>Acquisition Related (Chapter 3)</th><th>Relating to First Year Following Acquisition (Chapter 4)</th><th>Relating to Following Years (Chapter 5)</th><th>General Approach (Chapter 6)</th></tr>
<tr><td>1. Measure</td><td colspan="3">• Calculate cost and fair-value increments (FVI)
• Allocate FVI
• Determine NCI balance</td><td>1. Measure
• Calculate cost and FVI
• Allocate FVI
• Determine NCI balance</td></tr>
<tr><td rowspan="3">2. Eliminate and Recognize</td><td colspan="3">• Eliminate parent's investment account and sub's share equity accounts</td><td rowspan="3">2. Eliminate and Recognize
• Eliminate parent's investment account and sub's share equity accounts
• Eliminate intercompany transactions & balances
• Eliminate unrealized profits cumulative & current
• Recognize realized profits</td></tr>
<tr><td></td><td colspan="2">• Eliminate intercompany transactions & balances
• Eliminate unrealized profits</td></tr>
<tr><td></td><td></td><td>• Recognize realized profits</td></tr>
<tr><td rowspan="2">3. Amortize</td><td rowspan="2"></td><td colspan="2">• Amortize FVIs
• Recognize impairments</td><td rowspan="2">3. Amortize
• Amortize FVIs cumulative & current
• Recognize impairments cumulative & current</td></tr>
<tr><td></td><td>• Recognize cumulative amortization of FVIs
• Recognize cumulative impairments</td></tr>
<tr><td>4. Recognize NCI share of earnings</td><td></td><td colspan="2">• Recognize NCI share of earnings
• Calculate NCI SFP balance
• Calculate RE balance</td><td>4. Recognize NCI share of earnings
• Update NCI balance
• Update RE balance</td></tr>
<tr><td colspan="4">5. Check
• Independent calculation of RE balances
• Independent calculation of NCI balances</td><td></td></tr>
</table>

EXHIBIT 6-3

Parent Corp. buys 80% of Sub Ltd.

Fair-Value Increments, Date of Acquisition
December 31, 20X4

		Excess of fair value over carrying value [Dr/(Cr)]
		100%
Inventories		$ 10,000
Machinery		75,000
Investments		10,000
Total fair-value increments		$ 95,000
Goodwill calculation:		
Purchase price		$ 800,000
Implied fair value of 100% of Sub ($800,000 × (100% ÷ 80%))		$1,000,000
Carrying value of assets of Sub	$855,000	
Plus fair-value increments as above	95,000	
Fair-value of 100% of Sub's net identifiable assets		950,000
Goodwill at 100%		$ 50,000

Basic Information

On December 31, 20X4, Parent Corp. acquired 80% of the outstanding common shares of Sub Ltd. by issuing Parent shares worth $800,000. At the date of acquisition, Sub's shareholders' equity totalled $855,000, consisting of $300,000 in the common share account and $555,000 in retained earnings.

Some of Sub's assets had a fair value that differed from carrying value as shown in Exhibit 6-3. The implied fair value of Sub Ltd. is $1,000,000 and the goodwill at 100% is $50,000 as shown in Exhibit 6-3. Exhibit 6-4 shows the calculation of the NCI's share of goodwill of $10,000 and the NCI value of $200,000 under the entity method.

Exhibit 6-5 shows the separate-entity financial statements for Parent and Sub at December 31, 20X10, six years after Parent's acquisition of its 80% interest in Sub. Other relevant information is as follows:

1. Sub's machinery had an estimated remaining useful life of 10 years from December 31, 20X4. At the date of acquisition, the balance in Sub's accumulated depreciation (on

EXHIBIT 6-4

Calculation of NCI

Goodwill at 100% as calculated in Exhibit 6-3 above	$ 50,000
NCI's goodwill at 20% = [$50,000 × 20%]	10,000
100% of Sub's fair value as calculated in Exhibit 6-3 above:	1,000,000
Non-controlling interest:	
Entity method [($1,000,000) × 20%]	200,000

EXHIBIT 6-5

Parent Corp. and Sub Ltd. Condensed Separate-Entity Financial Statements

Statements of Financial Position
December 31, 20X10

	Parent	Sub
Assets		
Cash	$ 50,000	$ 20,000
Accounts receivable	150,000	160,000
Inventories	180,000	100,000
Machinery	5,000,000	2,700,000
Accumulated depreciation	(1,770,000)	(1,240,000)
Investment in Sub Ltd. (at cost)	800,000	—
Other investments	100,000	—
TOTAL ASSETS	$4,510,000	$ 1,740,000
Liabilities and shareholders' equity		
Accounts payable	$ 450,000	$ 200,000
Bonds payable	300,000	500,000
Total liabilities	750,000	700,000
Common shares	1,200,000	300,000
Retained earnings	2,560,000	740,000
Total shareholders' equity	3,760,000	1,040,000
TOTAL LIABILITIES AND SHAREHOLDERS' EQUITY	$4,510,000	$ 1,740,000

Statements of Comprehensive Income
Year Ended December 31, 20X10

	Parent	Sub
Sales revenue	$2,000,000	$ 1,500,000
Royalty revenue	150,000	—
Dividend income	75,000	—
Total revenue	2,225,000	1,500,000
Cost of sales	1,200,000	900,000
Other expenses	560,000	411,000
Total expenses	1,760,000	1,311,000
NET INCOME AND COMPREHENSIVE INCOME	$ 465,000	$ 189,000

Statements of Changes in Equity—Retained Earnings Section
Year Ended December 31, 20X10

Retained earnings, beginning of year	$2,395,000	$641,000
Net income	465,000	189,000
Dividends declared	(300,000)	(90,000)
Retained earnings, end of year	$2,560,000	$ 740,000

machinery) account was $575,000. Machinery is depreciated on a straight-line basis, assuming no residual value.

2. In 20X7, Sub sold its investments for a profit of $45,000 over carrying value.
3. During 20X10, intercompany sales were as follows:
   a) Parent had sales totalling $100,000$_D$ to Sub at a gross margin of 40% of selling price. On December 31, 20X10, $40,000 of the amount sold was still in Sub's inventory.
   b) Sub had sales of $700,000^U to Parent at a gross margin of 40% of sales. At year-end, $70,000 was still in Parent's inventory.
4. The inventories on January 1, 20X10, contained intercompany purchases as follows:
   a) Sub held goods purchased from Parent for $20,000; and
   b) Parent held goods purchased from Sub for $100,000.

   The gross margin on intercompany sales held in the beginning inventories was 40% of selling price for both companies. All of the beginning inventories were sold to third parties during 20X10.
5. Parent collects royalties from Sub (as well as from other companies). Between January 1, 20X5, and December 31, 20X9 (that is, prior to the current year), Sub paid a total of $500,000 in royalties to Parent. During 20X10, Sub paid $90,000 to Parent for royalties.
6. In 20X8, Sub sold machinery to Parent for $91,000^U. The machinery had originally been acquired by Sub in 20X5 for $100,000. Sub had been depreciating the machinery on a straight-line basis over 10 years (i.e., at $10,000 per year), with a full year's depreciation in the year of acquisition and no depreciation in the year of disposal. Thus, the net carrying value of the machine to Sub was $70,000 at the time of the sale to Parent. After the sale from Sub to Parent, Parent continued to depreciate the machinery over the seven remaining years of its original useful life (i.e., at $13,000 per year beginning in 20X8).

A Caution for Students

Before we launch into an illustration of consolidation techniques, we would like to caution you about your problem-solving approach to complex consolidation problems.

When we prepare financial statements for a real enterprise, it is rather obvious that statements of financial position must balance, and that the full set of four financial statements must *articulate* or tie in to each other. However, when we are attempting consolidations for learning and practice, it may well be beneficial not to worry too much if our statements of financial position don't balance! It is possible to spend many hours in an attempt to find an error (or errors) that keep our statements from balancing or from articulating properly. This particularly is a problem when we are using the direct approach, in which the *ad hoc* nature of the adjustment process denies us the self-balancing feature of the worksheet approach.

Often, the error is very minor—sometimes only a simple arithmetic error. We generally recommend, therefore, that you not get too stressed if your problem solutions don't quite work. This is especially true in examination situations, where time wasted looking for small mistakes will consume valuable time that could be used to answer other questions and problems.

Therefore, we urge all users of this book not to get too upset if your statements don't balance. Even the authors of this book sometimes have trouble getting their solutions to balance!

Direct Approach

We will follow the MEAR steps under the column titled "General Approach," in Exhibit 6-2.

The first step of Measure requires us to calculate the cost of the acquisition and the FVIs, allocate the FVIs to the various assets and liabilities, including goodwill and lastly determine the NCI balance. The purchase price of $800,000 was already given. Exhibits 6-3 and 6-4 show the FVI attributable to the various assets and liabilities, with the reminder allocated to goodwill, and the calculation of the fair value of 100% of Sub at $1,000,000, and the NCI balance of $200,000.

As compared to our practice in prior chapters, Exhibit 6-3 accomplishes the goal of the Measure step somewhat differently. This is a result of the absence of full information in our example. The example does not provide the carrying values of the individual assets and liabilities of the subsidiary at the time of acquisition. In contrast, we are given the FVIs relating to each asset and the overall carrying value of the net assets of the subsidiary. Therefore, Exhibit 6-3 uses the provided information to calculate the parent's share of goodwill. However, the overall logic remains the same as in previous chapters. Now, we are ready to move to the next step of Eliminate.

Eliminate

Eliminate Intercompany Transactions and Balances There are four intercompany items in our example:

Upstream sale by Sub Ltd.	$(700,000)
Downstream sale by Parent Corp.	$(100,000)
Royalty paid by Sub Ltd. to Parent Corp.	$ (90,000)
Dividends declared by Sub Ltd.	$ (90,000)

1. Sub Ltd. sold $700,000^{U} worth of goods to Parent Corp. We need to eliminate $700,000^{U} from both sales and cost of goods sold.
2. Parent Corp. sold $100,000$_{D}$ worth of goods to Sub Ltd. We must eliminate $100,000$_{D}$ from both sales and cost of goods sold as well.
3. Sub Ltd. paid royalties of $90,000 to Parent Corp. We must eliminate $90,000 from both royalty revenue and other expenses.
4. Sub Ltd. declared dividends of $90,000. Of the $90,000 dividends declared by Sub Ltd., Parent Corp.'s share is only $72,000; the remaining $18,000 belongs to the NCI. Therefore, while we eliminate the dividends declared amount of $90,000, we need to eliminate only $72,000 from dividend income. The NCI's share of $18,000 will be subtracted from the NCI balance on the SFP.

Unrealized Profits and Realized Profits There are two realized gains relating to the intercompany sale of inventory in the previous year and two unrealized gains relating to the intercompany sale of inventory in 20X10.

Realized profit on downstream sale of inventory in previous year	$ 8,000
Realized profit on upstream sale of inventory in previous year	$ 40,000
Unrealized profit on downstream sale of inventory in the current year	$(16,000)
Unrealized profit on upstream sale of inventory in the current year	$(28,000)

1. The inventory sold downstream last year is now realized. Therefore, the associated cumulative adjustment required will decrease the opening consolidated retained earnings of 20X10 by $8,000_D$, while decreasing cost of goods sold of 20X10 by $8,000_D$. We encountered similar examples in earlier chapters of realized gains relating to intercompany sales of inventory in previous periods. The associated discussion applies to our present example as well, and therefore we have chosen not to repeat it here.
2. Since the $40,000^U$ realized gain pertains to an upstream sale of inventory in the previous year, the cumulative adjustment required in 20X10 will decrease opening consolidated retained earnings by $32,000^U$ *and* opening NCI by $8,000^U$, while decreasing cost of goods sold of 20X10 by $40,000^U$.
3. Cost of goods sold of 20X10 should be increased by $16,000_D$ while decreasing ending inventory by $16,000 to reflect the unrealized gain of $16,000_D$ on the unsold portion of the inventory sold downstream during the year. Only the ending consolidated retained earnings (not the ending NCI) should be adjusted by the $16,000_D$ unrealized gain, since it relates to a downstream sale of inventory.
4. Likewise, cost of goods sold of 20X10 should by increased by $28,000^U$ while decreasing ending inventory by $28,000^U$ to reflect the unrealized gain of $28,000^U$ on the upstream sale of inventory remaining unsold at year-end. However, both ending consolidated retained earnings and ending NCI should be adjusted by their portion of the $28,000^U$ unrealized gain since the sale is now upstream.

Our current example also features the upstream sale of machinery, a long-lived depreciable asset, in the prior year of 20X8. This machinery was originally acquired by Sub in 20X5. Sub depreciated the machinery for three years (in 20X5, 20X6 and 20X7) prior to selling it to Parent Corp. Therefore, the following types of adjustments need to be made in 20X10 relating to the upstream sale of machinery:

1. Eliminate the unrealized gain on the upstream sale of machinery in 20X8.
2. Eliminate the excess depreciation charged by Parent Corp. and recognize the portion of the gain realized in the prior years of 20X8 and 20X9.
3. Eliminate the excess depreciation charged by Parent Corp. and recognize the portion of the gain realized in the current year of 20X10.
4. Reinstate the original cost and accumulated depreciation at the time of the upstream sale back on the machinery account.

The following schedule calculates the various unrealized and realized gains relating to the upstream sale of machinery:

	Cost/ carrying value	Depreciation/ realized gains in prior years (20X8–20X9 (Cumulative adjustments)	Depreciation/ realized gain in 20X10 (Current adjustments)	Carrying value/ unrealized gain at the end of 20X10
In Parent's books	$91,000	$26,000	$13,000	$52,000
In consolidated statements	70,000	20,000	10,000	40,000
Unrealized/realized gain	$21,000	$ 6,000	$ 3,000	$12,000

We will now elaborate on the various eliminations now. The unrealized gain relating to the upstream sale of machinery in 20X8 is \$21,000^U, and thus must be eliminated. The corresponding cumulative adjustment in 20X10 will reduce the opening machinery account balance by \$21,000^U while reducing opening retained earnings by \$16,800^U and opening NCI by \$4,200^U.

The excess depreciation charged by Parent Corp. and the realized gains on the machinery each year is \$3,000^U. Therefore, Parent Corp. would have cumulatively charged excess depreciation of \$6,000^U in the prior years of 20X8 and 20X9. The \$6,000^U also represents the portion of the unrealized gain of \$21,000^U realized in the prior years. Therefore, a cumulative adjustment for \$6,000^U must be made in 20X10 to reverse the impact of the excess depreciation in prior years. The adjustment will increase opening consolidated retained earnings by \$4,800^U and opening NCI by \$1,200^U, while reducing accumulated depreciation by \$6,000^U.

A current year adjustment of \$3,000^U is also required to reverse the excess depreciation of \$3,000^U in 20X10. This adjustment will decrease the depreciation expense of 20X10 and accumulated depreciation respectively by \$3,000^U. The effect of this adjustment will be to increase ending consolidated retained earnings by \$2,400^U and ending NCI by \$600^U.

In our initial example on the intercompany sale of equipment in this chapter, the selling company sold the equipment immediately after purchase, without charging any depreciation on the equipment. However, in our present example, the machinery sold by Sub Ltd. had been depreciated by it during 20X5–20X7, prior to its sale in 20X8. Sub Ltd. would therefore have eliminated from its books both the original cost and accumulated depreciation of the machinery on its sale to Parent Corp.

However, given that the sale was not to an outside party, from the consolidated perspective, no sale of the machinery occurred. Therefore, we have to reinstate the original cost of \$100,000 and accumulated depreciation of \$30,000^U at the time of sale of the machinery back onto the consolidation-level SFP. Specifically, we need to add back \$30,000^U to both the machinery account and the accumulated depreciation account on the consolidated SFP.

You may wonder why the adjustment is only \$30,000 and not \$100,000 when our aim is to reinstate the original balance of \$100,000. For the answer, recall that by eliminating the \$21,000^U unrealized gain earlier we reduced the carrying value of the machinery from \$91,000 to \$70,000, the net carrying value of the machinery in the books of Sub at the time of its sale. Therefore, to increase the value of the machinery from \$70,000 to \$100,000, we need to adjust the machinery value further by only \$30,000, not \$100,000.

Amortize FVIs The third step (Amortize) in our MEAR approach to consolidation requires us to amortize FVIs and recognize any impairment. The schedule below shows the calculations relating to the amortization of the FVIs, allocated to the various assets and liabilities at the time of acquisition.

	100% FVI	Amortization period	Amortization per year	Amortization/ impairment loss during previous periods (Cumulative adjustments)	Amortization/ impairment loss during 20X10 (Current adjustments)	Balance of FVI remaining at the end of 20X10
Inventories	\$ 10,000	—		\$10,000	—	\$ —
Machinery	75,000	10	\$7,500	37,500	\$7,500	30,000
Investment	10,000	—	—	10,000	—	—
Goodwill	50,000	—		—	—	50,000
Total	\$145,000			\$57,500	\$7,500	\$80,000

Remember that even though Parent Corp. owns only 80% of Sub Ltd., under the entity method, 100% of the fair values of the assets and liabilities of Sub Ltd., including goodwill, are included in the consolidated financial statements. Therefore, the schedule above calculates the amortization of the full 100% FVI, not just the portion owned by Parent Corp.

Inventory Typically in consolidation problems it is assumed that the subsidiary's inventory at the time of acquisition is fully sold by the end of the subsequent year. In our example, that would be 20X5. Sub Ltd. would have expensed only the carrying cost of the inventory in its books as cost of goods sold in 20X5. However, the FVI of $10,000 relating to inventory indicates that the cost of the inventory to the consolidated entity is $10,000 higher. Therefore, to reflect the true cost of the inventory to the consolidated entity, the FVI of $10,000 would have been amortized in the consolidated statements of 20X5. The adjustment in 20X5 would have reduced net income by $10,000 and, by extension, also reduced ending consolidated retained earnings of 20X5 by $8,000 and ending NCI of 20X5 by $2,000.

Remember that consolidation adjustments do not carry over to later years. We are now in 20X10. Therefore, to capture the impact of the prior year amortization of the $10,000 FVI relating to inventory, we need to make a cumulative adjustment in 20X10 reducing beginning inventory by $10,000 (that is, to eliminate the $10,000 FVI) while reducing opening retained earnings by $8,000 and NCI by $2,000.

Machinery The machinery had a future useful life of 10 years at the time of acquisition. Therefore, the FVI relating to machinery should be amortized as additional depreciation over this 10-year period on a straight-line basis. Five years are past since the time of acquisition. Therefore, the FVI amortized in prior years must be $7,500 × 5 = $37,500. A cumulative adjustment for this amount is required in 20X10 increasing accumulated depreciation by $37,500 while reducing opening retained earnings by $30,000 and opening NCI by $7,500.

An additional $7,500 current-year depreciation expense has to be recognized in 20X10. The current year adjustment will increase accumulated depreciation by $7,500 while reducing ending consolidated retained earnings by $6,000 and ending NCI by $1,500. The unamortized balance of the FVI relating to machinery at the end of 20X10 is $30,000.

Investment Sub Ltd. sold its investment in 20X7 for a profit of $45,000. However, the true cost of the investment to the consolidated entity is $10,000 higher as reflected by the FVI of $10,000 allocated to investment. Therefore, the true profit on the sale of the investment to the consolidated entity is $10,000 lower at $35,000. The $10,000 FVI would have been treated as part of the cost of the investment while calculating the gain on the sale of the investment at the consolidated level in 20X7. We must make a cumulative adjustment in 20X10 to recognize the decrease in the gain of $10,000 in 20X7. The adjustment will decrease the investment value by $10,000 (i.e., to eliminate the $10,000 FVI) while reducing opening consolidated retained earnings by $8,000 and opening NCI by $2,000.

Goodwill Finally, there is no impairment in the acquisition-related goodwill. Therefore, the goodwill balance will continue to be at $50,000.

Recognize NCI Share of Earnings

Recognize NCI Share of Current Year Earnings The calculation of the NCI's share of the adjusted income of Sub Ltd. for 20X10 is provided in the schedule below.

Details	Amount
Net income of Sub Ltd. for 20X10 (from separate-entity financial statement)	$189,000
Add:	
Realized profit on upstream sale of inventory in previous year	40,000
Excess depreciation charged by Parent Corp. on machinery purchased from Sub Ltd.	3,000
Less:	
Unrealized profit on upstream sale of inventory in the current year	(28,000)
Amortization of purchase price discrepancy during the year	(7,500)
Adjusted net income of Sub Ltd. for 20X10	**$196,500**
NCI's share @ 20%	**$ 39,300**

The adjusted net income of Sub Ltd. for 20X10 after making all the above adjustments is $196,500. Therefore, the NCI's share is $39,300, while Parent Corp.'s share will be $157,200. However, note that we also need to adjust Parent Corp.'s separate-entity net income by increasing it by $8,000 and decreasing it by $16,000, which is the realized and unrealized gain respectively in 20X10 from the downstream sale of inventory.

Recognize NCI Share of Prior Years' Earnings The change in the retained earnings of Sub Ltd. from the time of acquisition until the beginning of 20X10 is $86,000 (i.e., $641,000 beginning retained earnings balance of Sub Ltd. minus $555,000 retained earnings balance of Sub Ltd. at the time of acquisition). The NCI's share of this change at 20% is therefore $17,200. Adding the $17,200 to the NCI balance at the time of acquisition results in the NCI balance at the beginning of 20X10 of $217,200. The $217,200 is before allocating to the NCI its share of the consolidation adjustments relating to previous years.

In our current example, we must adjust the opening consolidated retained earnings and the opening NCI for the impact of the prior years' adjustments:

Amortization of machinery during 20X5–20X9	$ (37,500)
Unrealized profit on upstream sale of inventory in 20X9	(40,000)
Unrealized gain on upstream sale of machinery in 20X8	(21,000)
Realized gain on upstream sale of machinery in 20X8–20X9	6,000
Amortization of FVI relating to inventory	(10,000)
Amortization of FVI relating to investment	(10,000)
Total	**$(112,500)**
NCI's share (20% × $112,500)	**$ (22,500)**

Note that the opening retained earnings of 20X10 should also be adjusted for the unrealized gains in 20X9 of $8,000_D$ from the downstream sale of inventory.

Actual Consolidation Now we have all the information necessary to prepare the consolidated statement of income and the retained earnings section of the consolidated statement of changes in equity and consolidated SFP for Parent Corp. for the year 20X10. We can start the consolidation process by adding the carrying values of both companies and making the various adjustments identified in the previous steps. We also need to remember to eliminate the shareholders' equity of $855,000, consisting of $300,000 in the common share account and $555,000 in retained earnings, and the investment at cost of $800,000.

To do the above, following our practice in earlier chapters, we can go down the SCI, the SCE/RE and SFP and insert the correct amounts on a line-by-line basis. In Exhibits 6-6 and 6-7, we have added together the separate-entity amounts and made the required additional adjustments and eliminations. The adjustments and eliminations are listed below once again, now by each financial statement starting with the statement of comprehensive income. Exhibits 6-6 and 6-7 illustrate consolidation under the entity method.

Statement of Comprehensive Income and SCE/RE Following the practice under the direct method, the calculation of each consolidated item of revenue and expense is shown in brackets in Exhibit 6-6.

- *Sales revenue*. The consolidated sales are reduced by the intercompany sales during 20X10 of $\$100{,}000_D$ plus $\$700{,}000^U$.
- *Royalty revenue*. Royalties are reduced by the intercompany royalties of $90,000 paid by Sub to Parent during 20X10.

EXHIBIT 6-6

Parent Corp.

Condensed Consolidated Statement of Comprehensive Income
Year Ended December 31, 20X10

Revenues	
Sales revenue [2,000,000 + 1,500,000 − **$100{,}000_D$** − **$700{,}000^U$**]	$2,700,000
Royalty revenue [150,000 − **90,000**]	60,000
Dividend Income [75,000 − **72,000**]	3,000
	2,763,000
Expenses	
Cost of sales [1,200,000 + 900,000 − **$100{,}000_D$** − **$700{,}000^U$** + **$16{,}000_D$** + **$28{,}000^U$** − **$8{,}000_D$** − **$40{,}000^U$**]	1,296,000
Other expenses [560,000 + 411,000 − **90,000** + **7,500** − **$3{,}000^U$**]	885,500
	2,181,500
Net Income and Comprehensive Income	$ 581,500
Net income attributable to:	
Owners of the parent	542,200
Non-controlling interests	39,300

Statement of Changes in Equity—Retained Earnings Section
Year Ended December 31, 20X10

Retained earnings, December 31, 20X9 [2,395,000 − **21,200** − **8,000**]	$2,365,800
Net income	542,200
Dividends declared [300,000 + 90,000 − **90,000**]	(300,000)
Retained earnings, December 31, 20X10	$2,608,000

- *Dividend income*. Sub paid dividends of \$90,000 during 20X10. Of this amount, Parent received \$90,000 × 80% = \$72,000. The dividend income of Parent is reduced by the amount of the intercompany dividends of \$72,000.
- *Cost of sales*. The cost of sales of the two companies is adjusted for (1) the intercompany sales; (2) the unrealized profits in the ending inventories; and (3) the realization of the previously unrealized profits in the beginning inventories.
- The intercompany sales are $\$100{,}000_D$ and $\$700{,}000^U$, which are deducted from cost of sales as the offset to the deduction from sales, above.
- The unrealized profits in the ending inventories are $\$16{,}000_D$ for the downstream sales (\$40,000 × 40%) and $\$28{,}000^U$ for the upstream sales (\$70,000 × 40%). These amounts are added to cost of sales.
- The now-realized profits from the beginning inventory are \$20,000 × 40% = $\$8{,}000_D$ for downstream sales (in Sub's inventory) and are \$100,000 × 40% = $\$40{,}000^U$ for upstream sales (in Parent's inventory). These now-realized amounts are subtracted from cost of sales, thereby increasing consolidated net income.
- *Other expenses*. Operating expenses are adjusted for (1) the intercompany royalty expense; (2) the amortization of the fair-value increments; and (3) the over-depreciation of the machinery that was sold by Sub to Parent.
  1) Intercompany royalty payments of \$90,000 are eliminated.
  2) On a straight-line basis, the \$75,000 fair-value increment on the machinery is amortized over 10 years at \$7,500 per year.
  3) The depreciation expense relating to the machinery sold intercompany must be adjusted. Parent recorded \$13,000 of depreciation on the asset during 20X10, but the depreciation based on the cost of the machinery to Sub is only \$10,000. Therefore, depreciation expense must be reduced by $\$3{,}000^U$.
- *Non-controlling interest in earnings of Sub Ltd*. Exhibit 6-5 shows that Sub's separate-entity net income is \$189,000. Parent has equity in only 80% of this amount. The remaining 20% is equity of the non-controlling interest. Before taking the 20%, we must adjust Sub's separate-entity earnings for the realized and unrealized profits from upstream sales. There are four adjustments.

  Parent's *opening* inventory contains $\$100{,}000^U$ of goods that had been purchased from Sub. The gross profit percentage was 40%, which yields an unrealized gross profit at the beginning of the year of \$100,000 × 40% = $\$40{,}000^U$. This amount has been sold to outsiders, and therefore has now been realized. We must add the $\$40{,}000^U$ in now-realized profit to Sub's nominal earnings.

  Parent's *ending* inventory contains unrealized profit of \$70,000 × 40% = $\$28{,}000^U$. We must subtract this amount from Sub's separate-entity net income.

  Parent also is depreciating the machinery that had been purchased from Sub in 20X4. Parent's depreciation is \$91,000 ÷ 7 = \$13,000. Depreciation based on the historical cost of the asset to Sub would have been \$100,000 ÷ 10 = \$10,000. Parent has charged an extra $\$3{,}000^U$ in depreciation. Remember that amortization or depreciation constitutes recognition of the benefits of using a capital asset. Therefore, the extra $3,000^U$ represents the realization of part of the previously unrealized intercompany profit. This $3,000^U$ is added to Sub's nominal net income.

The fair value increment of $75,000 allocated to machinery at the time of acquisition is being amortized over 10 years. Therefore, an extra amortization expense of $7,500 should be added to the other expense line item.

After these four adjustments are made, we can simply multiply the result by 20% to find the non-controlling interest's share of the Sub earnings that are included in Parent's consolidated net income.

- *Retained earnings*. Once the net income for the year has been determined, the ending retained earnings can be calculated. First, however, we must determine the consolidated retained earnings at the beginning of the current year, January 1, 20X10. The opening balance of retained earnings will include Parent's separate-entity retained earnings, plus Parent's share of Sub's retained earnings *since the date of acquisition*, plus and minus adjustments for amortization, unrealized profits, and sale of fair-valued assets. The opening retained earnings on January 1, 20X10 on the separate-entity financial statements of Parent Corp. is $2,395,000. It needs to be adjusted for Parent's Corp.'s share of the adjusted change in retained earnings of Sub Ltd. of $21,200. We will provide the calculations leading to the $21,200 amount accompanied by detailed explanations later in the chapter in the section titled Check. Therefore, we will not provide the calculations or explanations here.
- *Dividends declared*. Parent's consolidated statements show only the dividends paid by Parent Corp.

Note that there is no need to adjust for the royalties paid by Sub to Parent prior to the beginning of 20X10. The $500,000 in prior-year royalties has reduced Sub's retained earnings, but has increased Parent's retained earnings by the same amount. On consolidation, the effects are directly offsetting. No adjustment needs to be made for intercompany expenses in prior years, only for unrealized profits.

Statement of Financial Position Exhibit 6-7 shows the consolidated statement of financial position for Parent Corp. at December 31, 20X10. Cash, accounts receivable, investments, and accounts payable are simply the sum of the two companies' balances. The common share amount is for Parent only, since this is Parent's statement of financial position. The calculations of the other amounts are summarized below.

- *Inventories*. The inventories are reduced by the full amount of the unrealized earnings in the ending inventories, both downstream ($16,000_D$) and upstream ($28,000^U$). In addition, we added and subtracted the acquisition-related FVI allocated to inventory.
- *Machinery*. First, Sub's accumulated depreciation at the date of acquisition ($575,000) must be offset against the asset account. Then we add the fair-value increment of $75,000. This adjustment assumes that all of the machinery to which the fair-value increment applies is still held by Sub.

  Next, we must adjust for the intercompany sale of machinery. The total upstream unrealized profit of $21,000^U$ is deducted to reduce the carrying value of the machinery from the $91,000 reflected on Parent's books to the $70,000 net carrying value that had been on Sub's books. However, the machinery should not be shown in the consolidated machinery account at its net carrying value to Sub at the time of the intercompany sale, but rather at the full historical cost ($100,000) to Sub. Therefore, the $30,000^U accumulated depreciation that existed on Sub's books at the time of the sale must be restored; $30,000^U is added to the machinery account and is also added to the accumulated depreciation account, below.

- *Accumulated depreciation*. First, Sub's accumulated depreciation at the date of Parent's acquisition ($575,000) is eliminated. Next, the amortization of the fair-value increment

EXHIBIT 6-7

Parent Corp.

Condensed Consolidated Statement of Financial Position
December 31, 20X10

ASSETS	
Current assets:	
Cash [50,000 + 20,000]	$ 70,000
Accounts receivable [150,000 + 160,000]	310,000
Inventories [180,000 + 100,000 + **(10,000 − 10,000)** − **16,000$_D$** − **28,000^U**]	236,000
	616,000
Capital assets:	
Machinery [5,000,000 + 2,700,000 − **575,000** + **75,000** − **21,000^U** + **30,000^U**]	7,209,000
Accumulated depreciation [1,770,000 + 1,240,000 − **575,000** + **(7,500 × 6)** + **30,000^U** − **(3,000 × 3)^U**]	(2,501,000)
	4,708,000
Other assets:	
Investments [800,000 + 100,000 + 0 − **800,000** + **(10,000 − 10,000)**]	100,000
Goodwill	50,000
	150,000
TOTAL ASSETS	$5,474,000
LIABILITIES AND SHAREHOLDERS' EQUITY	
Liabilities:	
Current: accounts payable [450,000 + 200,000]	$ 650,000
Long-term: bonds payable [300,000 + 500,000]	800,000
Total liabilities	1,450,000
EQUITY:	
Common shares **[Parent Corp. shares only]**	1,200,000
Retained earnings [see calculation later in text]	2,608,000
	3,808,000
Non-controlling interest in Sub Ltd. **[1,040,000 − (70,000 × 40%) − (21,000 × 4/7) + 80,000] × 20%**	216,000
Total equity	4,024,000
TOTAL LIABILITIES AND SHAREHOLDERS' EQUITY	$5,474,000

over the six years between the date of acquisition and the current statement of financial position date is added ($7,500 × 6 = $45,000). In addition, the accumulated depreciation of $30,000^U that existed on the machinery sold intercompany is restored, as explained in the preceding paragraph. Deducted from accumulated depreciation is three years' annual depreciation adjustment on the intercompany machinery sale (3 years @ $3,000 per year = $9,000^U).

- *Non-controlling interest*. The non-controlling interest starts out as 20% of Sub's net assets (i.e., shareholders' equity) at the statement of financial position date. On December 31, 20X10, Sub's net assets amount to $1,040,000. The non-controlling interest's share of the net asset value at 20% is $208,000. From that amount must be subtracted the non-controlling interest's share of the unrealized profit from the upstream sales at the end of the year: $70,000 × 40% × 20% = $5,600^U.

  Also, we must deduct the non-controlling interest's share of the remaining unrealized profit from the upstream sale of machinery. Three years have elapsed since the sale, leaving 4/7 of the profit unrealized: $21,000 × 4/7 × 20% = $2,400^U.

  Finally, we should allocate to the NCI its share of the time-of-acquisition FVIs that are still unamortized by the end of 20X10. From the Amortize step we know that the unamortized FVI balance is $80,000. The NCI share therefore is $16,000. After accounting for all the adjustments the ending NCI balance is $216,000. Note that we will use a different calculation while checking the NCI balance later in the chapter. This has been done deliberately and is aimed at improving your understanding of the concepts underlying the consolidation process.

- *Retained earnings*. The year-end retained earnings could be obtained from Exhibit 6-6, but that would take all the fun out of our consolidation. Instead, we should attempt to derive the year-end consolidated retained earnings directly. The year-end consolidated retained earnings consists of:

  1. the parent's year-end separate-entity retained earnings;
  2. plus the subsidiary's year-end separate-entity retained earnings;
  3. minus the subsidiary's date-of-acquisition retained earnings;
  4. minus the non-controlling interests' share of the subsidiary's retained earnings *since the date of acquisition*;
  5. less the cumulative amortization on fair-value increments from the date of acquisition to the current year-end; and
  6. less unrealized profits (net of non-controlling interest, where appropriate) at the *end* of the year.

We will illustrate the independent derivation of the ending consolidated retained earnings balance in the following section.

Check The NCI and consolidated retained earnings balances have been calculated below to provide independent checks of our calculations of these balances on the SFP. We will first calculate the opening NCI and consolidated retained earnings and next calculate the ending NCI and consolidated retained earnings:

NCI Balance at the Beginning of 20X10

Balance of NCI at the time of acquisition		$ 200,000
Add: NCI's share of the adjusted change in retained earnings in prior years		
Retained earnings balance of Sub Ltd. at the end of 20X9	$641,000	
Retained earnings balance of Sub Ltd. at the time of acquisition	555,000	
Change in carrying value of Sub Ltd. in previous years*	86,000	
Less:		
Total of cumulative adjustments pertaining to previous years	(112,500)	
Adjusted change in retained earnings of Sub Ltd. in prior years	(26,500)	
NCI's share @ 20%		(5,300)
Opening balance of NCI on Jan. 1, 20X10		$ 194,700

*See calculations under previous section titled "Recognize NCI Share of Prior Years' Earnings."

Opening Consolidated Retained Earnings Balance at the Beginning of 20X10

Opening retained earnings balance from separate-entity FS of Parent Corp. on Jan. 1, 20X10		$2,395,000
Add: Parent Corp.'s share of the adjusted change in retained earnings in prior years:		
Adjusted change in retained earnings of Sub Ltd. in prior years (as calculated in the section just above)	(26,500)	
Parent Corp.'s share @ 80%		(21,200)
Unrealized gain on downstream sale of inventory in 20X9		(8,000)
Opening consolidated retained earnings balance on Jan. 1, 20X10		$2,365,800

The calculations of the ending NCI and consolidated retained earnings are provided in Exhibit 6-8 below:

EXHIBIT 6-8

Ending NCI and Retained Earnings Balance at the End of 20X10

NCI Balance at the End of 20X10

Balance of NCI at the beginning of 20X10		$ 194,700
Add: NCI's share of Sub Ltd.'s adjusted net income in 20X10		39,300
Less: NCI's share of dividends declared by Sub Ltd. in 20X10		(18,000)
Ending balance of NCI in 20X10		$ 216,000

Consolidated Retained Earnings Balance at the End of 20X10

20X10 separate-entity ending retained earnings balance of Parent Corp.		$2,560,000
Less unrealized profit on downstream sale of inventory		(16,000)
Less dividend income from Sub Ltd.		(72,000)
Add realized profit on downstream sale of inventory in 20X9		8,000
Adjusted separate entity retained earnings balance of Parent Corp.		2,480,000
Add: Parent Corp.'s share of the adjusted change in retained earnings in prior years:		
Adjusted change in retained earnings of Sub Ltd. in prior years	$(26,500)	
Parent Corp..'s share @ 80%		(21,200)
Less: Unrealized gain on downstream sale of inventory in 20X9		(8,000)
Add Parent Corp.'s share of Sub Ltd.'s adjusted Income:		
Adjusted net income of Sub Ltd. for 20X10*	196,500	
Parent Corp.'s share @ 80%		157,200
20X10 ending consolidated retained earnings balance of Parent Corp.		$2,608,000

* See calculations in previous section titled "Recognize NCI Share of Current Year Earnings."

Parent-Company Extension Method

The SFP under the parent-company extension method differs from the SFP under the entity method in two respects—the balances of (1) goodwill; and (2) non-controlling interest. Under the parent-company extension method only the parent's portion of the goodwill is reported on the consolidated SFP, while the NCI balance does not include its share of the goodwill. In our example, therefore, under the parent-company extension method, at the time of acquisition the goodwill balance will be $40,000 instead of $50,000 and the NCI balance will be $190,000 instead of $200,000.

Since there was no impairment in the value of goodwill during 20X10, the statements of comprehensive income under both methods will be identical. Further, since there was no impairment in the value of goodwill from the time of acquisition until the end of 20X10, the same $10,000 difference will persist at the 20X10 year-end on the SFP. Therefore, on December 31, 20X10 under the parent-company extension method the goodwill balance will remain at $40,000, while the NCI balance will be $206,000 instead of $216,000.

Worksheet Approach

As usual, for the illustration of how the worksheet approach applies to our example, please refer to the textbook's Companion Website.

EQUITY-BASIS REPORTING

To determine Parent's equity in Sub's 20X10 earnings, we start with Parent's 80% share of Sub's reported net income of $189,000, or $151,200. This amount must then be adjusted for (1) amortization of fair-value increments; (2) previously unrealized profits now realized in 20X10; and (3) unrealized profits at the end of 20X10. The top section of Exhibit 6-9 illustrates the necessary calculations.

After making all the necessary adjustments, including the adjustment relating to the "excess" depreciation taken on the machinery that had been sold intercompany, Parent's equity in Sub's earnings is $149,200. If we take this amount and add it to Parent's net income less the dividends received from Sub, we obtain $542,200, which is exactly the same as the consolidated net income derived on Exhibit 6-6:

Parent separate-entity net income (Exhibit 6-5)	$465,000
Less dividends received from Sub	(72,000)
Plus equity in earnings of Sub (Exhibit 6-9)	149,200
Consolidated net income	$542,200

At the end of 20X10, Parent's investment in Sub should amount to:

1. the original purchase price to acquire the 80% share;
2. plus 80% of the increase in Sub's retained earnings since the date of acquisition;

EXHIBIT 6-9

Parent Corp.'s Equity in Sub Ltd.

December 31, 20X10		
Parent Corp.'s Equity in the Earnings of Sub Ltd.		
Parent's share of Sub's reported net income: $189,000 × 80%		$151,200
Adjustments:		
Amortization of fair value increment:		
Machinery ($7,500 × 80%)		($6,000)
Unrealized profit in opening inventories:		
Downstream ($8,000 × 100%)	8,000	
Upstream: ($40,000 × 80%)	32,000	40,000
Unrealized profit in ending inventories:		
Downstream ($16,000 × 100%)	(16,000)	
Upstream: ($28,000 × 80%)	(22,400)	(38,400)
Profit realized through depreciation on machinery sold intercompany: $3,000 × 80%		2,400
Parent Corp.'s equity in the 20X10 earnings of Sub Ltd.		**$149,200**
Parent Corp.'s Investment in Sub Ltd.		
Initial investment (cost)		$800,000
Equity in unremitted earnings (net of dividends received from Sub):		
Parent's share of the change in Sub's retained earnings since the date of acquisition: ($740,000 − $555,000) × 80%		148,000
Less amortization of fair-value increment through 20X10:		
Inventories (80% of the amount realized)	$(8,000)	
Investments (80% of the amount realized)	(8,000)	
Machinery: $75,000 × 80% × 6/10	(36,000)	(52,000)
Less remaining unrealized profits, December 31, 20X10:		
Inventory, downstream ($16,000 × 100%)	(16,000)	
Inventory, upstream: $28,000 × 80%	(22,400)	
Machinery: $21,000 × 80% × 4/7	(9,600)	(48,000)
Investment in Sub Ltd. (equity basis), December 31, 20X10		**$848,000**

3. less amortization and realization of fair-value increments and goodwill between the date of acquisition and year-end 20X10; and
4. less any unrealized profits at year-end 20X10.

The lower section of Exhibit 6-9 illustrates this calculation.

The increase in the balance of the investment account since acquisition (that is, $848,000 − $800,000 = $48,000), plus Parent's separate-entity retained earnings of $2,560,000 at the end of 20X10, equals the consolidated retained earnings of $2,608,000. Thus the equity method can be used to double-check the results of the consolidation process.

Equity-Basis Reporting of Investment in Associate/Interest in Joint Venture

Recall from Chapter 5 that IAS 28 *Investments in Associates* and IAS 31 *Interests in Joint Ventures* require the application of the proprietary theory when reporting investments in associates and joint ventures respectively under the equity method. Therefore, Parent's equity in the 20X10 earnings of Sub Ltd. and the balance in its Investment in Sub Ltd. account on December 31, 20X10 will both be different if Sub Ltd. is instead an associate or joint venture of Parent Corp.

The difference will stem from the difference in treatment accorded to the realized and unrealized gains/losses arising from downstream sales. Using the entity method, 100% of downstream unrealized and realized gains/losses are attributed to Parent Corp. when Sub Ltd. is its subsidiary. In contrast, using the proprietary method, only 80% of the unrealized and realized gains/losses are attributed to Parent Corp. when Sub Ltd. is Parent's associate or is a joint venture. These differences and their impact on the equity in the earnings of Sub Ltd. and Parent Corp.'s Investment in Sub Ltd. account respectively are summarized below:

Parent's equity in the 20X10 earnings of Sub Ltd.	**$149,200**
Reversal of difference due to 100% instead of 80% adjustment relating to unrealized profit in opening inventories [$8,000*(100%–80%)]:	(1,600)
Reversal of difference due to 100% instead of 80% adjustment relating to unrealized profit in ending inventories [$16,000*(100%–80%)]:	3,200
Parent Corp.'s equity in the 20X10 earnings of associate/joint venture	**$150,800**
Investment in Sub Ltd. (equity basis), December 31, 20X10	**$848,000**
Reversal of 100% instead of 80% adjustment relating to unrealized profit in ending inventories [$16,000*(100%–80%)]:	3,200
Investment in associate/joint venture (equity basis), December 31, 20X10	**$851,200**

CONSOLIDATION WITH EQUITY-BASIS RECORDING

Throughout this book, we have focused on consolidation when the parent company records its investment in the subsidiary at cost. This is the normal practice, since the cost method simplifies both parent-company bookkeeping and consolidation.

If the parent *records* its investment on the equity basis instead of the cost basis, the consolidation process must be modified accordingly. This is not a big problem. The only differences in the parent's separate-entity accounts between cost-basis and equity-basis reporting are that:

- the investment account includes the parent's share of the subsidiary's unremitted earnings to date (that is, the subsidiary's accumulated net incomes since the date of acquisition minus the dividends paid), in addition to the cost of the acquisition;
- the parent's opening retained earnings includes the cumulative amount of unremitted earnings to the beginning of the year;
- "Equity in earnings of subsidiary" will appear on the parent's separate-entity statement of comprehensive income; and
- the parent will show no dividend income from the subsidiary.

To prepare consolidated statements when the parent uses the equity basis of recording the investment, we must first remove the effects of the equity basis from the parent's accounts or trial balance. Once that is done, we can consolidate the accounts exactly as we have above.

Exhibit 6-10 shows Parent Corp.'s separate entity financial statements for 20X10 using both the cost method and the equity method. The accounts that show a difference

EXHIBIT 6-10

Comparison of Cost-Basis vs. Equity-Basis Recording of Investment

Parent Corp.
Statement of Financial Position
December 31, 20X10

	Cost	Equity	Difference Debit/(Credit)
ASSETS			
Cash	$ 50,000	$ 50,000	
Accounts receivable	150,000	150,000	
Inventories	180,000	180,000	
Machinery	5,000,000	5,000,000	
Accumulated depreciation	(1,770,000)	(1,770,000)	
Investment in Sub Ltd.	**800,000**	**848,000**	$ 48,000
Other investments	100,000	100,000	
TOTAL ASSETS	$4,510,000	$4,558,000	
LIABILITIES AND SHAREHOLDERS' EQUITY			
Accounts payable	$450,000	$450,000	
Bonds payable	300,000	300,000	
Total liabilities	750,000	750,000	
Common shares	1,200,000	1,200,000	
Retained earnings	**2,560,000**	**2,608,000**	$ 48,000
Total shareholders' equity	3,760,000	3,808,000	
TOTAL LIABILITIES AND SHAREHOLDERS' EQUITY	$4,510,000	$4,558,000	

Statement of Comprehensive Income
Year Ended December 31, 20X10

	Cost	Equity	
Sales revenue	$2,000,000	$2,000,000	
Royalty revenue	150,000	150,000	
Dividend income	**75,000**	**3,000**	$ 72,000
Equity in earnings of Sub Ltd.	—	149,200	$(149,200)
Total revenue	2,225,000	2,302,200	
Cost of sales	1,200,000	1,200,000	
Other expenses	560,000	560,000	
Total expenses	1,760,000	1,760,000	
Net income and comprehensive income	$ 465,000	$ 542,200	

Statement of Changes in Equity—Retained Earnings Section
Year Ended December 31, 20X10

Retained earnings, beginning of year	$2,395,000	$2,365,800	$ 29,200
Net income	465,000	542,200	
Dividends declared	(300,000)	(300,000)	
Retained earnings, end of year	$2,560,000	$2,608,000	

are highlighted. All other accounts are the same regardless of which recording method is used.

The first step in consolidation when Parent uses the equity basis of recording its investment is simply to reverse the differences between the two bases by undoing the equity recording. Using the amounts in the "difference" column of Exhibit 6-10, the reversal requires us to make the following changes:

Equity in earnings of Sub Ltd.	Decrease by	$149,200
Investment in Sub Ltd.	Decrease by	$ 48,000
Dividend income	Increase by	$ 72,000
Retained earnings (opening)	Increase by	$ 29,200

A slight variation is to leave the subsidiary's dividends received in the equity in earnings account, since they will be eliminated in the consolidation process anyway:

Equity in earnings of Sub Ltd.	Decrease by	$77,200
Investment in Sub Ltd.	Decrease by	$48,000
Retained earnings (opening)	Increase by	$29,200

Either adjustment will work equally well. The equity-reversal entry can be made either before starting the consolidation process by adjusting the parent's separate-entity accounts, or by entering the reversing amounts in the consolidation working papers—either direct method or worksheet approach—as the first step after entering the separate entity amounts.

DISCONTINUED OPERATIONS

In Chapter 4 we pointed out that the discontinued operations of a subsidiary should be reported separately, *only if the items represent discontinued operations to the parent* by satisfying the requirements at the level of the parent.

A subsidiary may decide to discontinue a separable line of business and thus report a discontinued operation. But if that type of discontinued business still remains within the broader economic entity, it will not qualify for reporting as a discontinued operation in a consolidated statement of comprehensive income. The profit or loss of a subsidiary's discontinued operations, which qualifies for being reported as a discontinued operation at the consolidated level, is reported separately from continuing operations. The non-controlling interest's share of such profit or loss is attributed to it on a separate line item.

As is always the case with these items, they are reported net of any related income tax. If an item loses its special status and becomes an operating item in the consolidated statements, the tax effect must be added back (to *gross up* the item) and the tax effect is included in operating income tax expense.

Since we are now at the end of the consolidation-related chapters, it is worthwhile to see what empirical research has to say about the usefulness of consolidated statements. Reality Check 6-1 provides findings from academic studies on the usefulness of consolidated statements and the value relevance of NCI reporting.

REALITY CHECK 6-1

Usefulness of Consolidated Statements and Value Relevance of NCI Reporting

The question of whether consolidated financial statements provide superior information to investors can be answered by comparing the information presented in them against the information presented in the separate entity financial statements of the parent. However, many countries (including Canada and the US) do not permit parent companies to publicly issue non-consolidated separate-entity financial statements in addition to issuing consolidated financial statements. Consequently, evidence regarding the superiority of consolidated financial statements is sparse. One study using data on the period between 1980 and 1994 on German-listed firms finds that consolidated financial statements provide information that is more useful for valuing those firms.[a] Another study using Spanish data during 1991–1997 also reaches a similar conclusion.[b] These results are comforting, reassuring us that the time and effort we've spent in learning the consolidation process is indeed worthwhile.

Note, however, that the above studies look at the usefulness of accounting information from the investors' perspective. In contrast, from a lender's point of view, consolidated statements obscure the credit-worthiness of the individual legal entities that are part of the consolidated group. Therefore, creditors may find the separate-entity financial statements to be more informative as compared to the consolidated financial statements.

a. T. S. Harris, M. H. Lang, and H. P. Moller, "Unconsolidated versus consolidated accounting measures: Evidence from German companies." Paper presented at the 20th Annual Congress European Accounting Association at Graz (1997).
b. C. J. Abad, L. A. Garcia-Borbolla, M. Larran, J.M. Pinero, and N. Garrod, "An evaluation of the value relevance of consolidated versus unconsolidated accounting information: Evidence from quoted Spanish Firms." *Journal of International Financial Management and Accounting* 11 (2000), p. 156.

Relevant Standards

IASB

Standards

- **IAS 27** Consolidated and Separate Financial Statements
- **IAS 28** Investments in Associates
- **IAS 31** Interests in Joint Ventures
- **IAS 36** Impairment of Assets
- **IFRS 3** Business Combinations

Exposure Drafts

- **ED 10** Consolidated Financial Statements

Summary of Key Points

1. When amortizable capital assets are sold between related companies, any unrealized profit must be eliminated. Intercompany *losses* on unrealized sales may or may not be eliminated, depending on whether the loss reflects a true decline in the recoverable benefit of the asset. The amount of *unrealized* profit declines as the asset is amortized because amortization reflects the use of the asset and thus the realization of its benefits.
2. For downstream sales, the full amount of unrealized profit is eliminated if such sales are to a controlled entity and only to the extent of the investor's share if such sales are to an associate or joint venture. For upstream sales (or lateral sales between subsidiaries/associates/joint ventures), the non-controlling interest absorbs its share of unrealized profit in the case of sales from controlled entities, and unrealized gains are eliminated only to the extent of the investor's share in the case of sales from associates or joint ventures.
3. An asset that was acquired via an intercompany sale may be sold to outside third parties. When that happens, any remaining unrealized gain must be combined with the recorded gain or loss on the sale.
4. In general, consolidation adjustments fall into three categories: (1) acquisition adjustments; (2) cumulative operations adjustments; and (3) current operations adjustments. For problems that are to be solved by a student, these three may be combined to arrive at a year-end statement of financial position or for a single-year statement of comprehensive income. In practice, however, comparative statements are always required and the distinction between beginning and ending statement of financial position amounts must be preserved.
5. The acquisition adjustments stay the same over time. There is no need to alter them, although they may be modified to reflect changes in asset structure, such as the disposition of fair-valued assets that were acquired but no longer held. In effect, this is a combination of acquisition and cumulative adjustments.
6. The theory underlying the cumulative operations adjustments is that date-of-acquisition balances must be updated to reflect amortizations and intercompany transactions to the *beginning* of the reporting year. Amounts such as opening inventories and opening retained earnings must be correctly stated.
7. Current operations adjustments have two basic functions: (1) to correctly state consolidated end-of-period balances; and (2) to adjust the year's earnings to reflect only transactions with non-related entities.
8. Equity-basis reporting of subsidiaries will result in the same parent-company net income and retained earnings as will consolidation. Calculations for equity-basis earnings therefore can provide a useful check on the accuracy of consolidated results.
9. If the parent company records its investment on the equity basis, the first step in consolidation is to reverse the impact of the entity-basis adjustments. Then, consolidation can proceed as has been described throughout this textbook.

10. A parent company normally will report a subsidiary's discontinued operations as such in its consolidated financial statements *only if the items represent discontinued operations to the parent* by satisfying the requirements at the level of the parent. All discontinued items are reported separate from continuing operations on a net of tax basis. The non-controlling interest's share of such discontinued operations are attributed to it in a separate line item.

Companion Website

Visit the text's website at www.pearsoned.ca/beechy for practice quizzes, additional problems, Excel® templates, answers to Concept Check questions, and important IFRS updates.

Self-Study Problem 6-1

Sparrow Limited is an 80%-owned subsidiary of Parks Corporation, a manufacturer of industrial equipment. In 20X7, Sparrow purchased a grummling machine from Parks for $100,000. Parks had manufactured the machine at a cost of $60,000. Sparrow uses straight-line depreciation over a 10-year period for its grummling machines, and follows the practice of depreciating its assets by one-half year in both the year of acquisition and the year of disposal. No residual value is assumed. Single asset accounting (that is, not group depreciation) is used. Sparrow used the machine in its productive operations from 20X7 to 20X20, in which year it was sold for scrap for $1,000.

Required

Prepare the adjustments that would be necessary in each of 20X7, 20X8, 20X12, 20X19, and 20X20 for the grummling machine when preparing Parks Corporation's consolidated financial statements.

Self-Study Problem 6-2

On January 1, 20X5, Power Corporation purchased 80% of the outstanding shares of Spencer Corporation for $2,500,000 in cash. On that date, Spencer Corporation's common shares had a carrying value of $2,000,000 and retained earnings of $1,000,000. On January 1, 20X5, all of Spencer's identifiable assets and liabilities had fair values that were equal to their carrying values except for:

1. a building that had an estimated fair value of $600,000 less than its carrying value; its remaining useful life was estimated to be 10 years; and
2. a long-term liability with a fair value of $500,000 less than its carrying value; the liability matures on December 31, 20X12.

EXHIBIT 6-11

Separate-Entity Statements of Comprehensive Income

Year Ended December 31, 20X9	Power	Spencer
Sales	$2,000,000	$ 900,000
Investment income	1,000,000	100,000
Gain on sale of land	—	68,000
Total revenue	3,000,000	1,068,000
Cost of goods sold	1,300,000	500,000
Other operating expenses	960,000	320,000
Total expenses	2,260,000	820,000
Net income and comprehensive income	$ 740,000	$ 248,000

The statements of comprehensive income of Power Corporation and Spencer Corporation for the year ended December 31, 20X9, are shown in Exhibit 6-11. Additional information is as follows:

1. On January 1, 20X6, Spencer sold a machine to Power for $210,000. Spencer originally paid $400,000 for the machine on January 2, 20X1. At the original date of purchase by Spencer, the machine had an estimated useful life of 20 years with no estimated residual value. There has been no change in these estimates—the machine still retains its value in use.
2. Both companies use the straight-line method for all depreciation and amortization.
3. During 20X8, the following intercompany inventory sales occurred:
   - Power sold $500,000 of merchandise to Spencer, $100,000 of which is in Spencer's inventory at 20X8 year-end.
   - Spencer sold $300,000 of merchandise to Power, $70,000 of which is in Power's inventory at the end of 20X8.
4. During 20X9, the following intercompany inventory sales occurred:
   - Power sold $400,000 of merchandise to Spencer, $90,000 of which is in Spencer's inventory at 20X9 year-end.
   - Spencer sold $250,000 of merchandise to Power, $60,000 of which is in Power's inventory at the end of 20X9.
5. Intercompany inventory transactions are priced to provide Power with 30% gross margin (on sales price) and Spencer with 40% gross profit (on sales). Both companies use the first-in first-out inventory cost flow assumption.
6. On September 1, 20X9, Spencer sold a parcel of land to Power Company for $133,000 that it had originally purchased for $65,000.
7. During 20X9, Power declared and paid $250,000 in dividends, while Spencer declared and paid $40,000 in dividends.
8. Power accounts for its investment in Spencer on the cost basis.
9. There was no impairment of goodwill at the end of 20X9.

Required

1. Prepare a consolidated SCI for Power Corporation for the year ended December 31, 20X9. Show supporting calculations for each amount in the consolidated SCI.
2. Independently, calculate Power Corporation's net income using equity-basis reporting. [SMA, adapted]

Review Questions

6-1 Under what conditions is a profit on an intercompany sale considered to be *unrealized*?

6-2 A capital asset is sold by a subsidiary to its parent company at the asset's fair market value, which is less than the asset's carrying value on the subsidiary's books. Would the unrealized loss on the sale be eliminated upon consolidation? Explain.

6-3 Company P owns 60% of Company S1 and 90% of Company S2. S1 sells inventory to S2 at a profit of $20,000. All the goods are still in S2's inventory at year-end. By what amount should consolidated net income be adjusted to eliminate the unrealized profit?

6-4 Company IR owns 30% of Company IE1 and 40% of Company IE2. IE1 sells inventory to IE2 at a profit of $20,000. All the goods are still in IE2's inventory at year-end. By what amount should IR's equity-basis investment income be adjusted to eliminate the unrealized profit?

6-5 In what way is the profit on intercompany sales of depreciable assets *realized*?

6-6 What happens if a company sells a long-lived asset that is part of its *inventory* to another company in the consolidated group instead of one that is shown as a *capital asset* on the books of the selling company?

6-7 How does the adjustment differ when there is a sale of an intangible asset; e.g., patent with limited life instead of a capital asset from the subsidiary to the parent?

6-8 Explain the composition of consolidated retained earnings in terms of the parent's and subsidiary's separate-entity retained earnings.

6-9 When a fair-valued asset is sold by a subsidiary to its parent, how does the amount of the fair-value increment affect the unrealized profit elimination?

6-10 When a fair-valued asset is sold to outsiders, what is the disposition of the fair-value increment when the statements are consolidated in the year of the sale? What is the disposition of the increment in years following the sale?

6-11 Explain briefly how the process of consolidation differs when the equity method is used by the parent for recording the investment account as compared to the cost method.

6-12 What does the equity-basis balance of the investment account for a subsidiary represent (e.g., cost of the investment, market value of the investment, etc.)?

6-13 Under equity reporting, why are unrealized profits from *downstream* sales deducted from the investor's equity in the earnings of the investee instead of from the parent's own earnings?

CASES

CASE 6-1 ALRIGHT BEVERAGES LTD.

Alright Beverages Ltd. (ABL) was federally incorporated in 19X0. In the initial years, the company produced a cranberry drink for sale at sporting and entertainment events in eastern Canada. In 19X7, operations were expanded to include sales to bars, restaurants, and fast-food outlets. To penetrate additional markets, ABL started manufacturing a wide variety of fruit beverages and acquired the distributorship of another company's fruit concentrate. Sold under the brand name "Fruit Brite," the fruit beverage sales were only moderately successful.

In 20X0, a management review indicated that while sales of the new fruit beverage line had increased, ABL's cost to manufacture was also greater than that of its competitors. Much of the profit was being made on the distribution of the fruit concentrate.

In an attempt to improve profitability, the company entered the retail market in 20X1. To finance the expansion, ABL obtained funds from two sources, bank loans and its first public issue of shares. The funds were used to purchase a bottling plant in Toronto and to provide working capital during the first year of operation. The retail operation was administered by a newly incorporated, wholly owned subsidiary, Fruitbrite Flavours Ltd. (FFL). In the first year the company incurred a loss on its retail operations, but subsequent years were profitable.

FFL continued to expand until it had a nationwide bottling and distribution network. In major cities the bottlers were wholly owned subsidiaries of FFL; in smaller cities, the bottlers were independents who bottled other products as well. In all cases, ABL sold its fruit concentrate to the bottlers.

In 20X4, ABL acquired 70% of the shares of Concentrated Vending Ltd. (CVL), a manufacturer of fruit beverage vending machines located in Windsor, Ontario. ABL purchased CVL at a price well below its proportionate carrying value, since CVL had encountered financial difficulties. ABL lent CVL funds to finance a plant modernization program. ABL contracted with the founders of CVL to continue as senior management since ABL had no experience in the equipment manufacturing industry. The management contract stipulated that a bonus would be paid, amounting to 20% of CVL's income before taxes, in each of the next five consecutive years. Although the plant modernization was successful, CVL had difficulty selling enough machines to achieve a break-even point.

Sales of fruit beverages through vending machines were growing rapidly with the increased awareness of the importance of a healthier lifestyle. This was a segment of the market in which the ABL group did not participate. Therefore, early in 20X6, ABL created a wholly owned subsidiary, VendSell Ltd. (VSL). VSL buys the machines from CVL at regular retail price and then sells them to local operators with the condition that only ABL products be sold in the machines. The intent was to place machines in as many locations as possible.

VSL sells the majority of machines under conditional sales contracts, in which the buyer agrees to make an initial payment of $500 and payments of $75 per month for the next

48 months, for a total of $4,100. Machine maintenance is the responsibility of the operator. The payment plan was devised with three objectives in mind:

1. to place the maximum number of machines by the use of an easy payment plan;
2. to defer payment of income tax by deducting the full cost of the machines when sold and deferring recognition of the revenue until the cash was collected; and
3. to ensure that only ABL products were used during the payment period, since title to the machine would not transfer until all payments had been made.

The fruit concentrate for the machines is purchased by the local operators from the bottler in the particular area, who in turn had purchased the fruit concentrate from ABL. The operator is charged an amount equal to the cost to the bottler plus 20%.

During 20X6, VSL expects to buy 8,000 machines from CVL at a price of $5,000 each. The machines currently cost CVL $3,000 each to manufacture. This cost to CVL is significantly lower than in previous years. To supply VSL, the volume of production in 20X7 is expected to be twice that of 20X5. As a result, CVL expects to show a profit in 20X6.

By the end of 20X6, VSL expects to sell 6,800 machines. The revenue from initial payments will amount to $3,400,000 and VSL expects to receive total revenues of $5,100,000 from initial payments and instalments in 20X6.

In its annual report for 20X5, ABL reported after-tax earnings of $4,575,000 on consolidated revenue of $77,970,000. Since CVL accounted for less than 10% of ABL's consolidated assets, revenues, and income, no segmented information was presented in the 20X5 annual report.

Within the management of ABL there is disagreement over the proper accounting treatment for the activities of ABL, VSL, FFL, and CVL for 20X6 and the effect on consolidation and reporting.

Required

In August 20X6, you were engaged as an independent advisor. Prepare a report in which you:

1. outline the major accounting and reporting issues faced by the company and its subsidiaries;
2. identify alternative policies to deal with the issues outlined; and
3. provide recommendations on the preferred policies.
   [CICA]

CASE 6-2 LE GOURMAND

Le Gourmand is one of Canada's most famous French restaurants. Located 20 kilometres north of Toronto, it draws diners from all over the province to enjoy its fare. One of the attractions at the restaurant is its private-label brand of wines—produced, bottled, and aged by Ombre Wines Ltd., located in the Niagara Peninsula.

The owner of Le Gourmand, Francois LeClerc, decided on New Year's Eve to increase the ties between Ombre Wines Ltd. and Le Gourmand Inc.; Le Gourmand is Ombre Wines' largest customer. On January 2, 20X5, Le Gourmand Inc. purchased 3,000 common shares of Ombre Wines Ltd. on the open market for $207,000. This left very few common shares still available to the public. The preferred shares were owned by the founders of Ombre Wines, but their children owned many of the common shares and were gradually selling them because none of them wished to take over the business.

Ombre Wines Ltd.'s owners' equity at January 2, 20X5, was:

Preferred shares:	
Cumulative, 6%, non-voting;	
2,000 authorized, 1,000 issued	$ 20,000
Common shares:	
7,000 authorized, 6,000 issued	137,000
Retained earnings	170,000
	$327,000

At January 1, 20X5, the carrying values of Ombre Wines Ltd.'s assets approximated fair values except as follows:

	Carrying value	Fair value
Two identical parcels of land, purchased in January 19X3 as an investment; each parcel cost $20,000 and the fair value of each parcel was identical	$40,000	$60,000
The land on which Ombre Wines' factory was located	$70,000	$85,000
Grape press, purchased in January 20X0 (useful life when the press was purchased was 10 years, no residual value)	$20,000	$24,000

In September 20X5, Ombre Wines sold one of the parcels of land that it had been holding as an investment (both lots had been put on the market but only one had sold). The proceeds were $18,000. The real estate market had declined badly in 20X5. The purchaser, however, had also discovered that Ombre Wines had been using the vacant lots to dump some residue from the wine processing; the land would not be ready to produce crops for at least five years. The purchaser had originally been willing to offer $24,000, but reduced this to $18,000 when the land use was confirmed by his lawyer.

Sales from Ombre Wines to Le Gourmand totalled $100,000 and $120,000 in 20X4 and 20X5, respectively. At December 31, 20X4, Le Gourmand's inventory contained $45,000 of Ombre Wines' wine. A year later, the inventory included $60,000 of Ombre Wines' wine. Of the ending inventory acquired from Ombre Wines, $20,000 had not been paid for as at December 31, 20X5. In settlement of part of this payable, Le Gourmand sent some old office equipment to Ombre Wines. The equipment had cost $10,000 and had a net carrying value at December 31, 20X5, of $1,000. Ombre Wines agreed to accept the equipment and to forgive $5,000 of the receivable from Le Gourmand, leaving a balance of $15,000 due from the restaurant. Ombre Wines did not depreciate this office equipment during 20X5.

Ombre Wines' most recent dividend declaration was December 31, 20X3.

The amortization policy for all capital assets is straight-line.

Francois LeClerc is looking forward to the cash flow from dividends that he hopes his company will receive from Ombre Wines Ltd. each year.

The statements of financial position of the two companies at December 31, 20X5, and the statements of comprehensive income for the year then ended are presented in Exhibit A below.

Exhibit A

Statements of Financial Position
December 31, 20X5

	Le Gourmand Inc.	Ombre Wines Ltd.
Assets		
Cash	$ 1,750	$ 16,400
Accounts receivable	—	66,000
Inventory	85,500	134,000
Investment in Ombre Wines	207,000	—
Land	30,000	90,000
Building	40,000	60,000
Equipment	25,000	75,000
	$389,250	$441,400
Liabilities and owners' equity		
Accounts payable	$ 34,000	$ 13,000
Taxes payable	2,150	15,000
Long-term debt	—	10,000
Deferred income taxes	1,600	—
Preferred shares	—	20,000
Common shares	155,000	137,000
Retained earnings	196,500	246,400
	$389,250	$441,400

Statements of Comprehensive Income
For the Year Ended December 31, 20X5

	Le Gourmand Inc.	Ombre Wines Ltd.
Sales	$400,000	$300,000
Gain on transfer of office equipment	4,000	—
Loss on sale of land	—	(2,000)
Cost of goods sold	(275,000)	(100,000)
Salaries	(78,000)	(55,000)
General and administration	(4,500)	(3,000)
Depreciation, building	(2,500)	(3,600)
Depreciation, equipment	(3,000)	(8,000)
Interest expense	—	(1,000)
Tax expense	(16,000)	(51,000)
Net income and comprehensive income	$ 25,000	$ 76,400

Required

Describe the alternative accounting treatments available to Le Gourmand Inc. for its investment in Ombre Wines Ltd. Describe why each alternative is an option and conclude which treatment is appropriate based on your description. Calculate Le Gourmand Inc.'s net income for the year ended December 31, 20X5. Show details of all calculations.

CASE 6-3 CONSTRUCTIVE INSPIRATIONS INC.

OVERVIEW

Jennifer Lu is a world-renowned architect. She is in the midst of a divorce with her husband, Johnnie Nu. On the whole the separation has been amicable and civil. Jennifer and Johnnie have agreed to divide the value of their assets equally. One of these assets is her architectural consulting company, Constructive Inspirations Inc. They have agreed that Jennifer would continue to own Constructive Inspirations (CI), but her husband would instead get other assets owned by them of equal value. The two of them have decided that the value of Constructive Inspirations will be based on the higher of CI's ending owner's equity, or six times its net income before taxes (but after all expenses) in 20X9. The calculation of both amounts will be guided by current IFRS standards for publicly accountable enterprises (i.e., public companies) as long as the end results are logical and fair to both parties. Both Jennifer and Johnnie are important clients of Accounting Experts LLP. They have approached Accounting Experts LLP for advice on the accounting methods to be adopted for the purpose of valuing CI in relation to their divorce settlement.

Further details about Constructive Inspirations, including items about which the two disagree, are provided below.

CUTTING EDGE DESIGN SUPPLIES

Constructive Inspiration purchased 40 percent of the shares of Cutting Edge Design Supplies (CEDS) on January 1, 20X7. The remaining 60 percent of CEDS's shares were purchased on that date by a group of 15 friends of Jennifer. These friends have no architectural background. Their reasons for investing in CEDS are their belief in Jennifer's vision, and their conviction that their investment in CEDS will payoff handsomely in the long run. They play no part in the day-to-day operations of CEDS, and have, via a written agreement dated January 1, 20X7, given Constructive Inspirations the authority to make operating and financing decisions in relation to CEDS. One of the employees of CI is on the board of CEDS. On the date of acquisition of CEDS, the carrying values of its assets and liabilities were equal to their fair values except for inventory and a patent. The balance of the purchase price discrepancy of $100,000 was allocated to goodwill. The table below provides details on the carrying and fair values of inventory and the patent.

	Carrying value	Fair value
Inventory	$150,000	$100,000
Patent	$200,000	$300,000

The patent had a remaining useful life of 10 years on January 1, 20X7.

A test for impairment at the end of 20X8 indicated that the acquisition-related goodwill had a value of $80,000 at that time. There was no further impairment of this goodwill in 2009.

From the beginning, CI has not charged any management fee to CEDS for the time spent by CI's employees on CEDS operations. Johnnie estimates that the management fee that should have been charged is $100,000, $125,000, and $150,000 for 20X7, 20X8, and 20X9 respectively.

On July 1, 20X8, CI provided a loan of $100,000 to CEDS via a 10 percent interest-bearing note payable. CEDS has been prompt in paying the interest on the note to CI. The loan is still outstanding at the end of 20X9.

CEDS sold a piece of equipment purchased by it on February 1, 20X7 to CI on January 1, 20X8. CEDS had recorded the full year's depreciation of $75,000 on the equipment in 20X7. No depreciation was recorded by CEDS for 20X8. The equipment was originally purchased by CEDS for $300,000 and sold to CI for $270,000. The equipment had a remaining useful life of 3 years with zero residual value on January 1, 20X8. CI charged a full year's depreciation in 20X8.

CEDS sold $80,000 and $90,000 worth of supplies to CI in 20X8 and 20X9 respectively. 20% of the supplies sold in 20X8 and 30% of the supplies sold in 20X9 by CEDS remained in CI's inventory at year-end. CEDS gross margin on these sales is 40%.

CI has from inception used the cost method to account for its investment in CEDS. CEDS has not declared any dividends since its acquisition by CI.

OTHER ISSUES

- CI's employees have a bonus based on the net income of CI before taxes.
- CI uses a line of credit with a local bank for its working capital needs. The bank bases the terms of the line of credit on the financial statements of CI. CI's receivables and assets act as collateral for the line of credit.

Required

After having recently graduated with a business degree from university you are presently working for Accounting Experts LLP. The partner of Accounting Experts LLP has asked you to analyze the above case and prepare a report for him. He will be using the report to prepare himself for an upcoming meeting with Jennifer and Johnnie.

In your report discuss how the different accounting alternatives available impact the financial affairs of CI, and support your accounting choice by discussing how it serves the users ranked by you as the most important and the objectives of such users. You should also discuss any concerns about the formula used for valuing CI and the "fairness" of using IFRS-based financial statements for determining CI's value. Ignore income taxes.

Problems

P6-1

Dudes Outfitters Ltd., is a 70%-owned subsidiary of Trail Ltd. On January 10, 20X2, Dudes sold some display cases to Trail Ltd. for $95,000, recognizing a gain of $45,000 before tax on the transaction. Trail Ltd. depreciated the cases on a straight-line basis over six years, taking a full year's depreciation in 20X2.

On February 12, 20X5, Trail sold the display cases to an unaffiliated company for $55,000.

Required

Prepare the appropriate consolidated adjustments relating to the display cases for each year ended December 31, 20X2 through 20X5.

[CICA]

P6-2

On January 1, 20X3, Sub Ltd., 80% owned by Par Ltd., sold a building to Par Ltd. for $1,800,000. The building cost Sub $800,000 and was 70% depreciated (at 5% per year). Par will depreciate the building over the six remaining years, straight-line.

Required

Give the consolidation eliminations required in relation to this transaction for the years ended:

a) 20X3
b) 20X5

[CGA–Canada, adapted]

P6-3

Parent Corp. owns 70% of the voting shares of Sub Ltd. During 20X4, Sub Ltd. sold inventory costing $640,000 to Parent Corp. for $800,000. At December 31, 20X4, Parent Corp. still had $300,000 of these goods in its inventory, and had not yet paid for $480,000 of the goods. All of the remaining goods were sold in 20X5.

Sub Ltd. also sold a piece of land (cost of $188,000) to Parent Corp. on July 1, 20X4, for $260,000, for which Parent Corp. had issued Sub Ltd. a five-year, 10% per annum note. The interest will be paid on July 1, 20X5.

Required

1. Prepare the consolidation related eliminations required in 20X4 and 20X5 respectively.
2. Assuming that Sub Ltd. earned $680,000 during 20X4 and $880,000 during 20X5, calculate the non-controlling interest in the earnings of Sub Ltd.

[CGA–Canada, adapted]

P6-4

Adam Ltd. owns 80% of the outstanding shares of Bob Ltd. Adam Ltd. also owns 70% of the shares of Xena Ltd. During the year 20X5, Adam sold $500,000 (cost) of goods (widgets) to Bob at a 30% markup. Xena sold $400,000 (cost) of goods (gadgets) to Adam at a 25% markup.

Adam sold a piece of land (cost $100,000) to Bob for $50,000.

On October 1, 20X5, Xena sold land (cost $80,000) and a building (cost $110,000) to Adam for $400,000; 40% of the price was allocated to land and 60% of the price was allocated to building. The building had five years of expected life at October 1, 20X5, and was 30% depreciated at that time.

The $400,000 was unpaid at year-end and Adam had agreed to pay $10,000 interest on the unpaid amount.

An inventory count showed that 20% of the widgets that Bob had purchased from Adam were unsold at December 31, 20X5; 70% of the gadgets that Adam had purchased from Xena were also unsold.

Required

Assume that Adam Ltd. uses the cost method of keeping its accounts.

1. Prepare the consolidation-related eliminations that would be required at December 31, 20X5, to prepare the consolidated financial statements.
2. Calculate the effect on the non-controlling interest. By how much would the income to each non-controlling interest be changed? Keep the two subsidiaries separate. [CGA–Canada, adapted]

P6-5

On January 1, 20X2, Peter Limited purchased 70% of the outstanding voting common shares of Susan Limited at a cost of $139,200. At acquisition date, the carrying value of Susan Limited was $161,000, inventory was undervalued by $2,500, and depreciable capital assets were undervalued by $7,500. Relevant information for 20X5 is shown below.

Required

1. Calculate non-controlling interest in net income for 20X5 assuming consolidation is appropriate.
2. Calculate non-controlling interest in the consolidated statement of financial position as of the end of 20X5.
3. Calculate consolidated net income for 20X5, assuming a 10-year remaining life at acquisition date for capital assets and straight-line depreciation. Note that Peter Limited uses the cost method and that Susan Limited paid dividends during the year.

Reported at End of 20X5

	Peter	Susan
Net income and comprehensive income	$ 44,000	$ 11,000
Dividends paid	4,000	1,000
Current assets	$170,800	$ 40,000
Investment in S (at cost)	139,200	—
Capital assets (net)	330,000	160,000
	$640,000	$200,000
Liabilities	$140,000	$ 30,000
Common shares	400,000	150,000
Retained earnings (end)	100,000	20,000
	$640,000	$200,000

[CGA–Canada, adapted]

P6-6

Anita Company owns a controlling interest in Brian Company and Gabriel Company. Anita purchased an 80% interest in Brian at a time when Brian reported retained earnings of

$450,000. Anita purchased a 60% interest in Gabriel at a time when Gabriel reported retained earnings of $100,000. In each acquisition, the purchase price was equal to the proportionate net carrying value of the acquired company's shares, and the fair values of the assets and liabilities approximated their carrying values.

An analysis of the changes in retained earnings of the three companies during the year 20X5 gives the following results:

	Anita Company	Brian Company	Gabriel Company
Retained earnings, January 1, 20X5	$ 742,000	$ 686,000	$ 475,000
Net income for the year	550,000	348,000	310,000
Dividends paid	(250,000)	(200,000)	(150,000)
Retained earnings, December 31, 20X5	$1,042,000	$ 834,000	$ 635,000

Gabriel sells some raw materials to Anita. After further processing and assembly, these parts are sold by Anita to Brian where they become a part of the finished products sold by Brian. Intercompany profits included in inventories at the beginning and end of the current year are estimated as follows:

	January 1, 20X5 Inventory	December 31, 20X5 Inventory
Intercompany profit included on sales from Gabriel to Anita	$70,000	$50,000
On sales from Anita to Brian	60,000	80,000

Brian also rents a building to Gabriel. Gabriel is paying $5,000 per month according to the lease contract. Anita carries its investments on a cost basis. Ignore the impact of income taxes.

Required

1. Compute the consolidated net income for 20X5.
2. Prepare the retained earnings section of the statement of changes in equity for 20X5.
3. What change would there be in consolidated net income if the three companies had engaged in the same transactions, but all purchases, sales, and lending had been with firms outside the affiliated group? Give the amount of the difference and explain how it is derived. [SMA, adapted]

P6-7

On June 30, 20X1, Punt Corporation acquired 70% of the outstanding common shares of Slide Ltd. for $3,326,000 in cash plus Punt Corporation common shares estimated to have a fair market value of $1,200,000. On the date of acquisition, the fair market value and carrying value of each of Slide Ltd.'s assets were generally equal, except for inventory, which was undervalued by $225,000, and capital assets (net), which was overvalued by $1,000,000. The shareholders' equity of Slide at that time was $3,440,000, consisting of:

Common shares	$2,900,000
Retained earnings	540,000
	$3,440,000

Statements of financial position at June 30, 20X5, are as follows:

	Punt Corp.	Slide Ltd.
Assets		
Cash and marketable securities	$ 4,432,000	$ 321,000
Accounts and other receivables	2,153,000	950,000
Inventory	2,940,000	1,206,000
Capital assets (net)	17,064,000	7,161,000
Other long-term investments	3,038,000	2,240,000
Investment in Slide Ltd.	4,526,000	—
TOTAL ASSETS	$34,153,000	$11,878,000
Liabilities		
Current liabilities	$ 3,025,000	$ 2,090,000
Mortgage note payable	12,135,000	4,000,000
Total liabilities	15,160,000	6,090,000
Shareholders' equity		
Common shares	10,000,000	2,900,000
Retained earnings	8,993,000	2,888,000
Total shareholders' equity	18,993,000	5,788,000
TOTAL LIABILITIES AND SHAREHOLDERS' EQUITY	$34,153,000	$11,878,000

Additional Information

1. Slide Ltd. had income of $1,460,000 for the year ended June 30, 20X5. Dividends of $480,000 were declared during the fiscal year but were not paid until August 12, 20X5.
2. Slide Ltd. has had an average inventory turnover of four times per year over the past decade.
3. The capital assets that were overvalued on the date of acquisition had a remaining useful life of 20 years.
4. Slide sold goods to Punt during the year ended June 30, 20X4 at a gross profit margin of 25%. The opening inventory of Punt at July 1, 20X4 included items purchased from Slide in the amount of $160,000. There were no sales from Slide to Punt during the year ended June 30, 20X5
5. Punt sold goods to Slide Ltd. during the current fiscal year at a gross profit margin of 30%. Of the $750,000 of sales, goods worth $200,000 were in Slide's closing inventory at June 30, 20X5. None of these intercompany sales still in inventory had been paid for at the fiscal year-end.
6. Both companies follow the straight-line method for depreciating capital assets.
7. The controller of Punt has informed you that, to date, there has been no impairment in goodwill.

Required

Prepare the consolidated statement of financial position for Punt Corporation and its subsidiary, Slide Ltd., at June 30, 20X5.

[SMA, adapted]

P6-8

On January 1, 20X1, ABC Limited purchased 90% of the outstanding common shares of XYZ Limited for $150,000. At that date, XYZ Limited's condensed statement of financial position and fair values were as follows:

	Carrying value	Fair value
Cash	$ 20,000	$20,000
Land	40,000	60,000
Building (net)	40,000	50,000
	$100,000	
Liabilities	$ 20,000	20,000
Common shares	20,000	
Retained earnings	60,000	
	$100,000	

Assume a 10-year amortization period for any capital assets.

Required

1. Assume the following information regarding net income and dividends for XYZ Limited:

Year	Net Income	Dividends
20X1	$20,000	$ 4,000
20X2	24,000	4,000
20X3	18,000	4,000
20X4	(20,000)	4,000*
20X5	20,000	52,000

*The 20X4 dividend was a stock dividend.

   Calculate the balance in the investment account in ABC's books at the end of 20X5 assuming that ABC uses the equity method of accounting in its books.

2. Assume that ABC uses the cost method of accounting for its investment. Prepare a journal entry or entries to reflect the information previously provided for 20X4 and 20X5. [CGA–Canada, adapted]

P6-9

On April 2, 20X4, Curry Ltd. acquired 40% of the outstanding common shares of Jasmine Ltd. by issuing one share of Curry plus $5 cash for each of Jasmine's shares acquired. At the time of purchase, Curry's shares were trading at $25 per share and Jasmine's shares were trading at $28. Jasmine had a total of 1 million shares outstanding.

At the date of acquisition, the shareholders' equity of Jasmine totalled $18,000,000. The fair values of Jasmine's assets and liabilities were the same as their net carrying values, except for the following capital assets:

	Carrying value	Fair value
Land	$5,000,000	$8,000,000
Building	6,000,000	5,000,000
Equipment	5,000,000	7,000,000

The building and equipment have estimated remaining useful lives of ten years and five years respectively. Jasmine uses straight-line amortization.

For the year ended March 31, 20X5, Jasmine reported net income of $1,500,000. Jasmine's dividend payout was 60% for fiscal 20X5.

Required

For the year ended March 31, 20X5, compute: (1) Curry's equity in the earnings of Jasmine, and (2) the balance of the investment account at the fiscal year-end, using the equity method. Provide supporting calculations.

P6-10

At the 20X5 annual meeting for Jasmine's shareholders, Curry nominated seven directors for Jasmine's 12-person board of directors. After some negotiation, five of Curry's nominees were accepted onto the board. During fiscal year 20X6 the following occurred:

1. Curry shifted a substantial amount of business to Jasmine. Jasmine became the major supplier of one of Curry's raw materials and had sales totalling $7,000,000 to Curry. Of that total, $1,000,000 was in Curry's raw materials inventory at year-end. The other $6,000,000 had been utilized in finished goods, of which one-third was still in inventory on March 31, 20X6.
2. Curry began selling some products to Cinnamon Corp., a wholly owned subsidiary of Jasmine. Fiscal 20X6 sales totalled $2,500,000, all within the last two months of the year. At year-end, 60% of the sales were still in Cinnamon's inventory.
3. Operating results for fiscal 20X6 were reported as follows:

	Curry	Jasmine
Sales	$80,000,000	$20,000,000
Cost of sales	(56,000,000)	(12,000,000)
	24,000,000	8,000,000
Operating expenses	(6,000,000)	(4,000,000)
Income tax expense	(7,200,000)	(1,600,000)
Net income and comprehensive income	$10,800,000	$ 2,400,000

Required

Using the information above and in P6-9, prepare a schedule(s) in which you:

1. Compute the amount of investment income that Curry should recognize in fiscal 20X6 from its investment in Jasmine.
2. Compute the balance of Curry's investment account for its investment in Jasmine at March 31, 20X6.

P6-11

On January 1, 20X2, Porter Inc. purchased 80% of the outstanding voting shares of Sloan Ltd. for $3,000,000 in cash. On this date, Sloan had common shares outstanding in the amount of $2,200,000 and retained earnings of $1,100,000. The identifiable assets and liabilities of Sloan had fair values that were equal to their carrying values except for the following:

a) Capital assets (net) had a fair value $200,000 greater than its carrying value. The remaining useful life on January 1, 20X2, was 20 years with no anticipated residual value.

b) Accounts receivable had a fair value $75,000 less than carrying value.

c) Long-term liabilities had a fair value $62,500 less than carrying value. These liabilities mature on June 30, 20X10.

It is the policy of Porter to test all goodwill balances for impairment on an annual basis. To date, there has been no impairment in goodwill. Both Porter and Sloan use the straight-line method for depreciation. Porter Inc. is a public company.

Additional Information

1. Between January 1, 20X2, and December 31, 20X4, Sloan earned $345,000 and paid dividends of $115,000.
2. On January 1, 20X4, Sloan sold a patent to Porter for $165,000. On this date, the patent had a carrying value on the books of Sloan of $185,000, and a remaining useful life of five years.
3. On September 1, 20X4, Porter sold land to Sloan for $103,000. The land had a carrying value on the books of Porter of $82,000. Sloan still owned this land on December 31, 20X5.
4. For the year ended December 31, 20X5, the statements of comprehensive income revealed the following:

	Porter	Sloan
Total revenues	$2,576,000	$ 973,000
Cost of goods sold	1,373,000	467,000
Depreciation expense	483,000	176,000
Other expenses	352,000	153,000
Total expenses	2,208,000	796,000
Net income and comprehensive income	$ 368,000	$ 177,000

Porter records its investment in Sloan using the cost method and includes dividend income from Sloan in its total revenues.

5. Porter and Sloan paid dividends of $125,000 and $98,000 respectively in 20X5.
6. Sloan issued no common shares subsequent to January 1, 20X2. Selected statement of financial position accounts for the two companies at December 31, 20X5, were:

	Porter	Sloan
Accounts receivable (net)	$ 987,000	$ 133,000
Inventories	1,436,000	787,000
Capital assets (net)	3,467,000	1,234,000
Patents (net)	263,000	—
Land	872,000	342,000
Long-term liabilities	1,876,000	745,000
Retained earnings	4,833,000	1,409,000

7. During 20X5, Porter's merchandise sales to Sloan were $150,000. The unrealized profits in Sloan's inventory on January 1 and December 31, 20X5, were $14,000 and $10,000, respectively. At December 31, 20X5, Sloan still owed Porter $5,000 for merchandise purchases.

8. During 20X5, Sloan's merchandise sales to Porter were $55,000. The unrealized profits in Porter's inventory on January 1 and December 31, 20X5, were $1,500 and $2,500 respectively. At December 31, 20X5, Porter still owed Sloan $2,000 for merchandise purchases.

Required

1. Compute the balances that would appear in the consolidated statement of financial position of Porter and Sloan as at December 31, 20X5, for the following:
   a. Patent (net)
   b. Non-controlling interest
   c. Retained earnings
2. Porter has decided not to prepare consolidated financial statements and will report its investment in Sloan by the equity method. Calculate the investment income that would be disclosed in the statement of comprehensive income of Porter for the year ended December 31, 20X5. [SMA]

P6-12

On January 1, 19X8, Partial Company acquired 80% of the outstanding voting shares of the Sum Company for $3,900,000 in cash. On this date, Sum Company had $2,000,000 in common shares outstanding and $2,000,000 in retained earnings. Any excess of cost over carrying value is to be recorded in the consolidated financial statements as goodwill and is tested annually for impairment. On December 31, 20X5, the statements of financial position of the two companies are as follows:

Statements of Financial Position
December 31, 20X5

	Partial Company	Sum Company
Cash	$ 3,000,000	$ 1,000,000
Accounts receivable	7,000,000	2,000,000
Inventories	4,100,000	3,000,000
Investment in Sum	3,900,000	—
Capital assets (net)	7,000,000	5,000,000
TOTAL ASSETS	$25,000,000	$11,000,000
Liabilities	$ 5,000,000	$ 3,000,000
Common shares	7,000,000	2,000,000
Retained earnings	13,000,000	6,000,000
TOTAL LIABILITIES AND EQUITIES	$25,000,000	$11,000,000

Additional Information

1. Sum Company sells merchandise to Partial Company at a price that provides Sum with a gross margin of 50% of the sales price. During 20X5, these sales amounted to $1,000,000. The December 31, 20X5, inventories of Partial contain $200,000 of these purchases while the December 31, 20X4, inventories of Partial contained $100,000 in merchandise purchased from Sum.
2. At the end of 20X5, Partial owes Sum $60,000 for merchandise purchased on account. The account is non-interest-bearing.

3. On December 31, 20X2, Partial Company sold equipment to Sum Company for $550,000. At the time of the sale, the equipment had a net carrying value in Partial's records of $450,000. The remaining useful life of the asset on this date was 10 years.
4. There has been no impairment in goodwill since January 1, 19X8.

Required

Prepare a consolidated statement of financial position for Partial Company and its subsidiary, Sum Company, at December 31, 20X5. Ignore the impact of income taxes.

[SMA, adapted]

P6-13

In January 20X3, Paris Ink Company (Paris) purchased 80% of the common shares of Slade Paper Ltd. (Slade) by issuing common shares worth $800,000. At that date, Slade's common shares and retained earnings totalled $250,000 and $340,000 respectively. The net carrying values and fair values of the net identifiable assets of Slade were the same except for the following:

1. The fair market value (FMV) of inventory was greater than carrying value by $50,000.
2. The FMV of capital assets had replacement cost that exceeded net carrying value (NCV) by $120,000, although net realizable value exceeded NCV by only $60,000 (management planned to retain the capital assets throughout their remaining useful life of 12 years).
3. Although the NCV of Slade's bonds payable was $400,000, the FMV was $460,000, due to a decline in the interest rates since the bonds were originally issued. The bonds payable mature on December 31, 20X8, and have a nominal rate of interest of 12%. The companies use straight-line amortization for bond premiums and discounts.

The financial statements for Paris and Slade for the year ended December 31, 20X5, are presented in Exhibit B. Additional information on transactions between Paris and Slade is presented in Exhibit C.

Exhibit B Financial Statements

Statements of Comprehensive Income
For the Year Ended December 31, 20X5

	Paris	Slade
Sales	$3,850,000	$1,650,000
Cost of goods sold	2,550,000	1,120,000
Gross profit	1,300,000	530,000
EXPENSES		
Administration & selling	550,000	384,000
Amortization	136,000	74,000
Interest	—	56,000
	686,000	514,000
OTHER INCOME		
Interest & dividends	76,000	4,000
Gain on sale of land	—	100,000
	76,000	104,000
Income before income taxes	690,000	120,000
Income tax expense	260,000	30,000
Net income and comprehensive income	$ 430,000	$ 90,000

Statements of Financial Position
As at December 31, 20X5

	Paris	Slade
ASSETS		
Current assets:		
Cash	$ 45,000	$ 80,000
Accounts receivable	655,000	455,000
Inventory	420,000	350,000
Marketable securities	380,000	45,000
Due from Slade	200,000	—
	1,700,000	930,000
Capital assets—net	1,450,000	690,000
Investment in Slade	800,000	—
	$3,950,000	$1,620,000
LIABILITIES		
Current liabilities:		
Accounts payable	$ 665,000	$ 280,000
Note payable to Paris	—	200,000
	665,000	480,000
Bonds payable	—	400,000
Shareholders' Equity		
Common shares	2,500,000	250,000
Retained earnings	785,000	490,000
	$3,950,000	$1,620,000

Exhibit C

Additional Information

1. On July 1, 20X5, Paris advanced Slade $200,000, due on July 1, 20X6. Interest of 8% is due at maturity.
2. Intercompany sales from Slade to Paris were as follows for 20X3–20X5:

	20X3	20X4	20X5
Sales	$200,000	$240,000	$250,000
Gross profit margin	32.00%	33.33%	30.00%
Amount remaining in inventory at year-end	$ 60,000	$ 75,000	$100,000

All amounts in closing inventory at the end of each year were sold during the first four months of the following year.

3. On March 1, 20X5, Slade sold land to Paris for $300,000. The original cost of the land was $200,000. Assume this transaction was taxed at the company's normal tax rate.
4. During 20X5, Paris sold inventory to Slade for $108,000, which represented a markup of 35% above cost. At December 31, 20X5, 20% of these goods remained in inventory.
5. During 20X5, Paris paid dividends of $250,000 and Slade paid dividends of $50,000.
6. Paris and Slade pay taxes at 40% and 25% rates, respectively.

Required

1. Calculate the carrying value of the goodwill on the consolidated financial statements of Paris Ink Company at December 31, 20X5. Paris tests goodwill for impairment on an annual basis.
2. Prepare a consolidated SCI for Paris Ink Company for the year ended December 31, 20X5.
3. Calculate the following balances for Paris Ink Company's consolidated statement of financial position as at December 31, 20X5:
   a) Inventory
   b) Non-controlling interest

[ICAO]

P6-14

Pop Company acquired 70% of Son Limited on January 1, 20X4, for $345,000. On the acquisition date, common shares and retained earnings of Son Limited were $100,000 and $200,000 respectively. The fair market values of Son's identifiable net assets were equivalent to their carrying value except for capital assets, which were undervalued by $50,000, and long-term debt, which was overvalued by $100,000. The undervalued capital assets have a remaining life of 10 years. The long-term debt matures on December 31, 20X8. Any goodwill is tested for impairment on an annual basis. Both companies use the straight-line method of amortization.

Intercompany transactions include the downstream sale of a capital asset in 20X4, which included an unrealized profit of $30,000 to be amortized over five years. During 20X5, there was an intercompany upstream sale of land for $120,000. The original cost of the land was $95,000.

For the year ended December 31, 20X5, Pop Company had net income of $244,000 and declared dividends of $10,000. Son Limited had 20X5 net income of $85,000 and paid dividends of $10,000. All dividends have been declared and paid on December 31. Pop Company uses the cost method to account for its investment in Son Limited. Shown below are the statements of financial position for the parent company and its subsidiary on December 31, 20X5.

Statements of Financial Position
December 31, 20X5

	Pop Company	Son Limited
Current assets	$1,200,000	$250,000
Investment in Son Limited	345,000	—
Capital assets—net	900,000	450,000
Goodwill	—	—
TOTAL ASSETS	$2,445,000	$700,000
Current liabilities	$1,045,000	$ 75,000
Long-term debt	500,000	200,000
Non-controlling interest	—	—
Common shares	500,000	100,000
Retained earnings	400,000	325,000
TOTAL LIABILITIES AND EQUITIES	$2,445,000	$700,000

Required

1. Determine consolidated net income for the year ended December 31, 20X5. Show all your calculations.

2. Calculate the balances of the following accounts as they would appear in the consolidated statement of financial position on December 31, 20X5:
   a) Capital assets, net
   b) Non-controlling interest
   c) Retained earnings
3. Prepare the required December 31, 20X5, journal entry to eliminate the Investment in Son Limited account.
   [CGA–Canada, adapted]

P6-15

Note: All dollar amounts in the question are in 000s.

On December 31, 19X9, Hari Company (Hari) purchased 70% of the outstanding common shares of Amin Limited (Amin) for $7,000. On that date, Amin's shareholders' equity consisted of common shares of $250 and retained earnings of $4,500. The financial statements for Hari and Amin for 20X5 were as follows:

Statements of Financial Position
December 31, 20X5

	Hari	Amin
Cash	$ 1,340	$ 780
Accounts receivable	2,800	1,050
Inventory	3,400	2,580
Capital assets—net	4,340	3,010
Investment in Amin	7,000	—
Total	$18,880	$7,420
Current liabilities	$ 4,200	$ 540
Long-term liabilities	3,100	1,230
Common shares	1,000	250
Retained earnings	10,580	5,400
Total	$18,880	$7,420

Statements of Comprehensive Income
Year Ended December 31, 20X5

	Hari	Amin
Sales	$21,900	$7,440
Cost of sales	14,800	3,280
Gross profit	7,100	4,160
Other revenue	1,620	—
Amortization expense	(840)	(420)
Other expenses	(5,320)	(2,040)
Income before income taxes	2,560	1,700
Income tax expense	800	680
Net income and comprehensive income	$ 1,760	$1,020

Statements of Changes in Equity—Retained Earnings Section
Year Ended December 31, 20X5

	Hari	Amin
Retained earnings, beginning	$10,420	$5,180
Net income	1,760	1,020
Dividends paid	(1,600)	(800)
Retained earnings, ending	$10,580	$5,400

Other Information

1. In negotiating the purchase price at the date of acquisition, it was agreed that the fair values of all of Amin's assets and liabilities were equal to their carrying values, except for the following:

	Carrying value	Fair value
Inventory	$2,100	$2,200
Equipment	2,500	3,000

2. Both companies use FIFO to account for their inventory and the straight-line method for amortizing their capital assets. Amin's capital assets had a remaining useful life of ten years at the acquisition date.
3. Each year, goodwill is evaluated to determine if there has been permanent impairment. It was determined that goodwill on the consolidated statement of financial position should be reported at $1,100 on December 31, 20X4, and at $1,030 on December 31, 20X5.
4. During 20X5, inventory sales from Amin to Hari were $10,000. Hari's inventories contained merchandise purchased from Amin for $2,000 on December 31, 20X4 and $2,500 at December 31, 20X5. Amin earns a gross margin of 40% on its intercompany sales.
5. On January 1, 20X1, Hari sold some equipment to Amin for $1,000 and recorded a gain of $200 before taxes. This equipment had a remaining useful life of eight years at the time of the purchase by Amin.
6. Hari charges $50 per month to Amin for consulting services.
7. Hari uses the cost method in accounting for its long-term investment.
8. Both companies pay taxes at the rate of 40%. Ignore future taxes when allocating and amortizing the purchase price.

Required

1. Prepare a consolidated statement of income for the year ended December 31, 20X5.
2. Calculate consolidated retained earnings at January 1, 20X5, and then prepare the retained earnings section of the consolidated statement of changes in equity for the year ended December 31, 20X5.
3. Explain how the historical cost principle supports the adjustments made on consolidation when there has been an intercompany sale of equipment.
[CGA–Canada, adapted]

P6-16

On January 1, 20X0, Mariachi Corporation acquired 70% of the outstanding shares of Sombrero Company for $85,000 cash. On that date, Sombrero Company had $35,000 of common shares outstanding and $25,000 of retained earnings. On January 1, 20X0, the carrying values of each of Sombrero Company's identifiable assets and liabilities were equal to their fair value except for the following:

	Carrying value	Fair value
Inventory	$25,000	$35,000
Equipment	10,000	30,000

The equipment had a useful life of 10 years as at January 1, 20X0, and all inventory was sold during 20X0. The following are the separate entity financial statements for Mariachi and Sombrero at December 31, 20X5:

Statements of Financial Position
December 31, 20X5

	Mariachi	Sombrero
Cash	$120,000	$ 20,000
Accounts receivable	90,000	65,000
Inventory	250,000	90,000
Capital assets—net	225,000	150,000
Investment in Sombrero	85,000	—
Total	$770,000	$325,000
Accounts payable	$230,000	$180,000
Deferred income taxes	70,000	60,000
	300,000	240,000
Common shares	200,000	35,000
Retained earnings	270,000	50,000
Total	$770,000	$325,000

Statements of Comprehensive Income
Year Ended December 31, 20X5

	Mariachi	Sombrero
Sales	$750,000	$600,000
Cost of goods sold	(500,000)	(450,000)
Gross margin	250,000	150,000
Dividend income	21,000	—
Gain on sale of trademark	—	12,000
Amortization expense	(35,000)	(20,000)
Other expenses	(86,000)	(62,000)
Income tax expense	(60,000	(32,000)
Net income and comprehensive income	$ 90,000	$ 48,000

Statements of Changes in Equity—Retained Earnings Section
Year Ended December 31, 20X5

	Mariachi	Sombrero
Retained earnings, beginning of year	$180,000	$ 32,000
Net income	90,000	48,000
Dividends paid	—	(30,000)
Retained earnings, end of year	$270,000	$ 50,000

Additional Information

1. On January 1, 20X2, Mariachi sold Sombrero a trademark with a net carrying value of $20,000 for cash consideration of $28,000. The trademark has an indefinite useful life. On July 1, 20X5, Sombrero sold the trademark to an unrelated company for cash consideration of $40,000.
2. Sombrero sells goods to Mariachi at 25% above cost. Total sales from Sombrero to Mariachi during 20X5 were $50,000, of which $20,000 remained in Mariachi's inventory at year end. Mariachi still owed Sombrero $18,000 for this inventory at December 31, 20X5. In 20X4, total sales from Sombrero to Mariachi were $40,000, of which $10,000 remained in Mariachi's inventory at year end.

3. Mariachi uses the cost method to account for its investment in Sombrero. Both companies pay income taxes at a rate of 40%, and have done so since 19X9. None of the transactions detailed above are considered capital gains for tax purposes. Ignore future taxes when calculating the purchase price discrepancy.
4. Each year, goodwill is evaluated to determine if there has been permanent impairment. To date there has been no impairment in value.

Required

1. Prepare a calculation for the purchase price discrepancy and goodwill as of January 1, 20X0.
2. Prepare a consolidated statement of income for the year ended December 31, 20X5.
3. What would the balance be for each of the following consolidated statement of financial position accounts as at December 31, 20X5?
   a) accounts receivable
   b) inventory
   c) equipment
   d) non-controlling interest

[CGA–Canada, adapted]

P6-17

Aztec Corporation purchased 70% of the outstanding shares of Inca Limited on January 1, 20X2, at a cost of $80,000. Aztec has always used the cost method to account for its investments. On January 1, 20X2, Inca had common shares of $50,000 and retained earnings of $30,000, and fair values were equal to carrying value for all of its net assets except for inventory (fair value was $9,000 less than carrying value) and equipment (fair value was $24,000 greater than carrying value). The equipment had an estimated remaining life of six years on January 1, 20X2.

The following are the separate-entity financial statements of Aztec and Inca at December 31, 20X5:

Statements of Financial Position
December 31, 20X5

	Aztec	Inca
Cash	$ —	$ 10,000
Accounts receivable	40,000	30,000
Note receivable	0	40,000
Inventory	66,000	44,000
Capital assets—net	220,000	76,000
Land	150,000	30,000
Investment in Inca	80,000	—
Total	$556,000	$230,000
Accounts payable	$140,000	$ 60,000
Notes payable	40,000	—
Common shares	150,000	50,000
Retained earnings	226,000	120,000
Total	$556,000	$230,000

Statements of Comprehensive Income
Year Ended December 31, 20X5

	Aztec	Inca
Sales	$798,000	$300,000
Management fee revenue	24,000	—
Investment income	14,000	3,600
Gain on sale of land	—	20,000
	836,000	323,600
Cost of sales	480,000	200,000
Amortization expense	40,000	12,000
Interest expense	10,000	—
Other expenses	106,000	31,600
Income tax expense	80,000	32,000
	716,000	275,600
Net income and comprehensive income	$120,000	$ 48,000

Statements of Changes in Equity—Retained Earnings Section
Year Ended December 31, 20X5

	Aztec	Inca
Retained earnings, beginning of year	$106,000	$ 92,000
Net income	120,000	48,000
Dividends paid	—	(20,000)
Retained earnings, end of year	$226,000	$120,000

Additional Information

1. During 20X5, Inca made a cash payment of $2,000 per month to Aztec for management fees, which is included in Inca's "other expenses."
2. During 20X5, Aztec made intercompany sales of $100,000 to Inca. The December 31, 20X5, inventory of Inca contained goods purchased from Aztec amounting to $30,000. These sales had a gross profit of 35%.
3. On April 1, 20X5, Aztec acquired land from Inca for $40,000. This land had been recorded on Inca's books at a net carrying value of $20,000. Aztec paid for the land by signing a $40,000 note payable to Inca, bearing interest at 8%. Interest for 20X5 was paid by Aztec in cash on December 31, 20X5. This land was still being held by Aztec on December 31, 20X5.
4. The fair value of the consolidated goodwill remained unchanged from January 1, 20X2, to July 1, 20X5. On July 1, 20X5, a valuation was performed, indicating that the fair value of consolidated goodwill was $3,500.
5. Inca and Aztec pay taxes at a 40% rate. Assume that none of the gains or losses were capital gains or losses. Ignore the impact of future taxes for all transactions.

Required

1. Prepare a calculation of goodwill and any unamortized purchase price discrepancy as at December 31, 20X5.
2. Prepare Aztec's consolidated SCI for the year ended December 31, 20X5.

3. Calculate the following balances that would appear on Aztec's consolidated statement of financial position as at December 31, 20X5:
   a) inventory
   b) land
   c) notes payable
   d) non-controlling interest
   e) common shares

   [CGA–Canada, adapted]

P6-18

On January 1, 19X9, Apache Company purchased 80% of the outstanding voting shares of Navaho Company for $300,000. Navaho's assets and liabilities all had fair values that were equal to their carrying values. The $80,000 excess of purchase price over 80% of the carrying values of Navaho Company's net assets was allocated to goodwill. Goodwill is tested for impairment on an annual basis. Between January 1, 19X9, and January 1, 20X5, Navaho Company earned $200,000 and paid dividends of $40,000. Both companies use the straight-line method to calculate depreciation and amortization.

Additional Information

1. On January 1, 19X5, Navaho Company purchased a machine for $100,000 that had an estimated useful life of 20 years; on January 1, 20X0, Navaho Company sold the machine to Apache Company for $60,000. The estimated useful life of the machine remains unchanged at a total of 20 years (15 years from January 1, 20X0).
2. During 20X5, Navaho Company had sales of merchandise in the amount of $400,000 to Apache Company, of which $60,000 remains in the December 31, 20X5, inventories of Apache Company. Apache Company had no sales to Navaho Company during 20X5, but had sales of $200,000 to Navaho Company in 20X4. Of these sales, $40,000 remained in the December 31, 20X4, inventories of Navaho Company. Intercompany sales are priced to provide the selling company with a 40% gross profit on sales prices.
3. On September 1, 20X5, Navaho Company sold a piece of land to Apache Company for $50,000. The land had been purchased for $35,000.
4. During 20X5, Navaho Company declared dividends of $6,000 and Apache Company declared dividends of $35,000.
5. During 20X5, Navaho Company paid Apache Company $10,000 in management fees.
6. On July 1, 20X5, Apache Company lent Navaho Company $100,000 for five years at an annual interest rate of 10%. Interest is paid on July 1 of each year for which the loan is outstanding.
7. To date, there has been no impairment in the value of goodwill.

Apache Company carries its investment in Navaho Company by the cost method. On this date, the statements of comprehensive income of Apache Company and Navaho Company for the year ended December 31, 20X5, are as follows:

	Apache	Navaho
Merchandise sales	$3,000,000	$2,000,000
Investment income	60,000	—
Other revenue	50,000	70,000
Total revenues	3,110,000	2,070,000
Cost of goods sold	1,800,000	1,400,000
Depreciation expense	400,000	400,000
Selling and administrative	500,000	200,000
Loss on sales of investments	—	26,000
Total expenses	2,700,000	2,026,000
Net income and comprehensive income	$ 410,000	$ 44,000

Required

1. Prepare the consolidated SCI for Apache Company and its subsidiary, Navaho Company, for the year ended December 31, 20X5.
2. Assume that Apache Company prepares separate-entity statements for its bank and uses the equity method of reporting its investment in Navaho. Provide a detailed calculation of Apache Company's investment income for the year ended December 31, 20X5.
   [SMA, adapted]

P6-19

On April 1, 20X5, Marsh Ltd. purchased 25% of the outstanding common shares of King Corp. for $6,000,000. The carrying value of King's net assets was $16,000,000, an amount that also approximated their fair value. For the year ended December 31, 20X5, King reported net income of $800,000 and Marsh reported net income of $10,200,000. King paid dividends of $50,000 in each of the first two quarters of 20X5, and $75,000 in each of the last two quarters. There were no intercompany transactions during the year. Both companies generate their incomes fairly evenly throughout the year. Assume no goodwill impairment.

Required

Compute the amounts that would appear on Marsh's 20X5 SCI as income from investment in King, and the balance of the investment account on the December 31, 20X5, statement of financial position, assuming that Marsh uses:

1. the cost method
2. the equity method

P6-20

[Copyright © 1984 by the American Institute of Certified Public Accountants Inc. Reprinted with permission.]

North Company has supplied you with information regarding two investments that were made during 20X5 as follows:

1. On January 1, 20X5, North purchased for cash 40% of the 500,000 shares of voting common shares of Young Company for $2,800,000, representing 40% of the net worth of Young. The carrying value of Young's net assets was $6,000,000 on January 1, 20X5, and this amount approximated the fair value of the net assets. Young's net income for the year ended

December 31, 20X5, was $900,000. Young paid dividends of $0.80 per share in 20X5. The market value of Young's common shares was $15 per share on December 31, 20X5. North exercised significant influence over the operating and financial policies of Young.

2. On July 1, 20X5, North purchased for cash 20,000 shares representing 5% of the voting common shares of the Mak Company for $500,000. Mak's net income for the six months ended December 31, 20X5, was $400,000, and for the year ended December 31, 20X5, it was $650,000. Mak paid dividends of $0.40 per share each quarter during 20X5 to shareholders of record on the last day of each quarter. The market value of Mak's common shares was $30 per share on January 1, 20X5, and $35 per share on December 31, 20X5.

Required

As a result of these two investments, determine the following:

1. What should be the balance in the investment account for North at December 31, 20X5?
2. What should be the investment income reported by North for the year ended December 31, 20X5?

   Show all supporting calculations. The equity method of recording investments is used when appropriate for reporting purposes.

   [AICPA, adapted]

P6-21

To maintain closer ties with associated companies in the oil business, King Oil Company decided to purchase holdings of common shares in several companies. The following is a list of activities associated with these acquisitions during 20X5.

February 15	Acquired 80,000 shares of Lub Oil Co. at $8 per share, representing 70% of the outstanding shares. At date of acquisition, carrying value of the Lub Oil Co.'s net assets was $800,000. Assets were considered to be valued at market.
April 13	Acquired 140,000 shares of Richman Refineries at $11 per share representing 60% of the outstanding shares. The purchase price corresponds to the underlying carrying value.
May 17	Acquired 50,000 shares of Discovery Co. Ltd. at $5 per share representing 2% of the outstanding shares.
June 30	Lub Oil Co. announced a loss of $50,000 for the first six months of 20X5. Richman Refineries announced earnings of $120,000 for the first six months of 20X5 and declared a dividend of $0.10 per share.
August 15	Dividend received from Richman Refineries.
October 11	Dividend of $0.05 per share received from Discovery Co. Ltd. with a statement of earnings for the six months ended September 30 indicating net earnings of $60,000.
December 31	Lub Oil Co. announced a loss of $40,000 for the year. Richman Refineries announced earnings of $200,000 for the year, including a gain of $40,000. Discovery Co. Ltd. announced earnings of $90,000 for the nine months ended December 31.

To date, there has been no goodwill impairment.

Required

1. Investments in shares could be recorded and/or reported using either the equity method or the cost method. Distinguish between the two methods, indicating under what circumstances each method should be used.
2. Prepare journal entries to record the above transactions in the books of King Oil Company, assuming the use of the equity method of accounting where appropriate for reporting purposes. [SMA, adapted]

P6-22

Slater Company purchased 30% of the outstanding voting shares of Rogan Company for $1,500,000 in cash on January 1, 20X3. On that date, Rogan Company's shareholders' equity was made up of common shares of $3 million and retained earnings of $1 million. There were no differences between the carrying values and the fair values of any of its net identifiable assets or liabilities. The net income and dividends declared and paid by Rogan Company for the two years subsequent to its acquisition were as follows:

	20X3	20X4
Net income (loss)	($200,000)	$180,000
Dividends	50,000	60,000

The statements of comprehensive income for the year ended December 31, 20X5, prior to the recognition of any investment income, for Slater and Rogan Companies are as follows:

	Slater	Rogan
Sales	$3,000,000	$550,000
Other revenues	200,000	—
Total revenues	3,200,000	550,000
Cost of goods sold	1,500,000	300,000
Other expenses	300,000	50,000
Loss	—	30,000
Total expenses	1,800,000	380,000
Net income and comprehensive income	$1,400,000	$170,000

During 20X5, Slater Company declared and paid dividends of $120,000, while Rogan Company declared and paid dividends of $80,000. Rogan Company declares and pays its dividends on December 31 of each year.

Required

1. Assume that Slater can exercise significant influence over the affairs of Rogan. Provide the following:
   a) The SCI of Slater Company, including recognition of any investment income or loss, for the year ended December 31, 20X5.
   b) The balance in the investment in Rogan Company account as it would appear on the December 31, 20X5, statement of financial position of Slater Company.
   Assume no impairment in the value of goodwill.
2. Assume that Slater cannot exercise significant influence over the affairs of Rogan. Provide the journal entry of Slater Company related to its investment in Rogan Company for 20X5. [SMA, adapted]

7

Segment and Interim Reporting

LEARNING OBJECTIVES

After studying this chapter, students should be able to:

1. describe segmented reporting and identify and distinguish between operating segments and reportable segments;
2. state the segment information and entity-wide disclosures that are required to be reported;
3. describe the scope, content, and periods covered in interim reports;
4. explain the different theoretical approaches to recognition and measurement for interim reporting; and
5. apply the recognition and measurement principles for interim reporting.

INTRODUCTION

Thomson Reuters Corporation is a world leader in the provision of information to businesses and professionals. The company operates in 93 countries around the world. In fiscal year 2009, the company reported revenue of almost $13 billion on its consolidated financial statements. Consolidated statements give a good overview of the Thomson Reuters economic entity, but they obscure information about the sources of the company's revenues and profits. Investors will want to know which market segments and which geographic markets are driving Thomson Reuters' profitability. Fortunately, securities regulators and standard setters have recognized this shortcoming of consolidated statements. To help investors better understand where and how they were able to generate their profits, public companies are required to disclose key financial information by operating and geographic segment.

Thomson Reuters has two key lines of business—*markets* and *professional*. "Markets" includes revenue generated from information provided to financial services professionals such as stock brokers and investment bankers. "Professional" includes revenue generated from information provided to agencies, organizations, and companies in the accounting, legal, scientific, and healthcare professions. Thomson Reuters also operates across the globe, in the Americas, the Asia–Pacific region, and a broad "EMEA" area—Europe, Middle East, and Africa.

Investors also find that annual financial reports are too far apart; they want more timely financial information. Therefore, public companies also supplement their annual reports with interim financial reports. Thomson Reuters issues quarterly unaudited financial statements in May, August, and November in addition to its annual financial statements which are usually issued in March.

The previous chapters have discussed only "the big picture" in the form of annual consolidated statements. This chapter looks at two types of information that a public company provides to its shareholders that are intended to remedy some of the shortcomings of annual consolidated information:

- disaggregated reporting for *segments* of the enterprise, as supplementary information; and
- reporting for shorter, *interim* periods of time, normally quarterly for public reporting in Canada and the United States (semi-annually in most other countries).

The requirements for segment and interim reporting are imposed by securities regulators and thus apply only to public companies. IFRS has developed standards to guide preparation of this information to enhance comparability.

SEGMENT REPORTING

Consolidated statements conceal the financial position and results of operations for the separate entities and business lines comprising the consolidated whole. A financial statement user cannot see the relative importance and profitability of a consolidated entity's different lines of business. Nor can a user determine the company's risk exposure in its various types of activities.

Each type of business will be affected by different factors relating to markets, supply, competition, etc. Analysts and investors need such information to make predictions about the companies they follow, but such information is not available in the consolidated financial statements.

The response of securities regulators (and securities laws) to this need has been to require segment reporting as a mandatory disclosure to accompany consolidated statements. **Segment reporting** is the disaggregation of consolidated results into the major different types of businesses in which a consolidated entity engages. Also known as **line of business reporting**, segmented reporting helps financial statement users understand the risks and rewards inherent in different lines of business and different geographic areas. National and regional economic and political environments differ, and exchange rate fluctuations add an additional dimension to risk analysis.

Segment reporting is not the same as reporting by separate legal entity. Segment reporting addresses the problems cited above for consolidated statements, but it does not directly address the need of some users (such as a company's bankers) for reporting by a separate legal entity. Only if there is a correspondence between corporate entities and segments in the consolidated financial statements can a minority shareholder or a creditor gain insight into the viability of the individual corporation in which she or he has a stake.

The IFRS 8 requirements for segment reporting are quite broad and permit substantial flexibility in reporting. The *core principle* is that a company should disclose information that helps users evaluate the nature and financial results of its various principal activities, as well as understand the economic environments in which it operates. Therefore, IFRS 8 also requires disclosure of information relating to products and services, geographic areas, and major customers.

Applicability

IFRS 8 applies only to *public* companies—those that have shares and/or bonds traded in the public capital markets, either on a regulated exchange or over the counter. Segment reporting therefore does not apply to most companies in Canada, although the requirements can be used as a guideline for private companies if they choose to provide segment reporting either voluntarily or at the request of major creditors. More commonly, however, banks require borrowers to supply separate legal-entity statements rather than segmented breakdowns of consolidated results.

In formulating the requirements in IFRS 8, the IASB was conscious of the benefit–cost relationship in presenting segmented information. In general, the IASB preferred to recommend disclosure only of information that was already readily available within the reporting enterprise, mainly from the management accounting system. Thus, some of the variability that exists in practice is the result of differing management accounting systems.

The focus of the segment disclosure requirements is on reportable operating segments. There are two key words here—*reportable* and *operating*. Not all operating segments are reportable. We will clarify the distinction in the following discussion.

In addition to reporting on their definable operating segments, enterprises should report additional companywide information about:

- products and services;
- geographic areas; and
- major customers.

The requirements also apply to publicly accountable fiduciary entities such as cooperative business enterprises, deposit-taking institutions (e.g., banks and credit unions), and mutual life insurance companies.

Operating Segments

Identifying Operating Segments The first step is to identify the segments to be reported. In some instances, identifying operating segments is not a problem. If a telephone company buys a gas pipeline company, it is clear that those are two distinct segments; they share no resources, markets, management expertise, or common costs, except at the top corporate level. Operationally, there is no similarity.

In other instances, however, it is more difficult to identify operating segments than one perhaps might expect. IFRS 8 cites three aspects to defining an operating segment:

1. It is a component of the enterprise that is expected to generate revenues and incur expenses. A segment need not be generating revenues currently, but should be expected to do so in the normal future course of its activity.
2. Financial information on the business component is regularly available through the company's internal financial reporting system.
3. The business component's operating results are reviewed regularly by the enterprise's "chief operating decision maker," which normally will be the COO (chief operating officer), the CEO (chief executive officer), or the president; this function also could be exercised by a

group of executive officers. This decision maker uses the various business components' financial information to make resource allocation decisions and assess performance within the enterprise.

Clearly, the guidelines focus on the decision-making process within the enterprise. The accounting system must provide the information as a matter of routine, and that information must be used by senior management for allocating resources and assessing performance within the company. Thus **operating segments** are the businesses in a company that regularly provide separate financial information for review to the chief operating decision maker who, in turn, uses the information to allocate resources and assess performance.

Normally there will be a manager in charge of a business component, and that manager will interact and negotiate directly with the chief operating decision maker about the segment's plans, results, and resources. In a matrix organization, where one manager is responsible for geographic areas and another is responsible for products or services across the entire enterprise, IFRS recommends that the operating segments be determined by referring to the core principle of enabling users to best understand and evaluate the entity's operating results and prospects.

Although some operating segments may be quite separable when defined by the criteria described above, they may nevertheless be combined for segment reporting. Separately identifiable segments may be combined if they have similar economic characteristics and are similar with respect to certain *aggregation criteria*. These criteria include the nature of the product or service, the nature of the production processes, the type or class of customer, the methods of distribution, and the regulatory environment (if applicable). In addition to meeting *all* of the aggregation criteria, any combining of segments must be consistent with the core principle of segment reporting. For example, two business components may serve the same general market, although not necessarily the same customers. If the products are complementary, or are substitutes for each other, then the enterprise may simply be horizontally integrated in the same market rather than being in two different segments. More specifically, consider an example where a winery is owned by a beer company. Beer and wine are likely to have different segment managers and distinct financial reporting, and may be viewed by senior management as two different segments. But since both beer and wine serve the same general market, it may make sense to report only one alcoholic beverages segment rather than two segments.

The degree of vertical integration can also be used as a criterion for segmentation. A company may produce a raw material, refine it, convert it into manufactured products, and sell the products through its own chain of stores. Each of these activities may have different future prospects and therefore users may find information about each of these activities important. However, the question arises as to whether the company is in three segments (resources, manufacturing, and retailing) or in one vertically integrated segment.

The answer depends on the relative independence of the various levels of the business and the degree of reliance by each on the others. If almost all of the raw material goes into the enterprise's own manufacturing plants, and the output of the plants is sold mainly through the company's stores, then the high level of interdivisional product flows suggests that there is only one integrated segment. This would be especially true if many of the divisions are treated as cost centres or revenue centres rather than as profit centres (remember that this would likely cause them to fail the first criterion for identifying an operating segment, that is, the revenue/expense criterion).

On the other hand, if the three levels of business operate fairly autonomously, buying materials from external suppliers and selling intermediate outputs on the open market, then the enterprise would seem to be in separate segments rather than in just one.

Different companies with seemingly comparable operations could quite legitimately segment their results differently. One company may report several related operating segments, while another company with seemingly similar segments may choose to report the segments together as a single, dominant, integrated segment. Therefore, users should be cautious when comparing segment information of seemingly similar companies.

Reportable Segments There is a difference between an *identifiable* segment and a *reportable* segment. To be reportable, a segment must be separately identifiable, but in addition must satisfy at least one of three quantitative criteria or guidelines. The general guidelines for reporting an operating segment are that a segment is considered **reportable** if it comprises 10% or more of the enterprise's:

- total revenues, including sales between segments; *or*
- operating profits; *or*
- combined assets of all operating segments.

Only one of the 10% tests needs to be met. The 10% test prevents companies from being forced to provide segment information on those segments that have relatively insignificant operations but nevertheless are identifiable separately. After applying the quantitative criteria, if an operating segment does not meet any of these criteria, it can be combined with another related segment provided the two segments have similar economic characteristics and meet a *majority* of the aggregation criteria listed earlier. If at least 75% of the enterprise's consolidated external revenues are disclosed by separate operating segments, then any remaining segments that did not meet the quantitative criteria can be combined into an "other" category.

Management can choose to report segments that do not meet any of the 10% criteria. However, IFRS 8 suggests that 10 segments may be a reasonable upper limit for disclosure. Exhibit 7-1 presents a diagram for identifying reportable segments.

In applying the 10% guideline for profits, a problem arises when some of the operating segments operate at a loss while others are profitable. The offsetting effect of profits and losses reduces the size of the company's total profit (or loss), and thereby reduces the level of segment profit or loss that would satisfy the 10% criterion. The approach to dealing with the offsetting effect is that the 10% profit guideline should be applied to the *larger* of:

1. 10% of the combined profits of all of the segments that reported profits, *or*
2. 10% of the combined losses of all of the segments that operated at a loss for the period.

For example, suppose that a company has six operating segments:

Segment	Operating Profit (Loss)
A	$25,000
B	(10,000)
C	15,000
D	30,000
E	(35,000)
F	40,000
Total	$65,000

EXHIBIT 7-1

Identifying Reportable Segments*

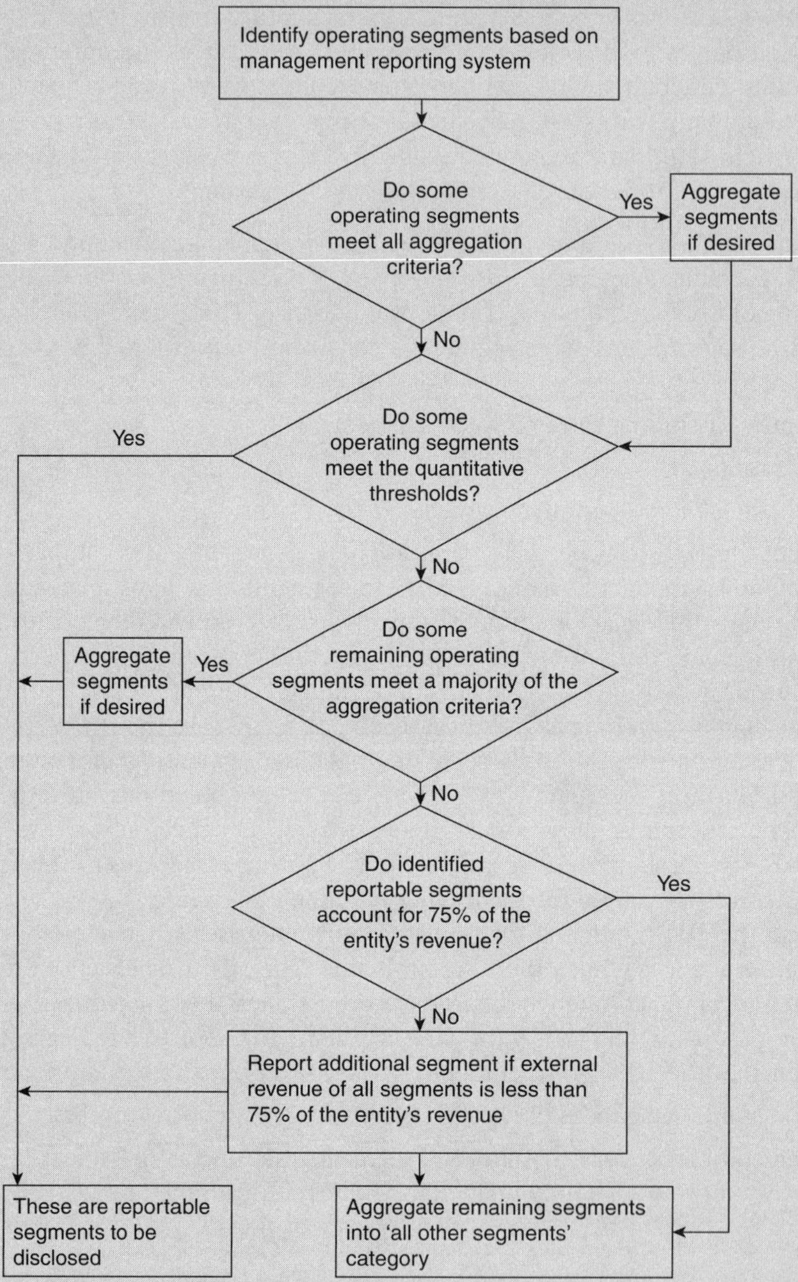

*Source: IFRS 8, Operating Segments, Implementation Guidance, p. 888. Accessed September 2009 at http://eifrs.iasb.org/eifrs/files/115/ifrs08_bv2009_190.pdf

The total profit is $65,000, and all of the segments have profits or losses that are higher than 10% of that amount. However, the sum of the profitable segments is $110,000 while the sum of the losses is $45,000. The basis for applying the 10% guideline is the larger of those two amounts, or $110,000. Any segment that has a profit or a loss larger than $11,000 is reportable. Under that criterion, segment B ceases to be a reportable segment (although it still may meet one of the other criteria).

The definition of "profit" is intentionally ambiguous. The requirements make no reference as to how profit is measured. It may be pre-tax or after-tax, and it may or may not include costs such as interest expense, allocated head office expenses, etc. The profit measure is simply the one used by the chief operating decision maker in allocating resources to the segment and assessing its performance. In other words, segment profit is measured on the same basis as the company measures it in its internal reporting system. If more than one measure is used by the chief operating decision maker, then the reported measure should be the one that is measured in a manner that is the most consistent with the measurement of profit in the company's financial statements. Again, a financial statement reader must be extremely cautious in trying to compare segment profits between different enterprises.

It is quite possible for an identifiable segment to satisfy one of the 10% criteria in one year and not the next, or vice versa. Therefore, the determination of reportable segments must be based on more than a one-year view. If a segment is likely to exceed a 10% guideline more often than not or if management believes that the segment is of continuing significance, then it probably should be reported *each* year even if it may not meet the guideline every year.

The qualitative criterion of *consistency* suggests that the same segment breakdown should be reported each year until a significant shift in relative importance of lines of business causes a segment to drop below the 10% guidelines more or less permanently. The guidelines should also be used to identify emerging segments, those that are increasing in importance in the consolidated enterprise.

Information to Be Reported The three basic pieces of information that should be reported for each segment are:

- a measure of profit or loss;
- total assets, if regularly provided; and
- a measure of liabilities, if regularly provided.

Remember that the requirement is specifically for "a" measure of profit—there is no suggestion as to how profit should be measured. The profit measure is whatever the company's senior management uses to evaluate the segment.

IFRS 8 lists the items to be disclosed for each reportable segment. However, these items are reported only *if* they are reviewed regularly by the chief operating decision maker. Regular review can be either (1) by their inclusion in the measure of segment profit that is used by senior management, or (2) by being separately reported and reviewed. The information to be disclosed is as follows:

- revenues, separately disclosed by:
  - sales to external customers;

REALITY CHECK 7-1

How does Thomson Reuters determine and report operating segment performance? The company's 2009 interim financial statements disclose that:

> In accordance with IFRS 8, Operating Segments, the Company discloses information about its reportable segments based upon the measures used by management in assessing the performance of those reportable segments. The Company uses segment operating profit to measure the operating performance of its segments. Segment operating profit is defined as operating profit before (i) amortization of other intangible assets, (ii) other operating gains and losses and (iii) asset impairment charges. Management uses this measure because amortization of other intangible assets, other operating gains and losses and asset impairment charges are not considered to be controllable operating activities for purposes of assessing the current performance of the segments. While in accordance with IFRS, the Company's definition of segment operating profit may not be comparable to that of other companies.

Source: Thomson Reuters Corporation, Third Quarter Report, (period ended September 30, 2009), p. 53.

  - intersegment sales;
  - interest revenue and interest expense, normally disclosed separately
- income tax expense or benefit;
- amortization and depreciation;
- significant non-cash items other than amortization and depreciation;
- nature and amount of material revenues, expenses, gains, or losses (such as discontinued operations; inventory and property, plant, and equipment write-downs or reversals; disposal of property, plant, and equipment or investments; restructuring costs or reversals; litigation settlements; other reversals of provisions);
- total expenditures for additions to non-current assets (other than financial instruments, deferred tax assets, post-employment benefit assets, and rights arising under insurance contracts);
- information about associates and joint ventures accounted for by the equity method:
  - equity in earnings;
  - amount of investment.

IFRS 8 requires that the reporting enterprise should explain in the notes the basis for determining reportable segments. Also, the company should present a general description of the products and services from which each segment derives its revenues.

The basis for reporting segment information to the chief operating decision maker will often be based on non-consolidated data. Therefore, a reconciliation of the segmented revenues, profits, assets, liabilities if reported, and any other reported material item to the amounts in the consolidated financial statements is also required.

Entity-wide Disclosures

As noted earlier, to achieve the objective of improving information through disaggregation, IFRS 8 requires that key information on products and services, geographic areas, and major customers should be provided if it is not already disclosed in the reportable segment information.

Products and Services We stated above that the company should disclose the nature of each segment's products and services. However, a company may not have separate reportable segments but still may have a series of different product types or services. In that case, the company should disclose the revenues from each group of similar products and services.

Geographic Areas One of the primary tasks of a financial statement reader is to assess the potential business risks that are facing an enterprise. Several aspects of business risk are related to the countries or geographic areas in which the company does business. Risks relate to both revenue potential and asset exposure.

If a Canadian company generates significant amounts of revenue in Europe, for example, European revenues (and profits) will be threatened if the euro weakens in relation to the Canadian dollar. As the euro declines, Canadian services and products become more expensive in terms of euros. Or, if the company maintains its prices in euros, the Canadian-dollar profit margin will decline as the euro declines. Similarly, assets located in certain geographic areas may be a source of risk. The risk can arise either politically (e.g., political instability) or economically (e.g., high inflation).

To help investors assess risk, companies should disclose the extent to which their sales are to foreign versus domestic customers, and also the breakdown between domestic and foreign assets. The specific required disclosures *for each geographic area* are as follows:

- revenues from external customers in foreign countries;
- revenues from external customers in the company's home country;
- non-current assets that are located in foreign countries; and
- non-current assets that are located in the company's home country.

Note that if the revenues or assets in an individual foreign country are material, they are to be disclosed separately. In many cases, the domestic–foreign breakdown is provided as part of the segment disclosure. If the segment disclosures contain all of the appropriate information, then no additional reporting is necessary. Otherwise, the company should disclose these four pieces of information for the consolidated enterprise as a whole.

Major Customers Another major risk factor is the extent to which a corporation is dependent upon one or a few major customers. What will happen to the company if 45% of its services are provided to a customer that goes bankrupt?

Because of the risk inherent in relying on major customers, a reporting enterprise should disclose information about the extent of its reliance on its major customers. Not too surprisingly, the guideline is 10%. If the company relies on a single customer for 10% or more of its revenue, the company should disclose the total amount of revenues from each such customer and the segment or segments that generate those total revenues. Customers under common control are considered to be a single customer.

Note that there is no requirement to disclose the *name* of the important customer or customers. This may be viewed as a shortcoming. If one or more companies in the retail clothing business is in financial jeopardy, it may not be terribly helpful to a financial-statement reader to know that a significant part of a clothing manufacturer's revenue comes from a retail clothing chain without knowing the name of the chain.

CONCEPT CHECK 7-1

Companion Website

1. What is segment reporting?
2. What risks does segment reporting help financial statements users assess?
3. What is the core principle that underlies segment reporting?
4. What three key items of information should be reported for each segment?

Examples of Segment Reporting

There is no prescribed format for the reporting of information by segments; the method of presentation is left entirely up to the preparers. In the following paragraphs, we will discuss two quite different examples of segment disclosure.

Agrium Inc. Our first example of segmented financial reporting is shown in Exhibit 7-2, for Calgary-based Agrium Inc. Agrium is a major supplier of agricultural products and services, as well as a global producer of agricultural nutrients and industrial products. Agrium segments its operations by product or service (as opposed to geography, which we will see in our second example). It has three reportable business segments: Wholesale, Retail, and Advanced Technologies. The company gives a brief description of its segments in Note 1, and then in Note 28 reports each of the pieces of information required under segment reporting.

First, the company provides net sales by reportable operating segment and, in addition, it also provides the net sales by major product categories for the retail and wholesale segments. The company thereby fulfills two requirements; in addition to reporting on the reportable operating segments, it also provides information about its products and services. Note also that the "other" category of sales for a negative $523 million is an elimination of intersegment sales. The resulting total segment sales ($10,031 million) is the same amount shown for net sales on the company's SCI. Thus it is reconciled to the corresponding amount on the consolidated financial statement as required.

Second, note that the operating income number ($1,911) that is reported is defined as "Net earnings before income taxes." The total reported is easily reconciled to the relevant item on the consolidated financial statements. Although not shown here, the difference of $30 million is due to the non-controlling interest.

Third, note that total assets are reported for all three segments and there is a substantial intersegment elimination. The total asset balance of $9,818 reconciles to the total assets reported on the SFP (not shown here). Interestingly, a measure of liabilities is not reported, which is not surprising as the Canadian standards at the time of this annual report did not require it.

EXHIBIT 7-2

Agrium Inc., Segmented Financial Reporting, December 31, 2008

1. Description Of Business

Agrium Inc. (with its subsidiaries, collectively, the "Company" or "Agrium") is a leading global producer and marketer of agricultural products.

Agrium operates three strategic business units:

- **Wholesale** operates in North and South America and Europe producing, marketing and distributing three primary groups of nutrients: nitrogen, potash, and phosphate for agricultural and industrial customers around the world.
- **Retail** operates in North and South America and sells crop nutrients, crop protection products, seed, and services directly to growers.
- **Advanced Technologies** produces and markets controlled-release nutrients, micronutrients, and plant protection products for sale to the agriculture, professional turf, and ornamental markets, primarily in North America.

28. Segmentation

	2008	2007	2006
Net sales			
Retail			
Crop nutrients	2,718	1,453	1,065
Crop protection products	2,115	619	591
Seed, services, and other	683	394	319
	5,516	2,466	1,975
Wholesale			
Nitrogen	1,815	1,535	1,280
Potash	816	305	213
Phosphate	847	466	298
Product purchased for resale	971	339	382
Other	237	200	96
	4,686	2,845	2,269
Advanced Technologies	352	249	101
Other	(523)	(290)	(152)
	10,031	5,270	4,193
Net earnings before income taxes			
Retail	480	177	95
Wholesale	1,478	667	91
Advanced Technologies	33	13	(1)
Other	25	(142)	(113)
	2,016	715	72
Interest on long-term debt	82	52	47
Other interest	23	18	16
	1,911	645	9
Total assets			
Retail	6,951	1,850	1,104
Wholesale	8,851	4,298	2,911
Advanced Technologies	340	372	277
Other	(6,324)	(688)	(1,027)
	9,818	5,832	3,265

EXHIBIT 7-2 *(continued)*

Agrium Inc., Segmented Financial Reporting, December 31, 2008

The Other segment is a non-operating segment for inter-segment eliminations and corporate functions. Net sales between segments are accounted for at prices that approximate fair market value.

	2008			2007			2006		
	Net Sales	PP&E	Goodwill	Net Sales	PP&E	Goodwill	Net Sales	PP&E	Goodwill
Canada	1,704	682	17	1,033	824	17	652	706	17
United States	7,296	535	1,762	3,659	381	161	2,954	400	157
Argentina	477	230	—	373	221	—	251	226	—
Europe	480	4	4	—	—	—	—	—	—
Egypt	—	585	—	—	346	—	—	—	—
Other	74	—	—	205	—	—	336	—	—
	10,031	2,036	1,783	5,270	1,772	178	4,193	1,332	174

Source: Agrium Inc. 2008 Annual Report.

Finally, the company discloses its sales and non-current assets (capital assets and goodwill) by major geographic area as required under segment reporting in a separate table. The totals all correspond to the totals on the company's SFP. It should be noted that the company discloses additional segment information in its management discussion and analysis (MD&A). For example, gross profit by segment and product line is discussed in addition to major expenses (e.g., amortization, asset impairment, inventory write-downs, selling, and general and administrative expenses). Incidentally, the requirements under IFRS 8 do not extend to the discussion in the MD&A.

Magna International Inc. A more extensive example using geographic segment disclosure can be found in Magna International Inc. Magna is a major Canada-based global supplier of automobile parts and systems, generating 78% of its revenue outside of Canada. The segmented reporting note for Magna is shown in Exhibit 7-3, slightly shortened from the original.

You should observe several points in this exhibit.

- In the first table, the company reports three geographic regions: North America, Europe, and Rest of World, since Magna's internal reporting system provides information at the level of these three regions for assessing performance and allocating resources. Canada is included in the "North America" region in the first table. No other region (e.g., Asia or Africa) meets the reporting criteria, and therefore Magna lumps all other regions into "Rest of World." Magna discloses total sales, both including and excluding intersegment sales. (The difference between the totals of each segment for these two measures is likely due to intersegment fees.) Magna's measure of operating profit is *operating income before interest*. Finally, the totals at the bottom all equal the corresponding accounts in the consolidated financial statements.
- In the second table, Magna discloses its major customers *by name* (something our first company did not do). The five customers disclosed account for roughly 76% of Magna's sales in 2008. Note also that Daimler AG is still disclosed even though it is slightly less than 10% of total revenues in both 2007 and 2008. This is for comparative consistency, since Daimler did meet the 10% guideline in 2006, the earliest comparative period presented in Magna's statements.
- In the third table, Magna discloses its sales for similar products and services.

EXHIBIT 7-3

Magna International Inc.

Segmented Financial Reporting (excerpts)
December 31, 2008

25. SEGMENTED INFORMATION

[a] Magna, a leading global supplier of technologically advanced automotive systems, assemblies, modules and components, follows a corporate policy of functional and operational decentralization. It conducts its operations through divisions, which function as autonomous business units. As at December 31, 2008, Magna had 240 manufacturing divisions and 86 product development, engineering and sales centres in 25 countries. Magna designs, develops and manufactures automotive systems, assemblies, modules and components, and engineers and assembles complete vehicles, primarily for sale to OEMs of cars and light trucks in North America, Europe, Asia, South America and Africa ["Rest of World"]. The Company's product capabilities span a number of major automotive areas including: the design, engineering, testing and manufacture of automotive interior systems; seating systems; closure systems; body and chassis systems; vision systems; electronic systems; exterior systems; powertrain systems; roof systems; as well as complete vehicle engineering and assembly.

Given the differences between the regions in which the Company operates. Magna's operations are segmented on a geographic basis between North America, Europe and Rest of World. A Co-Chief Executive Officer heads management in each of the Company's two primary markets, North America and Europe. The role of the North American and European management teams is to manage Magna's interests to ensure a coordinated effort across the Company's different product capabilities. In addition to maintaining key customer, supplier and government contacts in their respective markets, the regional management teams centrally manage key aspects of the Company's operations while permitting the divisions enough flexibility through Magna's decentralized structure to foster an entrepreneurial environment.

Consistent with the above, the Company's internal financial reporting separately segments key internal operating performance measures between North America, Europe and Rest of World for purposes of presentation to the chief operating decision maker to assist in the assessment of operating performance, the allocation of resources, and the long-term strategic direction and future global growth of the Company.

The accounting policies of each segment are the same as those set out under "Significant Accounting Policies" *[note 1]* and intersegment sales and transfers are accounted for at fair market value.

The following table shows certain information with respect to segment disclosures:

	2008						
	Total sales	External sales	Depreciation and amortization	EBIT[1]	Goodwill	Fixed asset additions	Fixed assets, net
North America							
Canada	$5,480	$ 5,134				$ 87	$ 682
United States	5,250	5,043				139	806
Mexico	1,840	1,649				56	374
Eliminations	(653)	—				—	—
North America	11,917	11,826	$535	$(106)	$ 675	282	1,862
Europe							
Euroland [ii]	9,608	9,383				278	1,107
Great Britain	1,160	1,157				13	66
Other European countries	903	761				53	191
Eliminations	(240)	—				—	—

EXHIBIT 7-3 *(continued)*

Magna International Inc.

	2008						
	Total sales	External sales	Depreciation and amortization	EBIT[1]	Goodwill	Fixed asset additions	Fixed assets, net
Europe	11,431	11,301	291	241	409	344	1,364
Rest of World	611	560	23	32	75	47	173
Corporate and Other [iii], [iv]	(255)	17	24	99	1	66	302
Total reportable segments	$23,704	$23,704	$873	$ 266	$1,160	$739	3,701
Current assets							7,351
Investments, goodwill and other assets							2,137
Consolidated total assets							$13,189

Notes:

[i] EBIT represents operating income before interest income or expense

[ii] For purposes of segmentation, Euroland has been defined as those European countries that have adopted the euro as their common currency.

[iii] Included in Corporate and Other EBIT are intercompany fees charged to the automotive segments.

[iv] During the year ended December 31, 2008, equity income of $19 million is included in the Corporate and Other segment [2007 - $11 million; 2006 - $13 million].

[b] The following table aggregates external revenues by customer as follows:

	2008	2007	2006
General Motors	$ 5,008	$ 6,341	$ 6,078
BMW	4,442	5,006	4,313
Ford Motor Company	3,286	3,860	3,477
Chrysler Group	2,866	3,380	3,236
Daimler AG	2,335	1,962	2,444
Other	5,767	5,518	4,632
	$23,704	$26,067	$24,180

[c] The following table summarizes external revenues generated by automotive products and services:

	2008	2007	2006
Exterior and interior systems	$ 7,806	$ 8,112	$ 7,438
Body systems and chassis systems	4,616	5,274	4,279
Powertrain systems	3,357	3,809	3,446
Complete vehicle assembly	3,306	4,008	4,378
Tooling, engineering and other	1,856	1,735	2,026
Vision and electronic systems	1,650	1,811	1,458
Closure systems	1,113	1,318	1,155
	$23,704	$26,067	$24,180

Source: Magna International Inc. 2008 Annual Report.

INTERIM REPORTING

All enterprises issue financial reports at least once a year. One of the basic postulates of accounting is *periodicity*—whether it is feasible to break the life of an organization into discrete time periods and to report meaningfully on financial performance during that period. However, periodicity is usually applied within the context of an annual reporting cycle.

Interim statements are financial statements issued for any period of time of *less* than one year. Interim statements may be prepared for external use or for management's internal use only. Public companies are required by securities regulations or corporations acts to issue interim statements. In Canada and the United States, quarterly statements are required. In most other counties, interim statements need only be semi-annual. Interim reports of public companies must comply with IFRS, but they do not need to be audited.

Private enterprises may issue interim statements (1) for their own use or (2) at the request of stakeholders such as banks or private equity investors. Internal interim reports may be monthly rather than quarterly, and will almost certainly be more detailed than those prepared for external release. Since the reports are for management's use only, they may be prepared on a basis that is consistent with the internal decision-making process rather than the basis on which the annual statements are prepared.

Interim reports issued at the request of other stakeholders fall under the broad category of special-purpose financial reporting. The statements may follow the general format and reporting principles that the company uses for the annual financial statements. Alternatively, the statements may be specially designed to satisfy specific needs of external users—e.g., to satisfy bank covenants concerning the fair value of collateral.

For public reporting, consistency between annual and interim reports is essential. Although interim reports may be prepared in less detail than annual statements and necessarily will include more estimates, it would be a rude shock to managers and shareholders alike if the annual statements were not consonant with the operations as described by the interim statements. Thus interim statements should be prepared by using accounting and reporting approaches that are consistent with those used for preparing the annual statements.

General Principles of Application

Scope IFRS specifies the minimum content of interim statements and specifies the recognition and measurement principles that are to be used in interim statements. Since the requirement for interim statements is a function of national securities regulators, IFRS does not indicate how frequently they should be prepared (quarterly or half-yearly).

Content of Interim Reports IFRS requires that interim reports contain condensed statements of (1) financial position; (2) comprehensive income; (3) changes in equity; and (4) cash flows, along with selected note disclosures. What is meant by "condensed statements"? IAS 34 suggests that, at a minimum, condensed statements should include the same headings and subtotals that were used in the annual financial statements. This should not be interpreted too literally. Too much aggregation will result in statements that are not useful. Some aggregation, however, is acceptable. For example, a company's SFP may have several lines for different types of depreciable capital assets and these may be collapsed into a single line for interim statements. Further, on the interim SCI, some expenses may be collapsed into a single line: "operating expenses."

There is also no need to repeat most note disclosures on interim financial statements. A statement reader has access to the previous year-end financial statements, and much of the information in the notes thereto will not be significantly different for the interim periods. Given this, an *exception reporting* principle is used for note disclosure—to the extent that there are significant changes, the company should provide note disclosure. Thus, new or changed accounting policies are disclosed.

In addition, the notes should disclose any material events or transactions that affect interpretation of the current interim period's financial results. Examples would include changes in strategic investments, restructurings, and/or discontinued operations. Subsequent-event disclosure is also required.

Finally, the notes to the interim statements should also indicate that they should be read in conjunction with the company's previous annual financial statements, since fuller information is available in the annual statements than in the interim statement.

Periods Covered in Interim Reports The period covered by the interim statements varies somewhat depending on the type of statement. Interim SCIs should report on both the individual interim period and on the year to date. For example, the third-quarter SCI will show operating results both for the third quarter and for the year-to-date cumulative amounts for the first three quarters.

The retained earnings statement and the cash flow statements, in contrast, report only on a year-to-date basis. The SFP will be as of the reporting date, of course; there is no such thing as a year-to-date SFP, since that statement reports on financial condition at a point in time.

All financial statements need a basis for comparison. Interim statements produced for external users are normally prepared on a comparative basis. In most statements, the comparison is with the same period of the preceding year. For the SFP, however, the comparison is with the previous year-end SFP. Exhibit 7-4 summarizes these requirements. For internal reports, budgeted figures for the period may provide a more relevant basis for comparison.

Segment Information Segment information should also be presented in the interim statements. Segment information should include at least the following:

- segment revenues, segregated between intersegment revenues and those to external customers;
- segment profit (loss);
- segment assets if there has been a significant change from the amounts reported in the previous annual statements;
- any changes in the basis of segmentation or the method of reporting segment profit; and
- reconciliation of segment earnings to consolidated earnings for the interim period.

The interim segment information is essentially the same as that required in the annual financial statements.

EXHIBIT 7-4

Statements Required for Interim Reporting*

Type of Statement	Current reporting	Comparative reporting
Statement of financial position		
• At a point in time	Sep 30, 20X3	Dec 31, 20X2
Statement of comprehensive income		
• Interim period (3 months ended)	Sep 30, 20X3	Sep 30, 20X2
• Year-to-date (9 months ended)	Sep 30, 20X3	Sep 30, 20X2
Statement of cash flows		
• Year-to-date (9 months ended)	Sep 30, 20X3	Sep 30, 20X2
Statement of changes in equity		
• Year-to-date (9 months ended)	Sep 30, 20X3	Sep 30, 20X2

* Assuming that quarterly reporting is required, that the company is reporting for its third quarter, and that the fiscal year-end is December 31, 20X3.

The Periodicity Problem

At first glance, it may appear that the preparation of interim statements poses no special problems. After all, interim reports use the same accounting policies that are used for the annual statements, so what's the big deal? Just use the same policies, and interim reporting is a no-brainer, right? Wrong! Interim reporting is not quite so simple.

When we prepare annual financial statements, we face many challenges of estimation and inter-period allocation. Revenue recognition can present significant difficulties, the costs of tangible and intangible capital assets must be allocated, and future costs must be estimated to achieve matching. When these accounting problems are confronted for a period shorter than a year, their significance increases proportionately.

Estimation errors will have a much larger impact on the operating income for a month or a quarter than they will on the operating income for a year. Cut-off procedures will not be as stringent for the unaudited interim statements, and interim inventories are most likely to be estimated or to be taken from perpetual inventory records whose accuracy has not been verified by a physical count.

Not only will estimation errors have a greater impact, but also the materiality threshold will be lower because the amounts on the quarterly SCI and cash flow statement will be only about one-fourth of the annual amounts. Estimation variances that might be ignored in the annual statements (with the higher materiality threshold) become significant in the quarterly statements. The result is that interim statements will be intrinsically and significantly less reliable than annual statements.

Additional estimation and allocation problems arise because of the shorter accounting period. Some costs and revenues are seasonal or annual in nature, and interim statements require allocations that are not necessary for annual statements.

For example, annual insurance costs pose no problems if the accounting period is a year, but how should the cost be allocated if the period is a month? An easy answer would be to allocate one-twelfth of the cost to each month. However, suppose that the insurance is an

REALITY CHECK 7-2

How does seasonality affect financial results for a company like Thomson Reuters? The company's 2009 third-quarter report discloses that traditionally the company's revenues and margins were smallest in the first quarter and largest in the fourth quarter. The addition of Reuters has reduced the seasonality of the results but the trend is still present. Hence they advise that:

Accordingly, performance remains not comparable quarter to consecutive quarter and is best considered on the basis of results for the whole year or by comparing results in a quarter with the results in the same quarter for the previous year.

Source: Thomson Reuters Corporation, Third Quarter Report, Period Ended September 30, 2009, p.3.

expensive public liability policy for an amusement park that is open all year, but that does the bulk of its business in the summer months. Should the cost be allocated by time or by volume of activity to match the cost with the revenue?

Another example is a factory that shuts down in the month of August for a vacation for all production employees. The fixed costs of the factory during August could be viewed as a cost to be allocated to all of the interim periods, or as a cost of the individual period in which August falls. Similarly, annual costs such as once-a-year major maintenance costs could either be allocated, or could be allowed to fall into the interim period in which they occur.

Some costs are determined not only on an annual basis, but also *after* the end of the year. Customer rebates, sales bonuses, and income taxes are examples of these costs. Should an attempt be made to estimate and allocate these costs, or should they be allowed to fall into the last interim period?

As the preceding examples suggest, there are two basic approaches to the preparation of interim statements. The interim period can be viewed either as a distinct and separate accounting period of its own (the *discrete approach*), or as a part of a year (the *integral approach*).

Discrete Approach

Under the **discrete** or *separate-period* **approach**, each interim period is accounted for by using the company's normal accounting policies applied to the interim period as though it were a year. A company's policy may be to immediately expense all costs that may have future benefits that are difficult to measure such as development costs. Under this accounting policy, deferred charges and credits are normally not carried on the SFP.

A company that follows this policy will also apply it to the interim periods under the discrete approach. Costs will be permitted to fall into the period in which they are incurred, even though they may be annual costs that benefit other interim periods.

The discrete approach implicitly recognizes that since revenues and expenses are likely to be "lumpy," the interim earnings are also going to be lumpy, and are not just a proportionate part of the annual earnings. This approach treats the insurance costs, vacation costs, or maintenance costs as period costs for the quarter rather than allocating them to the other periods.

Under the discrete approach, income taxes are viewed as cumulative. Income taxes are accrued for the first period based on the net operating income for the period. Income taxes for the second period will be based on the *additional* taxes payable as a result of the operations for the second period, and so forth. If a loss occurred in the first period, no benefit will be recognized. Future income taxes would be provided for all temporary differences arising during the interim period, even if the temporary difference is expected to reverse within the taxation year.

Integral Approach

Under the **integral approach**, the interim period is viewed simply as a part of the longer period of a year. Expenses are allocated across the interim periods in such a way as to portray the company's likely annualized operating results. Theoretically, if a company is heading for a year in which the operating margin (net income divided by sales) is 10%, then the interim statements should reflect that fact. Under this view, the interim statements should be the best predictor available of the company's operating results for the year.

For the examples cited above, the integral approach will allocate the insurance costs proportionately to the volume of business, and will allocate the costs of the plant closing, the annual maintenance costs, and the estimated bonuses and rebates to all of the interim periods.

Income taxes are viewed as an annual expense to be allocated to interim periods in proportion to the pre-tax interim net income. There will be no separate computation of income taxes for the interim period as though it were a separate taxation period. Temporary differences will be determined on an annual basis and allocated to the interim periods. An income tax benefit will be recognized for a first-quarter loss if the company expects to earn a profit for the tax year as a whole.

Recognition and Measurement in Practice

Internal Reporting For *internal* interim reports, the discrete approach is almost always used in practice. The comparative amounts for internal users are likely to be budgeted figures for the period (perhaps supplemented by the previous year's figures), and budgets generally include major costs as expenses of the period in which they occur. Controllability is a concern in budgeting, and costs allocated from previous periods are not controllable in the later periods to which they are allocated. Also, internal reports frequently do not include any income tax estimates, thereby removing one major estimation problem.

Public Reporting—General Approach For measuring interim period operating results, IAS 34 generally favours the discrete approach—a company should apply the same accounting policies to its interim statements as it used in its annual statements. However, the recommendations also contain some aspects of the integral approach because they suggest that the frequency of reporting should not affect the measurement of the annual results. Therefore, the IAS 34 approach might be characterized as a "modified discrete" approach.

As you can imagine, the presence of two differing approaches can lead to potential conflicts in the application of this standard. To assist users, IAS 34 provides some further guidance for particular revenues and costs and also provides examples of recognition and measurement applications in an appendix.

Revenues and Costs As we noted earlier under the periodicity problem, revenues and costs may not be earned/incurred evenly throughout the year. Some revenues may be affected by seasons or cycles or may only be received occasionally. Further costs such as maintenance may be incurred unevenly throughout the year. The question arises as to how to handle these types of revenues and costs. Should they be anticipated? For example, if maintenance is typically performed in the third quarter, should we anticipate it by accruing for it in the first quarter? IAS 34 recommends that costs and revenues should be accrued or deferred at the end of interim periods *only if those same costs or revenues would normally be accrued or deferred at the end of the fiscal year*.

Specific Examples

General Application Generally the discrete approach will be used in interim reporting for most revenues and costs. A general exception to the use of the discrete approach arises for costs that are determined only on an annual basis. IAS 34 specifically discusses year-end bonuses, contingent lease payments, and income taxes. The section uses the terminology of "constructive obligation" to rationalize these exceptions, but the basic point is simply that companies can estimate or project the determining factors for the entire year and accrue the costs in the interim statements.

For example, contingent rents may be based on annual sales in excess of a contractual minimum. In a strict application of the discrete approach, no accrual for contingent rent is made until the threshold level of sales is achieved. IAS 34, however, permits this type of cost to be spread out over several interim periods—an application of the integral approach.

As another example, consider purchases made under an annual volume rebate or discount scheme. If attainment of the required level of sales to qualify for the rebate is probable, the buyer and the seller should recognize the associated asset and liability respectively—another application of the integral approach.

In contrast, consider major planned periodic maintenance. A company may have a policy of shutting down its manufacturing plant every August for planned maintenance. IAS 34 suggests that these costs should not be anticipated unless there is a legal or constructive obligation. The argument is that the intention or necessity to incur maintenance costs in the future cannot give rise to an obligation, therefore, no liability should be recognized.

Income Tax Reporting Income tax expense presents a special problem. Under the discrete approach, income tax for each quarter would be calculated on the year-to-date taxable income. The increase (or decrease) in income tax from the previous quarter would be that quarter's tax expense.

Amounts of income and expenses reported in the current interim period will reflect any changes in estimates of amounts reported in prior interim periods of the fiscal year. The amounts reported in prior interim periods are not retroactively adjusted.

However, IFRS recommends that interim income tax expense be estimated by using the estimated average annual effective income tax rate (an integral approach). The average rate will differ from the marginal rate only under a two-rate tax system or a progressive tax system, in which higher levels of income are taxed at a different rate than lower levels. Instead of accruing income tax at the lower rate in the early quarters, the average rate applicable to management's estimate of the full year's earnings should be used. The average rate should be used even if the early quarters show a loss and even if the overall earnings for the year are expected to be zero.

The benefits of an income tax loss in an interim period are recognized in that period if:

- the loss will be offset by taxable income in the other interim periods of that year;
- the loss can be used as a tax loss carryback to a prior year; or
- it is probable that the benefit of the loss will be realized as a tax loss carryforward.

For example, suppose that a company expects to earn \$800,000 evenly over the year (i.e., \$200,000 each quarter). Also suppose that the company pays tax at 20% on the first \$400,000 of earnings and 50% on any amount above. What would be reported for income tax expense for the first quarter? Under the discrete approach, the tax would be \$40,000 (\$200,000 × 20%). IAS 34, however, recommends the use of the integral approach, wherein an average rate is calculated and then used to estimate income tax expense. In this scenario, an average tax rate of 35% would be used and the income tax expense reported would be \$70,000 (\$200,000 × 35%).

As another example, suppose that a company has a loss of \$50,000 in the first quarter but expects to earn \$120,000 over the following three quarters. If the expected average tax rate is 30%, the first quarter interim SCI will show an income tax *benefit* or recovery (i.e., a negative tax expense, or a credit) of \$50,000 × 30% = \$15,000. The following quarters will show a positive income tax expense totalling \$120,000 × 30% = \$36,000. The total income tax expense for the year will be \$36,000 − \$15,000 = \$21,000, based on cumulative net income of \$70,000 for the year (i.e., \$120,000 − \$50,000).

CONCEPT CHECK 7-2

Companion Website

1. Which condensed financial statements must be reported in interim reports under IFRS? What is meant by the term *condensed statements*?
2. What segment disclosures should be presented in interim financial statements?
3. What is the periodicity problem?
4. What is the discrete approach to interim reporting? What is the integral approach to interim reporting?

Illustrative Interim Statement

Exhibit 7-5 shows interim statements for Sportscene Group Inc. These are the third-quarter statements for fiscal year 2009. Sportscene is the operator of a chain of sports bars and restaurants in Quebec. The company's interim statements appear to comply with the IAS 34 recommendations. In Exhibit 7-5, we have omitted the statement of cash flows and most of the notes for brevity, but the following points should be noted:

- The financial statements shown in Exhibit 7-5 contain all the current and comparative information required. However, the *consolidated statements of variations in shareholders' equity* (and the statement of cash flows, not presented) also contain additional information. In addition to the required year-to-date information, they also contain information on the most recent three-month interim period. This additional disclosure is common in Canada.

EXHIBIT 7-5

Interim Financial Statements (Excerpts)

SPORTSCENE GROUP INC.

Consolidated statements of earnings and comprehensive income

(amounts are expressed in thousands of dollars except for per-share amounts and number of shares)
(unaudited)

	13 weeks ended		39 weeks ended	
	May 31, 2009	May 25, 2008	May 31, 2009	May 25, 2008
	$	$	$	$
Revenue	20,586	21,087	63,478	58,404
Cost of sales, selling, general and administrative expenses	17,562	17,681	54,335	49,302
Earnings before other items	3,024	3,406	9,143	9,102
Interest on long-term debt	146	136	406	383
Other interest expense	58	55	165	131
Amortization of deferred financing costs	—	—	2	—
Amortization of capital assets	893	816	2,612	2,371
Amortization of intangibles and other assets	126	139	400	380
Loss on disposal of assets	58	9	80	30
Gain on business disposals	(10)	—	(10)	(246)
	1,271	1,155	3,655	3,049
Earnings before income taxes and non-controlling interest	1,753	2,251	5,488	6,053
Income taxes	531	724	1,597	1,801
Earnings before non-controlling interest	1,222	1,527	3,891	4,252
Non-controlling interest	3	(7)	26	(13)
Net earnings and comprehensive income	1,225	1,520	3,917	4,239
Earnings per share:				
Basic	$0.29	$0.36	$0.94	$1.01
Diluted	$0.29	$0.36	$0.94	$1.01
Weighted average number of Class A shares outstanding (in thousands):				
Basic	4,178	4,188	4,182	4,188
Diluted	4,178	4,195	4,182	4,195

EXHIBIT 7-5 *(continued)*

Interim Financial Statements (Excerpts)

SPORTSCENE GROUP INC.
Consolidated balance sheets
(amounts are expressed in thousands of dollars)

	As at May 31, 2009	As at August 31, 2008
	(unaudited)	(audited)
	$	$
Assets		
Current assets:		
Cash and cash equivalents	7,056	6,867
Restricted cash	86	260
Temporary investment	—	100
Accounts receivable	4,103	5,169
Inventories	1,239	1,766
Prepaid expenses	688	679
Current portion of notes receivable	38	36
Total current assets	13,210	14,877
Notes receivable	951	959
Capital assets	31,280	29,265
Intangibles and other assets	1,062	1,381
Future income taxes	380	380
Goodwill	2,607	2,363
Total assets	49,490	49,225
Liabilities and shareholders' equity		
Current liabilities:		
Accounts payable and accrued liabilities	5,125	9,337
Income taxes payable	740	29
Future income taxes	116	116
Deferred income and credits	1,584	1,307
Current portion of long-term debt	1,838	1,791
Total current liabilities	9,403	12,580
Long-term debt	10,962	9,510
Deferred income and credits	796	927
Future income taxes	322	569
Non-controlling interest	491	517
Total liabilities	21,974	24,103
Shareholders' equity:		
Share capital	3,543	3,499
Contributed surplus	187	171
Retained earnings	23,786	21,452
	27,516	25,122
Total liabilities and shareholders' equity	49,490	49,225

EXHIBIT 7-5 (*continued*)

Interim Financial Statements (Excerpts)

SPORTSCENE GROUP INC.
Consolidated statements of variations in shareholders' equity
(amounts are expressed in thousands of dollars)
(unaudited)

	13 weeks ended		39 weeks ended	
	May 31, 2009	May 25, 2008	May 31, 2009	May 25, 2008
	$	$	$	$
Share capital, beginning of period	3,480	3,494	3,499	3,255
Issuance of stock	14	—	14	182
Redemption of stock	—	—	(23)	—
Transfer from contributed surplus	—	—	—	45
Retraction of notes receivable	49	4	53	16
Share capital, end of period	3,543	3,498	3,543	3,498
Contributed surplus, beginning of period	181	143	171	166
Stock-based compensation	6	14	17	36
Less:				
Excess of the purchase price over the carrying amount of the Class A shares redeemed	—	—	(1)	—
Transfer to share capital	—	—	—	(45)
Contributed surplus, end of period	187	157	187	157
Retained earnings, beginning of period	22,561	20,421	21,452	18,964
Net earnings	1,225	1,520	3,917	4,239
Less:				
Excess of the purchase price over the carrying amount of the Class A shares redeemed	—	—	(330)	—
Dividends on Class A shares	—	—	(1,253)	(1,262)
Retained earnings, end of period	23,786	21,941	23,786	21,941

Notes to the unaudited interim consolidated financial statements (excerpt)

1. **Basis of presentation:**

   The consolidated financial statements have been prepared in accordance with Canadian generally accepted accounting principles. The Company used the same accounting policies as described in the annual consolidated financial statements. These consolidated financial statements, however, do not include all information required in accordance with Canadian generally accepted accounting principles and, accordingly, should be read in connection with the consolidated financial statements and the notes thereto for the fiscal year ending at August 31, 2008.

EXHIBIT 7-5 *(continued)*

Interim Financial Statements (Excerpts)

11. Segmented information

					39 weeks ended May 31, 2009
	Restauration	Real estate	Other activities	Eliminations	Total
Third party revenues	49,709	1,447	10,098		61,254
Franchise revenues	2,224	—	—		2,224
Intersegment revenues	—	516	3,791	(4,307)	—
Total revenues	51,933	1,963	13,889	(4,307)	63,478
Earnings before other items	8,410	424	309		9,143
Amortization	2,485	326	201		3,012
Financial expenses	416	150	7		573
Earnings before income taxes	5,462	(58)	110		5,514
Total assets	33,777	11,387	4,326		49,490
Goodwill	2,507	—	100		2,607
Additions to capital assets	2,322	1,625	18		3,965

					13 weeks ended May 31, 2009
	Restauration	Real estate	Other activities	Eliminations	Total
Third party revenues	17,050	391	2,388		19,829
Franchise revenues	757	—	—		757
Intersegment revenues	—	176	1,027	(1,203)	—
Total revenues	17,807	567	3,415	(1,203)	20,586
Earnings before other items	3,061	71	(108)		3,024
Amortization	832	119	68		1,019
Financial expenses	159	41	4		204
Earnings (loss) before income taxes	2,035	(91)	(188)		1,756
Goodwill	3	—	—		3
Additions to capital assets	815	—	7		822

- Note 1 points out that the interim statements should be read in conjunction with the annual statements.
- Note 11 is a good example of why the most recent annual financial statements are needed. The note on segmented information contains only tabular information—no descriptive information on the segments is presented. Excerpts for 2009 showing the most recent quarter and the three quarters (year-to-date) are included in Exhibit 7-5 but the comparative information for 2008 is omitted. The reader has to use the most

recent annual financial statements to find the description of the company segments reproduced below.

The Company operates in the three reportable segments described below. Each segment offers different products and services and requires different marketing strategies. The Restauration segment is active in the operation, franchising and development of the "La Cage aux Sports" theme restaurants network. The Real Estate Holding segment focuses on managing buildings that generate rental revenues. The Other activities segment includes companies involved in the renovation of existing restaurants and the construction of new "La Cage aux Sports" restaurants, organization of travel and sport events and technology development.

Source: Sportscene Group, 2008 Annual Financial Statements, Note 19.

ACCOUNTING STANDARDS FOR PRIVATE ENTERPRISES

There are no standards for either segmented reporting or interim reporting in the *CICA Handbook, Part II*. Any such reporting is purely voluntary, although specific stakeholders may request (or demand) interim or segmented information. This absence is consistent with earlier Canadian standards—private enterprises were exempt from all earlier Canadian standards on interim reporting and segmented disclosure.

Private enterprises that do wish to prepare interim statements or disclose segment information may use the principles in IAS 34 and IFRS 8 as guidelines for reporting.

Relevant Standards

IASB

IFRS 8 Operating Segments
IAS 34 Interim Financial Reporting

Summary of Key Points

1. Segment reporting is the disaggregation of consolidated results into the major different types of businesses in which a consolidated entity engages. Segment reporting is intended to provide information to enable financial-statement readers to assess the risk and

return that a company generates in its different lines of business. Segment information reveals performance aspects that are concealed by the aggregated nature of consolidated statements. The requirements for segment reporting apply only to public companies, with a few exceptions. Basically, segment information is provided for reportable operating segments. An *operating* segment is one that has a separate reporting line directly to the company's chief operating officer for evaluation and resource allocation. A *reportable* segment is an operating segment that accounts for at least 10% of the consolidated company's revenues, profits, or assets.

2. The corporation should report a measure of profit or loss, total assets (if regularly provided), and a measure of liabilities (if regularly provided) for each reportable segment. Detail, as prescribed by IFRS 8, should be provided for specific SCI line items *if* those items are reviewed regularly by the chief operating decision maker. As well, the corporation should report certain entity-wide information on products and services, on the geographic distribution of revenues and assets, and on customers that account for 10% or more of the company's revenues.
3. Interim financial statements are those that are issued for any period less than a year. Public companies are required to issue interim statements—quarterly in the United States and Canada, semi-annually in most other countries. The IAS 34 recommendations on interim reporting apply only to companies that are required to prepare interim statements by law or regulation. Interim statements should consist of a statement of financial position, statement of comprehensive income, statement of cash flow, statement of changes in equity, and notes that explain major estimates and deviations from or exceptions to the accounting policies that are used for the annual statements. The statements can be condensed, but should include all of the subtotals and totals that the company uses in its annual statements, and should include those line items specifically required by IFRS. The company should also disclose in its notes major changes such as discontinued operations, restructurings, acquisitions, and other changes in strategic investments.
4. There are two basic approaches to interim reporting. The underlying philosophy of interim reporting is the *discrete* approach, in which each interim period is treated as a distinct time period. Under the discrete approach, costs will be permitted to fall into the period in which they are incurred, even though they may be annual costs that benefit other interim periods. Exceptions exist, however, for certain types of expense that are calculated only on an annual basis. For these items, the *integral* or *part-of-year* approach is used. The annual amount is estimated and apportioned to the interim periods.
5. Applying the recognition and measurement principles for interim reporting, expenses such as periodic maintenance are recognized in the quarter in which they are incurred. These costs should not be anticipated unless there is a legal or constructive obligation. The argument is that the intention or necessity to incur maintenance costs in the future cannot give rise to an obligation, therefore, no liability should be recognized. In contrast, some expenses such as bonuses, contingent rent, income tax, and quantity discounts are viewed as constructive obligations. Companies are seen to be capable of estimating the determining factors for the entire year. Given that these expenses are determined on an annual basis, these costs are estimated and spread out over the interim periods.

Companion Website

Visit the text's website at www.pearsoned.ca/beechy for practice quizzes, additional problems, Excel® templates, answers to Concept Check questions, and important IFRS updates.

Self-Study Problem 7-1

The CFO for Acme Inc. has identified four segments under IFRS 8. She has gathered the following information on those segments:

Operating segment	External sales	Operating profit (loss)	Total assets
East	760	50	1,000
West	60	80	680
North	90	10	160
South	100	(15)	150

There were no intersegment revenues during the year.

Required

Identify which segments are reportable segments.

Self-Study Problem 7-2

Tim Smith is the new controller for Widget Corporation, a company traded on the TSX venture exchange. It is his first time working for a public company. He is preparing the preliminary financial statements for the first quarter. Widget Corporation lost $100,000 in the first quarter and expects to lose $1,200,000 in the second quarter, earn $600,000 in the third quarter, and earn $900,000 in the fourth quarter. A large part of the loss in the second quarter is because of $800,000 in maintenance costs that are incurred when the factory is shut down as part of its annual maintenance program. The maintenance costs in the first quarter were $50,000 and are expected to be $50,000 for the third and fourth quarters also. The company is subject to an income tax rate of 30% on the first $100,000 of income and 50% on any income above $100,000.

Required

Assume that tax losses cannot be carried back or forward to another taxation year.

1. How should Tim account for the maintenance costs?
2. What is the income tax expense to be reported for the first quarter? What is the estimated income tax expense for each of the remaining three quarters?

Review Questions

7-1 What are the objectives of segmented reporting?

7-2 When a corporation reports financial information by segments, do the segments correspond to specific subsidiaries?

7-3 What type of company is required to provide segmented reporting?

7-4 How does the IASB consider benefit–cost relationships for segmented reporting?

7-5 How can an operating segment be identified?

7-6 What are the guidelines for determining whether an operating segment is *reportable*?

7-7 Companies L and D both operate food processing plants, and both operate a chain of retail food stores. Company L transfers all of the output from its processing plants to its stores, while Company D's processing plants produce private-label products for other retailers. How might the segment reporting of the two companies differ?

7-8 How is *profit* defined for determining operating segments?

7-9 How much of the consolidated enterprise's business activity must be reported in operating segments to satisfy IFRS requirements?

7-10 When some operating segments operate at a loss and others are profitable, how is the 10% reporting guideline applied?

7-11 What is the reason for requiring companies to report geographic segments?

7-12 What data must be reported for each geographic segment? How do these data differ from the data reported for industry segments?

7-13 How is the risk of relying on major customers considered in segmented reporting?

7-14 Explain briefly why interim reporting poses problems different from those of annual reporting.

7-15 What types of companies does IAS 34 apply to for interim reporting?

7-16 What does the *exception reporting* principle mean for note disclosure in interim reporting?

7-17 What comparative period(s) are used for interim financial statements?

7-18 What are the two basic approaches to the preparation of interim statements? Which approach is recommended by IAS 34?

7-19 Under the discrete or separate-period approach to interim statements, how would an annual, one-time expenditure such as plant maintenance be reported? How would the reporting differ under the integral or part-of-a-year approach?

7-20 How does the measurement of income tax expense differ between the two approaches to interim reporting?

CASES

CASE 7-1 ERMINE OIL LIMITED

Ermine Oil Limited (Ermine) is a fully integrated Canadian oil company. Ermine commenced operations as a petroleum exploration company and was very successful in its oil field discoveries. To attain market security and improve profits, Ermine was forced to embark on a program of vertical integration. It first acquired a refining division and then marketing and transportation divisions. From the beginning, management appreciated the integrated nature of the business, and production was transferred between divisions at standard cost. The management control system recognized the exploration, refining, and transportation divisions as cost centres and the marketing division as a revenue centre. While the exploration, refining, and transportation divisions did make external sales, historically none of these divisions' external sales accounted for 10% of Ermine's total sales. However, in the last fiscal year, due to unusual world market conditions, the transportation division's sales accounted for 11% of Ermine's total sales. Over 90% of Ermine's sales were within Canada, with the balance spread over many countries worldwide. Ermine did not feel it was necessary to disclose segmented information in its annual financial statements.

Beluga Petroleum Limited (Beluga) was similar to Ermine in size and also in scope of operations except that, in addition, it had a chemical division. However, Beluga was a subsidiary of a foreign oil company and its divisions were each organized as profit centres with products transferred between divisions at world market prices. Each division purchased and sold products extensively to outside companies. In addition, about 15% of Beluga's sales were exported, almost exclusively to the United States. In its annual financial statements, Beluga showed segmented information by the five divisions (exploration, refining, transportation, chemical, and marketing) and sales were divided between domestic and export operations.

Required

Discuss how both Ermine and Beluga could report differently with respect to disclosure of segmented information, and yet be in accordance with generally accepted accounting principles.

[SMA, adapted]

CASE 7-2 INTERIM REPORTING

In today's rapidly changing financial markets, financial-statement users are demanding more information, released more promptly than in the past. To respond to these needs, the IASB issued IAS 34.

At a professional development session, two members engaged in a lively discussion. One member is a controller of an international public company, while the other member is a senior financial analyst in a securities firm.

Financial Analyst: My review of IAS 34 leads me to conclude that the objectives of interim reporting should be the same as those of annual reporting.

Controller: I disagree. Interim reports are aimed at different users, serve different purposes, and must be published more quickly than annual reports. It follows that the underlying objectives should also differ.

Financial Analyst: Regardless of the content of interim reports, the interim operating results should be measured on the same basis as the annual results because the interim period is an integral part of the annual period.

Controller: I agree that there is a measurement problem for interim reporting, but I don't see that there is a simple solution. For example, I find it difficult to make interim estimates for various expenses given the cyclical nature of our business. After all, the interim period is only a portion of the annual period.

Required

Prepare a memo discussing the main issues raised in the preceding conversation.
[CICA, adapted]

CASE 7-3 SHAW NAVIGATIONAL COMPANY

The Shaw Navigational Company is a public Canadian corporation that operates a fleet of ships on the Great Lakes. In common with other Great Lakes shipping companies, rates are quoted and revenues are collected in U.S. dollars, regardless of the location or nationality of the shipper. Over 90% of Shaw's consolidated gross revenues, operating profits, and identifiable capital assets relate to the shipping business, and thus Shaw's management claims exemption from segmented reporting requirements on the grounds that shipping represents its only operating segment. In 20X3, Shaw's consolidated net income was $1,200,000.

Shaw does have two subsidiaries that are not in the shipping business. One is a bus company that operates on intercity routes in Manitoba, and that is consolidated with the shipping operation. The bus fleet has recently been modernized, and the new buses have been acquired by means of leases rather than by an outright purchase.

The other subsidiary is a casualty insurance company located in Michigan. About 20% of the insurance company's business involves Great Lakes shipping, although mainly for shipping companies other than Shaw. Shaw's earnings from the insurance company amounted to $180,000 in 20X3.

Required

Comment on management's assertion that Shaw is exempt from segment reporting because it operates in one line of business.

Problems

P7-1

JCN Company sells laptop computers, desktop computers, and software in more than seven countries. The company is required to file financial statements annually with a securities commission. The controller has just compiled the following information on last year's revenues:

	Revenue (in millions)
Laptop computers	$ 90
Desktop computers	12
Software	50
	$152
United States	$ 40
Canada	45
South America	25
Asia	19
Africa	13
Europe	10
	$152

Required

Which of the above should be reported as an operating segment and which as a geographic segment in a note to the financial statements?

[CICA, adapted]

P7-2

The Auto Corporation has internal reporting for four divisions. The following data have been gathered for the year just ended.

	Div. A	Div. B	Div. C	Div. D
Interdivisional sales	$ —	$ —	$50,000	$ 10,000
External sales	75,000	200,000	5,000	100,000
Direct divisional expenses	15,000	50,000	25,000	60,000
Allocated joint costs	35,000	55,000	–	–
Depreciation	12,500	22,500	17,500	20,000
Capital expenditures	40,000	80,000	10,000	30,000
Identifiable assets	62,500	122,500	92,500	107,500
Liabilities	17,500	27,500	22,500	52,500

1. Divisions A and B share production facilities. Joint product costs, depreciation, capital expenditures, and much of the identifiable assets are allocated one-third to Division A and the remainder to Division B.
2. Division C sells over 90% of its output to Division D on a cost-plus basis.
3. Unallocated corporate expenses not included above amount to $57,500.

Required

1. From the preceding information, what are the operating segments that should be reported by the Auto Corporation? Explain your recommendation fully.

2. Prepare a schedule of supplementary financial information by segments, in accordance with IFRS 8 recommendations, based on the information provided above, together with a condensed consolidated SCI.

P7-3

The controller for Saskatoon Potash Inc. has determined that her company has five identifiable segments under IFRS 8. She has gathered the following information on those segments:

Operating segment	External sales	Inter-segment sales	Operating profit (loss)	Total assets
Red	800	100	75	900
Green	500	300	60	680
Blue	150	—	5	200
Grey	160	—	(14)	150
Yellow	90	—	(12)	170

Required
Identify which segments are reportable segments.

P7-4

The following information is available for Export Corporation's operating subsidiaries throughout the world, in thousands of Canadian dollars:

	External sales	Sales to operating regions	Identifiable assets	After-tax profit
Canada	$ 60,000	$300,000	$ 30,000	$ 7,500
South America	285,000	60,000	120,000	6,750
United States	225,000	30,000	105,000	13,500
Asia	45,000	—	22,500	5,250
Europe	60,000	—	30,000	7,500
General Corporate	—	—	45,000	4,500*
Consolidated	$675,000		$352,500	$45,000

*Investment income, less general corporate expenses

Required
Determine which regions you would suggest reporting as geographic areas, as part of the entity-wide disclosures in IFRS 8. Identify the characteristics that led to your choices.

P7-5

This year, for the first time, CTR Corporation must report supplementary information by operating segment. The controller has prepared the following note for inclusion in the annual report.

Segmented Data

Your company operates in several different operating segments. Selected financial data by division are provided below, in Canadian dollars.

	Hardware	Tires	Other	Consolidated
Sales to outsiders	$400,000	$200,000	$300,000	$ 900,000
Sales between divisions	50,000	10,000	60,000	120,000
Total sales	$450,000	$210,000	$360,000	$1,020,000
Operating profit	15,000	40,000	20,000	62,000
Capital expenditures	5,000	25,000	30,000	70,000
Assets	65,000	240,000	90,000	455,000

During the year, your company had export sales that resulted in gross profit of $50,000.

Required

Criticize the note as prepared by the controller. Identify any missing information, either numerical or verbal, and indicate errors in presentation.

P7-6

The Aspen Company is a retail department store chain. The company's fiscal year ends on the Saturday closest to January 31 of each year. The company is publicly held and submits quarterly financial statements to the shareholders.

Like most retail establishments, Aspen operates at a loss for most of the year, but generally recovers the losses in the fourth quarter to finish the year with a profit. In fiscal year 20X5, the company reported pre-tax net income of $3,000,000, and paid taxes at a rate of 45%.

In the first quarter of 20X6 the company suffered a loss of $2,250,000 before taxes. In the second quarter, economic conditions improved slightly, but the cumulative six-month loss was $3,900,000, the worst in the company's history. Nevertheless, management predicted that the losses would be recovered as the economy improved, and forecast a break-even performance for the year as a whole.

The loss did decline in the third quarter, to a cumulative loss of $1,950,000; the fourth quarter almost completely wiped out the loss, ending the year with a fiscal pre-tax loss of only $150,000.

Required

Assume that tax losses can be carried back for only one year. Determine the provision for income taxes that should be reported on Aspen's interim SCIs for fiscal year 20X6, assuming that each quarter is reported:

1. using the discrete approach;
2. using the integral approach.

P7-7

Labels Ltd. experienced the following events during the first quarter of 20X3:

1. The annual sales catalogue was developed and provided online, at a cost of $3,500,000.
2. Programming and consulting fees were incurred for annual updates of the internet site, at a cost of $1,750,000.

3. Owing to a strike at the principal supplier's factory, Labels' inventory fell to the lowest level in 14 years. Labels uses the LIFO method for financial reporting.
4. A notice of assessed value for property taxes was received. The tax assessment will be received and be due in the second quarter. Taxes for 20X3 are estimated at $1,400,000.
5. Labels uses the declining-balance method for depreciation. The total depreciation for 20X3 on assets held at the start of the year will be $5,600,000.
6. The company's top management receives annual bonuses based on 10% of annual net income after taxes.

Required

For each event reported above, indicate what impact it would have on the first-quarter interim report under each approach to interim statements:

1. the integral or part-of-year approach;
2. the discrete or separate-period approach.

8

Foreign Currency Transactions and Hedges

LEARNING OBJECTIVES

After studying this chapter, students should be able to:

1. describe the conceptual alternatives to account for foreign currency transactions and balances;[1]
2. describe the practice of hedging;
3. define and describe hedge accounting and explain when it can be used; and
4. explain the accounting for fair-value hedges and cash-flow hedges.

INTRODUCTION

Bombardier is a large Canadian manufacturer of railcars and small aircraft. The company operates in 23 countries including the United States, China, Ireland, France, and Germany. In fiscal year 2009, the company had revenue of $20 billion, 96% of which was generated from outside Canada. With such wide-spread global operations, even small fluctuations in foreign currency rates can have a significant impact on Bombardier's financial results.

In its 2009 annual report, Bombardier estimates that a $0.01 change in the Canada–US exchange rate can affect 2010 costs by $23 million. This is a major factor affecting its operations. In Bombardier's 2009 fiscal year the Canadian dollar declined 19% relative to the US dollar as compared to an increase of 18% in 2008. Clearly, this volatility has a direct impact on the company's earnings.

Fortunately there are ways to minimize or eliminate the risk posed by fluctuating exchange rates. As we will see in this chapter, a company can use currency hedges to offset these potential gains or losses. Indeed, Bombardier also reports (in the same sensitivity analysis) that after considering the effects of its hedging program, a 1% change in the Canada–US exchange rate is not expected to have a material impact on costs.

Many Canadian corporations engage in some form of international activity, ranging from occasional transactions to highly complex and interrelated international operations. In this chapter we will address the two major accounting issues that arise from a company's transactions in foreign

1. Accounting for financial instruments is an intermediate accounting topic and therefore is not addressed directly in this chapter. However, it will help the reader to be familiar with the IFRS 7 reporting requirements for financial assets.

currencies: (1) accounting for the transactions themselves on the company's books; and (2) accounting for currency hedging activities to protect the company from the adverse consequences of exchange rate fluctuations.

The next chapter will deal with situations in which a company has operating subsidiaries in foreign countries; this issue is known as *accounting for foreign operations*. Bombardier has both foreign currency transactions and foreign operations.

FOREIGN CURRENCY CONCEPTS

Definitions

Transactions that are denominated in a foreign currency are called **foreign currency transactions**. A transaction is **denominated** in a foreign currency whenever the monetary value of the transaction is specified in a currency that is *not* the company's functional currency.[2] For most Canadian companies the functional currency is the Canadian dollar; any transaction that is stated in a different currency is a foreign currency transaction. Such transactions include (1) borrowing or lending money, and (2) buying or selling products at an amount stated in a foreign currency (e.g., US dollars, Japanese yen, or euros). All foreign currency transactions must be translated into the functional currency for accounting purposes, using the exchange rate in effect at the date of the transaction, known as the **spot exchange rate**.

On the other hand, if a Canadian company's functional currency is the US dollar, all transactions in Canadian dollars are foreign currency transactions for that company's financial reporting. The Canadian dollar transactions must be converted to US dollars.

Causes of Exchange Rate Changes

Why do exchange rates fluctuate? Some short-run changes in exchange rates are the result of speculation in the money markets. Over the longer run, however, exchange rates are related to differential inflation rates.

If Country A experiences inflation that is in excess of inflation in Country B, then the currency in Country A will decline in value relative to Country B's currency. The relative change in exchange rates will be approximately equal to the relative change in purchasing power of the currency; a fixed nominal amount of Country A's currency will buy less after a period of inflation than the equivalent nominal amount of Country B's currency, and therefore the relative values of the two currencies will be adjusted through the money markets to recognize the fact that Country A's currency will not buy as much any more. This is known as the **purchasing power parity** (PPP) concept.

2. As we will see in Chapter 9, a firm's functional currency is the currency of the primary economic environment in which the company operates.

Other theories have also been proposed to explain the changes in exchange rates, but it has been difficult to gather evidence in support of these different theories. Research over the past 25 years supports purchasing power parity as the best explanation of the direction of exchange rate changes over the long term. In the short term, however, this research has found that exchange rate changes are very difficult to explain. This is especially true for explaining changes between countries with low inflation rates and free capital markets.[3]

In addition, other factors often come into play. Some countries do not allow their currency to float freely. Their currencies are either pegged to a particular currency (usually the US dollar) or targeted to a narrow trading range. For example, prior to July 21, 2005, China pegged the exchange rate of its currency, the renminbi, against the US dollar. Since 2005, the Chinese government has managed the exchange rate for its currency within a very narrow band. One of the major reasons for the use of fixed or controlled exchange rates by countries like China is that it assists their companies who are exporting into markets like the United States' by reducing foreign currency risk. However, the management of exchange rates often fails or is ineffective when the official exchange rates bear no relationship to the underlying purchasing power parity between currencies. This leads to widespread trading of such currencies in the illicit or underground market.

Foreign Currency Transactions

Example: Sale Denominated in Euros Suppose that on December 5, 20X5, Domestic Corporation sells 100 units of its product in Germany for €100,000. To record this sale on its books, Domestic Corporation must translate the euro-denominated sale into the equivalent amount in Canadian dollars. If we assume that the exchange rate on the date of sale was €1 = C$1.25 (that is, that each euro is worth $1.25, or that one dollar is worth €0.80), then the Canadian equivalent is $125,000. The sale can be recorded as follows, assuming that it was a sale on account:

Accounts receivable	125,000	
Sales		125,000

The amount of the sale in its Canadian equivalent will then be added to the other domestic and foreign sales without further difficulties.

If the German customer pays the amount owing on December 21, Domestic Corporation will receive €100,000. If the exchange rate is €1 = $1.27 on the payment date, Domestic will receive $127,000 when the euros are converted to Canadian dollars. Domestic will debit cash for $127,000 and credit accounts receivable for $125,000. The $2,000 difference represents a gain that has been realized by Domestic because the value of the euro went up while Domestic was holding a receivable that was denominated in euros. If the exchange rate had gone down instead of up, Domestic would have realized a loss instead of a gain.

Alternatives Theoretically, the gain on the exchange rate change could be treated in either of two ways: (1) by increasing the amount of revenue recognized by $2,000; or (2) by crediting

3. Kenneth Rogoff, "Exchange rates in the modern floating era: what do we really know?", *Review of World Economics* (2009), 145:1–12.

a separate gain account. The difference may seem minor, since both treatments will result in an increase in net income in the same period. The alternative treatments can have a substantive impact, however, when a company buys inventory or capital assets in a foreign currency and the exchange rate changes between the date of purchase and the date of payment. Any exchange gain or loss realized by holding the liability could, in theory, either be (1) added to the cost of the assets acquired or (2) treated as a gain or loss of the period.

The first approach, to attach exchange gains and losses to the asset or the revenue that results from the initial transaction, is known as the **one-transaction theory** because the accrual and the cash settlement are viewed as a single economic event. The second approach is called the **two-transaction theory**—the accrual (i.e., the sale or purchase) is viewed as one economic event while the eventual cash settlement (collection of the receivable or payment of the liability) is treated as a separate financing activity. Under the two-transaction theory, exchange gains and losses normally flow directly through to net income in the period that they occur.

Current Practice The two-transaction theory underlies the IASB approach to foreign currency transactions. The financing component of a foreign currency transaction is separated from the purchase or sale itself because the cash flow is controlled by the domestic company, and the results of such essentially speculative activity should not be hidden in gross revenue or in the cost of assets. The financing component can be controlled because the company has many options—purchases can be paid for by bank drafts at the time of the transaction; receivables can be sold to banks or finance companies, or can be financed by the sale of credit "paper" denominated in the same currency; the foreign-currency-denominated payable or receivable can be hedged (which is the subject of the second part of this chapter); and so forth.

Under the two-transaction approach, the collection by Domestic of the €100,000 receivable will be recorded as follows:

Cash (€100,000)	127,000	
Accounts receivable		125,000
Foreign currency exchange gain		2,000

The two-transaction approach also applies to purchases. Companies frequently buy inventory or other assets at a price that is fixed in foreign currency. The cost of the asset is measured at the exchange rate in effect at the date of the purchase. If the liability is settled later at a higher or lower exchange rate, the exchange gain/loss has no impact on the carrying value of the asset.

Foreign Currency Balances

Monetary Balances Now assume instead that the receivable is not collected until June 5, 20X6, and that the fiscal year of Domestic Corporation ends on December 31. The receivable was initially recorded on Domestic's books at $125,000, but actually the receivable is for €100,000. We will also assume that the euro is worth $1.28 on December 31. The $1.28 is referred to as the **closing rate**, that is, the foreign exchange rate on the date of the SFP. On December 31, the value of the €100,000 receivable is $128,000, $3,000 greater than the original recorded amount of the transaction. How should accounts receivable be reported and how should the $3,000 gain be reported in the year-end financial statements?

In theory, we could translate foreign currency-denominated monetary assets and liabilities on the SFP using either (1) the historical rate or (2) the closing rate. Use of the historical rate means translating the foreign currency amount into our functional currency at the rate in effect when the monetary balance was created. If that approach were used, gains and losses from exchange rate fluctuations would be recognized only when realized—at the settlement or payment date. The historical approach ignores objectively measurable changes in the value of assets and liabilities, and enables management to manipulate earnings through the timing of cash settlement.

Thus, accounting practice uses the closing rate as the only feasible approach for reporting foreign currency monetary assets and liabilities. IFRS defines **monetary assets and liabilities** as currency held (i.e., cash) and assets and liabilities that are to be received or paid in a fixed or determinable amount of currency. The balances of monetary assets and liabilities, both current and long-term, are translated at the exchange rate at the SFP date. Because exchange rates change over time, the change will cause a Canadian dollar translation gain or loss. Now that we have resolved that monetary balances should be shown at the closing rate, we need to answer the related question of how the associated gains should be reported. There are two possible alternatives:

1. defer the unrealized gain or loss until the asset or liability is *settled* (that is, paid); or
2. recognize the gain or loss in 20X5 net income.

Proponents of deferral argue that exchange rates go up and down, and that the 20X5 gain may well be cancelled out by a loss in 20X6. Further, long-term foreign currency-denominated monetary assets and liabilities may not be settled for years. They argue that there is no point in recognizing gains and losses that may never be realized. In addition, if it is debt-related, the old debt may well be replaced by new debt (i.e., refinanced) at the end of its term. If the debt is refinanced, these proponents argue that no gain or loss needs to be recognized.

However, exchange gains and losses don't generally bounce up and down without reason. Exchange rates are subject to longer-term trends caused by changing relative economic performance between countries. Granted, exchange rates do not always behave in accordance with economic theory in the short run, but exchange rate changes are not random events.

In the example above, the gain reflects the increase in asset value and therefore should be included in income. The exchange rate change is an economic event affecting the company in 20X5. The company's receivable is worth more (in Canadian dollars) at the end of 20X5. This change in the company's net assets therefore should be recognized in net income. Indeed, the general rule is that all gains and losses on monetary assets and liabilities should be recognized in earnings.

Now we will turn our attention to two other issues: (1) accounting for non-monetary balances; and (2) practical ways of dealing with a large volume of foreign currency transactions.

Non-monetary Balances The foregoing discussion has focused on the translation of *monetary* balances. If the foreign currency transaction was not a sale but was, for example, a purchase of inventory, then the transaction will result in *two* SFP amounts—(1) an account payable and

(2) inventory. The account payable is a monetary balance and will be treated exactly as the account receivable discussed above.

The inventory, however, is a *non-monetary balance*. A **non-monetary balance** is, by definition, an amount that is *not* fixed in terms of a currency and does not represent a claim against monetary resources. Therefore, non-monetary balances are not affected by changes in the exchange rate if carried at historical cost. If inventory is carried at historical cost, then the historical cost of inventory that was purchased with a foreign currency is simply the domestic currency equivalent of the foreign currency *at the date of the purchase*. Non-monetary balances are carried at historical exchange rates because that is the historical cost.

An exception arises when a non-monetary asset is reported on the SFP at fair value rather than at historical cost. For example, suppose that Domestic Corporation purchased biological assets in US dollars and that Domestic reports its inventory of biological assets at fair value. If the current fair value is quoted in US dollars, it makes no sense to take a current value and translate it at a historical rate. To report the current value of the investment in Canadian dollars, the current value in US dollars must be converted into Canadian dollars at the current exchange rate. IFRS actually requires the use of the exchange rate in effect on the date fair value was determined. In most cases, such as the biological asset example above, this will be the spot exchange rate at the end of the reporting period (i.e., the closing rate).

Practical Expedients As a practical matter, companies that engage in a large volume of foreign currency transactions may not actually use the current rate for translating each transaction. If, for example, a company has thousands of sales transactions in US dollars during a year, it is impractical to check on the current exchange rate (the *spot rate*) every time a sale occurs. Instead, the sales may be accumulated for a period of time and a single rate applied to the aggregate. A company might use the average rate for each week or each month for that period's transactions. Each of these approaches is an expedient for accounting for a large volume of transactions. Minor differences between the actual spot rate and the rate used for translation of the transactions will be adjusted when the accounts are settled, or when still-outstanding monetary account balances are adjusted to the current rate on the reporting date.[4]

General Accounting Principles for Foreign Exchange-Denominated Items

Consistent with our discussion above, the appropriate accounting for foreign exchange transactions and balances can be summarized by the following three simple principles:

General Principle 1—All *monetary items* are translated using the exchange rate on the SFP date and the associated gains and losses are recognized in earnings. The exchange gains and losses are recognized in earnings regardless of whether the monetary assets and liabilities are carried at amortized value or fair value.

4. Some companies use a pre-determined standard rate for translating foreign currency transactions. If a company uses a profit-centre approach for evaluating its managers, it may be desirable to remove the effects of uncontrollable currency fluctuations from the profit centre's operating results so that the managers are not held accountable for factors beyond their control. The total amount of current monetary balances will then be adjusted to the current rate for external reporting.

EXHIBIT 8-1

General Principles for Accounting for Foreign Exchange Transactions in the Absence of Hedging

Type of financial asset or liability	Exchange rate for translation	Existence of exchange gain or loss	Disposition of exchange gains and losses	Exceptions in the absence of hedging
Monetary assets or liabilities	Exchange rate on reporting date	Yes	Profit and loss	n/a
Non-monetary assets and liabilities at historical cost	Historical rate	No	n/a	n/a
Non-monetary assets and liabilities at fair value	Exchange rate on date fair value is determined	Yes	Profit and loss	Equity investments using OCI election: foreign exchange gain/loss taken to OCI (with fair value change).

General Principle 2—All *non-monetary items carried at historical cost* are measured using the historical exchange rate. There are no exchange gains or losses, so accounting for foreign exchange changes is not an issue.

General Principle 3—All *non-monetary items carried at fair value* are measured using the exchange rate on the date that fair value is determined. Exchange gains and losses are recognized in earnings with one exception. For non-monetary assets where the changes in fair value are recognized in other comprehensive income (i.e., investments in equity securities), the associated foreign exchange gains and losses are also recognized in other comprehensive income.

These principles are summarized in Exhibit 8-1.

CONCEPT CHECK 8-1

Companion Website

1. What is the spot exchange rate?
2. Explain the "two-transaction" theory.
3. What options are available to handle unrealized gains and losses from changes in foreign exchange rates?

NATURE AND USE OF HEDGING

Hedging is any tactic used to reduce or eliminate commodity risk (e.g., risk of non-availability or change in value of the commodity) or financial risk (e.g., currency or interest rate risk). In this chapter we are specifically interested in hedging related to the financial risk arising from currency or foreign-exchange fluctuations. When a company holds a receivable denominated in a foreign currency, there will be a loss if the foreign currency falls in value relative to the Canadian dollar. Conversely, a loss on a foreign currency-denominated liability will occur if the foreign currency strengthens or increases in value relative to the Canadian dollar. To protect against foreign-currency losses, companies frequently *hedge* their monetary foreign-currency balances.

Hedging is the creation of an offsetting balance in the same foreign currency. If a company is holding a receivable of 1 million Japanese yen, the risk of gain or loss can be neutralized by incurring a liability of ¥1,000,000 for an equal term.

There are several ways of hedging. The most common is to enter into a *forward contract* with a bank or currency dealer. If a receivable is being hedged, then the company will contract to pay a bank an equivalent amount of foreign currency in exchange for Canadian dollars at a specified rate at a specified time in the future.

Some major currencies are also traded in a *futures* market. Futures markets for agricultural products are well known. Wheat, oats, and corn are traded on the commodities exchanges, as are cattle, cotton, copper, coffee, orange juice, plywood, and heating oil. The commodity that is of immediate concern here is money. On the Chicago Mercantile Exchange, for example, one can buy a futures contract for Canadian dollars, US dollars, euros, British pounds, or Japanese yen, among others. Futures contracts are for standard terms (e.g., 30, 60, 90, and 180 days) and for limited denominations.

Options are also available on most major currencies. A call option gives a holder the right to buy the currency while a put option gives a holder the right to sell the currency. The terms of the option are often standardized as to the quantity of a foreign currency, the price, and the expiry of the option. Depending on its nature, the option may be exercisable at any point during its life or only at the end of its life.

Another example of a hedging instrument is a *currency swap*, wherein corporations in two different countries agree to guarantee the payment of each other's interest and principal on foreign currency-denominated long-term debt. A Canadian company with outstanding British pound sterling debt may enter into a currency swap agreement with a British company that has outstanding Canadian-dollar debt.[5] Each party to the agreement thereby converts its foreign currency exposure to a fixed domestic equivalent, effectively eliminating exchange rate risk.

There are many different types of hedging instruments (see Reality Check 8-1). In this text, we will focus on forward contracts because they are the most common in Canada and

5. In practice, swaps are usually more complicated than this example and may involve more than two companies. Swaps normally are arranged through financial intermediaries, usually banks.

REALITY CHECK 8-1

What Derivatives Does Bombardier Use?

> Derivative financial instruments are mainly used to manage the Corporation's exposure to foreign exchange and interest-rate market risks. They consist of forward foreign exchange contracts, interest rate swap agreements, cross-currency interest-rate swap agreements, and interest-rate cap agreements. Derivative financial instruments are measured at fair value, including those derivatives that are embedded in financial or non-financial contracts that are not closely related to the host contracts . . . .Derivative financial instruments are classified as HFT, unless they are designated as hedging instruments for which hedge accounting is applied.

Source: Bombardier Inc., 2008–2009 Annual Report, pp. 158–159.

generally the most effective form of foreign currency hedge. Forward contracts are individually negotiated and thus can be tailored to suit the needs of the hedger in terms of currency type and contract duration.

Forward contracts, futures contracts, options, and swaps are examples of *secondary* or *derivative instruments*. **Derivative instruments** are contracts that derive their value from transferring one or more of the financial risks inherent in an underlying primary financial instrument. A derivative must possess three characteristics:

1. its value must change as a result of changes in a foreign exchange rate, a specified interest rate, a financial instrument price, a commodity price, etc.;
2. it must require very little or no initial investment; and
3. it must be settled in the future.

An example of a forward contract would be an agreement by a company to pay a bank $150,000 Canadian for the delivery of €100,000 in 90 days. In this case, the contracted amount of Canadian dollars is fixed, as is the contracted amount of euros, but the value of this contract will change over the next 90 days as the exchange rate between the Canadian dollar and the euro changes. Thus (1) the value of the forward contract changes in response to changes in the value of the euro (i.e., the underlying); (2) the forward contract has zero value when initiated (as we will see); and (3) the contract is settled in 90 days. Thus a forward contract possesses all three characteristics of a derivative.

Hedging Practice

To illustrate the practice of hedging, suppose that on November 1, 20X3, Domestic Corporation sells some of its product in Germany for €100,000. At the date of the sale, the euro is selling at a current or spot rate of $1.2717 in Canadian funds. As a result of the sale, Domestic has acquired a foreign currency monetary balance (account receivable) of $127,170. If Domestic wishes to protect itself against a possible exchange loss caused by a fall in the value of the euro, Domestic can buy a forward contract for an equivalent amount of euros. Assuming that the receivable will be collected in 90 days (on January 30, 20X4), Domestic can buy a contract for the *payment* of €100,000 90 days hence. The commitment to pay €100,000 will offset the commitment to receive €100,000 from the German customer.

On November 1, 20X3, a 90-day forward contract for euros is available for $1.2702. Domestic contracts to deliver or pay €100,000 in 90 days and the contract will be for $127,020. The $150 difference between the current value of €100,000 ($127,170) and the price of the forward contract ($127,020) reflects the anticipated change in the exchange rate over the next three months. In effect, Domestic is selling the euros that it will receive from the German customer. But since Domestic will not receive the euros for 90 days, the contract to deliver the euros will not be executed until then.

As a result, Domestic will have a *receivable* (from the customer) that is denominated in euros, but will also have a *payable* that is denominated in euros. The euro receivable and the euro payable are due at the same time. The two financial instruments will fluctuate in tandem as the euro exchange rate changes—a gain on one instrument will be exactly offset by a loss on the other.

Gross Method There are two ways to record the sale and associated hedge: (1) the gross method and (2) the memorandum method. Under the **gross method of recording a hedge**, the full amounts of both the hedge and the monetary item being hedged are recorded. First, we will use the *gross method* to illustrate the basic underlying economics of a hedge because the full economic values are more clearly illustrated than under the memorandum method. Thereafter, we will demonstrate the memorandum method.

Using the gross method, the entries to record **1a)** the sale of the merchandise and **1b)** the sale of the euros for delivery in the future are as follows:

November 1, 20X3

1a)		
Accounts receivable (€100,000)	127,170	
Sales		127,170
[sale of merchandise for €100,000 on account]		
1b)		
Forward contract receivable (in C$)	127,020	
Forward contract payable (€100,000)		127,020
[purchase of a forward contract to deliver €100,000]		

In the second entry, both the receivable and the payable in the forward contract are recorded at the gross amount at the time of entering into the contract.[6] It appears that the receivable and the payable for the forward contract are offsetting. However, this is not really

6. The memorandum alternative, as we will see, offsets the receivable with the payable and records the net amount. For financial statement presentation, only the *net* value of the contract is presented (i.e., the forward contract receivable is netted against the forward contract payable) even when the gross method is used.

the case. The receivable is fixed in terms of Canadian dollars and represents the amount to be received by Domestic when Domestic delivers the euros. The payable, on the other hand, is denominated in euros; the actual dollar equivalent will change as the price of the euro changes.

As is evident from the two entries, an effective hedge now exists because the account receivable from the customer is for the same amount and denominated in the same currency (euros) as the forward contract payable. Further, the forward contract receivable fixes the Canadian dollar value of the euros that Domestic will receive when it collects on its accounts receivable and, in turn, remits to the bank the euros to settle its forward contract.

Assume that Domestic's fiscal year ends on January 31. On January 30, 20X4, the customer pays €100,000 to Domestic, and Domestic delivers the euros in execution of the forward contract. Also assume that the spot rate for the euro is $1.2500 on the settlement date. The receipt of the €100,000 from the customer **1c)** will be recorded as follows:

January 30, 20X4

1c)

Cash (€100,000 @ 1.2500)	125,000	
Exchange gains and losses	2,170	
Accounts receivable (€100,000 @ 1.2717)		127,170
[receipt of €100,000 from customer, on account]		

There is a loss of $2,170 due to the fact that the exchange rate fell during the 90-day period.

To execute the forward contract that is now due, Domestic will **1d)** deliver €100,000 and **1e)** receive the contracted amount of $127,020 in return. The entries to record this transaction will appear as follows:

January 30, 20X4

1d)

Forward contract payable	127,020	
Exchange gains and losses		2,020
Cash (€100,000 @ 1.2500)		125,000
[payment of €100,000 to fulfill the forward contract obligation]		

1e)

Cash	127,020	
Forward contract receivable (in C$)		127,020
[receipt of cash from the buyer of the forward contract]		

Domestic recognizes a *loss* of $2,170 on the receivable and a *gain* of $2,020 on the forward contract. The net amount is a loss of $150. The fact that we end up with a net loss may suggest that the forward contract was not completely successful at eliminating risk, but that is not the case. The $150 loss is the difference between the spot rate and the forward rate on the date of the original sale, multiplied by the amount of the foreign currency balance being hedged: €100,000 × ($1.2717 − $1.2702).

What the hedge really does is limit any possible gain or loss to a known amount, the spread between the spot rate and the forward rate. The same net loss will exist in our example regardless of the actual exchange rate at the settlement date.

For example, suppose that instead of a rate of $1.2500, the actual spot rate on the settlement date was $1.2850. The three entries to record the receipt from the customer and the settlement of the forward contract will then be as follows:

1c2)

Cash (€100,000 @ 1.2850)	128,500	
Exchange gains and losses		1,330
Accounts receivable (€100,000 @ 1.2717)		127,170
[receipt of €100,000 from customer, on account]		

1d2)

Forward contract payable	127,020	
Exchange gains and losses	1,480	
Cash (€100,000 @ 1.2850)		128,500
[payment of €100,000 to fulfill the forward contract obligation]		

1e2)

Cash	127,020	
Forward contract receivable (in C$)		127,020
[receipt of cash from the buyer of the forward contract]		

Settlement of **1c2)** (the customer receivable) and **1d2)** (the forward contract) results in a gain of $1,330 and a loss of $1,480 respectively, for a net loss of $150, exactly as when the spot rate was $1.2500.

In the example that we have used above, the forward rate happened to be *lower* than the spot rate, resulting in a net *loss*. Forward rates may be either higher or lower than the spot rate. The spread between the spot and forward rates depends on (1) the interest rate differential between the two countries; and (2) how the market predicts the rate will move.

If the forward rate is *lower* than the spot rate, the hedge of a receivable would lock the hedger into a *loss*. But the loss would be quite minor in comparison to the potential loss from an unprotected position. The day-to-day change in the spot rate can easily be larger than the spread between the spot and forward rates. Thus the small certain loss can be viewed as the cost of insurance against a possibly substantial speculative loss. Of course, hedging also eliminates the possibility of realizing a gain as well.

When the forward rate is higher than the spot rate, the contract has a premium. When the forward rate is less, then a discount exists. If the hedge is of a foreign currency *receivable*, as above, a premium results in a gain while a discount results in a loss.

Conversely, if the hedge is of a foreign currency *liability*, a premium results in a loss while a discount causes a gain. The following table summarizes this relationship:

	Net result if a forward contract is priced at a:	
Item being hedged	Premium	Discount
Monetary assets	gain	loss
Monetary liability	loss	gain

In the example above, the forward contract was recorded by means of a journal entry that assigned equal values to the receivable and the payable. In addition to this method of recording, we will examine one other method of recording the hedge that yields the same result and that may be more appropriate.

Memorandum Entry or Net Method A second method of accounting for the forward contract is the **memorandum entry method**. Under this method, the forward contract is not recorded at all on November 1, 20X3. At the time of entering into the forward contract, the forward contract receivable is equal to the forward contract payable. The receivable is simply netted against the payable and, because the contract has zero value, only a memorandum entry is used. We will refer to this method as the *net method*.

A forward contract is an executory contract as well as a financial instrument. You already know (from previous courses) that an executory contract is an agreement by two parties to perform in the future. For accounting purposes, no liability or receivable is normally deemed to exist for an executory contract until one of the parties has actually performed, or *executed*, the contract. Usually the contract enters the accounting records only when it is settled. However, a forward contract is also a financial instrument, and as a result the accounting for forward contracts differs from the usual non-recognition of executory contracts.

Recognition for financial instruments like forward contracts occurs when the entity becomes party to the contractual provisions of the instrument rather than when performance occurs. Conceptually, the forward contract should be recognized on November 1, 20X3. However, since there is no cost at the beginning of the contract, there is no explicit cost that we can recognize and record. Thus it can be argued that there should be no entry on November 1, 20X3.

As a result, the net method of accounting for the forward contract makes no entry for the contract on November 1, 20X3. Unlike the gross method, the liability and the receivable relating to the contract are not recorded on the day that Domestic enters into the forward contract. The journal entries are as follows:

November 1, 20X3

2a)

Accounts receivable (€100,000)	127,170	
Sales		127,170
[sale of merchandise for €100,000 on account]		

2b)

No entry for forward contract

January 30, 20X4

2c)

Cash (€100,000 @ 1.2500)	125,000	
Exchange gains and losses	2,170	
Accounts receivable (€100,000 @ 1.2717)		127,170
[receipt of €100,000 from customer, on account]		

2d)

Cash (re: C$ forward contract receivable)	127,020	
Exchange gains and losses		2,020
Cash (re: €100,000 forward contract payable)		125,000
[settlement of forward contract @ $1.25 spot rate]		

EXHIBIT 8-2

Alternative Recording Methods for Hedging Contracts

	Gross Method		Net Method	
November 1, 20X3				
a) Accounts receivable (euros)	127,170		127,170	
Sales		127,170		127,170
b) Forward contract receivable (C$)	127,020			
Forward contract payable (euros)		127,020		
January 30, 20X4				
c) Cash (euros)	125,000		125,000	
Exchange gains and losses	2,170		2,170	
Accounts receivable (euros)		127,170		127,170
d) Cash (C$)			127,020	
Forward contract payable (euros)	127,020			
Exchange gains and losses		2,020		2,020
Cash (euros)		125,000		125,000
e) Cash (C$)	127,020			
Forward contract receivable (C$)		127,020		

*The gross method records the forward contract when initiated; the net method records the forward contract at settlement. A January 31 fiscal year-end is assumed.

The disadvantage of this approach is that since the forward contract has not been explicitly recognized on the books, it is easy to overlook when adjustments are made at year-end. At a conceptual level, however, the second approach (i.e., net method) is superior since it is difficult to record an asset (or liability) that has no cost. This is despite the fact that the forward contract meets the IFRS recognition criterion. In practice, the most common method is to treat the forward contract as an executory contract and thus not formally record it.

This example described an asset exposure. A liability exposure (e.g., a foreign-currency account payable) is treated similarly. However, the company will then enter into a forward contract to *receive* instead of *deliver* the foreign currency.

The two methods of recording the hedge are shown in Exhibit 8-2. The two entries for the sale and the collection of the customer receivable are identical under both methods. The accounting for the hedge does not affect the transactions for the primary instrument.

We also saw that regardless of the spot rate on the settlement date, the hedge offsets any gains or losses in the corresponding receivable. The cost was a small exchange loss of $150 in both scenarios. The accounting reflects the economics behind management's decision to enter into the hedge. Any exchange loss (gain) is matched with the related exchange gain (loss) and this is reflected in the financial statements for the period.

There are several issues still to be addressed. The accounting for an intervening year-end will be examined next. We will also discuss how we handle accounting for hedges when normal accounting does not allow the matching of related exchange gains and losses.

Intervening Year-End

The foregoing illustration dealt with the simplest situation, in which all of the related events occurred within the same accounting period. More commonly, a hedging relationship spans more than one accounting period, especially if the reporting enterprise is a public company that must report quarterly. When a foreign currency hedge spans two or more accounting periods, we continue to follow the general principles that were introduced earlier in the chapter.

A receivable is typically measured at amortized cost (or cost, if the difference is not material). If denominated in a foreign currency, it will be translated at the year-end spot rate and any exchange gains and losses will be included in net income. A forward contract is a derivative and gains and losses from derivatives are reported in earnings. Forward contracts (unless formally designated as hedges under hedge accounting) are therefore reported at fair value at the SFP date and the change in fair value is recognized in net income, regardless of whether the change has been realized or not.

To illustrate, we can slightly modify the previous example by assuming that Domestic's fiscal year ends on *December 31* instead of January 31. There will be a financial statement reporting date between the November 1 sale and the January 30 settlement date. Assume also that the spot rate for the euro on December 31 is $1.2600.

If the receivable were *not* hedged, the entries relating to a) the sale at a rate of $127,170; b) the year-end adjustment of the account receivable balance to $126,000 at the December 31 spot rate of $1.2600; and c) the settlement at $1.2500 would be as follows:

a) *November 1, 20X3*		
Accounts receivable (€100,000)	127,170	
Sales		127,170
[sale for €100,000 when the spot rate = $1.2717]		
b) *December 31, 20X3*		
Exchange gains and losses	1,170	
Account receivable		1,170
[reduce receivable to year-end spot rate: €100,000 × ($1.2600 − $1.2717)]		
c) *January 30, 20X4*		
Cash (€100,000 @ $1.25)	125,000	
Exchange gains and losses	1,000	
Account receivable		126,000
[receipt of cash to settle the €100,000 receivable at the January 30 spot rate of $1.25]		

In the absence of a hedge, the exchange gain/loss is recognized in the period in which it occurred. Of the total $2,170 exchange loss, $1,170 occurred in 20X3 and $1,000 occurred in 20X4.

If the receivable is hedged, however, the exchange gain/loss will be offset by a loss/gain on the forward contract liability on the settlement date. These gains and losses naturally offset using "normal" accounting for both the receivable balance and the forward contract on the SFP date. The use of *hedge accounting*, a specific IFRS term that we will explain shortly, is not

EXHIBIT 8-3

Recording Hedging Contracts with Intervening Year-End

	Gross Method		Net Method	
November 1, 20X3				
a) Accounts receivable (euros)	127,170		127,170	
Sales		127,170		127,170
b) Forward contract receivable (C$)	127,020			
Forward contract payable (euros)		127,020		
December 31, 20X3				
c) Exchange gains and losses	1,170		1,170	
Accounts receivable (euros)		1,170		1,170
d) Forward contract (payable - euros)	1,080		1,080	
Exchange gains and losses		1,080		1,080
January 30, 20X4				
e) Cash (euros)	125,000		125,000	
Exchange gains and losses	1,000		1,000	
Accounts receivable (euros)		126,000		126,000
f) Cash (C$)			127,020	
Forward contract (payable - euros)	125,940			1,080
Exchange gains and losses		940		940
Cash (euros)		125,000		125,000
g) Cash (C$)	127,020			
Forward contract receivable (C$)		127,020		

*The gross method formally records the forward contract when initiated; the net method formally records the forward contract only at settlement. A December 31 fiscal year-end is assumed.

necessary. The entries are shown in Exhibit 8-3 for both methods and the following comments are provided on the journal entries.

November 1, 20X3

a) An entry is made to record the sale and associated receivable.

b) Under the gross method, the forward contract is recorded using the forward rate of $1.2702.

December 31, 20X3

c) At year-end, accounts receivable are re-valued to $126,000 by crediting accounts receivable for $1,170 and recognizing an exchange loss of $1,170 [€100,000 × ($1.2600 − $1.2717)].

d) In addition, the forward contract must be valued at fair value. The forward rate for delivery of euros in 30 days is 1.2594. We will use this rate to value the forward contract since there are 30 days remaining until delivery is required. The value of the €100,000 payable under the forward contract declined from $127,020 to $125,940 for a gain of $1,080 [€100,000 × ($1.2702 − $1.2594)].

January 30, 20X4
e) When the customer's account is settled, an entry is made to record the receipt of €100,000 (at the January spot rate of $1.2500).
f and g) The settlement of the forward contract is also recorded to reflect both the payment of €100,000 to satisfy the forward contract payable and the receipt of C$127,020 in settlement of the forward contract receivable.

In 20X3, the exchange loss of $1,170 on the customer's account is offset against the $1,080 exchange gain on the forward contract. The net result is a loss of $90 in 20X3. In 20X4, the exchange loss of $1,000 on the customer receivable is offset by the $940 gain on the forward contract and the result is a $60 loss in 20X4. The net cost of the hedge is $150, the same as above, but it is now distributed across two periods.

CONCEPT CHECK 8-2

Companion Website

1. What is hedging?
2. Identify three instruments that can be used for hedging.
3. What is a derivative instrument?

HEDGE ACCOUNTING

Hedging allows management to limit their exposure to certain risks such as changes in currency exchange rates. In the example above, normal accounting rules reflected well the ability of a forward contract (the hedging item) to offset exchange gains and losses on monetary items such as trade accounts receivable (the hedged item). But this is not always the case. Assume that a company issues a purchase order to buy a machine. If the machine is priced in a foreign currency and if the lead time to delivery is several months or more, the company would be exposed to potentially large exchange losses (or gains).

To limit its exposure, the company may decide to enter into a forward contract. While this would be good business practice, normal accounting rules may not reflect the substance of this transaction. For example, if there was an intervening year-end, under normal accounting the company would be required to value the forward contract at fair value at year-end and to recognize the associated gain/loss in net income. Because we do not normally recognize the purchase order on the financial statements, there would be no offsetting loss/gain. The financial statements would not reflect the intent of the hedge as the gains and losses would not be matched. To overcome this problem, IFRS provides special rules for hedging activities (i.e., hedge accounting). **Hedge accounting** allows gains and losses on the hedged item to be matched with losses and gains on the hedging instrument in the same period. *It is important to note that hedge accounting is optional.*

Requirements for Hedge Accounting

Hedge accounting is a formal accounting designation and not simply a net result. For example, a Canadian company may have a substantial amount of receivables that are denominated in euros and may also have a large amount of payables in the same currency. Effectively, the currency risks from the receivables and the payables offset each other. This sort of offsetting position is sometimes called a **natural (implicit) hedge**—any gain or loss from the receivables will be offset by the loss or gain from the payables. The foreign exchange gains and losses will flow through to net income and naturally tend to offset each other. While this is a form of hedge in substance, it is not what the IFRS calls *hedge accounting*!

Under IFRS hedge accounting, a hedging relationship qualifies for special accounting rules only if it meets *all* of the following five conditions:

1. the hedging relationship is formally designated and documented at inception within the company's overall risk management strategy;
2. the hedge is anticipated to be highly effective;
3. for cash-flow hedges, the forecast transaction is highly probable;
4. the effectiveness of the hedge can be determined reliably; and
5. the hedge is assessed regularly on an ongoing basis and has been highly effective in the past.

Other points that underlie the concept of hedge accounting are as follows.

- A *hedged item* can be an asset or liability, an unrecognized *firm commitment* such as a purchase order, a highly probable forecast transaction such as a future revenue stream, or a net investment in a foreign operation. A derivative instrument cannot normally be a hedged item. Our focus in this chapter is on hedging changes in the future cash flows or fair value that result from exposure to changes in foreign currency exchange rates.
- A *hedging instrument* (that is, the offsetting risk) is normally a derivative. For currency hedges only, it also can be a non-derivative financial asset or liability.

Hedge accounting gives companies the ability to change the timing of recognition in net income of certain unrealized foreign currency gains and losses. Exchange gains and losses on hedging instruments (usually derivatives) are normally recognized in income in the current period. To match the gains and losses between a hedging instrument and a hedged item, a company can either:

- speed up recognition of the offsetting loss or gain on the hedged item into the current period; or
- defer recognition on the loss or gain on the hedging instrument to correspond with the hedged item.

REALITY CHECK 8-2

Bombardier's Use of Hedge Accounting

The Corporation formally documents all relationships between the hedging instruments and hedged items, as well as its risk management objectives and strategy for undertaking various hedge transactions. This process includes linking all derivatives to forecasted foreign currency cash flows or to a specific asset or liability. The Corporation also formally documents and assesses, both at the hedge's inception and on an ongoing basis, whether the derivative financial instruments that are used in hedging transactions are highly effective in offsetting the changes in the fair value or cash flows of the hedged items.

Source: Bombardier Inc., 2008–2009 Annual Report, p.159.

Three types of hedging relationships are identified in hedge accounting:

1. *Fair-value hedge*: the hedging of potential changes in fair value that result from changes in foreign exchange rates and that affect profit or loss. Fair-value hedges can be for the exposure to changes in exchange rates that affect recognized assets or liabilities and unrecognized firm commitments.
2. *Cash-flow hedge*: the hedging of the variability in cash flows that results from changes in foreign exchange rates and that affects profit or loss. Cash-flow hedges can be for the exposure to changes in exchange rates that affect recognized assets or liabilities and highly probable forecast transactions.
3. *Hedge of a net investment in a foreign operation*: we will discuss this type of situation in the next chapter.

In this chapter we focus on fair-value hedges and cash-flow hedges. In both cases the specific risk that could affect profit or loss is potential changes in foreign currency exchange rates. It is also important to remember that hedge accounting may not be applied until and unless the company has made a formal designation of a hedging relationship. The objective of the formal declaration is to keep companies from loosely defining their hedging relationships and thereby exercising choice of reporting options at reporting dates—net income versus OCI.

CONCEPT CHECK 8-3

Companion Website

1. Why do companies need hedge accounting?
2. Is hedge accounting optional or required? Explain.
3. What are the three possible hedging relationships found in hedge accounting?

ACCOUNTING FOR FAIR-VALUE AND CASH-FLOW HEDGES

Hedge accounting can be used in a variety of circumstances. However, for our discussions of foreign currency exposure, the most relevant and practical issues concern anticipated transactions. **Anticipated transactions** are those that are expected to occur in the future but for which no asset or liability has been recognized. Companies often have a foreign currency risk exposure for anticipated transactions. For example, a Canadian airline is exposed to risk on its anticipated purchases of aircraft fuel. The risk takes two forms: (1) a *fair-value risk* that the US dollar price will increase, and (2) a *currency risk* that the US–Canada exchange rate will change. Both types of risk can be hedged against. The airline can hedge the fair-value risk on fuel prices by buying futures options for oil. But the hedge won't solve the currency risk because the options are in US dollars. Therefore, the airline may also hedge against adverse exchange rate changes through a currency hedge. Projected future purchases of oil are one example of the kind of anticipated transactions that we will concern ourselves with for the remainder of the chapter.

In discussing anticipated transactions, IFRS distinguishes between a *firm commitment* and a *forecasted transaction*:

- A **firm commitment** is a binding agreement for the exchange of resources where the quantity, price, and dates are specified. An example of a firm commitment would be a purchase order that has been accepted by the source company.
- A **forecasted transaction** is an anticipated transaction for which no firm commitment exists. Examples of a forecasted transaction would be a projected future revenue stream or a projected future inventory purchase.

The distinction between a firm commitment and a forecasted transaction is important. Under IFRS, the hedge of a firm commitment is accounted for using a fair-value hedge, and the hedge of a highly probable forecasted transaction is accounted for using a cash-flow hedge. Interestingly, because a firm commitment is by definition a highly probable forecasted transaction and because the foreign currency exposure of a firm commitment impacts both fair values and cash flows, under IFRS a hedge of the foreign currency risk of a firm commitment can be accounted for as either a fair-value hedge or a cash-flow hedge.

Anticipated transactions do not immediately cause any financial assets or liabilities to be recorded, because by definition the transactions are *anticipated* future transactions. Nevertheless, a company often hedges the anticipated cash flow to offset the currency risk. Normal accounting for an anticipated transaction and hedge in this situation would not result in the associated exchange gains and losses being matched. The use of hedge accounting resolves this problem.

Fair-Value Hedge

The accounting for a fair-value hedge is straightforward. The foreign currency gain or loss (i.e., the particular risk) on the hedging instrument is recognized in current period net income as would normally occur. The foreign currency gain or loss (i.e., the same particular risk) on

REALITY CHECK 8-3

A recent study of US firms finds that firms often decide not to use hedge accounting despite its ability to reduce earnings volatility. This is surprising given that the reduction of earnings volatility is often an important preparer objective. The study found four reasons for the lack of use of hedge accounting:

> (1) the substantial cost (time and money) of documentation and ongoing monitoring of designated hedges; (2) the availability of natural hedges that can be highly effective; (3) new accounting standards that broaden the range of natural or economic hedges; and (4) qualifying hedges are not available or are too costly, or documentation is untimely, inadequate, or unavailable.[a]

The authors also suggest that an increased risk of restatements may be another reason that deters the use of hedge accounting.

a. E.E. Comiskey and C.W. Mulford, "The Non-designation of Derivatives as Hedges for Accounting Purposes" *The Journal of Applied Research in Accounting and Finance*, Volume 3, Issue 2, 2008, p. 11.

the hedged item is also recognized in current period net income and the carrying value of the hedged item is adjusted. The gains and losses of the hedged item and hedging instrument will then offset one another in the same period.

From the perspective of hedging foreign currency gains and losses on recognized assets or liabilities, hedge accounting using fair-value hedges will usually not be necessary to offset gains and losses. Foreign exchange gains and losses are already recognized in current period net income for all classes of financial assets and liabilities with one exception—equity investments where the entity has elected the fair value through other comprehensive income (FVTOCI) option. Exchange gains and losses from derivatives are also included in current period net income. The exchange gains and losses, therefore, are already matched for most financial assets and liabilities. For many businesses, it takes considerable time and effort to go through the formal designation and documentation process for hedge accounting. It is unlikely they would use hedge accounting if the foreign exchange gains and losses were naturally offsetting (see Reality Check 8-3).

From the perspective of hedging foreign currency gains and losses, fair-value hedges can be used for (1) FVTOCI equity investments; and (2) firm commitments. A fair-value hedge can be useful for FVTOCI equity investments because the foreign exchange gain or loss is normally recognized in OCI. Using a fair-value hedge under hedge accounting allows for the immediate recognition of the foreign exchange gain or loss so that it can be matched with the loss or gain on the hedging instrument.

A fair-value hedge is more commonly used for a firm commitment such as a purchase order. Because a purchase order is not normally recognized on the financial statements, there would be no foreign exchange gain/loss to offset the loss/gain on the hedging instrument. Using a fair-value hedge allows for the foreign exchange gain/loss on the purchase order to be recognized immediately so that it can offset the loss/gain on the hedging instrument.

Example: Fair-Value Hedge of a Commitment to Purchase a Machine To illustrate accounting for a fair-value hedge, assume that Domestic Corporation issues a purchase order to Français Ltée. on November 1, 20X7, to purchase a machine for €200,000. The machine is delivered on January 30, 20X8, and payment is made on March 1, 20X8. Domestic has a December 31 fiscal year-end.

Domestic Corp. finalized the decision to purchase the machine on November 1, based on the Canadian-dollar equivalent cost of the machine at that time. If the euro appreciates significantly in value between November 1 and the payment date, Domestic will incur substantial additional cost for the machine. Therefore, it is common for a purchaser to hedge a commitment as soon as the purchase contract is signed and the foreign currency cost of the asset or service is established.

Suppose that on November 1, 20X7, the spot rate for the euro is €1 = C$1.5000. The €200,000 initial commitment is equivalent to C$300,000. Domestic Corp. hedges its euro commitment by entering into a forward contract to *receive* €200,000 on March 1, 20X8. Assume that the March 1 forward rate for the euro is $1.5100 on November 1. The relevant exchange rates are summarized in the table below:

Date	Event	Spot rate	Forward rate to March 1, 20X8
November 1, 20X7	Purchase order issued	1.5000	1.5100
December 31, 20X7	SFP date	1.5050	1.5130
January 30, 20X8	Machine delivered	1.5300	1.5340
March 1, 20X8	Forward contract settled	1.5400	n/a—settlement date

We will also assume that this transaction qualifies as a fair-value hedge under hedge accounting. The entries to record these transactions are summarized in Exhibit 8-4 and the following comments are provided on the journal entries.

November 1, 20X7

a) No entry is made to record the purchase order.

b) Under the gross method, the forward contract is recorded using the forward rate of $1.51.

December 31, 20X7

c) At year-end the hedge is adjusted to (recorded at) fair value and the gain is recognized in net income. The adjustment to the hedge ($600) is determined using the forward rate on December 31 [€200,000 × (1.513 − 1.510)].

d) In addition, an exchange loss on the purchase order is recognized in net income and a liability is recognized to reflect the increase in the cost of the purchase order commitment. The amount of the loss and associated liability ($1,000) is determined using the spot rate on December 31 [€200,000 × (1.505 − 1.500)]. The net exchange loss from November 1 to December 31 is $400 ($1,000 − $600).

January 30, 20X8

e) The forward contract is re-valued by making an entry for $4,200, the change in the value of the contract [€200,000 × (1.534 − 1.513)]. The gain is recognized in net income.

f) An additional exchange loss on the purchase order is recognized in net income. The increase in the cost of the purchase order commitment is also recognized as an increased liability. The amount of the loss and associated liability ($5,000) is determined using the spot

EXHIBIT 8-4

Recording a Fair-Value Hedge

	Gross method		Net method	
November 1, 20X7				
a) Issue P.O.—no entry				
b) Forward contract receivable (euros)	302,000			
Forward contract payable (C$)		302,000		
[to record the forward contract using forward rate: (€200,000 × 1.51)]				
December 31, 20X7				
c) Forward contract receivable (euros)	600		600	
Exchange gains and losses		600		600
[€200,000 × (1.513 − 1.510)]				
d) Exchange gains and losses	1,000		1,000	
P.O. commitment liability		1,000		1,000
[€200,000 × (1.505 − 1.500)]				
January 30, 20X8				
e) Forward contract receivable (euros)	4,200		4,200	
Exchange gains and losses		4,200		4,200
f) Exchange gains and losses	5,000		5,000	
P.O. commitment liability		5,000		5,000
g) Machine	300,000		300,000	
P.O. commitment liability	6,000		6,000	
Accounts payable		306,000		306,000
March 1, 20X8				
h) Forward contract payable	302,000			
Cash (C$)		302,000		
i) Cash (euros)	308,000		308,000	
Forward contract receivable (euros)		306,800		4,800
Exchange gains and losses		1,200		1,200
Cash (C$)				302,000
j) Accounts payable	306,000		306,000	
Exchange gains and losses	2,000		2,000	
Cash (euros)		308,000		308,000

*The gross method records the forward contract when initiated; the net method records the forward contract only at settlement. A December 31 fiscal year-end is assumed.

rate on January 30 [€200,000 × (1.530 − 1.505)]. The net exchange loss from January 1 to January 30 is $800 ($5,000 − $4,200).

g) On delivery, accounts payable are recorded at the spot rate ($306,000 = €200,000 × 1.530) to reflect the value of the obligation to pay €200,000 to the supplier. The P.O. commitment liability is reversed as the increase in the liability is now captured in accounts payable. Finally, the machine is recorded at $300,000 to balance the journal entry. This results in the equipment being recorded at the spot rate (1.500) that was in effect when the purchase order was issued.

March 1, 20X8

h and i) The forward contract is settled on March 1, 20X8. Domestic Corp. pays the $302,000 it contracted to pay (€200,000 × 1.510) and in return receives €200,000 valued at $308,000. The difference is a gain of $6,000 on the contract of which $4,800 was recognized earlier. The remaining $1,200 is the gain that occurred between January 30 and March 1 [€200,000 × (1.540 − 1.534)].

j) Domestic Corp. uses the €200,000 (worth C$308,000) it received from its forward contract to settle the payable for the machine. As a result of the change in the exchange rate, the company incurs an exchange loss of $2,000 [€200,000 × (1.540 − 1.530)]. The net exchange loss from January 30 to March 1 is $800 ($2,000 − $1,200).

Observe the following about this transaction:

- The cost of the hedge was $2,000 [€200,000 × (1.510 − 1.500)], the difference between the spot rate and the forward rate at the time the machine was ordered; $400 was recognized as an exchange loss in 20X7 and $1,600 was recognized as an exchange loss in 20X8, $800 between January 1 and January 30 and $800 between January 30 and March 1, 20X8.
- The cost of the machine was $300,000, which can be calculated using the spot rate (€200,000 × 1.500) at the time it was ordered. None of the cost of the hedge was included in the cost of the machine.

Cash-Flow Hedge

The accounting for a cash-flow hedge achieves matching by deferring the recognition of the gains and losses on the hedging instrument in other comprehensive income. In addition to disclosing exchange gains/losses as a component of OCI, the cumulative gains/losses are also disclosed as a separate component of equity in the statement of changes in equity. Any ineffective portion of the hedging instrument is recognized in net income.

The accounting for the hedged item proceeds as normal. When *non-financial* assets are subsequently recognized, the gains or losses can be removed from other comprehensive income and included in the initial cost of the asset or liability. If the length of the forward contract was to the delivery date, then the terms of the hedge establish the cost of the anticipated goods or services.

Alternatively, for both *non-financial* and *financial* assets, the associated gains and losses in other comprehensive income can be left in the equity account and only reclassified into income in the same period(s) that the asset acquired or liability assumed affects net income.

Example: Cash-Flow Hedge of a Commitment to Purchase a Machine To illustrate accounting for a cash-flow hedge, we will re-use our Domestic Corp. example. A cash-flow hedge can be used by Domestic because, as a firm commitment, the purchase order automatically meets the criteria of being a highly probable future transaction. Further, the foreign exchange risk on the purchase order exposes Domestic to variability in cash flows. Thus cash-flow hedge accounting is appropriate. To continue our example, assume that Domestic Corporation issues a purchase order to Français Ltée. on November 1, 20X7, to purchase a machine for €200,000. The machine is delivered on January 30, 20X8, and payment is made on March 1, 20X8. Domestic has a December 31 fiscal year-end.

Domestic Corp. hedges the commitment as soon as the purchase contract is signed. We will assume that this transaction qualifies as a cash-flow hedge under hedge accounting. Of course, Domestic will not recognize a liability on the SFP until the machine has been delivered.

Suppose that on November 1, 20X7, the spot rate for the euro is €1 = C$1.5000. The €200,000 initial commitment is equivalent to C$300,000. Domestic Corp. hedges its euro commitment by entering into a forward contract to *receive* €200,000 on March 1, 20X8. Assume that the March 1 forward rate for the euro is $1.5100 on November 1. The relevant exchange rates are summarized in the table below:

Date	Event	Spot rate	Forward rate to March 1, 20X8
November 1, 20X7	Purchase order issued	1.5000	1.5100
December 31, 20X7	SFP date	1.5050	1.5130
January 30, 20X8	Machine delivered	1.5300	1.5340
March 1, 20X8	Forward contract settled	1.5400	n/a—settlement date

The entries to record these transactions are summarized in Exhibit 8-5 and the following comments are provided on the journal entries.

November 1, 20X7

a) No entry is made to record the purchase order.

b) Under the gross method, the forward contract is recorded using the forward rate of $1.51.

December 31, 20X7

c) At year-end the hedge is adjusted to (recorded at) fair value and the gain is deferred in other comprehensive income. The increase in the fair value of the hedge ($600) is determined using the forward rate on December 31 [€200,000 × (1.513 − 1.510)].

January 30, 20X8

d) The forward contract is re-valued by making an entry for the change in the value of the contract, $4,200 [€200,000 × (1.534 − 1.513)]. The gain is deferred in other comprehensive income.

e) On delivery, the machine and associated payable are recorded at the spot rate ($306,000 = €200,000 × 1.530).

f) Next, the gain deferred in other comprehensive income is now reclassified. We have chosen to adjust the cost of the machine. As such, the deferred gain will be amortized into income over the life of the machine through its effect on the depreciation expense of the machine. The carrying value of the machine is $301,200. This is slightly more than the $300,000 cost using the spot rate at the time the machine was ordered but is much less than the $306,000 cost if there had been no hedge.

March 1, 20X8

g and h) The forward contract is settled on March 1, 20X8. Domestic Corp. pays the $302,000 it contracted to pay (€200,000 × 1.510) and in return receives €200,000 valued at $308,000. The difference is a gain of $6,000 on the contract of which $4,800 was recognized earlier. The remaining $1,200 is the gain that occurred between January 30 and March 1 [€200,000 × (1.540 − 1.534)].

EXHIBIT 8-5

Recording a Cash-Flow Hedge

	Gross method		Net method	
November 1, 20X7				
a) Issue P.O.—no entry				
b) Forward contract receivable (euros)	302,000			
Forward contract payable (C$)		302,000		
[to record the forward contract using forward rate: (€200,000 × 1.51)]				
December 31, 20X7				
c) Forward contract receivable (euros)	600		600	
Other comprehensive income		600		600
[€200,000 × (1.513 − 1.510)]				
January 30, 20X8				
d) Forward contract receivable (euros)	4,200		4,200	
Other comprehensive income		4,200		4,200
e) Machine	306,000		306,000	
Accounts payable		306,000		306,000
f) Other comprehensive income	4,800		4,800	
Machine		4,800		4,800
March 1, 20X8				
g) Forward contract payable	302,000			
Cash (C$)		302,000		
h) Cash (euros)	308,000		308,000	
Forward contract receivable (euros)		306,800		4,800
Exchange gains and losses		1,200		1,200
Cash (C$)				302,000
i) Accounts payable	306,000		306,000	
Exchange gains and losses	2,000		2,000	
Cash (euros)		308,000		308,000

*The gross method records the forward contract when initiated; the net method records the forward contract at settlement. A December 31 fiscal year-end is assumed.

i) Domestic Corp. uses the €200,000 (worth C$308,000) it received from its forward contract to settle the payable for the machine. As a result of the change in the exchange rate, the company incurs an exchange loss of $2,000 [€200,000 × (1.540 − 1.530)]. The net exchange loss from January 30 to March 1 is $800 ($2,000 − $1,200).

The following can be noted about this transaction:

- No gains or losses were recognized in net income in 20X7.
- The cost of the hedge was $2,000 [€200,000 × (1.510 − 1.500)]; $800 was recognized as an exchange loss in 20X8 (between January 30 and March 1, 20X8) and $1,200 was included in the cost of the machine.

REALITY CHECK 8-4

How significant are the gains and losses deferred in other comprehensive income using cash-flow hedge accounting rules?

In their 2009 financial statements, Bombardier reported net income of $1.008 billion. In their statement of comprehensive income they also reported a loss on cash-flow hedges of $865 million. These losses almost equal their reported income. Clearly, the magnitude of amounts involved using cash-flow hedge accounting can be very significant. However, it is important to remember that there are unrealized and unrecognized economic gains offsetting these losses. Cash-flow hedge accounting provides Bombardier with the ability to defer these losses and subsequently match them with the corresponding economic gains. Thus hedge accounting allows the financial reporting to reflect the original intention of management in entering into the hedges.

- The cost of the machine was $301,200, which consists of two components: $300,000 calculated using the spot rate ($1.50) at the time it was ordered and $1,200, which is the cost of the hedge that was allocated to the machine for the price protection it provided from November 1, 20X7, to January 30, 20X8.

This example illustrated the purchase of an asset. The same principles apply if the purchase is of services rather than of an asset. If the company were *selling* assets or services priced in a foreign currency, the same procedures would apply, except that the recognized monetary item would be a receivable instead of a payable; any discount or premium on the forward contract would be reflected in sales revenue.

Finally, because a firm commitment can be accounted for as either a fair-value or cash-flow hedge, when a forecast transaction becomes a firm commitment (e.g., inventory purchases) the cash-flow hedge does not have to be re-designated as a fair-value hedge.

CONCEPT CHECK 8-4

Companion Website

1. What is a firm commitment?
2. What is a forecast transaction?
3. How are gains and losses on cash-flow hedges treated?

Effective Hedges

The question arises as to how to assess the effectiveness of a hedge. This is important because a hedge must be expected to be highly effective for it to be designated as a hedge under IFRS. Two conditions must be met for a hedge to be deemed highly effective with respect to foreign exchange risk:

1. The hedge is expected to be highly effective in offsetting the changes in fair value or cash flows due to foreign exchange risk. This expectation must exist at the inception of the hedge and in subsequent periods.

2. The actual results are such that the gain or loss on the hedging instrument falls within a range of 80% to 125% of the loss or gain on the hedged item.

Companion Website

This test has both a forward-looking component (it is expected to be effective) and a backward-looking component (it has been effective). The actual mechanics of different possible tests are beyond the scope of this chapter but this test is very important. To the extent that a hedge is deemed to be ineffective, the timing of the recognition of exchange gains and losses will change and the impact on income will be immediate.

PROPOSED CHANGE

The IASB has proposed significant changes to the standards dealing with financial instruments and hedge accounting. The purpose of the new standards is to streamline and simplify the accounting for financial instruments. The project consists of three phases: Phase 1 addresses the classification and measurement of financial instruments; Phase 2 addresses the impairment of financial instruments; and Phase 3 addresses hedge accounting. As of the date of writing this textbook, IFRS 9 had been issued to address the classification and measurement of financial assets. The IASB hopes to issue final standards addressing the classification and measurement of financial liabilities and the remaining issues in Phases 2 and 3 in 2010 and 2011, with a required adoption date likely for years beginning on or after January 1, 2013. It is possible that the use of fair-value hedges may be eliminated in the proposed changes.

ACCOUNTING STANDARDS FOR PRIVATE ENTERPRISES

The accounting for foreign currency transactions and hedges for private enterprises is prescribed in Sections 1651 and 3856 of the *CICA Handbook, Part II*.

The general principles for accounting for foreign exchange transactions and balances for private enterprises are very similar to IFRS. All *monetary items* are translated using the exchange rate on the SFP date and the associated gains and losses are recognized in net income. All *non-monetary items carried at historical cost* are measured using the historical exchange rate. There are no exchange gains or losses, so accounting for foreign exchange changes is not an issue.

The accounting for *non-monetary items carried at fair value* is slightly different from IFRS. These items are measured using the exchange rate in effect on the balance sheet date and not the exchange rate on the date that the fair value was determined as used by IFRS. Exchange gains and losses are also recognized in net income.

A much simpler hedge accounting model with more limited application is used for private enterprises. As with IFRS, hedge accounting is optional. From the perspective of hedging foreign currency exposures, hedge accounting can be used for the hedging of anticipated transactions and the hedging of the net investment in a foreign operation.[7] The documentation required for the use of hedge accounting is not as extensive as the IFRS requirements but the critical

7. Additionally, hedge accounting can also be used for "a foreign currency-denominated interest-bearing asset or liability hedged with a cross-currency interest rate swap to mitigate the effect of changes in interest rates and foreign currency exchange rates" (*CICA Handbook, Part II*. Section 3856.32(d)).

terms of the forward contract and the hedged item must be the same. An example of "matched" critical terms is the requirement that the forward contract must mature within two weeks of the date of the anticipated transaction.

Further, under ASPE only forward contracts can be used as hedging instruments; options and futures contracts are not allowed as hedging instruments under hedge accounting. The forward contract is only recognized at maturity and, at that time, any gains and losses are used to adjust the carrying value of the hedged item.

Finally, private enterprises also have disclosure requirements to ensure that appropriate information is available about the use of hedge accounting. For example, private enterprises are required to disclose key terms of the anticipated transaction and the forward contract and the net effect of using hedge accounting.

Relevant Standards

IASB

IAS 21 The Effects of Changes in Foreign Exchange Rates
IAS 32 Financial Instruments: Presentation
IAS 39 Financial Instruments: Recognition and Measurement
IFRS 7 Financial Instruments: Disclosures
IFRS 9 Financial Instruments

ASPE

1651 Foreign Currency Translation
3856 Financial Instruments

Summary of Key Points

1. Exchange rates change for several reasons. Some changes, especially short-term fluctuations, are the result of the speculative activities of money market traders. Longer-term, the fundamental cause for changes in exchange rates is differential inflation rates between countries. Differential inflation rates cause exchange rates to change to compensate for the changing purchasing power between currencies.
2. Many, if not most, Canadian corporations engage in international activities to some extent. Foreign currency transactions are very common; a foreign currency transaction is one where the value of the transaction is fixed in a currency other than the enterprise's functional currency. Foreign currency transactions must be recorded on the corporation's

books at their equivalent in Canadian dollars at the time of the transaction. For revenues, expenses, and non-monetary balances, the amounts that are established by the initial transaction are not changed at subsequent reporting dates. For monetary items denominated in a foreign currency, the balances are translated using the current or spot rate and any exchange gains and losses are recognized in net income at subsequent reporting dates.

3. Financial assets and liabilities that are denominated in a foreign currency may be hedged. Hedging involves incurring a foreign currency liability to offset a foreign currency financial asset, or an asset to offset a liability. Derivative instruments are most commonly used for hedging. In Canada, the most common derivative instrument for foreign currency hedges is a forward contract. Futures, options, and currency swaps are other types of derivatives for hedging a foreign currency risk exposure. The accounting for hedges is usually straightforward because the normal rules for accounting for financial instruments allow the gain or loss on the hedged item to be recognized in the same period as the offsetting loss or gain on the hedging instrument. In those cases where the gains and losses do not offset, hedge accounting can be used to match the gains and losses.
4. *Hedge accounting* is a formal accounting designation that allows gains and losses on the hedged item to be matched with losses and gains on the hedging instrument in the same period. It is important to note that hedge accounting is optional. A hedging relationship must be specifically designated and documented by management within the company's risk management strategy. Hedge accounting may not be used prior to explicit designation and documentation of the hedge.
5. When hedge accounting is used, a foreign currency exposure is hedged using either a fair-value hedge or a cash-flow hedge (coverage of hedges of a net investment in a foreign operation is deferred to the next chapter). In a fair-value hedge, the foreign currency gain or loss on the hedged item and the hedging instrument are recognized in current period net income.
6. In a cash-flow hedge, the exchange gains/losses on the hedging instrument are deferred as a component of *other comprehensive income* on the SCI and as a separate component of shareholders' equity in the statement of changes in equity. When the asset or liability is recognized, the accumulated exchange gain/loss is removed from accumulated other comprehensive income and recognized in net income in a manner that reflects the effect of the associated asset or liability on net income.
7. Once the hedging relationship has been established, management must evaluate the effectiveness of the hedge. Hedge accounting can continue to be used only if the hedge continues to be effective. To the extent that a hedging relationship is not effective, gains and losses arising from the portion of the exposure that is not effectively hedged must be recognized in net income.

Companion Website

Visit the text's website at www.pearsoned.ca/beechy for practice quizzes, additional problems, Excel® templates, answers to Concept Check questions, and important IFRS updates.

Self-Study Problem 8-1

On December 31, 20X5, Debtor Limited issued €5,000,000 in debentures to a private investment company located in Frankfurt, Germany. The debentures are due on December 31, 20X8. Debtor Limited is a privately held Alberta company that reports to its shareholders and creditors in Canadian dollars using IFRS. Debtor did not hedge its euro-denominated debt. Over the life of the bonds, the exchange rates for the euro were as follows:

Date	Canadian dollar equivalent
December 31, 20X5	$1.27
December 31, 20X6	$1.30
December 31, 20X7	$1.34
December 31, 20X8	$1.35

Required

Calculate the amount of gain or loss that will appear on Debtor Limited's net income for each of 20X6, 20X7, and 20X8.

Self-Study Problem 8-2

On December 2, 20X1, Domestic Corporation sold merchandise to a Taiwanese customer for 1 million New Taiwan Dollars (NTD). The NTD was worth C$0.0500 on the date of the sale. On December 3, 20X1, Domestic entered into a forward contract with its bank to deliver NTD1,000,000 in 60 days at a rate of $0.0520.

Domestic's fiscal year ended on December 31, 20X1. The NTD was worth $0.0510 at year-end and the forward rate for settlement of a February 1 contract was $0.0516 at year-end. On February 1, 20X2, the customer paid the balance owing, and Domestic also settled the forward contract. The exchange rate on the settlement date was $0.0525.

Required

1. In general journal form, record the entries in 20X1 and 20X2 relating to the account receivable and to the forward contract, assuming the hedge is recorded as an executory contract.
2. How would the entries relating to the account receivable differ if Domestic had not hedged the receivable?

Self-Study Problem 8-3

On October 14, 20X7, Buycorp signed a contract with Sellco, a US company, to purchase a piece of equipment for US$200,000. The equipment was to be delivered on December 1, 20X7, with payment to be made (in US dollars) no later than January 30, 20X8.

Having signed the contract, Buycorp immediately arranged a forward contract through the company's bank for US$200,000 as a hedge against the commitment. The spot rate for the US dollar was $1.20 on October 14; the forward rate was $1.22.

Sellco delivered the equipment to Buycorp on December 1, 20X7. The spot rate on that date was $1.19 and the forward rate was $1.215. On December 31, 20X7, the spot rate was $1.19 and the forward rate was $1.21. Buycorp paid the amount due on January 30, 20X8, per the contract. The spot rate was $1.24 on January 30.

Required

Prepare journal entries to record the acquisition of the equipment and the related hedge on Buycorp's books through January 30, 20X8. Assume Buycorp's fiscal year ends on December 31 and assume that the hedge is designated as a cash-flow hedge.

Review Questions

8-1 What is a foreign currency transaction?

8-2 What causes changes in exchange rates?

8-3 CarpCorp, a Canadian company, bought a machine from the United States for US$100,000 when the exchange rate was C$1.20. The liability for the machine was paid when the exchange rate was C$1.25. At what cost should the machine be recorded in the accounts, assuming (a) the one-transaction theory, and (b) the two-transaction theory?

8-4 CarpCorp bought inventory from the United Kingdom when the pound was worth C$1.80. When the year-end SFP was prepared, the pound was worth C$1.70. If the account payable for the inventory was unpaid at year-end, and the amount of the purchase was £5,000, how should the liability be reported on the SFP? How should the change in the value of the pound be reported (if at all)?

8-5 Explain the difference between a *monetary balance* and a *non-monetary balance*.

8-6 Why would some companies decide to use an average rate for each week or month for translating foreign currency transactions?

8-7 What is the purpose of *hedging*?

8-8 What are the three characteristics of a derivative?

8-9 CarpCorp has a liability of €400,000. If CarpCorp wants to hedge the liability, should the company enter into a forward contract to *buy* euros or to *sell* euros?

8-10 Does hedging eliminate all gains and losses arising from a foreign currency exposure? Explain.

8-11 Why is a forward contract viewed as an executory contract?

8-12 What is hedge accounting?

8-13 How does hedging an *anticipated transaction* differ from hedging a liability?

8-14 Explain the term "cash-flow hedge."

8-15 What is the difference between a hedged item and a hedging instrument?

8-16 What is a fair-value hedge?

8-17 What conditions must a hedging relationship meet for hedge accounting to be applied?

8-18 What are the two conditions necessary for a hedge to be deemed effective?

CASES

CASE 8-1 GRAHAM ENTERPRISES LIMITED

Graham Enterprises Limited (Graham) has just negotiated the purchase of an office building for £20 million in London, England, to be used as the head office of its newly incorporated, wholly owned European operating subsidiary, Graham Overseas Limited (GOL). Transfer of ownership to GOL is to be made on January 1, 20X6. Graham has arranged a loan for £20 million to finance the purchase through its bankers. The loan, to be dated January 1, 20X6, is at 12% and is repayable in 20 equal annual installments commencing January 1, 20X7. The loan would be made to GOL, which would make all interest and principal payments in pounds sterling.

The building will be depreciated on a straight-line basis over 20 years. Assume the following exchange rates: January 1, 20X6, £1 = $2.00; December 31, 20X6, £1 = $1.50.

Required

1. Discuss the nature of the relationship between the building and the loan and evaluate the alternatives available to Graham.
2. Discuss fully the options available to Graham in structuring its relationship to GOL, and evaluate the impact of each alternative on the consolidated financial statements. Show all supporting calculations.
   [SMA, adapted]

CASE 8-2 VIDEO DISPLAYS, INC.

Video Displays, Inc. (VDI) is a privately held corporation chartered under the *Canada Business Corporations Act*. The corporation was formed in 20X1 by four engineers who found themselves jobless after their previous employer (Argo Corporation) discontinued the production of television sets in Canada.

One of the sidelines of Argo had been the assembly of video display units (VDUs). A VDU is the basic chassis containing the liquid crystal display (LCD) screen and related components that are used in computers and in video game sets. When Argo discontinued production, the four engineers purchased some of Argo's assembly and testing equipment and formed VDI.

VDI has been fairly successful because it is the only Canadian producer of VDUs. Some computer manufacturers have a policy of obtaining their components in the country in which they manufacture the computers and thus VDI has enjoyed the benefits of local-sourcing policies since it is the only Canadian producer.

In 20X4, VDI needed additional debt financing. After being refused by several Canadian banks, the executives of VDI went to New York where, on March 1, they quickly obtained a five-year, 12% term loan of $3,000,000 (US) from Citibank, with interest payable annually on the anniversary date of the loan. The US dollar was worth C$1.10 on March 1, 20X4. By the end of 20X4, the exchange rate had slipped to $1.06.

In 20X5, VDI extended its operations into the United States by contracting with an electronic component distributor in Cambridge, Massachusetts. The US distributor supplies component assemblies to small manufacturers, and saw an opportunity to sell VDI's VDUs to independent manufacturers of computers. The December 31, 20X5, VDI unadjusted trial balance showed a balance due from the US distributor of $449,000. The 20X5 shipments to and payments from the distributor are shown in Exhibit A. VDI gave the distributor US$60,000 on April 4 as an accountable advance for financing promotional expenses. By December 31, 20X5, the distributor had spent and accounted for $40,000 of this advance. At the end of 20X5, the exchange rate was C$1.15 to US$1.00.

Required

Explain the impact of the transactions described above on VDI's financial statements on December 31, 20X5.

Exhibit A Current Account with US Distributor 20X5*

		Dr	Cr	Balance
Feb. 1: Shipment	(US$100,000)		$105,000	$105,000
April 1: Shipment	(US$180,000)		189,000	294,000
May 1: Payment	(US$100,000)	108,000		186,000
July 1: Shipment	(US$200,000)		204,000	390,000
Aug. 30: Payment	(US$150,000)	171,000		219,000
Nov. 15: Shipment	(US$200,000)		230,000	449,000

* In Canadian dollars.

[CGA–Canada, adapted]

CASE 8-3 CANADA COLA INC.

Canada Cola Inc. (CCI) is a public company engaged in the manufacture and distribution of soft drinks across Canada. Its primary product is CanaCola ("Fresh as a Canadian stream"), which is a top seller in Canada and generates large export sales.

You, CA, met with Jim MacNamara, the partner in charge of the CCI engagement, to commence planning for the upcoming audit of CCI.

During this meeting, the partner informed you that early this year CCI entered into an agreement with the government of Russia and has commenced the manufacture and sale of CanaCola in Russia. A short summary of the agreement is contained in Exhibit B. The partner would like you to prepare a detailed report that discusses the accounting and auditing implications of this new division of CCI for this engagement.

Exhibit B Summary of Agreement

1. The Russian government will provide the land and the building for the plant. It will make no further investment.
2. CCI will install bottling machinery costing $5 million in the Russian plant. Once installed, the machinery may not be removed from Russia.

3. CCI will be required to provide the funds for the initial working capital. CCI will sell US dollars to the Russian government in exchange for local currency (rubles).
4. CCI will be wholly responsible for the management and daily operations of the plant. Canadian managers will be transferred to Russia.
5. CCI will be permitted to export its cola syrup to Russia at CCI's Canadian cost.
6. CCI and the Russian government will share equally in the profits from the sale of CanaCola in Russia.
7. Although foreign currency can be converted into rubles, rubles cannot be converted back into any foreign currency. Therefore, the Russian government will sell vodka to CCI (at the prevailing export price in Russia) in exchange for the rubles CCI earns in profits. CCI will be permitted to export this vodka to Canada, where it may be sold in the Canadian domestic market only.

Required

1. Prepare the report for the partner.
   [CICA]

Problems

P8-1

NWT Ltd. is an outfitter based in Yellowknife that caters mainly to American clients. On January 1, 20X1, NWT Ltd. borrows US$300,000 from Norsebank of St. Paul, Minnesota. The annual interest rate is 5%, the term of the loan is four years, and interest is payable annually on December 31. Principal is to be repaid on December 31, 20X4. The relevant foreign exchange rates for 20X1 and 20X2 are:

January 1, 20X1	C$1.10 = US$1.00
December 31, 20X1	C$1.13 = US$1.00
December 31, 20X2	C$1.07 = US$1.00

Required

Calculate the exchange gain/loss on the loan principal for 20X1 and 20X2 that will appear on the financial statements of NWT Ltd.

P8-2

Weyburn Corp., a Canadian company, sells its products to customers in the United Kingdom at prices quoted in pounds sterling. On November 14, 20X1, Weyburn sold and shipped goods that had cost $65,000 to produce to an English company for £100,000. On December 20, Weyburn received an international draft for part of the amount due, £40,000. At year-end (December 31), the remaining £60,000 was unpaid.

On February 12, 20X2, Weyburn received payment of the remaining £60,000.

Required

In general journal form, prepare journal entries to record the above events, and any adjustments necessary at year-end. Exchange rates (Canadian-dollar equivalent to £1) are as follows:

November 14	$1.51
December 20	$1.56
December 31	$1.58
February 12	$1.55

P8-3

At the end of the fiscal year, December 31, 20X2, Avonlea Ltd. finds itself with two accounts receivable in pesos:

1. From a sale on July 1, 20X2, and due to be collected on December 1, 20X3, for 1,000,000 pesos.
2. From a sale on September 1, 20X2, and due to be collected on February 1, 20X4, for 2,000,000 pesos.

Exchange rates (spot):

July 1, 20X2	$1 = 16 pesos
September 1, 20X2	$1 = 17 pesos
December 31, 20X2	$1 = 18 pesos
December 1, 20X3	$1 = 11 pesos
December 31, 20X3	$1 = 9 pesos

Required

Prepare the journal entries for December 31, 20X2, and December 1 and December 31, 20X3, assuming that the foreign exchange risk is *not* hedged.

[CGA–Canada, adapted]

P8-4

Polar Limited is a Canadian company that recently completed two large transactions with companies based in Germany:

1. On July 1, 20X4, Polar acquired equipment at a cost of €500,000 from Bier Ltd. Polar received reasonable terms regarding this purchase acquisition. The €500,000 was in the form of a note payable to be paid on June 30, 20X7, at an interest rate of 6% per year, the interest to be paid semi-annually on December 31 and June 30.
2. On October 1, 20X4, Polar also sold inventory that cost C$100,000 to another German company, Wein Ltd., for €87,500. Payment is due from Wein on March 1, 20X5. Polar uses a perpetual inventory system. The spot rates for the euro were as follows:

July 1, 20X4	C$1.00 = €0.650
October 1, 20X4	C$1.00 = €0.750
December 31, 20X4	C$1.00 = €0.800
Average rate July 1 – December 31, 20X4	C$1.00 = €0.770
Average rate 20X4	C$1.00 = €0.700
March 1, 20X5	C$1.00 = €0.850

Required

1. Prepare all journal entries regarding Polar's notes payable and interest-related transactions on July 1, 20X4, and December 31, 20X4.
2. Prepare all journal entries regarding Polar's sales, cost of sales, and accounts receivable transactions on October 1, 20X4; December 31, 20X4; and March 1, 20X5.
[CGA–Canada, adapted]

P8-5

FX Corporation provides special effects for movies filmed in Manitoba. The company needs a sophisticated piece of equipment that can only be sourced from the United States. FX submitted a purchase order for US$50,000 for the equipment on July 1, 20X8, and received the equipment on October 31, 20X8. The company paid US$30,000 to the supplier on December 1, 20X8. The company will amortize the equipment starting in the month of acquisition. The equipment has an expected useful life of five years and the company uses the straight-line method for amortization. FX Corporation has a December 31, 20X8, year-end.

The relevant exchange rates are:

July 1, 20X8	C$1.00 = US$0.9500
October 31, 20X8	C$1.00 = US$0.9600
December 1, 20X8	C$1.00 = US$0.9900
December 31, 20X8	C$1.00 = US$1.0000

Required

1. Prepare all relevant journal entries for 20X8 relating to the above activities.
2. Calculate the carrying value of FX's equipment and accounts payable on its December 31, 20X8, SFP.

P8-6

Refer to P8-5 and assume that the remaining payment of US$20,000 is due on January 1, 20X9. FX enters into a forward contract with a bank on December 1, 20X8, to buy US$20,000 for delivery on January 1, 20X9. The relevant forward rate on December 1, 20X8, was C$1 = US$0.9950. Assume that the forward rate and spot rate on December 31, 20X8, and the spot rate on January 1, 20X9, were the same (i.e., US$1.0000).

Required

1. Should FX Corporation use hedge accounting in this situation? Why or why not?
2. Prepare all relevant journal entries related to the purchase of the equipment and the hedge for 20X8 and 20X9.

P8-7

On September 7, 20X5, Labrador Limited signed a contract to buy equipment from a US manufacturer. The price of the equipment was US$500,000. On the same date, Labrador entered into a forward contract with the bank to buy US$400,000 on February 1, 20X6.

Labrador designated the forward contract as a hedge of the outstanding purchase commitment on the equipment.

The equipment is to be delivered no later than December 1, 20X5. Labrador made a 20% down payment on September 7, 20X5, and signed a promise to pay the balance on or before February 1, 20X6. The exchange rates are:

	Spot	Forward
September 7, 20X5	C$1.00 = US$0.92	C$1.00 = US$0.91
December 1, 20X5	C$1.00 = US$0.90	C$1.00 = US$0.893
December 31, 20X5	C$1.00 = US$0.85	C$1.00 = US$0.845
February 1, 20X6	C$1.00 = US$0.88	n/a

The equipment was delivered on schedule. Labrador paid the manufacturer and closed out the forward contract on February 1, 20X6.

Required

1. Assume the hedge was designated as a fair-value hedge. Record the journal entries to record the purchase and the related hedge for 20X5 and 20X6. Labrador's fiscal year ends on December 31. Ignore amortization of the equipment.
2. Assume the hedge was designated as a cash-flow hedge. Record the journal entries to record the purchase and the related hedge for 20X5 and 20X6. Labrador's fiscal year ends on December 31. Ignore amortization of the equipment.

P8-8

Diamond Limited began purchasing parts from China. The Chinese currency is the renminbi (RMB). Diamond entered into the following transactions in 20X1 and 20X2:

November 1, 20X1	Ordered machine parts from the Chinese supplier for RMB2,000,000. The supplier promised to deliver the machine parts at the beginning of December, and payment is expected on January 15, 20X2.
December 1, 20X1	Received shipment of the machine parts.
December 31, 20X1	Acquired a forward contract to receive RMB2,000,000 on January 15, 20X2, as a hedge of the account payable to the Chinese supplier. The forward contract rate was RMB1 = C$0.16. Diamond treats all forward contracts as executory contracts.
January 15, 20X2	Received RMB2,000,000 on the forward contract; paid RMB2,000,000 to the Chinese supplier in settlement of the payable.

Spot rates were as follows:

November 1, 20X1	RMB1 = C$0.15
December 1, 20X1	RMB1 = C$0.18
December 31, 20X1	RMB1 = C$0.17
January 15, 20X2	RMB1 = C$0.19

Required

Prepare the journal entries for these transactions, including any adjusting entries needed at the December 31, 20X1, fiscal year-end. Specify if no entry is required on any specific date(s).

[CGA–Canada, adapted]

P8-9

At the beginning of 20X2, Skeena Industries Ltd. obtained a four-year loan of US$400,000 from a bank in New York City. At the time of the loan, the US dollar was worth C$1.10. At the end of 20X2, the exchange rate had changed to US$1.00 = C$1.14. By the end of 20X3, the US dollar was worth C$1.20.

During 20X3, Skeena Industries Ltd. sold goods to a French customer for €800,000. At the time of the sale, the euro was worth C$1.50. The customer paid one-fourth of the amount due later in the year, when the euro was worth C$1.41. By the end of 20X3, the euro had declined in value to C$1.35.

Required

Determine the impact of the transactions described above on Skeena Industries' financial statements for the year ended December 31, 20X3.

P8-10

Salluit Limited purchased a capital asset from a French company for €200,000. The asset was delivered to Salluit Limited on November 1, 20X7. Salluit Limited agreed to pay the supplier in full on February 1, 20X8. The payment was made as agreed. The exchange rates were as follows:

November 1, 20X7	C$1.00 = €0.70
December 31, 20X7	C$1.00 = €0.60
February 1, 20X8	C$1.00 = €0.62

Required

1. Prepare journal entries for 20X7 and 20X8 to record the above information.
2. Assume that Salluit Limited hedged the obligation on November 1, 20X7. The forward rate was C$1.00 = €0.64 on November 1, 20X7, and C$1.00 = €0.63 on December 31, 20X7. Prepare the appropriate journal entries for 20X7 and 20X8.
   [CGA–Canada, adapted]

P8-11

On May 5, 20X5, Sugluk Corp. purchased inventory from a Japanese supplier and gave the supplier a 90-day note for ¥40,000,000. On the same date, Sugluk entered a forward contract with its bank to receive ¥40,000,000 in 90 days. The spot rate for the yen was $0.0095. The forward rate was $0.0100.

Required

Prepare general journal entries to record the purchase, the hedge, and final settlement of both the note and the hedge, assuming each of the following spot rates at the settlement date:

a) $0.0095
b) $0.0100
c) $0.0093
d) $0.0102
   [CGA–Canada, adapted]

P8-12

On October 15, 20X1, Nahanni Limited sold merchandise to two companies in Sweden. In the first transaction, the price was 3,000,000 kronor and was to be paid in 90 days. Worried about the exposure to the exchange risk, the company hedged the receivable for a 90-day period with a forward contract.

In the second transaction, the price was 3,600,000 kronor and the date of payment was November 15, 20X4. Due to the difficulty of getting a forward contract to match the date payment was due, the company decided to remain in an "unhedged" position on this receivable.

Exchange rates:

October 15, 20X1, spot rate	\$1 = 8.00 kronor
October 15, 20X1, forward 90-day rate	\$1 = 9.26 kronor
December 31, 20X1, spot rate	\$1 = 9.10 kronor
December 31, 20X1, forward rate to January 13, 20X2	\$1 = 9.30 kronor
January 13, 20X2, spot rate	\$1 = 9.45 kronor
December 31, 20X2, spot rate	\$1 = 7.75 kronor

Required

Ignoring closing entries:

1. Prepare all the related journal entries required for the first sale for 20X1 *and* 20X2.
2. Assuming instead that the company had not hedged the receivable from the first sale in any way, prepare the appropriate journal entries for 20X1 *and* 20X2 to record this situation.
3. Prepare all the related journal entries for the *second* sale for 20X1 *and* 20X2.
   [CGA–Canada, adapted]

P8-13

Pinware Wholesalers Inc. (Pinware) imports high quality goods from select European countries. On May 1, 20X3, Pinware purchased Swiss watches from a supplier in Switzerland for 400,000 Swiss francs (CHF). Payment of the invoice was due on August 31, 20X3. On May 1, 20X3, Pinware also entered into a forward contract that was a perfect hedge of the full amount of the invoice price at a rate of CHF1 = C\$0.945. Pinware's year-end is June 30 and, on June 30, the August 31, 20X3, forward rate is CHF1 = C\$0.925. On August 31, 20X3, the forward contract was settled and the Swiss supplier was paid. The relevant spot rates were as follows:

May 1, 20X3	CHF1 = C\$0.930
June 30, 20X3	CHF1 = C\$0.920
August 31, 20X3	CHF1 = C\$0.915

Required

Prepare all relevant journal entries to record the transactions related to the purchase of the watches. Be sure to include any year-end adjustments required on June 30, 20X3.

[CGA–Canada, adapted]

P8-14

Assume the same facts as in P8-13 except that Pinware Wholesalers Inc. (Pinware) must order the watches two months in advance of expected delivery. On March 1, 20X3, Pinware ordered Swiss watches from a supplier in Switzerland for 400,000 Swiss francs (CHF) when the spot rate was CHF1 = C$0.95. The invoice called for payment to be made on August 31, 20X3. On March 1, 20X3, Pinware also entered into a forward contract with a bank to hedge the commitment by agreeing to purchase CHF400,000 on August 31, 20X3, at a rate of CHF1 = C$0.955. Pinware takes delivery of the watches on May 1, 20X3. All other information is the same as in P8-13.

Required

1. Prepare journal entries to record all of the transactions, including any adjustments required on June 30, 20X3, assuming that Pinware does not use hedge accounting.
2. Prepare journal entries to record all of the transactions, including any adjustments required on June 30, 20X3, assuming that Pinware designates the hedge a fair-value hedge.
3. Prepare journal entries to record all of the transactions, including any adjustments required on June 30, 20X3, assuming that Pinware designates the hedge a cash-flow hedge.

P8-15

Following are transactions of L'Anse Ltd., a company engaged in importing products into Canada.

September 1, 20X3:	Incurred a liability for 1,000,000 pesos, due February 1, 20X4, for purchasing inventory.
October 1, 20X3:	Incurred a liability for 6,000,000 yen, due November 1, 20X4, for purchasing inventory.
November 1, 20X3:	Incurred a liability for 22,000 Brazilian reals, due March 1, 20X5, for purchasing inventory.

Exchange rates:

September 1, 20X3	
$1 = 15 pesos	Spot rate
$1 = 12 pesos	Forward contract rate
October 1, 20X3	
$1 = 80 yen	Spot rate
$1 = 95 yen	Forward contract rate
November 1, 20X3	
$1 = 1.80 reals	Spot rate
$1 = 1.60 reals	Forward contract rate
December 31, 20X3, spot rates:	
$1 = 10 pesos	
$1 = 100 yen	
$1 = 1.50 reals	
Relevant December 31, 20X3, forward rates:	
$1 = 9 pesos	
$1 = 105 yen	
$1 = 1.45 reals	

Required

Parts (1) and (2), below, are based on different policies regarding hedging. Answer each part as an independent problem.

1. L'Anse Ltd. did not hedge or cover its exchange risk position. Prepare the journal entries for 20X3. The company has a December 31 year-end.
2. At the time of each transaction, L'Anse Ltd. entered into a forward contract, which was a perfect and complete hedge against the foreign exchange risk. Prepare the journal entries for 20X3. The company has a December 31 year-end.
   [CGA–Canada, adapted]

P8-16

Muskoka Furniture Inc. (Muskoka) imports pine furniture from factories around the world for sale to retailers in Canada. On October 31, 20X4, Muskoka bought a bedroom furniture set from a supplier in the United States for US$2,000. The invoice called for payment to be made on February 28, 20X5. On November 1, 20X4, Muskoka entered into a forward contract with a bank to hedge the existing monetary position by agreeing to buy US$2,000 on February 28, 20X5, at a rate of US$1 = C$1.15. Muskoka's year-end is December 31. On February 28, 20X5, Muskoka settled the forward contract with the bank and the US supplier was paid.

Spot rates were as follows:

October 31, 20X4	US$1 = C$1.14
November 1, 20X4	US$1 = C$1.14
December 31, 20X4	US$1 = C$1.16
February 28, 20X5	US$1 = C$1.19

The February 28, 20X5, forward rate on December 31, 20X4, was US$1 = C$1.165.

Required

Prepare journal entries to record all of the transactions, including any adjustments required on December 31, 20X4. Show your supporting calculations.

[CGA–Canada, adapted]

P8-17

Muskoka Furniture Inc. (Muskoka) can also import custom pine furniture but it must be ordered several months in advance as it is only manufactured after a specific request is made. Assume that on September 1, 20X4, Muskoka orders custom bedroom furniture from a supplier in the United States for US$2,000. The invoice called for payment to be made on February 28, 20X5. On September 1, 20X4, Muskoka entered into a forward contract with a bank to hedge the commitment by agreeing to buy US$2,000 on February 28, 20X5, at a rate of US$1 = C$1.13. Muskoka takes delivery of the furniture on November 1, 20X4 when the February 28, 20X5 forward rate is US$1 = C$1.15. Muskoka's year-end is December 31. On February 28, 20X5, Muskoka settled the forward contract with the bank and the US supplier was paid.

Spot rates were as follows:

September 1, 20X4	US$1 = C$1.11
November 1, 20X4	US$1 = C$1.14
December 31, 20X4	US$1 = C$1.16
February 28, 20X5	US$1 = C$1.19

The February 28, 20X5, forward rate on December 31, 20X4, was US$1 = C$1.165.

Required

1. Prepare journal entries to record all of the transactions for 20X4 and 20X5, including any adjustments required on December 31, 20X4, assuming that Muskoka does not use hedge accounting. Show your supporting calculations.
2. Assume that Muskoka Furniture Inc. designates the hedge as a fair-value hedge of a commitment, documents the relationship, and assesses the hedge as effective. Prepare journal entries to record all of the transactions for 20X4 and 20X5, including any adjustments required on December 31, 20X4, assuming that Muskoka can use hedge accounting.
3. Assume that Muskoka Furniture Inc. designates the hedge as a cash-flow hedge of a commitment, documents the relationship and assesses the hedge as effective. Prepare journal entries to record all of the transactions for 20X4 and 20X5, including any adjustments required on December 31, 20X4.

P8-18

Terrace Ltd., a manufacturer of motorcycles located in Burnaby, British Columbia, successfully negotiated a contract to sell 100 small motorcycles to the police department of Fairbanks, Alaska. The contract price for the cycles was US$10,000 each. The contract was signed on May 12, 20X6, with payment to be made by October 1. Terrace then entered into a forward contract to hedge against changes in the US dollar exchange rate.

Delivery of the motorcycles began on July 5 and continued in 20-cycle lots at two-week intervals until the last delivery on August 30, 20X6. The buyer then paid the US$1,000,000 contract price when due, and Terrace settled with the bank.

The exchange rates were as follows:

Canadian equivalent of US$1.00:	Spot rate	Forward rate
May 12, 20X6	$1.15	$1.18
May 31–August 30, 20X6	1.10	1.08
October 1, 20X6	1.12	n/a

Required

1. What amounts relating to the sale and the hedge would appear on Terrace's SCI and SFP for the year ended December 31, 20X6?
2. Assume instead that Terrace's year-end was May 31. What amounts would appear on Terrace's financial statements at May 31, 20X6?
3. Assume that Terrace's year-end was May 31 and Terrace designated the hedge as a cash-flow hedge. What amounts would appear on Terrace's financial statements at May 31, 20X6?

P8-19

Espanola Corporation, a Canadian corporation, engaged in the following transactions in late 20X7 and early 20X8:

December 2	Purchased sheet aluminum from a US subsidiary of a Canadian aluminum company for US$160,000, payable in 60 days.
December 2	Acquired a forward contract to receive US$160,000 in 60 days, as a hedge of the account payable. The forward contract rate was C$1.10.
December 20	Sold large cans to a Buffalo canner for US$200,000, due in 60 days.
January 31	Received US$160,000 on the forward contract; paid US$160,000 to the aluminum company.
February 18	Received US$200,000 from the Buffalo canner.

Spot rates for the US dollar were as follows:

December 2	$1.07
December 20	$1.12
December 31	$1.14
January 31	$1.20
February 18	$1.17

The January 31, 20X8, forward rate on December 31, 20X7, was $1.15.

Required

Prepare journal entries for these transactions, including any adjusting entries needed at the December 31, 20X7, year-end.

9

Reporting Foreign Operations

LEARNING OBJECTIVES

After studying this chapter, students should be able to:

1. describe the conceptual alternatives to translate the financial statements of foreign operations;
2. distinguish between accounting exposure and economic exposure to exchange rate changes;
3. explain the conceptual alternatives for reporting translation gains and losses;
4. determine a company's functional currency after considering the relevant factors identified by IFRS; and
5. translate a company's financial statements and properly handle any translation gain or loss in preparation for consolidation.

INTRODUCTION

Montreal-based CGI Group Inc. (CGI) is a large Canadian provider of information technology (IT) services such as outsourcing, business process services, and systems integration and consulting to companies around the world. CGI operates in 16 countries including the United States, India, Poland, and Australia, either directly or through its subsidiaries. In fiscal year 2009 the company had revenues of $3.8 billion, 43% of which was generated from outside Canada. The company's strategy is to grow both organically and through acquisitions. Currently, it sees future growth coming from international markets such as the United States and Europe.

The company conducts its international business through operating entities in foreign countries. These entities are likely to be companies that were either created or purchased by CGI. As we will see, many of these companies will keep their books in the local currency of the country in which they are operating. The issue that arises is how to translate these financial statements into Canadian dollars to allow CGI to consolidate them. This issue is known as accounting for foreign operations.

The previous chapter illustrated the accounting for foreign-currency transactions. A somewhat different problem arises when a Canadian corporation actually has one or more active, self-contained, operations located in a foreign country. In that case, the company is not merely selling its products in US dollars and/or buying inventory in Japanese yen; instead the foreign operation will need to prepare financial statements, usually in the operation's host-country currency.

This chapter examines the problems of accounting for foreign operations. We begin with a brief discussion of the possible forms of organization for a foreign operation. Then, we discuss:

- the reasons for preparing separate financial statements for foreign operations and why that presents a problem for the parent corporation;
- the two methods that can be used for translating foreign operations—(1) the temporal method and (2) the current-rate method—and their relationship with foreign-currency transaction accounting;
- the competing concepts of foreign exchange risk exposure—(1) accounting exposure and (2) economic exposure;
- the alternative treatments of gains and losses that arise from translating a foreign operation;
- the determination of a foreign operation's functional currency as a necessary condition for deciding which method to use; and
- a final summary comparison of the two translation methods.

Of course, we will provide illustrations as we proceed through the discussion.

FORMS OF ORGANIZATION FOR FOREIGN OPERATIONS

In theory, a Canadian parent company could organize its foreign operations in any way that it wants. Possible options are:

- branch office of the parent;
- unincorporated partnership involving officers or directors of the parent corporation;
- unincorporated partnership with an unrelated partner;
- incorporated joint venture with one or more unrelated corporate co-venturers;
- incorporated subsidiary, with minority shareholdings by unrelated shareholders; or
- wholly owned incorporated subsidiary.

The most common approach is the last one—to incorporate its foreign operations as a wholly owned subsidiary. A foreign operation is subject to the laws of its host country, including its tax laws. An incorporated subsidiary is best able to comply with host-country regulations and tax law. In addition, if the foreign operation gets into financial difficulty, an incorporated subsidiary can be kept separate from the parent and can be sold or liquidated without endangering the health of the parent. Unincorporated branches, partnerships, and joint ventures, on the other hand, may leave the parent company vulnerable to adverse situations in the host country.

Sometimes the foreign subsidiary is not wholly owned by the parent. This may be either by choice or by law. A local shareholder can provide local knowledge, political contacts, access to capital, or other intellectual capital. It can be quite foolish for a parent company to venture into a market that it does not understand, and a local "partner" can be very valuable. In some host countries, foreign companies are *required* to have local participation. These

REALITY CHECK 9-1

Modelo Molson Imports, L.P., is a partnership formed on January 1, 2008, between Grupo Modelo S.A.B. de C.V. (the producer of well-known Mexican brands of beer like Corona) and Molson "to import, distribute, and market the Modelo beer brand portfolio across all Canadian provinces and territories." Each company owns 50% of the partnership, which makes it an unincorporated joint venture. In the news release the following was noted:

> The joint venture board will consist of 6 directors, half from Grupo Modelo and half from Molson. . . . The 50/50 joint venture will be headquartered in Toronto and led by Robert Armstrong, previously CEO for Modelo's office in Canada.

Source: Molson Coors, "Grupo Modelo and Molson Create a Joint Venture for Beer Importation Into Canada," press release, January 2, 2008, http://www.molsoncoors.com/newsroom/press-releases/article/155/.

mandatory legal arrangements are often called "joint ventures," but be careful here—the arrangement often is not a joint venture in an accounting sense.

Generally speaking, unincorporated foreign operations are not practical. An exception that occasionally arises is an unincorporated joint venture between two corporations—one foreign and one Canadian. These are often either marketing or production arrangements. The two companies pool their resources to operate in either or both countries.

The accounting for foreign operations is not affected by the form of organization. The accounting standards that we discuss in the remainder of this chapter are applicable to all forms of organization.

THE TRANSLATION PROBLEM

To illustrate the nature of the problem, assume that Domestic Corporation decides to establish a sales subsidiary in the country of Pantania. Domestic's legal representatives in Pantania draw up the papers for a corporation in that country, to be named Forsub Ltd. The founding board of directors of Forsub is nominated (by Domestic) and Forsub begins operating. One hundred common shares of Forsub are issued to Domestic Corporation for 500 pants per share, the pant being the local currency of Pantania. Forsub will record the investment *in Pantanian pants* (P) as follows:

Cash	P50,000	
Common shares		P50,000

If the pant is worth C$2 at the time of the transaction, P50,000 will be worth C$100,000. Domestic will record the investment on its books at cost, as it would any initial investment:

Investment in Forsub Ltd	$100,000	
Cash		$100,000

Now, suppose that after receiving the cash, Forsub buys inventory for P20,000 (P5,000 on account) and land for P40,000. To finance this purchase, Forsub issues five-year bonds amounting to P25,000. The transactions will be recorded as follows on Forsub's books:

Cash	P25,000	
Bonds payable		P25,000
Inventory	P20,000	
Cash		P15,000
Accounts payable		P 5,000
Land	P40,000	
Cash		P40,000

At the time of these transactions, the exchange rate is still P1 = C$2. Forsub's SFP will then appear as follows:

Cash	P20,000	Accounts payable	P 5,000
Inventory	20,000	Bonds payable	25,000
Land	40,000	Common shares	50,000
TOTAL ASSETS	P80,000	TOTAL LIABILITIES AND SHAREHOLDERS' EQUITY	P80,000

A short while later, Domestic Corporation's fiscal year ends. Since Forsub is a subsidiary of Domestic, Domestic will consolidate Forsub. As with any subsidiary that is consolidated, the investment account is eliminated and Forsub's assets and liabilities are added to those of the parent company in Domestic's SFP.

However, Forsub's assets and liabilities are expressed in pants, not dollars. We can't add pants to dollars, and therefore we must translate all of Forsub's financial statement elements from pants to Canadian dollars.

In the previous chapter, we translated individual foreign-currency *transactions*. When we are trying to consolidate a foreign *operation*, however, we need to translate the whole set of foreign-currency financial statements before we can consolidate. The problem is how to translate the financial statements. IFRS adopts a *functional currency* approach to solve the translation problem. However, before we learn about the functional currency approach, we need to understand several other concepts:

1. The two methods of translation used under the functional currency approach.
2. The difference between accounting exposure and economic exposure.
3. The different alternatives available for disposing of the gains and losses arising from foreign exchange translations.

After discussing these concepts, we will explain how to determine the functional currency of a subsidiary and how to use that information to translate the financial statements.

Translation Methods

There are two translation methods permitted by IFRS:

- temporal method
- current-rate method

The following sections will explain and illustrate these two methods.

Temporal Method *Temporal* means "related to time." The temporal method uses multiple rates for translating a foreign operation's financial statement elements:

- All *monetary* assets and liabilities are translated at the current rate and any *non-monetary* assets or liabilities reported at fair value are translated at the rate at the date on which the fair value is determined (usually it is the current rate on the SFP date).
- All *non-monetary* assets and liabilities reported at historical cost are translated at the exchange rate that existed when the element was first recognized.

On the SFP, the year-end spot rate (i.e., the current rate or closing rate) is used to translate cash, accounts receivable, accounts payable, long-term debt, and all other monetary items. The current spot rate is also used for assets or liabilities that are reported on the SFP at fair value. For example, some inventories (such as precious metals) and some held-for-sale assets may be reported on the subsidiary's SFP at fair value rather than at historical cost. These balances are reported at the current rate because their carrying value represents an amount that can be converted to cash.

On Forsub's SFP, the monetary items are cash, accounts payable, and long-term debentures. These three elements are translated at the current spot rate. If the spot rate at the SFP date is P1 = C$2.30, the P20,000 cash balance is translated to C$46,000 for consolidation purposes.

Non-monetary items that are reported at historical cost are translated at the exchange rate in effect at the date of the transaction that created the non-monetary items. The rate on the date of the transaction is known as the historical rate. In essence, the temporal approach uses the same translation rules as we described in the previous chapter for monetary and non-monetary balances arising from foreign-currency transactions.

For Forsub Ltd., the non-monetary items are inventory and land, both purchased when the rate was P1 = C$2.00. Thus, these two assets will be translated at the $2.00 historical rate, while the cash, payables, and bonds will be translated at the $2.30 current rate.

Note that the historical rate is $2.00 because that was the rate existing at the time that the inventory and land were purchased. The fact that the rate was also $2.00 when the original investment in Forsub was made by Domestic is coincidental. If the land had been purchased when the rate was $2.10 and the inventory bought when the rate was $2.15, then those would be the historical rates used for translating each account balance.

The only account on the Forsub SFP that we have not yet discussed is the common shares. Since this is a non-monetary item, it is logical that it should be translated at the historical rate of $2.00. This account will be eliminated when Forsub is consolidated. Since the offsetting account in Domestic's SFP is the investment in Forsub account, the subsidiary's common

EXHIBIT 9-1

Translation of Statement of Financial Position, Temporal Method

Forsub Ltd.
December 31, 20X5

Exchange rate, December 31, 20X5: P1.00 = Cdn$2.30

	Balance on Forsub's books	Exchange rate	Translated amount
Cash	P20,000	$2.30	$ 46,000
Inventory	20,000	2.00	40,000
Land	40,000	2.00	80,000
Total assets	P80,000		$166,000
Accounts payable, current	P 5,000	2.30	$ 11,500
Bonds payable, long term	25,000	2.30	57,500
Common shares	50,000	2.00	100,000
Translation gain (loss)	—		(3,000)
	P80,000		$166,000

Calculation of net translation loss:

Cash	P 20,000	asset × ($2.30 – $2.00) =	$ 6,000	gain
Accounts payable	(5,000)	liability × ($2.30 – $2.00) =	(1,500)	loss
Bonds payable	(25,000)	liability × ($2.30 – $2.00) =	(7,500)	loss
Net	P(10,000)	liability × ($2.30 – $2.00) =	$(3,000)	loss

share account should be translated at the historical rate to facilitate the elimination on consolidation.

In summary, the accounts on Forsub's SFP will be translated as follows under the temporal method:

Item	Rate
Cash	Current
Inventory	Historical
Land	Historical
Accounts payable	Current
Bonds payable	Current
Common shares	Historical

Since the various accounts are not being translated with a uniform measurement approach, the translated SFP will not balance until we allow for a *translation gain or loss*. The total gain or loss will be the amount needed to balance the translated SFP, and it is a loss of $3,000 in this example. With this addition to the SFP, the translated SFP of Forsub Ltd. will appear as shown in the last column of Exhibit 9-1.

Composition of Translation Loss The $3,000 translation loss may appear to be a "plug"—just an amount necessary to balance the SFP. However, the translation loss is not a random event.

It can be derived directly from the information given about Forsub's transactions. There are three components to the loss:

1. **The first is a gain of $6,000 on the balance of cash.** Forsub originally received P50,000 in cash when the exchange rate was $2.00, and obtained another P25,000 from the issuance of bonds. While the rate was still $2.00, the company purchased land and inventory, thereby reducing the cash balance to P20,000. The company then held this balance of cash while the exchange rate rose to $2.30. The increase in the exchange rate meant that the P20,000 balance was worth $46,000 at the end of the fiscal year (P20,000 × $2.30) as compared to only $40,000 (P20,000 × $2.00) when the cash was received. Thus, holding a cash balance when the exchange rate rose resulted in an increase in the equivalent amount in Canadian dollars, a gain of $46,000 − $40,000 = $6,000.
2. **The second component of the $3,000 translation loss is a loss of $1,500 on the accounts payable.** Forsub still owes P5,000 to its trade creditors, but the dollar equivalent of this amount has changed from $10,000 (P5,000 × $2.00) to $11,500 (P5,000 × $2.30). In Canadian dollar terms, the value of the debt has risen, thereby resulting in a loss.
3. **The third component of the overall translation loss arises from the bonds payable.** The P25,000 in bonds were issued when the exchange rate was $2.00, or a Canadian equivalent of $50,000. At year-end, the Canadian equivalent of the bond indebtedness is $57,500, at the year-end exchange rate of $2.30. Therefore, a loss of $7,500 ($50,000 − $57,500) has arisen as a result of holding a liability that is denominated in pants as the Canadian equivalent increased because of changes in the exchange rate.

By breaking the translation loss down into its component amounts, we can see that the loss of $3,000 is really a net amount arising from a loss of $9,000 ($1,500 + $7,500) on monetary liabilities less a gain of $6,000 on holding cash, a monetary asset. This information is summarized at the bottom of Exhibit 9-1. We will examine the nature of this loss and its accounting implications more extensively later in the chapter. For the moment, however, note that the only items that give rise to translation gains or losses are those account balances that are translated at the *current* rate.

The extent of the foreign operation's **accounting exposure** *to currency rate fluctuations is equal to the net amount of balances that are translated at the current rate.* In Exhibit 9-1, the accounting exposure is a net monetary liability balance of P10,000: (P20,000 − P5,000 − P25,000). The translation loss is:

P10,000 × ($2.30 − $2.00) = $3,000

Balances that are translated at historical rates do not give rise to translation gains or losses because the rate at which they are translated does not change. The net amount of the exchange gain or loss can be calculated by looking only at the net changes in those balances that are translated at the current rate.

Relationship of Temporal Method to Transaction Accounting In Exhibit 9-1, we translated Forsub's year-end balances by using the temporal method, and we calculated a gain on the balance of cash and a loss on the balance of bonds and accounts payable. An important characteristic to note about the temporal method is that *it yields exactly the same results in terms of the translated*

EXHIBIT 9-2

Direct Transactions Equivalent to Forsub's Transactions

If the parent company had engaged in the transactions directly instead of through Forsub, the transactions would have been recorded on Domestic's books as follows:

		Dr.	Cr.
a	Cash (in Bank of Pantania)	100,000	
	Cash (in Canadian bank)		100,000
	[to record transfer of cash for Pantanian bank account]		
b	Cash (in Pantania)	50,000	
	Bonds payable		50,000
	[to record issuance of bonds in Pantania]		
c	Inventory (cost = P20,000)	40,000	
	Cash (in Pantania)		30,000
	Accounts payable (P5,000)		10,000
	[to record purchase of inventory in Pantania, paid in pants]		
d	Land (cost = P40,000)	80,000	
	Cash (in Pantania: P40,000)		80,000
	[to record purchase of land in Pantania, paid in pants]		
	Year-end adjusting entries, December 31, 20X5:		
e	Cash [P20,000 × (2.30 – 2.00)]	6,000	
	Foreign currency gains/losses		6,000
	[to adjust the cash balance to the year-end current rate]		
f	Foreign currency gains/losses	1,500	
	Accounts payable [P5,000 × (2.30 – 2.00)]		1,500
	[to adjust the accounts payable balance to the year-end current rate]		
g	Foreign currency gains/losses	7,500	
	Bonds payable [P25,000 × (2.30 – 2.00)]		7,500
	[to adjust the bonds payable balance to the year-end current rate]		

amounts as would have resulted from translating each transaction separately, as we discussed in Chapter 8. In substance, the temporal method views the operations of the foreign company as though the transactions had been carried out directly by Domestic Corporation operating from its home base in Canada.

Exhibit 9-2 illustrates the individual transactions as they would have been recorded by Domestic if they had been direct transactions. The first transaction shows the depositing of $100,000 in the Bank of Pantania—this amount is translated to P50,000 by the bank. The remaining transactions record the issuance of the bonds and the purchase of the inventory and land, recorded in the equivalent amount of Canadian dollars.

At year-end, it is necessary to record the monetary foreign currency-denominated balances at their current equivalents. These adjustments (for cash, accounts payable, and bonds payable) result in a net foreign-currency loss of $3,000. The impact of these individual transactions on Domestic Corporation's SFP would be exactly the same as translating Forsub's SFP by the temporal method and consolidating.

EXHIBIT 9-3

Translation of Statement of Financial Position, Current-Rate Method

Forsub Ltd.
December 31, 20X5

Exchange rate, December 31, 20X5: P1.00 = Cdn$2.30

	Balance on Forsub's books	Exchange rate	Translated amount
Cash	P20,000	$2.30	$ 46,000
Inventory	20,000	2.30	46,000
Land	40,000	2.30	92,000
Total assets	P80,000		$184,000
Accounts payable, current	P 5,000	2.30	$ 11,500
Bonds payable, long term	25,000	2.30	57,500
Shareholders' equity	50,000	2.00	100,000
Translation gain (loss)*	—		15,000
	P80,000		$184,000

* *Calculation of net translation gain:*

Translation gain = net asset position × change in exchange rate
= P50,000 × ($2.30 – $2.00)
= $15,000 gain

Current-Rate Method An alternative approach to the translation of the results of foreign operations is to translate *all* of the asset and liability balances at the current rate. The historical rate is used only for the shareholders' equity accounts. The current-rate SFP is shown in Exhibit 9-3.

Under the current-rate method, the total assets of Forsub translate to $184,000 as compared to $166,000 under the temporal method. The much larger amount is due to the fact that under the temporal method, the large non-monetary assets were translated at the lower historical rate. Conversely, if the exchange rate had declined during the period, the translated total assets would be less under the current-rate method than under the temporal method.

Every solvent corporation has more assets than liabilities. When all the assets and liabilities are translated at the current rate, the translated assets will always exceed the translated liabilities. As a result, the translated net assets will always be positive—the excess of assets over liabilities. Thus, when the current-rate method is used, the net balance of those SFP accounts that are translated at the current rate will always be a net *asset* balance.

Comparison of Methods The two different methods of translation will yield different accounting exposures and different amounts of gain or loss. Indeed, as we will demonstrate shortly, a translation loss that arises under one method often becomes a gain under the other method. The accounting exposure to foreign-currency fluctuations under the two methods can be summarized as follows:

- Under the current-rate method, the accounting exposure to currency fluctuations is always measurable as the net assets of the foreign subsidiary—almost always a positive net asset value.
- Using the temporal method, the accounting exposure can be either a net asset or net liability balance, depending on whether monetary assets and non-monetary assets measured at fair value exceed monetary liabilities and non-monetary liabilities measured at fair value (for a net asset exposure) or vice versa (for a net liability exposure).

A distinct characteristic of the current-rate method is that the proportionate amounts of the various asset and liability accounts do not change when the SFP is translated. For example, bonds are 31% of Forsub's total assets in pants (P25,000 ÷ P80,000), and they continue to be 31% of total assets in dollars ($57,500 ÷ $184,000). Under the temporal method, however, the proportion changes from 31% to 35% ($57,500 ÷ $166,000).

Many people feel that this characteristic is an advantage of the current-rate method—the "true" financial position of Forsub is that shown by the SFP in pants, and the process of currency translation should not change this picture of the foreign operation.

Summary of Translation Methods

The two translation methods can be summarized as follows:

1. Temporal method
   a) translates all monetary items at the current exchange rate and fair-value items at the exchange rate on the date the fair value is determined; translates all non-monetary historical cost items at their individual historical rate;
   b) yields an accounting exposure to exchange rate fluctuations of the net balance of monetary and fair-value assets and liabilities, depending on the financial structure of the company; and
   c) does not give effect to implicit hedges of monetary and fair-value items by offsetting non-monetary items.
2. Current-rate method
   a) translates all assets and liabilities at the current rate, whether current or non-current and whether monetary or non-monetary;
   b) yields an exposure to exchange rate changes that is always a net asset position, equivalent to the owners' equity in the foreign operation;[1] and
   c) preserves the proportionate relationships between the various SFP items and does not "distort" the statement as compared to the way it would appear in local currency.

So far, we have been treating the net translation gain or loss under each of the methods as a SFP item. However, there actually are various treatments possible *under each method* of translation. Before we consider these alternative treatments of the translation gain or loss, however, we should further address the issue of *exposure*.

CONCEPT CHECK 9-1

Companion Website

1. What is usually the best way to structure a company's operations in a foreign country? Why?
2. How are foreign currency denominated non-monetary assets that are carried at fair value translated under the temporal method?
3. What characteristic of translation is the main advantage of the current-rate method?

1. This is true unless the foreign operation has more liabilities than assets, in which case the owners' equity will be a deficit and there will be a net liability position rather than a net asset position.

ACCOUNTING EXPOSURE VS. ECONOMIC EXPOSURE

Throughout the foregoing discussion, we have pointed out that under each translation method, we can anticipate the nature of the translation gain or loss. We know which items will be translated at the current exchange rate, and only those amounts will give rise to a translation gain or loss. If we know which way the exchange rate is moving, then we can predict whether the translation will result in a gain or a loss for the current period.

We have also observed that since the different methods translate different accounts at the current exchange rate, a given movement in the exchange rate may cause a gain under one method but may cause a loss under another method. In the case of Forsub, above, we calculated a loss of $3,000 under the temporal method and a gain of $15,000 under the current-rate method.

The net balance of those SFP amounts that we translated at the current exchange rate is the *accounting exposure* to fluctuations in the foreign exchange rate. This exposure arises as the result of the accounting method of translation that we are using at the time. If a translation gain or loss is to be reported on the financial statements of the parent corporation, then the qualitative characteristic of "representational faithfulness" should be present. In other words, is there really an *economic* gain to the parent when an accounting gain is reported?

It might seem that when a Canadian company holds an asset that is denominated in a foreign currency and that currency rises in value against the Canadian dollar, the company experiences an economic gain because the asset increases in value as measured in dollars. Since a Canadian company's equity in a foreign operation is almost always a net asset position, one could argue that an increase in the exchange rate will result in a gain to the parent because that net investment will be worth more as a result of the change in the rate.

Such an argument, however, does not consider the impact of exchange rate changes on the earnings ability of the foreign subsidiary. In most instances, the foreign operation exists as a going concern that is expected to contribute favourably to the profits of the parent. Therefore, it makes sense to evaluate the impact of currency realignments on the earnings ability of the foreign operation. This impact is known as the *economic exposure* of the foreign operation. The economic exposure is much more complicated than the accounting exposure because many more factors are involved than simply the mechanical aspects of the translation method and the direction of change in the exchange rates.

Example of Economic Exposure

Suppose, for example, that the business of Forsub Ltd. is to import a product from Canada and to sell it in Pantania. The cost to produce the product is $10.00, and it is sold in Pantania at P6. When the exchange rate is P1 = $2.00, the value of the sale is $12.00 (P6 × $2), resulting in a gross profit of $2.00 ($12 − $10) to Domestic Corporation.

If the exchange rate goes up to P1 = $2.30, the value of each sale will then be $13.80, for an increased gross profit of $3.80. In such a situation, the increase in the value of the pant is a real gain in economic terms. Forsub will either have a larger profit on its sales (if it maintains the same selling price in pants), or it may decrease its price and increase its volume of sales in Pantania (owing to the price elasticity of demand). Either way, Domestic may be better off as a result of the increase in the value of the pant.

Now, suppose instead that the business of Forsub is to produce a product from materials in Pantania and then to transfer the product to Domestic Corporation for sale in Canada. The product costs P10 to produce in Pantania, and sells for $25 in Canada. When the exchange rate is P1 = $2.00, the cost of production is the equivalent of $20, yielding a gross margin of $5. An increase in the value of the pant to $2.30 will cause the production cost to rise to $23 in Canadian dollars, thereby lowering the gross margin to $2.00. In this situation, an increase in the value of the pant can be disadvantageous to Forsub and Domestic Corporation. Instead of being a gain, a rise in the value of the pant is actually a loss in earnings ability.

Of course, things are not really all that simple. Exchange rates do not change autonomously, but are the result of other economic factors, such as relative rates of inflation and interest rate differentials in the various countries. If the value of the pant increased because of high inflation in Canada, then Domestic may be able to charge a higher price for the product and maintain or possibly even increase its relative gross margin.

The economic impact of changes in exchange rates is quite complex and will vary from company to company and situation to situation.

Past vs. Future

Economic exposure is a result of the economic characteristics of the foreign operation, such as the sources of its raw materials, the sources of its debt financing, the market in which its products are sold, the price elasticity of demand for its products, and much more. *Economic exposure is the impact of an exchange rate change on the present value of future cash flows*—it is forward-looking.

In contrast, accounting exposure is historically oriented. It measures the mechanical impact of translating the results of past transactions. The economic exposure is not determinable from the accounting exposure, since the accounting exposure is mechanical in origin and is not necessarily indicative of the future earnings impact of a change in exchange rates.

However, application of the concept of representational faithfulness leads to the conclusion that, in any situation, the preferred accounting translation method is the one that yields an accounting exposure that best reflects the economic exposure. If an increase in the exchange rate is likely to have a beneficial economic impact on the foreign operation and the consolidated subsidiary, then the accounting translation method should yield a translation gain when the exchange rate goes up, rather than a loss.

CONCEPT CHECK 9-2

1. Does an increase in the value of a foreign currency always increase the value of a subsidiary in the same foreign country?
2. Why are reported translation gains and losses said to be focussed on the past?

ALTERNATIVES FOR REPORTING TRANSLATION GAINS AND LOSSES

So far in this chapter, we have treated the gain or loss arising from the translation of the SFP of a foreign operation simply as a balancing figure on the subsidiary's translated SFP. However, several theoretical alternatives are available for the disposition of these gains or losses. The broad alternatives are:

1. Immediate recognition of the net gain or loss in consolidated net income (applied to all companies).
2. Limited recognition of gains and losses in a manner that is consistent with the treatment of similar types of *transaction* gains or losses.
3. Deferred recognition of gains and losses until realized, the deferral to be shown as a balancing amount in the consolidated SFP (e.g., as a separate component of shareholders' equity).

Each of these alternatives can be applied under either method of translation. However, some of the alternatives are more logical under one method than the other, as we shall see later.

Immediate Recognition

Once upon a time, US standards required immediate recognition of all translation gains and losses. For many companies, immediate recognition had a significant effect on net income from operations and therefore affected earnings per share, dividend payout ratios, and profit-sharing and bonus calculations, as well as certain debt-covenant calculations such as times-interest-earned. As a result, the managers of some of these companies engaged in massive hedging operations to offset possible losses from an accounting exposure in a foreign operation. Others reorganized the financial affairs of their foreign subsidiaries to reduce the accounting exposure. In the process, the companies incurred significant "real" costs in an attempt to eliminate "fictional" accounting losses.

In response to this undesirable economic impact of immediate recognition, US standards were changed so that, in certain circumstances, the translation gains and losses would instead be reported on a cumulative basis as a separate component of shareholders' equity.

The experience in the United States clearly indicated the practical inadvisability of mandating the current recognition of translation gains and losses in all cases. Those instances in which current recognition seems particularly inappropriate are when the foreign operation is substantially autonomous in its activities. If a foreign operation functions independently of its parent, then recognition of a translation gain or loss is apt to be misleading because the accounting exposure is not at all indicative of the economic exposure.

Limited Recognition

The second broad approach to the disposition of translation gains and losses is to limit recognition only to gains and losses arising from monetary items so that they are treated in the same manner as foreign-currency *transactions*, as described in the preceding chapter.

This approach probably works best if it is limited to certain types of companies. Some foreign operations operate in the same primary economic environment as the parent. These operations are often extensions of the parent's domestic business. Examples include foreign sales offices and foreign production centres that have no real economic autonomy. Since the parent is directly involved in the foreign operation, the parent is, in effect, using the subsidiary as a facilitating mechanism for a series of foreign-currency transactions. Therefore, it is logical to apply the same recognition principles to foreign operations that are interdependent with the parent as would be applied to foreign-currency transactions.

The limited recognition alternative is inappropriate for foreign operations that operate in a different primary economic environment from the parent as relatively autonomous operations. Recognition implies that the parent will be directly affected by the subsidiary. However, it is not clear that future operating cash flows will be affected by exchange rate changes if the subsidiary is operating independently.

Deferred Recognition

The third alternative is to defer recognition of the translation gain or loss *indefinitely* so that it doesn't affect earnings at all. The cumulative translation gain or loss will be reported as an SFP item. The gain or loss would be recognized only if it is realized if the parent sells the subsidiary (or a significant enough portion to lose control).

This alternative seems appropriate for subsidiaries that operate in a different primary economic environment from the parent and, as a result, are essentially autonomous of the parent. The main argument for deferral of cumulative translation gains and losses is that a gain or loss is the result of a mechanical process of translating from a foreign currency into the parent's functional currency, and thus has little direct effect on the present and future cash flows from operations. Recognition of these gains and losses in income may not be reflective of the economic exposure to exchange rate changes.

Translation gains and losses clearly do not fit within the current definitions of assets and liabilities. To be shown on the SFP, they can only be placed directly in shareholders' equity. Thus the cumulative foreign-currency adjustment is treated as a separate component of consolidated shareholders' equity under this alternative.

CONCEPT CHECK 9-3

Companion Website

1. What are three alternatives for handling translation gains and losses?
2. When is the recognition of translation gains and losses in current year net income inappropriate?

THE FUNCTIONAL CURRENCY APPROACH

To summarize, we have discussed two possible methods to convert foreign currency denominated financial statements into another currency—the temporal method and the current-rate method. To apply the two different approaches, we must define the circumstances under which they are used. The determination is essentially made on the basis of the foreign operation's functional currency (IAS 21).

The **functional currency** is the currency of the primary economic environment in which the entity operates, which is normally the country in which it generates and expends cash. If Canada is the primary economic environment in which the parent operates, then the parent's functional currency is the Canadian dollar.

To illustrate, let us continue our example regarding Domestic Corporation and its subsidiary, Forsub. We will assume that the Canadian dollar is the *functional currency* of Domestic Corporation and that it is also the *presentation currency* on its financial statements. If it is determined that Canada is the primary economic environment in which Forsub operates then the Canadian dollar will also be the functional currency of Forsub. For example, this would be the case if Forsub buys most of its materials in Canadian dollars and also sells its output in Canadian dollars, such as an off-shore manufacturing subsidiary that imports parts from the parent for assembly and then sells the finished product back to the parent or to other customers in Canadian dollars.

Because Forsub's transactions have been recorded in terms of pants, the local currency, the goal will be to re-measure them in terms of its functional currency, that is, the Canadian dollar. Since the subsidiary is operating in the same economic environment as the parent, the results should be the same as if the parent had engaged in the transactions. Further, the goal is to produce the same financial statements that would have resulted if we had used the functional currency to record all the transactions. To accomplish this re-measuring, the temporal method will be used to translate the financial statements. With the temporal method, only gains and losses on monetary items (and fair-value non-monetary items) are recognized in net income.

If, however, it is determined that Pantania is the primary economic environment in which Forsub operates, then the pant will be the functional currency of Forsub. There will be no need to re-measure the transactions but the statements will still need to be translated to Canadian dollars, the presentation currency, before they can be consolidated. To accomplish this translation, the current-rate method will be used.

With the current-rate method, translation gains and losses are not recognized in earnings but instead are reported on the SCI as a component of other comprehensive income. The cumulative amount is reported as a separate component of shareholders' equity, as mentioned above. The decision to defer gains and losses is a reflection of the ambiguity surrounding the economic impact of exchange rate changes.

The above illustrations are the two basic scenarios encountered in translating financial statements and therefore are the focus of our discussions in this chapter. Other scenarios are possible.

EXHIBIT 9-4

Translation Decisions Where Accounting Records Are Maintained in a Currency Other Than Canadian Dollars

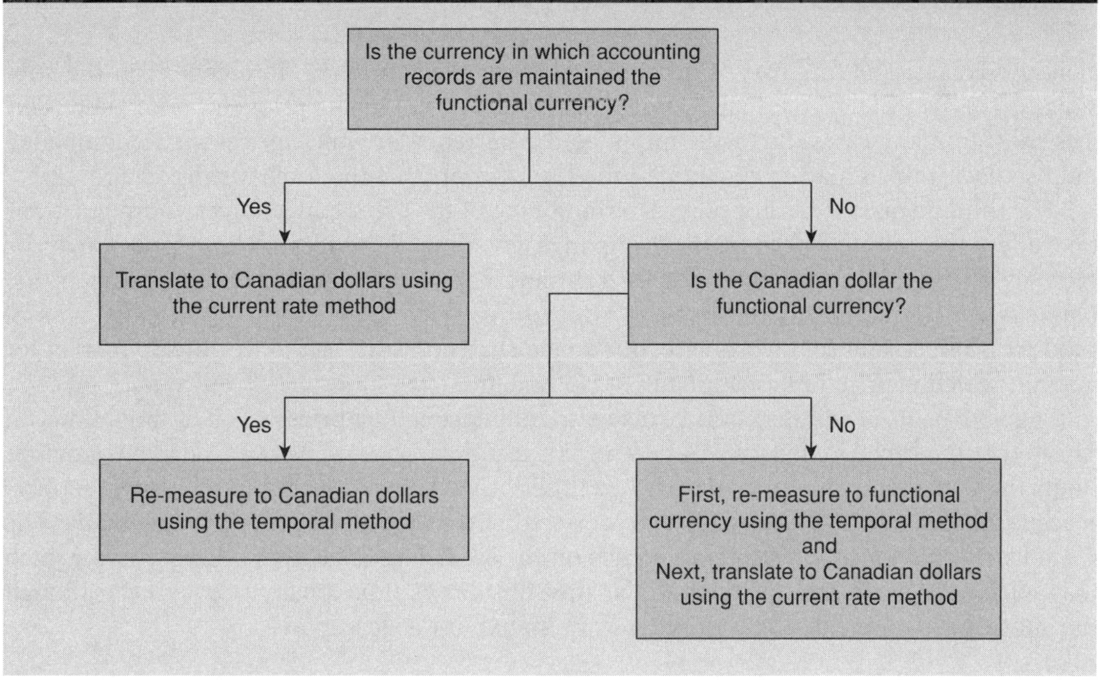

For example, Forsub, although a Pantanian subsidiary of a Canadian parent, may nonetheless identify the United States as its primary economic environment because most of its revenue and some of its expenses are in US dollars. In this case its functional currency would be the US dollar. If Forsub's transactions are recorded in pants, they will first have to be re-measured in terms of its functional currency, the US dollar, using the temporal method. Next, since the presentation currency for the group is the Canadian dollar, the re-measured transactions will have to be translated into Canadian dollars using the current-rate method.

An interesting aspect of dual concepts of *functional* currency and *presentation* currency is that the reporting (for consolidation purposes) may not reflect the geographic location of the subsidiary at all. However, never lose sight of the fact that we're talking only about statements prepared for consolidation. The Pantanian subsidiary will most likely prepare its separate-entity financial statements in pants for reporting to stakeholders in Pantania, such as bankers, tax authorities, regulators, and local "joint venture" partners.

Exhibit 9-4 should help you identify the steps to be followed during translation when the accounting records are maintained in a currency other than the Canadian dollar.

Determining the Functional Currency

As we have noted, the functional currency is the currency of the primary economic environment in which the company operates. This environment is normally the one where it generates and spends its cash. The determination of a company's functional currency is not always easy. To assist companies in determining their functional currency, IFRS discusses several primary and secondary indicators.

Primary Indicators The first two primary indicators are the currency "influences" on the subsidiary's (1) costs of the goods and services acquired, and (2) selling prices for goods and services sold. In many cases, this will simply be the currency in which prices are denominated (and settled), which may or may not be the local currency of the foreign subsidiary.

The third primary indicator relates to the source of the competitive forces and regulations that affect the selling prices of the company's goods and services. Selling prices may be strongly affected by competitive forces from another country, such as competition in the parent's home country. Another type of competitive force arises when a particular type of product is priced and sold worldwide in a single currency, such as the worldwide market for aircraft, which is priced internationally in US dollars.

Regulations from another country may also influence selling prices, such as limitations on prices that the buying country will permit. For example, suppose that a Canadian province limits the Canadian dollar price that its health service will pay for prescription drugs. A pharmaceutical company has a subsidiary in Mexico that sells most of its product to Canada. The Canadian regulations are a strong influence on the Mexican subsidiary's selling prices, which may effectively make the Canadian dollar the subsidiary's functional currency, even though the subsidiary's nominal selling prices may be stated in Mexican pesos.

Secondary Indicators If the functional currency is not easily determined from the primary factors, the following factors should also be considered in determining the functional currency:

1. The currency in which financing activities are conducted, including the issuance of debt and equity instruments.
2. The currency in which cash from operating activities is kept. That is, if currencies from operating activities are routinely converted to another currency before being held in the bank, then that other currency may be the company's functional currency.
3. Whether the activities of the foreign operation are conducted independently of the parent or as an extension of the parent.
4. Whether the foreign operation conducts a low or high proportion of its activities with the parent.
5. Whether the cash flows of the foreign operation directly affect the cash flows of the parent and are readily available to the parent.
6. Whether the cash flows of the foreign operation are sufficient to service its debt obligations without the need for funds from the parent.

Often, the functional currency is not obvious. Selecting a functional currency in these situations is a matter of professional judgment. The choice should be the one that most faithfully represents the economic impact of the activities of the company. In the following section, we will briefly review the nature of foreign operations that typically have functional currencies that are the same as or different from that of the parent.

REALITY CHECK 9-2

CGI Group Inc. offers the following explanation of its accounting for subsidiaries that have the same functional currency as the parent—the Canadian dollar:

> The accounts of foreign subsidiaries, which are financially or operationally dependent on the Company, are accounted for using the temporal method. Under this method, monetary assets and liabilities are translated at the exchange rates in effect at the balance sheet date, and non-monetary assets and liabilities are translated at historical exchange rates. Revenue and expenses are translated at average rates for the period. Translation exchange gains or losses of such subsidiaries are reflected in net earnings.

This disclosure tells us that CGI uses the temporal method for financially or operationally dependent subsidiaries, no matter where they are physically located. Notice that the disclosure does refer to the technical accounting name "temporal method," but then explains what that means for the benefit of readers who are not fortunate enough to be professional accountants.

Source: CGI Group Inc., 2009 Annual Report, p. 46.

Entities with the Same Functional Currency as the Parent

If an entity has the same functional currency as the parent, it typically operates as an extension of the parent company in the foreign country. Such operations are usually treated as revenue centres or cost centres from a management accounting standpoint. These operations are largely or entirely dependent on the parent, either for a source of product or for disposition of production. Interdependent foreign operations are a direct arm of the parent and the parent controls the assets and liabilities of the subsidiary.

Therefore, their operations are viewed simply as a series of foreign-currency *transactions*. If the financial statements are prepared in the local currency, they will have to be re-measured into the functional currency to be consolidated with the parent. The results obtained by re-measuring the financial statements of the foreign operation should appear as though the parent had engaged in the foreign-currency transactions directly, rather than through a foreign subsidiary.

The method used for re-measuring such integrated operations should be the same as the method used by the parent for reporting the results of its foreign-currency *transactions*. The method that accomplishes this objective is the *temporal method*. The translation gains and losses that arise from re-measuring foreign operations using the temporal method are treated in the same manner as for foreign-currency transactions. That is, the gains or losses on monetary transactions and balances are reported in the current year's net income.

We will demonstrate the application of this method in the following sections.

Entities with a Different Functional Currency from the Parent

An entity with a different functional currency from the parent is often viewed as being an individual, autonomous foreign business entity. The parent company's accounting exposure to

REALITY CHECK 9-3

How does CGI account for subsidiaries that have a different functional currency than it does?

> Self-sustaining subsidiaries, with economic activities largely independent of the Company, are accounted for using the current rate method. Under this method, assets and liabilities of subsidiaries denominated in a foreign currency are translated into Canadian dollars at exchange rates in effect at the balance sheet date. Revenue and expenses are translated at average exchange rates prevailing during the period. Resulting unrealized gains or losses are reported as net unrealized gains (losses) on translating financial statements of self-sustaining foreign operations in the consolidated statements of comprehensive income.

"Self sustaining" is a pre-2011 term (not currently used in IFRS) that essentially means a company that is operationally and financially independent of its parent.

Source: CGI Group Inc., 2009 Annual Report, p. 46.

exchange rate changes is limited to the net investment of the parent in the foreign subsidiary. Therefore, under IFRS the current-rate method is used for translating the financial statements.

The net gain or loss that arises from translating these operations is not recognized in net income, but is reported as other comprehensive income. As we explained above, this treatment is recommended because:

1. the accounting exposure may not be indicative of the economic exposure, and
2. this exchange gain or loss has no direct effect on the cash flows of the parent.

The cumulative gain or loss will be reported as part of equity in the shareholders' equity section of the SFP. Only on loss of control of the subsidiary is the cumulative gain or loss brought into income.

The parent may choose to hedge its net investment in a foreign entity. This option is only available for **foreign entities**, that is, entities that have a different functional currency from the parent. Any gains or losses from the hedge will be deferred (similar to a cash-flow hedge) and offset against the cumulative translation loss or gain in equity.

Although IFRS permits hedge accounting for a parent's net investment in a foreign subsidiary, it is rather difficult to find a rationale for actually engaging in such a hedge. It would make sense only if both of two conditions exist:

1. the net investment is a reasonable approximation of the fair value of the investment, which is highly unlikely, *and*
2. the parent intends to sell the subsidiary in the near future and wants to guard against value loss through currency fluctuations.

The second condition can arise when one company buys another with the intent of reselling (also known as *flipping*) the acquired company to another buyer.

REALITY CHECK 9-4

The cumulative impact of exchange gains and losses on net investments in foreign entities can be substantial. For example, CGI reports cumulative net unrealized losses on translating foreign entities of approximately $359 million in their 2009 Annual Report. In addition, they had also hedged some of their net investment as they also report cumulative "net unrealized gains on translating long-term debt designated as a hedge of net investments in self-sustaining foreign operations" of approximately $61 million.

Source: CGI Group Inc., 2009 Annual Report, p. 56, note 15.

Operations in Hyper-Inflationary Economies

An exception to the general recommendations given above occurs when a country has a high inflation rate. Some countries historically have had very high rates of inflation, sometimes well over 100% per year. This creates a problem as historical-cost financial statements will show long-term non-monetary assets at a cost that is expressed in currency of a far different purchasing power than the current exchange rate suggests.

The solution recommended in IFRS is to adjust the foreign operation's financial statements for changes in the price level in the foreign country. The adjusted statements are then translated using the closing rate for all amounts (assets, liabilities, equities, revenues, and expenses). IFRS provides several guidelines as to what constitutes a "highly inflationary" economy. It suggests that an inflation rate of 100% over a three-year period (that is, averaging 26% per year, compounded) would be highly inflationary. In addition, IAS 29 also provides several behavioural guidelines based on the actions of the general population and businesses that would be indicative of hyperinflation. We will not discuss this issue any further in this text.

CONCEPT CHECK 9-4

Companion Website

1. What are the three primary indicators that a company should use to determine its functional currency?
2. Why are the translation gains and losses resulting from the use of the current-rate method not recognized in net income?

APPLICATION OF IFRS RECOMMENDATIONS

Let's return to the introductory example of Domestic Corporation and its Pantanian subsidiary, Forsub Ltd. We determined earlier in the chapter that under the temporal method of translation, there was a net translation loss of $3,000 in the first year. If Forsub's functional currency is the Canadian dollar, the temporal method is used to re-measure the operations of Forsub in Canadian dollars. The net re-measurement or translation loss of $3,000 will be included *in Domestic Corporation's net income*. (For convenience, we will use the more common term "translate" instead of "re-measure" from here on.)

Instead, suppose that Forsub's functional currency is the pant. Then the current-rate method is appropriate—the entire translation gain or loss will be reported as a separate component of Domestic Corporation's shareholders' equity. Exhibit 9-3 shows that the current-rate method yields a net translation gain of $15,000, none of which is included in net income.

Obviously, a key facet of applying the IFRS recommendations is the determination of the functional currency of the foreign operation. Bear in mind, however, that if the foreign operations are relatively minor or if the parent is not otherwise constrained to follow GAAP for publicly accountable enterprises, it may be simpler and no less informative to apply the current-rate method across the board to all foreign subsidiaries and to report the translation gains or losses in other comprehensive income.

EXTENDING THE EXAMPLE

Earlier in this chapter, we described the initial transactions for the establishment of Forsub Ltd. by Domestic Corporation. After Forsub was established, the subsidiary purchased land and inventory and issued bonds. Exhibits 9-1 and 9-3 illustrate translation of Forsub's SFP accounts under two different translation methods. For simplicity, we assumed that Forsub had no operating revenues or expenses for the first year, 20X5 (even though, strictly speaking, there should have been some bond interest accrued). While we did point out that the translation gain or loss may be taken into income in 20X5, it is taken into income by the *parent* company and reported on the consolidated SCI.

Now let us make the example more realistic by looking at Forsub's financial statements for the next year, 20X6. Forsub Ltd.'s separate-entity SFP and SCI are shown in Exhibit 9-5. Additional information is as follows:

1. At the beginning of 20X6, Forsub purchased some equipment for P30,000; the equipment has an expected useful life of six years.
2. The ending inventory was purchased in the last quarter of the year, when the exchange rate was $2.45.
3. The exchange rate at December 31, 20X6, was $2.50; the average rate during the year was $2.40.

Current-Rate Method The translation of Forsub's account balances by using the current-rate method is shown in Exhibit 9-6. All of the assets and liabilities are translated at the year-end exchange rate of $2.50. The shareholders' equity accounts are translated at the historical rates:

- common shares at the rate that existed at the time of the initial investment, and
- retained earnings at the rate that existed at the time the earnings were recognized.

EXHIBIT 9-5

Forsub Ltd. Financial Statements, 20X6

Statement of Financial Position
December 31, 20X6

Assets		**Liabilities and shareholders' equity**	
Cash	P 15,000	Accounts payable, current	P 22,000
Accounts receivable	15,000	Bonds payable, long term	25,000
Inventory	10,000		47,000
Land	40,000	Common shares	50,000
Equipment	30,000	Retained earnings*	8,000
Accumulated depreciation	(5,000)		58,000
Total assets	P105,000		P105,000

* No revenues or expenses were recognized in 20X5, the only previous year.

Statement of Comprehensive Income
Year Ended December 31, 20X6

Sales revenue		P 60,000
Cost of sales:		
Beginning inventory	P20,000	
Purchases	30,000	
Ending inventory	(10,000)	40,000
Gross margin		20,000
Operating expenses:		
Depreciation	5,000	
Interest expense	3,000	
Other expenses	4,000	12,000
Net income		P 8,000

In this example, the only amount in retained earnings is the current earnings for 20X6, and thus the translated amount is the same as that shown on the translated SCI. The balancing figure for the SFP is the cumulative translation gain of $25,800.

Under a pure application of the current-rate method, the SCI would also be translated at the year-end rate. However, Exhibit 9-6 shows the SCI being translated at the average rate for the year rather than at the year-end rate. This is known as the *average-rate approach to the current-rate method*, and is used primarily to ensure additivity of the interim earnings figures of the parent company. IFRS recommends the use of exchange rates at the dates of the transactions rather than the year-end rate for SCI amounts. For practical reasons, a rate that approximates the dates of the transactions rates (i.e., an average rate) can be used if the exchange rates do not fluctuate significantly.

On the SCI, all items are translated at the current (average) rate, regardless of the type of revenue or expense, assuming that the revenue and expense accrued evenly through the year. Allocations of past costs, such as depreciation and amortization, are translated the same as are current costs such as interest expense. As a result, the translated amount of net income is also equal to the current (average) rate times the net income as expressed in pants.

EXHIBIT 9-6

Translation by Current-Rate Method, 20X6

Exchange rate, December 31, 20X6: P1.00 = Cdn$2.50
Average exchange rate for 20X6: P1.00 = Cdn$2.40

Statement of Financial Position
December 31, 20X6

	Local currency (pants)	Exchange rate	Translated amounts (C$)
Assets			
Cash	P 15,000	$2.50	$ 37,500
Accounts receivable	15,000	2.50	37,500
Inventory	10,000	2.50	25,000
Land	40,000	2.50	100,000
Equipment	30,000	2.50	75,000
Accumulated depreciation	(5,000)	2.50	(12,500)
Total assets	P105,000		$262,500
Liabilities and shareholders' equity			
Accounts payable, current	P 22,000	2.50	$ 55,000
Bonds payable, long term	25,000	2.50	62,500
	47,000		117,500
Common shares	50,000	2.00	100,000
Retained earnings	8,000	(below)	19,200
Cumulative translation gain (loss)*	—		**25,800**
	58,000		145,000
Total liabilities and shareholders' equity	P105,000		$262,500

Statement of Comprehensive Income
Year Ended December 31, 20X6

	Local currency (pants)	Exchange rate	Translated amounts (C$)
Sales	P 60,000	$ 2.40	$144,000
Cost of sales:			
Beginning inventory	20,000		
Purchases	30,000		
Ending inventory	(10,000)		
	40,000	2.40	96,000
Gross margin	20,000		48,000
Operating expenses:			
Depreciation	5,000	2.40	12,000
Interest expense	3,000	2.40	7,200
Other expenses	4,000	2.40	9,600
	12,000		28,800
Net income	P 8,000		$ 19,200

* *Cumulative exchange gain*:

2005 gain on P50,000 net investment: P50,000 × ($2.30 – $2.00) =	$15,000
2006 gain on P50,000 net investment: P50,000 × ($2.50 – $2.30) =	10,000
2006 gain on retained earnings: P8,000 × ($2.50 – $2.40) =	800
Cumulative translation gain	$25,800

EXHIBIT 9-7

Current-Rate Method—Analysis of Cumulative Translation Gain 20X6

	Local currency (pants)	Exchange rate	Translated amounts (C$)
AMOUNTS ARISING IN 20X6:			
Net assets:			
Balance January 1, 20X6	P50,000	2.30	$115,000
Changes during 20X6			
Net income	8,000	2.40	19,200
Dividends	n/a		
Derived balance			134,200
Actual balance	P58,000	2.50	145,000
Net translation gain for 20X6			10,800
Amounts relating to previous periods			
Gain from 20X5			15,000
Cumulative translation gain, December 31, 20X6			$ 25,800

The cumulative translation gain of $25,800 that arises under the current-rate method can be broken down into three components:

1. the $15,000 gain arising from the first year's change in the exchange rate from $2.00 to $2.30 (Exhibit 9-3);
2. an additional $10,000 gain in the current year, 20X6, caused by a further increase in the exchange rate from $2.30 to $2.50; and
3. an $800 gain on the retained earnings from the period of their generation (mid-20X6) to the end of 20X6, during which period the exchange rate changed from $2.40 to $2.50.

These components of the cumulative gain are summarized at the bottom of Exhibit 9-6. In addition, the gain for the current year can also be calculated directly by examining the change in net assets for the year. Starting with the beginning of year balance of these net assets, we can add the inflows (usually net income) and subtract the outflows (usually dividends) to arrive at the year-end balance of net assets expressed in pants. We then need only convert each balance or flow at the exchange rate in effect at the time of the balance or flow, and find the difference at year-end between the balance in foreign currency and the derived amount in domestic currency. Such a statement is shown in Exhibit 9-7.

Temporal Method If, instead, the accounts of Forsub Ltd. are translated by using the temporal method, then the procedure is somewhat more complicated. Exhibit 9-8 illustrates the application of the temporal method for 20X6.

The monetary assets and liabilities are translated by using the current rate. The non-monetary assets are translated at their historical rates. It is assumed that the ending inventory was purchased when the exchange rate was $2.45, and thus that is the historical rate for inventory. The specific historical rate for land is $2.00 and for the equipment is $2.30. The accumulated depreciation must be translated at the same rate as was used for the gross asset cost.

EXHIBIT 9-8

Translation by Temporal Method, 20X6

Exchange rate, December 31, 20X6: P1.00 = Cdn$2.50
Average exchange rate for 20X6: P1.00 = Cdn$2.40

Statement of Financial Position
December 31, 20X6

	Local currency (pants)	Exchange rate Type	Exchange rate Amount	Translated amounts (Cdn$)
Assets				
Cash	P 15,000	C	$ 2.50	$ 37,500
Accounts receivable	15,000	C	2.50	37,500
Inventory	10,000	H	2.45	24,500
Land	40,000	H	2.00	80,000
Equipment	30,000	H	2.30	69,000
Accumulated depreciation	(5,000)	H	2.30	(11,500)
Total assets	P105,000			$237,000
Liabilities and shareholders' equity				
Accounts payable, current	P 22,000	C	2.50	$ 55,000
Bonds payable, long term	25,000	C	2.50	62,500
	47,000			117,500
Common shares	50,000	H	2.00	100,000
Retained earnings	8,000			28,200
	58,000			128,200
Total liabilities and shareholders' equity	P105,000			$245,700
Cumulative translation gain (loss) [Exhibit 9-9]				**$ (8,700)**

Statement of Comprehensive Income
Year Ended December 31, 20X6

	Local currency (pants)	Exchange rate Type	Exchange rate Amount	Translated amounts (Cdn$)
Sales	P 60,000	H/A	$2.40	$144,000
Cost of sales:				
Beginning inventory	20,000	H	2.00	40,000
Purchases	30,000	H/A	2.40	72,000
Ending inventory	(10,000)	H	2.45	(24,500)
	40,000			87,500
Gross margin	20,000			56,500
Operating expenses:				
Depreciation	5,000	H	2.30	11,500
Interest expense	3,000	H/A	2.40	7,200
Other expenses	4,000	H/A	2.40	9,600
	12,000			28,300
Net income	P 8,000			$ 28,200

Exchange rate types:
C = current, year-end rate
H = historical rate for the individual item
H/A= historical rate, assumed to be the average for the year

On the SCI, the revenues and expenses are translated at the rates that were in effect at the time that the revenues were realized or the costs incurred. For many revenue and expense items, realization coincides with recognition, so that the historical rate is essentially the same as the average rate for the period as was used in the current-rate method. Although the result is the same for some SCI items, the concept is quite different.

Under the current-rate method, cost of sales could be translated simply by taking the cost of sales in pants and multiplying it by the average exchange rate for the period. Under the temporal method, however, the cost of sales amount must be derived by multiplying the beginning inventory by its historical rate of $2.00, adding the purchases at the historical/average rate of $2.40, and subtracting the ending inventory at its historical rate of $2.45. The resulting figure for cost of sales, $87,500, *cannot be derived directly by multiplying any exchange rate by the cost of sales in pants, P40,000*.

Similarly, any depreciation or amortization expense must be translated at the exchange rates that existed at the time the original costs were incurred. In this example, the only such expense is the depreciation of the equipment. Since the equipment was purchased when the rate was $2.30, the depreciation expense must be translated at $2.30. Other expenses are translated at the rate that existed when they were *accrued*. It does not matter whether they have been paid in cash or not. Thus interest expense and other expenses have been translated at the average rate for the year.

The net income that results from using the temporal method amounts to $28,200 before considering any components of the translation loss. This amount cannot be derived directly from the original net income of P8,000—it must be obtained by working through the SCI and translating all of its individual components by the appropriate historical rates. Note that the temporal method net income of $28,200 is quite different from the current-rate method net income of $19,200. This difference is due to the lags in expense recognition of two types of costs: inventory and depreciable capital assets.

Translation of Forsub Ltd.'s accounts to dollars results in total assets of $237,000, as compared to total liabilities and equities of $245,700. The cumulative translation loss therefore is $8,700. In Exhibit 9-8, the cumulative translation loss is shown as a single amount pending disposition, rather than being distributed to the SCI, the SFP, or both. The reason is that when the foreign operation's statements are translated, the translation gain or loss is not part of the statements of the subsidiary, but is an amount that must be allocated or assigned *on the parent's consolidated statements*.

Allocating the Accumulated Translation Loss—Temporal Method We know from Exhibit 9-1 that $3,000 of the $8,700 cumulative translation loss arose in 20X5, and therefore that the loss arising in 20X6 must be the remainder, or $5,700.

The gain or loss from holding monetary assets and liabilities can be computed by analyzing the flow of these items. Unlike the bonds payable in this example, monetary assets and liabilities may not be constant throughout the year. The impact of the exchange gains and losses must be measured only for the period of time that the current monetary items are in the enterprise.

For example, sales revenue increased monetary assets, either as cash or as accounts receivable, by P60,000. Assuming that the sales were even throughout the year, we can measure the gain from holding monetary assets resulting from the sales by multiplying the P60,000 by the change in the exchange rate from the average for the year ($2.40) to the end of the year ($2.50). Similarly, the current expenses (or expenditures) that caused either a decline in monetary assets or an increase in monetary liabilities must be taken into account.

EXHIBIT 9-9

Temporal Method—Analysis of Cumulative Translation Loss 20X6

	Local currency (pants)	Exchange rate	Translated amounts (C$)
Amounts arising in 20X6:			
Monetary Items:			
Balance January 1, 20X6	P(10,000)	2.30	$(23,000)
Changes during 20X6			
Sales revenue	P 60,000	2.40	144,000
Inventory purchases	(30,000)	2.40	(72,000)
Interest expense	(3,000)	2.40	(7,200)
Other expenses	(4,000)	2.40	(9,600)
Purchase of equipment	(30,000)	2.30	(69,000)
Derived balance			(36,800)
Actual balance	(17,000)	2.50	(42,500)
Net translation loss for 20X6			5,700
Amounts relating to previous periods			
Loss from 20X5 on monetary items			3,000
Cumulative translation loss, December 31, 20X6			$ 8,700

The easiest way to measure the net gain or loss from the monetary assets and liabilities is to construct a funds-flow statement, with funds defined as net monetary assets. Starting with the beginning-of-year balance of these net monetary assets, we can add the inflows and subtract the outflows, to arrive at the year-end balance of net monetary assets expressed in pants. We then need only to convert each balance or flow at the exchange rate in effect at the time of the balance or flow, and find the difference at year-end between the balance in foreign currency and the derived amount in domestic currency.

Such a funds-flow statement is shown at the top of Exhibit 9-9. The ending balance in pants is a P17,000 net monetary liability, as can be verified by referring to Exhibit 9-5. The year-end balance is equivalent to a $42,500 net monetary liability at the SFP date. The sum of the inflows and outflows, however, when translated at the rates in effect during the year, amounts to a $36,800 net monetary liability.

In effect, the $36,800 shows what the ending balance of the net monetary liabilities would have been if Domestic Corporation had maintained all of its Pantanian balances in dollars rather than in pants, and had converted to and from dollars only on the transaction dates. Since the actual dollar-equivalent balance of the accounts in pants is $42,500, Domestic Corporation has suffered a loss of $5,700 by having Forsub Ltd. hold balances in pants.

The remainder of Exhibit 9-9 summarizes the remaining amounts included in the $8,700 cumulative translation loss at December 31, 20X6. As we stated above, a total of $3,000 of the loss pertains to 20X5, while the remaining loss of $5,700 pertains to 20X6.

When Domestic Corporation consolidates Forsub Ltd., the total cumulative translation loss of $8,700 must be included somewhere in Domestic's consolidated financial statements. The temporal method is intended to yield the same result as if Domestic had carried out the foreign transactions directly. Therefore, the *translation* loss must be reported in Domestic's

EXHIBIT 9-10

Comparison of Methods for Translating Foreign Operations

	Current-rate method	Temporal method
When to use	Use when presentation currency differs from functional currency	Use when functional currency differs from currency in which accounts maintained
Extent of accounting exposure	Net asset position (usually) or net liability position	Net monetary & non-monetary items carried at fair value (most often a net liability position)
Most likely translation gain/loss:		
If foreign currency is strengthening	Exchange gain	Exchange loss
If foreign currency is weakening	Exchange loss	Exchange gain
Accounting treatment of gain/loss:		
Arising from previous years	Report in equity	Include in opening consolidated retained earnings
Arising in the current year	Report in other comprehensive income	Report in consolidated net income
Indication of true economic exchange risk exposure?	No relationship	No relationship

consolidated statements in a way that duplicates the treatment of gains and losses from foreign-currency *transactions*.

The consolidation process is quite straightforward:

- The portion of the cumulative translation gain or loss that relates to *prior years* is included in opening consolidated retained earnings.
- The portion of the gain or loss that relates to the *current year* is reported in the consolidated SCI, along with any foreign-currency gains and losses of the parent.

For Domestic, the $8,700 year-end 20X6 cumulative translation loss will be reported as follows:

- The $3,000 loss that arose in 20X5 will be included in consolidated retained earnings for January 1, 20X6.
- The $5,700 loss pertaining to 20X6 will be reported as an expense (i.e., foreign exchange loss) in Domestic's consolidated SCI for the year ended December 31, 20X6.

Comparison of Accounting Implications

Exhibit 9-10 compares the reporting implications of using the current-rate or temporal method. The decision to use a particular translation method will depend on the functional currency of the entity. The translation method used, in turn, will decide (1) whether the translation effect will be a gain or a loss, and (2) how that gain or loss will be reported in the parent's consolidated financial statements.

Remember, however, that the accounting exposure does not reflect the economic exposure. There is no necessary relationship between the direction of change in a foreign currency and its impact on the economic contribution of the foreign operation to its parent's welfare.

CONCEPT CHECK 9-5

1. Explain briefly how the translation gain or loss can be calculated directly when the current-rate method is being used.
2. How would revenue be translated under the current-rate method and the temporal method? How would unearned revenue be translated under both methods?

ACCOUNTING STANDARDS FOR PRIVATE ENTERPRISES

Canadian private-entity accounting standards use the same two methods of translating financial statements as IFRS: the temporal method and the current-rate method. However, Canadian standards do not use the concept of functional currency to determine which method to use. Instead they look at the nature of the foreign operation's relationship to its parent—the foreign operation is either integrated with the parent or is independent of the parent (i.e., self-sustaining). Integrated operations use the temporal method to translate their financial statements and self-sustaining operations use the current-rate method. The factors used to determine whether an operation is either integrated or self-sustaining are similar to the factors used to determine the functional currency of an operation. As a result, it is unlikely that there will be major translation differences for most foreign operations under ASPE as compared to IFRS.

There is no statement of comprehensive income for Canadian private enterprises, and thus no such category as "other comprehensive income" in which to report translation gains or losses. The translation gains or losses on "self-sustaining" operations (i.e., using the current rate method) flow directly into the separate component of shareholders' equity.

The translation of financial statements for operations in highly inflationary environments is also different for private enterprises. ASPE recommends the use of the temporal method for translating these operations and does not allow the adjustment of the foreign operation's financial statements for changes in the general price level of the foreign country.

Relevant Standards

IASB

IAS 21 The Effects of Changes in Foreign Exchange Rates
IAS 29 Financial Reporting in Hyperinflationary Economies

Accounting Standards for Private Enterprises

Sec 1651 Foreign Currency Translation

Summary of Key Points

1. A domestic Canadian corporation may establish a subsidiary in another country. When that happens, the parent has a foreign operation. The separate-entity financial statements of the foreign operation will be stated in terms of the host country's local currency. To prepare consolidated financial statements, the parent must translate the foreign-currency statements of the subsidiary into the parent's functional currency (normally Canadian dollars).
2. There are two methods for translating foreign operations: the temporal method and the current-rate method. The temporal method translates all monetary assets and liabilities at the exchange rate at the SFP date, known as the current rate or closing rate. Non-monetary assets and liabilities are translated at historical rates, except for those that are carried at fair value. For fair-valued non-monetary assets, the rate at the date on which such fair value is determined is used. The temporal method achieves the same translated amounts as would have arisen if the parent corporation had carried out all of the foreign operations directly, as a series of foreign-currency transactions, instead of through a foreign subsidiary. The current-rate method translates all assets and liabilities at the current rate (i.e., closing rate) as of the SFP date.
3. In a world of fluctuating exchange rates, all translation methods will yield a translation gain or loss. The apparent foreign-currency gain or loss is not a real economic gain or loss, however. Accounting gains and losses are the result of the *accounting exposure* to foreign-currency fluctuations, and are a mechanical result of the translation method used.
4. Economic exposure to foreign-currency fluctuations is the result of real economic impacts on the foreign subsidiary's operations, and cannot be measured by accounting methodologies. Any correspondence between accounting exposure and economic exposure is purely coincidental.
5. Translation gains and losses can be accorded (1) immediate recognition, (2) limited recognition in accordance with the treatment given to *transaction* gains and losses, or (3) deferred recognition. Immediate recognition of all translation gains and losses has been tried (in the United States) and subsequently rejected. The two remaining methods are both in use, even though they give diametrically opposed results. Limited recognition is the approach applied to foreign operations that have the same functional currency as the parent. Deferral, as a separate component of the parent's shareholders' equity, is the approach used for foreign operations that have a different functional currency from the parent.
6. The IFRS defines functional currency as the currency of the primary economic environment in which the entity operates, which is normally the environment in which it generates and expends cash. If the functional currency of the subsidiary is the same as the parent's, and if the foreign subsidiary's transactions have been recorded in a currency other than the functional currency, then the goal will be to re-measure them in terms of the functional currency. If the subsidiary is operating in the same economic environment as the parent, the results should be the same as if the parent had engaged in the transactions. This is best

accomplished by the temporal method. If, however, it is determined that the currency in the primary economic environment in which the foreign subsidiary operates is a foreign currency, then that foreign currency will be the functional currency of the subsidiary. There will be no need to re-measure the transactions but the statements will still need to be translated to Canadian dollars before they can be consolidated. The current-rate method is used to translate these statements.

7. Using the temporal method, the items in the SCI of a subsidiary are translated using the historical rates for all items. For many items the historical rate is essentially the same as the average rate for the period. Using the current-rate method, the items in the SCI of a subsidiary are translated using the average rate for the period. The treatment of the translation gain or loss that arises from translating the statements of a foreign operation depends on whether it has the same functional currency as the parent. If it has the same functional currency as the parent (i.e., the temporal method is being used), the translation gain or loss is reported in the consolidated statements in net income, that is, in a manner that is consistent with reporting foreign-currency transactions. If it has a different functional currency from the parent (i.e., the current-rate method is being used), the translation gain or loss is reported in the consolidated financial statements in other comprehensive income.

Companion Website

Visit the text's website at www.pearsoned.ca/beechy for practice quizzes, additional problems, Excel® templates, answers to Concept Check questions, and important IFRS updates.

Self-Study Problem 9-1

Early in 20X1, Irene Corporation established a subsidiary in Simonia. The subsidiary was named Gordon Limited, and Irene's investment was $1,250,000. When this investment was translated into Simonian frasers (SF), the currency of Simonia, the initial capitalization amounted to SF500,000.

Gordon Limited negotiated a three-year bank loan of SF200,000 from a Simonian bank when the exchange rate was $2.40. The company purchased depreciable capital assets for SF600,000 (exchange rate = $2.30).

The company then began operations. Due to an accumulation of cash through operations, Gordon invested SF200,000 in land during 20X2. The exchange rate at the time of the investment was $1.90. At the end of 20X2, Gordon's comparative SFP and SCI are as shown in Exhibit 9-11. Assume that any dividends are declared and paid at year-end.

Other exchange rate information for the Simonian fraser is as follows:

20X1 average	$2.20
20X1 year-end	$2.00
20X2 average	$1.70
20X2 year-end	$1.50

EXHIBIT 9-11

Gordon Limited

Statement of Comprehensive Income
Years Ended December 31

	20X2	20X1
Revenue	SF300,000	SF220,000
Depreciation expense	60,000	60,000
Interest expense	40,000	40,000
Other expenses	120,000	80,000
	220,000	180,000
Net income	SF 80,000	SF 40,000

Statement of Financial Position
December 31

	20X2	20X1
Assets		
Cash	SF 30,000	SF160,000
Accounts receivable	40,000	30,000
Land	200,000	—
Tangible capital assets	600,000	600,000
Accumulated depreciation	(120,000)	(60,000)
Total assets	SF750,000	SF730,000
Liabilities and shareholders' equity		
Accounts payable, current	SF 10,000	SF 20,000
Notes payable, due January 1, 20X4	200,000	200,000
	210,000	220,000
Common shares	500,000	500,000
Retained earnings	40,000	10,000
	540,000	510,000
Total liabilities and shareholders' equity	SF750,000	SF730,000

Required

Assume that Gordon Limited's functional currency is the Simonian fraser. Determine how the financial statement amounts shown in Gordon's SFP and SCI will affect Irene Corporation's consolidated statements for *each* of 20X1 and 20X2, including disposition of the cumulative translation gain or loss.

Self-Study Problem 9-2

Refer to the information in SSP9-1 and Exhibit 9-11. Assume instead that Gordon Limited's functional currency is the Canadian dollar.

Required

1. Translate Gordon's 20X1 financial statements.
2. Determine the amount of translation gain or loss for 20X1.
3. Translate Gordon's 20X2 financial statements.
4. Determine the amount of translation gain or loss for 20X2.

Review Questions

9-1 Distinguish between foreign-currency *transactions* and foreign-currency *operations*.

9-2 Explain the differences between these two translation methods:

a) temporal

b) current-rate

9-3 Which translation method views the foreign subsidiary's operations as though they were foreign-currency transactions of the parent?

9-4 Why is the common share account of a foreign subsidiary translated at the historical rate under both translation methods?

9-5 What is meant by the *accounting exposure* of a foreign operation? How is the accounting exposure measured?

9-6 How does the accounting exposure under the temporal method differ from the accounting exposure under the current-rate method?

9-7 For a given foreign operation for a given accounting period, is it possible for the accounting exposure under the temporal method to result in a translation loss, while the accounting exposure under the current-rate method results in a translation gain? Explain.

9-8 Define *economic exposure*. Distinguish between economic exposure and accounting exposure.

9-9 Forop Ltd. is a foreign subsidiary of Domop Inc. Domop's accounting exposure to exchange rate changes when translating the accounts of Forop is a substantial net liability exposure. Domop's management expects the foreign currency in which Forop operates to increase in value relative to the Canadian dollar; such an increase will result in a large translation loss. The management of Domop proposes to enter into a forward contract to receive an equivalent amount of foreign currency to hedge against the potential translation loss. Would you recommend that Domop's management follow their proposed course of action? Explain.

9-10 What is meant by the term *functional currency*?

9-11 What translation method is recommended for foreign operations with the same functional currency as the parent? Why is this method recommended?

9-12 What recommendation is made regarding the financial statement disposition of translation gains or losses for foreign operations with the same functional currency as the parent? Why?

9-13 How can management determine the functional currency of a foreign operation?

9-14 Mammoth Corporation has subsidiaries in 13 different countries, operating in 10 different currencies. Do all 13 have to be viewed the same way? Explain.

9-15 What translation method is recommended for foreign operations with a different functional currency from the parent?

9-16 Under the current-rate method, why are the revenue and expense accounts translated at average exchange rates, rather than at the current rate at the SFP date?

9-17 How does the translation of cost of goods sold differ between the current-rate method and the temporal method?

9-18 How does the translation of depreciation and amortization differ under the current-rate method as opposed to the temporal method?

9-19 Explain how the translation gain or loss on monetary items can be computed. Is the amount of gain or loss affected by the translation method used?

9-20 What is the impact of hyperinflation on the translation method for a foreign operation with a functional currency different from its parent?

CASES

CASE 9-1 ELITE DISTRIBUTORS LIMITED

Elite Distributors Limited is a Canadian public company that has been undergoing rapid expansion. The company is based in a major Canadian seaport, and several years ago found it necessary to open a sales office in the United States to transact business directly in that country.

Elite also has a wholly owned subsidiary, located in Singapore, that manufactures one of the main products that Elite sells in Canada. Substantially all of the Singapore subsidiary's sales are to Elite. There is a second (80% owned) subsidiary in the Republic of Ireland that was acquired in an attempt to diversify. This company sells exclusively through its own sales offices throughout Northern Europe, and has very few transactions with Elite, except for the regular payment of dividends.

Required

Recommend the appropriate accounting policies for Elite to follow with respect to each of these foreign operations. Support your recommendations.

[SMA, adapted]

CASE 9-2 CARE INC.

Care Inc. (CI), a national manufacturer and retailer of women's shoes, purchased 100% of the common shares of ShoeCo, a footwear manufacturing company located in a foreign country.

CI financed the purchase of ShoeCo's shares through a loan from a Canadian bank. To obtain this financing, CI had to offer one of its Canadian manufacturing plants as security. ShoeCo will continue to be managed and operated by locals and be responsible for obtaining operational loans.

ShoeCo sells most of its production to its domestic market. Previously a supplier of CI's, ShoeCo will continue to supply about 10% of its production to CI. CI has established a contract with ShoeCo fixing the quantity and the price in Canadian dollars.

Required

1. What is ShoeCo's functional currency? Explain how you reached your conclusion.
2. Describe both the temporal and current-rate translation methods. Which method would CI use?

[CICA]

CASE 9-3 MULTI-COMMUNICATIONS LTD.

Multi-Communications Ltd. (MCL) is a Canadian-owned public company operating throughout North America. Its core business is communications media, including newspapers, radio, television, and cable. The company's year-end is December 31.

You, CA, have recently joined MCL's reporting office as a finance director, reporting to the chief financial officer, Robert Allen. It is October 20X8. Mr. Allen has asked you to prepare a report discussing the accounting and auditing issues that may arise with the auditors during their visit in November.

MCL's growth in 20X8 was achieved through expansion into the United States by acquiring a number of newspaper, television, and cable operations. Since the US side of MCL's operations is now significant, management will be reporting its financial statements in US dollars. Shareholders' equity at the beginning of the period was $220 million, including a separately disclosed cumulative foreign exchange gain of $45 million. Management merged this balance with retained earnings because "the operations it relates to are no longer considered foreign for accounting purposes, and as a result no foreign-currency exposure will arise."

With recent trends to international free trade, MCL decided to position itself for future expansion into the South American market. Therefore, in 20X8 MCL bought a company that owns a radio network in a country in South America that has high inflation. MCL was willing to incur losses in the start-up since it was confident that in the long run it would be profitable. The South American country has had a democratic government for the past two years. Its government's objectives are to open the country's borders to trade and lower its inflation rate. The government was rather reluctant to let a foreign company purchase such a powerful communication tool. In exchange for the right to buy the network, MCL agreed, among other conditions, not to promote any political party, to broadcast only pre-approved public messages, and to let the government examine its books at the government's convenience. Management has recorded its investment in the books using the cost method.

In 20X8, MCL acquired a conglomerate, Peter Holdings (PH), which held substantial assets in the communications business. Over the past three months, MCL has sold off 80% of PH's non–communications-related businesses. In the current month, MCL sold PH's hotel and recreational property business for $175 million, realizing a gain of $22 million ($14.5 million after tax). The assets related to the non-communications businesses were scattered throughout the United States and MCL lacked the industry expertise to value them accurately. Management therefore found it difficult to determine the net realizable value of each of these assets at the time PH was acquired.

In 20X8, MCL decided to rationalize its television operations. Many of PH's acquisitions in the television business included stations in areas already being served by other stations operated by MCL. MCL systematically identified stations that were duplicating services and did not fit with MCL's long-range objectives. These assets have been segregated on the SFP and classified as current. The company anticipates generating a gain on the disposal of the entire pool of assets, although losses are anticipated on some of the individual stations. Operating results are capitalized in the pool. Once a particular station is sold, the resulting gain or loss is reflected in income.

Nine stations are in the pool at the present time. In 20X8, three were sold, resulting in gains of $65,000 after tax. Losses are expected to occur on several of the remaining stations. Although serious negotiations with prospective buyers are not underway at present, the company hopes to have disposed of them in early 20X9. To facilitate the sale of these assets, MCL is considering taking back mortgages.

In 20X8, MCL estimated the fair market value of its intangible assets at $250 million. Included as intangibles are newspaper and magazine circulation lists, cable subscriber lists, and broadcast licences. Some of these assets have been acquired through the purchase of existing businesses; others have been generated internally by operations that have been part of MCL for decades.

Amounts paid for intangibles are not difficult to determine; however, it has taken MCL staff some time to determine the costs of internally generated intangibles. To increase subscriptions for print and electronic media, MCL spends heavily on subscription drives by way of advertisements, cold calls, and free products. For the non-acquired intangibles, MCL staff have examined the accounting records for the past 10 years and have identified expenditures totalling $35 million that were expensed in prior years. These costs relate to efforts to expand customer bases. In addition, independent appraisers have determined the fair market value of these internally generated intangibles to be in the range of $60 million to $80 million. To be conservative, management has decided to reflect these intangibles on the December 31, 20X8, SFP at $60 million.

The market values of companies in the communications industry have been escalating in the past few years, indicating that the value of the underlying assets (largely intangibles) is increasing over time. MCL management stated that these licences do not lose any value, and in this industry, actually increase in value over time.

MCL has invested in the installation of fibre optic cable, which can transmit far more, far faster than conventional cable. The cost of the cable itself is negligible. MCL will be using it for transmission between its stations in two major Canadian cities. MCL needed only six cables to link all its television and radio stations between the two cities, but it decided to put in 36 cables since it was doing the digging anyway. To date, MCL has sold six cables and charges a monthly fee to new owners to cover their share of maintenance expenses. MCL is leasing 10 other cables for 15-year periods.

Required

Prepare the report.

[CICA]

CASE 9-4 JOHNSTON CO. LTD.

Johnston Co. Ltd. is a medium-sized Canadian company, incorporated in 20X1, whose shares are traded on the Toronto Stock Exchange. It began its operations as a processor and distributor of frozen herbs, but quickly branched out until it provided a full line of Canadian specialty foods. Some of these products were processed by Johnston itself, while others were processed by Johnston under contract with other Canadian companies.

The company's strategic plan calls for steady growth in sales and earnings. Accordingly, expansion into the lucrative United States market in 20X7 is under serious consideration. A major concern is changes in the exchange rate of the Canadian and American dollar because the company has received very different predictions from various analysts with respect to this.

Johnston is considering the following proposals. The first proposal involves setting up sales offices in the United States with orders filled from Johnston's Canadian warehouses. The sales offices would be responsible for sales, billing, and collections. All transactions would be in US dollars.

Alternatively, Johnston is considering establishing a wholly owned subsidiary in the United States to process and distribute a full line of specialty foods. It has not yet decided how to finance the purchase of the plant and equipment for this subsidiary.

The president has asked you, the controller, to prepare a report for possible use at a meeting of the board of directors. Specifically, he wants you to recommend which of the above proposals is preferable with respect to the impact of each on current and future income. He wants you to fully support your recommendation and to limit your discussion to foreign-currency translation issues, ignoring hedging and income tax considerations.

Required

Prepare the report for the president.

[SMA, adapted]

CASE 9-5 BUY CARTIER LTD.

Buy Cartier Ltd. (BCL) is a Canadian public company that operates primarily in the commercial and recreational transportation sector. Worldwide, the commercial transportation business is growing strongly, fuelled in part by rapid rates of urbanization. Traffic congestion, pollution, and commuting times are rising in major cities. Rail transportation represents an efficient, cost-effective solution to these problems. Analysts expect that the global passenger rail equipment market will grow at a compounded annual rate of more than 5%. Constraints on government ability to finance new transportation systems have resulted in the contracting of services to private companies such as BCL.

BCL has three divisions. The rail and transit operation offers a full range of urban, suburban, and intercity vehicles as well as complete rail transit systems. The recreational products division designs, builds, and distributes personal recreational transportation vehicles such as snowmobiles and watercraft. The capital services division oversees the financing activities for the company and provides secured financing for customer purchases of recreational product inventories and railcar leasing and management services for commercial customers.

Despite an uneasy economy, BCL has expanded its operations considerably in fiscal year 20X5. This expansion is consistent with management's published objective to double the corporation's revenues, profits, and earnings per share over the next five years.

It is now June 20X5 and BCL's fiscal year ends on September 30. You, CA, have recently accepted the position of assistant to the chief financial officer of BCL, Dave Butler. Your duties at BCL include overseeing the external reporting process and coordinating the external audit function.

BCL is an audit client of Rankin & Rankin (R&R), your previous employer. Mr. Butler has scheduled a meeting with the R&R audit partner and manager. In preparation for this meeting, Mr. Butler has asked you to prepare a report that discusses the major accounting and audit issues that might arise during the meeting with respect to the rail and transit division. Mr. Butler has provided you with information about new developments in this division (see Exhibit A). Mr. Butler would also like to know what information should be gathered to help the audit go as smoothly as possible. He is hopeful that your previous experience as an auditor at R&R will help reduce disagreements (which have been a problem between management and the auditors) and the current year's audit fee.

Required

Prepare your report for Mr. Butler.

Exhibit A Current Activities in Rail and Transit Division

1. On May 1, 20X5, BCL announced that it had signed an agreement to purchase all of the shares of Alltrans Rail Systems Inc., a US transportation company, for US$300 million (approximately C$500 million). A summary of the SFP items of Alltrans at April 30, 20X5 (in thousands of US$), is as follows:

Assets	
Receivables	$ 80,500
Inventories	100,200
Capital assets	500,100
Goodwill	20,000
Other assets	50,000
	$750,800
Liabilities	
Short-term borrowings	$ 20,500
Accounts payable and accrued liabilities	62,300
Long-term debt	330,000
Deferred income taxes	80,200
	$493,000

Alltrans has a contract with a US city to provide inter-city bus transit until December 1, 20X9. To ensure adequate continuation of services, key members of Alltrans have been retained under management contracts, which provide bonuses for the next two years based on Alltrans' operating results. The fiscal year-end of Alltrans is June 30. Management of Alltrans does not want to change the year-end and wishes to retain its current auditors, Patterson & Cole.

The Alltrans purchase is the single largest acquisition in BCL's history. As a result of this acquisition, US operations are now the largest part of BCL's global operations. Management has decided to report its financial statements in US dollars. The existing cumulative foreign exchange gain on other US operations of $16 million was transferred to retained earnings because reporting in US dollars means there is no longer any exposure to the Canadian/US dollar exchange rate.

2. In accordance with its intention to position itself in the growing international markets, BCL incorporated a company in Peru, South America, Transcom SA. The intent is to develop a citywide transit system in the country's capital city, Lima. To secure government approval and licences for the system, BCL agreed to invest C$50 million in the company. The government has agreed to provide subsidies for the purchase of the transit vehicles. These subsidies will become repayable if Transcom SA does not meet government-imposed quotas for hiring local employees to service the rail system.

   BCL engineers will design the transit system and BCL will provide the transit vehicles. BCL engineers have been seconded to oversee the design stage of the project. The engineers are working with local government officials and construction of the rail system and manufacture of the transit vehicles is expected to commence in February 20X6. The local government must approve all stages of the rail system design and will also approve the design of the transit vehicles. Once the system is complete, Transcom SA will operate it; however, the services provided would be rate-regulated by local government. The local government will also approve transit schedules. BCL agreed to allow government officials to review all books and records of Transcom SA at the convenience of the government. BCL expects that Transcom SA will incur losses in the start-up of the operations. Management of BCL has recorded its $50 million investment in Transcom SA using the cost method.

[ICAO adapted]

Problems

P9-1

Efren Ltd. is a foreign subsidiary of a Canadian parent and is located in the country of Matos. The SFP accounts of Efren are as follows, stated in mats (M):

Cash	M 20,000
Accounts receivable	10,000
Inventory (at market)	60,000
Capital assets	200,000
Accumulated depreciation	(80,000)
Long-term note receivable	50,000
Total assets	M260,000
Accounts and notes payable	M 40,000
Bonds payable	150,000
Common shares	70,000
Total liabilities and equities	M260,000

Additional Information

1. Efren Ltd. is wholly owned by Hialea Corp. Hialea established Efren when the mat was worth $1.00.
2. The capital assets were purchased when the mat was worth $1.20.
3. The bonds payable were issued when the exchange rate for the mat was $1.15.
4. The long-term note receivable arose when the mat was worth $1.30.
5. The inventory was purchased when the mat was worth $1.40.
6. The current exchange rate for the mat is $1.50.

Required

1. Translate the SFP accounts of Efren Ltd. into Canadian dollars, using each of the following methods:
   a) current-rate
   b) temporal

   In each case, treat the translation gain or loss as a single, balancing figure.
2. For each method, calculate the:
   a) accounting exposure
   b) additional gain or loss that would result if the exchange rate one year hence were $1.75, assuming no change in the SFP accounts in mats.

P9-2

The SCI for 20X3 for Hilary Co., expressed in Coker francs (CF), is as follows:

Sales revenue	CF3,000,000
Cost of goods sold:	
Beginning inventory	200,000
Purchases	1,000,000
	1,200,000
Ending inventory	400,000
	800,000
Depreciation	300,000
Other operating expenses	900,000
Interest expense	200,000
Total expenses	2,200,000
Net income	CF 800,000

Hilary Co. is 100% owned by Bryan Inc., a Canadian corporation.

Sales revenue, purchases of inventory, and operating expenses (except depreciation) all occurred evenly through the year. Interest expense accrued throughout the year, but was all paid at the end of the year. The beginning inventory was purchased on October 1, 20X2, when the exchange rate was $0.86; the ending inventory was purchased on November 1, 20X3, when the exchange rate was $0.97. The capital assets were acquired when the exchange rate was $0.74. Other exchange rate information is as follows:

December 31, 20X2	$0.89
Average for 20X3	$0.94
December 31, 20X3	$0.99

Required

Translate the SCI into Canadian dollars, using the:

1. current-rate method
2. temporal method

P9-3

Investco Ltd. is a Canadian real estate and property developer that decided to hold a parcel of land in downtown Munich, Germany, for speculative purposes. The land, costing

€12,000,000, was financed by a five-year bond (€9,000,000), which is repayable in euros, and an initial equity injection by Investco of €3,000,000. These transactions took place on January 1, 20X5, at which time a German subsidiary company was created to hold the investment. Investco plans to sell the land at the end of five years and use the euro proceeds to pay off the bond. In the interim, rent is being collected from another company, which is using the land as a parking lot.

The 20X5 year-end draft financial statements of the German subsidiary company are shown below (assume that rental revenue is collected and interest and other expenses are paid at the end of each month).

German Subsidiary
Statement of Comprehensive Income
For the Year Ended December 31, 20X5

Rental revenue		€ 1,000,000
Interest expense	€ 990,000	
Other expenses	10,000	1,000,000
Net income		€ 0

Statement of Financial Position
December 31, 20X5

Cash	—
Land	€ 12,000,000
	€ 12,000,000
Bond (due December 31, 20X9)	€ 9,000,000
Common shares	3,000,000
	€12,000,000

Assume the following exchange rates:

January 1, 20X5	€1 = $1.40
December 31, 20X5	€1 = $1.85
Average, 20X5	€1 = $1.60

Required

1. Prepare the translated 20X5 SCI and SFP at December 31, 20X5, following GAAP and assuming the German subsidiary's functional currency is the:
   a) Canadian dollar; and
   b) euro.
2. Which translation method better reflects Investco's *economic exposure* to exchange rate movements? Explain.
3. Which translation method would Investco be required to use? Explain.
   [SMA, adapted]

P9-4

Birch Limited is a 100%-owned foreign subsidiary with operations in England. Birch was acquired by its Canadian parent on January 1, 20X7. The financial records of Birch are maintained in pounds sterling (£) and provide the following information related to its equipment:

Date of Purchase	Cost of Purchase
January 1, 20X7	£1,000
January 1, 20X8	£1,500

The equipment is being amortized on a straight-line basis over its estimated useful life of 10 years.

Foreign exchange rates were as follows:

January 1, 20X6	£1 = C$1.50
Average for 20X6	£1 = C$1.51
January 1, 20X7	£1 = C$1.55
Average for 20X7	£1 = C$1.58
January 1, 20X8	£1 = C$1.63
Average for 20X8	£1 = C$1.47
December 31, 20X8	£1 = C$1.40

Birch's financial statements must be translated into Canadian dollars so that they can be consolidated with the financial statements of the Canadian parent.

Required

1. Assume that Birch's functional currency is the pound sterling. Calculate the translated Canadian-dollar balances for the following accounts for 20X8:
   a) Equipment
   b) Accumulated amortization—equipment
   c) Amortization expense
2. Assume that Birch's functional currency is the Canadian dollar. Calculate the translated Canadian-dollar balances for the following accounts for 20X8:
   a) Equipment
   b) Accumulated amortization—equipment
   [CGA–Canada adapted]

P9-5

On December 31, 20X3, Oak Company (Oak), a Canadian corporation, purchased 100% of the outstanding common shares of Maple Limited (Maple). Maple was incorporated on January 2, 20X0, and began operations immediately in the southwestern United States. Common shares were issued on the date of incorporation and no more common shares have been issued since then. The SFP for Maple at December 31, 20X9, was as follows:

Maple Limited
Statement of Financial Position
December 31, 20X9

Cash	US$ 100,000
Accounts receivable (note 1)	200,000
Inventory (note 2)	300,000
Equipment-net (note 3)	1,100,000
	US$1,700,000
Accounts payable	US$ 250,000
Bonds payable (note 4)	700,000
Common shares	100,000
Retained earnings	650,000
	US$1,700,000

Other Information

1. The accounts receivable relating to sales occurred evenly throughout the month of December 20X9.
2. Maple uses the FIFO method to account for its inventory. The inventory available for sale during the year was purchased as follows:

Date of Purchase	Cost of Purchase	Exchange Rate
December 31, 20X8	US$ 100,000	US$1.00 = C$1.31
March 1, 20X9	1,000,000	US$1.00 = C$1.35
November 1, 20X9	180,000	US$1.00 = C$1.38

3. The equipment was purchased on May 26, 20X3.
4. Bonds of US$700,000 were issued on May 26, 20X3, to finance the purchase of the equipment.
5. Maple reported net income of US$200,000, which was earned evenly throughout the year, and paid dividends of US$160,000 on July 1, 20X9.
6. Foreign exchange rates were as follows:

January 2, 20X0	US$1.00 = C$1.05
May 26, 20X3	US$1.00 = C$1.15
December 31, 20X3	US$1.00 = C$1.17
December 31, 20X8	US$1.00 = C$1.31
July 1, 20X9	US$1.00 = C$1.36
December 31, 20X9	US$1.00 = C$1.40
Average for December 20X9	US$1.00 = C$1.39
Average for 20X9	US$1.00 = C$1.34

Required

1. Translate the SFP of Maple at December 31, 20X9, into Canadian dollars using the temporal method. Assume the translated SFP will be consolidated with Oak's SFP. For retained earnings, simply use the amount required to balance your SFP.
2. Calculate the foreign exchange gain or loss on the bonds payable for the year ended December 31, 20X9.

3. Prepare an independent calculation of the translation gain or loss for 20X9, assuming that Maple's functional currency is the US dollar.
4. "Since the current-rate method uses the current rate to translate capital assets, the translated amount should represent the current value of the capital assets in Canadian dollars." Is this a valid statement? Briefly explain.
[CGA–Canada adapted]

P9-6

On January 1, 20X5, Pop Company of Regina, Saskatchewan, purchased 80% of the outstanding shares of Soda Limited of Switzerland. Soda's statements of financial position as at December 31, 20X4, and December 31, 20X5, and Soda's 20X5 statement of comprehensive income and retained earnings follow:

Soda Ltd.
Statement of Financial Position
at December 31

	20X5	20X4
Assets		
Cash	SF120,000	SF 50,000
Accounts receivable	85,000	75,000
Inventory	80,000	60,000
Equipment, net	250,000	300,000
	SF535,000	SF485,000
Liabilities and shareholders' equity		
Accounts payable	SF 60,000	SF 90,000
Bonds payable	200,000	200,000
Common shares	100,000	100,000
Retained earnings	175,000	95,000
	SF535,000	SF485,000

Soda Ltd.
Statement of Comprehensive Income and Retained Earnings
Year ended December 31, 20X5

Sales	SF500,000
Cost of sales	(280,000)
Amortization	(50,000)
Other expenses	(20,000)
Net income	150,000
Retained earnings, January 1, 20X5	95,000
	245,000
Dividends paid	70,000
Retained earnings, December 31, 20X5	SF175,000

Additional Information

1. Soda was incorporated on January 1, 20X2, at which time it acquired all of its equipment and issued its 10-year bonds.

2. Soda's purchases and sales occurred evenly during 20X5. Soda's December 31, 20X4, and December 31, 20X5, inventory was acquired evenly over the final six months of 20X4 and 20X5, respectively.
3. Dividends were paid on July 1, 20X5. Ignore income taxes.
4. Foreign exchange rates were as follows:

January 1, 20X2	SF1 = C$0.90
Average for July–December 20X4	SF1 = C$0.92
December 31, 20X4/January 1, 20X5	SF1 = C$0.94
July 1, 20X5	SF1 = C$0.98
December 31, 20X5	SF1 = C$1.02
Average for July–December 20X5	SF1 = C$1.00
Average for 20X5	SF1 = C$0.99

Required

1. Translate the liabilities and shareholders' equity of Soda as at December 31, 20X5, assuming that Soda's functional currency is the Swiss franc. Include a calculation of the cumulative translation adjustment.
2. Translate the following accounts from the financial statements of Soda for the year ended December 31, 20X5, assuming that Soda's functional currency is the Canadian dollar:
   a) Cost of sales
   b) Amortization expense
   c) Bonds payable

   [CGA–Canada]

P9-7

On December 31, 20X14, Pepper Company of Winnipeg acquired 100% of the outstanding shares of Salt Company of Switzerland. On this date, the fair values of Salt's identifiable assets and liabilities were equal to their carrying value. Salt's statements of financial position as at December 31, 20X14, and December 31, 20X15, and Salt's 20X15 statement of comprehensive income and retained earnings follow:

Salt Co.
Statement of Financial Position
December 31

	20X15	20X14
Assets		
Cash	SF 80,000	SF 60,000
Accounts receivable	140,000	80,000
Inventory	110,000	80,000
Equipment, net	250,000	280,000
	SF 580,000	SF 500,000
Liabilities and shareholders' equity		
Accounts payable	SF 150,000	SF 115,000
Bonds payable	120,000	120,000
Common shares	140,000	140,000
Retained earnings	170,000	125,000
	SF 580,000	SF 500,000

Salt Co.
Statement of Comprehensive Income and Retained Earnings
Year ended December 31, 20X15

Sales	SF 850,000
Cost of sales	(500,000)
Gross margin	350,000
Amortization expense	(30,000)
Other expenses	(245,000)
Net income	75,000
Retained earnings, January 1, 20X15	125,000
	200,000
Dividends paid	(30,000)
Retained earnings, December 31, 20X15	SF 170,000

Additional Information

1. Inventory on hand as at December 31, 20X14, and December 31, 20X15, was purchased evenly over the final three months of 20X14 and 20X15, respectively, from suppliers in Switzerland. Sales and purchases occurred evenly throughout the year.
2. The plant and equipment on hand at December 31, 20X14, was originally acquired for SF450,000 on January 1, 20X8, the date of Salt's incorporation. No plant and equipment was acquired or sold during fiscal 20X15.
3. Dividends were declared and paid on September 30, 20X15.
4. The bonds were issued on January 1, 20X10, and mature on December 31, 20X19. The Swiss franc has changed over time relative to the Canadian dollar, but the foreign exchange trend has little effect on Salt's sales prices, which are largely determined by local competition. Foreign exchange rates were as follows:

January 1, 20X8	SF1 = C$0.66
January 1, 20X10	SF1 = C$0.76
December 31, 20X14/January 1, 20X15	SF1 = C$0.86
July 1, 20X15	SF1 = C$0.92
September 30, 20X15	SF1 = C$0.94
December 31, 20X15	SF1 = C$0.96
Average for October–December 20X14	SF1 = C$0.84
Average for October–December 20X15	SF1 = C$0.95
Average for 20X15	SF1 = C$0.91

Required

1. Determine Salt's functional currency. State three facts from the problem to support your conclusion.
2. Ignore your answer in part 1 and assume that Salt's functional currency is the Canadian dollar. Translate the statement of comprehensive income and retained earnings for the year ended December 31, 20X15, to Canadian dollars. Include an independent calculation of any exchange gains/losses.
3. Ignore your answers to parts 1 and 2 and assume that Salt's functional currency is the Swiss franc. Calculate the cumulative translation adjustment on its December 31, 20X15, translated SFP.

   [CGA–Canada]

P9-8

On December 31, 20X5, KTR Corporation acquired 80% of the outstanding shares of SJC Limited for $5,000,000. KTR is a Vancouver-based company, while SJC is based in Las Vegas, in the US. SJC's financial statements follow:

SJC Ltd.
Statement of Financial Position
as of December 31

	20X6	20X5
Assets		
Cash	US$ 300,000	US$ 250,000
Accounts receivable	1,350,000	1,100,000
Inventory	2,100,000	1,800,000
Equipment, net	3,250,000	3,000,000
	US $7,000,000	US $6,150,000
Liabilities and shareholders' equity		
Accounts payable	US$ 560,000	US$ 400,000
Bonds payable	3,000,000	3,000,000
Common shares	1,500,000	1,500,000
Retained earnings	1,940,000	1,250,000
	US $7,000,000	US $6,150,000

SJC Ltd.
Statement of Comprehensive Income and Retained Earnings
Year ended December 31, 20X5

Sales	US $5,000,000
Cost of sales	(3,200,000)
Amortization expense	(350,000)
Bond interest expense	(240,000)
Other expenses	(470,000)
Net income	740,000
Retained earnings, January 1, 20X5	1,250,000
	1,990,000
Dividends paid	(50,000)
Retained earnings, December 31, 20X5	US $1,940,000

Additional Information

1. Inventory on hand as at December 31, 20X5, and December 31, 20X6, was purchased when the exchange rates were US$1.00 = C$1.10 and US$1.00 = C$1.28, respectively. Sales and purchases occurred evenly throughout 20X6.
2. Of the $3,000,000 plant and equipment (net) recorded on the December 31, 20X5, SFP, $2,000,000 (net) was purchased on December 31, 20X1, and $1,000,000 (net) was purchased on December 31, 20X5. Plant and equipment costing an additional $600,000 was purchased on December 31, 20X6. The plant and equipment purchased in 20X1 and 20X5 is being amortized at $250,000 per year and $100,000 per year respectively.
3. Dividends were declared and paid on October 31, 20X6.
4. The bonds were issued at par on December 31, 20X1, with an 8% interest rate, and they mature on December 31, 20X11. They pay interest semi-annually.

5. Ignore the impact of income taxes in the question.
6. Foreign exchange rates were as follows:

December 31, 20X1	US$1.00 = C$1.00
December 31, 20X5	US$1.00 = C$1.20
October 31, 20X6	US$1.00 = C$1.27
December 31, 20X6	US$1.00 = C$1.30
Average for 20X6	US$1.00 = C$1.25

Required

1. You are the controller of KTR. Assuming that SJC's functional currency is the Canadian dollar, translate the SCI for the year ended December 31, 20X6, into Canadian dollars. Include an independent calculation of any foreign exchange gains/losses.
2. Assuming that SJC's functional currency is the Canadian dollar, translate the following SFP accounts for SJC into Canadian dollars as at December 31, 20X6:
   a) Accounts receivable
   b) Plant and equipment (net)
   c) Bonds payable
3. Assuming that SJC's functional currency is the US dollar, translate the following SFP accounts for SJC into Canadian dollars as at December 31, 20X6:
   a) Plant and equipment (net)
   b) Common shares
   c) Retained earnings
4. Assume that you have just been hired at KTR and you are discussing the operations of SJC with the chief executive officer. List two questions about the operations of SJC that you could ask the CEO to help you establish SJC's functional currency.
   [CGA–Canada]

P9-9

FranCo Corporation is a foreign subsidiary of Desk Company, a Canadian company. FranCo was acquired on January 1, 20X6, and manufactures furniture for sale based on sales prices determined by worldwide competition. The chief financial officer of FranCo emailed the following December 31, 20X7, financial statements, stated in euros (€), to you, the CFO of Desk:

Franco Corporation
Statement of Financial Position

	December 31, 20X7	December 31, 20X6
Assets		
Cash	€ 300,000	€ 250,000
Accounts receivable	350,000	325,000
Inventory	500,000	425,000
Equipment, net	575,000	300,000
	€1,725,000	€1,300,000
Liabilities and shareholders' equity		
Accounts payable	€ 145,000	€ 200,000
Bonds payable	400,000	400,000
Common shares	900,000	500,000
Retained earnings	280,000	200,000
	€1,725,000	€1,300,000

Franco Corporation
Statement of Comprehensive Income
Years ended December 31, 20X7 and 20X6

	20X7	20X6
Sales	€ 2,100,000	€ 2,000,000
Cost of goods sold	1,600,000	1,500,000
Gross profit	500,000	500,000
Selling and administrative	145,000	120,000
Bond interest expense	30,000	30,000
Amortization	125,000	100,000
Income before income taxes	200,000	250,000
Income taxes	80,000	100,000
Net income	€ 120,000	€ 150,000

Additional Information

1. The following exchange rates were noted:

January 1, 20X1	€1 = C$1.55
January 1, 20X6	€1 = C$1.52
Average for October 1 – December 31, 20X6	€1 = C$1.48
Average for 20X6	€1 = C$1.50
December 31, 20X6	€1 = C$1.45
July 1, 20X7	€1 = C$1.44
Average for October 1 – December 31, 20X7	€1 = C$1.43
November 1, 20X7	€1 = C$1.41
Average for 20X7	€1 = C$1.42
December 31, 20X7	€1 = C$1.40

2. On January 1, 20X1, FranCo acquired equipment for €900,000 with an expected useful life of nine years. On July 1, 20X7, it acquired €400,000 of new equipment with an expected useful life of eight years. FranCo amortizes its equipment on a straight-line basis, calculated monthly.
3. FranCo partly financed its acquisition of equipment on January 1, 20X1 by issuing €400,000, 8-year, 5% bonds payable. Similarly, FranCo financed its acquisition of equipment in 20X7 by issuing €400,000 of common shares on July 1, 20X7.
4. Inventory on hand on December 31, 20X6 and December 31, 20X7 includes a significant amount of wood imported from western Canadian timber firms. It was purchased evenly over the last three months of 20X6 and 20X7.
5. Dividends of €40,000 were declared and paid on November 1, 20X7. No dividends were paid in 20X6.
6. All other sales, purchases, and expenses occurred evenly each year.

Required

1. Should FranCo's financial statements be translated into Canadian dollars using the temporal method or the current-rate method? Provide two facts from the question to support your answer.

2. Disregard your response to part 1. Using the current-rate method, translate the following accounts from FranCo's 20X7 financial statements into Canadian dollars.
   a) Accounts receivable
   b) Inventory
   c) Bonds payable
   d) Common shares
   e) Amortization expense
3. Disregard your responses to parts 1 and 2. Using the temporal method, translate the following accounts into Canadian dollars at December 31, 20X7.
   a) Accounts receivable
   b) Bond interest expense
   c) Accounts payable
   d) Inventory
   e) Amortization expense
   f) Cost of goods sold
4. Using the temporal method, calculate the exchange gain or loss that would result from the translation of FranCo's 20X7 financial statements.
   [CGA–Canada adapted]

P9-10

On January 2, 20X2, EL Limited established a subsidiary in Mexico City, Mexico. The subsidiary was named GC Company and the cost of EL's investment was C$500,000. When this investment was translated into Mexican pesos, the cost of the investment was *p*5,000,000. On January 2, 20X2, GC obtained long-term debt of *p*1,000,000 from a bank in Mexico City when the exchange rate was *p*1.00 = C$0.10.The long-term debt must be repaid at the end of four years. The opening SFP for GC on January 2, 20X2, is shown below:

GC Company
Statement of Financial Position
January 2, 20X2

Current monetary assets	*p* 6,000,000
Long-term debt	1,000,000
Common shares	5,000,000
	p 6,000,000

The December 31, 20X2, SFP and SCI for GC are shown below:

GC Company
Statement of Comprehensive Income
December 31, 20X2

Revenues	*p*3,200,000
Amortization expense	300,000
Operating expenses	2,200,000
Total expenses	2,500,000
Net income	*p* 700,000

GC Company
Statement of Financial Position
December 31, 20X2

Current monetary assets	p2,800,000
Capital assets	4,900,000
Accumulated amortization	(300,000)
	p7,400,000
Current monetary liabilities	p 900,000
Long-term debt	1,000,000
Common shares	5,000,000
Retained earnings	500,000
	p7,400,000

The relevant exchange rates for the Mexican peso were as follows:

January 2, 20X2	p1.00 = C$0.10
Average for 20X2	p1.00 = C$0.12
December 31, 20X2	p1.00 = C$0.14

During 20X2, GC purchased capital assets when the exchange rate was p1.00 = C$0.11. Dividends were declared and paid when the exchange rate was p1.00 = C$0.13. Revenues and other expenses were incurred evenly throughout the year.

Required

1. Calculate the exchange gains/losses for the temporal and current-rate methods to be disclosed on the December 31, 20X2, SFP and SCI.
2. Translate the 20X2 SFP and SCI for GC assuming GC's functional currency is the:
   a) Mexican peso
   b) Canadian dollar

[CGA–Canada]

P9-11

On January 1, 20X6, Woods Ltd. formed a foreign subsidiary that issued all of its currently outstanding common shares on that date. Selected captions from the SFPs, all of which are shown in local currency units (LCU), are as follows:

	20X7	20X6
Accounts receivable, net of allowance for uncollectable accounts of 2,200 LCU at December 31, 20X7, and 2,000 LCU at December 31, 20X6	40,000	35,000
Inventories, at cost	80,000	75,000
Capital assets, net of accumulated depreciation of 31,000 LCU at December 31, 20X7, and 14,000 LCU at December 31, 20X6	163,000	150,000
Long-term debt	100,000	120,000
Common stock, authorized shares par value 10 LCU per share, issued and outstanding 5,000 shares at December 31, 20X7, and December 31, 20X6	50,000	50,000

Additional Information:

Exchange Rates

January 1, 20X6 to July 31, 20X6	2.1 LCU to $1
August 1, 20X6 to October 31, 20X6	1.9 LCU to $1
November 1, 20X6 to June 30, 20X7	1.8 LCU to $1
July 1, 20X7 to December 31, 20X7	1.6 LCU to $1
Average rate for 20X6	2.0 LCU to $1
Average rate for 20X7	1.7 LCU to $1

Accounts Receivable—Analysis

	20X7	20X6
	(in LCUs)	
Balance beginning of year	37,000	—
Sales (36,000 LCU per month in 20X7 and 31,000 per month in 20X6)	432,000	372,000
Collections	(423,600)	(334,000)
Write-offs (May 20X7 and December 20X6)	(3,200)	(1,000)
	42,200	37,000

Allowance for Uncollectable Accounts

	20X7	20X6
	(in LCUs)	
Balance beginning of year	2,000	—
Provision for uncollectables	3,400	3,000
Write-offs	(3,200)	(1,000)
	2,200	2,000

Inventory, FIFO Basis

	20X7	20X6
	(in LCUs)	
Balance beginning of year	75,000	—
Purchases (June 20X7 and June 20X6)	335,000	375,000
Less: Inventory at year-end	(80,000)	(75,000)
Cost of goods sold	330,000	300,000

On January 1, 20X6, Woods' foreign subsidiary purchased land for 24,000 LCU and capital assets for 140,000 LCU. On July 1, 20X7, additional equipment was purchased for 30,000 LCU. Capital assets are being depreciated on a straight-line basis over a 10-year period with no salvage value. A full year's depreciation is taken in the year of purchase.

On January 15, 20X6, 7% bonds with a face value of 120,000 LCU were sold. The bonds pay interest on July 15 and January 15 each year. The first payment was made on July 15, 20X6.

Required

Prepare a schedule translating the selected captions above into Canadian dollars at December 31, 20X6, and December 31, 20X7, using the temporal method. Show supporting computations in good form.

[CGA–Canada adapted]

P9-12

Refer to **P9-2**. The comparative year-end SFPs for Hilary Co. were as follows:

	20X3	20X2
Cash	CF 200,000	CF 500,000
Accounts receivable	400,000	300,000
Inventory	400,000	200,000
Land	500,000	—
Equipment (net)	1,700,000	2,000,000
Total assets	CF3,200,000	CF3,000,000
Accounts payable	CF 500,000	CF 400,000
Bonds payable	1,800,000	1,800,000
Common shares	500,000	500,000
Retained earnings	400,000	300,000
Total liabilities and equities	CF3,200,000	CF3,000,000

The common shares were issued when the exchange rate was $0.64.

The land was purchased at the end of 20X3. The bonds were issued at the end of 20X1, and mature at the end of 20X7. The exchange rate at the end of 20X1 was $0.74. Dividends are declared and paid at the end of each year. The retained earnings at the end of 20X2 were earned at an average rate of $0.79.

Required

1. Translate the 20X2 and 20X3 SFPs, using the current-rate method. (Note that each year's SFP is translated at the current rate *at that year's SFP date.*)
2. Translate the 20X2 and 20X3 SFPs, using the temporal method.
3. Calculate the translation gain or loss for 20X3, under each translation method.

P9-13

SEQEA Company was incorporated on January 2, 20X4, and commenced active operations immediately. Common shares were issued on the date of incorporation and no new common shares have been issued since then. On December 31, 20X12, RST Company purchased 70% of the outstanding common shares of SEQEA for 1,500,000 Swedish kronor (SEK).

SEQEA's main operations are located in Sweden. It manufactures and sells fine Swedish furniture. Approximately 40% of its sales are to RST, 40% to companies throughout Western Europe, and 20% to China. To satisfy the extra demand from RST, SEQEA built a new manufacturing plant in Sweden in 20X14. The plant was financed with retained earnings and a loan from a Swedish bank. Most of the material and labour for the manufacturing operation are obtained from local sources in Sweden.

For the year ended December 31, 20X15, the SCI for SEQEA was as follows:

Sales and other revenue	SEK 8,500,000
Cost of goods sold	4,000,000
Amortization expense	150,000
Other expenses	3,850,000
Net income	SEK 500,000

The comparative SFP in condensed form for SEQEA was as follows:

	20X15	20X14
Inventory (Note 1)	SEK 200,000	SEK 180,000
Property, plant, and equipment—net (Note 2)	1,700,000	1,850,000
Monetary assets	2,400,000	2,170,000
	SEK 4,300,000	SEK 4,200,000
Monetary liabilities	SEK 2,400,000	SEK 2,500,000
Non-monetary liabilities (Note 3)	195,000	170,000
Common shares	100,000	100,000
Retained earnings	1,605,000	1,430,000
	SEK 4,300,000	SEK 4,200,000

Additional Information

1. The ending inventory for 20X14 and 20X15 was manufactured evenly throughout the last month of each year. The additions to inventory, sales and other revenue, and other expenses occurred evenly throughout the year.
2. The property, plant, and equipment on hand at the end of 20X12 had been purchased by SEQEA on January 10, 20X9. The new manufacturing plant was completed on December 31, 20X14 for a total cost of SEK 100,000. The amortization on the new plant in 20X15 was SEK 5,000. There have been no other purchases or sales of capital assets since 20X12.
3. The non-monetary liabilities represent obligations for SEQEA to provide services over the next 12 months. The obligations arose evenly throughout the last 6 months of 20X15.
4. Dividends were declared and paid on December 31, 20X15.
5. SEQEA's financial statements must be translated to Canadian dollars so that they can be consolidated with the financial statements of RST.
   Foreign exchange rates were as follows:

January 2, 20X4	SEK 1 = C$0.30
January 10, 20X9	SEK 1 = C$0.25
December 31, 20X12	SEK 1 = C$0.24
Average for 20X14	SEK 1 = C$0.23
Average for December 20X14	SEK 1 = C$0.21
December 31, 20X14	SEK 1 = C$0.20
Average for 20X15	SEK 1 = C$0.18
Average for July to December 20X15	SEK 1 = C$0.17
Average for December 20X15	SEK 1 = C$0.16
December 31, 20X15	SEK 1 = C$0.15

Required

1. The CFO is wondering whether SEQEA's financial statements should be translated into Canadian dollars using the current-rate or the temporal method. What is your recommendation? Why?

2. Ignore your answer to part 1 and determine the Canadian dollar amount for the following items on the financial statements for the year ended December 31, 20X15, under the current-rate method:
   a) Other expenses
   b) Inventory at end of year
   c) Common shares
   d) The translation gain or loss for 20X15
3. Ignore your answers to parts 1 and 2 and determine the Canadian dollar amount for the following items on the financial statements for the year ended December 31, 20X15, under the temporal method:
   a) Cost of goods sold
   b) Amortization expense
   c) Monetary assets
   d) Non-monetary liabilities
   e) The translation gain or loss for 20X15.

   [CGA–Canada adapted]

10

Financial Reporting for Not-for-Profit Organizations

LEARNING OBJECTIVES

After studying this chapter, students should be able to:

1. identify the characteristics of not-for-profit organizations (NFPs) and explain how NFPs differ from business enterprises;
2. explain the primary reporting issues that arise from the special characteristics of NFPs;
3. describe the two GAAP methods of accounting for NFPs: the deferral method and the restricted fund method; and
4. describe the application and use of budgetary control accounts and encumbrance accounting.

INTRODUCTION

The Canadian Cancer Society (CCS) is a national organization dedicated to finding a cure for cancer and to supporting people living with cancer. CCS is a registered charity that operates through a national office and 10 provincial divisions. In its 2009 annual report, CCS reported revenue in excess of $200 million. Significant sources of this revenue include well-known campaigns such as the "Relay for Life" campaign and a more traditional annual giving campaign.

Not-for-profit organizations such as the Canadian Cancer Society differ significantly from profit-oriented business organizations. For example, the Canadian Cancer Society is a corporation "without share capital." Since there are no shareholders, the typical primary user of a business's financial statements is non-existent. Another difference is that there are legal restrictions on how some of CCS's revenues can be used. The donors of CCS's restricted funds have needs that differ from the needs of users of business financial statements. The different needs of different users of an organization like CCS lead to different reporting objectives. Different reporting objectives lead to different accounting issues. In this chapter we will examine the unique accounting issues that arise for not-for-profit organizations.

Most study of accounting focuses on business enterprises. However, there are many organizations in Canada that are not businesses. The non-business sector includes not-for-profit organizations and the government, i.e., the entire public sector. Schools, universities, hospitals, social service agencies, performing arts organizations, museums, trade associations, unions, political parties, and philanthropic foundations are a few examples of the *not-for-profit organizations* that have an important place in our society. Municipal, territorial, provincial, and federal governments are examples of the different levels of *governments* that exist in Canada.

Overall, close to 20% of all Canadian employment is in not-for-profit organizations or governments. The larger segments are health care, education, and the various levels of government and government services. Indeed, *non-business organizations* comprise a larger component of the Canadian economy than manufacturing.

Given the importance of non-business organizations, not only in Canada but worldwide, it is somewhat surprising that so little attention is given to this important segment of the economy in accounting courses. Generally, it is only when students reach the advanced level that they are introduced to the particular problems faced by not-for-profit organizations and by governments. Well, better late than never! In this chapter, we discuss not-for-profit organizations. We discuss governmental accounting in Chapter 11, "Public Sector Financial Reporting."

OVERVIEW OF NON-BUSINESS ORGANIZATIONS

As a first step, we must make a distinction between *non-business* and *not-for-profit* organizations. A **non-business organization** is any organization that is not a private enterprise operating for profit. Non-business organizations can be roughly divided into three groups: (1) governments, (2) governmental units, and (3) not-for-profit organizations.

Governments are the governing bodies (legislatures, councils, etc.) at the federal, provincial, territorial, regional, and municipal levels. **Governmental accounting** is the body of principles and practices that has been developed for recordkeeping and reporting by the various levels of government. Governmental accounting is usually regulated by law. The accounting and reporting principles on which the law is based were developed by governments and by professional organizations. In Canada, the pronouncements of the CICA's Public Sector Accounting Board influence financial reporting by governments. As we will see in the next chapter, governments have quite different financial statement objectives because of the sources of their funds, their ability to tax, and their legal reporting obligations.

Governmental units are organizations that are set up by governments to carry out some aspect of their policy. Governmental units include school boards, public housing authorities, parking authorities, public cemeteries, water systems, and electric utilities. Such units may be incorporated, but they are corporations without share capital. *Governmental units* are not the same as **crown corporations**, such as VIA Rail Canada or the Liquor Control Board of Ontario, which are business corporations *with share capital* but that have the government as the only shareholder. Some governmental units do carry on some type of business (e.g., local transportation systems), but they are public-sector organizations rather than private enterprises. Therefore, they fall within the general classification of non-business organizations.

Not-for-profit organizations (NFPs) are neither business nor governmental organizations. not-for-profit organizations function as educational, scientific, charitable, artistic, or social agencies. They can be incorporated or unincorporated—if incorporated, they are *corporations without share capital*, such as the Canadian Cancer Society cited above. The term "social agency" covers a lot of ground, since a social agency can range anywhere from an amateur baseball club to a major hospital, with the Salvation Army, the Liberal Party of Canada, and the Kiwanis Club in between.

It is neither possible nor necessary to draw a clear line between governmental units and not-for-profit organizations. Canadian universities, for example, usually are established as independent corporate entities. But they are dependent on governments for most of their funding and they carry out part of government's educational policy. Similarly, hospitals and public utilities are semi-independent corporations that have some characteristics of governmental units. For accounting purposes, the distinction between not-for-profit organizations and governmental units is not crucial. The objectives of both are similar.

Terms other than *not-for-profit organization* are often used to describe the widely diverse types of organizations that are in this sector of the economy. The most popular alternative term is **non-profit** organization, usually abbreviated as NPO.[1] Another alternative is "volunteer organization," because they frequently use the services of volunteers for delivering the organization's services. Also, the directors of not-for-profit organizations are generally prohibited from being paid, and thus are volunteer directors. In this book we will use the term *not-for-profit organization*. In this chapter, we focus on not-for-profit organizations, including governmental units that are government not-for-profit organizations.

ACCOUNTING STANDARDS FOR NOT-FOR-PROFIT ORGANIZATIONS

Accounting for NFPs has been a concern among accounting standard-setters across the world. There have been attempts to create international standards, but those have come to naught. Instead, NFP accounting has been addressed by each nation (or region, in the case of the European Union) individually. This "go it alone" approach is largely due to national differences in NFP economic environments and legislation.

In Canada, GAAP for NFPs is contained in the *CICA Handbook, Part III*. Generally speaking, the *CICA Handbook* requires NFPs to comply with ASPE reporting—*CICA Handbook, Part II, except* as otherwise specified in *Part III*.

In practice, NFPs are "required" to follow Canadian GAAP, but this is an effective requirement only when the NFP is audited and is required to get a "clean" audit opinion. An audit usually is required by provincial legislation for large NFPs such as universities and hospitals. Small NFPs seldom have an audit unless it is required by a funding organization, such as a government ministry.

NFPs often provide special-purpose financial statements for specific users. For example, provincial Ministries of Social Services usually require an NFP to submit both its budget request and its financial statements in a format that complies with Ministry regulations (which may differ from CICA standards); from the Ministry's point of view, the main purpose of an audit is to provide assurance that the NFP has an effective internal control system and that the managers aren't subverting the money for unauthorized (or personal) purposes.

1. This is the more traditional term for a not-for-profit organization and is in common use (eg., government departments such as the Canada Revenue Agency still use the term non-profit organization).

NFPs are quite different from business enterprises. The following sections will explain the many fundamental differences. Once we understand just how different NFPs can be from businesses, we then can examine NFP accounting options.

CHARACTERISTICS OF NOT-FOR-PROFIT ORGANIZATIONS

Canada's not-for-profit sector, as a proportion of the country's total workforce, is the second largest in the world—the largest is the Netherlands. Not-for-profit organizations employ approximately 2 million individuals, representing 11.1% of the economically active population in Canada. The not-for-profit sector represents $79.1 billion or 7.8% of Canada's GDP.[2] A recent study estimated that there were 161,000 not-for-profit organizations in Canada. The distribution of these organizations is skewed to many small organizations and very few large organizations (see Exhibit 10-1). As Exhibit 10-1 shows, 41% of organizations in the not-for-profit sector had less than $30,000 in revenue, 88% had less than $500,000 in revenue—only 1% had more than $10 million in revenue.

EXHIBIT 10-1

Distribution of Organizations and Not-for-profit Sector Revenues by Organization Size

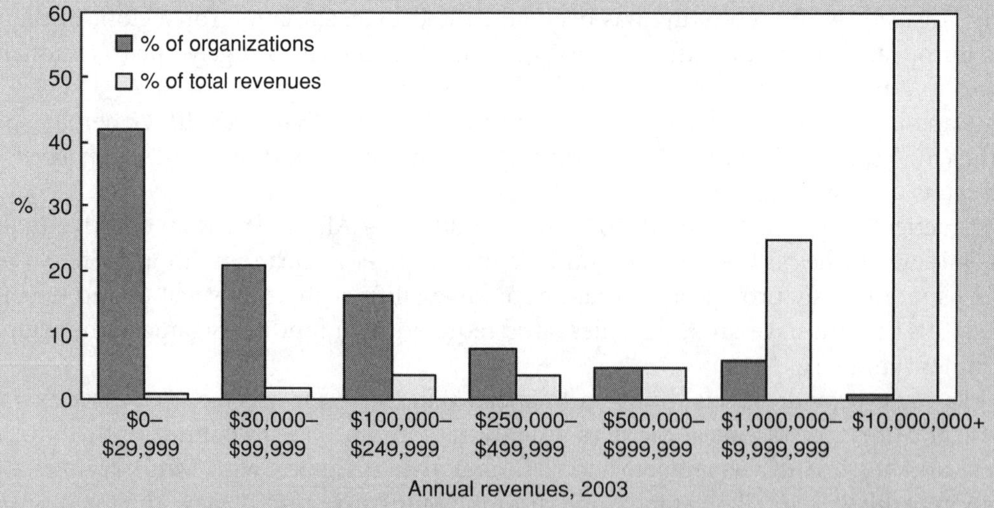

Source: Adapted from Statistics Canada, Cornerstones of Community: Highlights from the National Survey of Nonprofit and Voluntary Organizations 61-533-XIE2004001 2003, Revised, Released June 30, 2005.

2. Imagine Canada, *The Canadian Nonprofit and Voluntary Sector in Comparative Perspective*, 2005.

The not-for-profit sector can be divided into two groups: (1) a core group consisting of a large number of relatively small organizations; and (2) a smaller group consisting of a few relatively large organizations. The primary constituents of this second group are hospitals, colleges, and universities.

Clearly there will be differences between these two groups. For example, it is estimated that government funding makes more than 70% of the revenue of hospitals, colleges, and universities but makes up only about 20% of the funding of small NFPs.[3] These organizations will also differ in terms of need for and understanding of sophisticated accounting.

With this in mind we will first examine how NFPs differ from business enterprises. Later, we will consider how the differences among NFPs may affect the accounting choices made by NFPs.

There are four very fundamental ways in which not-for-profit organizations (NFPs) differ from business enterprises:

1. NFPs have *members* instead of owners; there are no residual economic interests.
2. The organization has a different "bottom line." The organization's objectives may be to serve the common good rather than to maximize net income or generate a return on investment.
3. The nature of revenues and the relationship between revenues and costs differs significantly from those of businesses. As well, the sources of revenue often sharply restrict the flexibility of the organization to use that revenue.
4. The suppliers of funds (who are the primary users of the financial statements) are not providing capital to earn a return on their investment. Therefore, financial reporting objectives often differ significantly from the profit sector.

These four characteristics profoundly affect the nature of NFP financial reporting. We will expand upon each of these characteristics in the following sections.

No Owners

Not-for-profit organizations have no owners. Regardless of whether an NFP is incorporated or unincorporated, no one has a right to the residual earnings of the organization. As we have already mentioned, incorporated NFPs are legally defined as *corporations without share capital*. Since NFPs have no owners, they have no transferable ownership interest.

Although NFPs have no shareholders, they do have *members* who elect the board of directors.[4] The constitution of the organization specifies the conditions for membership. Membership may be either *open* or *closed*.

In an open membership, the conditions for membership are clearly specified in the constitution or bylaws of the organization, and membership is available to anyone who is able to fulfill the membership requirements. A closed membership exists when the members are

3. *Satellite Account of Not-for-profit Institutions and Volunteering*, Statistics Canada, December 2008.
4. In some NFPs, the members elect only some of the directors, while other directors are appointed by stakeholder groups, such as government or constituency groups.

designated by the board of directors. Membership is *closed* in the sense that it is not automatically open to all otherwise-qualified individuals who apply, and because the board has the power to change the requirements for membership at any board meeting. In some not-for-profit organizations, the directors are the *only* members of the organization—in effect, the board elects itself.

A Different "Bottom Line"

NFPs exist to perform a service. Since there are no residual economic interests, financial performance on its own is not a primary objective. Obviously, an NFP must remain financially viable to continue to operate and to fulfill its service objectives, but financial viability is a *means to an end* rather than being the end itself as is the case with business enterprises.

Businesses provide goods and services to individuals (or to organized groups such as other businesses) at a price. Price is the rationing mechanism, but it also provides the revenue that finances the cost of providing the goods and services. Goods and services that are consumed by individuals (and thus unavailable to others) and that are rationed are referred to as **private goods and services**.

Not-for-profit organizations may also provide private goods and services. This is particularly true in NFPs such as sports or social clubs, wherein the primary objective of the organization is to provide services to its members. Private goods are also provided by organizations such as trade unions and professional organizations.

However, an NFP may provide goods and services that are not intended to benefit specific individuals but instead to benefit groups within society at large, or the common welfare. Greenpeace, for example, is engaged in environmental awareness activities that benefit society as a whole. The Canadian Cancer Society is engaged in supporting cancer research and in increasing public awareness of cancer (and understanding for those who are afflicted with it). The benefits of the activities of organizations such as Greenpeace and the Canadian Cancer Society are available to all individuals within the "target" group either free or at a nominal charge—these benefits are known as **collective goods and services** or **public goods and services**. Other examples of collective goods include accounting standard-setting, AIDS awareness programs, anti-racism campaigns, and museum exhibitions.

Collective goods are not provided by business enterprises; collective goods are provided *only* by governments and by not-for-profit organizations. Because there is no parallel in the private sector, proprietary accounting is of little help in designing financial reports for providers of collective goods. Accounting standard setters have implicitly acknowledged this fact in providing for different accounting principles for governments (as we will discuss in Chapter 11) as well as for NFPs.

The accounting policies of an NFP are not driven foremost by a need to determine residual interest, as is the case with shareholders in a business corporation. NFPs do, of course, have a residual of net assets. NFPs also have recognized costs, but the residual "bottom line" of revenues minus recognized costs is more of a true *residual*, *what is left over*, rather than a business-type net income measure.

Relationship Between Revenue and Costs

In business enterprises, the providers of revenue are the beneficiaries of the businesses' goods and services. There is a direct link between the service performed, the beneficiary of the service, and the generation of revenue. Therefore, much of business accounting focuses on *matching* to revenue the costs incurred to generate that revenue.

In some NFPs, there is a similar link. Clubs, private societies, and religious organizations generate revenue primarily from their members and spend that revenue primarily on activities and services that benefit their members. For convenience, we can refer to those organizations wherein the members are the primary (or only) beneficiary of the organization's goods and services as being **self-beneficial organizations**. The members provide the primary revenues, and they receive the benefits of the goods and services.

However, many other types of NFPs do not derive their primary revenues from the beneficiaries of their services. Instead, most social service agencies and arts organizations obtain the bulk of their revenue from governments or private donors, or both. When the beneficiaries of the goods and services are different from the providers of the resources, the NFP is a **public-beneficial organization**.[5]

A key aspect of public-beneficial NFPs is that their revenue is largely independent of the costs. The revenue comes from one group, but the money is spent on serving a different group. This is very different from businesses, where the costs are incurred to earn the revenue. Therefore, not-for-profit organizations (and governments) need expenditure controls that are markedly different from those normally encountered in private enterprise.

Businesses measure their expenses in relation to revenue, thereby using the cost/revenue relationship as a control device. In contrast, when revenues are received by an NFP from individual donors or as a block grant from government, the relationship between costs and revenues is broken and costs must be controlled directly. Therefore, the budgetary and management reporting system of NFPs is often designed to prevent managers from exceeding their *spending* authority—*expenditures* become more of a focus than *expenses*.

Some or all of the donations or grants received by a not-for-profit organization may be restricted for particular uses or programs. The donor wants assurance that the funds were used for the intended purpose. The accounting and reporting system must be able to match expenditures to specific programs or purposes. Funds are not transferable from one program to another; therefore, it may not be meaningful to combine revenues and expenditures relating to different programs into a single operating statement for the NFP as a whole.

For example, a school or university will have a large amount of operating funds (grants from government and fees received from students) that are specifically designated for operating the educational programs. The operating funds cannot be used for buildings or for ancillary activities such as providing free parking for faculty or low-cost meals for students. The school will receive separate capital grants that can be used only for capital projects such as new buildings or substantial renovations, and there will also be scholarship funds that must be used only for student aid. Therefore, the accounting and financial reporting system of

5. Charitable organizations are sometimes called "beneficial organizations," which is the same idea.

many NFPs must be able to distinguish between the various funds and be able to show that the various restrictions have been observed.

Objectives of Financial Reporting

The primary users of the financial statements of a not-for-profit organization are the suppliers of its funds. Funds are derived from (1) members, (2) granting agencies, (3) the general public, and (4) creditors. The objectives of financial statements for not-for-profit organizations are focussed on the needs of users. In general, the financial reporting objectives for not-for-profit organizations are:

- stewardship;
- measuring the cost of services rendered;
- cash-flow prediction; and
- management evaluation.

The first two are the primary objectives; the others tend to flow from satisfying the first two objectives. The relevance and priority of the primary objectives depends on the characteristics of the not-for-profit organization.

If a public-beneficial organization provides collective goods and services using funds donated by the public, *stewardship reporting* of the resources provided by the contributors is most likely to be the primary objective. Greenpeace is a good example. Measurement of the cost of Greenpeace's environmental protection activities is of limited usefulness; there is no meaningful measure of output and thus no useful cost of providing services can be determined. The emphasis in NFP reporting often is on disposition of the resources provided for specific purposes or programs rather than on the costs of services provided. This is an *input* base of reporting rather than the *output* basis that we are accustomed to in business reporting.

On the other hand, a public-beneficial organization may provide private goods and services on a *cost recovery basis*. An overnight hostel for homeless people may be supported by reimbursement on a fee-for-service basis from the city government. The city is the source of funds, and the city will want to know the cost per bed per night; the city may support several such programs and will want to compare the efficiency of the services provided. In such a case, measuring the cost of service becomes the primary reporting objective, and an output base of reporting similar to that used by business enterprises is appropriate.

A distinctive feature of NFP financial reporting is a strong commonality of interests among the various users of the statements. Members, managers, directors, and creditors need to see the organization and its programs in the same light as do the major providers of the resources. Managers and directors are accountable to the resource providers for the disposition of resources entrusted to their care. Creditors are also aware that future cash flows may be coming from the suppliers of resources (e.g., government ministries) rather than from the sale of goods and services.

Therefore, there often is a strong dominant influence by the providers of the resources in shaping financial reporting objectives and thereby determining accounting policies. This is particularly true of public-beneficial organizations that are providing goods and services (either private or collective) with a fixed revenue base.

CONCEPT CHECK 10-1

Companion Website

1. Describe four ways in which NFPs differ from business enterprises.
2. What are *collective goods and services*? What types of organizations offer collective goods and services?
3. What is a *public-beneficial organization*? Explain how a public-beneficial organization differs from a *self-beneficial organization*.
4. What are the financial reporting objectives for NFPs?

PRIMARY REPORTING ISSUES

There are several important reporting issues that shape the financial reporting of not-for-profit organizations. The primary reporting issues for an NFP are:

1. expense versus expenditure reporting;
2. capital assets;
3. segregation of resources and expense allocations;
4. defining the reporting entity; and
5. revenue recognition.

We will discuss these issues first, and then we will examine the basic reporting options that are available to NFPs. An NFP should choose the option that best meets its users' needs.

Expense Versus Expenditure Reporting

There are three different bases on which the resource outflows of any organization can be recognized in the statement of operations:

- *Disbursement* basis: outflows are recognized only when the cash is paid out or disbursed (i.e., a strict cash basis of reporting).
- *Expenditure* basis: outflows are recognized when liabilities are incurred or cash is paid out (i.e., accrual accounting applied to liabilities).
- *Expense* basis: outflows are recognized when goods and services are used in the operations (i.e., a "full accrual" basis of reporting).

Not-for-profit organizations must decide whether they are going to recognize their costs on the basis of disbursements, expenditures, or expenses. If they have a GAAP constraint[6] the *CICA*

6. Some not-for-profit organizations may have a GAAP constraint imposed by their funding body. Most not-for-profit organizations, however, will only have a GAAP constraint if they voluntarily choose to follow GAAP.

Handbook requires the expense basis. However, many of the small NFPs may not have a GAAP constraint and further, their members may not have the expertise to prepare or understand GAAP-compliant statements. Therefore, it is worthwhile to undertake a brief examination of alternatives to GAAP.

Disbursement Basis A disbursement (i.e., strict cash) basis may be suitable for small organizations with few accrued expenses or payables. The use of a strict cash basis, however, may result in reported expenditures that do not properly reflect the commitments made by the organization during the reporting period. Strict cash basis reporting can cause an organization to lose control of its resource management and to lose track of what it owes.

The real choice therefore is between recognizing costs in the statement of operations on the basis of *expenditures* or of *expenses*. The expenditure basis has little equivalency in the private sector, where we normally think in terms of expenses. But the notion of expenses is related to the concept of profit, which generally does not exist in the not-for-profit sector.

Expenditure Basis An expenditure occurs when a liability is incurred or cash (or other asset) is paid out to obtain goods or services. Note that the emphasis is on *obtaining* goods and services instead of on *using* goods and services, which is the focus of expense.

The expenditure basis means that costs are recorded in operations when incurred, either by disbursing cash or by incurring a liability. Supplies, for example, would be recognized in the statement of operations when acquired rather than when used—no supplies inventory would appear on the SFP. In contrast, the expense basis means that goods and services are recognized in the statement of operations when they are used in performing the organization's service.

An expenditure basis is most appropriate when service and program outputs are difficult to measure and therefore there is no clear basis for allocating expenses or measuring efficiency. A clear example would be any form of public or collective good wherein there is no specific beneficiary and no revenue derived from the costs incurred. Specific activities may be clearly defined but the general operations of the organization cannot be specifically related to programmatic goals with measurable outputs. An expenditure basis is also appropriate for programs wherein fixed-grant revenues are intended to finance variable-cost services, as in public-beneficial organizations that derive their primary revenues from block grants by government ministries or foundations.

Expense Basis In contrast, the expense basis is likely to be most appropriate when the NFP is delivering goods or services to individuals and the organization needs to measure the cost of providing those goods or services. For example, hospitals may use an expense basis so that they know the cost of specific services. Revenue providers, such as the provincial governments, often use comparative cost information (that is, from many different hospitals) to evaluate the efficiency of individual hospitals.

On the other hand, it may be useful to exclude certain costs from the cost-of-services calculation when those costs fall outside of the funding guidelines that have been established by the funding agency (i.e., the provincial Ministry of Health). The most notable such cost is the cost of capital assets, which leads us directly to our next major reporting issue—capital assets.

Capital Assets

Capital-asset accounting is controversial largely because of the various methods that NFPs use to finance asset acquisitions. Some NFPs must fund their asset acquisitions through operating revenue (including non-restricted donations), while others may acquire major long-term assets only by special grants or donations. As a result, three different approaches used for accounting for capital assets have developed:

1. charge to operations immediately (an expenditure basis);
2. capitalize and depreciate (an expense basis); or
3. capitalize but *not* depreciate.

Expenditure Basis Charging the cost of capital assets to operations when incurred is the expenditure basis as applied to capital assets. It is possible to use an expenditure basis for capital assets while using an expense basis for other costs. In the past, this approach was by far the most commonly used. The main reason for its popularity relates to the nature of the revenue used to acquire the assets.

Many funding organizations (especially government granting agencies and ministries) restrict NFPs' use of operating revenues to operating expenditures, *excluding* capital-asset acquisition. Separate grants are given as capital grants for the acquisition of capital assets, and the funding organizations usually prohibit the inclusion of depreciation in the operating accounts. When a capital grant is given, the revenue from the grant is matched to the cost of acquiring the asset in the period of acquisition, and no capitalization or depreciation occurs.

Sometimes capital grants are given only for major assets such as buildings, while smaller acquisitions (such as furniture or computers) must be financed through the operating grants. In that case, different accounting policies sometimes have been used for the two types of assets due to the differing relationship to revenues.

Even in organizations where revenue comes from general donations rather than from government grants, expenditures for major depreciable capital assets may be financed by means of special capital fundraising campaigns. There is no intent on the part of either the organization or the donors that part of the cost of assets be charged against operations. If depreciation expense is charged in periods following the acquisition, then the organization will show a deficit in those periods even if fundraising activities are sufficient to cover the expenditures for the period (or, conversely, if expenditures are held to the level of the revenue raised).

It can be argued that when an organization receives separate funding for its capital acquisitions and replacements, it is a form of double-counting to deduct depreciation from operating funds. The usual approach in such circumstances is to charge the full cost of the acquisition against the capital grant when it is received; this approach achieves matching of the revenues and related expenditures. However, the disadvantage of immediate write-off is that the assets do not appear on the SFP.

Expense Basis The argument for the expense approach is that depreciation is a cost of providing services and that depreciation should therefore be recorded regardless of the way in which the assets were financed. For example, the FASB has argued that "using up assets in providing services . . . has a cost whether those assets have been acquired in prior periods or in the current period and whether acquired by paying cash, incurring liabilities, or by contribution."[7] Similarly, the *CICA Handbook* recommends that capital assets of limited life should be amortized, and that amortization should be included in the NFP's operating statement as an expense.

Depreciation accounting makes sense under either of two circumstances:

1. the cost of replacing capital assets must be recovered from general revenues, or
2. evaluation of efficiency requires that the cost of *all* inputs, including capital assets, be included in the measurement of outputs.

The expense basis would seem to be appropriate for hospitals, colleges, and universities (HCU), which account for 64% of the value of activity in the NFP sector. Users of HCU financial statements, such as governments, would be very interested in being able to evaluate the efficiency of the HCUs' operations to aid them in their resource allocation decisions. An expense basis that includes depreciation also seems appropriate for self-beneficial organizations and for private goods that are paid for on a fee-for-service basis, regardless of whether the payer is the direct beneficiary or is an outside funder (e.g., a hostel that receives reimbursement from a city for overnight accommodation of homeless people).

Capitalization Only The third approach to reporting capital assets is to capitalize the assets and never charge the cost to operations. This approach makes sense when (1) asset replacement or renewal is separately funded or (2) the assets do not decline in value or in usefulness.

Canadian Standards for Capital Assets The *CICA Handbook, Part III* requires that NFPs capitalize and amortize all capital assets (although land is not amortized, of course). Smaller NFPs need not comply with this recommendation. The exemption applies to any organization whose average gross annual consolidated revenues of the preceding and current years is less than $500,000. From our review of the NFP sector earlier in the chapter it appears that over 85% of organizations in the NFP sector could take advantage of this exemption.

Collections—A Special Issue A related issue is the capitalization of **collections** in museums and galleries. Collections are worth a great deal of money, and they are acquired through the use of donors' funds. Since the AcSB requires the capitalization of capital assets, they also would like to see collections capitalized. However, the Board realizes that this is impractical in most situations as the cost of capitalizing the collections would be more than any benefit gained by it.

Thus, for collections, capitalizing the cost of collections is *permissible* but not *required*. To assist preparers in determining whether their assets qualify as a collection of works of art or historical treasures, the CICA requires that the following three criteria be met:

1. The asset(s) must be available to be seen or used (e.g., for education or research) by the public.
2. The collection needs to be maintained and protected.
3. If an asset from the collection is sold, the proceeds from its sale cannot be used for the operations of the NFP. The funds must be used to acquire new pieces for the collection or to help in meeting the second criterion—to care for the collection.

7. *Statement of Financial Accounting Standard No. 93, Recognition of Depreciation by Not-for-Profit Organizations* (FASB, 1987), ¶20.

Classification as a *collection* is important because the *CICA Handbook* recommendation to capitalize capital assets does not apply to collections. Instead, the NFP has three options:

- capitalize with no depreciation;
- capitalize and depreciate; or
- disclose only.

The most common alternative is simply to disclose the *existence* of a collection. Although reporting or disclosing the *value* of a collection may be desirable, the practice is not generally followed. Estimates of the value of assets inevitably are unreliable, are difficult to verify, and may not be free from bias. In addition, there is a cost associated with having independent appraisals made, and most institutions would prefer not to incur that cost.

Segregation of Resources and Expense Allocations

NFPs often receive revenue grants that are earmarked for specific purposes. When the use of the revenue is specified by the donor, the revenue is called a **restricted contribution** or grant. To maintain proper control over restricted funds, the NFP must have a way of segregating restricted funds from its other resources. This is important for two reasons:

- the donor and other external users need to see that the funds are being used for the donor-designated purposes; and
- the NFP needs to show financial-statement users that restricted funds are not available for general purposes and cannot be transferred to general operations.

One way of accomplishing segregated reporting of restricted funds is through the use of *fund accounting*. **Fund accounting** is a set of accounting procedures that are used in a particular fund to record the transactions of that fund and that result in a set of self-balancing accounts. The focus of fund accounting is on keeping track of resources that are designated for specific purposes. The purpose is to avoid mixing up resources that are intended for diverse purposes and to ensure that management fulfills its stewardship responsibility for proper disposition of the resources. A single non-business organization can have several (or many) such accounting entities. The extent to which funds need to be segregated in an organization is largely a matter of common sense, based on the types of contributions they receive and the users' needs. Appendix 10A on the Companion Website describes the basic principles of fund accounting.

Expense Allocations In addition to ensuring that their donations are used in the manner specified, donors are often interested in the efficiency of the organization in accomplishing its mission. In particular, donors will often focus on the costs reported for fundraising and general support (i.e., non-program costs). NFPs are acutely aware of the fact that they are often evaluated on their ability to control the costs of these two functions. As a result, they have an incentive to minimize the costs reported in these two functions. One practice that has developed is that costs are sometimes allocated out of one of these functions to another function such as education. To help ensure that these allocations are legitimate, the AcSB introduced a new standard for required disclosures for allocated expenses by NFPs.

If amounts are allocated from fundraising and general support to other areas, the standard requires the following disclosures:

- explanation of allocation policies;
- explanation of the nature of the expenses allocated;
- the allocation basis;
- the amounts allocated from fundraising and general support; and
- the amounts and areas the expenses are allocated towards.

In addition, the standard provides three specific criteria that must be met before an amount can be allocated to the education function. Finally, changes to the bases for allocations are to be treated as changes in accounting policy.

Defining the Reporting Entity

There are many types of relationships that may exist between legally distinct but operationally similar NFPs that are under common control. As a result, the definition of the reporting entity is not as simple as it is for business enterprises.

For example, some arts organizations and social service organizations have a *foundation* that serves primarily to raise money for the main organization. The foundation usually has a board of trustees that is drawn directly from the board of directors of the principal operating arts or social service organization that it controls. Therefore, both the foundation and the operating agency are under common control.

Since the foundation is a legally separate organization, it could report separately from the operating agency. If reporting were done on this basis it would be difficult to evaluate the operations of the operating agency because a large part of the revenues (or the expenses) would be "hidden" in the foundation's statements. Unless the reader of the operating agency knows that the foundation exists, he or she will have difficulty evaluating the agency's financial position or the results of its operations.

Control and Significant Influence To reduce this problem, the *CICA Handbook, Part III* recommends that an organization report each controlled NFP either by consolidating that entity or by providing specific disclosures of key financial statement information of that entity. The obvious issue is what constitutes "*control*."

The most common indicator that control exists is when one organization has the right to appoint the majority of another NFP's board of directors. However, there may be other factors that indicate control for an NFP, including (1) significant economic interest; (2) provisions in the organization's charter or bylaws; or (3) common or complementary objectives. Clearly, professional judgment is required for determining whether control exists.

An NFP may also exercise significant influence over another NFP. In these cases the reporting NFP should describe its relationship with the entity and disclose the nature and extent of its economic interest. Finally, the reporting NFP may not exercise control or significant influence, but may still have an economic interest in another NFP. In these cases the reporting NFP should disclose the nature and extent of its economic interest in the notes to the financial statements.

REALITY CHECK 10-1

The Canadian Cancer Society has a close relationship with the National Cancer Institute of Canada (NCIC). In fact, subsequent to the 2009 fiscal year, the operations and related assets and liabilities of the NCIC were integrated with the CCS. The CCS disclosed its economic interest in NCIC in the following note in its 2009 financial statements:

> The Society has an economic interest in the activities of the NCIC by virtue of significant funds contributed to the NCIC for research in support of the Society's mission. The Society contributed 22% (2008 – 24%) of its revenue to the NCIC. The contribution for the fiscal year was $45,413 (2008 – $48,046).

Source: Canadian Cancer Society, Financial Statements for the year ended January 31, 2009, p. 19.

Investments in Profit-Seeking Enterprises An NFP may also own shares in a profit-oriented enterprise. If the NFP controls the enterprise, then it has two options: it can consolidate the enterprise or it can account for the enterprise using the equity method, but additional disclosure is required when the equity method is used. If the NFP can exercise significant influence over the enterprise, then the equity method is used. Finally, if no significant influence can be exerted, the cost method is used to account for the investment in the profit-oriented enterprise. These requirements are summarized in Exhibit 10-2.

Related-Party Transactions Our discussion above focussed on the issue of consolidation of related entities, which is the usual connotation of consolidation, as we have seen in Chapters 2 through 7 of this text. However, there are two other issues that we need to

EXHIBIT 10-2

Summary of Accounting for Economic Interests in NFPs and Investments in Profit-Oriented Enterprises

Type of organization	Extent of influence	Recommended accounting
Not-for-profit organization	Control	Consolidate; or Provide specific and extensive disclosure
	Significant influence	Describe relationship and disclose nature and extent of economic interest
	Economic interest	Disclose nature and extent of economic interest
Profit-oriented enterprise	Control	Consolidate; or Use equity method with supplemental disclosure
	Significant influence	Use equity method
	No significant influence	Use cost method

address briefly. The first is the concept of related parties and related-party transactions. To the extent that control, significant influence, or an economic interest exists, the parties are related. In this case, if there are transactions between the related parties, the financial statements must contain disclosure on the relationship, and the nature and amount of the transaction(s).

Consolidation vs. Combination There is another aspect of consolidation that is unique to non-business organizations: if an organization has restricted funds and is using fund accounting, to what extent should separate funds and restricted resources be *consolidated* or *combined* on the organization's financial statements?

If there is a large number of separate funds under control of management, separate reporting of the operations and SFP of each fund would result in quite a voluminous report, even though columnar formats could be used for conciseness. Separate reporting by funds may clarify the status of each individual fund for stewardship reporting purposes, but may obscure the overall financial position of the organization and the results of its operations.

On the other hand, consolidation of the various funds may hide important characteristics of individual funds, and may impede stewardship reporting.

The AcSB supports consolidated reporting. The *CICA Handbook, Part III* recommends that the *statement of financial position* show a total for each financial statement item that includes all funds. The recommendation for a consolidated total does not rule out separate reporting of funds (or of programs), but simply states that everything should be added together at the end.

Note that the requirement for a total applies only to the statement of financial position. The operating statement need not have a "total" column under the restricted fund approach (one of the two methods permitted by the *CICA Handbook*, as we will see soon) because to provide a total for the operating statement would suggest that the money is interchangeable between funds, which clearly is not the case when restricted funds exist.

While this recommendation for aggregating all of the resources on the SFP may seem relatively innocuous, reporting of organization-wide totals implicitly suggests that resources can be moved from fund to fund or program to program. Many NFPs oppose the recommendation for consolidated reporting for that reason.

There is a middle ground between fully detailed fund reporting and full consolidation. Similar types of funds or funds with similar objectives can be combined for reporting purposes. All of the ancillary, self-supporting activities of a university—such as the bookstore, food services, parking, and residences—can be grouped together because they are similar types of funds. Also, all the student aid funds can be combined for reporting purposes since they serve a similar objective.

The funds do not need to have the same treatment for reporting on all the financial statements. Funds (or groups of funds) can be reported separately on the statement of operations, but combined on the statement of financial position. Conversely, the funds may be combined on the statement of operations, but reported separately on the statement of financial position and the cash flow statement. As we will discuss below, an NFP may account in different ways for different funds or programs. When such is the case, it is impossible to meaningfully consolidate the various funds or programs.

Revenue Recognition

Contributions are a major source of revenue for most NFPs. A **contribution** is defined as a non-reciprocal transfer of cash (or other assets) to the NFP. The typical example would be a donation. It is non-reciprocal because the individual providing the donation does not receive anything back in exchange for the donation.

This is an important point, as you recall, from our earlier discussion on the relationship between revenues and costs. In a business enterprise, an individual gives money to the business in exchange for a product or service. Thus the focus of accounting is on the exchange (or reciprocal transfer). Revenue is recognized when the earnings process is complete (for example, upon delivery of the good). Furthermore, performance is measured by matching costs to the revenue generated.

With contributions, the connection between revenues and expenses is severed because the contribution is non-reciprocal. Therefore contribution revenue is not recognized when earned (because it is never earned) but rather it is recognized when received. Thus revenue recognition for contributions is relatively easy when compared to revenue recognition for businesses. There is one exception. Contributions are sometimes received with restrictions attached as to how the money is to be spent. In these cases, to help ensure that the money is spent appropriately (i.e., meet the stewardship objective), the revenue may be recognized by matching it to the related expense, where possible. This of course is the exact opposite of businesses where expenses are matched to the revenue. We will explore when and how this occurs in more detail below.

The *CICA Handbook, Part III* recommends two alternative methods of accounting for contributions: the *deferral method* or the *restricted fund method*. Before we discuss and demonstrate these two methods, we must first explain the three different types of contributions—restricted contributions, endowment contributions, and unrestricted contributions.

Three Categories of Contributions **Externally restricted contributions** are contributions that are *restricted by the donor* for specific purposes or uses. They may not be used for other purposes, and the system of accounts must maintain the integrity of the donation and its purpose. Externally restricted contributions must be distinguished from **board-designated funds (internally restricted)**, which are funds that the board of directors has earmarked for a specific purpose. The board can decide to reverse its internal restriction, and therefore internal restrictions do not have the same importance for financial reporting as do true restricted funds.

An **endowment contribution** is a special type of restricted contribution. Not only is the contribution restricted in purpose, but also the principal amount of the contribution cannot be spent. The contribution must be invested in an endowment fund and only the earnings on the investment can be spent for the intended purposes. An example is a scholarship fund within a university. The principal amount to establish the scholarship is maintained and interest earned on that principal is used to provide scholarships.

An **unrestricted contribution** is provided without any restrictions on its use by the organization. Basically, it is any contribution that does not meet the definition of either a restricted contribution or an endowment contribution.

It is critical to remember the differences between these types of contributions as we discuss the NFP reporting options. The recognition and presentation of different types of contributions on the financial statement differs among these methods.

REALITY CHECK 10-2

The Canadian Cancer Society uses the deferral method to account for externally restricted contributions that relate to their regular operations. With regards to the deferred contributions that arise, they state in the financial statement notes that:

Deferred contributions are recognized as revenue when the related expenses are incurred.

Source: Canadian Cancer Society, Financial Statements for the year ended January 31, 2009, p. 7.

Deferral Method: Business-Type Accounting This method is conceptually similar to that used by business enterprises, at least on the surface. The concept behind this method is to match the revenues with the associated expenses. The revenue is recognized as the related expenses are incurred, at least for restricted contributions.

Unrestricted contributions are recognized as revenues in the current period. They are available for any use by the organization.

The treatment of *restricted contributions* depends on the purpose for which they have been restricted by the donor. If the contribution is for expenses of the current period, the contribution should be recognized as revenue in the current period. If the contribution is for expenses of a future period, it is recorded as *deferred contributions or deferred revenue* until the related expense is recognized.

Note that this matching process is reversed from our normal expectation in business enterprise accounting. For businesses, the usual focus is on recognizing revenue first, and then matching expenses to that revenue. If there are related costs that will be incurred in the future (e.g., warranty expense), those future costs are estimated and recognized in the period in which the revenue has been recognized to achieve matching.

Under the deferral method of NFP accounting, first, the expenses are recognized, and then the revenue is matched. If revenue is received prior to the expense, the revenue must be deferred until the expense is recognized. Note that the deferral is until the *expense* is recognized, not the *expenditure*. If a restricted contribution is for a capital asset, the treatment depends on whether or not that asset will be amortized. If the asset is amortized, the revenue will be deferred and recognized on the same basis as the amortization of the specific asset that has been purchased.

Example: Deferral Method For example, suppose that a donor contributes $30,000 to a social agency on December 13, 20X5. The donation is restricted for the purchase of a new van. The van will be purchased in 20X6. The van will be depreciated over three years, straight-line. When the contribution is received, the credit will be to deferred revenue:

December 13, 20X5

Cash	30,000	
Deferred revenue (restricted—van)		30,000

If the van is purchased on January 27, 20X6, the transaction will have no immediate impact on the statement of operations:

January 27, 20X6		
Capital asset—van	30,000	
Cash		30,000

At the end of 20X6, the agency will record $10,000 in depreciation. Simultaneously, the same amount of revenue will be recognized:

December 31, 20X6		
Depreciation expense	10,000	
Accumulated depreciation		10,000
Deferred revenue (restricted—van)	10,000	
Revenue		10,000

Under the deferral method, all revenues are added together in the statement of operations. If the restricted revenue were recognized when it is received or when the van is purchased, the agency would show restricted revenue that is not matched by an expense; and any unmatched revenue will lead financial statement readers to believe that the NFP has more revenue available for unrestricted purposes than it really does.

To avoid showing revenue without any related expenses, *endowment contributions* are recognized as direct increases in net assets in the current period because they will never be available to meet expenses of the organization. This is also true for assets that are not amortized (e.g., land). If a contribution is received that is restricted for the purchase of land, the revenue will be shown as a direct increase in net assets. These kinds of contributions are shown on the statement of changes in net assets, which may be in a separate statement or combined with the statement of operations.

Restricted-Fund Method The second method is based on the concepts of fund accounting[8] that have been used in not-for-profit organizations for many years. A number of separate funds (i.e., self-balancing sets of accounts) are used to segregate the three basic different types of contributions: (1) restricted funds, (2) endowment funds, and (3) the general fund (or operating fund) for unrestricted contributions.

Unrestricted contributions are recognized as revenue in the general fund. The accounting for restricted contributions depends on whether or not there is a separate restricted fund for that contribution. If there is a separate restricted fund, it is recognized as revenue in the current period in that fund. If there is no separate fund, it is *recognized in the general fund using the deferral method* of accounting for contributions. Therefore, restricted contributions are treated differently depending on whether or not they are shown in a separate fund.

Endowment contributions are recognized as revenues in the *endowment fund* in the current period. Note the difference here between the two reporting methods. The restricted-fund method shows the contributions as *revenue* in a separate fund. In contrast, the deferral method shows endowment contributions as a direct increase in net assets—there is no revenue recognition on the statement of operations.

Companion Website

8. Fund accounting is discussed briefly in Appendix 10A on the Companion Website.

EXHIBIT 10-3

Summary of Revenue Recognition of Contributions

Method	Type of contribution	Accounting
Deferral method	Unrestricted	Recognize as revenue in the current period
	Restricted	
	• To pay for (or repay debt incurred for) current-period expenses	Recognize as revenue in the current period
	• To pay for (or repay debt incurred for) future-period expenses	Defer, match revenues to expenses
	• To pay for (or repay debt incurred for) capital asset – amortizable	Defer, match revenues to expenses (amortization)
	• To pay for (or repay debt incurred for) capital asset – non-amortizable	Recognize as direct increase to net assets
	Endowment	Recognize as direct increase to net assets
Restricted-fund method	Unrestricted	Recognize as revenue in the general fund
	Restricted	
	• Appropriate restricted fund exists	Recognize as revenue in restricted fund
	• No appropriate restricted fund	Recognize as revenue in general fund using the deferral method
	Endowment	Recognize as revenue in the endowment fund

Notice also that under the restricted-fund method, contributions in separate restricted and endowment funds are recognized currently. When restricted funds are shown separately, there will be no confusion about whether excess revenue is available for general use. The use of a restricted fund makes it clear to users that those resources are not available for general operations. Matching of revenues to expenses is not of concern in this reporting framework, and therefore there is no need to defer recognition of the revenue.

The restricted-fund method of accounting tends to result in a higher level of revenue than does the deferral method. The reasons are that (1) restricted revenues often are recognized earlier because there is no need to defer recognition of the revenue until the expense has been recognized; and (2) contributions to endowment funds are recognized as revenue under the restricted-fund method but not under the deferral method. Therefore, the selection of accounting method may place an organization over the size test for capitalizing capital assets (i.e., average revenues of less than $500,000) if the restricted-fund method is used, but not if the deferral method is used. The accounting for the different types of contributions under the two systems is summarized in Exhibit 10-3.

Pledges How should pledges be recognized in the financial statements of NFPs? A **pledge** is a promise to give cash (or other assets) to the NFP. A promise to pay could be viewed as a receivable. However, a donor may give a pledge, but may subsequently decide not to actually

REALITY CHECK 10-3

The accounting policy note on pledges for the Canadian Cancer Society is consistent with the practices of most NFPs.

> Revenue from donations is recognized on a cash basis, with no accrual being made for amounts pledged but not received.

Source: Canadian Cancer Society, Financial Statements for the year ended January 31, 2009, p. 10.

give the money. Unlike a business transaction, for an NFP donor, there is no exchange, but only a one-way promise that can be rescinded, retracted, or ignored by the donor.

An NFP can recognize a pledge as a receivable on its SFP if both of two criteria are met: (1) the amount can be reasonably estimated, and (2) ultimate collection is reasonably assured.

The amount is not usually in doubt. Most pledges are for cash, and are payable within a fairly short period of time. Cash pledges may be uncertain in amount, however, if they depend on future events. For example, a business may promise to contribute 1% of its revenue from sales of a certain product. Even though the contribution will be in cash, the amount will not be known until the sales results are known.

The estimation criterion may also not be met when the pledge is not in cash but is in the form of a non-cash asset. It may be impossible to get a reasonable estimate of the value of the asset until it is in the NFP's hands and can be reliably assessed. As well, the donation may be contingent on some future event, such as the donor's death, which makes both the timing *and* value of the donation uncertain.

The dual criteria of measurability and collectability often are difficult to achieve for many not-for-profit organizations. Most NFPs prefer not to count their cash before it has been received. Therefore, revenue is usually recognized only when the amount is collected.

Donated Goods and Services It is not unusual for people and businesses to donate goods and services instead of (or in addition to) money. Indeed, the very nature of most NFPs and volunteer organizations means that much of the work is being carried out by volunteers through contributed services. As well, companies often choose to donate goods or services, such as an airline that provides free transportation to a sports organization to fly athletes to major competitions. An accounting issue arises from non-monetary donations—should the donated goods and services be assigned a value and reported in the statements?

In some cases, goods or services are donated as a way of helping the organization raise money. The goods or services are sold or auctioned off, and the organization ultimately receives cash in exchange for the donated goods or services. In such instances, the inflow of cash determines the value of the donation, and the amount of cash received must be recorded as a donation by the not-for-profit organization.

More commonly, however, the goods and services are donated to help the organization achieve its objectives. The United Way, for example, receives substantial donations of executive time from businesses to help manage its campaigns. Should the United Way assign a value to the donated time?

To Record or Not? When donated goods or services are assigned a value and recorded by the organization, the credit to revenues offsets the debit to expenditures and there is no impact on the net operating results. However, the absolute values of the revenues and expenses are affected, and it is possible that management's performance could be evaluated differently.

For example, one measure of the performance of a fundraising organization is the proportion of funds raised that are consumed as fundraising expenses. An organization that spends only 10% of the donations to obtain those donations is perceived as doing a better job than one that spends 40% of the funds it raises. But if the 40% organization is paying for all of the services it receives, while the 10% organization is using enormous amounts of volunteer effort, are the financial results of the two organizations really comparable? If the 10% organization were to record the value of its donated effort, its cost ratio may rise to 60%. Thus the recording of donated goods and services can have an impact on the perceptions of the readers of the statements, at least in terms of performance evaluation.

For stewardship reporting, the advantages of reporting the value of donated goods and services are not so clear. If the primary objective of the statements is to report on how management used the funds at its disposal, then reporting donated services on the statements may only impair the reporting objective, because it will appear that management had more funds at its disposal than was actually the case.

Guidance from Canadian Accounting Standards Practice has varied considerably. Recording and reporting the value of *donated goods and services* seems to have been the exception rather than the rule in the past. The requirements to record donated goods and services are:

- the value can be reasonably estimated; and
- the goods and services would otherwise have been purchased in the normal course of business.

While the general recommendation for donated goods and services is permissive (i.e., "may"), the suggested recommendation for *donated capital assets* is stronger. The *CICA Handbook* requires that donated capital assets "should" be recorded at fair value. When the fair value cannot be reasonably determined, the capital asset should be recorded at nominal value.

CONCEPT CHECK 10-2

Companion Website

1. When should the expense basis of reporting for capital assets be used?
2. What disclosures are required for expense allocations?
3. What indicators of control can be used to determine if one NFP controls another NFP?
4. Briefly explain how the recognition of contribution revenue by NFPs differs from the recognition of revenue by businesses.

REALITY CHECK 10-4

The accounting policies of the Canadian Cancer Society for donated time and donated capital assets are:

> The Society's programs benefit substantially from services in the form of volunteer time. The value of these services is not recorded in these financial statements.

Source: Canadian Cancer Society, Financial Statements for the year ended January 31, 2009, p. 13.

> Capital assets . . . donated to the Society are recorded at their fair market value at the date of acquisition when fair market value can be reasonably estimated.

Source: Canadian Cancer Society, Financial Statements for the year ended January 31, 2009, p. 7.

FINANCIAL REPORTING FOR NOT-FOR-PROFIT ORGANIZATIONS

In the sections above we have briefly described the substantial differences between NFPs and businesses. These differences include the nature of the organizations, the financial reporting objectives, and the specific reporting issues. Due to these differences, it is not surprising that GAAP for NFPs developed quite differently from that for business enterprises.

NFPs can use one of two different approaches:[9]

- the deferral method, in which all funds are combined in the financial statements without distinction between restricted and unrestricted funds, and
- the restricted-fund method, in which funds can be segregated for financial reporting.

If an NFP has at least one externally restricted fund (that is, restricted by the *donor*), management can choose either of the two methods. If there are no restricted funds, then the deferral method must be used.

Many NFPs are not constrained by GAAP and do not need to comply with the *CICA Handbook* recommendations. These organizations may use a reporting method that is mandated by their primary funding agency, such as the Ministry of Health or the Ministry of Social Services. Alternatively, they may follow a more traditional expenditure-based reporting system.

9. It is possible for NFPs that are using the deferral method to also use fund accounting concurrently. In this case, each fund would apply the deferral method and the funds would be reported separately on both the statement of financial position and statement of operations. We do not explore this option here although the principles would be the same.

In the following sections we will further explain the various methods of reporting. The first is the expenditure-based approach, which we are calling the "traditional" method. Then we will look at the two methods recommended by the *CICA Handbook, Part III*. It is important to understand that this is not a theoretical discussion—*all of these methods are used in practice*.

Some organizations use a dual-reporting approach. They may use one of the AcSB's recommended methods to obtain a clean audit opinion, and then use an expenditure-based set of statements to satisfy their primary user's needs. Such an approach is somewhat costly, since it involves extensive year-end adjustments to get from an expenditure approach to one of the *CICA* Handbook–recommended expense approaches.

Types of Financial Statements

The *CICA Handbook* recommends that NFPs prepare the following four financial statements:

1. statement of financial position
2. statement of operations
3. statement of changes in net assets, and
4. cash-flow statement.

The second and third statements will often be combined into a single statement of operations and fund balances. The statements should be in a comparative format, with comparisons to the previous year. There may also be comparisons to budgeted amounts. In addition to the statements themselves, there should be notes to the financial statements.

This list of statements looks deceptively simple. The statements do not look much different from those that we are accustomed to seeing for businesses. The differences can be great, however. As we will discuss shortly, the presentation will depend on whether the NFP has selected the *deferral method* or the *restricted-fund method* for recognizing contributions.

Reporting Options

Traditional Method In the sections above on reporting issues, we outlined the basic nature of NFP financial reporting as it developed throughout the twentieth century. Many NFPs use the following reporting practices:

- Revenues are recognized when received; accruals are rare.
- Resource *outflows* are recognized when the cost is incurred or when the liability is incurred. Accruals are seldom made for items such as pensions, leases, or vacation pay. The general tendency is to report on a flow-of-funds accrual basis, without inter-period allocations.
- Capital assets may or may not be recorded on the SFP, but depreciation is used only for funds that conduct activities that are expected to be self-supporting on a cost-recovery or profit-making basis.
- Funds are segregated on the SFP, and separate statements of operations are used for different funds (or for different groups of funds of similar nature).
- Funds rarely are totalled on the statement of operations; the SFP more often shows a total for all funds.
- Related organizations are not consolidated.

Many NFPs follow these practices, usually because their donors or funding agencies want to see what the organization's managers have done with the resources placed at their disposal during the year—a classic instance of applying the stewardship objective of financial reporting.

CICA Handbook Methods As mentioned previously, the *CICA Handbook, Part III* recommends two alternative methods of accounting: the *deferral method* or the *restricted-fund method.* The two methods can be briefly described as follows:

Deferral Method The deferral method can be used by any NFP. Under this method:

- no distinction is made between different funds or groups of resources in the SFP or the statement of operations;
- a full accrual basis is used, including the possible accrual of pledges and full inter-period allocation of revenues and expenses in accordance with the recommendations of the *CICA Handbook* for business enterprises;
- capital assets are capitalized and amortized; and
- restricted revenues are deferred and matched to the expenses that they were intended to fund.

Restricted-Fund Method The restricted fund method may be used by any NFP that has at least one fund or resource group that is restricted by an outside donor. Under this method:

- The NFP presents a separate operating statement for each fund (or group of similar funds)—no totals for the organization need appear on the statement of operations because the funds are not interchangeable.
- The statement of financial position should present totals for the organization as a whole.
- Accrual accounting is applied and capital assets are capitalized.
- Amortization does not have to be charged to general operations; amortization can be charged to a separate capital fund instead.
- Revenue is usually recognized in the appropriate fund when it is received (or accrued) rather than when the expenses are incurred.

Comparison of Methods The deferral method requires total columns for *both* the SFP and the statement of operations. All funds, by implication, may be perceived as transferable between activities or programs.

In contrast, under the restricted-fund method, the *CICA Handbook* does recommend that the resources and liabilities of the various funds be added together for a "total" column on the statement of financial position. However, there is no requirement that the various funds be added together on the statement of operations. The whole point of this method of accounting is to recognize that restricted and endowed funds are not interchangeable with unrestricted funds, and that a deficit in the operating fund cannot be remedied by transferring money from the restricted funds to the operating fund.

As a result, an NFP might show a surplus under the one-column operating statement of the deferral method, when all of the funds are added together. But under the restricted-fund method of reporting, the funds are segregated and it will be apparent to the financial-statement user that the restricted and endowment funds cannot be used for general operating purposes.

REALITY CHECK 10-5

In 1998, York University began using the deferral method for financial reporting. The university previously had used the traditional method, which in most regards is similar to the restricted fund method. To prepare its comparative1998 statements, the university had to restate its 1997 statements from restricted-fund to deferral, which gave a rare opportunity to compare the two methods. In the original (restricted fund) statements, the university reported an operating surplus of $3.5 million, and a total surplus in all funds of $27.5 million—the difference was largely due to surpluses in restricted trust and endowment funds. When restated, the total surplus of $27.5 million became a deficit of $4.1 million. A major cause was the provision of $19.8 million of depreciation. No results were reported for operating funds, since they were no longer separately reported. The performance of the restricted trust and endowment funds disappeared from view, as did the losses on ancillary services such as the bookstore and student residences. After 1998, the reader had no way of understanding the underlying causes of any deficit or surplus, whether from operations, restricted trust funds, ancillary services, or sponsored research.

Source: T. H. Beechy, "Turning a Surplus into a Deficit—'Improved' Accounting for Universities?" International Symposium on Public Sector Management, Universität Klagenfurt (Austria), June 25, 2007.

Another important distinction between the deferral method and the restricted-fund method is that, under the restricted-fund method, depreciation and amortization on capital assets need not be charged to the operating fund. Depreciation and amortization can be segregated in the capital asset fund instead. This eliminates one of the major objections that many NFPs have to the idea of business-style accounting—that depreciation is charged against operations that are not intended to recover the costs of capital assets, if the assets have been acquired through special grants or fundraising drives.

Number of Restricted Funds It is the organization's option as to how many restricted funds it wishes to have on its statements. An NFP may decide not to have a separate fund for smaller restricted contributions. Instead, smaller funds can be combined into a single larger restricted fund. For example, the many different scholarship and bursary endowments typically present in a college or university are combined into a single "financial aid endowment fund."

Even though funds may be combined, their distinct nature should be preserved. Restricted donations and endowment donations are not combined with unrestricted donations. Unrestricted contributions are recognized as revenue in the *general fund* in the current period. This is similar in treatment to the deferral method.

The choice of method depends primarily on the users and their needs. If the organization wants the simplest financial statements it may select the deferral method. If the primary purpose is to show information on specific activities or programs, or if there is a large number of external users who have imposed restrictions, the restricted-fund method may be more appropriate.

Exhibit 10-4 compares some of the fundamental characteristics of these two methods, as well as comparing them to the traditional method.

EXHIBIT 10-4

Alternative Approaches to NFP Financial Reporting

		CICA Handbook recommendations	
Accounting practice	**Traditional approach**	**Deferral method**	**Restricted-fund method**
Accrual of pledges	Not done	Recognition if criteria met	Recognition if criteria met
Revenue recognition	Recognize when realized	Match to expense recognition	Recognize when realized
Expense or expenditure basis	Expenditure	Expense	Expense
Capital assets:			
Capitalize	Sometimes	Required*	Required*
Charge to operations	Seldom	Required*	Not required (may use separate fund)
Combine funds in "total" column:			
Statement of operations	Seldom	Required	Not required
Statement of financial position	Seldom	Required	Required
Consolidation of related organizations	Not done	Required	Required
General application of *CICA Handbook* (e.g., pensions, leases, expense accruals)	Not done	Required	Required

*Not required for NFPs that are less than the $500,000 gross revenue test.

Illustration of GAAP Reporting Methods[10]

Deferral Method Exhibit 10-5 gives an illustration of a simple set of NFP financial statements prepared by using the deferral method. This organization receives three types of contributions—endowment, restricted, and unrestricted—but the statements do not have to be prepared on the restricted fund method. Any NFP can use the deferral method.

There are three statements:

- a statement of financial position;
- a statement of operations; and
- a statement of changes in net assets.

In the first two statements, no distinction is made between the resources in the various funds.

However, notice that on the statement of financial position, there is not just one amount for capital, shown here as "net assets" (other often-used headings are *fund balances*, *net resources*

10. For brevity of exposition, the statements of cash flows are omitted under both approaches.

EXHIBIT 10-5

Sample NFP Financial Statements—Deferral Method

Statement of Financial Position
December 31, 20X5
(in thousands)

	20X5	20X4
Assets		
Current assets:		
Cash and term deposits	$ 520	$ 280
Accounts receivable	150	160
Supplies	160	60
	830	500
Investments	570	200
Capital assets, net	1,000	1,100
Total assets	$2,400	$1,800
Liabilities, deferred contributions, and net assets		
Current liabilities:		
Accounts payable and accrued liabilities	$ 70	$ 10
Current portion mortgage payable	10	10
	80	20
Mortgage payable	120	130
	200	150
Deferred contributions:		
Capital	600	720
Other deferred contributions	110	—
	710	720
Net assets:		
Externally restricted	150	100
Invested in capital assets	280	250
Internally restricted	100	200
Endowments	570	200
Unrestricted	390	180
	1,490	930
Total liabilities, deferred contributions, and net assets	$2,400	$1,800

Statement of Operations
Year Ended December 31, 20X5
(in thousands)

	20X5	20X4
Revenues		
Grants and contributions	$2,140	$2,400
Amortization of capital contributions	120	100
Other revenue	1,400	1,200
	3,660	3,700
Expenses		
Salaries	2,790	2,800
Amortization of capital assets	200	260
Other expenses	480	460
	3,470	3,520
Excess of revenues over expenses	$ 190	$ 180

Statement of Changes in Net Assets
Year Ended December 31, 20X5
(in thousands)

Net assets	Externally restricted	Invested in capital assets	Internally restricted	Endow-ments	Unrestricted	Total
Balance, January 1	$100	$250	$ 200	$200	$ 180	$ 930
Excess (deficiency) of revenues over expenses	50	(80)			220	190
Investment in capital assets		110			(110)	—
Endowment contribution				370		370
Internally imposed restrictions			(100)		100	—
Balance, December 31	$150	$280	$ 100	$570	$ 390	$1,490

available, or *accumulated excess of revenues over expenditures*). Instead, there are five different fund balances shown. This is an important option in NFP accounting. Even when the deferral method is used, the net resources that relate to each fund may be shown separately on the statement of financial position. By using this approach, users can see that, although the total fund balances amount to $1,490, only $390 of that amount is unrestricted and is available for future operations.

The third statement reconciles the beginning and ending balances of each of the fund balances shown on the SFP. If the statement of financial position shows more than one fund balance, then the beginning balance must be reconciled to the ending balance for each fund.

On the statement of changes in net assets, observe that the total column shows a surplus of $190 (i.e., excess of revenues over expenses). In addition, this statement reveals that:

- the surplus in the unrestricted fund actually was $220
- the contributions to the endowment fund of $370 were not included in revenues on the statement of operations
- capital assets of $110 were purchased from unrestricted funds during the year; and
- the board reversed an internal restriction by $100, releasing those funds for general unrestricted use.

Restricted-Fund Method Exhibit 10-6 shows the same organization, but this time using the restricted fund method of reporting. Only two statements are presented—a statement of financial position and a combined statement of operations and changes in net assets. In this approach, detailed statements of financial position are presented for the operating fund, for each restricted fund (research and capital assets), and for the endowment fund. We can see, for example, that of the total current assets of $830, only $680 is for unrestricted use.

Revenue recognition also is quite different between the two methods. Notice that in the SFP in Exhibit 10-6, there is no liability for deferred revenue. That is because revenue is recognized when realized in the restricted-fund method. The endowment is in a separate fund,

EXHIBIT 10-6

Sample NFP Financial Statements—Restricted Fund Method

Statement of Financial Position
December 31, 20X5
(in thousands)

	Operating fund	Research fund	Capital asset fund	Endowment fund	20X5 Total	20X4 Total
Current assets						
Cash and term deposits	$370	$150			$ 520	$ 280
Accounts receivable	150				150	160
Supplies	160	—			160	60
	680	150			830	500
Investments				$570	570	200
Capital assets, net	200	—	$800	—	1,000	1,100
Total assets	$880	$150	$800	$570	$2,400	$1,800
Current liabilities						
Accounts payable and accrued liabilities	$ 70				$ 70	$ 10
Current portion, mortgage payable	10				10	10
	80				80	20
Mortgage payable	—		$120		120	130
Total liabilities	80		120		200	150
Fund balances						
Externally restricted	110	$150			260	100
Invested in capital assets	200		680		880	970
Internally restricted	100				100	200
Endowments				$570	570	200
Unrestricted	390	—	—	—	390	180
Total fund balances	800	150	680	570	2,200	1,650
Total liabilities and fund balances	$880	$150	$800	$570	$2,400	$1,800

Statement of Operations and Changes in Net Assets
Year Ended December 31, 20X5
(in thousands)

	Operating fund	Research fund	Capital asset fund	Endowment fund
Revenues				
Grants and contributions	$1,650	$640		$370
Other revenue	1,400	—		—
	3,050	640		370
Expenses				
Salaries	2,300	490		
Amortization of capital assets	200			
Other	480	—		
	2,980	490		
Excess (deficiency) of revenues over expenses	70	150		370
Fund balance, January 1	640		$770	200
Interfund transfers	90	—	(90)	—
Fund balance, December 31	$ 800	$150	$680	$570

and therefore the contributions to the endowment fund are recognized as revenue *for that fund* in the restricted-fund method. In the deferral method, the endowment contributions are not recognized as revenue.

Since revenue recognition is different, the total fund balances are different between the two methods. Notice that the total fund balances (or "net assets") shown in Exhibit 10-5 are $1,490, while in Exhibit 10-6 the total fund balances amount to $2,200.

To avoid complicating the presentation we have omitted the 20X4 comparative data for the statement of operations in Exhibit 10-6. In practice, comparative information would be presented either by putting more columns in the statement or by providing another statement in identical format for the prior year. The restricted-fund approach tends to present a lot of numbers. But the numbers are necessary to try to grasp the real operating situation of the organization.

The Chore of Users: Unravelling GAAP

We pointed out earlier in the chapter that the users of NFP financial statements often are interested in the organization's use of the resources given to help the organization accomplish its mandate. There are two aspects to this interest—(1) stewardship over the resources themselves, and (2) effectiveness in accomplishing the organization's objectives. Unfortunately, the annual financial statements of an NFP usually do not satisfy either goal very well.

Stewardship is difficult to assess because the expense basis of reporting that is recommended by the AcSB is often in conflict with users' interest in how the organization *spent* the money given to it—expenditures rather than expenses. Sometimes the organization tries to help users by pointing out the impact of major unfunded accruals.

The deferral method makes it especially difficult to unravel the financial performance of any NFP that has restricted funds. As we pointed out in Reality Check 10-5, above, some universities, for example, have chosen to use the deferral method, adding together unrestricted funds, restricted funds, endowment funds, and enterprise accounts into a single set of numbers. The "bottom line" in such a situation is meaningless. If there is a surplus, is it a surplus that can be used for future operations (i.e., unrestricted), or is the surplus due to restricted funds that hide a deficit in the general fund? If the university shows a deficit, is it a deficit in the operating funds or is it because the university is losing piles of money on its enterprises, such as the bookstore or food operations? It is impossible to unravel the reasons for either a surplus or a deficit when the deferral method is used in an NFP that has restricted donations.

The difficulty of evaluating *efficiency* in an NFP has led to a demand for a greater volume of non-financial data as supplementary information in non-business financial statements. Data on the level of services performed or activities accomplished, membership levels, contributors, etc., can be provided. For example, a CICA research study on NFPs recommended that not-for-profit organizations provide the following information along with their annual financial statements:[11]

- the nature and objectives of the organization;
- plans for the future;

11. Canadian Institute of Chartered Accountants, *Financial Reporting for Not-for-profit Organizations* (Toronto: CICA, 1980), pp. 41–42.

- significant events during the year and their relationship to or impact on the financial results;
- any unusual or important items or trends in the financial statements; and
- important non-financial information.

It would be most useful if quantitative supplementary information were audited. Sometimes the audit opinion does cover at least some such information, but normally the supplementary information is outside the scope of the audit opinion. Auditors find it difficult to independently verify most non-financial data unless it is directly tied into the accounting and reporting system. Therefore, financial statement readers have to accept supplementary information largely on trust.

Unfortunately, there have been instances of overenthusiastic managers issuing inflated performance data to enhance the apparent efficiency or effectiveness of the organization. For example, one Canadian film festival was alleged to have announced attendance figures that were in excess of the combined maximum seating capacities of its theatres! But this type of behaviour is undoubtedly the exception rather than the rule.

CONCEPT CHECK 10-3

Companion Website

1. Explain the distinction between the *restricted-fund method* and the *deferral method.*
2. What types of financial statements will an NFP normally issue?
3. Why is stewardship difficult to assess in an NFP?

BUDGETARY CONTROL AND ENCUMBRANCE ACCOUNTING

By now, you will have seen that accounting for not-for-profit organizations is quite different from accounting for business enterprises. But we are not done yet. There are two other special aspects of NFP accounting. We will conclude this chapter with an overview of these two special accounting techniques—*budgetary control accounts* and *encumbrance accounting.*

Budgetary Control Accounts

A unique characteristic that is often used in fund accounting is the practice of formally incorporating budgetary accounts into the accounting system. **Budgetary accounts** enable managers to keep a running comparison of budgeted with actual amounts of revenue and expenditure as well as to monitor expenditure levels.

It is quite possible to accomplish the same result without formally including the budget in the accounting system—many businesses routinely have budget vs. actual comparisons on their *internal* statements. The difference in non-business organizations, and especially in governments, is that when strict expenditure limits are in effect, a formalized system acts as an internal control so that managers are not permitted to issue purchase orders that will push the expenditure total above the budgeted limit. The comparison between the budget and the combined total of expenditures is constant and routine, rather than being occasional and special.

We will not go into the technical aspects of budgetary control accounts here. There are many books that explain the mechanics of fund accounting and budgetary accounts in exquisite detail. It will be sufficient to say simply that the nature of the budgetary accounts is to create a self-balancing set of accounts *within* the regular accounting system, normally within the general or operating fund.

In general, the bookkeeping approach that is used for budgetary accounts is as follows:

- Budgeted revenues are *debited* to an account that serves as an offset to actual revenues (which are credits). The difference between the budgeted and actual revenues is automatically shown within the system by netting the actual against the budgeted amounts. A net debit balance indicates that actual revenues are falling short of the budget, while a net credit balance shows that revenues are exceeding budget.
- Budgeted *expenditures* (not *expenses*) are shown as credits. The level of detail matches the level of expenditure control that has been mandated by the board of directors (or by the legislature, for governments). The budget balance is the upper limit of permitted expenditures. Managers and employees will not be permitted to make additional commitments once the budget limit has been met.

The budget limits on expenditure are enforced by means of an encumbrance system.

The Encumbrance System

The **encumbrance system** records the estimated cost of commitments in the formal accounting system when the commitments are made rather than when a legal liability has arisen. For example, purchase orders for supplies are recorded as an *encumbrance* at the estimated cost of the supplies when the purchase order is issued, even though no liability (in either a legal or an accounting sense) exists until the supplier delivers the supplies. In theory, an encumbrance system could be used in private enterprise accounting—encumbrances are not necessarily limited to fund accounting. In practice, encumbrance accounting is unique to governments and NFPs.

The objective of using an encumbrance system is to keep track of the commitments that an organization's managers have made for the acquisition of goods and services. If there is a budgetary or legislative limit on the expenditures that a manager can make during the year, then use of the encumbrance system keeps the manager from over-committing the organization and running up a large deficit.

Even in the absence of fixed budgetary limits, encumbrances can be used simply as an aid to planning and control. This is particularly true when commitments on the same budget amount can be made by several people within the organization. When control is decentralized, an encumbrance system improves regulation and communicates to managers and to the people making the expenditures just what the actual level of commitment is.

The encumbrance system is widely used in governmental accounting; budget amounts are legislated maxima that must not be exceeded. In NFPs, however, whether or not an encumbrance system is used depends on the nature of the organization and its operations. In fact, encumbrance accounting can be used in some parts of an organization and not in others, and for some types of expenditure (such as for supplies) and not others (such as salaries). The system is most appropriate when the following conditions are present:

1. the organization, fund, or activity is a cost centre with a maximum expenditure limit *or* has no relationship between costs and revenues;
2. goods and services acquired discretionally are a significant part of the total budget;
3. there is a significant lag between the commitment (e.g., purchase order) and the receipt of the purchased items;
4. levels of activity (and expenditure) within the organizational unit are not affected in the short run by an autonomous demand, either external to the organization or from other parts of the organization;
5. reporting is on an expenditure basis rather than an expense basis;
6. responsibility for making commitments and expenditures is decentralized throughout a large organization.

If, in contrast, a small organizational unit (1) must vary its level of activity in response to market demand for its services, (2) is able to generate revenues to cover expenses, and (3) considers externally acquired goods and services of little consequence or receives them very shortly after ordering, then there is little reason to use an encumbrance system.

Encumbrance systems are used to control costs when expenditure limits are basically fixed and are not tied to revenue or activity levels. If these conditions do not exist, then encumbrances are of limited usefulness. Also, if only a very small part of expenditures is discretionary rather than being tied to longer-term employment or supply contracts, then there is little point to using encumbrances.

CONCEPT CHECK 10-4

Companion Website

1. Explain the purpose of recording budgetary amounts in the accounts.
2. When is the use of an encumbrance system most appropriate for NFPs?

A FINAL EXAMPLE

We will end this chapter with an example of NFP financial statements. Exhibit 10-7 shows the basic 2009 statements for the Canadian Cancer Society. As is common in NFP reporting, the CCS takes a slightly eclectic approach. The SFP has only one column (for each year), which might lead one to believe that the statements are prepared on the deferral method.

EXHIBIT 10-7

Sample NFP Financial Statements, Canadian Cancer Society

Statement of Resources
(In thousands of dollars)
January 31, 2009, with comparative figures for 2008

	2009	2008 (Restated – note 2(a))
ASSETS		
Current Assets:		
Cash	$ 22,759	$ 20,634
Short-term investments (note 3)	52,903	48,582
Accounts receivable	3,734	3,155
Prepaid expenses	5,235	5,100
	84,631	77,471
Long-term investments (note 4)	32,950	33,963
Intangible assets (note 5)	1,476	1,504
Capital assets (note 6)	27,371	21,939
	$146,428	$134,877
LIABILITIES AND RESOURCES		
Current Liabilities:		
Accounts payable	$ 12,965	$ 10,492
Research contributions payable to National Cancer Institute of Canada (note 7)	212	285
Deferred contributions (note 8)	8,967	8,875
Current portion of credit facility (note 9)	1,428	600
	23,572	20,252
Credit facility (note 9)	—	878
Accrued pension benefit liability (note 10(a))	3,103	2,354
Liability for post-retirement benefits other than pensions (note 10(b))	13,884	12,348
Resources:		
Externally restricted (note 14)	5,038	6,304
Invested in capital assets (note 11)	27,117	21,965
Internally restricted	53,695	44,061
Unrestricted	20,019	26,715
	105,869	99,045
Commitments (notes 6 and 12)		
Guarantees and contingencies (note 16)		
Subsequent event (note 18)		
	$146,428	$134,877

Statement of Changes in Resources
(In thousands of dollars)
Year Ended January 31, 2009, with comparative figures for 2008

	2009					2008 (Restated – note 2(a))
	Externally restricted	Invested in capital assets	Internally restricted	Unrestricted	Total	Total
Resources, beginning of year	$6,304	$21,965	$44,061	$26,715	$ 99,045	$87,831
Change in accounting policy, net unrealized investment gain	—	—	—	—	—	780
Increase (decrease) in resources	2,910	(3,917)	(3,348)	11,179	6,824	10,434
Invested in capital assets	(4,212)	9,069	(1,923)	(2,934)	—	—
Appropriations (note 15)	36	—	14,905	(14,941)	—	—
Resources, end of year	$5,038	$27,117	$53,695	$20,019	$105,869	$99,045

See accompanying notes to financial statements

EXHIBIT 10-7 *(Continued)*

Sample NFP Financial Statements, Canadian Cancer Society

Statement of Financial Activities — Operations and Externally Restricted Resources
(In thousands of dollars)
Year Ended January 31, 2009, with comparative figures for 2008

	Operations		Externally restricted	
	2009	2008 (Restated – note 2(a))	2009	2008 (Restated – note 2(a))
Revenue:				
Relay for Life	$ 51,005	$ 44,279	$ —	$ —
Annual giving	49,279	50,987	5	61
Major and planned gifts	42,075	43,170	582	275
Special events	26,949	26,175	25	—
Tributes	12,290	12,866	—	—
Lotteries, net revenue (note 13)	2,003	4,068	—	—
Government sponsored projects	10,564	9,536	153	258
Investment income (expense)	1,200	4,147	(117)	14
Other income	8,155	2,707	3,615	1,516
	$203,520	$197,935	$4,263	$2,124
Expenditures:				
Cancer Control:				
Research (note 7)	$ 48,588	$ 49,536	$ 243	$ —
Support for people living with cancer	37,051	32,957	155	553
Prevention	20,352	16,828	93	297
Information	15,033	14,873	78	262
Advocacy	6,844	5,943	7	—
	127,868	120,137	576	1,112
Supporting:				
Fundraising	61,984	57,703	740	605
Management and general	9,754	9,929	37	139
	71,738	67,632	777	744
	199,606	187,769	1,353	1,856
Increase in resources	$ 3,914	$ 10,166	$2,910	$ 268

See accompanying notes to financial statements.

EXHIBIT 10-7 (*Continued*)

Sample NFP Financial Statements, Canadian Cancer Society

Statement of Cash Flows
(In thousands of dollars)
Year Ended January 31, 2009, with comparative figures for 2008

	2009	2008 (Restated – note 2(a))
Cash provided by (used in):		
Operating activities:		
Increase in resources	$ 6,824	$10,434
Non-cash items:		
Amortization of capital assets	2,554	2,692
Amortization of intangible assets	28	29
Gain on capital asset disposition	(3,414)	(33)
Post-retirement benefits expense	1,972	1,841
Defined benefit pension expense	3,807	3,104
Net unrealized losses on investments	3,045	1,968
Employer post-retirement benefits contributions	(436)	(380)
Employer defined benefit contributions	(3,058)	(3,038)
Change in non-cash operating working capital	1,778	(3,117)
	13,100	13,500
Financing activities:		
Increase (decrease) in credit facility	(50)	1,478
Investing activities:		
Capital asset additions	(9,330)	(10,801)
Capital asset disposal	4,758	38
Net increase in short-term investments	(4,321)	(966)
Net increase in long-term investments	(2,032)	(6,621)
	(10,925)	(18,350)
Increase (decrease) in cash	2,125	(3,372)
Cash, beginning of year	20,634	24,006
Cash, end of year	$22,759	$20,634

See accompanying notes to financial statements.

However, the statement of operations has two columns for each year—operations and externally restricted. There is no total column. Therefore, the CCS must be using the restricted-fund method. This is confirmed in the accounting policy note (not reproduced in Exhibit 10-7), which states that "the Society follows the restricted-fund method of accounting for contributions." The SFP, however, also presents "deferred contributions" of $8,967. The CCS must also be using the deferral method of accounting for some of the restricted contributions. This is also confirmed in the notes.

The consolidated statement of changes in resources contains the reconciliation of beginning fund balances (called "Resources" in the CCS statements) with the ending balances. In this statement, there are four columns for the current year as contrasted with two columns in the operating statement. The four-column reconciliation in the statement of changes corresponds with the four balances shown under "resources" on the statement of financial position.

Finally, in the CCS 2009 cash flow statement, the adjustments decrease the accrual-basis surplus of $6,824 to a cash flow surplus of $2,125.

Relevant Standards

Accounting Standards for Private Enterprises

4410 Contributions — revenue recognition
4420 Contributions receivable
4430 Capital assets held by not-for-profit organizations
4440 Collections held by not-for-profit organizations
4450 Reporting controlled and related entities by not-for-profit organizations
4460 Disclosure of related party transactions by not-for-profit organizations
4470 Disclosure of allocated expenses by not-for-profit organizations

Summary of Key Points

1. A non-business organization is any organization other than a private enterprise operating for profit. Non-business organizations can be roughly divided into three groups: (1) governments, (2) governmental units, and (3) not-for-profit organizations.
2. The primary differences between not-for-profit organizations and business enterprises are that (1) they have members, but no owners; (2) they do not exist to generate a return on investment; (3) expenses are not usually incurred to generate revenue; and (4) the suppliers of funds usually do not receive the benefits of an NFP's activities.
3. The objectives of NFP financial reporting tend to emphasize (1) stewardship and (2) measuring the cost of services. Most NFPs obtain their funding from members, external donors, and public or government granting agencies. These donors need to see how the

organization used the resources that were given to it during the year. Therefore, there often is a heightened interest in stewardship reporting—what did the managers do with the funds entrusted to their care?

4. Accounting for expenditures becomes an important reporting objective for many NFPs. Some NFPs provide goods and services to individuals on a cost-recovery basis. In such cases, a primary reporting objective is to measure the cost of providing those services. The emphasis then falls on expense accounting rather than expenditure accounting.
5. There are many reporting issues that are unique to NFPs. One of the first issues is to determine which of three different bases to use to recognize the resource outflows of any organization in the statement of operations: disbursement basis, expenditure basis, and expense basis. Second, because the majority of NFPs qualify for an exemption from the capitalize-and-amortize approach in the *CICA Handbook*, there is often an issue on how to account for capital assets. Third, determining the necessary disclosure required when an organization allocates costs from administrative and fundraising efforts to other expenses such as education is a new issue that many organizations are facing. Fourth, there is often a problem in simply identifying the reporting entity, identifying possible related-party transactions, and implementing consolidated reporting. Finally, NFPs must account for contributions from donors and funding partners. Unlike business enterprises, these contributions may be restricted for specific uses. NFPs also receive donated goods and services and donated capital assets.
6. The *CICA Handbook, Part III* recommends two methods of reporting: (1) the deferral method or (2) the restricted-fund method. The deferral method can be used by any NFP. The restricted-fund method can be used only by an NFP that has at least one externally restricted fund. The deferral method adds all of the various funds together into a single total column. No segregation is reported, except that separate fund balances may be reported in the statement of financial position. The individual reported-fund balances then are reconciled in a statement of changes in fund balances. The restricted-fund method permits segregated reporting for restricted and endowment funds. The funds do not need to be added together on the statement of operations, although a total column should be provided on the statement of financial position.
7. An accounting procedure that is unique to NFPs and governments is the use of budgetary accounts within the formal set of accounts. The purpose of budgetary accounts is to control the level of expenditure, and also to permit an automatic comparison of budget versus actual amounts at every reporting date. Expenditure limits are enforced by means of encumbrance accounting. Encumbrance accounting records an obligation as soon as a purchase order is issued, thereby reducing the amount of available funds that can be committed to other purchases.

Companion Website

Visit the text's website at www.pearsoned.ca/beechy for practice quizzes, additional problems, Excel® templates, answers to Concept Check questions, and important IFRS updates.

Self-Study Problem 10-1

You have been recruited to act as the treasurer on the board of directors of a not-for-profit organization. The board of directors has very limited accounting experience. The organization, Rose Plants Forever (RPF), receives an estimated $800,000 per year in regular contributions from the federal government.

RPF uses the deferral method of accounting for contributions and has no separate fund for restricted contributions. On January 1, 20X6, RPF received its first restricted cash contribution—$200,000 for the purchase and maintenance of land and a greenhouse building for its rare rose plant collection. On July 1, 20X6, RPF acquired land and a building for $44,000 and $120,000 cash, respectively. The building has an estimated useful life of 20 years and zero salvage value. On December 31, 20X6, the remaining $36,000 cash was paid to KJ Maintenance Ltd. for a three-year maintenance contract that requires KJ personnel to provide maintenance services four days per month until December 31, 20X9.

Required

Prepare the journal entries for the following dates:

1. January 1, 20X6
2. July 1, 20X6
3. December 31, 20X6

[CGA–Canada, adapted]

Self-Study Problem 10-2

The OPI Care Centre (OPI) is a not-for-profit organization funded by government grants and private donations. It prepares its annual financial statements using the deferral method of accounting for contributions, and it uses only the operations fund to account for all activities. It uses an encumbrance system as a means of controlling expenditures.

Required

The following summarizes some of the transactions that were made during 20X2. Assuming a GAAP constraint, prepare the journal entries to reflect the transactions.

1. The founding member of OPI contributed $100,000 on the condition that the principal amount be invested in marketable securities and that only the income earned from the investment be spent on operations.
2. During the year, purchase orders were issued to cover the budgeted cost of $1,400,000 for goods and contracted services.

3. During the year, a public campaign was held to raise funds for daily operations for the current year. Cash of $800,000 was collected, and pledges for an additional $100,000 were received by the end of the year. It is estimated that approximately 95% of these pledges will be collected early in the new year.
4. The provincial government pledged $600,000 for the year to cover operating costs and an additional $1,000,000 to purchase equipment and furniture. All of the grant money was received by the end of the year, except for the last $50,000 to cover operating costs for December.
5. OPI used the $1,000,000 received from the provincial government to purchase equipment and furniture for the care facility. The amortization of these assets amounted to $100,000 for the year. A purchase order has not been issued for this purchase.
6. Invoices totalling $1,450,000 were received for goods and contracted services. Of these invoices, 90% were paid by the end of the fiscal year. Purchase orders in the amount of $1,375,000 had been issued for these services.

   [CGA–Canada, adapted]

Review Questions

10-1 Who owns not-for-profit organizations?

10-2 What is the difference between *non-business* organizations and *not-for-profit* organizations?

10-3 Describe the population of NFPs in Canada. Are there any financial reporting implications given the skewness of the size distribution?

10-4 Distinguish between an *open membership* not-for-profit organization and a *closed membership* organization.

10-5 What types of organizations offer *private goods and services*?

10-6 Describe the ways in which the nature of revenue in not-for-profit organizations can differ from the nature of revenue in business enterprises.

10-7 Who are the primary users of the financial statements of not-for-profit organizations?

10-8 If the emphasis in accounting for many not-for-profit organizations is on the control of cash flows, why is the accrual basis recommended?

10-9 Explain the difference between the *expense basis*, the *expenditure basis*, and the *disbursements basis* of reporting.

10-10 What alternative approaches are there to accounting for capital assets in not-for-profit organizations?

10-11 What is a *pledge* and what are the criteria for recognizing pledges?

10-12 What is a *collection* and what criteria are required to be met for a group of items to be defined as a collection?

10-13 Explain the differences between an *externally restricted contribution*, a *board-designated (internally restricted) fund*, an *endowment contribution,* and an *unrestricted contribution.*

10-14 How are *externally restricted contributions* recognized in the deferral method compared to the restricted-fund method? What is the difference if there is no separate fund in the *restricted-fund method* for that contribution?

10-15 Does the restricted-fund method or the deferral method of accounting tend to result in a higher level of revenues?

10-16 How should an NFP account for a business enterprise that it controls?

10-17 Why is the allocation of expenses an issue for NFPs?

10-18 When budgetary accounts are used, why is the amount for estimated revenues a debit instead of a credit?

10-19 What is an *encumbrance*?

10-20 What is the purpose of an *encumbrance system*?

CASES

CASE 10-1 REPORTING OBJECTIVES

You have recently been appointed auditor of three different organizations. The first organization is a mining company that was formed a year ago to develop a gold mining site in northern Ontario. The largest single part of the initial investment was provided by a major, publicly held mining company in exchange for 36% of the common shares. The remaining shares were issued publicly in the over-the-counter market, where they are very thinly traded. The company is still in the development stage and does not expect to commence production for at least another year.

The second organization is a not-for-profit secondary school that provides courses for students who intend to pursue a career in one of the performing arts. The school is fully recognized by the provincial Ministry of Education, which provides about 50% of the school's operating budget. Another 20% of the operating funds are provided by the Ministry of Culture and Recreation, while the remainder is derived from student fees and by fundraising in the private sector. The school occupies an old public high school building that was no longer being used by the city; the school acquired the building on a 20-year lease from the city's board of education.

The third organization is a labour union for the graduate students at a major university. The union receives its funding from dues that are mandatorily deducted by the university from the earnings of all members of the bargaining unit, whether they are members of the union or not. A portion of the funds is sent to the union's parent national organization, and another part is set aside for the strike fund, which is held and invested by a trustee until such time as it is needed to pay striking union members.

Required

Explain how the objectives of financial reporting would likely differ for these three organizations.

CASE 10-2 GOLD DEVELOPMENT

Gold Development (GD), a newly incorporated not-for-profit organization with a December 31 year-end, will offer low-rent housing services for people with low income.

GD reports to Logimex, a government agency that requires audited annual financial statements to be filed. Mr. Bilodeau, the project originator and administrator of GD, is not familiar with the preparation of financial statements.

GD received a non-repayable grant from Logimex in February 20X2 for the construction of an eight-storey apartment building. Construction began in April 20X2.

Residents will start to move into the apartment building between October and December 20X2, although it will not be entirely completed until the end of December 20X2. By December 20X2 all the apartments should be rented.

GD receives donations from companies and individuals in the region. It has received pledges from large, well-known companies for the next five years, and pledges from individuals for the current and next year. Pledge amounts have been set out in writing on forms signed by the donors.

For a nominal salary, Mr. Bilodeau manages the organization with the help of his wife and the local priest, both of whom are volunteers.

Required

1. Explain to Mr. Bilodeau what is meant by "reporting on a restricted-fund accounting basis" according to the *CICA Handbook.*
2. Advise Mr. Bilodeau on the appropriate accounting for the above issues assuming that GD decides to report on a restricted-fund accounting basis.

CASE 10-3 PERTH HOUSING

Perth Housing Corporation (PHC) is a community-sponsored not-for-profit organization that was incorporated on September 1, 20X5. Its purpose is to provide residential accommodation for physically handicapped adults in the town of Perth.

The nature of PHC's operations is described in Exhibit A. The sources of funding are described in Exhibit B.

The executive director has asked for your assistance in establishing accounting policies for PHC for its general purpose year-end financial statements. The accounting policies should comply with GAAP.

Required

Provide recommendations for accounting policies for PHC for the year ended August 31, 20X6. Assume that PHC would want to set up two funds for reporting purposes—a general fund and a capital fund—and that annual revenues exceed $1,050,000.

Exhibit A Nature of Operations

In October 20X5, PHC purchased a 15-unit apartment building in downtown Perth for $1,125,000. It then spent $375,000 in renovations to upgrade the building and make it accessible for physically handicapped adults.

PHC offers 24-hour non-medical attendant care. Support care services are provided through a combination of staff members and volunteers. The staff members receive a monthly salary. As an inducement to recruit and retain qualified support care workers, each staff member is allowed 15 sick days per year. The employee can bank the sick days not used in any one year. Upon termination or retirement, the employee is paid for banked sick days at the wage rate in effect at that time.

Rental payments are due the first day of each month and are geared to tenant income. Most of the tenants are very good about making their rent payments on time. Some rental payments are received late. On August 31, 20X6, there was $19,500 of unpaid rent.

PHC plans to install central air conditioning in the building in April 20X7 at an expected cost of $75,000. This expenditure is being financed by a special fundraising drive, which, by August 31, 20X6, has raised $30,000 in cash and $22,500 in pledges from citizens in the local community.

Exhibit B **Sources of Funding**

The cost of acquiring and renovating the apartment building was financed by a $1,500,000 cash donation received from the estate of Mr. Smith. The provincial government funds approximately 70% of non-medical and support costs. Claims are made monthly for the previous month's eligible costs. PHC depends on outside fundraising efforts, primarily door-to-door canvassing and sponsored bingos, to cover the remaining non-medical care and support costs.

[CGA–Canada, adapted]

CASE 10-4 **YOUTH SINGERS**

Youth Singers (YS) is a not-for-profit organization that was formed in 20X1 by Nancy, a retired professional singer. Members of the choir range in age from 8 to 20. The choir has won a number of major singing competitions across North America and is producing its first CD next month. The choir plans to record an annual CD of its Christmas concert.

Nancy is in charge of YS's daily operations. All major decisions need to be approved by the board of directors. Initial financing for YS came solely from private donations, and a fundraising committee was recently formed to raise funds for special projects. Last year, YS qualified for two government grants that require audited financial statements to be submitted on an annual basis. YS has attached a set of financial statements to government grant applications in the past. The Canada Revenue Agency also requires financial statements to provide tax receipts for donors.

Your CA firm has a policy of supporting its staff in volunteering their time to NFP activities. You have recently joined YS as a member of its board of directors and have volunteered to assist with all accounting issues. Details on past accounting policies are provided in Exhibit C.

You have been asked to prepare a report identifying any changes you would make to the current accounting policies for the next board of directors' meeting.

Required

Prepare the draft report to the board of directors.

Exhibit C **Accounting Policies and Other Information**

1. Donation—Original Historic Sheet Music
   A donor recently died, leaving in her will a large selection of sheet music to YS. It is impossible to verify the value of this donation due to its historical value. The music will be performed by the choir during concerts. The original sheet music will be displayed in a glassed-in case.

2. Annual Pledges
   Every Christmas, YS holds an annual benefit concert. At this time, YS holds a major fundraising drive and asks all concert guests to provide a donation or pledge an amount. All pledges are recognized when the pledge is made by the donor.
3. Fundraising Costs
   YS is committed to having fundraising costs not exceed 5% of donation revenue. Nancy reviews all amounts expended for fundraising each year. Part of the advertising and promotion costs for fundraising are allocated to education each year because part of the purpose of these campaigns is to educate the public on the goals of YS.
4. Capital Assets
   All capital assets are recorded at their market value as determined by the finance director. During 20X7, a local music store provided sheet music stands at manufacturer's direct costs of $20,000. Purchasing these stands at retail prices would have cost $40,000.
5. Revenues
   Individual choir members started providing singing lessons during 20X7 as a source of fundraising. The revenue during 20X7 from lessons was $50,000. Annual revenue from all sources was $200,000 in 20X6 and $280,000 during 20X7.
6. Amortization
   Capital assets are not amortized.

CASE 10-5 FINEST ART GALLERY

Finest Art Gallery (Finest) is a major art gallery in Toronto. Finest has the largest collection of art in Canada and has five major exhibits a year. Finest is a not-for-profit organization with funding received primarily from private contributors and government grants.

The board of directors turns over its members every three years. A new board just announced for 20X3 to 20X5 has a number of younger members who have rejuvenated a previous idea to expand a new section of the gallery for the work of children. This would require major fundraising over the next few years. It is anticipated that this addition would attract a wider audience to the gallery and encourage young children to become interested in art at an early age.

The new board, although energetic and ambitious, lacks knowledge of accounting. Board members were recruited for their marketing skills and love of art. They have asked you, CA, to assist them over the next few months in selecting accounting policies and provide recommendations for changes to their existing policies. They want to comply with any *CICA Handbook* recommendations for not-for-profit organizations, but are not familiar with the *Handbook*'s content. You have committed to preparing a report for the next board meeting outlining specific accounting policies. If you recommend any changes, they must be fully supported. The board is concerned with the costs involved with preparing financial statements and wants to minimize these costs.

After the meeting with the board of directors you sat down and reviewed the financial statements for 20X3. Notes from your review are included in Exhibit D.

A set of financial statements has been provided to any donors who requested them in the past. In addition, government agencies require a set of audited financial statements as a requirement for government grants.

Required

Prepare the report for the board of directors.

Exhibit D

Notes: Taken from a Review of the 20X3 Financial Statements

1. The financial statements include a statement of income and expenditures and a statement of financial position. A cash flow statement was not prepared since it was felt that it does not provide meaningful information.
2. Revenues for 20X3 included the following:

Memberships	$ 600,000
Admission fees	800,000
Government grants	2,000,000
Contributions	450,000
Endowment fund revenue	950,000

3. Admission fees are recognized as money is collected. Contributions are recognized when a pledge is made by the donor. Notes to the financial statements segregate the number of restricted and unrestricted contributions. Restricted funds include any amounts donated for a specific purpose and amounts segregated by the board for future expansion or special projects.
4. All capital assets are recorded at a dollar value to have a nominal amount provided on the financial statements. No amortization is taken on these assets. A recent review of the capital assets indicated the following items. The amounts were estimated by one of the board of directors:

Office equipment	$ 500,000
Automobiles	70,000
Facilities	10,000,000
Artwork	unable to estimate

5. During 20X3, the roof was replaced on the art gallery at a cost of $260,000. This amount was expensed. In addition, a new air-conditioning unit was installed to protect the artwork from damages due to temperature changes. The cost was $300,000. To finance the purchase of the new air-conditioning system, a piece of artwork was sold.
6. Volunteer services are not recorded.
7. For fundraising, a portion of the advertising and promotion costs incurred are allocated to education expenditures each year.

CASE 10-6 TGF CARE FACILITY

The TGF Care Facility (TGF) is a not-for-profit organization dedicated to providing services in the care and rehabilitation of seniors with physical or mental disabilities. The main programs are the seniors' residence program and the home-care program. TGF also sponsors research activities and conducts educational activities for its clients, their relatives, and the general public.

TGF has an eight-person board of directors that sets policy and approves plans, but the day-to-day operations are left to Joe, the full-time, salaried executive director. At a recent meeting, Joe told you that he is not satisfied with the information provided in the annual financial statements. He does not see how he and the board can make useful decisions on the basis of information presented in the financial statements. He wants the financial statements to be audited as this may help improve financial reporting and provide credibility to the financial statements, which may, in turn, increase donor confidence and donations. The financial statements have never been audited in the past.

Revenues for TGF's activities exceeded $600,000 per year in 20X8 and 20X9. Revenues are obtained from a variety of sources. Approximately 50% of the total revenue is obtained from the residents in the form of a user fee. Approximately 30% of the total revenue is obtained from the Ministry of Social Services. Most of the remainder is obtained from bequests and from donations by foundations, corporations, and individuals.

The Ministry of Social Services provides funds on the basis of annual budgets prepared for each program. Many of the public donations are also designated for specific programs or purposes such as research. The bequests are usually given under the condition that the principal amount cannot be expended. The income from investing the bequest can be used for designated purposes. The board at its discretion can allocate unrestricted donations.

TGF has constructed several buildings over the years to house the various programs. All the buildings were paid for by a combination of specific capital grants from the municipal and provincial governments and funds raised for capital projects by public campaigns. The repair and maintenance of the furniture and equipment, as well as general maintenance of the buildings, are paid for out of operating funds as needed.

You are an accountant with a professional designation. You have been asked by Joe to prepare a memo to the board of directors. The memo should describe the changes in accounting policies necessary to ensure a clean audit opinion in accordance with GAAP for the December 31, 20X9, year-end. The memo should also explain how these accounting practices will better serve the needs of the users of TGF's financial statements. A description of current accounting practices for TGF is provided in Exhibit E.

Required

Prepare the memo to the board of directors. Revenue recognition policies should use the deferral method.

Exhibit E

Notes on Accounting System and Practices

1. The annual financial statements consist of a statement of financial position, a statement of cash receipts and disbursements, and a statement of changes in net assets. The statement of cash receipts and disbursements compares the actual results for the year against the original budget of the year.
2. The budget is prepared annually by the treasurer of the board in co-operation with the executive director. A monthly comparison of the year-to-date expenditure with the total budgeted amounts, on a line-by-line basis, is prepared by the bookkeeper and forwarded to the executive director and treasurer.
3. Grants from governments, foundations, and corporations are recorded as revenue when pledges are made or grants are announced. Donations from individuals are recorded as revenue when the cash, cheque, or credit card voucher is received, regardless of whether the cheque or voucher is current-dated or post-dated.
4. Expenditures are charged to accounts as paid, on the basis of the type of expenditure; for example, all salaries are charged to a single account, all furniture replacements and repairs are charged to a single account, and so forth.
5. The historical cost of the buildings and land is carried on the SFP. The buildings are not amortized. The cost of furniture and equipment is charged to operations when the expenditure is made.

[CGA–Canada, adapted]

CASE 10-7 CKER–FM ETHNIC RADIO

In the fall of 20X1, eight wealthy businesspeople from the same ethnic background formed a committee (CKER committee) to obtain a radio licence from the Canadian Radio-Television and Telecommunications Commission (CRTC). Their goal is to start a not-for-profit, ethnic community radio station for their area. They plan to call the station CKER–FM Ethnic Radio (CKER). It will broadcast ethnic music, news and sports from their country of origin, cultural information, ethnic cooking, and other such programs, seven days a week.

The station's capital requirements are to be financed by memberships, donations, and various types of loans. It is expected that the ongoing operations will be supported by advertising paid for by businesspeople from that ethnic community and by the larger business community targeting that ethnic audience, as well as by donations and memberships.

It is now March 20X2, and the CRTC has announced that hearings will start in one month on a number of broadcasting licence applications, including the CKER committee's application. The CKER committee members are fairly confident about the viability of their proposal; however, they have decided to seek the advice of a professional accounting firm to assist with the endeavour. The CKER committee has engaged Maria & Casano, Public Accountants, for the assignment, as three of the five partners of the firm are from the same ethnic community. The partner in charge of the assignment has stated that the firm will donate half its fee for the work.

You are a public accountant who works for Maria & Casano and have been put in charge of the assignment. You have met with the CKER committee and various volunteers associated with the project. Information gathered on station start-up is contained in Exhibit F. Exhibit G provides other information on the CKER committee's proposal. The partner has asked you to prepare a draft report to the committee members discussing the viability of the proposed radio station over the initial three-year period. Since the committee members are fairly confident that they will receive the licence, the partner has asked you to recommend accounting policies for the transactions that CKER is contemplating. Your report must also cover other significant issues that the station will face after it commences operations.

Required

Prepare the draft report.

Exhibit F Information on Station Start-Up

1. Costs to date have totalled $50,000 and are mostly transportation and meeting costs, as well as postage. These costs have been paid for personally by the CKER committee members.
2. To approve the licence application, the CRTC must see written commitments to finance the station's start-up costs and operating losses in the first two years. Remaining costs to obtain the licence, excluding donated legal work, are expected to be about $8,000, and will be paid by CKER committee members.
3. If the CRTC approves the licence application, the CKER committee will immediately set up a not-for-profit organization and apply to the Canada Revenue Agency (CRA) for charitable status, which it will likely receive.
4. Fairly exhaustive efforts to obtain commercial financing have failed. As a result, four wealthy individuals have volunteered to provide CKER with the financing for the start-up. They will each personally borrow $25,000 from financial institutions and give the funds to the station. These individuals expect the loan to be cost-free to them, as the station will make the interest and principal payments.
5. A "Reverse Lifetime Contribution" program will be instituted. Under this program a donor will pay the station a capital sum of at least $50,000. The station can do whatever it wants with the funds, but it will repay the donor an equal annual amount calculated as the capital sum divided by 90 years less the individual's age at the time of contribution. Upon the death of the donor, the station will retain the balance of the funds. Currently, a 64-year-old station supporter has committed $78,000, and seven other individuals are considering this method of assisting the station.
6. Initially the station is to broadcast with a 2,500-watt signal. Within three to four years it hopes to obtain commercial financing for a second transmitter that will boost the power of the signal and the broadcast range.

Exhibit G Other Information About Plans for the Station

1. The CKER committee has analyzed census and other data to determine the potential market for the station. Engineering studies have mapped out the area that will be covered by the broadcast signal. There are about 1.1 million people in the target listening area. The latest Canadian census shows that 14% of the population

comes from the target ethnic group. By applying a conservative factor of 40% to these findings, the CKER committee has arrived at a listenership figure of about 5.6% or about 62,000 people. The CKER committee has found that about one in five of the businesses in the area are run by members of the ethnic community, many of whom would like a medium for reaching their own people through direct advertising.

2. The amount of time expected to be devoted to commercials per hour is four minutes in year one, five minutes in year two, and six minutes in year three. Advertising cost per minute, discounted to 25% below the current market rate, will be:

Prime time (6 hours a day)	$40
Regular time (10 hours a day)	$30
Off-peak (8 hours a day)	$25

   Advertising time will be sold by salespeople whose remuneration will be a 15% commission.
3. Miscellaneous revenue from renting out the recording studio when not in use by CKER could approach $3,000 per month in year three, but will start out at about $2,200 per month.
4. At least 120 people have committed to pay a $125 annual membership fee. Membership carries no special privileges other than to be identified as a supporter of the station. Membership is expected to grow by 20% per year.
5. Start-up capital expenditures are as follows: transmission equipment $61,000; broadcast studio equipment $62,000; and production studio equipment $40,000. Administration and other costs, including rent, are expected to total about $1,237,000 per year and will not increase when advertising sales increase.
6. The committee believes that there are no GST implications related to running the station, since it is a not-for-profit venture.
7. About one-third of the person-hours needed to run the station are expected to come from volunteers.

[CICA]

CASE 10-8 SAFETY NET

Safety Net (SN) is a not-for-profit organization operating in Big Town, Canada. SN runs a shelter for the homeless, operates a soup kitchen, and provides counselling services to runaway teenagers and street kids. The demand for SN's services has expanded rapidly over the last few years, as has its operating budget. Exhibit H describes SN's operations.

SN's operations have changed substantially in the past year (Exhibit H). Fundraising has been much more aggressive, two government grants have been obtained, and the "bequest on death" campaign begun several years ago yielded one large bequest during the year. In dealing with these changes, the board of directors of SN realized that they need financial advice to ensure they are making informed business decisions. Accordingly, they recently approached your firm, Fortin & Larose, Public Accountants, to advise them on the reporting requests they should be making of management to provide relevant information. Where appropriate, the board would like advice on the selection of accounting policies and on financial statement disclosure and other matters of importance. In the past, SN has recorded revenue and expenses on a cash basis.

The board has asked your firm to perform an audit to meet the requirements of one of the government grants and to provide the certified documentation for both grants, for the year ended March 31, 20X8 (see Exhibit I).

It is now January 22, 20X8. The senior partner of Fortin & Larose has asked you to draft a report to the board of directors of SN providing them with the requested information. The partner has also requested a memo highlighting the various engagement issues. He believes that there are additional service opportunities, and he wants you to note in the memo the services that the firm could perform for SN.

Required

Prepare the report and the memo.

Exhibit H Description of Safety Net's Operations

SN has three core operations: a shelter for the homeless, a soup kitchen for the needy, and a drop-in counselling service for runaways and street kids. There are also administrative and fundraising activities.

SHELTER FOR THE HOMELESS

The shelter operates out of a former university residence. The residence was donated to SN several years ago when the university was closed as part of the provincial government's plan to rationalize higher education. No amount was recorded on SN's books for the donated residence. The shelter is run by a very small number of staff.

SOUP KITCHEN

The soup kitchen operates out of leased facilities: a former church in a rundown part of town. The signing of a 20-year lease on this property resulted in the dismissal of the previous executive director of SN after the board discovered the lease costs exceeded the fair market-value rent for similar properties and that the remaining useful life of the church, at the signing of the lease, was only 15 years.

Paid staff and volunteers prepare two meals a day. Volunteers include chefs from local restaurants, university food-service providers, and students from a local university's food sciences program.

Donated food supplies are a major component of operations, and the level of donations remains relatively constant. Corporations make donations throughout the year, and individuals donate large volumes of fresh produce in the summer and fall months. None of these donated goods or services is currently recorded.

COUNSELLING SERVICES FOR RUNAWAYS AND STREET KIDS

The drop-in centre has two paid counsellors who work closely with the kids and provide referrals to other programs, such as drug rehabilitation.

The centre has entered into several innovative arrangements to provide assistance to runaways needing transportation back home. A major airline has begun a frequent-flyer grant program whereby the members of its frequent-flyer program are asked to donate some or all of their frequent-flyer points to the drop-in centre. The centre can then use the donated points to acquire a plane ticket. Counsellors attempt to identify the kids most likely to benefit from free transportation back home.

ADMINISTRATION

The administrative staff consists of the executive director, a full-time fundraiser, a manager for each of the three operating areas, a bookkeeper, and an accounting clerk/receptionist. There is a relatively large number of volunteer fundraisers. In the past, fundraising consisted mainly of a door-to-door campaign by volunteers seeking donations and selling "I care" SN memberships. In SN's financial statements, the costs of the campaign are netted against total funds raised to present a single door-to-door fundraising total.

The bookkeeper handles all accounting and banking duties except for verifying accounts payable invoices for accuracy and filing documents. The two tasks are handled by a receptionist. The bookkeeper has a desktop computer system and uses an off-the-shelf computerized accounting package.

The executive director orally promised the full-time fundraiser a bonus of 10% of funds raised in excess of $500,000.

Exhibit I Changes to Safety Net's Operations

FUNDRAISING

The full-time fundraiser aggressively pursued fundraising opportunities. Among the new fundraising efforts was a Safety Net charity golf tournament put on by a local golf club. The net proceeds of the tournament received from the golf club were recorded on SN's books.

SN's annual telethon was held on a local cable television station during December 20X7. Its success was greatly enhanced when a country music superstar, in town for a series of concerts, saw the broadcast and volunteered to do a one-hour personal appearance as soon as five companies pledged $20,000 each. Five local car dealers responded by making pledges, although payment has yet to be received. News of this commitment increased the number of personal pledges by viewers. Even though the number of personal pledges increased, only a small percentage of them have been honoured to date. As a result, the bookkeeper is not sure how to record the pledges.

The "bequest on death" program began several years ago. There was one large bequest during the year, which left SN with a cash fund to be used for capital acquisitions only. During the years some of the money from the fund was used to acquire furniture for the shelter, at a cost substantially below fair market value.

Two grants were negotiated during the year. The first provides for the recovery of 50% of operating costs for the shelter and soup kitchen and 30% of other operating costs. The second government grant was a lump sum contribution of $200,000 to assist with capital costs related to the shelter for the next five years. SN must provide a minimum number of beds at the shelter during that period and create at least one full-time position or 33% of the grant becomes payable. Both grants include a clause that states, "Safety Net will provide certified documentation annually to support its claim of government funds." The second grant also requires annual audited financial statements to be submitted to the government.

During the year, SN began a campaign to raise funds to build a new shelter for runaway children. The shelter is expected to begin operations in three years. Thus far, $2 million in pledges has been raised, and construction of the building is scheduled to begin sometime in July 20X8. SN plans to apply most of the $200,000 grant from the government to the capital costs of the new shelter. The funds have therefore been set aside for this use.

[CICA]

CASE 10-9 EUROPEAN EXCHANGE CLUB

On August 15, 20X1, the European Exchange Club (EEC) was formed in an effort to create a united social group out of several separate regional clubs in the vicinity of the city of Decker, located in central Canada. The purpose of the group is to combine resources to meet the recreational, cultural, and social needs of their collective members. EEC was formed through the collaboration of the following clubs and their memberships:

Members	
The Canadian Russian Society	$12,300
The Italian Club of Canada	10,800
Portuguese Cultural Foundation	4,100
Association of Greeks of the World	2,700
The German Groups	1,100
Other	1,700
	$32,700

It is now December 20X7, and EEC's executives have spent the past few years planning and preparing for the club's operation. The club's community centre is expected to be fully completed next year. Its facilities will include the following:

- a multi-purpose building to house banquets, meetings, and arts activities;
- hiking trails;
- indoor/outdoor tennis facilities;
- bicycle trails;
- baseball diamonds;
- an indoor/outdoor pool; and
- a soccer field.

The multi-purpose building is 75% complete, and EEC's executives have stated that it is "approximately within budget." Estimated building costs were outlined in a 20X6 feasibility study as follows:

Construction cost	$2,300,000
Site preparation costs	400,000
Furniture and fixtures	550,000
Consulting fees	120,000
Miscellaneous	80,000
	$3,450,000

The four hectares of land on which the facility is built were provided by the provincial government by way of a five-year lease at $1 a year. The Italian Club of Canada contributed the 60 hectares of adjacent land. Previously, this land had been leased to a farmer for $54,000 a year. The 64 hectares will be used for the following projects, which will incur the additional costs listed below:

Hiking trails	$ 595,000
Baseball diamonds	30,000
Soccer field	22,000
Bicycle trails	95,000
Indoor/outdoor pool	700,000
Indoor/outdoor tennis facilities	300,000
	$1,742,000

In addition to these development costs, the club faces annual operating costs of approximately $740,000, outlined in Exhibit J. John Mendez-Smith, the newly elected president of the club, has approached your firm, Young and Kerr, Chartered Accountants, to prepare a report that provides recommendations on accounting, finance, and internal control issues. You took the notes appearing in Exhibit K at a meeting with the club's president and executive committee.

Required

Prepare the requested report for the president.

Exhibit J

EUROPEAN EXCHANGE CLUB YEARLY BUDGET

Operating revenues	
Membership fees	$ 91,000
Social rentals	185,000
Meeting rentals	50,000
Sports rentals	23,000
Concessions	61,000
Fund raising events	225,000
Total operating revenues	$635,000
Operating costs	
Salaries	$363,000
Administrative costs	39,000
Maintenance	126,000
Utilities	112,000
Educational scholarships	100,000
Total operating costs	$740,000

Exhibit K

Notes From Meeting

1. Under the lease agreement with the province, EEC is responsible for maintenance and all costs of improvements. The lease agreement provides for 20 renewal terms of five years' duration each. Renewal is based on the condition that EEC makes the club's services available to all present and future EEC member clubs and their membership.
2. EEC has requested an operating grant from the provincial government. Its proposal asks the province to provide EEC with annual funds to cover 50% of "approved" operating costs incurred to provide services to all club members. The city of Decker wishes to construct an arena and a swimming pool and has opposed the provincial operating grant. The city has asked to be the first in line for available provincial funds. The province has informed EEC that if funds are granted, EEC will have to supply audited financial statements of the organization for all future fiscal year-ends. The committee members suspect that they will have to compromise on their proposal and are having problems determining the minimum annual funds required by the club from the province.
3. The Russian and Italian clubs have been arguing with other clubs over the equalization payments required from each club. Currently, each club makes payments to EEC based upon its proportionate membership. Payments for each calendar year are made on February 1 of the following year.
4. The accounting function is a major concern of the member club representatives. In particular, they have raised the following issues:
   a) Several fundraising events are organized by individual member clubs.
   b) Any donations to EEC are received through the member clubs.
   c) No accounting has been made of services donated to EEC by the members of the individual clubs.
   d) EEC has approached a bank to assist in future phases of the club's development. The bank has informed EEC that it is interested in asset values and EEC's ability to repay the loans.

[CICA]

CASE 10-10 ART GALLERY

You have been hired to prepare a report for the board of directors of a large art gallery. The board has just reviewed the annual financial statements of the art gallery, and is dissatisfied with the financial information provided in the statements. You have been provided with the following information.

The principal activity of the art gallery is the acquisition and exhibition of modern and contemporary pieces of art. The gallery is open to the general public on a daily basis, and has special exhibits for specific interest groups. Each year the gallery has a number of fundraising activities to help defray operating costs and make the acquisition of art possible. These activities are organized by the support staff, but rely on volunteers to staff the various functions. The major fundraising activity is an Annual Rennaise Telethon (ART), which solicits pledges from corporations and individuals and has been very successful.

Capital assets, in addition to the pieces of artwork, include a building, maintenance equipment, office furniture, and fixtures. The building that houses the art gallery is a large Victorian mansion that was donated by a prominent local family several years ago. Because the building has been designated a heritage property, utilities are provided by the local utility companies for a nominal fee of one dollar a year. As well, the municipal government has exempted the gallery from paying property taxes. Funding for capital asset acquisitions comes from various granting agencies and from fundraising activities of the gallery.

The gallery also operates a gift shop on a break-even basis, with the objective of attracting visitors to the gallery. The gift shop has a small staff of salaried employees, but also operates with the assistance of a number of volunteers. The gift shop has an annual inventory of $175,000, and annual sales of approximately $1 million.

The gallery has a support staff of 17 employees, a curator, and a director who is responsible for the overall operation of the gallery. The total operating budget for the gallery is $4.2 million.

Required

Prepare a report addressing the concerns of the board of directors of the art gallery. Your report should include a brief description of the purpose and objective of a fund accounting system. As well, you have been asked to recommend the different types of funds that would be most appropriate for the gallery. A discussion of relevant accounting policies is also required.

[CGA–Canada]

Problems

P10-1

It has been a hectic year at Abdalla Lodge. In January 20X4, Myesha Kind incorporated Abdalla as a not-for-profit organization. Its mandate is to provide counselling services for troubled youth. During the year, the organization organized a fundraising drive, signed a 10-year lease for office space, and commenced offering services to the public. The organization looks forward to many years of improving the lives of troubled youths in the community.

The office space was found in a rundown building in an older area of Smallville. Most of the town's poorest people live in this area of town. Abdalla took possession of the space on April 1, 20X4, and completed leasehold improvements by June 30, 20X4, at a cost of $30,000. On July 2, 20X4, Myesha opened the doors for business. She took on the job of director of the organization at an annual salary of $48,000. However, she worked July and August of 20X4 for free. On September 1, 20X4, two social workers were hired to meet the demands of the growing organization.

It is now December 20X4. You, CGA, have been asked by Myesha to prepare the financial statements for Abdalla for the 10-month period ending October 31, 20X4. Myesha provided the following schedule of cash receipts and disbursements:

Cash receipts	
Donations from individuals and businesses	$60,000
Grant from provincial government	70,000
	130,000
Cash disbursements	
Leasehold improvements	30,000
Furniture and equipment	24,000
Rent	10,500
Office supplies	5,000
Wages and benefits	28,000
Other expenses	8,500
	106,000
Cash on hand at October 31, 20X4	$24,000

Of the $60,000 received from individuals and businesses, $10,000 was designated for the purchase of furniture and equipment and $15,000 was designated for the purpose of hiring a program director in 20X5. The remaining funds were unrestricted. The provincial government agreed to provide an annual grant equal to 70% of all expenses to a maximum of $200,000 a year. To maximize the grant received from the provincial government, Myesha wants to record the value of all donated goods and services and to claim the full cost of the leasehold improvements and furniture and equipment in the year when these assets are acquired.

The furniture and equipment is expected to have a useful life of five years. Revenue is to be recognized using the deferral method. At the end of October 20X4, $3,000 of wages and benefits had been earned but not yet paid for and $1,000 was owing for other expenses.

Required

Prepare a statement of operations and a statement of financial position for the 10-month period ended October 31, 20X4. Show supporting calculations.

[CGA–Canada]

P10-2

You have been appointed to the board of directors for a local not-for-profit organization called "Food for Friends" (FFF). This organization has been in operation for 12 months and has never prepared a set of financial statements. Operations started on July 1, 20X3, and FFF's first set of financial statements is now being prepared for the year just ended (at June 30, 20X4). A volunteer bookkeeper has done his best to keep track of the organization's financial affairs. Although he has taken an introductory accounting course, he has limited knowledge of reporting requirements for not-for-profit organizations. You have tried to explain the deferral method of accounting to him, but he still needs your help.

Required

Prepare the journal entries in response to each of the following questions from the bookkeeper:

1. On January 1, 20X4, a local business donated a van to FFF. This saved us from having to rent a van twice per week. The van has a fair market value of $20,000 but we obtained it for $1. It is expected to last four years. I want to record it and amortize it on a straight-line basis, if this is acceptable. What journal entries would I make for the year ended June 30, 20X4, related to this van, using the deferral method?
2. In September 20X3, one of our "friends" won $10 million in a lottery. She was so grateful to have been helped in her time of need that she provided us with a $2 million endowment on September 30, 20X3, with the requirement that the purchasing power of the endowment be maintained. We invested it in a government bond on October 1, 20X3 (at par). The bond pays 5% interest annually with the first payment to be received on September 30, 20X4. We are happy with this investment as it is quite secure and it protects us against inflation, which has been steady at 2% for years. What journal entries would I make for the year ended June 30, 20X4, for these transactions using the deferral method of accounting?
   [CGA–Canada, adapted]

P10-3

You have recently received an accounting designation and, to celebrate, you are out for dinner with a long-time friend, Sandy. Sandy feels that "the key to success is networking, because getting to know influential people can help your career." However, Sandy may be taking this a little too far.

Sandy recently joined the board of directors for two not-for-profit organizations (NFPs). Big Charity ("Big") has annual revenues of $850,000, 20 paid employees, and separate funds for its key activities (a capital fund, an endowment fund, and a general fund). Small Foundation ("Small") has average annual revenues of $75,000 and only one paid employee. It uses the deferral method of accounting. Sandy has been appointed as the treasurer at both organizations. "A great way to network!" says Sandy. Unfortunately, Sandy barely passed her high school accounting course and has not taken any accounting courses since that time. She knows that the boards of directors of both organizations want to comply with GAAP to ensure key donors will be confident about the NFPs' financial statements. However, Sandy is not sure what the specific guidelines are for NFPs under GAAP.

Required

Address each of Sandy's concerns, making sure your advice complies with GAAP.

1. Sandy stated that "Small received a piece of equipment on January 1, 20X8, valued at $32,000, which was donated by a friend of the charity. We want to record the $32,000 as contribution revenue and amortize the equipment on a straight-line basis over four years."

   Prepare the journal entries required for the contribution and amortization for the year ended December 31, 20X8.

2. "Small also received its first pledge ever, and it is a big one," said Sandy. "A local high-technology company has promised to pay us $30,000 per year for the next three years, starting July 1, 20X9. It put no restrictions on how we use the donation."

   Explain how the not-for-profit organizations should account for pledges. In particular, would the accounting for pledges differ for Small since this is its "first pledge ever"?

3. "Big received a $600,000 endowment donation on January 1, 20X8, to be used as follows: the principal is to remain intact but any interest earned can be used for charity for whatever purpose it chooses."

   Prepare the journal entries for the $600,000 and $30,000 interest earned and received in 20X8 on the endowment donation.

4. "I convinced the board of directors of Big to hold a vote next week to change our accounting for our head office building. It was acquired for $2,000,000 on January 1, 20X1, and was amortized over 25 years at $80,000 per year. However, buildings similar to ours are selling for close to $5,000,000 now. Therefore, I want to stop amortizing the building. Since we are an NFP, this is acceptable isn't it?" asks Sandy.

   State whether this would be acceptable and briefly explain.

   [CGA–Canada, adapted]

P10-4

Forest Hill Lodge (Lodge) is a seniors' residence operated as a not-for-profit organization. During 20X2, Lodge built a new bingo hall on its property at a cost of $1,200,000. The bingo hall was financed with $600,000 of donations from private individuals and a $600,000 grant from the provincial government. In addition, a $50,000 donation was received specifically to cover the cost of future maintenance of the bingo hall. The bingo hall commenced operations on September 1, 20X2. In the last four months of the year, $15,000 was spent on maintenance of the bingo hall. The estimated useful life of the bingo hall is 40 years. Lodge amortizes its capital assets using the straight-line method.

Among other things, Lodge has an excellent reputation for its bingo nights. Most of the callers and runners for the bingo nights are unpaid volunteers.

Required

1. Based on the information provided, prepare a partial SFP to capture all activities related to the bingo hall, assuming Lodge uses the deferral method and does not have a separate capital fund for the bingo hall.
2. Differentiate between expenditure accounting and expense accounting as they apply to the $1,200,000 cost of the bingo hall.
3. Identify the conditions that must be met to recognize the value of volunteers' time in the financial statements of a not-for-profit organization.
4. Prepare the journal entry that would be made under the deferral method if volunteers' services were to be recorded at a value of $10,000.
   [CGA–Canada, adapted]

P10-5

Sports for Kids (SFK) is a not-for-profit organization that provides sporting equipment for inner-city children who cannot otherwise afford it. SFK has been in operation since 20X1 and operated on a break-even basis from 20X1 to 20X4. In 20X5, SFK spent $120,000 on sporting equipment, similar to previous years. However, donations were reduced and SFK ended up with cash disbursements exceeding cash receipts by $30,000. In 20X6, SFK decided it needed to make some changes. You have recently obtained your professional accounting designation and have volunteered to provide advice on the following matters related to the December 31, 20X6, year-end financial statements.

Required

1. The directors of SFK have heard of encumbrance accounting, but are not sure how it works.
   a) Briefly explain the difference between encumbrance accounting and a budgetary accounting system.
   b) Briefly explain the difference between an encumbrance and a liability.
   c) If an encumbrance system is used, what journal entries would be made to record purchase orders issued for $130,000 for goods and services and the subsequent invoices of $129,600 received that related to those purchase orders?
2. SFK has decided to follow Canadian GAAP in 20X6 for the first time. The directors have heard about the deferral method of accounting for contributions, but are not sure how to implement it. Provide journal entries to record the following transactions under the deferral method for the December 31, 20X6, financial statements.

a) A former teacher donated $10,000 on July 1, 20X6, with the condition that 50% of it be spent on supplies to be provided to children by December 31, 20X6, and 50% to be spent on supplies to be provided to children in 20X7.

b) Another donor donated land to SFK for a future warehouse site in 20X6. The land originally cost $50,000 in 20X1, but had a fair value of $250,000 in 20X6.

3. As a small not-for-profit organization, SFK would like to simplify its accounting for capital assets.

   a) Briefly explain under what circumstances SFK would *not* have to capitalize and amortize its capital assets.

   b) How would capital assets be reflected on SFK's financial statements and notes to financial statements if SFK chose *not* to capitalize and amortize?

   c) One benefit of not capitalizing would be to simplify the preparation of SFK's financial statements. List *three* other arguments that support the adoption of a policy of *not* capitalizing and amortizing capital assets.

[CGA–Canada, adapted]

P10-6

Glendale College is a private girls' school and is operated as a not-for-profit organization. During 20X1 the school received $500,000 in private donations from individuals to establish a scholarship fund for its students. The principal amount of the fund must be invested in government bonds. Only the interest on the fund can be used to provide scholarships to students. For the year ended December 31, 20X1, the fund earned interest of $30,000, and scholarships totalling $20,000 were awarded to students in need. At the end of the year, the balance in the scholarship fund was $510,000.

On January 1, 20X1, a local businessperson donated a small bus to the school. The bus seats 20 people and was worth approximately $40,000 at the time of the donation. It has an estimated useful life of six years with a residual value of $10,000. The school amortizes its capital assets using the straight-line method.

Required

1. Prepare the journal entries to capture all activities related to the scholarship fund, assuming the school uses the deferral method and records all entries in the operating fund because it does not have a separate endowment fund for the scholarship.

2. Assume the school wishes to record the value of the donated bus. Prepare journal entries for 20X1 to capture all activities related to the donated bus, assuming the school uses the deferral method and does not have a separate fund for the donated bus.

[CGA–Canada, adapted]

P10-7

You have been hired as a consultant to provide accounting advice for a not-for-profit organization that wishes to improve its accounting system. In particular, the organization, Save the Ozone (STO), is considering changing its method for contributions and implementing a new budgeting and encumbrance accounting system. STO has a December 31 year-end.

Required

1. In November 20X4, STO issued a $1,000 purchase order for key chains to be provided as an incentive to donors who contribute to its Spring 20X5 fundraising drive. In December 20X4 the key chains were shipped to STO with an invoice price of $1,095. Prepare the journal entries for November 20X4 and December 20X4 using encumbrance accounting.
2. Briefly explain the difference between an encumbrance and a liability.
3. STO has always used the restricted-fund method of accounting for contributions, but other similar organizations have been using the deferral method. Briefly explain how STO would account for the following restricted contributions using the deferral method:
   a) Restricted contributions for expenses of future periods
   b) Restricted contributions for the acquisition of amortizable capital assets
   c) Restricted contributions for expenses of the current period

   [CGA–Canada, adapted]

P10-8

Zak Organization is a not-for-profit organization set up for famine relief. Zak has been operating for 25 years and has a December 31 year-end. Zak's policy with respect to capital assets is to capitalize and amortize the capital assets over their expected useful lives.

On June 30, 20X3, Zak received three donations from a former director:

- $30,000 cash for famine relief.
- $50,000 to be used solely for construction of the new administrative building. Of the $50,000, 70% was received in cash, with the remainder promised in February 20X4. (Note: construction is expected to commence in October 20X4.)
- $600,000 cash, which was invested on July 1, 20X3, in long-term Government of Canada bonds, with 10% interest to be paid semi-annually on December 31 and June 30. The $600,000 donation was given with the stipulation that it be invested in interest-bearing securities with the principal maintained by Zak, although interest earned on the securities is not restricted.

Required

1. Briefly explain (do not provide journal entries) how each of the three donations should be accounted for using the deferral method of accounting. In particular, should each of the donations be recognized as revenue for the year ended December 31, 20X3?
2. Despite the recent donations from its former director, Zak is increasingly faced with severe budgetary constraints. Zak is considering implementing encumbrance accounting in the coming year.
   a) Briefly describe the process of encumbrance accounting.
   b) Briefly describe how encumbrance accounting might serve as a device to help control spending when it is used in conjunction with a formal budgeting system.

   [CGA–Canada, adapted]

11

Public Sector Financial Reporting

LEARNING OBJECTIVES

After studying this chapter, students should be able to:

1. identify the characteristics of governments and governmental units;
2. discuss the objectives of financial reporting for the public sector and how they are reflected in government financial statements; and
3. discuss the major reporting and measurement issues.

INTRODUCTION

Nova Scotia is a small province of approximately 940,000 people on the east coast of Canada. In its 2009 public accounts (i.e., annual report), Nova Scotia reported revenue in excess of $9 billion and a small surplus of $190 million. The most significant revenue sources were income taxes (24%) and sales taxes (17%). Other sources included petroleum royalties (5%) and net income from government business enterprises (4%). The major expenses for the province were health (38%), education (23%), community services (10%), and debt servicing costs (10%). These types of revenues and expenses are typical for many provincial governments.

Governments like the Province of Nova Scotia are different from the traditional business organization. Their objective is not to make a profit but rather to provide services to the public. In addition, much of their revenue is derived not from exchange transactions, but from their ability to impose and collect taxes. Given differences like these, it is easy to understand why financial reporting for governments differs from that for businesses. In this chapter we will examine exactly how the financial reporting for government differs from businesses. In the process, we will explore many unique issues that arise in governmental accounting.

This chapter continues our discussion of accounting for *non-business organizations*. The preceding chapter discussed not-for-profit organizations. In this chapter, we focus on *public sector reporting*—that is, the financial reporting for governments and governmental units. It is important to note that unlike businesses and not-for-profits, for which accounting standards are set by the CICA's Accounting Standards Board, the accounting standards for governments are set by a separate board, the CICA's

Public Sector Accounting Board (PSAB). Public sector accounting standards are contained in a separate handbook, the CICA *Public Sector Accounting Handbook* (*PSA* Handbook).[1]

THE NATURE OF GOVERNMENT

Characteristics of Government

To properly understand public sector reporting, it is important to first understand the nature of government. In Canada, there is one national government, ten provincial governments, three territorial governments,[2] and approximately 4,000 municipal governments. The governing process usually starts with the government preparing a budget that reflects their spending priorities for the year. The budget must be approved by the elected members of the legislature or council, which thereby provides the authority for funds to be spent.[3] Because this budget portrays public policy, it forms a key part of the government's financial report and, as we will see, is explicitly incorporated into two of the financial statements. Including the budget in the financial report allows for a better evaluation of the government's fiscal management and thus serves to improve accountability.

Governments are generally characterized by a much broader user group than either businesses or not-for-profit organizations. The main users are the public (either directly or as represented by legislators and councillors), the civil service, other governments, debt investors such as pension funds, and analysts. People are often surprised to learn that the market for debt is substantially larger than the market for equities and further that governments, as a group, are by far the largest issuers of debt. Thus it is not surprising that analysts are often very interested in the financial statements of government.

Most governments generate the majority of their revenues from taxes. The ability to assess and collect taxes provides governments with a much more stable foundation than any business or not-for-profit organization could ever attain. Because of this, there is usually less worry about going concern issues for government. Thus it is not surprising that there is very little emphasis on working capital in government financial statements.

There is, however, an emphasis on debt. Due to their taxing authority, governments have a tremendous capacity to borrow. Still, debt bears interest and the principal must be repaid sometime

1. The *PSA Handbook* does not have the authority to force governments to adopt its recommendations. In this chapter, however, we will refer to the recommendations of the *PSA Handbook* as the necessary requirements for governments to comply with GAAP.
2. In Canada, the federal, provincial, and territorial governments are often referred to as the *senior levels* of government.
3. Given the political nature of legislatures and councils, arrangements are often in place that provide the authority to allow the government to function even if a budget has not been approved. For example, in Nova Scotia, if a budget has not passed, departments automatically have 50% of the previous year's budget to conduct ongoing business (but not new program spending).

in the future. The burden of rising debt servicing costs will affect a government's ability to provide services to the public in the future. As we will see, this lack of emphasis on working capital and increased emphasis on debt affects the structure of government financial statements.

Governments, like NFPs, do not have profit as their primary objective. Instead, their objectives are to provide services to the public and to redistribute wealth to meet legislated social goals. Given these objectives, governments generally do not engage in exchange transactions as a primary function. Like NFPs, the link between revenue and costs is severed. The provision of a service does not normally lead to revenue and furthermore, the payment of taxes does not entitle the taxpayer to a pre-determined level of service. This separation of revenue from expenses has implications in the accounting for certain government activities.

The objective to provide services rather than make a profit has implications for how tangible capital assets are viewed. These assets are seen as representing future service capability and not as a source of future cash flows (as in a business). The carrying value of these assets represents the unexpired service potential of the assets.

Note that the distinction between non-financial and financial assets will be important because non-financial assets are only used for providing services while financial assets can be used for both future services and debt payment. The lack of a profit motive also means that spending on capital assets may not be focussed on the financial return but rather on other objectives such as stimulating economic activity (i.e., providing incentives for private sector employment). This suggests that the impact of capital spending on debt in the current period should be highlighted because increases in debt will affect future service potential.

In designing the government reporting model, the CICA's Public Sector Accounting Board (PSAB) identified these and other unique characteristics of governments. PSAB cites nine unique characteristics that differentiate governmental reporting from private sector reporting:

- the goal is to provide services and redistribute resources, not to make a profit;
- public tangible capital assets are different in nature from business tangible capital assets;
- capital spending is *not* focussed on maximizing returns;
- the principal source of revenue is taxation;
- all assets acquired are held in the right of the Crown (i.e., the government);
- the environment is non-competitive;
- a budget shows public policy, establishes estimates and financing requirements, and is part of public accountability;
- governments have huge debt capacities; and
- there is a higher standard of public accountability.

We have already addressed most of these characteristics in our earlier discussion. We should note that governments often own assets because they "came with the territory", so to speak, such as "crown land" held by the government because it *is* the government. Crown property has no acquisition cost and is difficult to value; thus it is not recognized in the financial statements. Nevertheless, governments should disclose the *existence* of these assets.

In addition, governments should strive to disclose the costs of the services provided. While this information often is not sufficient to evaluate the efficiency or effectiveness of the service, it is necessary information in an environment of limited resources—the spending on one item in a budget will affect what is available for spending on other items in the same budget.

Finally, consistent with the theme of increased disclosure and a higher standard of accountability, governments will often need to provide additional non-financial disclosures to allow for an effective evaluation of their programs and services, similar to the non-financial measures that NFPs make.

Types of Government Organizations

The **public sector** is defined in the *PSA Handbook* as consisting of (1) the federal, provincial, territorial, and local governments; (2) government organizations; (3) government partnerships; and (4) school boards. The accounting for government organizations is complicated by the nature and variety of government organizations. Organizations are included as *government organizations* in the government reporting entity only if they are controlled by the government. Further, the accounting for government organizations depends on the underlying characteristics of the organization. In general, there are three types of government organizations:

- government business enterprises (GBEs);
- government not-for-profit organizations (GNPOs);
- other government organizations (OGOs)

PSAB defines a GBE as one that:

- is a separate legal entity that can contract in its own name and it can sue or be sued;
- has the financial and operational authority to operate as a business;
- engages in external exchange transactions (i.e., sells goods and services to parties outside of the government reporting entity) as its principal activity; and
- is capable of maintaining its operations and meeting its liabilities from external revenues through the normal operation of its business.

GBEs are deemed to be publicly accountable enterprises and as such are directed by PSAB to follow the recommendations of the *CICA Handbook, Part I*, and thus GBEs are expected to follow International Financial Reporting Standards (IFRS), effective in 2011. A GNPO is a government organization that meets the definition of an NFP in the *CICA Handbook*. Finally, an OGO is any organization not included in the first two categories. As a general rule, OGOs would base their accounting on the *PSA Handbook*. However, PSAB recognizes that there may be situations in which IFRS may be more appropriate. To help OGOs determine whether they are eligible to use IFRS, PSAB suggests that OGOs consider a number of factors, including (1) whether they possess the characteristics of a publicly accountable enterprise; (2) the nature of their operations, assets, and mandate; and (3) their dependence on government funding.

The accounting for governments and government organizations is summarized in Exhibit 11-1. Our concern in the remainder

PROPOSED CHANGE

In the past, GNPOs were directed by PSAB to follow the standards for NFPs contained in the *CICA Handbook*. This requirement is changing. The *CICA Handbook, Part III*, contains standards specific to NFP issues. In a March 2010 exposure draft, PSAB proposes to incorporate the 4400 series recommendations for NFPs that are in the *CICA Handbook* directly into the *PSA Handbook*. PSAB, however, plans to review these standards and make appropriate changes in the near future. Students should visit the text's website for updates on PSAB's plan for changes in accounting standards.

EXHIBIT 11-1

Financial Reporting Requirements for Governments and Government Organizations[4]

Organization	Source of accounting
Governments (federal, provincial, territorial, local)	CICA *PSA Handbook*
Government business enterprise (GBE)	IFRS (as directed by PSAB)
Government not-for-profit organization (GNPO)	Currently—*CICA Handbook, Part III* (Accounting for not-for-profit organizations) Effective January 1, 2012—*PSA Handbook*
Other government organization (OGO)	CICA *PSA Handbook* or IFRS (choose best option based on organization's objectives)

of the chapter will be with the governments and other government organizations (OGOs) that are subject to the *PSA Handbook*.

CONCEPT CHECK 11-1

Companion Website

1. Why is there very little emphasis on working capital in government financial statements?
2. How are tangible capital assets viewed in government financial statements?
3. Why is the distinction between financial and non-financial assets important?
4. What is a government business enterprise (GBE)?

FINANCIAL REPORTING FOR GOVERNMENTS

The Compliance Issue

Improvements to reporting standards for governments have occurred despite the fact that PSAB does not have the "clout" that the CICA's Accounting Standards Board has for public for-profit enterprises. PSAB recommendations are just that: *recommendations*, not *requirements* for most levels of government. Other types of organizations may have compelling reasons to comply with recommendations of the *CICA Handbook* (such as the requirements of securities acts), but such is not the case with governments and the recommendations of the PSAB.

For senior levels of government especially, there is no mechanism to compel compliance with the PSAB recommendations. Governmental financial reporting is governed by legislation,

4. Adapted from PSAB website.

which may be either extensive or virtually non-existent at different levels and in different provinces and territories. Senior governments are not audited by external auditors, but by the governments' auditors general. Auditors general are often not required to report in accordance with the recommendations of the PSAB, but rather in accordance with that government's legal reporting requirements. Local governments usually are audited by external auditors, although some major cities have their own city auditor. Local government auditors are required to report in accordance with provincial legislation governing municipal reporting. Interestingly, many local governments are now required by legislation in their individual provinces to report in compliance with the PSAB recommendations.[5,6]

While there is no compliance mechanism for the PSAB accounting recommendations for senior levels of government, the recommendations can serve as a useful guide to auditors general. The recommendations give the auditors an authoritative lever for persuading government authorities to improve their financial reporting. Ultimately, the PSAB recommendations can guide provincial legislatures in stipulating requirements for local and provincial governmental reporting.

A standard-setting body such as the PSAB can make progress only if its recommendations are accepted by its users. Changes or improvements in existing practice must be "eased" into practice. This process will result in a greater likelihood of acceptance, even when there is no legal compliance requirement. Part of the process of introducing a new standard must be to convince users of the benefits of the standard. For example, the change from cash accounting to accrual accounting was successful because it was perceived as providing three benefits:

- improved efficiency, transparency, quality of information, and priority setting;
- improved cash management, asset management, and financial management; and
- improved accountability.[7]

It is interesting to note that although no senior governments are *required* to follow PSAB recommendations, it is now very unlikely that a government would not follow PSAB. Progress continues to be made by PSAB through persuasion and consensus among governments.

Objectives of Governmental Reporting

What are the objectives of government financial statements? What are the information needs of the users? Several research studies have examined the users and uses of financial statements.[8] As a result of these studies, the PSAB issued PS 1100, "Financial Statement Objectives," which

5. Beauchamp, Tim, "Municipalities on the move" *CA Magazine*, September 2009, p. 50.
6. It appears that almost all municipalities are effectively compelled to comply with PSAB recommendations. All provinces either have a legislative requirement for municipalities to comply with PSAB or require compliance for the municipality to receive specific funds from the province. The result will likely be very high compliance with PSAB recommendations.
7. Roy, J. Paul-Emile, "Accounting bases used in Canadian government budgeting" *CA Magazine*, January/February 2005, p. 19.
8. For example, see *Financial Reporting by Governments* (CICA, 1980).

is applicable to all levels of government. PS 1100 provides the following four objectives for financial statements:

1. to provide an accounting of financial affairs and resources under the government's control;
2. to demonstrate government's ability to finance activities, meet liabilities, and provide future services;
3. to account for sources, allocation, and use of government resources; to evaluate how activities affect net debt; and to show how activities were financed and how cash requirements were met; and
4. to display the state of a government's finances and evaluate if the finances are in accordance with legislative requirements.

Objective 1: Defining the Entity The first objective defines the broad scope of government financial statements. The statements should capture the full extent of the activities undertaken by the government. The statements should therefore include not only government departments but also all the agencies, organizations, and enterprises that it controls. Only then will users be able to properly assess a government's policies and service delivery.

Objective 2: Statement of Financial Position The second objective suggests that government financial statements should allow users to assess a government's finances. This is accomplished through a statement of financial position (SFP).

Remember that debt is a very important issue for governments. The inability to pay their debt has forced governmental entities to file for bankruptcy or seek bankruptcy protection in the past, such as in the famous case of Orange County, California, in 1994 and more recently in the case of the city of Vallejo, California, in 2008. In 2010, the financial markets worldwide experienced extreme volatility given doubts about the ability of nations such as Greece and to some extent Portugal in the European Union to meet their debt obligations. While such cases do not exist in recent memory in Canada, to help users assess a government's ability to finance its activities and meet its liabilities, the government's "net debt" is presented in the SFP. **Net debt** is the total of government liabilities less the total of its financial assets. Net debt is important because debt has to be serviced and repaid and therefore will impact a government's ability to deliver programs and services in the future. For users, net debt is an important indicator of a government's financial position.

In addition, you will also recall that we said that tangible capital assets (and other nonfinancial assets) are viewed in terms of their unexpired or future service potential and not in terms of future cash flows. Thus, the total of tangible capital assets will help users assess a government's ability to deliver its services and programs in the future.

Net debt is thought of as *claims that could reduce future services*, while tangible capital assets can be thought of as *prepaid future service potential*. The two items are combined on the SFP to produce an **accumulated deficit or surplus**. For users, accumulated deficit or surplus is another important indicator of a government's financial position because it shows the recognized economic resources that a government has available.

Objective 3: Changes in Financial Position The third objective suggests that government financial statements should allow users to assess changes in a government's financial position. Government financial statements should focus on explaining the changes in three items: (1) the change in the accumulated deficit or surplus, (2) the change in net debt, and (3) the change in cash. We discussed the importance of the first two items above and, of course, understanding the change in cash is important for any organization whether business, not-for-profit, or government. The need for users to assess these changes in financial position requires three additional financial statements:

- statement of operations;
- statement of changes in net debt; and
- statement of cash flows.

Statement of Operations The change in the accumulated deficit or surplus is explained by a government's **statement of operations**. This statement explains (1) the source and nature of a government's revenues, and (2) the purpose and nature of a government's expenses. Measuring the cost of services is important to users because it will help them assess the efficacy of government programs (with the aid of additional non-financial information).

The relationship between revenues and expenses is also important. The purpose of government is not to make money but to provide services. To the extent that there may be excess revenues, it may allow a government to budget more for particular programs. To the extent that there is a deficiency of revenues, it may mean that a government has to raise taxes to cover the costs. In addition, the deficit or surplus indicates how successful the government was in maintaining its economic resources. If the economic resources declined (e.g., the accumulated deficit increased), then it is an indication that future services may be curtailed.

Statement of Changes in Net Debt The **statement of changes in net debt** reconciles the deficit or surplus for the period with the change in net debt. A difference exists between the two items because the cost of goods and services in a period will not exactly equal the expenditures on goods and services. A simple statement of net debt will start with the deficit or surplus for the period, subtract the cost of non-financial assets acquired (which will be mostly tangible capital assets), and add back the amortization of tangible capital assets to arrive at the **change in net debt**. This is an important indicator of performance for users because it will allow them to determine the capital expenditures for the period and the extent to which these expenditures were covered by the revenues of the period.

Statement of Cash Flows The rationale for the **statement of cash flows** is the same as it is for business—it is important to understand an organization's sources and uses of cash for the period. This statement is very similar to the statement of cash flows for a business with one major difference—the statement has a section for *capital transactions* to capture the effect of the acquisition or sale of capital assets on cash flows. To understand why these transactions are not included under investing activities (as in a business), recall our discussion of the nature of tangible capital assets for a government. Capital assets are seen as representing future service capability and not future cash flows (as in a business). Because they are not evaluated in terms of future cash flows, there is no financial "return," therefore they are not an investment in the classic sense. In fact, for governments, the only items that will appear under investing activities will be the buying and selling of financial assets.

Objective 4: Budget Comparison The fourth objective suggests that government financial statements should allow users to evaluate the financial results of the period. This is best accomplished if the results can also be compared to the budget that was initially approved by the legislature. This requirement reflects the principle that governments should be accountable for their spending. It is achieved by including the budget in the statement of operations and the statement of changes in net debt. Then, users can compare actual results to planned results, thereby improving the user's ability to evaluate the government's performance for the period.

Qualitative Characteristics

Standard setters have conducted research on the qualitative characteristics that the information in government financial reports should possess to be useful. An early study that interviewed various categories of users of governmental reports found a wide diversity of needs. Four qualities were stressed by the interviewees: (1) comparability among governments; (2) consistency between years; (3) completeness; and (4) timeliness. The users were particularly emphatic about *comparability*:

> Almost above everything else, users wanted to compare the reports of various governments. This meant they wanted consistency among governments in the basis for:
>
> - defining the reporting entity to make clear what kinds of government organizations were included and excluded;
> - classifying and reporting revenues, expenditures, assets and liabilities; and
> - reporting government debt including contingent debt.
>
> They also wanted consistency, to the extent possible, between the Public Accounts and various statistical compilations of government figures (e.g., the National Accounts) and the ability to reconcile two sets of figures where differences in basis are justified by the different purposes served by the two sets of figures.[9]

The PSAB incorporated qualitative criteria into PS 1000 that reflected these needs of users:

> Financial statements should communicate information that is relevant to the needs of those for whom the statements are prepared, reliable, comparable, understandable and clearly presented in a manner that maximizes its usefulness. [PS 1000.24]

While we will not review the qualitative characteristics in detail, we will note that the qualitative characteristics are similar to those in Section 1000 of the *CICA Handbook, Part I*. With respect to the characteristics of relevance and reliability, however, each contains an additional element that is not found in the *CICA Handbook*. These additional elements reflect the unique nature of governments. For example:

- For relevance to be achieved, information must possess the characteristics of predictive value, feedback value, timeliness, and *accountability value*. The addition of **accountability**

9. *Financial Reporting by Governments* (CICA, 1980), p. 31.

value reflects the importance of stewardship in governments. It is manifested in the inclusion of budget figures in the financial statements.

- For reliability to be achieved, the information must possess the characteristics of representational faithfulness, neutrality, conservatism, verifiability, and *completeness*. The addition of **completeness** directly reflects the concerns of users as discussed above. Sufficient information should be disclosed to allow for an accurate understanding of government finances. We will have more to say about completeness when we discuss how the government reporting entity is defined.

Illustration of Government Financial Statements

Following the government reporting model, the *PSA Handbook* recommends presentation of information on five issues about government finances:[10]

- accumulated surplus/deficit;
- annual surplus/deficit;
- net debt/net financial assets;
- change in net debt; and
- change in cash and cash flows that contributed to the change.

This information can be found in the following four statements required by PSAB:

- statement of financial position;
- statement of operations;
- statement of changes in net debt; and
- statement of cash flows.

Exhibit 11-2 gives an illustration of a simple set of government financial statements.

In these financial statements, *net debt* is an important indicator of the government's finances. Notice that the statement of financial position reports net debt of $650 for 20X2, and then deducts non-financial assets of $450 from net debt to measure the government's accumulated deficit of $200. Net debt is the difference between financial assets of $750 and liabilities of $1,400. Net debt provides an indicator of future revenues required to pay for past transactions. The *accumulated deficit* is an indication of the government's ability to provide future services. You will also notice that, unlike statements for NFPs and most businesses, there is no segregation of current and noncurrent assets and liabilities.

The financial statements also contain a statement of operations that shows an excess of revenues over expenses of $50. To help evaluate how well the government has done, the budget is also included. We can see that the government's surplus was $40 higher than forecast ($50 versus $10) and that this was entirely due to revenues being higher than forecast ($900 versus $860). This statement is prepared under full accrual accounting, not under an expenditure basis of accounting.

10. CICA, *20 Questions About Government Financial Reporting*, January 2003, p. 21.

EXHIBIT 11-2

Sample Government Financial Statements

New Government
Consolidated Statement of Financial Position
December 31, 20X2
($ millions)

	20X2	20X1
Financial assets		
Cash	200	230
Receivables	150	130
Investments	400	380
	750	740
Liabilities		
Payables	400	380
Unmatured debt	1000	910
	1400	1290
Net debt	(650)	(550)
Non-financial assets		
Tangible capital assets	400	250
Prepaids	50	50
	450	300
Accumulated deficit	(200)	(250)

New Government
Consolidated Statement of Operations and Accumulated Deficit
Year Ended December 31, 20X2
($ millions)

	20X2 Budget	20X2 Actual	20X1 Actual
Revenue			
Income tax	540	550	500
Sales tax	320	350	300
Total revenue	860	900	800
Expenses			
Health	355	360	350
Education	245	240	200
Debt service	50	50	40
Other	200	200	240
Total expenses	850	850	830
Surplus (deficit)	10	50	(30)
Accumulated deficit, beginning	(250)	(250)	(220)
Accumulated deficit, end	(240)	(200)	(250)

EXHIBIT 11-2 *(Continued)*

Sample Government Financial Statements

New Government
Consolidated Statement of Changes in Net Debt
Year Ended December 31, 20X2
($ millions)

	20X2 Budget	20X2 Actual	20X1 Actual
Net debt, beginning of year	(550)	(550)	(570)
Surplus	10	50	(30)
Acquisition of tangible capital assets	(200)	(220)	(15)
Amortization of tangible capital assets	70	70	65
(Increase) / decrease in net debt	(120)	(100)	20
Net debt, end of year	(670)	(650)	(550)

New Government
Consolidated Statement of Cash Flows
Year Ended December 31, 20X2
($ millions)

	20X2 Actual	20X1 Actual
Cash from operations	120	35
Cash received from (used for) capital	(220)	(15)
Cash received from (used for) investing	(20)	50
Cash received from (used for) financing	90	(50)
Increase (decrease) in cash	(30)	20
Cash, beginning of year	230	210
Cash, end of year	200	230

You may notice from these statements that, despite the surplus of $50, the net debt on the SFP increased $100 from $550 in 20X1 to $650 in 20X2. To understand why, we need to examine the statement of changes in net debt, which reconciles a government's total expenses for the period to its spending on operations (i.e., expenditures) for the period.

The statement reports that capital spending in the period was $220. This expenditure of $220 was only partially financed by operations. Operations provided $120 (surplus of $50 plus non-cash expenses of $70 added back), therefore net debt increased by $100 from $550 to $650. Notice that the budget information is also included here. In evaluating the performance of government, we can see that the increase in net debt was less than budgeted. It appears that the larger-than-budgeted surplus allowed the government to spend slightly more on capital assets and still keep the net debt below the budgeted figure.

The final statement is the statement of cash flows. This statement calculates the cash flows from operating activities ($120) using either the direct method or the indirect method. If the indirect method is used, the surplus or deficit for the accounting period will be adjusted to the amount of cash used or available from operations. The details of each section are not provided in this simple example. Note that the cash used to purchase capital assets ($220) is shown under a separate capital transactions section, which reflects the government's view of capital assets as representing future *service potential* and not necessarily future cash flows.

This model of financial reporting applies to all governments. The format of the statement of financial position and the inclusion of a statement of changes in net debt reflect the unique characteristics of government. The inclusion of the budget on the statement of operations and the statement of changes in net debt provides accountability—a measure of the government's achievement of its objectives.

CONCEPT CHECK 11-2

Companion Website

1. What five messages about government finances are contained in the government reporting model?
2. How does the SCF for governments differ from the SCF for businesses?
3. Why is the statement of changes in net debt important to users?

MAJOR REPORTING ISSUES

There are many reporting issues that are either unique to governments or sufficiently different from business accounting issues as to warrant separate discussion. We will only discuss several of the major issues and will highlight any that are similar to NFPs. The primary issues that we will discuss are:

- defining the reporting entity;
- revenue recognition;
- tangible capital assets;
- liability measurement;
- accrual accounting; and
- international harmonization.

We will briefly address these issues in the following sections.

Defining the Reporting Entity

In Chapter 10, we discussed the problem of defining the reporting entity for not-for-profit organizations. This problem actually is much more severe for governmental reporting.

PSAB defines a government organization as "an organization that is controlled by the government" (PS 2500.04(d)). It further defines a governmental unit as any government organization that is not a government business enterprise (GBE).

Government activities are carried out through a very complex set of ministries, agencies, Crown corporations, quasi-business enterprises, and not-for-profit organizations formed by government for the purpose of carrying out parts of government's policies. When financial statements are prepared for a government, which of the many bodies that are directly or indirectly related to the government are to be included in the statements? PSAB recommends that the **government reporting entity** include all organizations that are *controlled* by government (PS 1300).

Persuasive evidence of **control** may be indicated by the government having:

1. the power to appoint a majority of the members of a governing body;
2. access and control over the assets of the organization;
3. the majority of the voting shares; or
4. unilateral power to dissolve the organization.

These are not the only potential indicators. The *PSA Handbook* identifies seven other possible indicators of control.[11] While these indicators are not as persuasive as the four above, in combination with other indicators they may suggest that control is present.

It also is important to understand when control is *not* present. An organization that is financially dependent on the government is not necessarily controlled by the government. Further, an organization that is regulated by the government is also not considered to be controlled by virtue of the regulation. The regulated organization chooses to participate in the industry and is free to cease those operations or expand its operations in areas beyond the regulated operation. Finally, a government's constitutional responsibility for a sector does not mean that it controls organizations in that sector.[12] While the government may have influence over these organizations, it does not necessarily exercise *control*. These organizations are often instruments of government or are dependent on government, but if they are not directly accountable to government, they are excluded from the reporting entity. The criteria for control must be applied carefully. Decisions should be based on the preponderance of the evidence after considering all relevant factors.

For example, in some provinces, school boards are elected directly by the public. However, this is not sufficient evidence to conclude that they are *not* controlled by the province. The province may have control over revenue and may also be able to restrict expenditure, either by type (e.g., teachers' salaries) or by purpose (e.g., early childhood education). If the school boards were created by provincial legislation, they also can be dissolved the same way.

Another example is an art gallery that has 11 of its 18 board members appointed by the provincial government. The gallery was created by a special act, and although a majority of the board members are appointed by government, the gallery functions completely independently of government. Despite the fact that the directors are *appointed* by the province, they do not *represent* the province and therefore control may not be present.

Finally, consider how universities should be reported. Although they are an instrument of government (to assist in educating the public) and usually are financially dependent on government for the majority of their financing, in most situations they still would not be considered to be *controlled* by the government.

11. See PS1300.19 for the list of the other possible indicators of control.
12. PSAB, *20 Questions About the Government Reporting Entity*, p. 17.

EXHIBIT 11-3

Summary of Accounting for Government Organizations / Investments

Entity type	Control present	Accounting
Governmental unit	Yes	Consolidate
Government business enterprise	Yes	Modified equity method
Portfolio investment	No	Cost method

PSAB also addresses the question of how organizations that constitute parts of the reporting entity should be reported in the financial statements. In general, the conclusions of the statement are that:

1. investments in entities that are not controlled by the government (portfolio investments) should be reported on the *cost basis*;
2. investments in GBE (government business enterprises), such as a public utility, should be reported on a *modified equity basis*; and
3. the financial statements of all other organizations or agencies that are part of the reporting entity should be *consolidated* with the government's own financial statements.

Under the *modified equity method*, the net profit or loss of the business enterprise is included in the government's statement of operations (net of dividends or distributions) and is added to the investment account related to that enterprise. It is called a **modified equity method** because the accounting principles for the GBE are not changed to government accounting principles. The GBE's results are reported in the government's financial statements using GAAP for publicly accountable enterprises (i.e., IFRS). Exhibit 11-3 summarizes the reporting requirements for the different parts of the reporting entity.

Revenue Recognition

Revenue recognition for governments has been the source of considerable debate. As we noted earlier, revenues for governments are often characterized as non-exchange transactions. Government transfers and taxes are the two largest sources of non-exchange revenue. The discussion that follows is based on a re-exposure draft that was issued by PSAB in 2010 for government transfers and on the new PS 3510 on taxes.

Government Transfers The proposal for accounting for government transfers deals with revenue recognition by the *recipient* government and expense recognition by the transferring government (*transferor*). We will begin our discussion by first examining the nature of transfers and then examine transfers from the perspective of the transferor and finally from the perspective of the recipient government.

A **government transfer** is the provision of either monetary or tangible capital assets by a government entity to another entity (i.e., government, organization, or individual). The transferor does not receive any goods or services in return, or expect to be repaid or expect a financial return. The transfer is a non-exchange transaction.

The government transferring the resources can, however, impose **transfer terms**. There are two types of terms that can be imposed: *eligibility criteria* and *stipulations*. If a term of the transfer can be met before the transfer occurs, it is an **eligibility criterion**. Typically an eligibility criterion will specify who can receive the transfer or what must be done to receive the transfer.

If a term of the transfer can only be met after the transfer occurs, it is a **stipulation**. Typically, a stipulation describes how the resources must be used or what must be done to keep the transfer. The distinction between the two is important. Eligibility criteria will affect the timing of the recognition of the transfer (by both parties) while stipulations will affect the timing of the recognition of revenue by a recipient government.

Transferor Accounting The accounting for transfers for the transferor is straightforward regardless of whether the transfer is of an operating or capital nature. The transferring government (transferor) will recognize an expense when the transfer is fully authorized and the *eligibility criteria* have been met. The transfer is fully authorized when it has been approved by the legislature or council. In rare cases, the transferor may recognize the expense before it is fully authorized if two conditions are met. First, the preponderance of the evidence must suggest that the government is committed to the transfer and second, the transfer must receive approval from the legislature or council in the "stub" period (i.e., the period after the government's year-end but before it issues its financial statements). Finally, we should note that if the transferor transfers a tangible capital asset, its recorded expense will equal the net book value of the asset.

Recipient Accounting The accounting for the recipient government is more involved. We will discuss the accounting for operating transfers first and then discuss the accounting for capital transfers.

With an operating transfer, the first question that arises is, when should the transfer be recognized? It is recognized when the transfer has been fully authorized by the transferor and the *eligibility criteria* have been met.

Often revenue recognition will correspond with the receipt of cash from the transferor government but, if both criteria are present, the revenue and a related receivable could be accrued. Revenue is not recognized, however, if *stipulations* attached to the transfer create a liability for the recipient government. In this case, the transfer would be recognized as deferred revenue and then recognized as revenue as the *stipulations* are met. This will allow the recipient government to match its transfer revenue with the related costs to satisfy the stipulations.

The second type of transfer for a recipient government is a capital transfer (transfer of monetary assets for the purpose of acquiring capital assets) or the direct transfer of tangible capital assets. The issue of accounting for capital transfers is controversial and, at the time of writing this text, had not been resolved.

Two questions arise in dealing with capital transfers. The first is how to recognize the revenue. Currently, some senior governments recognize the revenue by matching it against the costs of the related capital asset. Usually then, the revenue is deferred and matched against the related amortization expense. Others defer the revenue only until the asset is available for use. The revenue is booked when the asset is completed and ready for use. This leads to higher amortization charges in later years with no revenue offset.

EXHIBIT 11-4

Summary of Accounting for Recipient Government Transfers

Transfer type	Holding account	Revenue recognition
Operating transfer	None	Immediate
Operating transfer with stipulations that create a liability	Deferred revenue	Recognize as stipulations met
Capital transfer	None	Immediate
Capital transfer with stipulations that create a liability	Deferred revenue	Recognize as stipulations met

The second question is, if a deferred revenue account is created, where will the related "deferred" revenue be held? If it is classified as deferred revenue, it would normally be recognized as a liability and included in the recipient government's calculation of net debt. It is difficult to see this as a reasonable result. If the federal government transferred an office building to a provincial government, it would not be an accurate representation of reality to suggest that the net debt of the province has increased.

Recently, to avoid the "deferred revenue" problem described above, PSAB is suggesting that all transfers be recognized as revenue when the transfer has been fully authorized by the transferor and the *eligibility criteria* have been met (that is, a deferred revenue account would not be created and amortized into income to offset the amortization charges associated with the capital asset). The revenue would only be deferred if the transfer created a liability for the recipient. This deferred revenue would then be recognized when the liability had been settled. As the recommendations are controversial, there may be changes before this issue is settled.

The likely accounting for government transfers for the recipient government is summarized in Exhibit 11-4. The proposals in the exposure draft are effective April 1, 2012.

Tax Revenues Tax revenue is measured using accrual accounting concepts. According to PS 3510, tax revenue and the related asset (cash or receivable) should be recognized in the government statements if three conditions are met:

1. it meets the definition of an asset;
2. the taxes are authorized by the legislature or council; and
3. the taxable event has occurred.

Examples of taxable events would be (1) the earning of income by an individual in regards to personal income taxes, or (2) the sale of a taxable good in regards to sales tax. The resulting asset is measured at its net realizable value.

The issue that arises with regards to taxes is, what should or should not be included in tax revenue? The answer is that it depends on the nature of the items being discussed. The two items that have received the most attention are (1) transfers made through the tax system, and (2) tax concessions. Transfers made through the tax system are amounts paid to entities through a reduction in taxes but which the taxpayer would have been able to receive even if they had not paid taxes.

An example is the child tax benefit. The monies are available to all individuals who have children of a particular age and who meet the conditions required for the benefit. While it is administered through the tax system, it is available to an individual even if they did not pay

REALITY CHECK 11-1

The accounting for government transfers for the province of Nova Scotia is summarized in the following excerpt.

> Government transfers are recognized as revenue in the period during which the transfer is authorized and any eligibility criteria are met. Transfers are recorded as deferred revenue if they are restricted for a stated purpose, such as a specific program or the purchase of tangible capital assets.

Source: 2009 Nova Scotia Public Accounts, Volume 1, p. 83.

taxes. PSAB recommends that these transfers should be shown as an expense and not as a reduction in tax revenue.

Tax concessions are amounts that affect the amount that an entity currently owes or previously owed. They are provided only to taxpayers and only through the tax system. They reduce the taxes that would otherwise be owed and result in forgone revenue for the government. As an example, a province may provide a property tax credit to resident landowners. The credit is available only to property tax payers and it directly reduces the property tax revenue of the government. As such it would qualify as a tax concession.

PSAB recommends that tax revenue be shown net of tax concessions, that is, tax revenue should not be shown at its gross amount before the tax concessions. In contrast, any costs related to tax collection (administrative costs or commissions) should be shown as expenses and not netted against tax revenues.

Restricted Revenue The reporting of restricted revenues by governments is similar to the reporting of restricted revenues by NFPs. Governments may also have restrictions by external parties that limit the use of revenues. PS 3100 makes similar distinctions to NFPs between external restrictions that are imposed by an external party and internal restrictions or internally restricted entities. The recommended method for external restrictions is similar to the deferral method of recognizing contributions. PS 3100.11 states that revenue subject to external restrictions should be recognized in the period in which the resources are used for the purpose specified. Internal restrictions are treated differently since the government can change its mind by changing legislation. To provide information to the users, disclosure is required of all internal restrictions.

It should be noted that if the re-exposure draft on government transfers is approved, government transfers would no longer fall under the recommendations of PS 3100.

Tangible Capital Assets

Historically, Canadian governments almost universally reported tangible capital assets on an expenditure basis except for enterprise activities that operated on a cost-recovery basis. In general, tangible capital assets were seldom capitalized and were almost never depreciated. This method of accounting created several problems, an important one being that the modified accrual or "expenditure" model created a bias against spending on tangible capital assets. If a government wanted to balance the budget, they would simply defer spending on tangible capital assets. This led to the problem of an "infrastructure deficit" in Canada.[13]

The government reporting model now requires that tangible capital assets be recorded as assets and depreciated (PS 3150). This has proven to be a major issue for municipalities, in particular. Municipalities provide many services that are capital intensive—water, sewer, public transit, garbage collection, sporting venues, etc.

However, the issue does not end there. Because of the importance of tangible capital assets in service delivery for many governments, financial statement users need to have an understanding of the physical condition of these assets. The condition of the assets will have direct implications for the need for or use of future revenues.

The problem is that traditional accounting information does not provide sufficient information to fully assess the government's stewardship of these assets. To assist preparers and users, PSAB has issued a statement of recommended practice (SORP 3 – *Assessment of tangible capital assets*) to provide guidance to governments in disclosing the condition of their various categories of assets. It is important to note that the SORP is voluntary disclosure.

Liability Measurement

Reporting the liabilities of government is a bigger problem than may be apparent on the surface. A major issue is the debate over what constitutes a government liability. PS 3200 suggests that liabilities can arise from a number of different kinds of obligations. In addition to the standard agreements or contracts and liabilities arising from legislation (issued by the reporting government or another government), liabilities can also arise from constructive obligations and equitable obligations.

The thorny issue in recognizing a liability is determining whether the government has little or no discretion to avoid the obligation. This issue can be especially difficult for certain constructive and equitable obligations and the determination will often require considerable professional judgment. If it is determined from the preponderance of the evidence that the government has little or no discretion to avoid the obligation, then it is recognized as a liability.

PSAB has also addressed the important issue of contingencies. Contingencies are important because users such as rating agencies tend to add outstanding guarantees to unmatured debt to assess the total debt capacity utilized by an entity. Senior governments often guarantee others' debts to achieve important policy objectives. Examples are legislated programs that offered guarantees for small business loans or student loans. The accounting for general contingencies is very similar to that found in the *CICA Handbook*.

Accrual Accounting

The cash versus accrual debate in government accounting was similar to that for NFPs. The choice was between cash, modified cash or modified accrual, and full accrual. *Modified*

13. CICA, *20 Questions About Government Financial Reporting*, January 2003, p. 20.

accrual means accrual of assets and liabilities without necessarily allocating the costs on an expense basis (usually called *full accrual*).

In previous years, the vast majority of governments used a modified accrual basis. Gradually, there has been a shift to full accrual. An example was the introduction of PS 3250, in which the Board recommended pension accounting that was consistent with the recommendations of Section 3461 of the *CICA Handbook*, an expense-basis recommendation.

The present government reporting model uses a full accrual basis. As we have seen, this model analyzes the characteristics of governments and reporting implications, and stresses the importance of identifying the net cost of services, net debt, and capital spending.

International Harmonization

We will conclude our section on accounting issues by commenting briefly on the international harmonization of public sector accounting standards. Although PSAB has no official policy regarding harmonization or convergence with international standards, the Board notes that international standards have become increasingly important. The PSA Board has stated:

> In the absence of clearly demonstrated unique Canadian public sector circumstances, PSAB will endeavour to adopt a new accounting standard in Canada that reflects that of its international colleagues. Consequently, the activities of international groups such as the International Public Sector Accounting Standards Board (IPSASB) can affect Canadian public sector standard setting.[14]

Clearly, the direction of international standards will be important for those interested in government accounting in Canada.

CONCEPT CHECK 11-3

Companion Website

1. What is the modified equity method of accounting?
2. When can a recipient government recognize a transfer?
3. Under what conditions should tax revenue and the related asset be recognized on government financial statements?

A Final Example

We will end this chapter with an example of a provincial government's financial statements. Exhibit 11-5 shows the basic statements for the Province of Nova Scotia. We will briefly highlight several of the items that we have discussed in this chapter.

The first statement is the consolidated statement of financial position. It reveals that the government's net debt increased from $12.1 billion to $12.3 billion, while the accumulated

14. PSAB website, http://pre.cica.ca/index.cfm/ci_id/1053/la_id/1.htm, accessed November 1, 2009.

EXHIBIT 11-5

Financial Statements of the Province of Nova Scotia

Consolidated Statement of Financial Position
As at March 31, 2009
($ thousands)

	2009	2008
Financial Assets		
Cash and Short-term Investments (Note 3)	974,592	609,998
Accounts Receivable and Advances	893,462	1,137,782
Inventories for Resale	3,725	4,461
Loans Receivable (Schedule 3)	1,304,299	1,138,779
Investments (Schedule 3)	42,845	44,363
Investment in Government Business Enterprises (Schedule 6)	40,520	26,826
	3,259,443	2,962,209
Liabilities		
Bank Advances and Short-term Borrowings	613,866	1,090,870
Accounts Payable and Accrued Liabilities	1,526,213	1,531,799
Deferred Revenue (Note 4)	918,366	1,054,282
Accrued Interest	205,923	188,610
Unmatured Debt of Governmental Units (Schedule 4)	10,224,796	9,292,334
Unamortized Foreign Exchange Translation Gains, Premiums, and Discounts	221,614	202,114
Federal Equalization Repayable Loan (Note 6)	84,225	96,258
Pension, Retirement and Other Obligations (Note 7)	1,787,948	1,620,705
	15,582,951	15,076,972
Net Direct Debt	(12,323,508)	(12,114,763)
Non-Financial Assets		
Tangible Capital Assets (Schedule 7)	4,069,592	3,850,387
Inventories of Supplies	56,499	51,898
Prepaid Expenses	30,285	25,645
	4,156,376	3,927,930
Accumulated Deficits	(8,167,132)	(8,186,833)
Trust Funds under Administration (Note 8)	6,729,124	8,357,688

Accounting Changes (Note 2)
Contingencies and Contractual Obligations (Note 12)
Subsequent Events (Note 13)
Comparative Figures (Note 14)

EXHIBIT 11-5 (*Continued*)

Financial Statements of the Province of Nova Scotia

Consolidated Statement of Operations and Accumulated Deficits
For the fiscal year Ended March 31, 2009
($ thousands)

	Estimate 2009	Actual 2009	Actual 2008
Revenue			
Provincial Sources	4,948,495	4,951,010	4,886,676
Federal Sources	3,052,363	2,956,451	3,035,703
Prior Years' Adjustments—Federal/Provincial Fiscal Arrangements	—	61,534	98,056
Other Revenue	535,961	743,011	775,114
Sinking Fund and Public Debt Retirement Fund Earnings	114,400	116,384	112,834
Total Revenue	8,651,219	8,828,390	8,908,383
Expenses			
Agriculture	59,563	65,884	75,971
Community Services	947,445	906,088	892,272
Economic and Rural Development	110,496	77,090	83,049
Education	1,552,702	1,635,452	1,586,129
Assistance to Universities	230,511	485,468	422,589
Energy	24,642	38,789	44,828
Environment	44,607	72,852	91,085
Finance	51,476	50,089	47,894
Fisheries and Aquaculture	7,743	7,571	6,934
Health	3,342,304	3,418,883	3,248,225
Health Promotion and Protection	55,196	40,969	48,230
Justice	262,177	261,639	235,881
Labour and Workforce Development	62,443	57,695	23,480
Natural Resources	87,820	96,893	94,866
Public Service	161,607	217,716	177,898
Seniors	2,127	1,693	1,576
Service Nova Scotia and Municipal Relations	256,297	244,713	237,921
Tourism, Culture, and Heritage	59,113	62,842	59,466
Transportation and Infrastructure Renewal	351,703	381,585	364,642
Restructuring Costs	177,690	72,208	33,643
Pension Valuation Adjustment	67,590	85,066	107,504
Loss (Gain) on Disposal of Crown Assets	—	(1,076)	(4,169)
Debt Servicing Costs	904,522	888,160	953,698
Total Expenses	19,774	9,168,269	8,833,612
Surplus (Deficit) from Governmental Units	(168,555)	(339,879)	74,771
Net Income from Government Business Enterprises	358,221	359,580	344,158
Provincial Surplus	189,666	19,701	418,929
Accumulated Deficits, Beginning of Year		(8,186,833)	(8,605,762)
Accumulated Deficits, End of Year		(8,167,132)	(8,186,833)

EXHIBIT 11-5 *(Continued)*

Financial Statements of the Province of Nova Scotia

Consolidated Statement of Change in Net Direct Debt
For the fiscal year Ended March 31, 2009
($ thousands)

	Estimate 2009	Actual 2009	Actual 2008
Net Direct Debt - Beginning of Year	(12,114,763)	(12,114,763)	(12,357,205)
Changes in the Year*			
Provincial Surplus	189,666	19,701	418,929
Acquisition of Tangible Capital Assets	(341,437)	(503,313)	(437,103)
Amortization of Tangible Capital Assets	191,954	280,384	267,360
Disposals and Adjustments to Tangible Capital Assets	—	3,724	7,473
(Increase) Decrease in Inventories of Supplies	—	(4,601)	(5,204)
(Increase) Decrease in Prepaid Expenses	—	(4,640)	(9,013)
Total Changes in the Year	40,183	(208,745)	242,442
Net Direct Debt - End of Year	(12,074,580)	(12,323,508)	(12,114,763)

*Except for the Provincial Surplus figure, the estimates for items shown as *Changes in the Year* reflect the activity of the Consolidated Fund only.

EXHIBIT 11-5 (*Continued*)

Financial Statements of the Province of Nova Scotia

Consolidated Statement of Cash Flow
For the fiscal year Ended March 31,2009
($ thousands)

	2009	2008
CASH INFLOW (OUTFLOW) FROM THE FOLLOWING ACTIVITIES:		
Operating:		
Provincial Surplus	19,701	418,929
Sinking Fund and Public Debt Retirement Fund Earnings	(116,384)	(112,834)
Foreign Exchange Amortization	1,295	2,039
Amortization of Tangible Capital Assets	280,384	267,360
Net Income from Government Business Enterprises	(359,580)	(344,158)
Profit Distributions from Government Business Enterprises	345,886	332,947
Loss on Disposal of Tangible Capital Assets	2,448	4,499
Net Change in Other Items	(198,135)	266,709
	(24,385)	835,491
Investing:		
Repayment of Loans	211,577	220,973
Advances and Investing	(375,579)	(252,592)
	(164,002)	(31,619)
Capital:		
Acquisition of Tangible Capital Assets	(503,313)	(437,103)
Proceeds from Disposal of Tangible Capital Assets	1,276	2,973
	(502,037)	(434,130)
Financing:		
Debentures Issued	1,541,909	156,580
Repayment of Federal Equalization Repayable Loan	(12,033)	(12,032)
Foreign Currency Swaps and Adjustments	(20,556)	(12,131)
Sinking Fund Installments	(63,688)	(55,912)
Repayment of Debentures and Other Long-term Obligations	(390,614)	(709,339)
	1,055,018	(632,834)
Cash (Outflows) Inflows	364,594	(263,092)
Cash Position, Beginning of Year	609,998	873,090
Cash Position, End of Year	974,592	609,998
Cash Position Represented by:		
Cash and Short-Term Investments	974,592	609,998

deficit decreased slightly. Note that a line item "Investment in Government Business Enterprises" is presented under financial assets. You should recall that this item is unique in that it is accounted for by using the modified equity method. In addition, note that a line item for deferred revenue is shown under liabilities. The details can be found in Note 4 (not included).

The second statement is the consolidated statement of operations and accumulated deficits. It contains three columns: two columns present the actual results for 2008 and 2009 while the third column presents the budgeted numbers (called "Estimate") for 2009. After the deficit from governmental units is calculated, the income from GBEs is added to give the provincial surplus. Recall that this income would have been calculated using the modified equity method.

The third statement is the consolidated statement of changes in net direct debt. Despite the surplus, the government's debt increased for 2009. The reasons are apparent when we examine this statement. The provincial surplus was less than budgeted and the acquisition of tangible capital assets was considerably higher than budgeted.

The final statement is the consolidated statement of cash flows. The item of interest is the section on capital transactions. The same $503 million that was present in the statement of change in net direct debt is also present under the section on cash flows used for capital transactions.

PROPOSED CHANGE

The accounting for government transfers has been particularly controversial. The PSAB issued a third re-exposure draft on government transfers in May 2010 (the original exposure draft was issued in June 2006). It proposed a significant change from the April 2009 re-exposure draft for accounting for capital transfers for the recipient government. It eliminates the use of a "deferred capital contributions account" that was contained in the April 2009 exposure draft. The revised standard proposes using the same general principles for capital transfers that are used for operating transfers.

The PSAB is also proposing (in a March 2010 exposure draft) to incorporate the 4400 series recommendations for NFPs that are in the *CICA Handbook* directly into the *PSA Handbook*. These standards will be effective for GNPOs starting in 2012. Students should visit the text's Website for updates on the status of proposed changes in accounting standards.

Relevant Standards

Public Sector Accounting Handbook

PS 1000 Financial Statement Concepts
PS 1100 Financial Statement Objectives
PS 1300 Government Reporting Entity
PS 2500 Basic Principles of Consolidation
PS 3100 Restricted Assets and Revenues
PS 3150 Tangible Capital Assets

PS 3200 Liabilities
PS 3410 Government Transfers
PS 3510 Tax Revenue

Summary of Key Points

1. Public sector reporting differs from private sector reporting in nine unique characteristics. The most important are: the objective of government, which is to provide a service rather than make a profit; the higher standard of accountability to a larger potential user group; and the ability to raise large amounts of money through taxes. These characteristics play an important role in shaping the public sector reporting model.
2. The public sector consists of the federal, provincial, territorial, and local governments; government organizations; government partnerships; and school boards. There are three types of government organizations: government business enterprises (GBEs); government not-for-profit organizations (GNPOs); and other government organizations (OGOs). This chapter focussed on the financial reporting for governments and other government organizations.
3. The Public Sector Accounting Board (PSAB) sets the standards in accounting for the public sector. The *PSA Handbook* (PS 1100) identifies the objectives of financial statements for governments. These objectives are (1) the need to define the entity, that is, what is under government's control; (2) the types of financial information needed by users, that is, the financial statements that will be required; and (3) if the results are in accordance with what was authorized by the legislature or council. Four qualitative characteristics of good financial reports for governments are also identified: comparability among governments, consistency between years, completeness, and timeliness.
4. PSAB recommendations require four financial statements: statement of financial position; statement of operations; statement of changes in net debt; and statement of cash flows. These statements will communicate five key messages: accumulated surplus or deficit; annual surplus or deficit; net debt or net financial assets; change in net debt; and change in cash and cash flows that contributed to the change.
5. Governments have a number of reporting issues, some that are unique to governments and some that are similar to those of an NFP. The major reporting issues are defining the reporting entity, revenue recognition, tangible capital assets, and liability measurement. The major issue in defining the reporting entity is determining whether the government controls an organization. Revenue recognition is concerned about two sources of revenue that are unique to governments: transfers and taxes. Finally, the position of international bodies such as the International Public Sector Accounting Standards Board (IPSASB) will likely influence PSAB's position on government accounting issues in Canada.

Visit the text's website at www.pearsoned.ca/beechy for practice quizzes, additional problems, Excel® templates, answers to Concept Check questions, and important IFRS updates.

Review Questions

11-1 Why is the budget important in public sector reporting?

11-2 How does the primary user group for government financial statements differ from that for NFP financial statements?

11-3 Why is the focus on debt important for government accounting?

11-4 What are the nine unique characteristics of government that influence the government reporting model?

11-5 How is the public sector defined by PSAB?

11-6 What are the three types of government organizations and where should each look for guidance in accounting?

11-7 What is the Public Sector Accounting Board? What is its role?

11-8 Are government auditors required to report in accordance with the PSAB's recommendations?

11-9 Are municipalities required to report in compliance with PSAB recommendations?

11-10 What are the objectives of governmental reporting?

11-11 Briefly explain the two key messages on the statement of financial position.

11-12 What additional elements were included in relevance and reliability by PSAB? Why were they included?

11-13 What types of financial statements does the government reporting model recommend for governments?

11-14 What indicators provide persuasive evidence of control by governments?

11-15 How should a government business enterprise be reported?

11-16 What is a government transfer? Describe the two kinds of transfer terms a government may impose on a transfer.

11-17 When can the transferring government (transferor) recognize a transfer as an expense?

11-18 How should the recipient government account for the transfer of a tangible capital asset?

11-19 What is a tax concession and how does it differ from a transfer made through the tax system?

11-20 How did the expenditure basis of accounting discourage reinvestment in long-lived assets?

CASES

CASE 11-1 PROVINCE OF MAJESTIC LAKES

You are a staff member in the finance department for the Province of Majestic Lakes. You have just completed a meeting with a new member of the provincial legislature. As part of the background material in preparing for this position, the member had been provided with a detailed reading on the "New Government Reporting Model." At your meeting, the member asked for a quick written briefing on the following questions:

- What characteristics are unique for governments and what are the reporting implications?
- What are the five key messages in the model?
- What are the required financial statements and what are they like?
- What key information should I look for in each of the statements?
- What is the key impact of the change to "accrual" accounting?
- Why is it important to have a comparison with budgeted numbers?
- Why is it important to account for capital assets?

Required

Provide the requested briefing for the member.

CASE 11-2 COMPARISON OF OBJECTIVES

William Witherspoon III is executive vice-president of Marble Industries Ltd., a publicly held industrial company. Mr. Witherspoon has just been elected to the city council of Turnwater, a major industrial city. Prior to assuming office as a city councillor, he asks you, as his accountant, to explain the major differences that exist in accounting and financial reporting for a large city when compared to a large industrial corporation.

Required

Describe the major differences that exist in the purpose of accounting and financial reporting and in the types of reports of a large city when compared to a large industrial corporation.

[CGA–Canada, adapted]

CASE 11-3 TOWN OF EVERGREEN

Ms. Hannah Morse is a councillor for the growing town of Evergreen. She has approached you, as a friend and a public accountant, with her concerns over the draft financial statements of Evergreen for their most recent year-end, March 31, 20X2. She is concerned by the dramatic increase in revenue shown in the financial statements for the town.

Her suspicions are based on her work on the town compensation committee over the past year. She informs you that the town controller had requested a raise, which had yielded a lot of discussion at the committee. He had indicated that his compensation had not kept up with his increased workload that had resulted from the growth that the town was experiencing. After considerable discussion, the compensation committee agreed to a modest raise to the base salary. In addition, to avoid falling behind again, it agreed to the controller's request to pay a bonus based on town revenues. The bonus would be based on the town's consolidated revenue as it was the best figure to track the town's growth. Each year the bonus would be paid on revenues in excess of 20X1's level of revenue.

Ms. Morse believes that the apparent increase in revenue may not be legitimate but is not sure where to look to determine what has occurred. To assist you, she provides you with a copy of the draft annual report for the town. She also informs you that last year their auditor had informed the audit committee that Evergreen's statements were conservative, high-quality financial statements.

Your review of the financial statements finds a substantial increase in property tax revenues and transfers from the provincial government. You find the following in the notes:

- Property taxes are recorded at their gross amount when the taxable event has occurred. Costs related to tax collection are recorded as expenses and not as a reduction in tax revenue.
- Government transfers from the province are recognized in Evergreen's financial statements only when the province has also recognized the transfer.

Further, in the discussion accompanying the statements you also note the following:

- Town revenues: The major sources of revenue for the town are property taxes and government transfers from the province. Transfers from the province are received to help subsidize the town's recreational programs and to assist in the capital costs of constructing new streets. Substantial funds are received in advance of construction projects.
- Town expenses: The town incurred a number of expenses in the operation of the town. Several of these expenses were to encourage business to set up and stay in the town. The major components of this program were an advertising campaign and a rebate on property taxes.

Required

Prepare your notes for your discussion with Ms. Morse on what you think may have happened. Also include any recommendations that you deem appropriate based on your preliminary review.

CASE 11-4 GREEN PROVINCE

The following is the trial balance for Green Province for the current year:

Green Province
Trial Balance

Account	Dr.	Cr.
Accumulated deficit	625	
Cash	500	
Education expense	600	
GBE income	25	
Health expense	900	
Income tax		1375
Investment in GBEs	250	
Investments	750	
Unmatured debt		2500
Other expenses	600	
Payables		1000
Prepaids	125	
Receivables	375	
Sales tax		875
Tangible capital assets	1000	
	5750	5750

Required

Prepare the consolidated statement of financial position and consolidated statement of operations and accumulated deficit for Green Province.

CASE 11-5 DISTRICT OF MAPLE RIDGE

The District of Maple Ridge is well known in Canada for its high-quality financial reporting. It recently won a prestigious award as described in the following news release:

> The Canadian Award for Financial Reporting has been awarded to The District of Maple Ridge by the Government Finance Officers Association of the United States and Canada (GFOA) for its latest annual financial report. The Canadian Award for Financial Reporting program was established to encourage municipal governments throughout Canada to publish high quality financial reports and to provide peer recognition and technical guidance for officials preparing these reports. Maple Ridge has been commended for its performance in all areas judged by the review committee. The CAnFR represents a significant accomplishment by a government and its management.
>
> The District has also received the Award for Outstanding Achievement in Popular Annual Financial Reporting (PAFR) for its Citizens Report. "I am very proud of the work done by our Finance Department and obviously their efforts are recognized well beyond the boundaries of Maple Ridge," said Paul Gill, General Manager: Corporate & Financial Services.
>
> The District has been granted the Canadian Award for Financial Reporting Achievement 19 years in a row and for the past 13 years, it has received the Popular Annual Financial Report Award. "I am used to hearing about the great achievements of our Finance folks," said Mayor Ernie Daykin. "I appreciate the sense of pride that they put into their work and recognize their ongoing efforts and due diligence."
>
> The Annual Financial and Citizens Reports were judged by impartial Review Committee members to meet the high standards of the program, including demonstrating a constructive "spirit of full disclosure" designed to clearly communicate the municipality's financial story and to motivate potential users and user groups to read the report.
>
> Source: The District of Maple Ridge, "Outstanding Recognition for Exceptional Financial Reporting," press release, March 8, 2010, http://www.mapleridge.ca/EN/main/municipal/media/archives/financial_reporting_award.html.

Required

Visit the website for the District of Maple Ridge at http://www.mapleridge.ca/EN/main/municipal/2300/2591/annual_report-09.html Examine the financial statements and notes for the most recent annual report and citizens report. Identify five strengths of Maple Ridge's reporting.

[Reprinted with permission from District of Maple Ridge]

Solutions to Self-Study Problems

SSP 2-1

Direct Method
Archie Corp. Consolidated Financial Statements

Statement of Financial Position
December 31, 20X6

ASSETS	
Current assets:	
Cash and current receivables [200,000 + 400,000 **− 80,000 − 200,000**]	$ 320,000
Inventories [900,000 + 500,000]	1,400,000
	1,720,000
Property, plant, and equipment:	
Furniture, fixtures, and equipment, net of accumulated depreciation [2,000,000 + 1,700,000]	3,700,000
Buildings under capital leases, net of related amortization [6,000,000 + 3,000,000]	9,000,000
	12,700,000
Other assets:	
Investment in Bunker Ltd. [1,000,000 − 1,000,000]	—
TOTAL ASSETS	$14,420,000
LIABILITIES AND SHAREHOLDERS' EQUITY	
Liabilities:	
Current liabilities [1,500,000 + 400,000 **− 80,000 − 200,000**]	$ 1,620,000
Long-term liabilities [4,000,000 + 2,000,000]	6,000,000
	7,620,000
Shareholders' equity:	
Common shares [1,500,000 + 1,000,000 − 1,000,000]	1,500,000
Retained earnings [3,100,000 + 2,200,000]	5,300,000
	6,800,000
TOTAL LIABILITIES AND SHAREHOLDERS' EQUITY	$14,420,000

Statement of Comprehensive Income
Year Ended December 31, 20X6

Sales revenue [13,000,000 + 5,000,000 **− 4,000,000**]	$14,000,000
Dividend income [500,000 **− 500,000**]	—
	14,000,000
Operating expenses:	
Cost of sales [7,000,000 + 3,200,000 **− 4,000,000**]	6,200,000
Other operating expenses [3,500,000 + 700,000]	4,200,000
	10,400,000
NET INCOME	$ 3,600,000

Statement of Changes in Equity—Retained Earnings Section
Year Ended December 31, 20X6

Retained earnings, December 31, 20X5 [2,100,000 + 1,600,000]	$ 3,700,000
Net income	$ 3,600,000
Dividends declared [2,000,000 + 500,000 **− 500,000**]	(2,000,000)
Retained earnings, December 31, 20X6	$ 5,300,000

Worksheet Method
Archie Corp. Consolidation Worksheet

	Trial balances: Archie Corp. Dr/(Cr)	Trial balances: Bunker Ltd. Dr/(Cr)	Adjustments Dr/(Cr)		Archie Corp. consolidated trial balance*
Cash and current receivables	$ 200,000	$ 400,000	$ (80,000)	b	
			(200,000)	c	$ 320,000
Inventories	900,000	500,000			1,400,000
Furniture, fixtures, and equipment (net)	2,000,000	1,700,000			3,700,000
Buildings under capital leases (net)	6,000,000	3,000,000			9,000,000
Investment in Bunker Ltd. (at cost)	1,000,000	—	(1,000,000)	a	—
Current liabilities	(1,500,000)	(400,000)	80,000	b	(1,620,000)
			200,000	c	
Long-term liabilities	(4,000,000)	(2,000,000)			(6,000,000)
Common shares	(1,500,000)	(1,000,000)	1,000,000	a	(1,500,000)
Retained earnings, December 31, 20X5	(2,100,000)	(1,600,000)			(3,700,000)
Dividends declared	2,000,000	500,000	(500,000)	d	2,000,000
Sales revenue	(13,000,000)	(5,000,000)	4,000,000	e	(14,000,000)
Dividend income	(500,000)	—	500,000	d	—
Cost of sales	7,000,000	3,200,000	(4,000,000)	e	6,200,000
Other expenses	3,500,000	700,000			4,200,000
	$ —	$ —	$ —		$ —

*The SFP and SCI must be prepared from the amounts in this column.

This worksheet does **not** constitute a set of financial statements!

SSP 2-2

Direct method (000 omitted)
Brad Corp. Consolidated Financial Statements

Statement of Financial Position
December 31, 20X7

ASSETS		
Cash & investments (1,500 + 450)	$ 1,950	
Current rec. and accruals (3,400 + 1,890 − 200 − 100 − 30)	4,960	
Inventories (10,640 + 5,210)	15,850	$ 22,760
Loan receivable (1,000 + 0 − 1,000)	0	
Land (18,000 + 0)	18,000	
Buildings and equipment (net) (37,700 + 22,450)	60,150	
Investment in Pitt (20,000 + 0 − 20,000)	0	78,150
TOTAL ASSETS		$100,910
LIABILITIES AND SHAREHOLDERS' EQUITY		
Current payables and accruals (2,820 + 1,540 − 200 − 100 − 30)	$ 4,030	
Income tax payable (180 + 85)	265	$ 4,295
Long-term debt payable (33,750 + 1,000 − 1,000)	33,750	
Deferred tax liability (2,650 + 375)	3,025	36,775
Total liabilities		41,070
Common shares (13,000 + 20,000 − 20,000)	13,000	
Retained earnings (39,840 + 7,000)	46,840	59,840
TOTAL LIABILITIES AND SHAREHOLDERS' EQUITY		$100,910

Consolidated Statement of Comprehensive Income Ended December 31, 20X7

Sales revenue (7,100 + 3,400 − 1,400)	$ 9,100
Other income (235 + 840 − 100 − 30)	945
Total revenue	10,045
Operating expenses:	
Cost of goods sold (4,175 + 1,900 − 1,400)	4,675
Selling expenses (435 + 560)	995
General and administrative expenses (995 + 770)	1,765
Interest and other expenses (1,015 + 30 − 30)	1,015
Total operating expenses	8,450
Earnings before income taxes	1,595
Income tax expense (215 + 290)	505
Net earnings	$ 1,090

Statement of Changes in Equity—Retained Earnings Section
Year Ended December 31, 20X7

Retained earnings, December 31, 20X6 (39,500 + 6,410)	$45,910
Net earnings	$ 1,090
Dividends declared (160 + 100 − 100)	(160)
Retained earnings, December 31, 20X7	$46,840

Worksheet method (000 omitted)

	Trial balances Dr/(Cr)		Adjustments Dr/(Cr)	Notes	Consolidated trial balance
	Brad	Pitt			
Cash & temp. investment	1,500	450			1,950
Receivables & accruals	3,400	1,890	(200)	c	
			(100)	d	
			(30)	f	4,960
Inventories	10,640	5,210			15,850
Loan receivable	1,000	—	(1,000)	e	—
Land	18,000	—			18,000
Buildings and equipment	37,700	22,450			60,150
Investment in Pitt	20,000	—	(20,000)	a	—
Current payables & accruals	(2,820)	(1,540)	200	c	
			100	d	
			30	f	(4,030)
Income tax payable	(180)	(85)			(265)
Long-term debt payable	(33,750)	(1,000)	1,000	e	(33,750)
Deferred tax liability	(2,650)	(375)			(3,025)
Common shares	(13,000)	(20,000)	20,000	a	(13,000)
Ret. earn., December 31, 20X6	(39,500)	(6,410)			(45,910)
Sales revenue	(7,100)	(3,400)	1,400	b	(9,100)
Other income	(235)	(840)	100	d	
			30	f	(945)
Cost of goods sold	4,175	1,900	(1,400)	b	4,675
Selling expenses	435	560			995
G&A expenses	995	770			1,765
Interest and other exp.	1,015	30	(30)	f	1,015
Income tax expense	215	290			505
Dividends	160	100	(100)	d	160
Totals	$ —	$ —	$ —		$ —

Notes:

a. Acquisition adjustment
b. Eliminate intercompany sales
c. Eliminate intercompany receivable and payable
d. Eliminate intercompany dividends, including intercompany dividend payable/receivable
e. Eliminate intercompany loan
f. Eliminate intercompany interest accrual: $1,000,000 × 6% × ½ year = $30,000

SSP 3-1

Analysis of Fair Value of Net Assets Acquired:

	Carrying value	Fair value	Fair value increment	FVI allocated
Cash and cash equivalents	$ 1,200,000	$ 1,200,000	$ —	$ —
Accounts receivable	1,800,000	1,800,000	—	—
Machinery and equipment, net	8,400,000	11,000,000	2,600,000	2,600,000
Deferred development costs	3,100,000	4,000,000	900,000	900,000
Accounts payable	(1,100,000)	(1,100,000)	—	—
Notes payable, long-term	(1,000,000)	(900,000)	100,000	100,000
	$12,400,000	$16,000,000	$3,600,000	$3,600,000

1. **Direct Purchase of Blue's Net Assets for $20,000,000:**

	Ace's carrying value	+ FV of Blue assets acq'd	+ Cost of purchase =	Ace SFP after purchase
Cash and cash equivalents	$ 2,350,000	$ 1,200,000	$ (2,000,000)	$ 1,550,000
Accounts receivable	2,000,000	1,800,000		3,800,000
Land	5,000,000	—		5,000,000
Machinery and equipment, net	13,500,000	11,000,000		24,500,000
Deferred development costs	600,000	4,000,000		4,600,000
Goodwill*		4,000,000		4,000,000
				$43,450,000
Accounts payable	(650,000)	(1,100,000)		$ 1,750,000
Notes payable, long-term	(2,000,000)	(900,000)	(18,000,000)	20,900,000
Common shares	(15,000,000)			15,000,000
Retained earnings	(5,800,000)			5,800,000
	$ —	$20,000,000	$(20,000,000)	$43,450,000

*20,000,000 purchase price − 16,000,000 fair value of net assets = 4,000,000 goodwill

2. **Purchase of 100% of Blue's shares by issuance of Ace shares worth $20,000,000:**

	Ace's carrying value	Blue's carrying value	Adjustments	Ace consolidated SFP
Cash and cash equivalents	$ 2,350,000	$ 1,200,000		$ 3,550,000
Accounts receivable	2,000,000	1,800,000		3,800,000
Land	5,000,000	—		5,000,000
Machinery and equipment, net	13,500,000	8,400,000	$ 2,600,000	24,500,000
Investment in Blue*	20,000,000		(20,000,000)	—
Deferred development costs	600,000	3,100,000	900,000	4,600,000
Goodwill			4,000,000	4,000,000
				$45,450,000
Accounts payable	(650,000)	(1,100,000)		$ 1,750,000
Notes payable, long-term	(2,000,000)	(1,000,000)	100,000	2,900,000
Common shares*	(35,000,000)	(6,950,000)	6,950,000	35,000,000
Retained earnings	(5,800,000)	(5,450,000)	5,450,000	5,800,000
	$ —	$ —	$ —	$45,450,000

*These accounts are **after** recording the purchase of Blue's shares. The common shares account is increased by 400,000 × $50 = $20,000,000

3. **Purchase of 100% of Blue's shares by shares and cash worth $14,500,000:**
Note: In this scenario, the purchase price is less than the fair value of Blue's net assets. Therefore, negative goodwill is $1,500,000. Negative goodwill is recognized as a gain on a bargain purchase in the consolidated financial statements issued by Ace.

	Ace's carrying value*	Blue's carrying value	Adjustments	Ace consolidated SFP
Cash and cash equivalents*	$ 1,350,000	$1,200,000		$ 2,550,000
Accounts receivable	2,000,000	1,800,000		3,800,000
Land	5,000,000	—		5,000,000
Machinery and equipment, net	13,500,000	8,400,000	$ 2,600,000	24,500,000
Investment in Blue*	14,500,000		(14,500,000)	0
Deferred development costs	600,000	3,100,000	900,000	4,600,000
				$40,450,000
Accounts payable	(650,000)	(1,100,000)		$ 1,750,000
Notes payable, long-term	(2,000,000)	(1,000,000)	100,000	2,900,000
Common shares*	(28,500,000)	(6,950,000)	6,950,000	28,500,000
Retained earnings	(5,800,000)	(5,450,000)	{ 5,450,000	
			(1,500,000) }	7,300,000
	$ —	$ —	$ —	$40,450,000

*These accounts are **after** recording the purchase of Blue's shares. Cash is reduced by $1,000,000;

Common shares is increased by $270,000 × $50 = $13,500,000; Investment in Blue is increased by $14,500,000.

SSP 3-2

Patricia Ltd.
Consolidated SFP
January 1, 20X6

ASSETS	
Cash (80,000 + 55,000)	$ 135,000
Accounts receivable (220,000 + 135,000)	355,000
Inventories (100,000 + 90,000)	190,000
Total current assets	680,000
Land (800,000 + 180,000 **+ 120,000**)	1,100,000
Buildings (net) (1,100,000 + 430,000 **+ 20,000**)	1,550,000
Equipment (net) (720,000 + 120,000 **+ 60,000**)	900,000
Investment in Shelly Inc. (850,000 + 0 − **850,000**)	—
Goodwill (**+200,000**)	200,000
TOTAL ASSETS	$4,430,000
LIABILITIES AND SHAREHOLDERS' EQUITY	
Accounts payable (120,000 + 140,000)	$ 260,000
Long-term debt payable (400,000 + 420,000)	820,000
Total liabilities	1,080,000
Common shares (1,000,000 + 850,000 + 200,000 − **200,000**)	1,850,000
Retained earnings (1,500,000 + 250,000 − **250,000**)	1,500,000
Total shareholders' equity	3,350,000
TOTAL LIABILITIES AND SHAREHOLDERS' EQUITY	$4,430,000

Note: The bolded amounts are adjustments that must be made to:
- recognize fair value increments;
- recognize goodwill;
- eliminate Patricia's investment account; and
- eliminate Shelley's date-of-acquisition shareholders' equity.

SSP 4-1

Analysis of the purchase transaction:

Purchase price		$10,000,000
Net assets acquired:		
Carrying value of Subco's net assets	$7,000,000	
Fair value increment on buildings	1,400,000	
		8,400,000
Goodwill		$ 1,600,000

a. Consolidated net income:

Separate-entity net incomes:		
Parco	$ 680,000	
Subco	350,000	
		$ 1,030,000
Adjustments:		
Eliminate dividend income from Subco	$ (150,000)	
Unrealized profit from upstream sales [200,000 × 20%]	(40,000)	
Amortization of fair value increment [1,400,000/14]	(100,000)	
		(290,000)
Consolidated net income, year ended December 31, 20X5		$ 740,000

b. Consolidated retained earnings:

	Parco	Subco	Consolidated
Separate-entity retained earnings, January 1, 20X5	$3,450,000	$1,250,000	
Separate-entity net incomes for 20X5	680,000	350,000	
Dividends declared in 20X5	(200,000)	(150,000)	
Carrying value of retained earnings, December 31, 20X5	$3,930,000	$1,450,000	$5,380,000
Consolidation adjustments:			
Eliminate Subco date-of-acquisition retained earnings			(1,250,000)
Unrealized profit from upstream sales [200,000 × 20%]			(40,000)
Amortization of fair value increment [1,400,000/14]			(100,000)
			(1,390,000)
Consolidated retained earnings, December 31, 20X5			$3,990,000

c. Parco's equity-basis earnings in Subco

Subco's unadjusted separate-entity net income		$ 350,000
Equity-basis adjustments:		
Unrealized profit from upstream sales [200,000 × 20%]	$ (40,000)	
Amortization of fair value increment [1,400,000/14]	(100,000)	
		(140,000)
Subco's adjusted equity-basis earnings		$ 210,000

SSP 4-2

Measure step at the time of acquisition:

100% Purchase of Subsidiary Inc., January 1, 20X8

Purchase price	$1,084,000
Less carrying value of Target's net identifiable assets (100%)	(687,000)
= Fair value increment, allocated below	$ 397,000

	Carrying value (a)	Fair value (b)	Fair value increment (c) = (b) − (a)	FVI allocated	
Cash	$ 80,000	$ 80,000	—		
Accounts receivable	99,000	99,000	—		
Inventory	178,000	195,000	$ 17,000	$ 17,000	
Property, plant, and equipment	800,000	740,000	140,000	140,000	
Accumulated depreciation	(200,000)	—			
Accounts payable	(70,000)	(70,000)	—		
Long-term notes payable	(200,000)	(200,000)	—		
Total fair value increment					157,000
Net asset carrying value	$687,000				
Fair value of assets acquired		$ 844,000			
Balance of FVI allocated to goodwill					$ 240,000

Eliminate and recognize steps:

Intercompany transactions and balances:	
Upstream sale by Subsidiary Inc.	$(150,000)
Downstream sale by Parent Ltd.	(390,000)
Unrealized and realized profits:	
Realized profit on upstream sale of inventory in previous year	$ 12,000
Unrealized profit on upstream sale of inventory in the current year	(20,000)
Unrealized profit on downstream sale of inventory in the current year	(18,000)
Unrealized gain on sale of land by Subsidiary Inc. to Parent Ltd.	(210,000)

Amortize FVIs

	FVI allocated	Amortization period	Amortization per year	Amortization/ impairment loss during previous periods	Amortization/ impairment loss during 20X9	Balance of FVI remaining at the end of 20X9
Inventory	$ 17,000	—		$17,000	—	—
Property, plant, and equipment	140,000	10	$14,000	14,000	$14,000	$112,000
Total	$157,000			$31,000	$14,000	$112,000

We also need to remember to eliminate the subsidiary's share equity account balances at the time of acquisition, as well as the Investment in the Subsidiary account during consolidation.

Consolidated Financial Statements (direct method)

Parent Ltd.
Statement of Comprehensive Income
Year Ended December 31, 20X9

Sales revenue [1,200,000 + 987,000 − **390,000 − 150,000**]	$1,647,000
Cost of goods sold [800,000 + 650,000 − **390,000 − 150,000 − 12,000 + (90,000 × 20%) + (50,000 × 40%)**]	936,000
Gross profit	711,000
Other operating expenses [235,000 + 147,000 **+ 210,000 + 14,000**]	606,000
NET INCOME	$ 105,000

Parent Ltd.
Statement of Changes in Equity—Retained Earnings Section
Year Ended December 31, 20X9

Retained earnings, December 31, 20X8 [1,153,000 + 330,000 − **437,000 − 17,000 − 12,000 − (140,000/10 × 1)**	$1,003,000
Net income	105,000
Retained earnings, December 31, 20X9	$1,108,000

Parent Ltd.
Statement of Financial Position
December 31, 20X9

ASSETS	
Current assets:	
Cash [120,000 + 110,000]	$ 230,000
Accounts receivable [150,000 + 135,000]	285,000
Inventory [240,000 + 195,000 − **(90,000 × 20%) − (50,000 × 40%)**]	397,000
	912,000
Property, plant, and equipment [1,400,000 + 910,000 − **60,000 − 210,000**]	2,040,000
Accumulated depreciation [510,000 + 320,000 − **200,000 + (140,000/10 × 2)**]	(658,000)
	1,382,000
Goodwill [76,000 **+ 240,000**]	316,000
TOTAL ASSETS	$2,610,000
LIABILITIES AND SHAREHOLDERS' EQUITY	
Liabilities:	
Accounts payable [142,000 + 60,000]	$ 202,000
Long-term notes payable [600,000 + 200,000]	800,000
	1,002,000
Shareholders' equity:	
Common shares	500,000
Retained earnings [1,318,000 + 520,000 − **437,000 − 17,000 − 210,000 − (90,000 × 20%) − (50,000 × 40%) − (140,000/10 × 2)**]	1,108,000
	1,608,000
TOTAL LIABILITIES AND SHAREHOLDERS' EQUITY	$2,610,000

SSP 5-1

Measure step under entity method:

60% Purchase of Dakota Ltd., January 10, 20X5

Purchase price	$150,000	
100% fair value based on purchase price [$150,000 × (100%/60%)]		$250,000
Less carrying value of Dakota's net identifiable assets		(165,000)
= Fair value increment, allocated below		$ 85,000

	Carrying value (a)	Fair value (b)	Fair value increment (c) = (b) − (a)	FVI allocated	
Cash	$ 10,000	$ 10,000	—	—	
Accounts and other receivables	20,000	20,000	—	—	
Inventories	30,000	30,000	—	—	
Land	45,000	80,000	$ 35,000	$ 35,000	
Buildings	150,000	130,000	(20,000)	(20,000)	
Accumulated depreciation	(50,000)		50,000	50,000	
Equipment	130,000	10,000	(120,000)	(120,000)	
Accumulated depreciation	(80,000)		80,000	80,000	
Current accounts payable	(40,000)	(40,000)	—	—	
Long-term liabilities	(50,000)	(50,000)	—	—	
Total fair value increment				25,000	25,000
Net asset carrying value	$165,000				
Fair value of assets acquired		$190,000			
Balance of FVI allocated to goodwill @ 100%					$60,000

Notes:

1. Under the entity method the NCI balance will be equal to 40% of the full fair value of Dakota Ltd., i.e., 40% of $250,000 or $100,000.
2. Under the parent-company extension theory, only the parent's share of the goodwill of $60,000 × 60%, or $36,000, is reported on the consolidated financial statements. Consequently, under this method, the NCI is valued at only its 40% share of the net identifiable assets of Dakota or $190,000 × 40% = $76,000.

Regina Ltd.
Consolidated SFP (direct method)
January 10, 20X5

ASSETS	
Current assets:	
Cash [50,000 + 10,000]	$ 60,000
Accounts and other receivables [70,000 + 20,000]	90,000
Inventories [80,000 + 30,000]	110,000
	260,000
Capital assets:	
Land [0 + 45,000 **+ 35,000**]	80,000
Buildings [260,000 + 150,000 **− 20,000**]	390,000
Accumulated depreciation [40,000 + 50,000 **− 50,000**]	(40,000)
Equipment [175,000 + 130,000 **− 120,000**]	185,000
Accumulated depreciation [70,000 + 80,000 **− 80,000**]	(70,000)
	545,000
Goodwill **[250,000 − 190,000]**	60,000
TOTAL ASSETS	$865,000
LIABILITIES AND SHAREHOLDERS' EQUITY	
Liabilities:	
Current accounts payable [80,000 + 40,000]	$120,000
Long-term liabilities [0 + 50,000]	50,000
	170,000
Shareholders' equity:	
Common shares [220,000 + **150,000**]	370,000
Retained earnings	225,000
Non-controlling interest [**250,000 × 40%**]	100,000
	695,000
TOTAL LIABILITIES AND SHAREHOLDERS' EQUITY	$865,000

Note:

The total for each asset and liability is arrived at as: Regina carrying value + Dakota carrying value + Dakota FVI.

Goodwill is the difference between the 100% fair value of Dakota of $250,000 arrived at based on the purchase price of $150,000 paid by Regina for its 60% share and the fair value of the net identifiable assets of $190,000, i.e., $60.000.

The Investment in Dakota account and the share equity accounts of Dakota need not be eliminated since they were not included in the calculation to start with.

SSP 5-2

For the Measure step see SSP5-1.

Eliminate and Recognize Steps:

Intercompany transactions and balances:	
Upstream sale by Dakota Ltd.	$(400,000)
Downstream sale by Regina Ltd.	(200,000)
Dividend declared by Dakota Ltd.	(40,000)
Interest expense of Dakota Ltd. and revenue of Regina Ltd. and interest receivable/payable at year-end.	(2,500)
Note receivable of Regina Ltd. and note payable of Dakota Ltd.	(50,000)
Unrealized and realized profits:	
Unrealized profit on upstream sale of inventory in the current year	$ (40,000)
Unrealized profit on downstream sale of inventory in the current year	(20,000)

Amortize FVIs

	FVI allocated	Amortization period	Amortization per year	Amortization impairment loss during 20X5	Balance of FVI remaining at the end of 20X5
Land	$ 35,000				$35,000
Building	30,000	10	$ 3,000	$ 3,000	27,000
Property, plant, & Equipment	(40,000)	5	(8,000)	(8,000)	(32,000)
Goodwill	60,000				60,000
Total	$(85,000)		$(5,000)	$(5,000)	$90,000

Recognize NCI share of earnings

Details	Amount
Net income of Dakota Ltd. for 20X5 (from separate-entity financial statement)	$110,000
Add:	
Amortization of FVI during the year	5,000
Less:	
Unrealized profit on upstream sale of inventory in the current year	(40,000)
Adjusted net income of Dakota Ltd. for 20X5	**$ 75,000**
NCI's share @ 40%	**$ 30,000**

NCI Balance at the End of 20X5

Balance of NCI at the beginning of 20X5	$100,000
Add: NCI's share of Dakota Ltd.'s adjusted net income in 20X5	30,000
Less: NCI's share of dividends declared by Dakota Ltd. in 20X5	(16,000)
Ending balance of NCI in 20X5	$114,000

Regina Ltd.
Consolidated Statement of Comprehensive Income (direct method)
Year Ended December 31, 20X5

Sales [2,000,000 + 1,000,000 − **400,000** − **200,000**]	$2,400,000
Dividend income [24,000 + 0 − **24,000**]	—
Other income [7,000 + 0 − **2,500**]	4,500
	2,404,500
Cost of sales [1,000,000 + 600,000 − **400,000** − **200,000** + **40,000** + **20,000**]	1,060,000
Other operating expenses [886,000 + 280,000 + **3,000** − **8,000**]	1,161,000
Interest expense [2,000 + 10,000 − **2,500**]	9,500
	2,230,500
Net income and comprehensive income	$ 174,000
NET INCOME ATTRIBUTABLE TO:	
Owners of the parent	$ 144,000
Non-controlling interest	$ 30,000

Regina Ltd.
Statement of Changes in Equity—Retained Earnings Section
Year Ended December 31, 20X5

Retained earnings, December 31, 20X4	$ 225,000
Net income	144,000
Dividends declared [20,000 + 40,000 − **40,000**]	(20,000)
Retained earnings, December 31, 20X5	$ 349,000

Regina Ltd.
Consolidated Statement of Financial Position (direct method)
December 31, 20X5

ASSETS	
Current assets:	
Cash [28,000 + 10,000]	$ 38,000
Accounts and other receivables [110,000 + 30,000 − **50,000** − **2,500**]	87,500
Inventories [160,000 + 60,000 − **40,000** − **20,000**]	160,000
	285,500
Capital assets:	
Land [0 + 135,000 + **35,000**]	170,000
Buildings [300,000 + 150,000 − **20,000**]	430,000
Accumulated depreciation [45,000 + 60,000 − **50,000** + **3,000**]	(58,000)
Equipment [200,000 + 130,000 − **120,000**]	210,000
Accumulated depreciation [80,000 + 90,000 − **120,000**]	(82,000)
	670,000
Goodwill [**250,000** − **190,000**]	60,000
TOTAL ASSETS	$1,015,500
LIABILITIES AND SHAREHOLDERS' EQUITY	
Liabilities:	
Current accounts payable and accrued liabilities [40,000 + 80,000 − **50,000** − **2,500**]	$ 67,500
Long-term liabilities [65,000 + 50,000]	115,000
	182,500
Shareholders' equity:	
Common shares	370,000
Retained earnings [348,000 + 135,000 − **65,000** − **(40,000 × 60%)** − **20,000** + **8,000** − **3,000** − **(75,000 × 40%)**]	349,000
Non-controlling interest [**(235,000** − **40,000** + **90,000)** × **40%**]	114,000
	833,000
TOTAL LIABILITIES AND SHAREHOLDERS' EQUITY	$1,015,500

SSP 5-3

For the Measure step see SSP 5-1.

1. **Non-controlling interest in earnings:**

Dakota's separate-entity net income for 20X6 (Exhibit 5-15)	$130,000
Plus unrealized upstream profit in opening inventory:	
$100,000 × 40% gross margin	40,000
Less unrealized upstream profit in ending inventory:	
$160,000 sales × 50% remaining in inventory × 40% gross margin	(32,000)
Add Amortization of FVI during the year	5,000
Adjusted Regina net income	143,000
Non-controlling interest share	× 40%
	$ 57,200

2. **Non-controlling interest:**

Dakota's shareholders' equity, December 31, 20X6 (Exhibit 5-15)	$305,000
Less unrealized upstream profit at year-end:	
Ending inventory, $160,000 × 50% × 40% gross margin	(32,000)
Add balance of FVI remaining at the end of 20X6	95,000
	368,000
Non-controlling interest share	× 40%
	$147,200

3. **Consolidated retained earnings:**

Alternative 1:

Regina's separate-entity retained earnings, December 31, 20X5 (Exhibit 5-15)		$348,000
Dakota's retained earnings, December 31, 20X5	$205,000	
Less Dakota's retained earnings at date of acquisition	(65,000)	
Change in Dakota's retained earnings since acquisition	140,000	
Regina's ownership share	× 60%	
Regina's share of Dakota's cumulative earnings		84,000
Less unrealized profits at December 31, 20X6:		
Upstream: $160,000 × 50% × 40% gross margin × 60% share		(19,200)
Downstream: $40,000 × 50% gross margin		(20,000)
Amortization of FVI:		
Less Building ($30,000 ÷ 10 × 2) × 60%	$ (3,600)	
Plus Equipment (− $40,000 ÷ 5 × 2) × 60%	9,600	6,000
Regina consolidated retained earnings		$398,800

Alternative 2:

Total retained earnings (348,000 + 205,000)	$553,000
Less Dakota's R/E at acquisition date	(65,000)
Less NCI's share of Dakota's cumulative earnings since acquisition (205,000 − 65,000) × 40%	(56,000)
Less Unrealized gains on inter-company sales:	
60% of upstream sales $160,000 × 50% × 40% gross margin	(19,200)
100% of downstream sales $40,000 × 50% gross margin	(20,000)
Amortization of FVI:	
Less Building ($30,000 ÷ 10 × 2) × 60%	(3,600)
Plus Equipment (− $40,000 ÷ 5 × 2) × 60%	9,600
Regina's consolidated retained earnings	$398,800

SSP 6-1

Note: This is a ***downstream*** sale; NCI is not affected, except by the gain from sale as scrap in 20X16.

20X7:		
Sales	100,000	
Cost of sales		60,000
Equipment		40,000
Accumulated depreciation	2,000	
Depreciation expense (40,000 ÷ 10 × 1/2 year)		2,000
20X8:		
Retained earnings [40,000 − (40,000 ÷ 10 × 1/2 year)]	38,000	
Accumulated depreciation	2,000	
Equipment		40,000
Accumulated depreciation	4,000	
Depreciation expense (40,000 ÷ 10)		4,000
20X12:		
Retained earnings [40,000 − (40,000 ÷ 10 × 4.5 years)]	22,000	
Accumulated depreciation	18,000	
Equipment		40,000
Accumulated depreciation	4,000	
Depreciation expense		4,000
20X19:		
Accumulated depreciation	40,000	
Equipment		40,000

20X20:

The NCI's share of $200 on the sale of the equipment as scrap will be attributed to it as part of its share of the adjusted earnings of Sparrow Ltd.

SSP 6-2

Measurement:

80% Purchase of Spencer Corp., January 1, 20X5

Purchase price		$2,500,000	
100% fair value based on purchase price [$2,500,000 × (100%/80%)]			$3,125,000
Less carrying value of Spencer's net identifiable assets			(3,000,000)
= Fair value increment, allocated below			125,000
	Fair value increment (c) = (b) − (a)	FVI allocated	
Buildings	$(600,000)	$(600,000)	
Long-term liabilities	500,000	500,000	
Total fair value increment			(100,000)
Balance of FVI allocated to goodwill @ 100%			$ 225,000

Eliminate and recognize steps:

Intercompany transactions and balances:	
Upstream sale by Spencer Ltd.	$(250,000)
Downstream sale by Power Ltd.	(400,000)
Dividends declared by Spencer Ltd.	(40,000)
Unrealized and realized profits:	
Unrealized gain from upstream sale in ending inventory	$ (24,000)
Unrealized gain from downstream sale in ending inventory	(27,000)
Unrealized gain from upstream sale of land	(68,000)
Realized gain from downstream sale in beginning inventory	30,000
Realized gain from upstream sale in beginning inventory	28,000

Note: unrealized gains have to be eliminated, while realized gains have to be recognized.

Amortize FVIs:

	FVI allocated	Amortization period	Amortization per year	Amortization/ impairment loss in prior years	Amortization/ impairment loss during 20X9	Balance of FVI remaining at the end of 20X9
Building	$(600,000)	10	$(60,000)	(240,000)	$(60,000)	$(300,000)
Long-term liability	500,000	8	62,500	250,000	62,500	187,500
Goodwill	225,000					225,000
Total	$ 125,000		$ 2,500	$ 10,000	$ 2,500	$ 112,500

Note: The FVI amortization on buildings will reduce the overall amortization per year on buildings, while the FVI amortization on long-term liabilities will be an additional expense/loss on SCI.

Unrealized loss on intercompany sale of machine:

	Cost/carrying value	Depreciation/ realized losses in prior years (20X6–20X8) (cumulative adjustments)	Depreciation/ realized loss in 20X9 (current adjustments)	Carrying value/ unrealized loss at the end of 20X9
In Power's books	$210,000	$ 42,000	$14,000	$154,000
In consolidated statements	300,000	60,000	20,000	220,000
Unrealized/realized loss	$ (90,000)	$(18,000)	$ (6,000)	$ (66,000)

Note: Since the loss of $90,000 is being realized over the remaining useful life of the asset, the $6,000 per year realized loss will increase the amortization on the machine over its useful life.

Non-controlling interest in earnings:

Spencer's separate-entity net income for 20X9 (Exhibit 6-11)	$248,000
Adjustments for gains/losses on upstream transactions:	
Add unrealized gain on upstream sale of land	(68,000)
Add realized gain on upstream sale of inventory in previous year (20X8)	28,000
Less unrealized gain on upstream sale of inventory in current year	(24,000)
Less realization of unrealized loss on upstream sale of machine in 20X6	(6,000)
Amortization of FVI allocated to buildings	60,000
Amortization of FVI allocated to long-term liability	(62,500)
Spenser net income adjusted for realized and unrealized gains	$175,500
Non-controlling interest share	× 20%
	$ 35,100

1. Consolidated Statement of Comprehensive Income:

Power Corporation Consolidated Statement of Comprehensive Income
Year Ended December 31, 20X9

Sales (2,000,000 + 900,000 **− 400,000 − 250,000)**	$2,250,000
Investment income (1,000,000 + 100,000 **− 32,000)**	1,068,000
Gain on sale of land (68,000 **− 68,000)**	—
Total revenues	3,318,000
Cost of goods sold [1,300,000 + 500,000 **− 400,000 − 250,000 − 30,000 − 28,000 + 27,000 + 24,000**]	1,143,000
Other operating expenses [960,000 + 320,000 **+ 6,000 − 60,000 + 62,500**]	1,288,500
Total expenses	2,431,500
Net income and comprehensive income	$ 886,500
Net income attributable to:	
Owners of the parent	$ 851,400
Non-controlling interest	$ 35,100

2. Check via equity-basis income:

Power Corporation separate-entity net income		$ 740,000
Equity in earnings of Spencer Corporation:		
Spencer separate-entity net income (248,000 × 80%)	$198,400	
Unrealized upstream profit from land sale (68,000 × 80%)	(54,400)	
Unrealized downstream profit, ending (90,000 × 30%)	(27,000)	
Unrealized upstream profit, ending (60,000 × 40% × 80%)	(19,200)	
Realized downstream profit, beginning (100,000 × 30%)	30,000	
Realized upstream profit, beginning (70,000 × 40% × 80%)	22,400	
Under-depreciation on intercompany sale of machine (6,000 × 80%)	(4,800)	
Amortization of FV decrement on building (600,000 ÷ 10) × 80%	48,000	
Amortization of FVD on long-term liabilities (500,000 ÷ 8) × 80%	(50,000)	
Spencer adjusted net income		143,400
Less dividends received from Spencer (40,000 × 80%)		(32,000)
Net income attributable to Power Corporation's shareholders		$ 851,400

SSP 6A-1

1. The total available votes and Numbers' share thereof are as follows:

	Total available votes			Numbers Inc.'s votes		
Class	Shares outstanding	Votes per share	Total votes	Shares held	Votes per share	Total votes
A	600,000	1	600,000	40,000	1	40,000
B	50,000	15	750,000	44,000	15	660,000
	650,000		1,350,000	84,000		700,000

Numbers Incorporated owns 700,000 ÷ 1,350,000 = 51.85% of the votes, and therefore controls 212°F Corporation.

2. The ownership share for consolidation purposes (or for equity-basis earnings) is the proportion of residual earnings that accrues to Numbers. Preferred shares are a prior claim, and therefore do not participate in residual earnings. The two classes of common shareholders participate equally in earnings. Therefore, Numbers' ownership share is simply the investor's proportionate share of the total shares outstanding: 84,000 ÷ 650,000 = 12.923%.
3. The amount of the non-controlling interest is the sum of the preferred share redemption value (call price) plus 87.077% of the residual shareholders' equity after deducting the prior claim of the preferred shares:

Preferred shares:		
1,000,000 shares × $12 per share call price		$ 12,000,000
Residual common equity:		
Total 212°F shareholders' equity	$125,000,000	
Less preferred share redemption value	(12,000,000)	
Residual common equity	113,000,000	
Non-controlling interest percentage	× 87.077%	98,397,010
Non-controlling interest amount		$110,397,010

SSP 6B-1

The $500,000 face value bonds were purchased by Passion for $479,000, a discount of $21,000. The discount will be amortized by Passion over the six years remaining to maturity at $3,500 per year. On Sweetness's books, the original issue discount (which also is $21,000) will be amortized over 10 years at $2,100 per year. Over the life of the bonds, the carrying value of the $500,000 bonds on the issuing (Sweetness, the subsidiary) and investing (Passion, the parent) companies' books will be as follows:

	Sweetness	Passion
Original issue price, January 1, 20X5	$479,000	
4 years' accumulated amortization	8,400	
Carrying value, December 31, 20X8	487,400	
Purchase price, December 31, 20X8		$479,000
2 years' amortization	4,200	7,000
Carrying value, December 31, 20X10	491,600	486,000
4 years' amortization	8,400	14,000
Carrying value, December 31, 20X14	$500,000	$500,000

The consolidation adjustments must dispose of the difference between the carrying values of the bonds on the two companies' books. Assuming that the bonds are carried ***net*** of the discount on each company's books, the adjustments under each method are as follows:

Agency method:

December 31, 20X8		
Bonds payable	487,400	
Bond investment		479,000
Gain on bond retirement		8,400

Note: 30% of the gain of $8,400, i.e., $2,520, is attributable to the NCI. Therefore, when the income summary account is being closed and net income is transferred to retained earnings and NCI, respectively, the NCI's share of the gain should be included in the amount transferred to the NCI account on the SFP.

December 31, 20X10		
Bonds payable	491,600	
Bond investment		486,000
Non-controlling interest (5,600 × 30%)		1,680
Retained earnings		3,920
Interest income (including $3,500 amortization)	63,500	
Interest expense (including $2,100 amortization)		62,100
Non-controlling interest [(3,500 − 2,100) × 30%]		420
Retained earnings		980
December 31, 20X14		
Bonds payable	500,000	
Bond investment		500,000
Interest income (including $3,500 amortization)	63,500	
Interest expense (including $2,100 amortization)		62,100
Non-controlling interest [(3,500 − 2,100) × 30%]		420
Retained earnings		980

Par-value method:

December 31, 20X8		
Bonds payable	487,400	
Bond investment		479,000
Gain on bond retirement		8,400

Note: 30% of the difference between $500,000 and $487,400, i.e., 30% of $12,600, which is $3,780, is attributable to the NCI. Therefore, when the income summary account is being closed and net income is transferred to retained earnings and NCI, respectively, the NCI's share of $3,780 should be part of the amount transferred to the NCI account on the SFP.

December 31, 20X10		
Bonds payable	491,600	
Bond investment		486,000
Non-controlling interest (8,400 × 30%)		2,520
Retained earnings		3,080
Interest income (including \$3,500 amortization)	63,500	
Interest expense (including \$2,100 amortization)		62,100
Non-controlling interest (2,100 × 30%)		630
Retained earnings		770
December 31, 20X14		
Bonds payable	500,000	
Bond investment		500,000
Interest income (including \$3,500 amortization)	63,500	
Interest expense (including \$2,100 amortization)		62,100
Non-controlling interest (2,100 × 30%)		630
Retained earnings		770

SSP 7-1

A segment is reportable if it comprises 10% or more of an enterprise's total revenues, operating profits, or combined assets. Only one of the 10% tests needs to be met.

1. Reportable segments under revenue test:

   Test: $\frac{\text{Segment revenues (including intersegment)}}{\text{Total revenues (including intersegment)}}$

   East = 760/1010 = 75.2%
   West = 60/1010 = 5.9%
   North = 90/1010 = 8.9%
   South = 100/1010 = 9.9%

   East is a reportable segment. The remaining segments are less than 10% and are not reportable under this test.
2. Reportable segments under profit test:
   Total profits (50 + 80 + 10) = \$140
   Total losses = \$15
   Apply 10% criteria to larger of total profits or total losses. Larger is total profits: \$140 × 10% = \$14. Therefore any segment reporting a profit or loss of \$14 or more is reportable. East, West and South are reportable under this test.
3. Total assets are \$1,990. Any segment reporting assets of \$199 (= 1,990 × 10%) or more is reportable. Segments East and West both have assets greater than \$199 and are reportable under this test.
   Other test: External revenues disclosed in separate operating segments must be at least 75% of consolidated external revenues. The three tests above identified East, West and South as the reportable segments. External revenues for the three segments are (760 + 60 + 100 =) \$920, which is 91% of total external revenues of \$1010.

Conclusion: Reportable segments are East, West and South.

SSP 7-2

1. Widget Corporation is a public company and therefore must comply with IAS 34. Under IAS 34, costs such as maintenance are recognized in the interim period in which they occur (consistent with the discrete approach). As such, the costs in the second quarter will be expensed in the second quarter (and cannot be accrued and allocated to other interim periods).

2. Under IAS 34, the integral approach is used to accrue income taxes. As such, an estimate is made of the weighted average annual tax rate and this tax rate is used to accrue the income tax expense for the interim periods. The average tax rate is calculated as follows:

(i) The estimated income for the year is $200,000 (= 900,000 + 600,000 − 1,200,000 − 100,000).
(ii) The tax payable on the $200,000 is $80,000 calculated as follows: [(100,000 × 30%) + (100,000 × 50%)]
(iii) The average tax rate is 40% (i.e., 80,000 ÷ 200,000).

Using the average tax rate, the income tax expense for each quarter is as follows:
1st quarter: (100,000) × 40% = (40,000)
2nd quarter: (1,200,000) × 40% = (480,000)
3rd quarter: 600,000 × 40% = 240,000
4th quarter: 900,000 × 40% = 360,000

SSP 8-1

Fiscal Year	Year-end FX rate	C$ value of bonds	FX gain (loss)
20X5	1.27	$ 6,350,000	n/a
20X6	1.30	$ 6,500,000	(150,000)
20X7	1.34	$ 6,700,000	(200,000)
20X8	1.35	$ 6,750,000	(50,000)

SSP 8-2

1. Assumes the receivable is hedged.

December 2, 20X1		
Accounts receivable (NTD)	50,000	
Sales		50,000
[NTD 1,000,000 × 0.0500]		
December 3, 20X1		
Forward contract receivable(C$)	52,000	
Forward contract payable (NTD)		52,000
[NTD 1,000,000 × 0.0520]		
December 31, 20X1		
Accounts receivable (NTD)	1,000	
Exchange gains and losses		1,000
[NTD 1,000,000 × (0.0510 − 0.0500)]		
Forward contract payable (NTD)	400	
Exchange gains and losses		400
[NTD 1,000,000 × (0.0520 − 0.0516)]		
February 1, 20X2		
Cash (NTD)	52,500	
Exchange gains and losses		1,500
Accounts receivable (NTD)		51,000
[NTD 1,000,000 × (0.0525 − 0.0510)]		
Forward contract payable (NTD)	51,600	
Exchange gains and losses	900	
Cash (NTD)		52,500
[NTD 1,000,000 × (0.0525 − 0.0516)]		
Cash (C$)	52,000	
Forward contract receivable (C$)		52,000

2. Assumes the receivable is *not* hedged

December 2, 20X1		
Accounts receivable (NTD)	50,000	
Sales		50,000
[NTD 1,000,000 × 0.0500]		
December 31, 20X1		
Accounts receivable (NTD)	1,000	
Exchange gains and losses		1,000
[NTD 1,000,000 × (0.0510 − 0.0500)]		
February 1, 20X2		
Cash (NTD)	52,500	
Exchange gains and losses		1,500
Accounts receivable (NTD)		51,000
[NTD 1,000,000 × (0.0525 − 0.0510)]		

SSP 8-3

October 14, 20X7		
Forward contract receivable (US$)	244,000	
Forward contract payable (C$)		244,000
[US $200,000 × 1.22]		
December 1, 20X7		
Purchase order commitment liability	2,000	
Exchange gains and losses		2,000

To recognize the exchange gain [US $200,000 × (1.20 − 1.19) = 2,000] on the hedged item (purchase order) in current period net income and to record the associated reduction in the liability.

Equipment	240,000	
Accounts payable (US$)		238,000
Purchase order commitment liability		2,000

On delivery, accounts payable are recorded at the spot rate ($238,000 = US $200,000 × 1.19) to reflect the value of the obligation to pay US $200,000 to the supplier. The P.O. commitment liability is reversed as the decrease in the liability is now captured in accounts payable. Finally, the machine is recorded at $240,000 to balance the journal entry. This results in the equipment being recorded at the spot rate (1.200) that was in effect when the purchase order was issued.

Exchange gains and losses	1,000	
Forward contract receivable (US$)		1,000
[US $200,000 × (1.220 − 1.215) = 1,000].		
To record the exchange loss on the forward contract at December 1, 20X7.		

This entry does not have to be recorded now but could be included in the year-end adjustment. We present it here to illustrate the offsetting of the exchange loss on the forward contract with the exchange gain on the purchase order commitment.

December 31, 20X7		
Exchange gains and losses	1,000	
Forward contract receivable (US$)		1,000

Hedge accounting would no longer be used as the exchange gains and losses on the US denominated accounts payable naturally offset the exchange losses and gains on the forward contract. The spot rate has not changed from December 1, therefore no entry is needed to adjust the carrying value of the accounts payable. The forward rate has changed so an entry is made to adjust the forward contract to its fair value. [US $200,000 × (1.215 − 1.210) = 1,000].

January 30, 20X8		
Forward contract payable (C$)	244,000	
Cash (C$)		244,000

To pay the $244,000 agreed to under the forward contract to be able to receive the US $200,000.

Cash (US$)	248,000	
Exchange gains and losses		6,000
Forward contract receivable (US$)		242,000

To recognize the exchange gain [US $200,000 × (1.24 − 1.21) = 6,000] on the forward contract and receipt of US $200,000 from settling the forward contract.

Accounts payable (US$)	238,000	
Exchange gains and losses	10,000	
Cash (US$)		248,000

To recognize the exchange loss [US $200,000 × (1.24 − 1.19) = 10,000] on the accounts payable and payment of US $200,000 to settle the accounts payable.

SSP 9-1

SCI translated at average rate for the year:

	20X2 @ $1.50	20X1 @ $2.00
Revenue	$510,000	$484,000
Depreciation expense	102,000	132,000
Interest expense	68,000	88,000
Other expenses	204,000	176,000
	374,000	396,000
NET INCOME	$136,000	$ 88,000

SFP translated at year-end rate (except for shareholders' equity):

	20X2 @ $1.50	20X1 @ $2.00
ASSETS		
Cash	$ 45,000	$ 320,000
Accounts receivable	60,000	60,000
Land	300,000	—
Tangible capital assets	900,000	1,200,000
Accumulated depreciation	(180,000)	(120,000)
	$1,125,000	$1,460,000
LIABILITIES AND SHAREHOLDERS' EQUITY		
Accounts payable, current	$ 15,000	$ 40,000
Notes payable, long term	300,000	400,000
	315,000	440,000
Common shares (note 1)	1,250,000	1,250,000
Retained earnings (note 2)	89,000	28,000
Translation loss, cumulative (note 3)	(529,000)	(258,000)
	810,000	1,020,000
	$1,125,000	$1,460,000

Notes:

1. SF500,000 × 2.50 = $1,250,000
2. The retained earnings are translated at the historical rate at which the subsidiaries earnings were included in the parent's net income.

20X1	
Beginning balance	$ —
Net income (40,000 × 2.20)	88,000
Less dividends (30,000 × 2.00)	(60,000)
Ending balance	$ 28,000
20X2	
Beginning balance	$ 28,000
Net income (80,000 × 1.70)	136,000
Less dividends (50,000 × 1.50)	(75,000)
Ending balance	$ 89,000

3. The translation loss can be calculated independently as follows:

	Local Currency (SF)	Exchange rate	Translated amounts (C$)
Amounts arising in 20X1:			
NET ASSETS:			
Balance January 1, 20X1	SF500,000	2.50	$1,250,000
Changes during 20X1			
Net Income	40,000	2.20	88,000
Dividends	(30,000)	2.00	(60,000)
Derived balance			1,278,000
Actual balance	SF510,000	2.00	1,020,000
Net translation loss for 20X1			258,000
Amounts relating to previous periods			0
Cumulative translation gain, December 31, 20X1			$ 258,000

	Local Currency (SF)	Exchange rate	Translated amounts (C$)
Amounts arising in 20X2:			
NET ASSETS:			
Balance January 1, 20X2	SF 510,000	2.00	$1,020,000
Changes during 20X2			
Net Income	80,000	1.70	136,000
Dividends	(50,000)	1.50	(75,000)
Derived balance			1,081,000
Actual balance	SF 540,000	1.50	810,000
Net translation loss for 20X2			271,000
Amounts relating to previous periods			
20X1			258,000
Cumulative translation gain, December 31, 20X2			$ 529,000

SSP 9-2

1. *Translated 20X1 financial statements (temporal method)*

Statement of Comprehensive Income

	Local currency	Exchange rate	Canadian dollars
Revenue	SF 220,000	2.20	$484,000
Depreciation expense	60,000	2.30	138,000
Interest expense	40,000	2.20	88,000
Other expenses	80,000	2.20	176,000
	180,000		402,000
NET INCOME	SF 40,000		$ 82,000

Statement of Financial Position

	Local currency	Exchange rate	Canadian dollars
Assets			
Cash	SF 160,000	2.00	$ 320,000
Accounts receivable	30,000	2.00	60,000
Tangible capital assets	600,000	2.30	1,380,000
Accumulated depreciation	(60,000)	2.30	(138,000)
	SF 730,000		$1,622,000
Liabilities and shareholders' equity			
Accounts payable, current	SF 20,000	2.00	$ 40,000
Note payable, long-term	200,000	2.00	400,000
	220,000		440,000
Common shares	500,000	2.50	1,250,000
Retained earnings	10,000	(Note 1)	22,000
Translation gain (loss)	—		(90,000)
	510,000		1,182,000
	SF 730,000		$1,622,000

Note 1

Net income, per income statement	SF 40,000	(as above)	$ 82,000
Less dividends declared and paid at year-end 20X1	(30,000)	2.00	(60,000)
Retained earnings	SF 10,000		$ 22,000

2.

	Local Currency (SF)	Exchange rate	Translated amounts (C$)
Amounts arising in 20X1:			
MONETARY ITEMS:			
Balance January 1, 20X1[1]	SF 500,000	2.50	$1,250,000
Changes during 20X1			
Sales revenue	220,000	2.20	484,000
Interest expense	(40,000)	2.20	(88,000)
Other expenses	(80,000)	2.20	(176,000)
Payment of dividends	(30,000)	2.00	(60,000)
Purchase of tangible capital assets	(600,000)	2.30	(1,380,000)
Derived balance			30,000
Actual balance (160 + 30 − 20 − 200)	SF (30,000)	2.00	(60,000)
Net translation loss for 20X1			(90,000)
Amounts relating to previous periods			0
Cumulative translation loss, December 31, 20X1			$ (90,000)

1. The initial investment was treated as the beginning balance. An alternative approach would be to set the beginning balance to zero and treat the initial investment as a sale of common shares that increased the monetary balance.

3. *Translated 20X2 financial statements (temporal method)*

Statement of Comprehensive Income

	Local currency	Exchange rate	Canadian dollars
Revenue	SF 300,000	1.70	$510,000
Depreciation expense	60,000	2.30	138,000
Interest expense	40,000	1.70	68,000
Other expenses	120,000	1.70	204,000
	220,000		410,000
NET INCOME	SF 80,000		$100,000

Statement of Financial Position

	Local currency	Exchange rate	Canadian dollars
Assets			
Cash	SF 30,000	1.50	$ 45,000
Accounts receivable	40,000	1.50	60,000
Land	200,000	1.90	380,000
Tangible capital assets	600,000	2.30	1,380,000
Accumulated depreciation	(120,000)	2.30	(276,000)
	SF 750,000		$1,589,000
Liabilities and shareholders' equity			
Accounts payable, current	SF 10,000	1.50	$ 15,000
Note payable, long-term	200,000	1.50	300,000
	210,000		315,000
Common shares	500,000	2.50	1,250,000
Retained earnings	40,000	(Note 1)	47,000
Translation gain (loss)	—		(23,000)
	540,000		1,274,000
	SF 750,000		$1,589,000

Note 1

Balance, January 1, 20X2	SF 10,000		$ 22,000
Net income, per income statement	80,000	(as above)	100,000
Less dividends declared and paid at year-end 20X2	(50,000)	1.50	(75,000)
Retained earnings	SF 40,000		$ 47,000

4.

	Local currency (SF)	Exchange rate	Translated amounts (C$)
Amounts arising in 20X2:			
MONETARY ITEMS:			
Balance January 1, 20X2	SF (30,000)	2.00	$ (60,000)
Changes during 20X2:			
Sales revenue	300,000	1.70	510,000
Interest expense	(40,000)	1.70	(68,000)
Other expenses	(120,000)	1.70	(204,000)
Payment of dividends	(50,000)	1.50	(75,000)
Purchase of land	(200,000)	1.90	(380,000)
Derived balance			(277,000)
Actual balance (30 + 40 − 10 − 200)	SF (140,000)	1.50	(210,000)
Net translation gain for 20X2			$ 67,000
Amounts relating to previous periods			
20X1			(90,000)
Cumulative translation loss, December 31, 20X2			$ (23,000)

SSP 10-1

1. *January 1, 20X6*		
Cash	200,000	
Deferred contribution revenue		200,000
2. *July 1, 20X6*		
Land	44,000	
Building	120,000	
Cash		164,000
Deferred contribution revenue	44,000	
Net assets invested in capital assets		44,000
3. *December 31, 20X6*		
Amortization expense	3,000	
Accumulated amortization		3,000
($120,000/20) × 6 ÷ 12 = $3,000		
Deferred contribution revenue	3,000	
Contribution revenue		3,000
Prepaid maintenance	36,000	
Cash		36,000

SSP 10-2

1. Cash or marketable securities	100,000	
Net assets		100,000
2. Encumbrances	1,400,000	
Estimated commitments		1,400,000
3. Cash	800,000	
Pledge receivable	95,000	
Donation revenue		895,000
4. Cash	1,550,000	
Grant receivable	50,000	
Deferred revenue		1,000,000
Grant revenue		600,000
5. Equipment and furniture	1,000,000	
Cash		1,000,000
Amortization expense	100,000	
Accumulated amortization		100,000
Deferred revenue	100,000	
Revenue		100,000
6. Goods and services expense	1,450,000	
Cash		1,305,000
Accounts payable		145,000
Estimated commitments	1,375,000	
Encumbrances		1,375,000

Index

C